# Selected Plays

## of

# Eugene O'Neill

# Selected

# Plays

# OF

# Eugene

# O'Neill ·

Random House · *New York*

# Contents

# The
# Emperor Jones

# Characters

BRUTUS JONES, *Emperor*

HENRY SMITHERS, *A Cockney Trader*

AN OLD NATIVE WOMAN

LEM, *A Native Chief*

SOLDIERS, *Adherents of Lem*

*The Little Formless Fears; Jeff; The Negro Convicts; The Prison Guard; The Planters; The Auctioneer; The Slaves; The Congo Witch-Doctor; The Crocodile God.*

The action of the play takes place on an island in the West Indies as yet not self-determined by White Marines. The form of native government is, for the time being, an Empire.

# Scenes

*Scene* I: In the palace of the Emperor Jones. Afternoon.

*Scene* II: The edge of the Great Forest. Dusk.

*Scene* III: In the Forest. Night.

*Scene* IV: In the Forest. Night.

*Scene* V: In the Forest. Night.

*Scene* VI: In the Forest. Night.

*Scene* VII: In the Forest. Night.

*Scene* VIII: Same as Scene Two—the edge of the Great Forest. Dawn.

# SCENE ONE

THE audience chamber in the palace of the Emperor—a spacious, high-ceilinged room with bare, white-washed walls. The floor is of white tiles. In the rear, to the left of center, a wide archway giving out on a portico with white pillars. The palace is evidently situated on high ground for beyond the portico nothing can be seen but a vista of distant hills, their summits crowned with thick groves of palm trees. In the right wall, center, a smaller arched doorway leading to the living quarters of the palace. The room is bare of furniture with the exception of one huge chair made of uncut wood which stands at center, its back to rear. This is very apparently the Emperor's throne. It is painted a dazzling, eye-smiting scarlet. There is a brilliant orange cushion on the seat and another smaller one is placed on the floor to serve as a footstool. Strips of matting, dyed scarlet, lead from the foot of the throne to the two entrances.

It is late afternoon but the sunlight still blazes yellowly beyond the portico and there is an oppressive burden of exhausting heat in the air.

As the curtain rises, a native negro woman sneaks in cautiously from the entrance on the right. She is very old, dressed in cheap calico, bare-footed, a red bandana handkerchief covering all but a few stray wisps of white hair. A bundle bound in colored cloth is carried over her shoulder on the end of a stick. She hesitates beside the doorway, peering back as if in extreme dread of being discovered. Then she begins to glide noiselessly, a step at a time, toward the doorway in the rear. At this moment, SMITHERS appears beneath the portico.

SMITHERS is a tall, stoop-shouldered man about forty. His bald head, perched on a long neck with an enormous Adam's apple, looks like an egg. The tropics have tanned his naturally pasty face with its small, sharp features to a sickly yellow, and native rum has

*painted his pointed nose to a startling red. His little, washy-blue
eyes are red-rimmed and dart about him like a ferret's. His expression is one of unscrupulous meanness, cowardly and dangerous. He
is dressed in a worn riding suit of dirty white drill, puttees, spurs,
and wears a white cork helmet. A cartridge belt with an automatic
revolver is around his waist. He carries a riding whip in his hand.
He sees the woman and stops to watch her suspiciously. Then, making up his mind, he steps quickly on tiptoe into the room. The
woman, looking back over her shoulder continually, does not see
him until it is too late. When she does* SMITHERS *springs forward
and grabs her firmly by the shoulder. She struggles to get away,
fiercely but silently.*

SMITHERS (*tightening his grasp—roughly*)   Easy! None o' that, me
   birdie. You can't wiggle out, now I got me 'ooks on yer.
WOMAN (*seeing the uselessness of struggling, gives way to frantic
   terror, and sinks to the ground, embracing his knees supplicatingly*)   No tell him! No tell him, Mister!
SMITHERS (*with great curiosity*)   Tell 'im? (*Then scornfully*) Oh,
   you mean 'is bloomin' Majesty. What's the gaime, any'ow? What
   are you sneakin' away for? Been stealin' a bit, I s'pose. (*He taps
   her bundle with his riding whip significantly*).
WOMAN (*shaking her head vehemently*)   No, me no steal.
SMITHERS   Bloody liar! But tell me what's up. There's somethin'
   funny goin' on. I smelled it in the air first thing I got up this
   mornin'. You blacks are up to some devilment. This palace of 'is
   is like a bleedin' tomb. Where's all the 'ands? (*The woman keeps
   sullenly silent.* SMITHERS *raises his whip threatingly*)   Ow, yer
   won't, won't yer? I'll show yer what's what.
WOMAN (*coweringly*)   I tell, Mister. You no hit. They go—all go
   (*She makes a sweeping gesture toward the hills in the distance*).
SMITHERS   Run away—to the 'ills?
WOMAN   Yes, Mister. Him Emperor—Great Father (*She touches
   her forehead to the floor with a quick mechanical jerk*) Him
   sleep after eat. Then they go—all go. Me old woman. Me left
   only. Now me go too.
SMITHERS (*his astonishment giving way to an immense, mean satisfaction*)   Ow! So that's the ticket! Well, I know bloody well
   wot's in the air—when they runs orf to the 'ills. The tom-tom 'll be
   thumping out there bloomin' soon. (*With extreme vindictiveness*)
   And I'm bloody glad of it, for one! Serve 'im right! Puttin' on airs,

the stinkin' nigger! 'Is Majesty! Gawd blimey! I only 'opes I'm
there when they takes 'im out to shoot 'im. (*suddenly*) 'E's still
'ere all right, ain't 'e?

WOMAN Him sleep.

SMITHERS 'E's bound to find out soon as 'e wakes up. 'E's cunnin'
enough to know when 'is time's come. (*He goes to the doorway
on right and whistles shrilly with his fingers in his mouth. The
old woman springs to her feet and runs out of the doorway, rear.*
SMITHERS *goes after her, reaching for his revolver*) Stop or I'll
shoot! (*Then stopping—indifferently*) Pop orf then, if yer like,
yer black cow. (*He stands in the doorway, looking after her*).
(JONES *enters from the right. He is a tall, powerfully-built, full-
blooded negro of middle age. His features are typically negroid,
yet there is something decidedly distinctive about his face—an
underlying strength of will, a hardy, self-reliant confidence in
himself that inspires respect. His eyes are alive with a keen,
cunning intelligence. In manner he is shrewd, suspicious, evasive.
He wears a light blue uniform coat, sprayed with brass buttons,
heavy gold chevrons on his shoulders, gold braid on the collar,
cuffs, etc. His pants are bright red with a light blue stripe down
the side. Patent leather laced boots with brass spurs, and a belt
with a long-barreled, pearl-handled revolver in a holster complete his make up. Yet there is something not altogether ridiculous
about his grandeur. He has a way of carrying it off*).

JONES (*not seeing anyone—greatly irritated and blinking sleepily
—shouts*) Who dare whistle dat way in my palace? Who dare
wake up de Emperor? I'll git de hide frayled off some o' you niggers sho'!

SMITHERS (*showing himself—in a manner half-afraid and half-
defiant*) It was me whistled to yer. (*As* JONES *frowns angrily*)
I got news for yer.

JONES (*putting on his suavest manner, which fails to cover up his
contempt for the white man*) Oh, it's you, Mister Smithers.
(*He sits down on his throne with easy dignity*) What news you
got to tell me?

SMITHERS (*coming close to enjoy his discomfiture*) Don't yer notice
nothin' funny today?

JONES (*coldly*) Funny? No. I ain't perceived nothin' of de kind!

SMITHERS Then yer ain't so foxy as I thought yer was. Where's
all your court? (*sarcastically*) the Generals and the Cabinet Ministers and all?

JONES (*imperturbably*) Where dey mostly runs to minute I closes my eyes—drinkin' rum and talkin' big down in de town. (*Sarcastically*) How come you don't know dat? Ain't you sousin' with 'em most every day?

SMITHERS (*stung but pretending indifference—with a wink*) That's part of the day's work. I got ter—ain't I—in my business?

JONES (*contemptuously*) Yo' business!

SMITHERS (*imprudently enraged*) Gawd blimey, you was glad enough for me ter take yer in on it when you landed here first. You didn' 'ave no 'igh and mighty airs in them days!

JONES (*his hand going to his revolver like a flash—menacingly*) Talk polite, white man! Talk polite, you heah me! I'm boss heah now, is you fergettin'? (*The Cockney seems about to challenge this last statement with the facts but something in the other's eyes holds and cows him*).

SMITHERS (*in a cowardly whine*) No 'arm meant, old top.

JONES (*condescendingly*) I accepts yo' apology. (*Lets his hand fall from his revolver*) No use'n you rakin' up ole times. What I was den is one thing. What I is now's another. You didn't let me in on yo' crooked work out o' no kind feelin's dat time. I done de dirty work fo' you—and most o' de brain work, too, fo' dat matter—and I was wu'th money to you, dat's de reason.

SMITHERS Well, blimey, I give yer a start, didn't I?—when no one else would. I wasn't afraid to 'ire you like the rest was—'count of the story about your breakin' jail back in the States.

JONES No, you didn't have no s'cuse to look down on me fo' dat. You been in jail you'self more'n once.

SMITHERS (*furiously*) It's a lie! (*Then trying to pass it off by an attempt at scorn*) Garn! Who told yer that fairy tale?

JONES Dey's some tings I ain't got to be tole. I kin see 'em in folk's eyes. (*Then after a pause—meditatively*) Yes, you sho' give me a start. And it didn't take long from dat time to git dese fool, woods' niggers right where I wanted dem. (*With pride*) From stowaway to Emperor in two years! Dat's goin' some!

SMITHERS (*with curiosity*) And I bet you got yer pile o' money 'id safe some place.

JONES (*with satisfaction*) I sho' has! And it's in a foreign bank where no pusson don't ever git it out but me no matter what come. You didn't s'pose I was holdin' down dis Emperor job for de glory in it, did you? Sho'! De fuss and glory part of it, dat's only to turn de heads o' de low-flung, bush niggers dat's here.

Dey wants de big circus show for deir money. I gives it to 'em an' I gits de money. (*With a grin*) De long green, dat's me every time! (*Then rebukingly*) But you ain't got no kick agin me, Smithers. I'se paid you back all you done for me many times. Ain't I pertected you and winked at all de crooked tradin' you been doin' right out in de broad day? Sho' I has—and me makin' laws to stop it at de same time! (*He chuckles*).

SMITHERS (*grinning*) But, meanin' no 'arm, you been grabbin' right and left yourself, ain't yer? Look at the taxes you've put on 'em! Blimey! You've squeezed 'em dry!

JONES (*chuckling*) No, dey ain't *all* dry yet. I'se still heah, ain't I?

SMITHERS (*smiling at his secret thought*) They're dry right now, you'll find out. (*Changing the subject abruptly*) And as for me breakin' laws, you've broke 'em all yerself just as fast as yer made 'em.

JONES Ain't I de Emperor? De laws don't go for him. (*Judicially*) You heah what I tells you, Smithers. Dere's little stealin' like you does, and dere's big stealin' like I does. For de little stealin' dey gits you in jail soon or late. For de big stealin' dey makes you Emperor and puts you in de Hall o' Fame when you croaks. (*Reminiscently*) If dey's one thing I learns in ten years on de Pullman ca's listenin' to de white quality talk, it's dat same fact. And when I gits a chance to use it I winds up Emperor in two years.

SMITHERS (*unable to repress the genuine admiration of the small fry for the large*) Yes, yer turned the bleedin' trick, all right. Blimey, I never seen a bloke 'as 'ad the bloomin' luck you 'as.

JONES (*severely*) Luck? What you mean—luck?

SMITHERS I suppose you'll say as that swank about the silver bullet ain't luck—and that was what first got the fool blacks on yer side the time of the revolution, wasn't it?

JONES (*with a laugh*) Oh, dat silver bullet! Sho' was luck. But I makes dat luck, you heah? I loads de dice! Yessuh! When dat murderin' nigger ole Lem hired to kill me takes aim ten feet away and his gun misses fire and I shoots him dead, what you heah me say?

SMITHERS You said yer'd got a charm so's no lead bullet'd kill yer. You was so strong only a silver bullet could kill yer, you told 'em. Blimey, wasn't that swank for yer—and plain, fat-'eaded luck?

JONES (*proudly*) I got brains and I uses 'em quick. Dat ain't luck.

SMITHERS  Yer know they wasn't 'ardly liable to get no silver bullets. And it was luck 'e didn't 'it you that time.

JONES (*laughing*)  And dere all dem fool bush niggers was kneelin' down and bumpin' deir heads on de ground like I was a miracle out o' de Bible. Oh, Lawd, from dat time on I has dem all eatin' out of my hand. I cracks de whip and dey jumps through.

SMITHERS (*with a sniff*)  Yankee bluff done it.

JONES  Ain't a man's talkin' big what makes him big—long as he makes folks believe it? Sho', I talks large when I ain't got nothin' to back it up, but I ain't talkin' wild just de same. I knows I kin fool 'em—I *knows* it—and dat's backin' enough fo' my game. And ain't I got to learn deir lingo and teach some of dem English befo' I kin talk to 'em? Ain't dat wuk? You ain't never learned ary word er it, Smithers, in de ten years you been heah, dough you knows it's money in yo' pocket tradin' wid 'em if you does. But you'se too shiftless to take de trouble.

SMITHERS (*flushing*)  Never mind about me. What's this I've 'eard about yer really 'avin' a silver bullet moulded for yourself?

JONES  It's playin' out my bluff. I has de silver bullet moulded and I tells 'em when de time comes I kills myself wid it. I tells 'em dat's 'cause I'm de on'y man in de world big enuff to git me. No use'n deir tryin'. And dey falls down and bumps deir heads. (*He laughs*) I does dat so's I kin take a walk in peace widout no jealous nigger gunnin' at me from behind de trees.

SMITHERS (*astonished*)  Then you 'ad it made—'onest?

JONES  Sho' did. Heah she be. (*He takes out his revolver, breaks it, and takes the silver bullet out of one chamber*) Five lead an' dis silver baby at de last. Don't she shine pretty? (*He holds it in his hand, looking at it admiringly, as if strangely fascinated*).

SMITHERS  Let me see. (*Reaches out his hand for it*).

JONES (*harshly*)  Keep yo' hands whar dey b'long, white man. (*He replaces it in the chamber and puts the revolver back on his hip*).

SMITHERS (*snarling*)  Gawd blimey! Think I'm a bleedin' thief, you would.

JONES  No, 'tain't dat. I knows you'se scared to steal from me. On'y I ain't 'lowin' nary body to touch dis baby. She's my rabbit's foot.

SMITHERS (*sneering*)  A bloomin' charm, wot? (*Venomously*) Well, you'll need all the bloody charms you 'as before long, s' 'elp me!

JONES (*judicially*)  Oh, I'se good for six months yit 'fore dey gits sick o' my game. Den, when I sees trouble comin', I makes my getaway.

SMITHERS   Ho! You got it all planned, ain't yer?

JONES   I ain't no fool. I knows dis Emperor's time is sho't. Dat why I make hay when de sun shine. Was you thinkin' I'se aimin' to hold down dis job for life? No, suh! What good is gittin' money if you stays back in dis raggedy country? I wants action when I spends. And when I sees dese niggers gittin' up deir nerve to tu'n me out, and I'se got all de money in sight, I resigns on de spot and beats it quick.

SMITHERS   Where to?

JONES   None o' yo' business.

SMITHERS   Not back to the bloody States, I'll lay my oath.

JONES (*suspiciously*)   Why don't I? (*Then with an easy laugh*) You mean 'count of dat story 'bout me breakin' from jail back dere? Dat's all talk.

SMITHERS (*skeptically*)   Ho, yes!

JONES (*sharply*)   You ain't 'sinuatin' I'se a liar, is you?

SMITHERS (*hastily*)   No, Gawd strike me! I was only thinkin' o' the bloody lies you told the blacks 'ere about killin' white men in the States.

JONES (*angered*)   How come dey're lies?

SMITHERS   You'd 'ave been in jail if you 'ad, wouldn't yer then? (*With venom*) And from what I've 'eard, it ain't 'ealthy for a black to kill a white man in the States. They burns 'em in oil, don't they?

JONES (*with cool deadliness*)   You mean lynchin' 'd scare me? Well, I tells you, Smithers, maybe I does kill one white man back dere. Maybe I does. And maybe I kills another right heah 'fore long if he don't look out.

SMITHERS (*trying to force a laugh*)   I was on'y spoofin' yer. Can't yer take a joke? And you was just sayin' you'd never been in jail.

JONES (*in the same tone—slightly boastful*)   Maybe I goes to jail dere for gettin' in an argument wid razors ovah a crap game. Maybe I gits twenty years when dat colored man die. Maybe I gits in 'nother argument wid de prison guard was overseer ovah us when we're wukin' de road. Maybe he hits me wid a whip and I splits his head wid a shovel and runs away and files de chain off my leg and gits away safe. Maybe I does all dat an' maybe I don't. It's a story I tells you so's you knows I'se

de kind of man dat if you evah repeats one word of it, I ends
yo' stealin' on dis yearth mighty damn quick!

SMITHERS (*terrified*)　Think I'd peach on yer? Not me! Ain't I
always been yer friend?

JONES (*suddenly relaxing*)　Sho' you has—and you better be.

SMITHERS (*recovering his composure—and with it his malice*)　And
just to show yer I'm yer friend, I'll tell yer that bit o' news I was
goin' to.

JONES　Go ahead! Shoot de piece. Must be bad news from de
happy way you look.

SMITHERS (*warningly*)　Maybe it's gettin' time for you to resign—
with that bloomin' silver bullet, wot? (*He finishes with a mocking
grin*).

JONES (*puzzled*)　What's dat you say? Talk plain.

SMITHERS　Ain't noticed any of the guards or servants about the
place today, I 'aven't.

JONES (*carelessly*)　Dey're all out in de garden sleepin' under de
trees. When I sleeps, dey sneaks a sleep, too, and I pretends
I never suspicions it. All I got to do is to ring de bell and dey
come flyin', makin' a bluff dey was wukin' all de time.

SMITHERS (*in the same mocking tone*)　Ring the bell now an' you'll
bloody well see what I means.

JONES (*startled to alertness, but preserving the same careless tone*)
Sho' I rings. (*He reaches below the throne and pulls out a big,
common dinner bell which is painted the same vivid scarlet
as the throne. He rings this vigorously—then stops to listen. Then
he goes to both doors, rings again, and looks out*).

SMITHERS (*watching him with malicious satisfaction, after a pause
—mockingly*)　The bloody ship is sinkin' an' the bleedin' rats 'as
slung their 'ooks.

JONES (*in a sudden fit of anger flings the bell clattering into a
corner*)　Low-flung, woods' niggers! (*Then catching* SMITHERS'
*eye on him, he controls himself and suddenly bursts into a low
chuckling laugh*)　Reckon I overplays my hand dis once! A man
can't take de pot on a bob-tailed flush all de time. Was I sayin' I'd
sit in six months mo'? Well, I'se changed my mind den. I cashes
in and resigns de job of Emperor right dis minute.

SMITHERS (*with real admiration*)　Blimey, but you're a cool bird,
and no mistake.

JONES　No use'n fussin'. When I knows de game's up I kisses it good-by widout no long waits. Dey've all run off to de hills, ain't dey?

SMITHERS   Yes—every bleedin' man jack of 'em.

JONES   Den de revolution is at de post. And de Emperor better git his feet smokin' up de trail. (*He starts for the door in rear*).

SMITHERS   Goin' out to look for your 'orse? Yer won't find any. They steals the 'orses first thing. Mine was gone when I went for 'im this mornin'. That's wot first give me a suspicion of wot was up.

JONES   (*alarmed for a second, scratches his head, then philosophically*)   Well, den I hoofs it. Feet, do yo' duty! (*He pulls out a gold watch and looks at it*) Three-thuty. Sundown's at six-thuty or dereabouts. (*Puts his watch back—with cool confidence*) I got plenty o' time to make it easy.

SMITHERS   Don't be so bloomin' sure of it. They'll be after you 'ot and 'eavy. Ole Lem is at the bottom o' this business an' 'e 'ates you like 'ell. 'E'd rather do for you than eat 'is dinner, 'e would!

JONES   (*scornfully*)   Dat fool no-count nigger! Does you think I'se scared o' him? I stands him on his thick head more'n once befo' dis, and I does it again if he comes in my way—(*Fiercely*) And dis time I leave him a dead nigger fo' sho'!

SMITHERS   You'll 'ave to cut through the big forest—an' these blacks 'ere can sniff and follow a trail in the dark like 'ounds. You'd 'ave to 'ustle to get through that forest in twelve hours even if you knew all the bloomin' trails like a native.

JONES   (*with indignant scorn*)   Look-a-heah, white man! Does you think I'se a natural bo'n fool? Give me credit fo' havin' some sense, fo' Lawd's sake! Don't you s'pose I'se looked ahead and made sho' of all de chances? I'se gone out in dat big forest, pretendin' to hunt, so many times dat I knows it high an' low like a book. I could go through on dem trails wid my eyes shut. (*With great contempt*) Think dese ign'rent bush niggers dat ain't got brains enuff to know deir own names even can catch Brutus Jones? Huh, I s'pects not! Not on yo' life! Why, man, de white men went after me wid bloodhounds where I come from an' I jes' laughs at 'em. It's a shame to fool dese black trash around heah, dey're so easy. You watch me, man. I'll make dem look sick, I will. I'll be 'cross de plain to de edge of de forest by time dark comes. Once in de woods in de night dey got a swell chance o' findin' dis baby! Dawn tomorrow I'll be out at de oder side and on de coast whar dat French gunboat is stayin'.

She picks me up, takes me to Martinique when she go dar, and dere I is safe wid a mighty big bankroll in my jeans. It's easy as rollin' off a log.

SMITHERS (*maliciously*) But s'posin' somethin' 'appens wrong an' they do nab yer?

JONES (*decisively*) Dey don't—dat's de answer.

SMITHERS But, just for argyment's sake—what'd you do?

JONES (*frowning*) I'se got five lead bullets in dis gun good enuff fo' common bush niggers—and after dat I got de siiver bullet left to cheat 'em out o' gittin' me.

SMITHERS (*jeeringly*) Ho, I was fergettin' that silver bullet. You'll bump yourself orf in style, won't yer? Blimey!

JONES (*gloomily*) You kin bet yo' whole roll on one thing, white man. Dis baby plays out his string to de end and when he quits, he quits wid a bang de way he ought. Silver bullet ain't none too good for him when he go, dat's a fac'! (*Then shaking off his nervousness—with a confident laugh*) Sho'! What is I talkin' about? Ain't come to dat yit and I never will—not wid trash niggers like dese yere. (*Boastfully*) Silver bullet bring me luck anyway. I kin outguess, outrun, outfight, an' outplay de whole lot o' dem all ovah de board any time o' de day er night! You watch me! (*From the distant hills comes the faint, steady thump of a tom-tom, low and vibrating. It starts at a rate exactly corresponding to normal pulse beat—72 to the minute—and continues at a gradually accelerating rate from this point uninterruptedly to the very end of the play*).

(JONES *starts at the sound. A strange look of apprehension creeps into his face for a moment as he listens. Then he asks, with an attempt to regain his most casual manner*) What's dat drum beatin' fo'?"

SMITHERS (*with a mean grin*) For you. That means the bleedin' ceremony 'as started. I've 'eard it before and I knows.

JONES Cer'mony? What cer'mony?

SMITHERS The blacks is 'oldin' a bloody meetin', 'avin' a war dance, gettin' their courage worked up b'fore they starts after you.

JONES Let dem! Dey'll sho' need it!

SMITHERS And they're there 'oldin' their 'eathen religious service —makin' no end of devil spells and charms to 'elp 'em against your silver bullet. (*He guffaws loudly*) Blimey, but they're balmy as 'ell!

JONES (*a tiny bit awed and shaken in spite of himself*) Huh! Takes more'n dat to scare dis chicken!

SMITHERS (*scenting the other's feeling—maliciously*) Ternight when it's pitch black in the forest, they'll 'ave their pet devils and ghosts 'oundin' after you. You'll find yer bloody 'air 'll be standin' on end before termorrow mornin'. (*Seriously*) It's a bleedin' queer place, that stinkin' forest, even in daylight. Yer don't know what might 'appen in there, it's that rotten still. Always sends the cold shivers down my back minute I gets in it.

JONES (*with a contemptuous sniff*) I ain't no chicken-liver like you is. Trees an' me, we'se friends, and dar's a full moon comin' bring me light. And let dem po' niggers make all de fool spells dey'se a min' to. Does yo' s'pect I'se silly enuff to b'lieve in ghosts an' ha'nts an' all dat ole woman's talk? G'long, white man! You ain't talkin' to me. (*With a chuckle*) Doesn't you know dey's got to do wid a man was member in good standin' o' de Baptist Church? Sho' I was dat when I was porter on de Pullmans, befo' I gits into my little trouble. Let dem try deir heathen tricks. De Baptist Church done pertect me and land dem all in hell. (*Then with more confident satisfaction*) And I'se got little silver bullet o' my own, don't forgit!

SMITHERS Ho! You 'aven't give much 'eed to your Baptist Church since you been down 'ere. I've 'eard myself you 'ad turned yer coat an' was takin' up with their blarsted witch-doctors, or whatever the 'ell yer calls the swine.

JONES (*vehemently*) I pretends to! Sho' I pretends! Dat's part o' my game from de fust. If I finds out dem niggers believes dat black is white, den I yells it out louder 'n deir loudest. It don't git me nothin' to do missionary work for de Baptist Church. I'se after de coin, an' I lays my Jesus on de shelf for de time bein'. (*Stops abruptly to look at his watch—alertly*) But I ain't got de time to waste on no more fool talk wid you. I'se gwine away from heah dis secon'. (*He reaches in under the throne and pulls out an expensive Panama hat with a bright multi-colored band and sets it jauntily on his head*) So long, white man! (*With a grin*) See you in jail sometime, maybe!

SMITHERS Not me, you won't. Well, I wouldn't be in yer bloody boots for no bloomin' money, but 'ere's wishin' yer luck just the same.

JONES (*contemptuously*) You're de frightenedest man evah I see! I tells you I'se safe's 'f I was in New York City. It takes dem

niggers from now to dark to git up de nerve to start somethin'.
By dat time, I'se got a head start dey never kotch up wid.

SMITHERS (*maliciously*)   Give my regards to any ghosts yer meets
up with.

JONES (*grinning*)   If dat ghost got money, I'll tell him never ha'nt
you less'n he wants to lose it.

SMITHERS (*flattered*)   Garn! (*Then curiously*) Ain't yer takin' no
luggage with yer?

JONES   I travels light when I wants to move fast. And I got tinned
grub buried on de edge o' de forest. (*Boastfully*) Now say dat I
don't look ahead an' use my brains! (*With a wide, liberal gesture*)
I will all dat's left in de palace to you—and you better grab all
you kin sneak away wid befo' dey gits here.

SMITHERS (*gratefully*)   Righto—and thanks ter yer. (*As* JONES
*walks toward the door in rear—cautioningly*) Say! Look 'ere, you
ain't goin' out that way, are yer?

JONES   Does you think I'd slink out de back door like a common
nigger? I'se Emperor yit, ain't I? And de Emperor Jones leaves de
way he comes, and dat black trash don't dare stop him—not yit,
leastways (*He stops for a moment in the doorway, listening to
the far-off but insistent beat of the tom-tom*) Listen to dat roll-
call, will you? Must be mighty big drum carry dat far. (*Then
with a laugh*) Well, if dey ain't no whole brass band to see me
off, I sho' got de drum part of it. So long, white man. (*He puts his
hands in his pockets and with studied carelessness, whistling a
time, he saunters out of the doorway and off to the left*).

SMITHERS (*looks after him with a puzzled admiration*)   'E's got
'is bloomin' nerve with 'im, s'elp me! (*Then angrily*) Ho—the
bleedin' nigger—puttin' on 'is bloody airs! I 'opes they nabs 'im an'
gives 'im what's what!

*Curtain*

# SCENE TWO

THE *end of the plain where the Great Forest begins. The fore-ground is sandy, level ground dotted by a few stones and clumps of stunted bushes cowering close against the earth to escape the buffeting of the trade wind. In the rear the forest is a wall of darkness dividing the world. Only when the eye becomes accustomed to the gloom can the outlines of separate trunks of the nearest trees be made out, enormous pillars of deeper blackness. A somber monotone of wind lost in the leaves moans in the air. Yet this sound serves but to intensify the impression of the forest's relentless immobility, to form a background throwing into relief its brooding implacable silence.*

(JONES *enters from the left, walking rapidly. He stops as he nears the edge of the forest, looks around him quickly, peering into the dark as if searching for some familiar landmark. Then, apparently satisfied that he is where he ought to be, he throws himself on the ground, dog-tired*).

Well, heah I is. In de nick o' time, too! Little mo' an' it'd be blacker'n de ace of spades heahabouts. (*He pulls a handkerchief from his hip pocket and mops off his perspiring face*) Sho'! Gimme air! I'se tuckered out sho' 'nuff. Dat soft Emperor job ain't no trainin' fo' a long hike ovah dat plain in de brilin' sun. (*Then with a chuckle*) Cheer up, nigger, de worst is yet to come. (*He lifts his head and stares at the forest. His chuckle peters out abruptly. In a tone of awe*) My goodness, look at dem woods, will you? Dat no-count Smithers said dey'd be black an' he sho' called de turn. (*Turning away from them quickly and looking down at his feet, he snatches at a chance to change the subject— solicitously*) Feet, you is holdin' up yo' end fine an' I sutinly hopes you ain't blisterin' none. It's time you git a rest. (*He takes off his shoes, his eyes studiously avoiding the forest. He feels of the soles of his feet gingerly*) You is still in de pink—on'y a little mite feverish. Cool yo'selfs. Remember you done got a long journey yit befo' you. (*He sits in a weary attitude, listening to the rhythmic beating of the tom-tom. He grumbles in a loud tone to cover up a growing uneasiness*) Bush niggers! Wonder dey wouldn't git sick o' beatin' dat drum. Sound louder, seem like. I wonder if dey's startin' after me? (*He scrambles to his feet, looking back across the plain*) Couldn't see dem now, nohow, if dey was hundred feet away. (*Then shaking himself like a wet dog to get rid of these depressing thoughts*) Sho', dey's miles an' miles behind. What you gittin' fidgety about? (*But he sits down and begins to lace up his shoes in great haste, all the time muttering reassuringly*) You know what? Yo' belly is empty, dat's what's de matter wid you. Come time to eat! Wid nothin' but wind on yo' stumach, o' course you feels jiggedy. Well, we eats right heah an' now soon's I gits dese pesky shoes laced up. (*He finishes lacing up his shoes*) Dere! Now le's see! (*Gets on his hands and knees and searches the ground around him with his eyes*) White stone, white stone, where is you? (*He sees the first white stone and crawls to it—with satisfaction*) Heah you is! I knowed dis was de right place. Box of grub, come to me. (*He turns over the stone and feels in under it—in a tone of dismay*) Ain't heah! Gorry, is I in de right place or isn't I? Dere's 'nother stone. Guess dat's it. (*He scrambles to the next stone and turns it over*) Ain't heah, neither! Grub, whar is you? Ain't heah. Gorry, has I got to go hungry into dem woods—all de night? (*While he is talking he scrambles from one stone to another, turning them over in frantic haste. Finally, he jumps to his feet excitedly*) Is I lost de place? Must have! But how dat happen when I was followin' de trail across de plain in broad daylight? (*Almost plaintively*) I'se hungry, I is! I gotta git my feed. Whar's my strength gonna come from if I doesn't? Gorry, I gotta find dat grub high an' low somehow! Why it come dark so quick like dat? Can't see nothin'. (*He scratches a match on his trousers and peers about him. The rate of the beat of the far-off tom-tom increases perceptibly as he does so. He mutters in a bewildered voice*) How come all dese white stones come heah when I only remembers one? (*Suddenly, with a frightened gasp, he flings the match on the ground and stamps on it*) Nigger, is you gone crazy mad? Is you lightin' matches to show dem whar you is? Fo' Lawd's sake, use yo' haid. Gorry, I'se got to be careful! (*He stares at the plain behind him apprehensively, his hand on his revolver*) But how come all dese white stones? And whar's dat tin box o' grub I hid all wrapped up in oilcloth?

(*While his back is turned, the* LITTLE FORMLESS FEARS *creep out from the deeper blackness of the forest. They are black, shapeless, only their glittering little eyes can be seen. If they have any describable form at all it is that of a grubworm about the size of a creeping child. They move noiselessly, but with deliberate, painful effort, striving to raise themselves on end, failing and sinking prone again.* JONES *turns about to face the forest. He stares up at the tops of the trees, seeking vainly to discover his whereabouts by their conformation*).

Can't tell nothin' from dem trees! Gorry, nothin' 'round heah looks like I evah seed it befo'. I'se done lost de place sho' 'nuff! (*With mournful foreboding*) It's mighty queer! It's mighty queer! (*With sudden forced defiance—in an angry tone*) Woods, is you tryin' to put somethin' ovah on me?

(*From the formless creatures on the ground in front of him comes a tiny gale of low mocking laughter like a rustling of leaves. They squirm upward toward him in twisted attitudes.* JONES *looks down, leaps backward with a yell of terror, yanking out his revolver as he does so—in a quavering voice*) What's dat? Who's dar? What is you? Git away from me befo' I shoots you up! You don't?—

(*He fires. There is a flash, a loud report, then silence broken only by the far-off, quickened throb of the tom-tom. The formless creatures have scurried back into the forest.* JONES *remains fixed in his position, listening intently. The sound of the shot, the reassuring feel of the revolver in his hand, have somewhat restored his shaken nerve. He addresses himself with renewed confidence*).

Dey're gone. Dat shot fix 'em. Dey was only little animals— little wild pigs, I reckon. Dey've maybe rooted out yo' grub an' eat it. Sho', you fool nigger, what you think dey is—ha'nts? (*Excitedly*) Gorry, you give de game away when you fire dat shot. Dem niggers heah dat fo' su'tin! Time you beat it in de woods widout no long waits. (*He starts for the forest—hesitates before the plunge—then urging himself in with manful resolution*) Git in, nigger! What you skeered at? Ain't nothin' dere but de trees! Git in! (*He plunges boldly into the forest*).

# SCENE THREE

IN THE *forest. The moon has just risen. Its beams, drifting through the canopy of leaves, make a barely perceptible, suffused, eerie glow. A dense low wall of underbrush and creepers is in the nearer foreground, fencing in a small triangular clearing. Beyond this is the massed blackness of the forest like an encompassing barrier. A path is dimly discerned leading down to the clearing from left, rear, and winding away from it again toward the right. As the scene opens nothing can be distinctly made out. Except for the beating of the tom-tom, which is a trifle louder and quicker than at the close of the previous scene, there is silence, broken every few seconds by a queer, clicking sound. Then gradually the figure of the negro,* JEFF, *can be discerned crouching on his haunches at the rear of the triangle. He is middle-aged, thin, brown in color, is dressed in a Pullman porter's uniform and cap. He is throwing a pair of dice on the ground before him, picking them up, shaking them, casting them out with the regular, rigid, mechanical movements of an automaton. The heavy, plodding footsteps of someone approaching along the trail from the left are heard and* JONES' *voice, pitched on a slightly higher key and strained in a cheery effort to overcome its own tremors.*

De moon's rizen. Does you heah dat, nigger? You gits more light from dis out. No mo' buttin' yo' fool head agin' de trunks an' scratchin' de hide off yo' legs in de bushes. Now you sees whar yo'se gwine. So cheer up! From now on you has a snap. (*He steps just to the rear of the triangular clearing and mops off his face on his sleeve. He has lost his Panama hat. His face is scratched, his brilliant uniform shows several large rents*) What time's it gittin' to be, I wonder? I dassent light no match to find out. Phoo'. It's wa'm an' dat's a fac'! (*Wearily*) How long I been makin' tracks in dese woods? Must be hours an' hours. Seems like fo'evah! Yit can't be, when de moon's jes' riz. Dis am a long night fo' yo', yo' Majesty! (*With a mournful chuckle*) Majesty! Der ain't much majesty 'bout dis baby now. (*With attempted cheerfulness*) Never min'. It's all part o' de game. Dis night come to an end like everything else. And when you gits dar safe and has dat bankroll in yo' hands you laughs at all dis. (*He starts to whistle but checks himself abruptly*) What yo' whistlin' for, you po' dope! Want all de worl' to heah you? (*He stops talking to listen*) Heah dat ole drum! Sho' gits nearer from de sound. Dey's packin' it along wid 'em. Time fo' me to move. (*He takes a step forward, then stops—worriedly*) What's dat odder queer clickety sound I heah? Dere it is! Sound close! Sound like—sound like— Fo' God sake, sound like some nigger was shootin' crap! (*Frightenedly*) I better beat it quick when I gits dem notions. (*He walks quickly into the clear space—then stands transfixed as he sees* JEFF—*in a terrified gasp*) Who dar? Who dat? Is dat you, Jeff? (*Starting toward the other, forgetful for a moment of his surroundings and really believing it is a living man that he sees— in a tone of happy relief*) Jeff! I'se sho' mighty glad to see you! Dey tol' me you done died from dat razor cut I gives you. (*Stopping suddenly, bewilderedly*) But how you come to be heah, nigger? (*He stares fascinatedly at the other who continues his mechanical play with the dice.* JONES' *eyes begin to roll wildly. He stutters*) Ain't you gwine—look up—can't you speak to me? Is you—is you—a ha'nt? (*He jerks out his revolver in a frenzy of terrified rage*) Nigger, I kills you dead once. Has I got to kill you ag'in? You take it den. (*He fires. When the smoke clears away* JEFF *has disappeared,* JONES *stands trembling—then with a certain reassurance*) He's gone, anyway. Ha'nt or not ha'nt, dat shot fix him. (*The beat of the far-off tom-tom is perceptibly louder and more rapid.* JONES *becomes conscious of it—with a start, looking back over his shoulder*) Dey's gittin' near! Dey's comin' fast! And heah I is shootin' shots to let 'em know jes' whar I is! Oh, Gorry, I'se got to run. (*Forgetting the path he plunges wildly into the underbrush in the rear and disappears in the shadow*).

# SCENE FOUR

IN THE *forest. A wide dirt road runs diagonally from right, front to left, rear. Rising sheer on both sides the forest walls it in. The moon is now up. Under its light the road glimmers ghastly and unreal. It is as if the forest had stood aside momentarily to let the road pass through and accomplish its veiled purpose. This done, the forest will fold in upon itself again and the road will be no more.* JONES *stumbles in from the forest on the right. His uniform is ragged and torn. He looks about him with numbed surprise when he sees the road, his eyes blinking in the bright moonlight. He flops down exhaustedly and pants heavily for a while. Then with sudden anger.*

I'm meltin' wid heat! Runnin' an' runnin' an' runnin'! Damn dis heah coat! Like a straitjacket! (*He tears off his coat and flings it away from him, revealing himself stripped to the waist*) Dere! Dat's better! Now I kin breathe! (*Looking down at his feet, the spurs catch his eye*) And to hell wid dese high fangled spurs. Dey're what's been a-trippin' me up an' breakin' my neck. (*He unstraps them and flings them away disgustedly*) Dere! I gits rid o' dem frippety Emperor trappin's an' I travels lighter. Lawd! I'se tired! (*After a pause, listening to the insistent beat of the tom-tom in the distance*) I must 'a' put some distance between myself an' dem—runnin' like dat—and yit— dat damn drum sounds jes' de same—nearer, even. Well, I guess I a'most holds my lead anyhow. Dey won't never catch up. (*With a sigh*) If on'y my fool legs stands up. Oh, I'se sorry I evah went in for dis. Dat Emperor job is sho' hard to shake. (*He looks around him suspiciously*) How'd dis road evah git heah? Good level road, too. I never remembers seein' it befo'. (*Shaking his head apprehensively*) Dese woods is sho' full o' de queerest things at night. (*With a sudden terror*) Lawd God, don't let me see no more o' dem ha'nts! Dey gits my goat! (*Then trying to talk himself into confidence*) Ha'nts! You fool nigger, dey ain't no such things! Don't de Baptist parson tell you dat many time? Is you civilized, or is you like dese ign'rent black niggers heah? Sho'! Dat was all in yo' own head. Wasn't nothin' dere. Wasn't no Jeff! Know what? You jus' get seein' dem things 'cause yo' belly's empty and you's sick wid hunger inside. Hunger 'fects yo' head and yo' eyes. Any fool know dat. (*Then pleading fervently*) But bless God, I don't come across no more o' dem, whatever dey is! (*Then cautiously*) Rest! Don't talk! Rest! You needs it. Den you gits on yo' way again. (*Looking at the moon*) Night's half gone a'most. You hits de coast in de mawning! Den you's all safe.

(*From the right forward a small gang of negroes enter. They are dressed in striped convict suits, their heads are shaven, one leg drags limpingly, shackled to a heavy ball and chain. Some carry picks, the others shovels. They are followed by a white man dressed in the uniform of a prison guard. A Winchester rifle is slung across his shoulders and he carries a heavy whip. At a signal from the* GUARD *they stop on the road opposite where* JONES *is sitting.* JONES, *who has been staring up at the sky, unmindful of their noiseless approach, suddenly looks down and sees them. His eyes pop out, he tries to get to his feet and fly, but sinks back, too numbed by fright to move. His voice catches in a choking prayer*).

Lawd Jesus!

(*The* PRISON GUARD *cracks his whip—noiselessly—and at that signal all the convicts start to work on the road. They swing their picks, they shovel, but not a sound comes from their labor. Their movements, like those of* JEFF *in the preceding scene, are those of automatons—rigid, slow, and mechanical. The* PRISON GUARD *points sternly at* JONES *with his whip, motions him to take his place among the other shovelers.* JONES *gets to his feet in a hypnotized stupor. He mumbles subserviently*).

Yes, suh! Yes, suh! I'se comin'.

(*As he shuffles, dragging one foot, over to his place, he curses under his breath with rage and hatred*).

God damn yo' soul, I gits even wid you yit, sometime.

(*As if there were a shovel in his hands he goes through weary, mechanical gestures of digging up dirt, and throwing it to the roadside. Suddenly the* GUARD *approaches him angrily, threaten-*

*ingly. He raises his whip and lashes* JONES *viciously across the shoulders with it.* JONES *winces with pain and cowers abjectly. The* GUARD *turns his back on him and walks away contemptuously. Instantly* JONES *straightens up. With arms upraised as if his shovel were a club in his hands he springs murderously at the unsuspecting* GUARD. *In the act of crashing down his shovel on the white man's skull,* JONES *suddenly becomes aware that his hands are empty. He cries despairingly*).

Whar's my shovel? Gimme my shovel 'til I splits his damn head! (*Appealing to his fellow convicts*) Gimme a shovel, one o' you, fo' God's sake!

(*They stand fixed in motionless attitudes, their eyes on the ground. The* GUARD *seems to wait expectantly, his back turned to the attacker.* JONES *bellows with baffled, terrified rage, tugging frantically at his revolver*).

I kills you, you white debil, if it's de last thing I evah does! Ghost or debil, I kill you agin!

(*He frees the revolver and fires point blank at the* GUARD's *back. Instantly the walls of the forest close in from both sides, the road and the figures of the convict gang are blotted out in an enshrouding darkness. The only sounds are a crashing in the underbrush as* JONES *leaps away in mad flight and the throbbing of the tom-tom still far distant, but increased in volume of sound and rapidity of beat*).

# SCENE FIVE

A LARGE *circular clearing, enclosed by the serried ranks of gigantic trunks of tall trees whose tops are lost to view. In the center is a big dead stump worn by time into a curious resemblance to an auction block. The moon floods the clearing with a clear light.* JONES *forces his way in through the forest on the left. He looks wildly about the clearing with hunted, fearful glances. His pants are in tatters, his shoes cut and misshapen, flapping about his feet. He slinks cautiously to the stump in the center and sits down in a tense position, ready for instant flight. Then he holds his head in his hands and rocks back and forth, moaning to himself miserably.*

Oh, Lawd, Lawd! Oh, Lawd, Lawd! (*Suddenly he throws himself on his knees and raises his clasped hands to the sky—in a voice of agonized pleading*) Lawd Jesus, heah my prayer! I'se a po' sinner, a po' sinner! I knows I done wrong, I knows it! When I cotches Jeff cheatin' wid loaded dice my anger overcomes me and I kills him dead! Lawd, I done wrong! When dat guard hits me wid de whip, my anger overcomes me, and I kills him dead. Lawd, I done wrong! And down heah whar dese fool bush niggers raises me up to the seat o' de mighty, I steals all I could grab. Lawd, I done wrong! I knows it! I'se sorry! Forgive me, Lawd! Forgive dis po' sinner! (*Then beseeching terrifiedly*) And keep dem away, Lawd! Keep dem away from me! And stop dat drum soundin' in my ears! Dat begin to sound ha'nted, too. (*He gets to his feet, evidently slightly reassured by his prayer—with attempted confidence*) De Lawd'll preserve me from dem ha'nts after dis. (*Sits down on the stump again*) I ain't skeered o' real men. Let dem come. But dem odders—(*He shudders—then looks down at his feet, working his toes inside the shoes—with a groan*) Oh, my po' feet! Dem shoes ain't no use no more 'ceptin' to hurt. I'se better off without dem. (*He unlaces them and pulls them off—holds the wrecks of the shoes in his hands and regards them mournfully*) You was real, A-one patin' leather, too. Look at you now. Emperor, you'se gettin' mighty low!

(*He sighs dejectedly and remains with bowed shoulders, staring down at the shoes in his hands as if reluctant to throw them away. While his attention is thus occupied, a crowd of figures silently enter the clearing from all sides. All are dressed in Southern costumes of the period of the fifties of the last century. There are middle-aged men who are evidently well-to-do plant-ers. There is one spruce, authoritative individual—the* AUCTIONEER. *There is a crowd of curious spectators, chiefly young belles and dandies who have come to the slave-market for diversion. All exchange courtly greetings in dumb show and chat silently to-gether. There is something stiff, rigid, unreal, marionettish about their movements. They group themselves about the stump. Finally a batch of slaves is led in from the left by an attendant —three men of different ages, two women, one with a baby in her arms, nursing. They are placed to the left of the stump, beside* JONES.

*The white planters look them over appraisingly as if they were cattle, and exchange judgments on each. The dandies point with their fingers and make witty remarks. The belles titter bewitch-ingly. All this in silence save for the ominous throb of the tom-tom. The* AUCTIONEER *holds up his hand, taking his place at the stump. The groups strain forward attentively. He touches* JONES *on the shoulder peremptorily, motioning for him to stand on the stump—the auction block.*

JONES *looks up, sees the figures on all sides, looks wildly for some opening to escape, sees none, screams and leaps madly to the top of the stump to get as far away from them as possible. He stands there, cowering, paralyzed with horror. The* AUCTIONEER *begins his silent spiel. He points to* JONES, *appeals to the planters to see for themselves. Here is a good field hand, sound in wind and limb as they can see. Very strong still in spite of his being middle-aged. Look at that back. Look at those shoulders. Look at the muscles in his arms and his sturdy legs. Capable of any amount of hard labor. Moreover, of a good disposition, intelligent and tractable. Will any gentleman start the bidding? The* PLANTERS *raise their fingers, make their bids. They are apparently all eager to possess* JONES. *The bidding is lively, the crowd interested. While this has been going on,* JONES *has been seized by the courage of desperation. He dares to look down and around him. Over his face abject terror gives way to mystification, to gradual realization—stutteringly).*

What you all doin', white folks? What's all dis? What you all lookin' at me fo'? What you doin' wid me, anyhow? (*Suddenly convulsed with raging hatred and fear*) Is dis a auction? Is you sellin' me like dey uster befo' de war? (*Jerking out his revolver just as the* AUCTIONEER *knocks him down to one of the planters—glaring from him to the purchaser*) And *you* sells me? And *you* buys me? I shows you I'se a free nigger, damn yo' souls! (*He fires at the* AUCTIONEER *and at the* PLANTER *with such rapidity that the two shots are almost simultaneous. As if this were a signal the walls of the forest fold in. Only blackness remains and silence broken by* JONES *as he rushes off, crying with fear—and by the quickened, ever louder beat of the tom-tom*)

# SCENE SIX

A CLEARED *space in the forest. The limbs of the trees meet over it forming a low ceiling about five feet from the ground. The interlocked ropes of creepers reaching upward to entwine the tree trunks give an arched appearance to the sides. The space thus enclosed is like the dark, noisome hold of some ancient vessel. The moonlight is almost completely shut out and only a vague wan light filters through. There is the noise of someone approaching from the left, stumbling and crawling through the undergrowth.* JONES' *voice is heard between chattering moans.*

Oh, Lawd, what I gwine do now? Ain't got no bullet left on'y de silver one. If mo' o' dem ha'nts come after me, how I gwine skeer dem away? Oh, Lawd, on'y de silver one left—an' I gotta save dat fo' luck. If I shoots dat one I'm a goner sho'! Lawd, it's black heah! Whar's de moon? Oh, Lawd, don't dis night evah come to an end! (*By the sounds, he is feeling his way cautiously forward*) Dere! Dis feels like a clear space. I gotta lie down an' rest. I don't care if dem niggers does cotch me. I gotta rest.

(*He is well forward now where his figure can be dimly made out. His pants have been so torn away that what is left of them is no better than a breech cloth. He flings himself full length, face downward on the ground, panting with exhaustion. Gradually it seems to grow lighter in the enclosed space and two rows of seated figures can be seen behind* JONES. *They are sitting in crumpled, despairing attitudes, hunched, facing one another with their backs touching the forest walls as if they were shackled to them. All are negroes, naked save for loin cloths. At first they are silent and motionless. Then they begin to sway slowly forward toward each and back again in unison, as if they were laxly letting themselves follow the long roll of a ship at sea. At the same time, a low, melancholy murmur rises among them, increasing*) *gradually by rhythmic degrees which seem to be directed and controlled by the throb of the tom-tom in the distance, to a long, tremulous wail of despair that reaches a certain pitch, unbearably acute, then falls by slow gradations of tone into silence and is taken up again.* JONES *starts, looks up, sees the figures, and throws himself down again to shut out the sight. A shudder of terror shakes his whole body as the wail rises up about him again. But the next time, his voice, as if under some uncanny compulsion, starts with the others. As their chorus lifts he rises to a sitting posture similar to the others, swaying back and forth. His voice reaches the highest pitch of sorrow, of desolation. The light fades out, the other voices cease, and only darkness is left.* JONES *can be heard scrambling to his feet and running off, his voice sinking down the scale and receding as he moves farther and farther away in the forest. The tom-tom beats louder, quicker, with a more insistent, triumphant pulsation*).

# SCENE SEVEN

THE *foot of a gigantic tree by the edge of a great river. A rough structure of boulders, like an altar, is by the tree. The raised river bank is in the nearer background. Beyond this the surface of the river spreads out, brilliant and unruffled in the moonlight, blotted out and merged into a veil of bluish mist in the distance.* JONES' *voice is heard from the left rising and falling in the long, despairing wail of the chained slaves, to the rhythmic beat of the tom-tom. As his voice sinks into silence, he enters the open space. The expression of his face is fixed and stony, his eyes have an obsessed glare, he moves with a strange deliberation like a sleepwalker or one in a trance. He looks around at the tree, the rough stone altar, the moonlit surface of the river beyond, and passes his hand over his head with a vague gesture of puzzled bewilderment. Then as if in obedience to some obscure impulse, he sinks into a kneeling, devotional posture before the altar. Then he seems to come to himself partly, to have an uncertain realization of what he is doing, for he straightens up and stares about him horrifiedly—in an incoherent mumble.*

What—what is I doin'? What is—dis place? Seems like I know dat tree—an' dem stones—an' de river. I remember—seems like I been heah befo'. (*Tremblingly*) Oh, Gorry, I'se skeered in dis place! I'se skeered. Oh, Lawd, pertect dis sinner!

(*Crawling away from the altar, he cowers close to the ground, his face hidden, his shoulders heaving with sobs of hysterical fright. From behind the trunk of the tree, as if he had sprung out of it, the figure of the* CONGO WITCH-DOCTOR *appears. He is wizened and old, naked except for the fur of some small animal tied about his waist, its bushy tail hanging down in front. His body is stained all over a bright red. Antelope horns are on each side of his head, branching upward. In one hand he carries a bone rattle, in the other a charm stick with a bunch of white cockatoo feathers tied to the end. A great number of glass beads and bone ornaments are about his neck, ears, wrists, and ankles. He struts noiselessly with a queer prancing step to a position in the clear ground between* JONES *and the altar. Then with a preliminary, summoning stamp of his foot on the earth, he begins to dance and to chant. As if in response to his summons the beating of the tom-tom grows to a fierce, exultant boom whose throbs seem to fill the air with vibrating rhythm.* JONES *looks up, starts to spring to his feet, reaches a half-kneeling, half-squatting position and remains rigidly fixed there, paralyzed with awed fascination by this new apparition. The* WITCH-DOCTOR *sways, stamping with his foot, his bone rattle clicking the time. His voice rises and falls in a weird, monotonous croon, without articulate word divisions. Gradually his dance becomes clearly one of a narrative in pantomime, his croon is an incantation, a charm to allay the fierceness of some implacable deity demanding sacrifice. He flees, he is pursued by devils, he hides, he flees again. Ever wilder and wilder becomes his flight, nearer and nearer draws the pursuing evil, more and more the spirit of terror gains possession of him. His croon, rising to intensity, is punctuated by shrill cries.* JONES *has become completely hypnotized. His voice joins in the incantation, in the cries, he beats time with his hands and sways his body to and fro from the waist. The whole spirit and meaning of the dance has entered into him, has become his spirit. Finally the theme of the pantomime halts on a howl of despair, and is taken up again in a note of savage hope. There is a salvation. The forces of evil demand sacrifice. They must be appeased. The* WITCH-DOCTOR *points with his wand to the sacred tree, to the river beyond, to the altar, and finally to* JONES *with a ferocious command.* JONES *seems to sense the meaning of this. It is he who must offer himself for sacrifice. He beats his forehead abjectly to the ground, moaning hysterically).*

Mercy, Oh, Lawd! Mercy! Mercy on dis po' sinner.

*(The* WITCH-DOCTOR *springs to the river bank. He stretches out his arms and calls to some God within its depths. Then he starts backward slowly, his arms remaining out. A huge head of a crocodile appears over the bank and its eyes, glittering greenly, fasten upon* JONES. *He stares into them fascinatedly. The* WITCH-DOCTOR *prances up to him, touches him with his wand, motions with hideous command toward the waiting monster.* JONES

*squirms on his belly nearer and nearer, moaning continually).*
Mercy, Lawd! Mercy!
(*The crocodile heaves more of his enormous hulk onto the land.*
JONES *squirms toward him. The* WITCH-DOCTOR's *voice shrills out*
*in furious exultation, the tom-tom beats madly.* JONES *cries out in*
*a fierce, exhausted spasm of anguished pleading).*
Lawd, save me! Lawd Jesus, heah my prayer!
(*Immediately, in answer to his prayer, comes the thought of the*
*one bullet left him. He snatches at his hip, shouting defiantly).*
De silver bullet! You don't git me yit!
(*He fires at the green eyes in front of him. The head of the*
*crocodile sinks back behind the river bank, the* WITCH-DOCTOR
*springs behind the sacred tree and disappears.* JONES *lies with his*
*face to the ground, his arms outstretched, whimpering with fear*
*as the throb of the tom-tom fills the silence about him with a*
*somber pulsation, a baffled but revengeful power).*

# SCENE EIGHT

DAWN. *Same as Scene Two, the dividing line of forest and plain. The nearest tree trunks are dimly revealed but the forest behind them is still a mass of glooming shadow. The tom-tom seems on the very spot, so loud and continuously vibrating are its beats.* LEM *enters from the left, followed by a small squad of his soldiers, and by the Cockney trader,* SMITHERS. LEM *is a heavy-set, ape-faced old savage of the extreme African type, dressed only in a loin cloth. A revolver and cartridge belt are about his waist. His soldiers are in different degrees of rag-concealed nakedness. All wear broad palm-leaf hats. Each one carries a rifle.* SMITHERS *is the same as in Scene One. One of the soldiers, evidently a tracker is peering about keenly on the ground. He points to the spot where* JONES *entered the forest.* LEM *and* SMITHERS *come to look.*

SMITHERS (*after a glance, turns away in disgust*)  That's where 'e went in right enough. Much good it'll do yer. 'E's miles orf by this an' safe to the Coast, damn 's 'ide! I tole yer yer'd lose im, didn't I?—wastin' the 'ole bloomin' night beatin' yer bloody drum and castin' yer silly spells! Gawd blimey, wot a pack!

LEM (*gutturally*)  We cotch him. (*He makes a motion to his soldiers who squat down on their haunches in a semi-circle*).

SMITHERS (*exasperatedly*)  Well, ain't yer goin' in an' 'unt 'im in the woods? What the 'ell's the good of waitin'?

LEM (*imperturbably—squatting down himself*)  We cotch him.

SMITHERS (*turning away from him contemptuously*)  Aw! Garn! 'E's a better man than the lot o' you put together. I 'ates the sight o' 'im but I'll say that for 'im. (*A sound comes from the forest. The soldiers jump to their feet, cocking their rifles alertly.* LEM *remains sitting with an imperturbable expression, but listening intently. He makes a quick signal with his hand. His followers creep quickly into the forest, scattering so that each enters at a different spot).*

SMITHERS   You ain't thinkin' that would be 'im, I 'ope?

LEM *(calmly)*   We cotch him.

SMITHERS   Blarsted fat 'eads! *(Then after a second's thought—wonderingly)* Still an' all, it might 'appen. If 'e lost 'is bloody way in these stinkin' woods 'e'd likely turn in a circle without 'is knowin' it.

LEM *(peremptorily)*   Ssh! *(The reports of several rifles sound from the forest, followed a second later by savage, exultant yells. The beating of the tom-tom abruptly ceases.* LEM *looks up at the white man with a grin of satisfaction)* We cotch him. Him dead.

SMITHERS *(with a snarl)*   'Ow d'yer know it's 'im an' 'ow d'yer know 'e's dead?

LEM   My mens dey got um silver bullets. Lead bullet no kill him. He got um strong charm. I cook um money, make um silver bullet, make um strong charm, too.

SMITHERS *(astonished)*   So that's wot you was up to all night, wot? You was scared to put after 'im till you'd moulded silver bullets, eh?

LEM *(simply stating a fact)*   Yes. Him got strong charm. Lead no good.

SMITHERS *(slapping his thigh and guffawing)*   Haw-haw! If yer don't beat all 'ell! *(Then recovering himself—scornfully)* I'll bet yer it ain't im they shot at all, yer bleedin' looney!

LEM *(calmly)*   Dey come bring him now. *(The soldiers come out of the forest, carrying* JONES' *limp body. He is dead. They carry him to* LEM, *who examines his body with great satisfaction.* SMITHERS *leans over his shoulder—in a tone of frightened awe)* Well, they did for yer right enough, Jonesey, me lad! Dead as a 'erring! *(Mockingly)* Where's yer 'igh an' mighty airs now, yer bloomin' Majesty? *(Then with a grin)* Silver bullets! Gawd blimey, but yer died in the 'eighth o' style, any'ow!

*Curtain*

# Anna
# Christie

# Characters

"JOHNNY-THE-PRIEST"

TWO LONGSHOREMEN

A POSTMAN

LARRY, *bartender*

CHRIS. CHRISTOPHERSON, *captain of the barge*
Simeon Winthrop

MARTHY OWEN

ANNA CHRISTOPHERSON, *Chris' daughter*

THREE MEN OF A STEAMER'S CREW

MAT BURKE, *a stoker*

JOHNSON, *deckhand on the barge*

# Scenes

# ACT ONE

SCENE—"JOHNNY-THE-PRIEST'S" *saloon near South Street, New York City. The stage is divided into two sections, showing a small back room on the right. On the left, forward, of the barroom, a large window looking out on the street. Beyond it, the main entrance—a double swinging door. Farther back, another window. The bar runs from left to right nearly the whole length of the rear wall. In back of the bar, a small showcase displaying a few bottles of case goods, for which there is evidently little call. The remainder of the rear space in front of the large mirrors is occupied by half-barrels of cheap whisky of the "nickel-a-shot" variety, from which the liquor is drawn by means of spigots. On the right is an open doorway leading to the back room. In the back room are four round wooden tables with five chairs grouped about each. In the rear, a family entrance opening on a side street.*

*It is late afternoon of a day in fall.*

*As the curtain rises,* JOHNNY *is discovered.* "JOHNNY-THE-PRIEST" *deserves his nickname. With his pale, thin, clean-shaven face, mild blue eyes and white hair, a cassock would seem more suited to him than the apron he wears. Neither his voice nor his general manner dispel this illusion which has made him a personage of the water front. They are soft and bland. But beneath all his mildness one senses the man behind the mask—cynical, callous, hard as nails. He is lounging at ease behind the bar, a pair of spectacles on his nose, reading an evening paper.*

*Two longshoremen enter from the street, wearing their working aprons, the button of the union pinned conspicuously on the caps pulled sideways on their heads at an aggressive angle.*

FIRST LONGSHOREMAN (*As they range themselves at the bar*)
Gimme a shock. Number Two. (*He tosses a coin on the bar.*)

SECOND LONGSHOREMAN  Same here. (JOHNNY *sets two glass of barrel whisky before them.*)

FIRST LONGSHOREMAN  Here's luck! (*The other nods. They gulp down their whisky.*)

SECOND LONGSHOREMAN  (*Putting money on the bar*)  Give us another.

FIRST LONGSHOREMAN  Gimme a scoop this time—lager and porter. I'm dry.

SECOND LONGSHOREMAN  Same here. (JOHNNY *draws the lager and porter and sets the big, foaming schooners before them. They drink down half the contents and start to talk together hurriedly in low tones. The door on the left is swung open and* LARRY *enters. He is a boyish, red-cheeked, rather good-looking young fellow of twenty or so.*)

LARRY  (*Nodding to* JOHNNY—*cheerily*)  Hello, boss.

JOHNNY  Hello, Larry. (*With a glance at his watch.*) Just on time. (LARRY *goes to the right behind the bar, takes off his coat, and puts on an apron.*)

FIRST LONGSHOREMAN  (*Abruptly*)  Let's drink up and get back to it. (*They finish their drinks and go out left.* THE POSTMAN *enters as they leave. He exchanges nods with* JOHNNY *and throws a letter on the bar.*)

THE POSTMAN  Addressed care of you, Johnny. Know him?

JOHNNY  (*Picks up the letter, adjusting his spectacles.* LARRY *comes and peers over his shoulders.* JOHNNY *reads very slowly.*)  Christopher Christopherson.

THE POSTMAN  (*Helpfully*)  Square-head name.

LARRY  Old Chris—that's who.

JOHNNY  Oh, sure. I was forgetting Chris carried a hell of a name like that. Letters come here for him sometimes before, I remember now. Long time ago, though.

THE POSTMAN  It'll get him all right then?

JOHNNY  Sure thing. He comes here whenever he's in port.

THE POSTMAN  (*Turning to go*)  Sailor, eh?

JOHNNY  (*With a grin*)  Captain of a coal barge.

THE POSTMAN  (*Laughing*)  Some job! Well, s'long.

JOHNNY  S'long. I'll see he gets it. (THE POSTMAN *goes out.* JOHNNY *scrutinizes the letter.*) You got good eyes, Larry. Where's it from?

LARRY  (*After a glance*)  St. Paul. That'll be in Minnesota, I'm thinkin'. Looks like a woman's writing, too, the old divil!

JOHNNY He's got a daughter somewheres out West, I think he told me once. (*He puts the letter on the cash register.*) Come to think of it, I ain't seen old Chris in a dog's age. (*Putting his overcoat on, he comes around the end of the bar.*) Guess I'll be gettin' home. See you tomorrow.

LARRY Good-night to ye, boss. (*As* JOHNNY *goes toward the street door, it is pushed open and* CHRISTOPHER CHRISTOPHERSON *enters. He is a short, squat, broad-shouldered man of about fifty, with a round, weather-beaten, red face from which his light blue eyes peer short-sightedly, twinkling with a simple good humor. His large mouth, overhung by a thick, drooping, yellow mustache, is childishly self-willed and weak, of an obstinate kindliness. A thick neck is jammed like a post into the heavy trunk of his body. His arms with their big, hairy, freckled hands, and his stumpy legs terminating in large flat feet, are awkwardly short and muscular. He walks with a clumsy, rolling gait. His voice, when not raised in a hollow boom, is toned down to a sly, confidential half-whisper with something vaguely plaintive in its quality. He is dressed in a wrinkled, ill-fitting dark suit of shore clothes, and wears a faded cap of gray cloth over his mop of grizzled, blond hair. Just now his face beams with a too-blissfull happiness, and he has evidently been drinking. He reaches his hand out to* JOHNNY.)

CHRIS Hello, Yohnny! Have drink on me. Come on, Larry. Give us drink. Have one yourself. (*Putting his hand in his pocket.*) Ay gat money—plenty money. . . .

JOHNNY (*Shakes* CHRIS *by the hand*) Speak of the devil. We was just talkin' about you.

LARRY (*Coming to the end of the bar*) Hello, Chris. Put it there. (*They shake hands.*)

CHRIS (*Beaming*) Give us drink.

JOHNNY (*With a grin*) You got a half snootful now. Where'd you get it?

CHRIS (*Grinning*) Oder fallar on oder barge—Irish fallar—he gat bottle vhisky and we drank it, yust us two. Dot vhisky gat kick, by yingo! Ay yust come ashore. Give us drink, Larry. Ay vas little drunk, not much. Yust feel good. (*He laughs and commences to sing in a nasal, high-pitched quaver.*)

"My Yosephine, come aboard de ship. Long time Ay vait for you.
De moon. she shi-i-i-ine. She looka yus like you.
Tchee-tchee, tchee-tchee, tchee-tchee, tchee-tchee."

(*To the accompaniment of this last he waves his hand as if he were conducting an orchestra.*)

JOHNNY (*With a laugh*) Same old Yosie, eh Chris?

CHRIS You don't know good song when you hear him. Italian fallar on oder barge, he learn me dat. Give us drink. (*He throws change on the bar.*)

LARRY (*With a professional air*) What's your pleasure, gentlemen?

JOHNNY Small beer, Larry.

CHRIS Vhisky—Number Two.

LARRY (*As he gets their drinks*) I'll take a cigar on you.

CHRIS (*Lifting his glass*) Skoal! (*He drinks.*)

JOHNNY Drink hearty.

CHRIS (*Immediately*) Have oder drink.

JOHNNY No. Some other time. Got to go home now. So you've just landed? Where are you in from this time?

CHRIS Norfolk. Ve make slow voyage—dirty vedder—yust fog, fog, fog, all bloody time! (*There is an insistent ring from the doorbell at the family entrance in the back room.* CHRIS *gives a start—hurriedly.*) Ay go open, Larry. Ay forgat. It vas Marthy. She come with me. (*He goes into the back room.*)

LARRY (*With a chuckle*) He's still got that same cow livin' with him, the old fool!

JOHNNY (*With a grin*) A sport, Chris is. Well, I'll beat it home. S'long. (*He goes to the street door.*)

LARRY So long, boss.

JOHNNY Oh—don't forget to give him his letter.

LARRY I won't. (JOHNNY *goes out. In the meantime,* CHRIS *has opened the family entrance door, admitting* MARTHY. *She might be forty or fifty. Her jowly, mottled face, with its thick red nose, is streaked with interlacing purple veins. Her thick, gray hair is piled anyhow in a greasy mop on top of her round head. Her figure is flabby and fat; her breath comes in wheezy gasps; she speaks in a loud, mannish voice, punctuated by explosions of hoarse laughter. But there still twinkles in her blood-shot blue eyes a youthful lust for life which hard usage has failed to stifle, a sense of humor mocking, but good-tempered. She wears a man's cap, doublebreasted man's jacket, and a grimy, calico skirt. Her bare feet are encased in a man's brogans several sizes too large for her, which gives her a shuffling, wobbly gait.*)

MARTHY (*Grumblingly*) What yuh tryin' to do, Dutchy—keep me standin' out there all day? (*She comes forward and sits at the table in the right corner, front.*)

CHRIS (*Mollifyingly*) Ay'm sorry, Marthy. Ay talk to Yohnny. Ay forgat. What you goin' take for drink?

MARTHY (*Appeased*) Gimme a scoop of lager an' ale.

CHRIS Ay go bring him back. (*He returns to the bar.*) Lager and ale for Marthy, Larry. Vhisky for me. (*He throws change on the bar.*)

LARRY Right you are. (*Then remembering, he takes the letter from in back of the bar.*) Here's a letter for you—from St. Paul, Minnesota—and a lady's writin'. (*He grins.*)

CHRIS (*Quickly—taking it*) Oh, den it come from my daughter, Anna. She live dere. (*He turns the letter over in his hands uncertainly.*) Ay don't gat letter from Anna—must be a year.

LARRY (*Jokingly*) That's a fine fairy tale to be tellin'—your daughter! Sure I'll bet it's some bum.

CHRIS (*Soberly*) No. Dis come from Anna. (*Engrossed by the letter in his hand—uncertainly.*) By golly, Ay tank Ay'm too drunk for read dis letter from Anna. Ay tank Ay sat down for a minute. You bring drinks in back room, Larry. (*He goes into the room on right.*)

MARTHY (*Angrily*) Where's my lager an' ale, yuh big stiff?

CHRIS (*Preoccupied*) Larry bring him. (*He sits down opposite her. LARRY brings in the drinks and sets them on the table. He and MARTHY exchange nods of recognition. LARRY stands looking at CHRIS curiously. MARTHY takes a long draught of her schooner and heaves a huge sigh of satisfaction, wiping her mouth with the back of her hand. CHRIS stares at the letter for a moment—slowly opens it, and, squinting his eyes, commences to read laboriously, his lips moving as he spells out the words. As he reads his face lights up with an expression of mingled joy and bewilderment.*)

LARRY Good news?

MARTHY (*Her curiosity also aroused*) What's that yuh got—a letter, fur Gawd's sake?

CHRIS (*Pauses for a moment, after finishing the letter, as if to let the news sink in—then suddenly pounds his fist on the table with happy excitement*) Py yiminy! Yust tank, Anna say she's comin' here right avay! She gat sick on yob in St. Paul, she say. It's short letter, don't tal me much more'n dat. (*Beaming.*) Py golly, dat's good news all at one time for ole fallar! (*Then turning to MARTHY, rather shamefacedly.*) You know, Marthy, Ay've tole you Ay don't see my Anna since she vas little gel in Sveden five year ole.

MARTHY How old'll she be now?

CHRIS She must be—lat me see—she must be twenty year ole, py Yo!

LARRY (*Surprised*) You've not seen her in fifteen years?

CHRIS (*Suddenly growing somber—in a low tone*) No. Ven she vas little gel, Ay vas bo'sun on vindjammer. Ay never gat home only few time dem year. Ay'm fool sailor fallar. My voman—Anna's mother—she gat tired vait all time Sveden for me ven Ay don't never come. She come dis country, bring Anna, dey go out Minnesota, live with her cousins on farm. Den ven her mo'der die ven Ay vas on voyage, Ay tank it's better dem cousins keep Anna. Ay tank it's better Anna live on farm, den she don't know dat ole davil, sea, she don't know fa'der like me.

LARRY (*With a wink at* MARTHY) This girl, now, 'll be marryin' a sailor herself, likely. It's in the blood.

CHRIS (*Suddenly springing to his feet and smashing his fist on the table in a rage*) No, py God! She don't do dat!

MARTHY (*Grasping her schooner hastily—angrily*) Hey, look out, yuh nut! Wanta spill my suds for me?

LARRY (*Amazed*) Oho, what's up with you? Ain't you a sailor yourself now, and always been?

CHRIS (*Slowly*) Dat's yust vhy Ay say it. (*Forcing a smile.*) Sailor vas all right fallar, but not for marry gel. No. Ay know dat. Anna's mo'der, she know it, too.

LARRY (*As* CHRIS *remains sunk in gloomy reflection*) When is your daughter comin'? Soon?

CHRIS (*Roused*) Py yiminy, Ay forgat. (*Reads through the letter hurriedly.*) She say she come right avay, dat's all.

LARRY She'll maybe be comin' here to look for you, I s'pose. (*He returns to the bar, whistling. Left alone with* MARTHY, *who stares at him with a twinkle of malicious humor in her eyes,* CHRIS *suddenly becomes desperately ill-at-ease. He fidgets, then gets up hurriedly.*)

CHRIS Ay gat speak with Larry. Ay be right back. (*Mollifyingly.*) Ay bring you oder drink.

MARTHY (*Emptying her glass*) Sure. That's me. (*As he retreats with the glass she guffaws after him derisively.*)

CHRIS (*To* LARRY *in an alarmed whisper*) Py yingo, Ay gat gat

Marthy shore off barge before Anna come! Anna raise hell if she find dat out. Marthy raise hell, too, for go, py golly!

LARRY (WITH A CHUCKLE) Serve ye right, ye old divil—havin' a woman at your age!

CHRIS (*Scratching his head in a quandary*) You tal me lie for tal Marthy, Larry, so's she gat off barge quick.

LARRY She knows your daughter's comin'. Tell her to get the hell out of it.

CHRIS No. Ay don't like make her feel bad.

LARRY You're an old mush! Keep your girl away from the barge, then. She'll likely want to stay ashore anyway. (*Curiously.*) What does she work at, your Anna?

CHRIS She stay on dem cousins' farm till two year ago. Dan she gat yob nurse gel in St. Paul. (*Then shaking his head resolutely.*) But Ay don't vant for her gat yob now. Ay vant for her stay with me.

LARRY (*Scornfully*) On a coal barge! She'll not like that, I'm thinkin'.

MARTHY (*Shouts from next room*) Don't I get that bucket o' suds, Dutchy?

CHRIS (*Startled—in apprehensive confusion*) Yes, Ay come, Marthy.

LARRY (*Drawing the lager and ale, hands it to* CHRIS—*laughing.*) Now you're in for it! You'd better tell her straight to get out!

CHRIS (*Shaking in his boots*) Py golly. (*He takes her drink in to* MARTHY *and sits down at the table. She sips it in silence.* LARRY *moves quietly close to the partition to listen, grinning with expectation.* CHRIS *seems on the verge of speaking, hesitates, gulps down his whisky desperately as if seeking for courage. He attempts to whistle a few bars of "Yosephine" with careless bravado, but the whistle peters out futilely.* MARTHY *stares at him keenly, taking in his embarrassment with a malicious twinkle of amusement in her eye.* CHRIS *clears his throat.*) Marthy——

MARTHY (*Aggressively*) Wha's that? (*Then, pretending to fly into a rage, her eyes enjoying* CHRIS' *misery.*) I'm wise to what's in back of your nut, Dutchy. Yuh want to git rid o' me, huh?—now she's comin'. Gimme the bum's rush ashore, huh? Lemme tell yuh, Dutchy, there ain't a square-head workin' on a boat man enough to git away with that. Don't start nothin' yuh can't finish!

CHRIS (*Miserably*) Ay don't start nutting, Marthy.

MARTHY (*Glares at him for a second—then cannot control a burst of laughter*) Ho-ho! yuh're a scream, Square-head—an honest-ter-Gawd knockout! Ho-ho! (*She wheezes, panting for breath.*)

CHRIS (*With childish pique*) Ay don't see nutting for laugh at.

MARTHY Take a slant in the mirror and yuh'll see. Ho-ho! (*Recovering from her mirth—chuckling, scornfully.*) A square-head tryin' to kid Marthy Owen at this late day!—after me campin' with barge men the last twenty years. I'm wise to the game, up, down, and sideways. I ain't been born and dragged up on the water front for nothin'. Think I'd make trouble, huh? Not me! I'll pack up me duds an' beat it. I'm quittin' yuh, get me? I'm tellin' yuh I'm sick of stickin' with yuh, and I'm leavin' yuh flat, see? There's plenty of other guys on other barges waitin' for me. Always was, I always found. (*She claps the astonished* CHRIS *on the back.*) So cheer up, Dutchy! I'll be offen the barge before she comes. You'll be rid o' me for good—and me o' you—good riddance for both of us. Ho-ho!

CHRIS (*Seriously*) Ay don' tank dat. You vas good gel, Marthy.

MARTHY (*Grinning*) Good girl? Aw, can the bull! Well, yuh treated me square, yuhself. So it's fifty-fifty. Nobody's sore at nobody. We're still good frien's, huh? (LARRY *returns to bar.*)

CHRIS (*Beaming now that he sees his troubles disappearing*) Yes, py golly.

MARTHY That's the talkin'! In all my time I tried never to split with a guy with no hard feelin's. But what was yuh so scared about—that I'd kick up a row? That ain't Marthy's way. (*Scornfully.*) Think I'd break my heart to lose yuh? Commit suicide, huh? Ho-ho! Gawd! The world's full o' men if that's all I'd worry about! (*Then with a grin, after emptying her glass.*) Blow me to another scoop, huh? I'll drink your kid's health for yuh.

CHRIS (*Eagerly*) Sure tang. Ay go gat him. (*He takes the two glasses into the bar.*) Oder drink. Same for both.

LARRY (*Getting the drinks and putting them on the bar*) She's not such a bad lot, that one.

CHRIS (*Jovially*) She's good gel, Ay tal you! Py golly, Ay calabrate now! Give me vhisky here at bar, too. (*He puts down money.* LARRY *serves him.*) You have drink, Larry.

LARRY (*Virtuously*) You know I never touch it.

CHRIS You don't know what you miss. Skoal! (*He drinks—then begins to sing loudly.*) "My Yosephine, come board de ship——" (*He picks up the drinks for* MARTHY *and himself and walks unsteadily into the back room, singing.*)

"De moon, she shi-i-i-ine. She looks yust like you.
Tchee-tchee, Tchee-tchee, tchee-tchee, tchee-tchee."

MARTHY (*Grinning, hands to ears*) Gawd!

CHRIS (*Sitting down*) Ay'm good singer, yes? Ve drink, eh? Skoal! Ay calabrate! (*He drinks.*) Ay calabrate 'cause Anna's coming home. You know, Marthy, Ay never write for her to come, 'cause Ay tank Ay'm no good for her. But all time Ay hope like hell some day she vant for see me and den she come. And dat's vay it happen now, py yiminy! (*His face beaming.*) What you tank she look like, Marthy? Ay bet you she's fine, good, strong gel, pooty like hell! Living on farm made her like dat. And Ay bet you some day she marry good, steady land fallar here in East, have home all her own, have kits—and dan Ay'm ole grand-fader, py golly! And Ay go visit dem every time Ay gat in port near! (*Bursting with joy.*) By yiminy crickens, Ay calabrate dat! (*Shouts.*) Bring oder drink, Larry! (*He smashes his fist on the table with a bang.*)

LARRY (*Coming in from bar—irritably*) Easy there! Don't be breakin' the table, you old goat!

CHRIS (*By way of reply, grins foolishly and begins to sing*) "My Yosephine, come board de ship——"

MARTHY (*Touching CHRIS' arm persuasively*) You're soused to the ears, Dutchy. Go out and put a feed into you. It'll sober you up. (*Then as CHRIS shakes his head obstinately.*) Listen, yuh old nut! Yuh don't know what time your kid's liable to show up. Yuh want to be sober when she comes, don't yuh?

CHRIS (*Aroused—gets unsteadily to his feet*) Py golly, yes.

LARRY That's good sense for you. A good beef stew'll fix you. Go round the corner.

CHRIS All right. Ay be back soon, Marthy. (*CHRIS goes through the bar and out the street door.*)

LARRY He'll come round all right with some grub in him.

MARTHY Sure. (*LARRY goes back to the bar and resumes his news-paper. MARTHY sips what is left of her schooner reflectively. There is the ring of the family entrance bell. LARRY comes to the door and opens it a trifle—then, with a puzzled expression, pulls it wide. ANNA CHRISTOPHERSON enters. She is a tall, blond, fully-developed girl of twenty, handsome after a large, Viking-daughter fashion but now run down in health and plainly show-ing all the outward evidences of belonging to the world's oldest profession. Her youthful face is already hard and cynical be-*

*neath its layer of make-up. Her clothes are the tawdry finery of peasant stock turned prostitute. She comes and sinks wearily in a chair by the table, left front.*)

ANNA  Gimme a whisky—ginger ale on the side. (*Then, as* LARRY *turns to go, forcing a winning smile at him.*) And don't be stingy, baby.

LARRY  (*Sarcastically*)  Shall I serve it in a pail?

ANNA  (*With a hard laugh*)  That suits me down to the ground. (LARRY *goes into the bar. The two women size each other up with frank stares.* LARRY *comes back with the drink which he sets before* ANNA *and returns to the bar again.* ANNA *downs her drink at a gulp. Then, after a moment, as the alcohol begins to rouse her, she turns to* MARTHY *with a friendly smile.*) Gee, I needed that bad, all right, all right!

MARTHY  (*Nodding her head sympathetically*)  Sure—yuh look all in. Been on a bat?

ANNA  No—traveling—day and a half on the train. Had to sit up all night in the dirty coach, too. Gawd, I thought I'd never get here!

MARTHY  (*With a start—looking at her intently*)  Where'd yuh come from, huh?

ANNA  St. Paul—out in Minnesota.

MARTHY  (*Staring at her in amazement—slowly*)  So—yuh're—— (*She suddenly bursts out into hoarse, ironical laughter.*) Gawd!

ANNA  All the way from Minnesota, sure. (*Flaring up.*) What you laughing at? Me?

MARTHY  (*Hastily*)  No, honest, kid. I was thinkin' of somethin' else.

ANNA  (*Mollified—with a smile*)  Well, I wouldn't blame you, at that. Guess I do look rotten—yust out of the hospital two weeks. I'm going to have another 'ski. What d'you say? Have something on me?

MARTHY  Sure I will. T'anks. (*She calls.*) Hey, Larry! Little service! (*He comes in.*)

ANNA  Same for me.

MARTHY  Same here. (*Larry takes their glasses and goes out.*)

ANNA  Why don't you come sit over here, be sociable. I'm a dead stranger in this burg—and I ain't spoke a word with no one since day before yesterday.

MARTHY  Sure thing. (*She shuffles over to* ANNA's *table and sits down opposite her.* LARRY *brings the drinks and* ANNA *pays him.*)

ANNA  Skoal! Here's how! (*She drinks.*)

MARTHY  Here's luck! (*She takes a gulp from her schooner.*)

ANNA  (*Taking a package of Sweet Caporal cigarettes from her bag*) Let you smoke in here, won't they?

MARTHY  (*Doubtfully*)  Sure. (*Then with evident anxiety.*) On'y trow it away if yuh hear someone comin'.

ANNA  (*Lighting one and taking a deep inhale*)  Gee, they're fussy in this dump, ain't they? (*She puffs, staring at the table top.* MARTHY *looks her over with a new penetrating interest, taking in every detail of her face.* ANNA *suddenly becomes conscious of this appraising stare—resentfully.*) Ain't nothing wrong with me, is there? You're looking hard enough.

MARTHY  (*Irritated by the other's tone—scornfully*)  Ain't got to look much. I got your number the minute you stepped in the door.

ANNA  (*Her eyes narrowing*)  Ain't you smart! Well, I got yours, too, without no trouble. You're me forty years from now. That's you! (*She gives a hard little laugh.*)

MARTHY  (*Angrily*)  Is that so? Well, I'll tell you straight, kiddo, that Marthy Owen never—— (*She catches herself up short—with a grin.*) What are you and me scrappin' over? Let's cut it out, huh? Me, I don't want no hard feelin's with no one. (*Extending her hand.*) Shake and forget it, huh?

ANNA  (*Shakes her hand gladly*)  Only too glad to. I ain't looking for trouble. Let's have 'nother. What d'you say?

MARTHY  (*Shaking her head*)  Not for mine. I'm full up. And you ——Had anythin' to eat lately?

ANNA  Not since this morning on the train.

MARTHY  Then yuh better go easy on it, hadn't yuh?

ANNA  (*After a moment's hesitation*)  Guess you're right. I got to meet someone, too. But my nerves is on edge after that rotten trip.

MARTHY  Yuh said yuh was just outa the hospital?

ANNA  Two weeks ago. (*Leaning over to* MARTHY *confidentially.*) The joint I was in out in St. Paul got raided. That was the start. The judge give all us girls thirty days. The others didn't seem to mind being in the cooler much. Some of 'em was used to it. But me, I couldn't stand it. It got my goat right—couldn't eat or sleep or nothing. I never could stand being caged up nowheres. I got good and sick and they had to send me to the hospital. It was nice there. I was sorry to leave it, honest!

MARTHY (*After a slight pause*) Did yuh say yuh got to meet some-one here?

ANNA Yes. Oh, not what you mean. It's my Old Man I got to meet. Honest! It's funny, too. I ain't seen him since I was a kid—don't even know what he looks like—yust had a letter every now and then. This was always the only address he give me to write him back. He's yanitor of some building here now—used to be a sailor.

MARTHY (*Astonished*) Janitor!

ANNA Sure. And I was thinking maybe, seeing he ain't never done a thing for me in my life, he might be willing to stake me to a room and eats till I get rested up. (*Wearily.*) Gee, I sure need that rest! I'm knocked out. (*Then resignedly.*) But I ain't ex-pecting much from him. Give you a kick when you're down, that's what all men do. (*With sudden passion.*) Men, I hate 'em —all of 'em! And I don't expect he'll turn out no better than the rest. (*Then with sudden interest.*) Say, do you hang out around this dump much?

MARTHY Oh, off and on.

ANNA Then maybe you know him—my Old Man—or at least seen him?

MARTHY It ain't old Chris, is it?

ANNA Old Chris?

MARTHY Chris Christopherson, his full name is.

ANNA (*Excitedly*) Yes, that's him! Anna Christopherson—that's my real name—only out there I called myself Anna Christie. So you know him, eh?

MARTHY (*Evasively*) Seen him about for years.

ANNA Say, what's he like, tell me, honest?

MARTHY Oh, he's short and——

ANNA (*Impatiently*) I don't care what he looks like. What kind is he?

MARTHY (*Earnestly*) Well, yuh can bet your life, kid, he's as good an old guy as ever walked on two feet. That goes!

ANNA (*Pleased*) I'm glad to hear it. Then you think he'll stake me to that rest cure I'm after?

MARTHY (*Emphatically*) Surest thing you know. (*Disgustedly.*) But where'd you get the idea he was a janitor?

ANNA He wrote me he was himself.

MARTHY Well, he was lyin'. He ain't. He's captain of a barge—five men under him.

ANNA (*Disgusted in her turn*) A barge? What kind of a barge?

MARTHY  Coal, mostly.

ANNA  A coal barge! (*With a harsh laugh.*) If that ain't a swell job to find your long lost Old Man working at! Gee, I knew something'd be bound to turn out wrong—always does with me. That puts my idea of his giving me a rest on the bum.

MARTHY  What d'yuh mean?

ANNA  I s'pose he lives on the boat, don't he?

MARTHY  Sure. What about it? Can't you live on it, too?

ANNA  (*Scornfully.*)  Me? On a dirty coal barge! What d'you think I am?

MARTHY  (*Resentfully*)  What d'yuh know about barges, huh? Bet yuh ain't never seen one. That's what comes of his bringing yuh up inland—away from the old devil sea—where yuh'd be safe—Gawd! (*The irony of it strikes her sense of humor and she laughs hoarsely.*)

ANNA  (*Angrily*)  His bringing me up! Is that what he tells people! I like his nerve! He let them cousins of my Old Woman's keep me on their farm and work me to death like a dog.

MARTHY  Well, he's got queer notions on some things. I've heard him say a farm was the best place for a kid.

ANNA  Sure. That's what he'd always answer back—and a lot of crazy stuff about staying away from the sea—stuff I couldn't make head or tail to. I thought he must be nutty.

MARTHY  He is on that one point. (*Casually.*) So yuh didn't fall for life on the farm, huh?

ANNA  I should say not! The old man of the family, his wife, and four sons—I had to slave for all of 'em. I was only a poor relation, and they treated me worse than they dare treat a hired girl. (*After a moment's hesitation—somberly.*) It was one of the sons —the youngest—started me—when I was sixteen. After that, I hated 'em so I'd killed 'em all if I'd stayed. So I run away—to St. Paul.

MARTHY  (*Who has been listening sympathetically*)  I've heard Old Chris talkin' about your bein' a nurse girl out there. Was that all a bluff yuh put up when yuh wrote him?

ANNA  Not on your life, it wasn't. It was true for two years. I didn't go wrong all at one jump. Being a nurse girl was yust what finished me. Taking care of other people's kids, always listening to their bawling and crying, caged in, when you're only a kid yourself and want to go out and see things. At last I got the chance—to get into that house. And you bet your life I took it! (*Defiantly.*) And I ain't sorry neither. (*After a pause—with bitter hatred.*) It was all men's fault—the whole business. It was men on the farm ordering and beating me—and giving me the wrong start. Then when I was a nurse, it was men again hanging around, bothering me, trying to see what they could get. (*She gives a hard laugh.*) And now it's men all the time. Gawd, I hate 'em all, every mother's son of 'em! Don't you?

MARTHY   Oh, I dunno. There's good ones and bad ones, kid. You've just had a run of bad luck with 'em, that's all. Your Old Man, now—old Chris—he's a good one.

ANNA (*Sceptically*)   He'll have to show me.

MARTHY   Yuh kept right on writing him yuh was a nurse girl still, even after yuh was in the house, didn't yuh?

ANNA   Sure. (*Cynically.*) Not that I think he'd care a darn.

MARTHY   Yuh're all wrong about him, kid. (*Earnestly.*) I know Old Chris well for a long time. He's talked to me 'bout you lots o' times. He thinks the world o' you, honest he does.

ANNA   Aw, quit the kiddin'!

MARTHY   Honest! Only, he's a simple old guy, see? He's got nutty notions. But he means well, honest. Listen to me, kid—— (*She is interrupted by the opening and shutting of the street door in the bar and by hearing* CHRIS' *voice.*) Ssshh!

ANNA   What's up?

CHRIS (*Who has entered the bar. He seems considerably sobered up*)   Py golly, Larry, dat grub taste good. Marthy in back?

LARRY   Sure—and another tramp with her. (*Chris starts for the entrance to the back room.*)

MARTHY (*To* ANNA *in a hurried, nervous whisper*)   That's him now. He's comin' in here. Brace up!

ANNA   Who? (*Chris opens the door.*)

MARTHY (*As if she were greeting him for the first time*)   Why hello, Old Chris. (*Then before he can speak, she shuffles hurriedly past him into the bar, beckoning him to follow her.*) Come here. I wanta tell yuh somethin'. (*He goes out to her. She speaks hurriedly in a low voice.*) Listen! I'm goin' to beat it down to the barge—pack up me duds and blow. That's her in there— your Anna—just come—waitin' for yuh. Treat her right, see? She's been sick. Well, s'long! (*She goes into the back room— to* ANNA.) S'long kid. I gotta beat it now. See yuh later.

ANNA (*Nervously*)   So long. (MARTHY *goes quickly out of the family entrance.*)

LARRY (*Looking at the stupefied* CHRIS *curiously*) Well, what's up now?

CHRIS (*Vaguely*) Nutting—nutting. (*He stands before the door to the back room in an agony of embarrassed emotion—then he forces himself to a bold decision, pushes open the door and walks in. He stands there, casts a shy glance at* ANNA, *whose brilliant clothes, and, to him, high-toned appearance, awe him terribly. He looks about him with pitiful nervousness as if to avoid the appraising look with which she takes in his face, his clothes, etc. —his voice seeming to plead for her forbearance.*) Anna!

ANNA (*Acutely embarrassed in her turn*) Hello—father. She told me it was you. I yust got here a little while ago.

CHRIS (*Goes slowly over to her chair*) It's good—for see you—after all dem years, Anna. (*He bends down over her. After an embarrassed struggle they manage to kiss each other.*)

ANNA (*A trace of genuine feeling in her voice*) It's good to see you, too.

CHRIS (*Grasps her arms and looks into her face—then overcome by a wave of fierce tenderness*) Anna lilla! Anna lilla! (*Takes her in his arms.*)

ANNA (*Shrinks away from him, half-frightened*) What's that— Swedish? I don't know it. (*Then as if seeking relief from the tension in a voluble chatter.*) Gee, I had an awful trip coming here. I'm all in. I had to sit up in the dirty coach all night— couldn't get no sleep, hardly—and then I had a hard job finding this place. I never been in New York before, you know, and——

CHRIS (*Who has been staring down at her face admiringly, not hearing what she says—impulsively*) You know you vas awful pooty gel, Anna? Ay bet all men see you fall in love with you, py yiminy!

ANNA (*Repelled—harshly*) Cut it! You talk same as they all do.

CHRIS (*Hurt—humbly*) Ain't no harm for your fader talk dat vay, Anna.

ANNA (*Forcing a short laugh*) No—course not. Only—it's funny to see you and not remember nothing. You're like—a stranger.

CHRIS (*Sadly*) Ay s'pose. Ay never come home only few times ven you vas kit in Sveden. You don't remember dat?

ANNA No. (*Resentfully.*) But why didn't you never come home them days? Why didn't you never come out West to see me?

CHRIS (*Slowly*) Ay tank, after your mo'der die, ven Ay vas avay on voyage, it's better for you you don't never see me! (*He sinks down in the chair opposite her dejectedly—then turns to her —sadly.*) Ay don't know, Anna, vhy Ay never come home in Sveden in old year. Ay vant come home end of every voyage. Ay vant see your mo'der, your two bro'der before dey vas drowned, you ven you vas born—but—Ay—don't go. Ay sign on oder ships —go South America, go Australia, go China, go every port all over world many times—but Ay never go aboard ship sail for Sveden. Ven Ay gat money for pay passage home as passenger den—(*He bows his head guiltily.*) Ay forgat and Ay spend all money. Ven Ay tank again, it's too late. (*He sighs.*) Ay don't know why but dat's vay with most sailor fallar, Anna. Dat ole davil sea make dem crazy fools with her dirty tricks. It's so.

ANNA (*Who has watched him keenly while he has been speaking— with a trace of scorn in her voice*) Then you think the sea's to blame for everything, eh? Well, you're still workin' on it, ain't you, spite of all you used to write me about hating it. That dame was here told me you was captain of a coal barge—and you wrote me you was yanitor of a building!

CHRIS (*Embarrassed but lying glibly*) Oh, Ay vork on land long time as yanitor. Yust short time ago Ay gat dis job cause Ay vas sick, need open air.

ANNA (*Sceptically*) Sick? You? You'd never think it.

CHRIS And, Anna, dis ain't real sailor yob. Dis ain't real boat on sea. She's yust old tub—like piece of land with house on it dat float. Yob on her ain't sea yob. No. Ay don't gat yob on sea, Anna, if Ay die first. Ay swear dat ven your mo'der die. Ay keep my word, py yingo!

ANNA (*Perplexed*) Well, I can't see no difference. (*Dismissing the subject.*) Speaking of being sick, I been there myself—yust out of the hospital two weeks ago.

CHRIS (*Immediately all concern*) You Anna? Py golly! (*Anxiously.*) You feel better now, dough, don't you? You look little tired, dat's all!

ANNA (*Wearily*) I am. Tired to death. I need a long rest and I don't see much chance of getting it.

CHRIS What you mean, Anna?

ANNA Well, when I made up my mind to come to see you, I thought you was a yanitor—that you'd have a place where, maybe, if you didn't mind having me, I could visit a while and rest up—till I felt able to get back on the job again.

CHRIS (*Eagerly*) But Ay gat place, Anna—nice place. You rest all you want, py yiminy! You don't never have to vork as nurse gel no more. You stay with me, py golly!

ANNA (*Surprised and pleased by his eagerness—with a smile*) Then you're really glad to see me—honest?

CHRIS (*Pressing one of her hands in both of his*) Anna, Ay like see you like hell, Ay tal you! And don't you talk no more about gatting yob. You stay with me. Ay don't see you for long time, you don't forgat dat. (*His voice trembles.*) Ay'm gatting ole. Ay gat no one in vorld but you.

ANNA (*Touched—embarrassed by this unfamiliar emotion*) Thanks. It sounds good to hear someone—talk to me that way. Say, though—if you're so lonely—it's funny—why ain't you ever married again?

CHRIS (*Shaking his head emphatically—after a pause*) Ay love your mo'der too much for ever do dat, Anna.

ANNA (*Impressed—slowly*) I don't remember nothing about her. What was she like? Tell me.

CHRIS Ay tal you all about everytang—and you tal me all tangs happen to you. But not here now. Dis ain't good place for young gel, anyway. Only no good sailor fallar come here for gat drunk. (*He gets to his feet quickly and picks up her bag.*) You come with me, Anna. You need lie down, get rest.

ANNA (*Half rises to her feet, then sits down again*) Where're you going?

CHRIS Come. Ve gat on board.

ANNA (*Disappointedly*) On board your barge, you mean? (*Dryly.*) Nix for mine! (*Then seeing his crestfallen look—forcing a smile.*) Do you think that's a good place for a young girl like me—a coal barge?

CHRIS (*Dully*) Yes, Ay tank. (*He hesitates—then continues more and more pleadingly.*) You don't know how nice it's on barge, Anna. Tug come and ve gat towed out on voyage—yust water all round, and sun, and fresh air, and good grub for make you strong, healthy gel. You see many tangs you don't see before. You gat moonlight at night, maybe; see steamer pass; see schooner make sail—see everytang dat's pooty. You need take rest like dat. You work too hard for young gel already. You need vacation, yes!

ANNA (*Who has listened to him with a growing interest—with an uncertain laugh*) It sounds good to hear you tell it. I'd sure like a trip on the water, all right. It's the barge idea has me stopped. Well, I'll go down with you and have a look—and maybe I'll take a chance. Gee, I'd do anything once.

CHRIS (*Picks up her bag again*) Ve go, eh?

ANNA What's the rush? Wait a second. (*Forgetting the situation for a moment, she relapses into the familiar form and flashes one of her winning trade smiles at him.*) Gee, I'm thirsty.

CHRIS (*Sets down her bag immediately—hastily*) Ay'm sorry, Anna. What you tank you like for drink, eh?

ANNA (*Promptly*) I'll take a—— (*Then suddenly reminded—confusedly.*) I don't know. What'a they got here?

CHRIS (*With a grin*) Ay don't tank dey got much fancy drink for young gel in dis place, Anna. Yinger ale—sas-prilla, maybe.

ANNA (*Forcing a laugh herself*) Make it sas, then.

CHRIS (*Coming up to her—with a wink*) Ay tal you, Anna, ve calabrate, yes—dis one time because ve meet after many year. (*In a half whisper, embarrassedly.*) Dey gat good port wine, Anna. It's a good for you, Ay tank—little bit—for give you appetite. It ain't strong, neider. One glass don't go to your head. Ay promise.

ANNA (*With a half hysterical laugh*) All right. I'll take port.

CHRIS Ay go gat him. (*He goes to the bar. As soon as the door closes,* ANNA *starts to her feet.*)

ANNA (*Picking up her bag—half-aloud—stammeringly*) Gawd, I can't stand this! I better beat it. (*Then she lets her bag drop, stumbles over to her chair again, and covering her face with her hands, begins to sob.*)

LARRY (*Putting down his paper as* CHRIS *comes up—with a grin*) Well, who's the blond?

CHRIS (*Proudly*) Dat vas Anna, Larry.

LARRY (*In amazement*) Your daughter, Anna? (CHRIS *nods.* LARRY *lets a long, low whistle escape him and turns away embarrassedly.*)

CHRIS Don't you tank she vas pooty gel, Larry?

LARRY (*Rising to the occasion*) Sure! A peach!

CHRIS You bet you! Give me drink for take back—one port vine for Anna—she calabrate dis one time with me—and small beer for me.

LARRY (*As he gets the drinks*) Small beer for you, eh? She's reformin' you already.

CHRIS (*Pleased*) You bet! (*He takes the drinks. As she hears him coming,* ANNA *hastily dries her eyes, tries to smile.* CHRIS *comes in and sets the drinks down on the table—stares at her for a second anxiously—patting her hand.*)  You look tired Anna. Vell, Ay make you take good long rest now. (*Picking up his beer.*) Come, you drink vine. It put new life in you. (*She lifts her glass—he grins.*) Skoal, Anna! You know dat Svedish word?

ANNA  Skoal! (*Downing her port at a gulp like a drink of whisky —her lips trembling.*) Skoal? Guess I know that word, all right!

*Curtain*

# ACT TWO

Scene—*Ten days later. The stern of the deeply-laden barge,* Simeon Winthrop, *at anchor in the outer harbor of Provincetown, Mass. It is ten o'clock at night. Dense fog shrouds the barge on all sides, and she floats motionless on a calm. A lantern set up on an immense coil of thick hawser sheds a dull, filtering light on objects near it— the heavy steel bits for making fast the tow lines, etc. In the rear is the cabin, its misty windows glowing wanly with the light of a lamp inside. The chimney of the cabin stove rises a few feet above the roof. The doleful tolling of bells, on Long Point, on ships at anchor, breaks the silence at regular intervals.*

*As the curtain rises,* ANNA *is discovered standing near the coil of rope on which the lantern is placed. She looks healthy, transformed, the natural color has come back to her face. She has on a black oilskin coat, but wears no hat. She is staring out into the fog astern with an expression of awed wonder. The cabin door is pushed open and* CHRIS *appears. He is dressed in yellow oilskins— coat, pants, sou'wester—and wears high sea-boots.*

CHRIS (*The glare from the cabin still in his eyes, peers blinkingly astern*) Anna! (*Receiving no reply, he calls again, this time with apparent apprehension.*) Anna!

ANNA (*With a start—making a gesture with her hand as if to impose silence—in a hushed whisper*) Yes, here I am. What d'you want?

CHRIS (*Walks over to her—solicitously*) Don't you come turn in, Anna? It's late—after four bells. It ain't good for you to stay out here in fog, Ay tank.

ANNA Why not? (*With a trace of strange exultation.*) I love this fog! Honest! It's so——(*She hesitates, groping for a word.*) Funny and still. I feel as if I was—out of things altogether.

CHRIS (*Spitting disgustedly*) Fog's vorst one of her dirty tricks, py yingo!

ANNA (*With a short laugh*) Beefing about the sea again? I'm getting so's I love it, the little I've seen.

CHRIS (*Glancing at her moodily*) Dat's foolish talk, Anna. You see her more, you don't talk dat vay. (*Then seeing her irritation, he hastily adopts a more cheerful tone.*) But Ay'm glad you like it on barge. Ay'm glad it makes you feel good again. (*With a placating grin.*) You like live like dis alone with ole fa'der, eh?

ANNA Sure I do. Everything's been so different from anything I ever come across before. And now—this fog—Gee, I wouldn't have missed it for nothing. I never thought living on ships was so different from land. Gee, I'd yust love to work on it, honest I would, if I was a man. I don't wonder you always been a sailor.

CHRIS (*Vehemently*) Ay ain't sailor, Anna. And dis ain't real sea. You only see nice part. (*Than as she doesn't answer, he continues hopefully.*) Vell, fog lift in morning, Ay tank.

ANNA (*The exultation again in her voice*) I love it! I don't give a rap if it never lifts! (CHRIS *fidgets from one foot to the other worriedly,* ANNA *continues slowly, after a pause.*) It makes me feel clean—out here—'s if I'd taken a bath.

CHRIS (*After a pause*) You better go in cabin read book. Dat put you to sleep.

ANNA I don't want to sleep. I want to stay out here—and think about things.

CHRIS (*Walks away from her toward the cabin—then comes back*) You act funny tonight, Anna.

ANNA (*Her voice rising angrily*) Say, what're you trying to do—make things rotten? You been kind as kind can be to me and I certainly appreciate it—only don't spoil it all now. (*Then, seeing the hurt expression on her father's face, she forces a smile.*) Let's talk of something else. Come. Sit down here. (*She points to the coil of rope.*)

CHRIS (*Sits down beside her with a sigh*) It's gatting pooty late in night, Anna. Must be near five bells.

ANNA (*Interestedly*) Five bells? What time is that?

CHRIS Half past ten.

ANNA Funny I don't know nothing about sea talk—but those cousins was always talking crops and that stuff. Gee, wasn't I sick of it—and of them!

CHRIS You don't like live on farm, Anna?

ANNA I've told you a hundred times I hated it. (*Decidedly.*) I'd rather have one drop of ocean than all the farms in the world! Honest! And you wouldn't like a farm, neither. Here's where you belong. (*She makes a sweeping gesture seaward.*) But not on a coal barge. You belong on a real ship, sailing all over the world.

CHRIS (*Moodily*) Ay've done dat many year, Anna, when Ay vas damn fool.

ANNA (*Disgustedly*) Oh, rats! (*After a pause she speaks musingly.*) Was the men in our family always sailors—as far back as you know about?

CHRIS (*Shortly*) Yes. Damn fools! All men in our village on coast, Sveden, go to sea. Ain't nutting else for dem to do. My fa'der die on board ship in Indian Ocean. He's buried at sea. Ay don't never know him only little bit. Den my tree bro'der, older'n me, dey go on ships. Den Ay go, too. Den my mo'der she's left all 'lone. She die pooty quick after dat—all 'lone. Ve vas all avay on voyage when she die. (*He pauses sadly.*) Two my bro'der dey gat lost on fishing boat same like your bro'ders vas drowned. My oder bro'der, he save money, give up sea, den he die home in bed. He's only one dat ole davil don't kill (*Defiantly.*) But me, Ay bet you Ay die ashore in bed, too!

ANNA Were all of 'em yust plain sailors?

CHRIS Able body seaman, most of dem. (*With a certain pride.*) Dey vas all smart seaman, too—A one. (*Then after hesitating a moment—shyly.*) Ay vas bo'sun.

ANNA Bo'sun?

CHRIS Dat's kind of officer.

ANNA Gee, that was fine. What does he do?

CHRIS (*After a second's hesitation, plunged into gloom again by his fear of her enthusiasm*) Hard vork all time. It's rotten, Ay tal you, for go to sea. (*Determined to disgust her with sea life—volubly.*) Dey're all fool fallar, dem fallar in our family. Dey all vork rotten yob on sea for nutting, don't care nutting but yust gat big pay day in pocket, gat drunk, gat robbed, ship avay again on oder voyage. Dey don't come home. Dey don't do anytang like good man do. And dat ole davil, sea, sooner, later she svallow dem up.

ANNA (*With an excited laugh*) Good sports, I'd call 'em. (*Then hastily.*) But say—listen—did all the women of the family marry sailors?

CHRIS (*Eagerly—seeing a chance to drive home his point*) Yes—
and it's bad on dem like hell vorst of all. Dey don't see deir
men only once in long while. Dey set and vait all 'lone. And
vhen deir boys grows up, go to sea, dey sit and vait some more.
(*Vehemently.*) Any gel marry sailor, she's crazy fool! Your
mo'der she tal you same tang if she vas alive. (*He relapses into
an attitude of somber brooding.*)

ANNA (*After a pause—dreamily*) Funny! I do feel sort of—nutty,
tonight. I feel old.

CHRIS (*Mystified*) Ole?

ANNA Sure—like I'd been living a long, long time—out here in the
fog. (*Frowning perplexedly.*) I don't know how to tell you yust
what I mean. It's like I'd come home after a long visit away some
place. It all seems like I'd been here before lots of times—on
boats—in this same fog. (*With a short laugh.*) You must think
I'm off my base.

CHRIS (*Gruffly*) Anybody feel funny dat vay in fog.

ANNA (*Persistently*) But why d'you s'pose I feel so—so—like I'd
found something I'd missed and been looking for—'s if this was
the right place for me to fit in? And I seem to have forgot—
everything that's happened—like it didn't matter no more. And
I feel clean, somehow—like you feel yust after you've took a
bath. And I feel happy for once—yes, honest!—happier than I
ever have been anywhere before! (*As* CHRIS *makes no comment
but a heavy sigh, she continues wonderingly.*) It's nutty for me
to feel that way, don't you think?

CHRIS (*A grim foreboding in his voice*) Ay tank Ay'm damn fool
for bring you on voyage, Anna.

ANNA (*Impressed by his tone*) You talk—nutty tonight yourself.
You act 's if you was scared something was going to happen.

CHRIS Only God know dat, Anna.

ANNA (*Half-mockingly*) Then it'll be Gawd's will, like the preach-
ers say—what does happen.

CHRIS (*Starts to his feet with fierce protest*) No! Dat ole davil,
sea, she ain't God! (*In the pause of silence that comes after his
defiance a hail in a man's husky, exhausted voice comes faintly
out of the fog to port.*) "Ahoy!" (CHRIS *gives a startled exclamation.*)

ANNA (*Jumping to her feet*) What's that?

CHRIS (*Who has regained his composure—sheepishly*) Py golly,
dat scare me for minute. It's only some fallar hail, Anna—loose

his course in fog. Must be fisherman's power boat His engine break down, Ay guess. (*The "ahoy" comes again through the wall of fog, sounding much nearer this time.* CHRIS *goes over to the port bulwark.*) Sound from dis side. She come in from open sea. (*He holds his hands to his mouth, megaphone-fashion, and shouts back.*) Ahoy, dere! Vhat's trouble?

THE VOICE (*This time sounding nearer but up forward toward the bow*) Heave a rope when we come alongside. (*Then irritably.*) Where are ye, ye scut?

CHRIS Ay hear dem rowing. Dey come up by bow, Ay tank. (*Then shouting out again.*) Dis vay!

THE VOICE Right ye are! (*There is a muffled sound of oars in oar-locks.*)

ANNA (*Half to herself—resentfully*) Why don't that guy stay where he belongs?

CHRIS (*Hurriedly*) Ay go up bow. All hands asleep 'cepting fallar on vatch. Ay gat heave line to dat fallar. (*He picks up a coil of rope and hurries off toward the bow.* ANNA *walks back toward the extreme stern as if she wanted to remain as much isolated as possible. She turns her back on the proceedings and stares out into the fog.* THE VOICE *is heard again shouting "Ahoy" and* CHRIS *answering "Dis vay." Then there is a pause—the murmur of excited voices—then the scuffling of feet.* CHRIS *appears from around the cabin to port. He is supporting the limp form of a man dressed in dungarees, holding one of the man's arms around his neck. The deckhand,* JOHNSON, *a young blond Swede, follows him, helping along another exhausted man similar fashion.* ANNA *turns to look at them.* CHRIS *stops for a second—volubly.*) Anna! You come help, vill you? You find vhisky in cabin. Dese fallars need drink for fix dem. Dey vas near dead.

ANNA (*Hurrying to him*) Sure—but who are they? What's the trouble?

CHRIS Sailor fallars. Deir steamer gat wrecked. Dey been five days in open boat—four fallars—only one left able stand up. Come, Anna. (*She precedes him into the cabin, holding the door open while he and* JOHNSON *carry in their burdens. The door is shut, then opened again as* JOHNSON *comes out.* CHRIS' *voice shouts after him.*) Go gat oder fallar, Yohnson.

JOHNSON Yes, sir. (*He goes. The door is closed again.* MAT BURKE *stumbles in around the port side of the cabin. He moves slowly, feeling his way uncertainly, keeping hold of the port bulwark with his right hand to steady himself. He is stripped to the waist, has on nothing but a pair of dirty dungaree pants. He is powerful, broad-chested six-footer, his face handsome in a hard, rough, bold, defiant way. He is about thirty, in the full power of his heavy-muscled, immense strength. His dark eyes are blood-shot and wild for sleeplessness. The muscles of his arms and shoulders are lumped in knots and bunches, the veins of his fore-arms stand out like blue cords. He finds his way to the coil of hawser and sits down on it facing the cabin, his back bowed, head in his hands, in an attitude of spent weariness.)*

BURKE (*Talking aloud to himself*) Row, ye divil! Row! (*Then lifting his head and looking about him.*) What's this tub? Well, we're safe anyway—with the help of God. (*He makes the sign of the cross mechanically.* JOHNSON *comes along the deck to port, supporting the fourth man, who is babbling to himself incoherently.* BURKE *glances at him disdainfully.*) Is it losing the small wits ye iver had, ye are? Deck-scrubbing scut! (*They pass him and go into the cabin, leaving the door open.* BURKE *sags forward wearily.*) I'm bate out—bate out entirely.

ANNA (*Comes out of the cabin with a tumbler quarter-full of whisky in her hand. She gives a start when she sees* BURKE *so near her, the light from the open door falling full on him. Then, overcoming what is evidently a feeling of repulsion, she comes up beside him.*) Here you are. Here's a drink for you. You need it, I guess.

BURKE (*Lifting his head slowly—confusedly*) Is it dreaming I am?

ANNA (*Half smiling*) Drink it and you'll find it ain't no dream.

BURKE To hell with the drink—but I'll take it just the same. (*He tosses it down.*) Ahah! I'm needin' that—and 'tis fine stuff. (*Looking up at her with frank, grinning admiration.*) But 'twasn't the booze I meant when I said, was I dreaming. I thought you was some mermaid out of the sea come to torment me. (*He reaches out to feel of her arm.*) Aye, rale flesh and blood, divil a less.

ANNA (*Coldly. Stepping back from him*) Cut that.

BURKE But tell me, isn't this a barge I'm on—or isn't it?

ANNA Sure.

BURKE And what is a fine handsome woman the like of you doing on this scow?

ANNA (*Coldly*) Never you mind. (*Then half-amused in spite of herself.*) Say, you're a great one, honest—starting right in kidding after what you been through.

BURKE (*Delighted—proudly*) Ah, it was nothing—aisy for a rale man with guts to him, the like of me. (*He laughs.*) All in the day's work, darlin'. (*Then, more seriously but still in a boastful tone, confidently.*) But I won't be denying 'twas a damn narrow squeak. We'd all ought to be with Davy Jones at the bottom of the sea, be rights. And only for me, I'm telling you, and the great strength and guts is in me, we'd be being scoffed by the fishes this minute!

ANNA (*Contemptuously*) Gee, you hate yourself, don't you? (*Then turning away from him indifferently.*) Well, you'd better come in and lie down. You must want to sleep.

BURKE (*Stung—rising unsteadily to his feet with chest out and head thrown back—resentfully*) Lie down and sleep, is it? Divil a wink I'm after having for two days and nights and divil a bit I'm needing now. Let you not be thinking I'm the like of them three weak scuts come in the boat with me. I could lick the three of them sitting down with one hand tied behind me. They may be bate out, but I'm not—and I've been rowing the boat with them lying in the bottom not able to raise a hand for the last two days we was in it. (*Furiously, as he sees this is making no impression on her.*) And I can lick all hands on this tub, wan be wan, tired as I am!

ANNA (*Sarcastically*) Gee, ain't you a hard guy! (*Then, with a trace of sympathy, as she notices him swaying from weakness.*) But never mind that fight talk. I'll take your word for all you've said. Go on and sit down out here, anyway, if I can't get you to come inside. (*He sits down weakly.*) You're all in, you might as well own up to it.

BURKE (*Fiercely*) The hell I am!

ANNA (*Coldly*) Well, be stubborn then for all I care. And I must say I don't care for your language. The men I know don't pull that rough stuff when ladies are around.

BURKE (*Getting unsteadily to his feet again—in a rage*) Ladies! Ho-ho! Divil mend you! Let you not be making game of me. What would ladies be doing on this bloody hulk? (*As* ANNA *attempts to go to the cabin, he lurches into her path.*) Aisy, now! You're not the old Square-head's woman, I suppose you'll be telling me next—living in his cabin with him, no less! (*Seeing the cold, hostile expression on* ANNA'S *face, he suddenly changes his tone to one of boisterous joviality.*) But I do be thinking, iver since the first look my eyes took at you, that it's a fool you are to be wasting yourself—a fine, handsome girl—on a stumpy runt of a man like that old Swede. There's too many strapping great lads on the sea would give their heart's blood for one kiss of you!

ANNA (*Scornfully*)  Lads like you, eh?

BURKE (*Grinning*)  Ye take the words out o' my mouth. I'm the proper lad for you, if it's meself do be saying it. (*With a quick movement he puts his arms about her waist.*) Whisht, now, me daisy! Himself's in the cabin. It's wan of your kisses I'm needing to take the tiredness from me bones. Wan kiss, now! (*He presses her to him and attempts to kiss her.*)

ANNA (*Struggling fiercely*)  Leggo of me, you big mutt! (*She pushes him away with all her might.* BURKE, *weak and tottering, is caught off his guard. He is thrown down backward and, in falling, hits his head a hard thump against the bulwark. He lies there still, knocked out for the moment.* ANNA *stands for a second, looking down at him frightenedly. Then she kneels down beside him and raises his head to her knee, staring into his face anxiously for some sign of life.*)

BURKE (*Stirring a bit—mutteringly*)  God stiffen it! (*He opens his eyes and blinks up at her with vague wonder.*)

ANNA (*Letting his head sink back on the deck, rising to her feet with a sigh of relief*)  You're coming to all right, eh? Gee, I was scared for a moment I'd killed you.

BURKE (*With difficulty rising to a sitting position—scornfully*)  Killed, is it? It'd take more than a bit of a blow to crack my thick skull. (*Then looking at her with the most intense admiration.*) But, glory be, it's a power of strength is in them two fine arms of yours. There's not a man in the world can say the same as you, that he seen Mat Burke lying at his feet and him dead to the world.

ANNA (*Rather remorsefully*)  Forget it. I'm sorry it happened, see? (*Burke rises and sits on bench. Then severely.*) Only you had no right to be getting fresh with me. Listen, now, and don't go getting any more wrong notions. I'm on this barge because I'm making a trip with my father. The captain's my father. Now you know.

BURKE (*Rising—peering at her face*)  Sure I might have known it, if I wasn't a bloody fool from birth. Where else'd you get that fine yellow hair is like a golden crown on your head.

ANNA (*With an amused laugh*)  Say, nothing stops you, does it? (*Then attempting a severe tone again.*) But don't you think you

ought to be apologizing for what you said and done yust a minute ago, instead of trying to kid me with that mush?

BURKE (*Indignantly*) Mush! (*Then bending forward toward her
with very intense earnestness.*) Indade and I will ask your
pardon a thousand times—and on my knees, if ye like. I didn't
mean a word of what I said or did. (*Resentful again for a second.*)
But divil a woman in all the ports of the world has iver made
a great fool of me that way before!

ANNA (*With amused sarcasm*) I see. You mean you're a lady-
killer and they all fall for you.

BURKE (*Offended. Passionately*) Leave off your fooling! 'Tis that
is after getting my back up at you. (*Earnestly.*) 'Tis no lie I'm
telling you about the women. (*Ruefully.*) Though it's a great
jackass I am to be mistaking you, even in anger, for the like
of them cows on the waterfront is the only women I've met up
with since I was growed to a man. (*As* ANNA *shrinks away from
him at this, he hurries on pleadingly.*) I'm a hard, rough man
and I'm not fit, I'm thinking, to be kissing the shoe-soles of a
fine, dacent girl the like of yourself. 'Tis only the ignorance of
your kind made me see you wrong. So you'll forgive me, for the
love of God, and let us be friends from this out. (*Passionately.*)
I'm thinking I'd rather be friends with you than have my wish
for anything else in the world. (*He holds out his hand to her
shyly.*)

ANNA (*Looking queerly at him, perplexed and worried, but moved
and pleased in spite of herself—takes his hand uncertainly*) Sure.

BURKE (*With boyish delight*) God bless you! (*In his excitement
he squeezes her hand tight.*)

ANNA Ouch!

BURKE (*Hastily dropping her hand—ruefully*) Your pardon, Miss.
'Tis a clumsy ape I am. (*Then simply—glancing down his arm
proudly.*) It's great power I have in my hand and arm, and I
do be forgetting it at times.

ANNA (*Nursing her crushed hand and glancing at his arm, not without a trace of his own admiration*) Gee, you're some strong,
all right.

BURKE (*Delighted*) It's no lie, and why shouldn't I be, with me
shoveling a million tons of coal in the stokeholes of ships since
I was a lad only. (*He pats the coil of hawser invitingly.*) Let
you sit down, now, Miss, and I'll be telling you a bit of myself,
and you'll be telling me a bit of yourself, and in an hour we'll

be as old friends, as if we was born in the same house (*He pulls at her sleeve shyly.*) Sit down now, if you plaze.

ANNA (*With a half laugh*) Well——(*She sits down.*) But we won't talk about me, see? You tell me about yourself and about the wreck.

BURKE (*Flattered*) I'll tell you, surely. But can I be asking you one question, Miss, has my head in a puzzle?

ANNA (*Guardedly*) Well—I dunno—what is it?

BURKE What is it you do when you're not taking a trip with the Old Man? For I'm thinking a fine girl the like of you ain't living always on this tub.

ANNA (*Uneasily*) No—of course I ain't. (*She searches his face suspiciously, afraid there may be some hidden insinuation in his words. Seeing his simple frankness, she goes on confidently.*) Well, I'll tell you. I'm a governess, see? I take care of kids for people and learn them things.

BURKE (*Impressed*) A governess, is it? You must be smart, surely.

ANNA Let's not talk about me. Tell me about the wreck, like you promised me you would.

BURKE (*Importantly*) 'Twas this way, Miss. Two weeks out we ran into the divil's own storm, and she sprang wan hell of a leak up for'ard. The skipper was hoping to make Boston before another blow would finish her, but ten days back we met up with another storm the like of the first, only worse. Four days we was in it with green seas raking over her from bow to stern. That was a terrible time, God help us. (*Proudly.*) And if 'twasn't for me and my great strength, I'm telling you—and it's God's truth—there'd been mutiny itself in the stokehole. 'Twas me held them to it, with a kick to wan and a clout to another, and they not caring a damn for the engineers any more, but fearing a clout of my right arm more than they'd fear the sea itself. (*He glances at her anxiously, eager for her approval.*)

ANNA (*Concealing a smile—amused by this boyish boasting of his*) You did some hard work, didn't you?

BURKE (*Promptly*) I did that! I'm a divil for sticking it out when them that's weak give up. But much good it did anyone! 'Twas a mad, fightin' scramble in the last seconds with each man for himself. I disremember how it came about, but there was the four of us in wan boat and when we raised high on a great wave I took a look about and divil a sight there was of ship or men on top of the sea.

ANNA (*In a subdued voice*) Then all the others was drowned?

BURKE They was, surely.

ANNA (*With a shudder*) What a terrible end!

BURKE (*Turns to her*) A terrible end for the like of them swabs does live on land, maybe. But for the like of us does be roaming the seas, a good end, I'm telling you—quick and clane.

ANNA (*Struck by the word*) Yes, clean. That's yust the word for—all of it—the way it makes me feel.

BURKE The sea, you mean? (*Interestedly.*) I'm thinking you have a bit of it in your blood, too. Your Old Man wasn't only a barge rat—begging your pardon—all his life, by the cut of him.

ANNA No, he was bo'sun on sailing ships for years. And all the men on both sides of the family have gone to sea as far back as he remembers, he says. All the women have married sailors, too.

BURKE (*With intense satisfaction*) Did they, now? They had spirit in them. It's only on the sea you'd find rale men with guts is fit to wed with fine, high-tempered girls (*then he adds half-boldly*) the like of yourself.

ANNA (*With a laugh*) There you go kiddin' again. (*Then seeing his hurt expression—quickly*) But you was going to tell me about yourself. You're Irish, of course I can tell that.

BURKE (*Stoutly*) Yes, thank God, though I've not seen a sight of it in fifteen years or more.

ANNA (*Thoughtfully*) Sailors never do go home hardly, do they? That's what my father was saying.

BURKE He wasn't telling no lie. (*With sudden melancholy.*) It's a hard and lonesome life, the sea is. The only women you'd meet in the ports of the world who'd be willing to speak you a kind word isn't woman at all. You know the kind I mane, and they're a poor, wicked lot, God forgive them. They're looking to steal the money from you only.

ANNA (*Her face averted—rising to her feet—agitatedly*) I think—I guess I'd better see what's doing inside.

BURKE (*Afraid he has offended her—beseechingly*) Don't go, I'm saying! Is it I've given you offense with the talk of the like of them? Don't heed it at all! I'm clumsy in my wits when it comes to talking proper with a girl the like of you. And why wouldn't I be? Since the day I left home for to go to sea punching coal, this is the first time I've had a word with a rale, dacent woman.

So don't turn your back on me now, and we beginning to be friends.

ANNA (*Turning to him again—forcing a smile*) I'm not sore at you, honest.

BURKE (*Gratefully*) God bless you!

ANNA (*Changing the subject abruptly*) But if you honestly think the sea's such a rotten life, why don't you get out of it?

BURKE (*Surprised*) Work on land, is it? (*She nods. He spits scornfully.*) Digging spuds in the muck from dawn to dark, I suppose? (*Vehemently.*) I wasn't made for it, Miss.

ANNA (*With a laugh*) I thought you'd say that.

BURKE (*Argumentatively*) But there's good jobs and bad jobs at sea, like there'd be on land. I'm thinking if it's in the stokehole of a proper liner I was, I'd be able to have a little house and be home to it wan week out of four. And I'm thinking that maybe then I'd have the luck to find a fine dacent girl—the like of yourself, now—would be willing to wed with me.

ANNA (*Turning away from him with a short laugh—uneasily*) Why, sure. Why not?

BURKE (*Edging up close to her—exultantly*) Then you think a girl the like of yourself might maybe not mind the past at all but only be seeing the good herself put in me?

ANNA (*In the same tone*) Why, sure.

BURKE (*Passionately*) She'd not be sorry for it, I'd take my oath! 'Tis no more drinking and roving about I'd be doing then, but giving my pay day into her hand and staying at home with her as meek as a lamb each night of the week I'd be in port.

ANNA (*Moved in spite of herself and troubled by this half-concealed proposal—with a forced laugh*) All you got to do is find the girl.

BURKE I have found her!

ANNA (*Half-frightenedly—trying to laugh it off*) You have? When? I thought you was saying——

BURKE (*Boldly and forcefully*) This night. (*Hanging his head—humbly.*) If she'll be having me. (*Then raising his eyes to hers—simply.*) 'Tis you I mean.

ANNA (*Is held by his eyes for a moment—then shrinks back from him with a strange, broken laugh*) Say—are you—going crazy? Are you trying to kid me? Proposing—to me!—for Gawd's sake! —on such short acquaintance? (*CHRIS comes out of the cabin and stands staring blinkingly astern. When he makes out* ANNA *in such intimate proximity to this strange sailor, an angry expression comes over his face.*)

BURKE (*Following her—with fierce, pleading insistence*) I'm telling you there's the will of God in it that brought me safe through the storm and fog to the wan spot in the world where you was! Think of that now, and isn't it queer——

CHRIS Anna! (*He comes toward them, raging, his fists clenched.*) Anna, you gat in cabin, you hear!

ANNA (*All her emotions immediately transformed into resentment at his bullying tone*) Who d'you think you're talking to—a slave?

CHRIS (*Hurt—his voice breaking—pleadingly*) You need gat rest, Anna. You gat sleep. (*She does not move. He turns on* BURKE *furiously.*) What you doing here, you sailor fallar? You ain't sick like oders. You gat in fo'c'stle. Dey give you bunk. (*Threateningly.*) You hurry, Ay tal you!

ANNA (*Impulsively*) But he is sick. Look at him. Look at him. He can hardly stand up.

BURKE (*Straightening and throwing out his chest—with a bold laugh*) Is it giving me orders ye are, me bucko? Let you look out, then! With wan hand, weak as I am, I can break ye in two and fling the pieces over the side—and your crew after you. (*Stopping abruptly.*) I was forgetting. You're her Old Man and I'd not raise a fist to you for the world. (*His knees sag, he wavers and seems about to fall.* ANNA *utters an exclamation of alarm and hurries to his side.*)

ANNA (*Taking one of his arms over her shoulder*) Come on in the cabin. You can have my bed if there ain't no other place.

BURKE (*With jubilant happiness—as they proceed toward the cabin*) Glory be to God, is it holding my arm about your neck you are! Anna! Anna! Sure it's a sweet name is suited to you.

ANNA (*Guiding him carefully*) Sssh! Sssh!

BURKE Whisht, is it? Indade, and I'll not. I'll be roaring it out like a fog horn over the sea! You're the girl of the world and we'll be marrying soon and I don't care who knows it!

ANNA (*As she guides him through the cabin door*) Ssshh! Never mind that talk. You go to sleep. (*They go out of sight in the cabin.* CHRIS, *who has been listening to* BURKE's *last words with open-mouthed amazement stands looking after them desperately.*)

CHRIS (*Turns suddenly and shakes his fist out at the sea—with bitter hatred*) Dat's your dirty trick, damn ole davil, you! (*Then in a frenzy of rage.*) But, py God, you don't do dat! Not vhile Ay'm living! No, py God, you don't!

*Curtain*

# ACT THREE

SCENE—*The interior of the cabin on the barge,* Simeon Winthrop
(*at dock in Boston*)—*a narrow, low-ceilinged compartment the
walls of which are painted a light brown with white trimmings.
In the rear on the left, a door leading to the sleeping quarters.
In the far left corner, a large locker-closet, painted white, on the
door of which a mirror hangs on a nail. In the rear wall, two
small square windows and a door opening out on the deck toward
the stern. In the right wall, two more windows looking out on the
port deck. White curtains, clean and stiff, are at the windows. A
table with two cane-bottomed chairs stands in the center of the
cabin. A dilapidated, wicker rocker, painted brown, is also by the
table.*

*It is afternoon of a sunny day about a week later. From the
harbor and docks outside, muffled by the closed door and windows,
comes the sound of steamers' whistles and the puffing snort of the
donkey engines of some ship unloading nearby.*

*As the curtain rises,* CHRIS *and* ANNA *are discovered.* ANNA *is
seated in the rocking-chair by the table, with a newspaper in her
hands. She is not reading but staring straight in front of her. She
looks unhappy, troubled, frowningly concentrated on her thoughts.*
CHRIS *wanders about the room, casting quick, uneasy side glances
at her face, then stopping to peer absent-mindedly out of the
window. His attitude betrays an overwhelming, gloomy anxiety
which has him on tenterhooks. He pretends to be engaged in setting
things ship-shape, but this occupation is confined to picking up some
object, staring at it stupidly for a second, then aimlessly putting
it down again. He clears his throat and starts to sing to himself
in a low, doleful voice:* "My Yosephine, come board de ship.
Long time Ay vait for you."

ANNA (*Turning on him, sarcastically*) I'm glad someone's feeling good. (*Wearily.*) Gee, I sure wish we was out of this dump and back in New York.

CHRIS (*With a sigh*) Ay'm glad vhen ve sail again, too. (*Then, as she makes no comment, he goes on with a ponderous attempt at sarcasm.*) Ay don't see vhy you don't like Boston, dough. You have good time here, Ay tank. You go ashore all time, every day and night veek ve've been here. You go to movies, see show, gat all kinds fun——(*His eyes hard with hatred.*) All with that damn Irish fallar!

ANNA (*With weary scorn*) Oh, for heaven's sake, are you off on that again? Where's the harm in his taking me around? D'you want me to sit all day and night in this cabin with you—and knit? Ain't I got a right to have as good a time as I can?

CHRIS It ain't right kind of fun—not with that fallar, no.

ANNA I been back on board every night by eleven, ain't I? (*Then struck by some thought—looks at him with keen suspicion—with rising anger.*) Say, look here, what d'you mean by what you yust said?

CHRIS (*Hastily*) Nutting but what Ay say, Anna.

ANNA You said "ain't right" and you said it funny. Say, listen here, you ain't trying to insinuate that there's something wrong between us, are you?

CHRIS (*Horrified*) No, Anna! No, Ay svear to God, Ay never tank dat!

ANNA (*Mollified by his very evident sincerity—sitting down again*) Well, don't you never think it neither if you want me ever to speak to you again. (*Angrily again.*) If I ever dreamt you thought that, I'd get the hell out of this barge so quick you couldn't see me for dust.

CHRIS (*Soothingly*) Ay wouldn't never dream—— (*Then after a second's pause, reprovingly*) You vas getting learn to svear. Dat ain't nice for young gel, you tank?

ANNA (*With a faint trace of a smile*) Excuse me. You ain't used to such language, I know. (*Mockingly.*) That's what your taking me to sea has done for me.

CHRIS (*Indignantly*) No, it ain't me. It's dat damn sailor fallar learn you bad tangs.

ANNA He ain't a sailor. He's a stoker.

CHRIS (*Forcibly*) Dat vas million times vorse, Ay tal you! Dem fallars dat vork below shoveling coal vas de dirtiest, rough gang of no-good fallars in vorld!

ANNA  I'd hate to hear you say that to Mat.

CHRIS  Oh, Ay tal him same tang. You don't gat it in head Ay'm scared of him yust 'cause he vas stronger'n Ay vas. (*Menacingly.*) You don't gat for fight with fists with dem fallars. Dere's oder vay for fix him.

ANNA  (*Glancing at him with sudden alarm*)  What d'you mean?

CHRIS  (*Sullenly*)  Nutting.

ANNA  You'd better not. I wouldn't start no trouble with him if I was you. He might forget some time that you was old and my father—and then you'd be out of luck.

CHRIS  (*With smoldering hatred*)  Vell, yust let him! Ay'm ole bird maybe, but Ay bet Ay show him trick or two.

ANNA  (*Suddenly changing her tone—persuasively*)  Aw come on, be good. What's eating you, anyway? Don't you want no one to be nice to me except yourself?

CHRIS  (*Placated—coming to her—eagerly*)  Yes, Ay do, Anna—only not fallar on sea. But Ay like for you marry steady fallar got good yob on land. You have little home in country all your own——

ANNA  (*Rising to her feet—brusquely*)  Oh, cut it out! (*Scornfully.*) Little home in the country! I wish you could have seen the little home in the country where you had me in jail till I was sixteen!
(*With rising irritation.*) Some day you're going to get me so mad with that talk, I'm going to turn loose on you and tell you—a lot of things that'll open your eyes.

CHRIS  (*Alarmed*)  Ay don't vant——

ANNA  I know you don't; but you keep on talking yust the same.

CHRIS  Ay don't talk no more den, Anna.

ANNA  Then promise me you'll cut out saying nasty things about Mat Burke every chance you get.

CHRIS  (*Evasive and suspicious*)  Vhy? You like dat fallar—very much, Anna?

ANNA  Yes, I certainly do! He's a regular man, no matter what faults he's got. One of his fingers is worth all the hundreds of men I met out there—inland.

CHRIS  (*His face darkening*)  Maybe you tank you love him, den?

ANNA  (*Defiantly*)  What of it if I do?

CHRIS (*Scowling and forcing out the words*) Maybe—you tank you—marry him?

ANNA (*Shaking her head*) No! (CHRIS' *face lights up with relief.* ANNA *continues slowly, a trace of sadness in her voice.*) If I'd met him four years ago—or even two years ago—I'd have jumped at the chance, I tell you that straight. And I would now—only he's such a simple guy—a big kid—and I ain't got the heart to fool him. (*She breaks off suddenly.*) But don't never say again he ain't good enough for me. It's me ain't good enough for him.

CHRIS (*Snorts scornfully*) Py yiminy, you go crazy, Ay tank!

ANNA (*With a mournful laugh*) Well, I been thinking I was myself the last few days. (*She goes and takes a shawl from a hook near the door and throws it over her shoulders.*) Guess I'll take a walk down to the end of the dock for a minute and see what's doing. I love to watch the ships passing. Mat'll be along before long, I guess. Tell him where I am, will you?

CHRIS (*Despondently*) All right, Ay tal him. (ANNA *goes out the doorway in rear.* CHRIS *follows her out and stands on the deck outside for a moment looking after her. Then he comes back inside and shuts the door. He stands looking out of the window— mutters—"Dirty ole davil, you." Then he goes to the table, sets the cloth straight mechanically, picks up the newspaper* ANNA *has let fall to the floor and sits down in the rocking-chair. He stares at the paper for a while, then puts it on table, holds his head in his hands and sighs drearily. The noise of a man's heavy footsteps comes from the deck outside and there is a loud knock on the door.* CHRIS *starts, makes a move as if to get up and go to the door, then thinks better of it and sits still. The knock is repeated—then as no answer comes, the door is flung open and* MAT BURKE *appears.* CHRIS *scowls at the intruder and his hand instinctively goes back to the sheath knife on his hip.* BURKE *is dressed up—wears a cheap blue suit, a striped cotton shirt with a black tie, and black shoes newly shined. His face is beaming with good humor.*)

BURKE (*As he sees* CHRIS—*in a jovial tone of mockery*) Well, God bless who's here! (*He bends down and squeezes his huge form through the narrow doorway.*) And how is the world treating you this afternoon, Anna's father?

CHRIS (*Sullenly*) Pooty goot—if it ain't for some fallars.

BURKE (*With a grin*) Meaning me, do you? (*He laughs.*) Well,

if you ain't the funny old crank of a man! (*Then soberly.*)
Where's herself? (CHRIS *sits dumb, scowling, his eyes averted.*
BURKE *is irritated by this silence.*) Where's Anna, I'm after asking
you?

CHRIS (*Hesitating—then grouchily*) She go down end of dock.

BURKE I'll be going down to her, then. But first I'm thinking I'll
take this chance when we're alone to have a word with you.
(*He sits down opposite* CHRIS *at the table and leans over toward
him.*) And that word is soon said. I'm marrying your Anna
before this day is out, and you might as well make up your mind
to it whether you like it or no.

CHRIS (*Glaring at him with hatred and forcing a scornful laugh*)
Ho-ho! Dat's easy for say!

BURKE You mean I won't? (*Scornfully.*) Is it the like of yourself
will stop me, are you thinking?

CHRIS Yes, Ay stop it, if it come to vorst.

BURKE (*With scornful pity*) God help you!

CHRIS But ain't no need for me do dat. Anna——

BURKE (*Smiling confidently*) Is it Anna you think will prevent
me?

CHRIS Yes.

BURKE And I'm telling you she'll not. She knows I'm loving her,
and she loves me the same, and I know it.

CHRIS Ho-ho! She only have fun. She make big fool of you,
dat's all!

BURKE (*Unshaken—pleasantly*) That's a lie in your throat, divil
mend you!

CHRIS No, it ain't lie. She tal me yust before she go out she
never marry fallar like you.

BURKE I'll not believe it. 'Tis a great old liar you are, and a
divil to be making a power of trouble if you had your way.
But 'tis not trouble I'm looking for, and me sitting down here.
(*Earnestly.*) Let us be talking it out now as man to man. You're
her father, and wouldn't it be a shame for us to be at each other's
throats like a pair of dogs, and I married with Anna? So out
with the truth, man alive. What is it you're holding against
me at all?

CHRIS (*A bit placated, in spite of himself, by* BURKE'S *evident
sincerity—but puzzled and suspicious*) Vell—Ay don't vant for
Anna get married. Listen, you fallar. Ay'm a ole man. Ay don't
see Anna for fifteen year. She vas all Ay gat in vorld. And

now ven she come on first trip—you tank Ay vant her leave me 'lone again?

BURKE (*Heartily*) Let you not be thinking I have no heart at all for the way you'd be feeling.

CHRIS (*Astonished and encouraged—trying to plead persuasively*) Den you do right tang, eh? You ship avay again, leave Anna alone. (*Cajolingly.*) Big fallar like you dat's on sea, he don't need vife. He gat new gel in every port, you know dat.

BURKE (*Angrily for a second*) God stiffen you! (*Then controlling himself—calmly.*) I'll not be giving you the lie on that. But divil take you, there's a time comes to every man, on sea or land, that isn't a born fool, when he's sick of the lot of them cows, and wearing his heart out to meet up with a fine dacent girl, and have a home to call his own and be rearing up children in it. 'Tis small use you're asking me to leave Anna. She's the wan woman of the world for me, and I can't live without her now, I'm thinking.

CHRIS You forgat all about her in one veek out of port, Ay bet you!

BURKE You don't know the like I am. Death itself wouldn't make me forget her. So let you not be making talk to me about leaving her. I'll not, and be damned to you! It won't be so bad for you as you'd make out at all. She'll be living here in the States, and her married to me. And you'd be seeing her often so—a sight more often than ever you saw her the fifteen years she was growing up in the West. It's quare you'd be the one to be making great trouble about her leaving you when you never laid eyes on her once in all them years.

CHRIS (*Guiltily*) Ay taught it vas better Anna stay away, grow up inland vhere she don't ever know ole davil, sea.

BURKE (*Scornfully*) Is it blaming the sea for your troubles ye are again, God help you? Well, Anna knows it now. 'Twas in her blood. anyway.

CHRIS And Ay don't vant she ever know no-good fallar on sea——

BURKE She knows one now.

CHRIS (*Banging the table with his fist—furiously*) Dat's yust it! Dat's yust what you are—no-good sailor fallar! You tank Ay lat her life be made sorry by you like her mo-der's vas by me! No, Ay svear! She don't marry you if Ay gat kill you first!

BURKE (*Looks at him a moment, in astonishment—then laughing*

*uproariously*)  Ho-ho! Glory be to God, it's bold talk you have
for a stumpy runt of a man!

CHRIS (*Threateningly*)  Vell—you see!

BURKE (*With grinning defiance*)  I'll see, surely! I'll see myself
and Anna married this day, I'm telling you. (*Then with contemptuous exasperation.*) It's quare fool's blather you have about
the sea done this and the sea done that. You'd ought to be
'shamed to be saying the like, and you an old sailor yourself.
I'm after hearing a lot of it from you and a lot more that
Anna's told me you do be saying to her, and I'm thinking
it's a poor weak thing you are, and not a man at all!

CHRIS (*Darkly*)  You see if Ay'm man—maybe quicker'n you tank.

BURKE (*Contemptuously*)  Yerra, don't be boasting. I'm thinking
'tis out of your wits you've got with fright of the sea. You'd
be wishing Anna married to a farmer, she told me. That'd
be a swate match, surely! Would you have a fine girl the
like of Anna lying down at nights with a muddy scut stinking
of pigs and dung? Or would you have her tied for life to the
like of them skinny, shriveled swabs does be working in cities?

CHRIS  Dat's lie, you fool!

BURKE  'Tis not. 'Tis your own mad notions I'm after telling. But
you know the truth in your heart, if great fear of the sea has
made you a liar and coward itself. (*Pounding the table.*) The
sea's the only life for a man with guts in him isn't afraid of
his own shadow! 'Tis only on the sea he's free, and him roving
the face of the world, seeing all things, and not giving a
damn for saving up money, or stealing from his friends, or any
of the black tricks that a landlubber'd waste his life on. 'Twas
yourself knew it once, and you a bo'sun for years.

CHRIS (*Sputtering with rage*)  You vas crazy fool, Ay tal you!

BURKE  You've swallowed the anchor. The sea gives you a clout
once, knocked you down, and you're not man enough to get
up for another, but lie there for the rest of your life howling
bloody murder. (*Proudly.*) Isn't it myself the sea has nearly
drowned, and me battered and bate till I was that close to
hell I could hear the flames roaring, and never a groan out of
me till the sea gave up and it seeing the great strength and
guts of a man was in me?

CHRIS (*Scornfully*)  Yes, you vas hell of fallar, hear you tal it!

BURKE (*Angrily*)  You'll be calling me a liar once too often, me
old bucko! Wasn't the whole story of it and my picture itself

in the newspapers of Boston a week back? (*Looking* CHRIS *up and down belittlingly.*) Sure I'd like to see you in the best of your youth do the like of what I done in the storm and after. 'Tis a mad lunatic, screeching with fear, you'd be this minute!

CHRIS Ho-ho! You vas young fool! In ole years when Ay vas on windyammer, Ay vas through hundred storms vorse'n dat! Ships vas ships den—and men dat sail on dem vas real men. And now what you gat on steamers? You gat fallars on deck don't know ship from mudscow. (*With a meaning glance at* BURKE.) And below deck you gat fallars yust know how for shovel coal—might yust as vell vork on coal vagon ashore!

BURKE (*Stung—angrily*) Is it casting insults at the men in the stokehole ye are, ye old ape? God stiffen you! Wan of them is worth any ten stock-fish-swilling Square-heads ever shipped on a windbag!

CHRIS (*His face working with rage, his hand going back to the sheath-knife on his hip*) Irish svine, you!

BURKE (*Tauntingly*) Don't ye like the Irish, ye old baboon? 'Tis that you're needing in your family, I'm telling you—an Irishman and a man of the stokehole—to put guts in it so that you'll not be having grandchildren would be fearful cowards and jackasses the like of yourself!

CHRIS (*Half rising from his chair—in a voice choked with rage*) You look out!

BURKE (*Watching him intently—a mocking smile on his lips*) And it's that you'll be having, no matter what you'll do to prevent; for Anna and me'll be married this day, and no old fool the like of you will stop us when I've made up my mind.

CHRIS (*With a hoarse cry*) You don't! (*He throws himself at* BURKE, *knife in hand, knocking his chair over backwards.* BURKE *springs to his feet quickly in time to meet the attack. He laughs with the pure love of battle. The old Swede is like a child in his hands.* BURKE *does not strike or mistreat him in any way, but simply twists his right hand behind his back and forces the knife from his fingers. He throws the knife into a far corner of the room—tauntingly.*)

BURKE Old men is getting childish shouldn't play with knives. (*Holding the struggling* CHRIS *at arm's length—with a sudden rush of anger, drawing back his fist.*) I've half a mind to hit you a great clout will put sense in your square head. Kape off me now, I'm warning you! (*He gives* CHRIS *a push with the*

*flat of his hand which sends the old Swede staggering back
against the cabin wall, where he remains standing, panting
heavily, his eyes fixed on* BURKE *with hatred, as if he were
only collecting his strength to rush at him again.*)

BURKE (*Warningly*) Now don't be coming at me again, I'm saying,
or I'll flatten you on the floor with a blow, if 'tis Anna's father
you are itself! I've not patience left for you. (*Then with an
amused laugh.*) Well, 'tis a bold old man you are just the
same, and I'd never think it was in you to come tackling me
alone. (*A shadow crosses the cabin windows. Both men start.*
ANNA *appears in the doorway.*)

ANNA (*With pleased surprise as she sees* BURKE) Hello, Mat.
Are you here already? I was down—— (*She stops, looking from
one to the other, sensing immediately that something has happened.*) What's up? (*Then noticing the overturned chair—in
alarm.*) How'd that chair get knocked over? (*Turning on*
BURKE *reproachfully.*) You ain't been fighting with him, Mat—
after you promised?

BURKE (*His old self again*) I've not laid a hand on him, Anna.
(*He goes and picks up the chair, then turning on the still questioning* ANNA—*With a reassuring smile.*) Let you not be worried
at all. 'Twas only a bit of an argument we was having to pass
the time till you'd come.

ANNA It must have been some argument when you got to throwing chairs. (*She turns on* CHRIS.) Why don't you say something? What was it about?

CHRIS (*Relaxing at last—avoiding her eyes—sheepishly*) Ve vas
talking about ships and fallars on sea.

ANNA (*With a relieved smile*) Oh—the old stuff, eh?

BURKE (*Suddenly seeming to come to a bold decision—with a
defiant grin at* CHRIS) He's not after telling you the whole of
it. We was arguing about you mostly.

ANNA (*With a frown*) About me?

BURKE And we'll be finishing it out right here and now in your
presence if you're willing. (*He sits down at the left of table.*)

ANNA (*Uncertainly—looking from him to her father*) Sure. Tell
me what it's all about.

CHRIS (*Advancing toward the table—protesting to* BURKE) No!
You don't do dat, you! You tal him you don't vant for hear
him talk, Anna.

ANNA But I do. I want this cleared up.

CHRIS (*Miserably afraid now*) Vell, not now, anyvay. You vas going ashore, yes? You ain't got time——

ANNA (*Firmly*) Yes, right here and now. (*She turns to* BURKE.) You tell me, Mat, since he don't want to.

BURKE (*Draws a deep breath—then plunges in boldly*) The whole of it's in a few words only. So's he'd make no mistake, and him hating the sight of me, I told him in his teeth I loved you. (*Passionately.*) And that's God's truth, Anna, and well you know it!

CHRIS (*Scornfully—forcing a laugh*) Ho-ho! He tal same tang to gel every port he go!

ANNA (*Shrinking from her father with repulsion—resentfully*) Shut up, can't you? (*Then to* BURKE—*feelingly.*) I know it's true, Mat. I don't mind what he says.

BURKE (*Humbly grateful*) God bless you!

ANNA And then what?

BURKE And then——(*Hesitatingly.*) And then I said——(*He looks at her pleadingly.*) I said I was sure—I told him I thought you have a bit of love for me, too. (*Passionately.*) Say you do, Anna! Let you not destroy me entirely for the love of God! (*He grasps both her hands in his two.*)

ANNA (*Deeply moved and troubled—forcing a trembling laugh*) So you told him that, Mat? No wonder he was mad. (*Forcing out the words.*) Well, maybe it's true, Mat. Maybe I do. I been thinking and thinking—I didn't want to, Mat, I'll own up to that—I tried to cut it out—but——(*She laughs helplessly.*) I guess I can't help it anyhow. So I guess I do, Mat. (*Then with a sudden joyous defiance.*) Sure I do! What's the use of kidding myself different? Sure I love you, Mat!

CHRIS (*With a cry of pain*) Anna! (*He sits crushed.*)

BURKE (*With a great depth of sincerity in his humble gratitude*) God be praised!

ANNA (*Assertively*) And I ain't never loved a man in my life before, you can always believe that—no matter what happens.

BURKE (*Goes over to her and puts his arms around her*) Sure I do be believing ivery word you iver said or iver will say. And 'tis you and me will be having a grand, beautiful life together to the end of our days! (*He tries to kiss her. At first she turns away her head—then, overcome by a fierce impulse of passionate love, she takes his head in both her hands and holds his face close to hers, staring into his eyes. Then she kisses him full on the lips.*)

ANNA (*Pushing him away from her—forcing a broken laugh*) Good-by. (*She walks to the doorway in rear—stands with her back toward them, looking out. Her shoulders quiver once or twice as if she were fighting back her sobs.*)

BURKE (*Too in the seventh heaven of bliss to get any correct interpretation of her word—with a laugh*) Good-by, is it? The divil you say! I'll be coming back at you in a second for more of the same! (*To* CHRIS, *who has quickened to instant attention at his daughter's good-by, and has looked back at her with a stirring of foolish hope in his eyes.*) Now, me old bucko, what'll you be saying? You heard the words from her own lips. Confess I've bate you. Own up like a man when you're bate fair and square. And here's my hand to you——(*Holds out his hand.*) And let you take it and we'll shake and forget what's over and done, and be friends from this out.

CHRIS (*With implacable hatred*) Ay don't shake hands with you fallar—not vhile Ay live!

BURKE (*Offended*) The back of my hand to you then, if that suits you better. (*Growling.*) 'Tis a rotten bad loser you are, divil mend you!

CHRIS Ay don't lose. (*Trying to be scornful and self-convincing.*) Anna say she like you little bit but you don't hear her say she marry you, Ay bet. (*At the sound of her name* ANNA *has turned round to them. Her face is composed and calm again, but it is the dead calm of despair.*)

BURKE (*Scornfully*) No, and I wasn't hearing her say the sun is shining either.

CHRIS (*Doggedly*) Dat's all right. She don't say it, yust same.

ANNA (*Quietly—coming forward to them*) No, I didn't say it, Mat.

CHRIS (*Eagerly*) Dere! You hear!

BURKE (*Misunderstanding her—with a grin*) You're waiting till you do be asked, you mane? Well, I'm asking you now. And we'll be married this day, with the help of God!

ANNA (*Gently*) You heard what I said, Mat—after I kissed you?

BURKE (*Alarmed by something in her manner*) No—I disremember.

ANNA I said good-by. (*Her voice trembling.*) That kiss was for good-by, Mat.

BURKE (*Terrified*) What d'you mane?

ANNA  I can't marry you, Mat—and we've said good-by. That's all.

CHRIS  (*Unable to hold back his exultation*)  Ay know it! Ay know dat vas so!

BURKE  (*Jumping to his feet—unable to believe his ears*)  Anna! Is it making game of me you'd be? 'Tis a quare time to joke with me, and don't be doing it, for the love of God.

ANNA  (*Looking him in the eyes—steadily*)  D'you think I'd kid you? No, I'm not joking, Mat. I mean what I said.

BURKE  Ye don't! Ye can't! 'Tis mad you are, I'm telling you!

ANNA  (*Fixedly*)  No, I'm not.

BURKE  (*Desperately*)  But what's come over you so sudden? You was saying you loved me——

ANNA  I'll say that as often as you want me to. It's true.

BURKE  (*Bewilderedly*)  Then why—what, in the divil's name—— Oh, God help me, I can't make head or tail to it at all!

ANNA  Because it's the best way out I can figure, Mat. (*Her voice catching.*)  I been thinking it over and thinking it over day and night all week. Don't think it ain't hard on me, too, Mat.

BURKE  For the love of God, tell me then, what is it that's preventing you wedding me when the two of us has love? (*Suddenly getting an idea and pointing at* CHRIS—*exasperatedly.*)  Is it giving heed to the like of that old fool ye are, and him hating me and filling your ears full of bloody lies against me?

CHRIS  (*Getting to his feet—raging triumphantly before* ANNA *has a chance to get in a word*)  Yes, Anna believe me, not you! She know her old fa'der don't lie like you.

ANNA  (*Turning on her father angrily*)  You sit down, d'you hear? Where do you come in butting in and making things worse? You're like a devil, you are! (*Harshly.*)  Good Lord, and I was beginning to like you, beginning to forget all I've got held up against you!

CHRIS  (*Crushed feebly*)  You ain't got nutting for hold against me, Anna.

ANNA  Ain't I yust! Well, lemme tell you—— (*She glances at* BURKE *and stops abruptly.*)  Say, Mat, I'm s'prised at you. You didn't think anything he'd said——

BURKE  (*Glumly*)  Sure, what else would it be?

ANNA  Think I've ever paid any attention to all his crazy bull? Gee, you must take me for a five-year-old kid.

BURKE  (*Puzzled and beginning to be irritated at her too*)  I don't know how to take you, with your saying this one minute and that the next.

ANNA  Well, he has nothing to do with it.

BURKE  Then what is it has? Tell me, and don't keep me waiting and sweating blood.

ANNA  (*Resolutely*)  I can't tell you—and I won't. I got a good reason—and that's all you need to know. I can't marry you, that's all there is to it. (*Distractedly.*) So, for Gawd's sake, let's talk of something else.

BURKE  I'll not! (*Then fearfully.*) Is it married to someone else you are—in the West maybe?

ANNA  (*Vehemently*)  I should say not.

BURKE  (*Regaining his courage*)  To the divil with all other reasons then. They don't matter with me at all. (*He gets to his feet confidently, assuming a masterful tone.*) I'm thinking you're the like of them women can't make up their mind till they're drove to it. Well, then, I'll make up your mind for you bloody quick. (*He takes her by the arms, grinning to soften his serious bullying.*) We've had enough of talk! Let you be going into your room now and be dressing in your best and we'll be going ashore.

CHRIS  (*Aroused—angrily*)  No, py God, she don't do that! (*Takes hold of her arm.*)

ANNA  (*Who has listened to* BURKE *in astonishment. She draws away from him, instinctively repelled by his tone, but not exactly sure if he is serious or not—a trace of resentment in her voice*)  Say, where do you get that stuff?

BURKE  (*Imperiously*)  Never mind, now! Let you go get dressed, I'm saying. (*Then turning to* CHRIS.)  We'll be seeing who'll win in the end—me or you.

CHRIS  (*To* ANNA—*also in an authoritative tone*)  You stay right here, Anna, you hear! (ANNA *stands looking from one to the other of them as if she thought they had both gone crazy. Then the expression of her face freezes into the hardened sneer of her experience.*)

BURKE  (*Violently*)  She'll not! She'll do what I say! You've had your hold on her long enough. It's my turn now.

ANNA  (*With a hard laugh*)  Your turn? Say, what am I, anyway?

BURKE  'Tis not what you are, 'tis what you're going to be this day—and that's wedded to me before night comes. Hurry up now with your dressing.

CHRIS (*Commandingly*) You don't do one tang he say, Anna! (ANNA *laughs mockingly.*)

BURKE She will, so!

CHRIS Ay tal you she don't! Ay'm her fa'der.

BURKE She will in spite of you. She's taking my orders from this out, not yours.

ANNA (*Laughing again*) Orders is good!

BURKE (*Turning to her impatiently*) Hurry up now, and shake a leg. We've no time to be wasting. (*Irritated as she doesn't move.*) Do you hear what I'm telling you?

CHRIS You stay dere, Anna!

ANNA (*At the end of her patience—blazing out at them passionately*) You can go to hell, both of you! (*There is something in her tone that makes them forget their quarrel and turn to her in a stunned amazement.* ANNA *laughs wildly.*) You're just like all the rest of them—you two! Gawd, you'd think I was a piece of furniture! I'll show you! Sit down now! (*As they hesitate—furiously.*) Sit down and let me talk for a minute. You're all wrong, see? Listen to me! I'm going to tell you something—and then I'm going to beat it. (*To* BURKE—*with a harsh laugh.*) I'm going to tell you a funny story, so pay attention. (*Pointing to* CHRIS.) I've been meaning to turn it loose on him every time he'd get my goat with his bull about keeping me safe inland. I wasn't going to tell you, but you've forced me into it. What's the dif? It's all wrong anyway, and you might as well get cured that way as any other. (*With hard mocking.*) Only don't forget what you said a minute ago about it not mattering to you what other reason I got so long as I wasn't married to no one else.

BURKE (*Manfully*) That's my word, and I'll stick to it!

ANNA (*Laughing bitterly*) What a chance! You make me laugh, honest! Want to bet you will? Wait 'n see! (*She stands at the table rear, looking from one to the other of the two men with her hard, mocking smile. Then she begins, fighting to control her emotion and speak calmly.*) First thing is, I want to tell you two guys something. You was going on 's if one of you had got to own me. But nobody owns me, see?—'cepting myself. I'll do what I please and no man, I don't give a hoot who he is, can tell me what to do! I ain't asking either of you for a living. I can make it myself—one way or other. I'm my own boss. So put that in your pipe and smoke it! You and your orders!

BURKE  (*Protestingly*)  I wasn't meaning it that way at all and well
you know it. You've no call to be raising this rumpus with me.
(*Pointing to* CHRIS.) 'Tis him you've a right——

ANNA  I'm coming to him. But you—you did mean it that way,
too. You sounded—yust like all the rest. (*Hysterically.*) But,
damn it, shut up! Let me talk for a change!

BURKE.  'Tis quare, rough talk, that—for a dacent girl the like of
you!

ANNA  (*With a hard laugh*)  Decent? Who told you I was?
(CHRIS *is sitting with bowed shoulders, his head in his hands. She
leans over him in exasperation and shakes him violently by the
shoulder.*)  Don't got to sleep, Old Man! Listen here, I'm talking
to you now!

CHRIS  (*Straightening up and looking about as if he were seeking a
way to escape—with frightened foreboding in his voice*)  Ay
don't vant for hear it. You vas going out of head, Ay tank,
Anna.

ANNA  (*Violently*)  Well, living with you is enough to drive anyone off their nut. Your bunk about the farm being so fine! Didn't
I write you year after year how rotten it was and what a dirty
slave them cousins made of me? What'd you care? Nothing!
Not even enough to come and see me! That crazy bull about
wanting to keep me away from the sea don't go down with me!
You yust didn't want to be bothered with me! You're like all the
rest of 'em!

CHRIS  (*Feebly*)  Anna! It ain't so——

ANNA  (*Not heeding his interruption—revengefully*)  But one
thing I never wrote you. It was one of them cousins that you
think is such nice people—the youngest son—Paul—that started
me wrong. (*Loudly.*) It wasn't none of my fault. I hated him
worse'n hell and he knew it. But he was big and strong—(*pointing to* BURKE)—like you!

BURKE  (*Half springing to his feet—his fists clenched*)  God blarst
it! (*He sinks slowly back in his chair again, the knuckles showing white on his clenched hands, his face tense with the effort
to suppress his grief and rage.*)

CHRIS  (*In a cry of horrified pain*)  Anna!

ANNA  (*To him—seeming not to have heard their interruptions*)
That was why I run away from the farm. That was what made
me get a yob as nurse girl in St. Paul. (*With a hard, mocking
laugh.*) And you think that was a nice yob for a girl, too, don't

you? (*Sarcastically.*) With all of them nice inland fellers yust looking for a chance to marry me, I s'pose. Marry me? What a chance! They wasn't looking for marrying. (*As* BURKE *lets a groan of fury escape him—desperately.*) I'm owning up to everything fair and square. I was caged in, I tell you—yust like in yail—taking care of other people's kids—listening to 'em bawling and crying day and night—when 1 wanted to be out—and I was lonesome—lonesome as hell! (*With a sudden weariness in her voice.*) So I give up finally. What was the use? (*She stops and looks at the two men. Both are motionless and silent.* CHRIS *seems in a stupor of despair, his house of cards fallen about him.* BURKE's *face is livid with the rage that is eating him up, but he is too stunned and bewildered yet to find a vent for it. The condemnation she feels in their silence goads* ANNA *into a harsh, strident defiance.*) You don't say nothing—either of you—but I know what you're thinking. You're like all the rest! (*To* CHRIS—*furiously.*) And who's to blame for it, me or you? If you'd even acted like a man—if you'd even had been a regular father and had me with you—maybe things would be different!

CHRIS (*In agony*) Don't talk dat vay, Anna! Ay go crazy! Ay von't listen! (*Puts his hands over his ears.*)

ANNA (*Infuriated by his action—stridently*) You will too listen! (*She leans over and pulls his hands from his ears—with hysterical rage.*) You—keeping me safe inland—I wasn't no nurse girl the last two years—I lied when I wrote you—I was in a house, that's what!—yes, that kind of a house—the kind sailors like you and Mat goes to in port—and your nice inland men, too—and all men, God damn 'em! I hate 'em! Hate 'em! (*She breaks into hysterical sobbing, throwing herself into the chair and hiding her face in her hands on the table. The two men have sprung to their feet.*)

CHRIS (*Whimpering like a child*) Anna! Anna! It's a lie! It's a lie! (*He stands wringing his hands together and begins to weep.*)

BURKE (*His whole great body tense like a spring—dully and gropingly*) So that's what's in it!

ANNA (*Raising her head at the sound of his voice—with extreme mocking bitterness*) I s'pose you remember your promise, Mat? No other reason was to count with you so long as I wasn't married already. So I s'pose you want me to get dressed and go ashore, don't you? (*She laughs.*) Yes, you do!

BURKE (*On the verge of his outbreak—stammeringly*)   God stiffen you!

ANNA (*Trying to keep up her hard, bitter tone, but gradually letting a note of pitiful pleading creep in*)   I s'pose if I tried to tell you I wasn't—that—no more you'd believe me, wouldn't you? Yes, you would! And if I told you that yust getting out in this barge, and being on the sea had changed me and made me feel different about things, 's if all I'd been through wasn't me and didn't count and was yust like it never happened—you'd laugh, wouldn't you? And you'd die laughing sure if I said that meeting you that funny way that night in the fog, and afterwards seeing that you was straight goods stuck on me, had got me to thinking for the first time, and I sized you up as a different kind of man—a sea man as different from the ones on land as water is from mud —and that was why I got stuck on you, too. I wanted to marry you and fool you, but I couldn't. Don't you see how I've changed? I couldn't marry you with you believing a lie—and I was shamed to tell you the truth—till the both of you forced my hand, and I seen you was the same as all the rest. And now, give me a bawling out and beat it, like I can tell you're going to. (*She stops, looking at* BURKE. *He is silent, his face averted, his features beginning to work with fury. She pleads passionately.*) Will you believe it if I tell you that loving you has made me— clean? It's the straight goods, honest! (*Then as he doesn't reply —bitterly.*) Like hell you will! You're like all the rest!

BURKE (*Blazing out—turning on her in a perfect frenzy of rage—his voice trembling with passion*)   The rest, is it? God's curse on you! Clane, is it? You slut, you, I'll be killing you now! (*He picks up the chair on which he has been sitting and, swinging it high over his shoulder, springs toward her.* CHRIS *rushes forward with a cry of alarm, trying to ward off the blow from his daughter.* ANNA *looks up into* BURKE'S *eyes with the fearlessness of despair.* BURKE *checks himself, the chair held in the air.*)

CHRIS (*Wildly*)   Stop, you crazy fool! You vant for murder her!

ANNA (*Pushing her father away brusquely, her eyes still holding* BURKE'S)   Keep out of this, you! (*To* BURKE—*dully.*) Well, ain't you got the nerve to do it? Go ahead! I'll be thankful to you, honest. I'm sick of the whole game.

BURKE (*Throwing the chair away into a corner of the room—help-lessly*)   I can't do it, God help me, and your two eyes looking at me. (*Furiously.*) Though I do be thinking I'd have a good right to smash your skull like a rotten egg. Was there iver a woman in the world had the rottenness in her that you have, and was there iver a man the like of me was made the fool of the world, and me thinking thoughts about you, and having great love for you, and dreaming dreams of the fine life we'd have when we'd be wedded! (*His voice high pitched in a lamentation that is like a keen.*) Yerra, God help me! I'm destroyed entirely and my heart is broken in bits! I'm asking God Himself, was it for this He'd have me roaming the earth since I was a lad only to come to black shame in the end, where I'd be giving a power of love to a woman is the same as others you'd meet in any hookershanty in port, with red gowns on them and paint on their grinning mugs, would be sleeping with any man for a dollar or two!

ANNA (*In a scream*) Don't, Mat! For Gawd's sake! (*Then raging and pounding on the table with her hands.*) Get out of here! Leave me alone! Get out of here!

BURKE (*His anger rushing back on him*) I'll be going, surely! And I'll be drinking sloos of whisky will wash that black kiss of yours off my lips; and I'll be getting dead rotten drunk so I'll not remember if 'twas iver born you was at all; and I'll be shipping away on some boat will take me to the other end of the world where I'll never see your face again! (*He turns toward the door.*)

CHRIS (*Who has been standing in a stupor—suddenly grasping* BURKE *by the arm—stupidly*) No, you don't go. Ay tank maybe it's better Anna marry you now.

BURKE (*Shaking* CHRIS *off—furiously*) Lave go of me, ye old ape! Marry her, is it? I'd see her roasting in hell first! I'm shipping away out of this, I'm telling you! (*Pointing to* ANNA—*passionately.*) And my curse on you and the curse of Almighty God and all the Saints! You've destroyed me this day and may you lie awake in the long nights, tormented with thoughts of Mat Burke and the great wrong you've done him!

ANNA (*In anguish*) Mat! (*But he turns without another word and strides out of the doorway.* ANNA *looks after him wildly, starts to run after him, then hides her face in her outstretched arms, sobbing.* CHRIS *stands in a stupor, staring at the floor.*)

CHRIS (*After a pause, dully*) Ay tank Ay go ashore, too.

ANNA (*Looking up, wildly*) Not after him! Let him go! Don't you dare——

CHRIS (*Somberly*) Ay go for gat drink.

ANNA (*With a harsh laugh*) So I'm driving you to drink, too, eh? I s'pose you want to get drunk so's you can forget—like him?

CHRIS (*Bursting out angrily*) Yes, Ay vant! You tank Ay like hear dem tangs. (*Breaking down—weeping.*) Ay tank you vasn't dat kind of gel, Anna.

ANNA (*Mockingly*) And I s'pose you want me to beat it, don't you? You don't want me here disgracing you, I s'pose?

CHRIS No, you stay here! (*Goes over and pats her on the shoulder, the tears running down his face.*) Ain't your fault, Anna, Ay know dat. (*She looks up at him, softened. He bursts into rage.*) It's dat ole davil, sea, do this to me! (*He shakes his fist at the door.*) It's her dirty tricks! It vas all right on barge with yust you and me. Den she bring dat Irish fallar in fog, she make you like him, she make you fight with me all time! If dat Irish fallar don't never come, you don't never tal me dem tangs, Ay don't never know, and everytang's all right. (*He shakes his fist again.*) Dirty ole davil!

ANNA (*With spent weariness*) Oh, what's the use? Go on ashore and get drunk.

CHRIS (*Goes into room on left and gets his cap. He goes to the door, silent and stupid—then turns*) You vait here, Anna?

ANNA (*Dully*) Maybe—and maybe not. Maybe I'll get drunk, too. Maybe I'll——But what the hell do you care what I do? Go on and beat it. (CHRIS *turns stupidly and goes out.* ANNA *sits at the table, staring straight in front of her.*)

*Curtain*

# ACT FOUR

SCENE—*Same as Act Three, about nine o'clock of a foggy night two days later. The whistles of steamers in the harbor can be heard. The cabin is lighted by a small lamp on the table. A suit case stands in the middle of the floor.* ANNA *is sitting in the rocking-chair. She wears a hat, is all dressed up as in Act One. Her face is pale, looks terribly tired and worn, as if the two days just past had been ones of suffering and sleepless nights. She stares before her despondently, her chin in her hands. There is a timid knock on the door in rear.* ANNA *jumps to her feet with a startled exclamation and looks toward the door with an expression of mingled hope and fear.*

ANNA (*Faintly*)  Come in. (*Then summoning her courage—more resolutely.*) Come in. (*The door is opened and* CHRIS *appears in the doorway. He is in a very bleary, bedraggled condition, suffering from the after-effects of his drunk. A tin pail full of foaming beer is in his hand. He comes forward, his eyes avoiding* ANNA's. *He mutters stupidly.*) It's foggy.

ANNA (*Looking him over with contempt*)  So you come back at last, did you? You're a fine looking sight! (*Then jeeringly.*) I thought you'd beaten it for good on account of the disgrace I'd brought on you.

CHRIS (*Wincing—faintly*)  Don't say dat, Anna, please! (*He sits in a chair by the table, setting down the can of beer, holding his head in his hands.*)

ANNA (*Looks at him with a certain sympathy*)  What's the trouble? Feeling sick?

CHRIS (*Dully*)  Inside my head feel sick.

ANNA  Well, what d'you expect after being soused for two days? (*Resentfully.*) It serves you right. A fine thing—you leaving me alone on this barge all the time!

CHRIS (*Humbly*) Ay'm sorry, Anna.

ANNA (*Scornfully*) Sorry!

CHRIS But Ay'm not sick inside head vay you mean. Ay'm sick from tank too much about you, about me.

ANNA And how about me? D'you suppose I ain't been thinking, too?

CHRIS Ay'm sorry, Anna. (*He sees her bag and gives a start.*) You pack your bag, Anna? You vas going——?

ANNA (*Forcibly*) Yes, I was going right back to what you think.

CHRIS Anna!

ANNA I went ashore to get a train for New York. I'd been waiting and waiting till I was sick of it. Then I changed my mind and decided not to go today. But I'm going first thing to morrow, so it'll all be the same in the end.

CHRIS (*Raising his head—pleadingly*) No, you never do dat, Anna!

ANNA (*With a sneer*) Why not, I'd like to know?

CHRIS You don't never gat to do—dat vay—no more, Ay tal you. Ay fix dat up all right.

ANNA (*Suspiciously*) Fix what up?

CHRIS (*Not seeming to have heard her question—sadly*) You vas vaiting, you say? You vasn't vaiting for me, Ay bet.

ANNA (*Callously*) You'd win.

CHRIS For dat Irish fallar?

ANNA (*Defiantly*) Yes—if you want to know! (*Then with a forlorn laugh.*) If he did come back it'd only be 'cause he wanted to beat me up or kill me, I suppose. But even if he did, I'd rather have him come than not show up at all. I wouldn't care what he did.

CHRIS Ay guess it's true you vas in love with him all right.

ANNA You guess!

CHRIS (*Turning to her earnestly*) And Ay'm sorry for you like hell he don't come, Anna!

ANNA (*Softened*) Seems to me you've changed your tune a lot.

CHRIS Ay've been tanking, and Ay guess it vas all my fault—all bad tangs dat happen to you. (*Pleadingly.*) You try for not hate me, Anna. Ay'm crazy ole fool, dat's all.

ANNA Who said I hated you?

CHRIS Ay'm sorry for everytang Ay do wrong for you, Anna. Ay vant for you be happy all rest of your life for make up! It make you happy marry dat Irish fallar, Ay vant it, too.

ANNA (*Dully*)  Well, there ain't no chance. But I'm glad you think different about it, anyway.

CHRIS (*Supplicatingly*)  And you tank—maybe—you forgive me sometime?

ANNA (*With a wan smile*)  I'll forgive you right now.

CHRIS (*Seizing her hand and kissing it—brokenly*)  Anna lilla! Anna lilla!

ANNA (*Touched but a bit embarrassed*)  Don't bawl about it. There ain't nothing to forgive, anyway. It ain't your fault, and it ain't mine, and it ain't his neither. We're all poor nuts, and things happen, and we yust get mixed in wrong, that's all.

CHRIS (*Eagerly*)  You say right tang, Anna, py golly! It ain't nobody's fault! (*Shaking his fist.*) It's dat ole davil sea!

ANNA (*With an exasperated laugh*)  Gee, won't you ever can that stuff? (CHRIS *relapses into injured silence. After a pause* ANNA *continues curiously.*) You said a minute ago you'd fixed something up—about me. What was it?

CHRIS (*After a hesitating pause*)  Ay'm shipping avay on sea again, Anna.

ANNA (*Astounded*)  You're—what?

CHRIS  Ay sign on steamer sail tomorrow. Ay gat my ole yob—bo'sun. (ANNA *stares at him. As he goes on, a bitter smile comes over her face.*) Ay tank dat's best tang for you. Ay only bring you bad luck, Ay tank. Ay make your mo'der's life sorry. Ay don't vant make yours dat way, but Ay do yust same. Dat ole davil, sea, she make me Yonah man ain't no good for nobody. And Ay tank now it ain't no use fight with sea. No man dat live going to beat her, py yingo!

ANNA (*With a laugh of helpless bitterness*)  So that's how you've fixed me, is it?

CHRIS  Yes, Ay tank if dat ole davil gat me back she leave you alone den.

ANNA (*Bitterly*)  But, for Gawd's sake, don't you see you're doing the same thing you've always done? Don't you see——? (*But she sees the look of obsessed stubbornness on her father's face and gives it up helplessly.*) But what's the use of talking? You ain't right, that's what. I'll never blame you for nothing no more. But how you could figure out that was fixing me——!

CHRIS  Dat ain't all. Ay gat dem fallars in steamship office to pay you all money coming to me every month vhile Ay'm avay.

ANNA (*With a hard laugh*) Thanks. But I guess I won't be hard up for no small change.

CHRIS (*Hurt—humbly*) It ain't much, Ay know, but it's plenty for keep you so you never gat go back——

ANNA (*Shortly*) Shut up, will you? We'll talk about it later, see?

CHRIS (*After a pause—ingratiatingly*) You like Ay go ashore look for dat Irish fallar, Anna?

ANNA (*Angrily*) Not much! Think I want to drag him back?

CHRIS (*After a pause—uncomfortably*) Py golly, dat booze don't go vell. Give me fever, Ay tank. Ay feel hot like hell. (*He takes off his coat and lets it drop on the floor. There is a loud thud.*)

ANNA (*With a start*) What you got in your pocket, for Pete's sake—a ton of lead? (*She reaches down, takes the coat and pulls out a revolver—looks from it to him in amazement.*) A gun? What were you doing with this?

CHRIS (*Sheepishly*) Ay forget. Ain't nothing. Ain't loaded, anyway.

ANNA (*Breaking it open to make sure—then closing it again—looking at him suspiciously*) That ain't telling me why you got it?

CHRIS Ay'm ole fool. Ay got it when Ay go ashore first. Ay tank den it's all fault of dat Irish fallar.

ANNA (*With a shudder*) Say, you're crazier than I thought. I never dreamt you'd go that far.

CHRIS (*Quickly*) Ay don't. Ay gat better sense right avay. Ay don't never buy bullets even. It ain't his fault, Ay know.

ANNA (*Still suspicious of him*) Well, I'll take care of this for a while, loaded or not. (*She puts it in the drawer of table and closes the drawer.*)

CHRIS (*Placatingly*) Throw it overboard if you vant. Ay don't care. (*Then after a pause.*) Py golly, Ay tank Ay go lie down. Ay feel sick. (ANNA *takes a magazine from the table.* CHRIS *hesitates by her chair.*) Ve talk again before Ay go, yes?

ANNA (*Dully*) Where's this ship going to?

CHRIS Cape Town. Dat's in South Africa. She's British steamer called Londonderry. (*He stands hesitatingly—finally blurts out.*) Anna—you forgive me sure?

ANNA (*Wearily*) Sure I do. You ain't to blame. You're yust—what you are—like me.

CHRIS (*Pleadingly*) Den—you lat me kiss you again once?

ANNA (*Raising her face—forcing a wan smile*) Sure. No hard feelings.

CHRIS (*Kisses her brokenly*) Anna lilla! Ay——(*He fights for words to express himself, but finds none—miserably—with a sob.*) Ay can't say it. Good-night, Anna.

ANNA Good-night. (*He picks up the can of beer and goes slowly into the room on left, his shoulders bowed, his head sunk forward dejectedly. He closes the door after him.* ANNA *turns over the pages of the magazine, trying desperately to banish her thoughts by looking at the pictures. This fails to distract her, and flinging the magazine back on the table, she springs to her feet and walks about the cabin distractedly, clenching and unclenching her hands. She speaks aloud to herself in a tense, trembling voice.*) Gawd, I can't stand this much longer! What am I waiting for anyway?—like a damn fool! (*She laughs helplessly, then checks herself abruptly, as she hears the sound of heavy footsteps on the deck outside. She appears to recognize these and her face lights up with joy. She gasps.*) Mat! (*A strange terror seems suddenly to seize her. She rushes to the table, takes the revolver out of drawer and crouches down in the corner, left, behind the cupboard. A moment later the door is flung open and* MAT BURKE *appears in the doorway. He is in bad shape—his clothes torn and dirty, covered with sawdust as if he had been grovelling or sleeping on barroom floors. There is a red bruise on his forehead over one of his eyes, another over one cheekbone, his knuckles are skinned and raw—plain evidence of the fighting he has been through on his "bat." His eyes are bloodshot and heavy-lidded, his face has a bloated look. But beyond these appearances—the results of heavy drinking—there is an expression in his eyes of wild mental turmoil, of impotent animal rage baffled by its own abject misery.*)

BURKE (*Peers blinkingly about the cabin—hoarsely*) Let you not be hiding from me, whoever's here—though 'tis well you know I'd have a right to come back and murder you. (*He stops to listen. Hearing no sound, he closes the door behind him and comes forward to the table. He throws himself into the rocking-chair— despondently.*) There's no one here, I'm thinking, and 'tis a great fool I am to be coming. (*With a sort of dumb, uncomprehending anguish.*) Yerra, Mat Burke, 'tis a great jackass you've become and what's got into you at all, at all? She's gone out of this long ago, I'm telling you, and you'll never see her face again. (ANNA *stands up, hesitating, struggling between joy and fear.* BURKE's *eyes fall on* ANNA's *bag. He leans over to examine it.*) What's this? (*Joyfully.*) It's hers. She's not gone! But where is she? Ashore? (*Darkly.*) What would she be doing ashore on this rotten night? (*His face suddenly convulsed with grief and rage.*) 'Tis that, is it? Oh, God's curse on her! (*Raging.*) I'll wait till she comes and choke her dirty life out. (ANNA *starts, her face grows hard. She steps into the room, the revolver in her right hand by her side.*)

ANNA (*In a cold, hard tone*) What are you doing here?

BURKE (*Wheeling about with a terrified gasp*) Glory be to God! (*They remain motionless and silent for a moment, holding each other's eyes.*)

ANNA (*In the same hard voice*) Well, can't you talk?

BURKE (*Trying to fall into an easy, careless tone*) You've a year's growth scared out of me, coming at me so sudden and me thinking I was alone.

ANNA You've got your nerve butting in here without knocking or nothing. What d'you want?

BURKE (*Airily*) Oh, nothing much. I was wanting to have a last word with you, that's all. (*He moves a step toward her.*)

ANNA (*Sharply—raising the revolver in her hand*) Careful now! Don't try getting too close. I heard what you said you'd do to me.

BURKE (*Noticing the revolver for the first time*) Is it murdering me you'd be now, God forgive you? (*Then with a contemptuous laugh.*) Or is it thinking I'd be frightened by that old tin whistle? (*He walks straight for her.*)

ANNA (*Wildly*) Look out, I tell you!

BURKE (*Who has come so close that the revolver is almost touching his chest*) Let you shoot, then! (*Then with sudden wild grief.*) Let you shoot, I'm saying, and be done with it! Let you end me with a shot and I'll be thanking you, for it's a rotten dog's life I've lived the past two days since I've known what you are, till I'm after wishing I was never born at all!

ANNA (*Overcome—letting the revolver drop to the floor, as if her fingers had no strength to hold it—hysterically*) What d'you want coming here? Why don't you beat it? Go on! (*She passes him and sinks down in the rocking-chair.*)

BURKE (*Following her—mournfully*) 'Tis right you'd be asking why did I come. (*Then angrily.*) 'Tis because 'tis a great weak fool of the world I am, and me tormented with the wickedness you'd told of yourself, and drinking oceans of booze that'd make me forget. Forget? Divil a word I'd forget, and your face grinning always in front of my eyes, awake or asleep, till I do be thinking a madhouse is the proper place for me.

ANNA (*Glancing at his hands and face—scornfully*) You look like you ought to be put away some place. Wonder you wasn't pulled in. You been scrapping, too, ain't you?

BURKE I have—with every scut would take off his coat to me! (*Fiercely.*) And each time I'd be hitting one a clout in the mug, it wasn't his face I'd be seeing at all, but yours, and me wanting to drive you a blow would knock you out of this world where I wouldn't be seeing or thinking more of you.

ANNA (*Her lips trembling pitifully*) Thanks!

BURKE (*Walking up and down—distractedly*) That's right, make game of me! Oh, I'm a great coward surely, to be coming back to speak with you at all. You've a right to laugh at me.

ANNA I ain't laughing at you, Mat.

BURKE (*Unheeding*) You to be what you are, and me to be Mat Burke, and me to be drove back to look at you again! 'Tis black shame is on me!

ANNA (*Resentfully*) Then get out. No one's holding you!

BURKE (*Bewilderedly*) And me to listen to that talk from a woman like you and be frightened to close her mouth with a slap! Oh, God help me, I'm a yellow coward for all men to spit at! (*Then furiously.*) But I'll not be getting out of this till I've had me word. (*Raising his fist threateningly.*) And let you look out how you drive me! (*Letting his fist fall helplessly.*) Don't be angry now! I'm raving like a real lunatic, I'm thinking, and the sorrow you put on me has my brains drownded in grief. (*Suddenly bending down to her and grasping her arm intensely.*) Tell me it's a lie, I'm saying! That's what I'm after coming to hear you say.

ANNA (*Dully*) A lie? What?

BURKE (*With passionate entreaty*) All the badness you told me two days back. Sure it must be a lie? You was only making game of me, wasn't you? Tell me 'twas a lie, Anna, and I'll be saying prayers of thanks on my two knees to the Almighty God!

ANNA (*Terribly shaken—faintly*) I can't Mat. (*As he turns away—imploringly.*) Oh, Mat, won't you see that no matter what I was I ain't that any more? Why, listen! I packed up my bag this afternoon and went ashore. I'd been waiting here all alone

for two days, thinking maybe you'd come back—thinking maybe
you'd think over all I'd said—and maybe—oh, I don't know what
I was hoping! But I was afraid to even go out of the cabin
for a second, honest—afraid you might come and not find me
here. Then I gave up hope when you didn't show up and
I went to the railroad station. I was going to New York. I
was going back——

BURKE (*Hoarsely*)    God's curse on you!

ANNA    Listen, Mat. You hadn't come, and I'd gave up hope. But
—in the station—I couldn't go. I'd bought my ticket and everything. (*She takes the ticket from her dress and tries to hold
it before his eyes.*) But I got to thinking about you—and I
couldn't take the train—I couldn't! So I come back here—to
wait some more. Oh, Mat, don't you see I've changed? Can't
you forgive what's dead and gone—and forget it?

BURKE (*Turning on her—overcome by rage again*)    Forget, is it?
I'll not forget till my dying day, I'm telling you, and me
tormented with thoughts. (*In a frenzy.*) Oh, I'm wishing I had
wan of them fornenst me this minute and I'd beat him with
my fists till he'd be a bloody corpse! I'm wishing the whole
lot of them will roast in hell till the Judgment Day—and yourself along with them, for you're as bad as they are.

ANNA (*Shuddering*)    Mat! (*Then after a pause—in a voice of
dead, stony calm.*) Well, you've had your say. Now you better
beat it.

BURKE (*Starts slowly for the door—hesitates—then after a pause*)
And what'll you be doing?

ANNA    What difference does it make to you?

BURKE    I'm asking you!

ANNA (*In the same tone*)    My bag's packed and I got my ticket.
I'll go to New York tomorrow.

BURKE (*Helplessly*)    You mean—you'll be doing the same again?

ANNA (*Stonily*)    Yes.

BURKE (*In anguish*)    You'll not! Don't torment me with that talk!
'Tis a she-devil you are sent to drive me mad entirely!

ANNA (*Her voice breaking*)    Oh, for Gawd's sake, Mat, leave me
alone! Go away! Don't you see I'm licked? Why d'you want
to keep on kicking me?

BURKE (*Indignantly*)    And don't you deserve the worst I'd say,
God forgive you?

ANNA    All right. Maybe I do. But don't rub it in. Why ain't you done what you said you was going to? Why ain't you got that ship was going to take you to the other side of the earth where you'd never see me again?

BURKE  I have.

ANNA  (*Startled*)  What—then you're going—honest?

BURKE  I signed on today at noon, drunk as I was—and she's sailing tomorrow.

ANNA  And where's she going to?

BURKE  Cape Town.

ANNA  (*The memory of having heard that name a little while before coming to her—with a start, confusedly*)  Cape Town? Where's that? Far away?

BURKE  'Tis at the end of Africa. That's far for you.

ANNA  (*Forcing a laugh*)  You're keeping your word all right, ain't you? (*After a slight pause—curiously.*)  What's the boat's name?

BURKE  The Londonderry.

ANNA  (*It suddenly comes to her that this is the same ship her father is sailing on*)  The Londonderry! It's the same—Oh, this is too much! (*With wild, ironical laughter.*)  Ha-ha-ha!

BURKE  What's up with you now?

ANNA  Ha-ha-ha! It's funny, funny! I'll die laughing!

BURKE  (*Irritated*)  Laughing at what?

ANNA  It's a secret. You'll know soon enough. It's funny. (*Controlling herself—after a pause—cynically.*)  What kind of a place is this Cape Town? Plenty of dames there, I suppose?

BURKE  To hell with them! That I may never see another woman to my dying hour!

ANNA  That's what you say now, but I'll bet by the time you get there you'll have forgot all about me and start in talking the same old bull you talked to me to the first one you meet.

BURKE  (*Offended*)  I'll not, then! God mend you, is it making me out to be the like of yourself you are, and you taking up with this one and that all the years of your life?

ANNA  (*Angrily assertive*)  Yes, that's yust what I do mean! You been doing the same thing all your life, picking up a new girl in every port. How're you any better than I was?

BURKE  (*Thoroughly exasperated*)  Is it no shame you have at all? I'm a fool to be wasting talk on you and you hardened in badness. I'll go out of this and have lave you alone forever. (*He starts for the door—then stops to turn on her furiously.*)  And I suppose 'tis the same lies you told them all before that you told to me?

ANNA (*Indignantly*) That's a lie! I never did!

BURKE (*Miserably*) You'd be saying that, anyway.

ANNA (*Forcibly, with growing intensity*) Are you trying to accuse me—of being in love—really in love—with them?

BURKE I'm thinking you were, surely.

ANNA (*Furiously, as if this were the last insult—advancing on him threateningly*) You mutt, you! I've stood enough from you. Don't you dare. (*With scornful bitterness.*) Love 'em! Oh, my Gawd! You damn thick-head! Love 'em? (*Savagely.*) I hated 'em, I tell you! Hated 'em, hated 'em, hated 'em! And may Gawd strike me dead this minute and my mother, too, if she was alive, if I ain't telling you the honest truth!

BURKE (*Immensely pleased by her vehemence—a light beginning to break over his face—but still uncertain, torn between doubt and the desire to believe—helplessly*) If I could only be believing you now!

ANNA (*Distractedly*) Oh, what's the use? What's the use of me talking? What's the use of anything? (*Pleadingly.*) Oh, Mat, you mustn't think that for a second! You mustn't! Think all the other bad about me you want to, and I won't kick, 'cause you've a right to. But don't think that! (*On the point of tears.*) I couldn't bear it! It'd be yust too much to know you was going away where I'd never see you again—thinking that about me!

BURKE (*After an inward struggle—tensely—forcing out the words with difficulty*) If I was believing—that you'd never had love for any other man in the world but me—I could be forgetting the rest, maybe.

ANNA (*With a cry of joy*) Mat!

BURKE (*Slowly*) If 'tis truth you're after telling, I'd have a right, maybe, to believe you'd changed—and that I'd changed you my-self till the thing you'd been all your life wouldn't be you any more at all.

ANNA (*Hanging on his words—breathlessly*) Oh, Mat! That's what I been trying to tell you all along!

BURKE (*Simply*) For I've a power of strength in me to lead men the way I want, and women, too, maybe, and I'm thinking I'd change you to a new woman entirely, so I'd never know, or you either, what kind of woman you'd been in the past at all.

ANNA  Yes, you could, Mat! I know you could!

BURKE  And I'm thinking 'twasn't your fault, maybe, but having that old ape for a father that left you to grow up alone, made you what you was. And if I could be believing 'tis only me you——

ANNA  (*Distractedly*) You got to believe it, Mat! What can I do? I'll do anything, anything you want to prove I'm not lying!

BURKE  (*Suddenly seems to have a solution. He feels in the pocket of his coat and grasps something—solemnly*) Would you be willing to swear an oath, now—a terrible, fearful oath would send your soul to the divils in hell if you was lying?

ANNA  (*Eagerly*) Sure, I'll swear, Mat—on anything!

BURKE  (*Takes a small, cheap old crucifix from his pocket and holds it up for her to see*) Will you swear on this?

ANNA  (*Reaching out for it*) Yes. Sure I will. Give it to me.

BURKE  (*Holding it away*) 'Tis a cross was given me by my mother, God rest her soul. (*He makes the sign of the cross mechanically.*) I was a lad only, and she told me to keep it by me if I'd be waking or sleeping and never lose it, and it'd bring me luck. She died soon after. But I'm after keeping it with me from that day to this, and I'm telling you there's great power in it, and 'tis great bad luck it's saved me from and me roaming the seas, and I having it tied round my neck when my last ship sunk, and it bringing me safe to land when the others went to their death. (*Very earnestly.*) And I'm warning you now, if you'd swear an oath on this, 'tis my old woman herself will be looking down from Hivin above, and praying Almighty God and the Saints to put a great curse on you if she'd hear you swearing a lie!

ANNA  (*Awed by his manner—superstitiously*) I wouldn't have the nerve—honest—if it was a lie. But it's the truth and I ain't scared to swear. Give it to me.

BURKE  (*Handing it to her—almost frightenedly, as if he feared for her safety*) Be careful what you'd swear, I'm saying.

ANNA  (*Holding the cross gingerly*) Well—what do you want me to swear? You say it.

BURKE  Swear I'm the only man in the world ivir you felt love for.

ANNA  (*Looking into his eyes steadily*) I swear it.

BURKE  And that you'll be forgetting from this day all the badness you've done and never do the like of it again.

ANNA (*Forcibly*) I swear it! I swear it by God!

BURKE And may the blackest curse of God strike you if you're lying. Say it now!

ANNA And may the blackest curse of God strike me if I'm lying!

BURKE (*With a stupendous sigh*) Oh, glory be to God, I'm after believing you now! (*He takes the cross from her hand, his face beaming with joy, and puts it back in his pocket. He puts his arm about her waist and is about to kiss her when he stops, appalled by some terrible doubt.*)

ANNA (*Alarmed*) What's the matter with you?

BURKE (*With sudden fierce questioning*) Is it Catholic ye are?

ANNA (*Confused*) No. Why?

BURKE (*Filled with a sort of bewildered foreboding*) Oh, God, help me! (*With a dark glance of suspicion at her.*) There's some divil's trickery in it, to be swearing an oath on a Catholic cross and you wan of the others.

ANNA (*Distractedly*) Oh, Mat, don't you believe me?

BURKE (*Miserably*) If it isn't a Catholic you are——

ANNA I ain't nothing. What's the difference? Didn't you hear me swear?

BURKE (*Passionately*) Oh, I'd a right to stay away from you— but I couldn't! I was loving you in spite of it all and wanting to be with you, God forgive me, no matter what you are. I'd go mad if I'd not have you! I'd be killing the world—— (*He seizes her in his arms and kisses her fiercely.*)

ANNA (*With a gasp of joy*) Mat!

BURKE (*Suddenly holding her away from him and staring into her eyes as if to probe into her soul—slowly*) If your oath is no proper oath at all, I'll have to be taking your naked word for it and have you anyway, I'm thinking—I'm needing you that bad!

ANNA (*Hurt—reproachfully*) Mat! I swore, didn't I?

BURKE (*Defiant, as if challenging fate*) Oath or no oath, 'tis no matter. We'll be wedded in the morning, with the help of God. (*Still more defiantly.*) We'll be happy now, the two of us, in spite of the divil! (*He crushes her to him and kisses her again. The door on the left is pushed open and* CHRIS *appears in the doorway. He stands blinking at them. At first the old expression of hatred of* BURKE *comes into his eyes instinctively. Then a look of resignation and relief takes its place. His face lights up with a sudden happy thought. He turns back into the bedroom—reappears immediately with the tin can of beer in his hand—grinning.*)

CHRIS Ve have a drink on this, py golly! (*They break away from each other with startled exclamations.*)

BURKE (*Explosively*) God stiffen it! (*He takes a step toward* CHRIS *threateningly.*)

ANNA (*Happily—to her father*) That's the way to talk! (*With a laugh.*) And say, it's about time for you and Mat to kiss and make up. You're going to be shipmates on the Londonderry, did you know it?

BURKE (*Astounded*) Shipmates—— Has himself——

CHRIS (*Equally astounded*) Ay vas bo'sun on her.

BURKE The divil! (*Then angrily.*) You'd be going back to sea and leaving her alone, would you?

ANNA (*Quickly*) It's all right, Mat. That's where he belongs, and I want him to go. You got to go, too; we'll need the money. (*With a laugh, as she gets the glasses.*) And as for me being alone, that runs in the family, and I'll get used to it. (*Pouring out their glasses.*) I'll get a little house somewhere and I'll make a regular place for you two to come back to—wait and see. And now you drink up and be friends.

BURKE (*Happily—but still a bit resentful against the old man*) Sure! (*Clinking his glass against* CHRIS'.) Here's luck to you! (*He drinks.*)

CHRIS (*Subdued—his face melancholy*) Skoal. (*He drinks.*)

BURKE (*To* ANNA, *with a wink*) You'll not be lonesome long. I'll see to that, with the help of God. 'Tis himself here will be having a grandchild to ride on his foot, I'm telling you!

ANNA (*Turning away in embarrassment*) Quit the kidding now. (*She picks up her bag and goes into the room on left. As soon as she is gone* BURKE *relapses into an attitude of gloomy thought.* CHRIS *stares at his beer absent-mindedly. Finally* BURKE *turns on him.*)

BURKE Is it any religion at all you have, you and your Anna?

CHRIS (*Surprised*) Vhy yes. Ve vas Lutheran in ole country.

BURKE (*Horrified*) Luthers, is it? (*Then with a grim resignation, slowly, aloud to himself.*) Well, I'm damned then surely. Yerra, what's the difference? 'Tis the will of God, anyway.

CHRIS (*Moodily preoccupied with his own thoughts—speaks with somber premonition as* ANNA *re-enters from the left*) It's funny. It's queer, yes—you and me shipping on same boat dat vay.

It ain't right. Ay don't know—it's dat funny vay ole davil sea do her vorst dirty tricks, yes. It's so. (*He gets up and goes back and, opening the door, stares out into the darkness.*)

BURKE (*Nodding his head in gloomy acquiescence—with a great sigh*) I'm fearing maybe you have the right of it for once, divil take you.

ANNA (*Forcing a laugh*)    Gee, Mat, you ain't agreeing with him, are you? (*She comes forward and puts her arm about his shoulder—with a determined gayety.*) Aw say, what's the matter? Cut out the gloom. We're all fixed now, ain't we, me and you? (*Pours out more beer into his glass and fills one for herself— slaps him on the back.*) Come on! Here's to the sea, no matter what! Be a game sport and drink to that! Come on! (*She gulps down her glass.* BURKE *banishes his superstitious premonitions with a defiant jerk of his head, grins up at her, and drinks to her toast.*)

CHRIS (*Looking out into the night—lost in his somber preoccupation—shakes his head and mutters*)    Fog, fog, fog, all bloody time. You can't see vhere you vas going, no. Only dat ole davil, sea—she knows! (*The two stare at him. From the harbor comes the muffled, mournful wail of steamers' whistles.*)

*Curtain*

# "The
# Hairy Ape"

# Characters

ROBERT SMITH, "YANK"

PADDY

LONG

MILDRED DOUGLAS

HER AUNT

SECOND ENGINEER

A GUARD

A SECRETARY OF AN ORGANIZATION

*Stokers, Ladies, Gentlemen, etc.*

# Scenes

# SCENE ONE

THE *firemen's forecastle of a transatlantic liner an hour after sailing from New York for the voyage across. Tiers of narrow, steel bunks, three deep, on all sides. An entrance in rear. Benches on the floor before the bunks. The room is crowded with men, shouting, cursing, laughing, singing—a confused, inchoate uproar swelling into a sort of unity, a meaning—the bewildered, furious, baffled defiance of a beast in a cage. Nearly all the men are drunk. Many bottles are passed from hand to hand. All are dressed in dungaree pants, heavy ugly shoes. Some wear singlets, but the majority are stripped to the waist.*

*The treatment of this scene, or of any other scene in the play, should by no means be naturalistic. The effect sought after is a cramped space in the bowels of a ship, imprisoned by white steel. The lines of bunks, the uprights supporting them, cross each other like the steel framework of a cage. The ceiling crushes down upon the men's heads. They cannot stand upright. This accentuates the natural stooping posture which shoveling coal and the resultant over-development of back and shoulder muscles have given them. The men themselves should resemble those pictures in which the appearance of Neanderthal Man is guessed at. All are hairy-chested, with long arms of tremendous power, and low, receding brows above their small, fierce, resentful eyes. All the civilized white races are represented, but except for the slight differentiation in color of hair, skin, eyes, all these men are like.*

*The curtain rises on a tumult of sound.* YANK *is seated in the foreground. He seems broader, fiercer, more truculent, more powerful, more sure of himself than the rest. They respect his superior strength—the grudging respect of fear. Then, too, he represents to them a self-expression, the very last word in what they are, their most highly developed individual.*

VOICES   Gif me trink dere, you!
  'Ave a wet!
  Salute!
  Gesundheit!
  Skoal!
  Drunk as a lord, God stiffen you!
  Here's how!
  Luck!
  Pass back that bottle, damn you!
  Pourin' it down his neck!
  Ho, Froggy! Where the devil have you been?
  *La Touraine.*
  I hit him smash in yaw, py Gott!
  Jenkins—the First—he's a rotten swine—
  And the coppers nabbed him—and I run—
  I like peer better. It don't pig head gif you.
  A slut, I'm sayin'! She robbed me aslape—
  To hell with 'em all!
  You're a bloody lair!
  Say dot again! (*Commotion. Two men about to fight are pulled
    apart*).
  No scrappin' now!
  Tonight—
  See who's the best man!
  Bloody Dutchman!
  Tonight on the for'ard square.
  I'll bet on Dutchy.
  He packa da wallop, I tella you!
  Shut up, Wop!
  No fightin', maties. We're all chums, ain't we?
  (*A voice starts bawling a song*).

  "Beer, beer, glorious beer!
  Fill yourselves right up to here."

YANK (*for the first time seeming to take notice of the uproar about
  him, turns around threateningly—in a tone of contemptuous authority*)   Choke off dat noise! Where d'yuh get dat beer stuff?
  Beer, hell! Beer's for goils—and Dutchmen. Me for somep'n wit
  a kick to it! Gimme a drink, one of youse guys. (*Several bottles
  are eagerly offered. He takes a tremendous gulp at one of them;*

*then, keeping the bottle in his hand, glares belligerently at the owner, who hastens to acquiesce in this robbery by saying)* All righto, Yank. Keep it and have another. (YANK *contemptuously turns his back on the crowd again. For a second there is an embarrassed silence. Then—)*

VOICES We must be passing the Hook.

She's beginning to roll to it.

Six days in hell—and then Southampton.

Py Yesus, I vish somepody take my first vatch for me!

Gittin' seasick, Square-head?

Drink up and forget it!

What's in your bottle?

Gin.

Dot's nigger trink.

Absinthe? It's doped. You'll go off your chump, Froggy.

Cochon!

Whisky, that's the ticket!

Where's Paddy?

Going asleep.

Sing us that whisky song, Paddy. (*They all turn to an old, wizened Irishman who is dozing, very drunk, on the benches forward. His face is extremely monkey-like with all the sad, patient pathos of that animal in his small eyes).*

Singa da song, Caruso Pat!

He's gettin' old. The drink is too much for him.

He's too drunk.

PADDY (*blinking about him, starts to his feet resentfully, swaying, holding on to the edge of a bunk)* I'm never too drunk to sing. 'Tis only when I'm dead to the world I'd be wishful to sing at all. (*With a sort of sad contempt)* "Whisky Johnny," ye want? A chanty, ye want? Now that's a queer wish from the ugly like of you, God help you. But no matther. (*He starts to sing in a thin, nasal, doleful tone):*

Oh, whisky is the life of man!

  Whisky! O Johnny! (*They all join in on this).*

Oh, whisky is the life of man!

  Whisky for my Johnny! (*Again chorus).*

Oh, whisky drove my old man mad!

  Whisky! O Johnny!

Oh, whisky drove my old man mad!
Whisky for my Johnny!

YANK (*again turning around scornfully*) Aw hell! Nix on dat old
sailing ship stuff! All dat bull's dead, see? And you're dead,
too, yuh damned old Harp, on'y yuh don't know it. Take it
easy, see. Give us a rest. Nix on de loud noise. (*With a cynical
grin*) Can't youse see I'm tryin' to t'ink?

ALL (*repeating the word after him as one with the same cynical
amused mockery*) Think! (*The chorused word has a brazen
metallic quality as if their throats were phonograph horns. It is
followed by a general uproar of hard, barking laughter*).

VOICES Don't be cracking your head wit ut, Yank.
You gat headache, py yingo!
One thing about it—it rhymes with drink!
Ha, ha, ha!
Drink, don't think!
Drink, don't think!
Drink, don't think! (*A whole chorus of voices has taken up this
refrain, stamping on the floor, pounding on the benches with
fists*).

YANK (*taking a gulp from his bottle—good-naturedly*) Aw right.
Can de noise. I got yuh de foist time. (*The uproar subsides.
A very drunken sentimental tenor begins to sing*):

"Far away in Canada,
    Far across the sea,
There's a lass who fondly waits
    Making a home for me—"

YANK (*fiercely contemptuous*) Shut up, yuh lousy boob! Where
d'yuh get dat tripe? Home? Home, hell! I'll make a home for
yuh! I'll knock yuh dead. Home! T'hell wit home! Where
d'yuh get dat tripe? Dis is home, see? What d'yuh want wit
home? (*Proudly*) I runned away from mine when I was a kid.
On'y too glad to beat it, dat was me. Home was lickings for me,
dat's all. But yuh can bet your shoit no one ain't never licked
me since! Wanter try it, any of youse? Huh! I guess not. (*In a
more placated but still contemptuous tone*) Goils waitin' for yuh,
huh? Aw, hell! Dat's all tripe. Dey don't wait for no one. Dey'd
double-cross yuh for a nickel. Dey're all tarts, get me? Treat

'em rough, dat's me. To hell wit 'em. Tarts, dat's what, de whole bunch of 'em.

LONG (*very drunk, jumps on a bench excitedly, gesticulating with a bottle in his hand*) Listen 'ere, Comrades! Yank 'ere is right. 'E says this 'ere stinkin' ship is our 'ome. And 'e says as 'ome is 'ell. And 'e's right! This is 'ell. We lives in 'ell, Comrades—and right enough we'll die in it. (*Raging*) And who's ter blame, I arsks yer? We ain't. We wasn't born this rotten way. All men is born free and ekal. That's in the bleedin' Bible, maties. But what d'they care for the Bible—them lazy, bloated swine what travels first cabin? Them's the ones. They dragged us down 'til we're on'y wage slaves in the bowels of a bloody ship, sweatin', burnin' up, eatin' coal dust! Hit's them's ter blame—the damned Capitalist clarss! (*There had been a gradual murmur of contemptuous resentment rising among the men until now he is interrupted by a storm of catcalls, hisses, boos, hard laughter*).

VOICES  Turn it off!

Shut up!

Sit down!

Closa da face!

Tamn fool! (*Etc.*).

YANK (*standing up and glaring at* LONG) Sit down before I knock yuh down! (LONG *makes haste to efface himself.* YANK *goes on contemptuously*) De Bible, huh? De Cap'tlist class, huh? Aw nix on/ dat Salvation Army-Socialist bull. Git a soapbox! Hire a hall! Come and be saved, huh? Jerk us to Jesus, huh? Aw g'wan! I've listened to lots of guys like you, see. Yuh're all wrong. Wanter know what I t'ink? Yuh ain't no good for no one. Yuh're de bunk. Yuh ain't got no noive, get me? Yuh're yellow, dat's what. Yellow, dat's you. Say! What's dem slobs in de foist cabin got to do wit us? We're better men dan dey are, ain't we? Sure! One of us guys could clean up de whole mob wit one mit. Put one of 'em down here for one watch in de stokehole, what'd happen? Dey'd carry him off on a stretcher. Dem boids don't amount to nothin'. Dey're just baggage. Who makes dis old tub run? Ain't it us guys? Well den, we belong, don't we? We belong and dey don't. Dat's all. (*A loud chorus of approval.* YANK *goes on*) As for dis bein' hell—aw, nuts! Yuh lost your noive, dat's what. Dis is a man's job, get me? It belongs. It runs dis tub. No stiffs need apply. But yuh're a stiff, see? Yuh're yellow, dat's you.

VOICES (*with a great hard pride in them*)

Righto!

A man's job!

Talk is cheap, Long.

He never could hold up his end.

Divil take him!

Yank's right. We make it go.

Py Gott, Yank say right ting!

We don't need no one cryin' over us.

Makin' speeches.

Throw him out!

Yellow!

Chuck him overboard!

I'll break his jaw for him!

(*They crowd around* LONG *threateningly*).

YANK (*half good-natured again—contemptuously*) Aw, take it easy. Leave him alone. He ain't woith a punch. Drink up. Here's how, whoever owns dis. (*He takes a long swallow from his bottle. All drink with him. In a flash all is hilarious amiability again, backslapping, loud talk, etc.*).

PADDY (*who has been sitting in a blinking, melancholy daze—suddenly cries out in a voice full of old sorrow*) We belong to this, you're saying? We make the ship to go, you're saying? Yerra then, that Almighty God have pity on us! (*His voice runs into the wail of a keen, he rocks back and forth on his bench. The men stare at him, startled and impressed in spite of themselves*) Oh, to be back in the fine days of my youth, ochone! Oh, there was fine beautiful ships them days—clippers wid tall masts touching the sky—fine strong men in them—men that was sons of the sea as if 'twas the mother that bore them. Oh, the clean skins of them, and the clear eyes, the straight backs and full chests of them! Brave men they was, and bold men surely! We'd be sailing out, bound down round the Horn maybe. We'd be making sail in the dawn, with a fair breeze, singing a chanty song wid no care to it. And astern the land would be sinking low and dying out, but we'd give it no heed but a laugh, and never a look behind. For the day that was, was enough, for we was free men—and I'm thinking 'tis only slaves do be giving heed to the day that's gone or the day to come—until they're old like me. (*With a sort of religious exaltation*) Oh, to be scudding south again wid the power of the Trade Wind driving her on steady through the nights and the days! Full sail on her! Nights and days! Nights when the foam of the wake would be flaming wid fire, when the sky'd be blazing and winking wid stars. Or the full of the moon maybe. Then you'd see her driving through the gray night, her sails stretching aloft all silver and white, not a sound on the deck, the lot of us dreaming dreams, till you'd believe 'twas no real ship at all you was on but a ghost ship like the *Flying Dutchman* they say does be roaming the seas forevermore widout touching a port. And there was the days, too. A warm sun on the clean decks. Sun warming the blood of you, and wind over the miles of shiny green ocean like strong drink to your lungs. Work—aye, hard work—but who'd mind that at all? Sure, you worked under the sky and 'twas work wid skill and daring to it. And wid the day done, in the dog watch, smoking me pipe at ease, the lookout would be raising land maybe, and we'd see the mountains of South Americy wid the red fire of the setting sun painting the white tops and the clouds floating by them! (*His tone of exaltation ceases. He goes on mournfully*) Yerra, what's the use of talking? 'Tis a dead man's whisper. (*To* YANK *resentfully*) 'Twas them days men belonged to ships, not now. 'Twas them days a ship was part of the sea, and a man was part of a ship, and the sea joined all together and made it one. (*Scornfully*) Is it one wid this you'd be, Yank—black smoke from the funnels smudging the sea, smudging the decks—the bloody engines pounding and throbbing and shaking—wid divil a sight of sun or a breath of clean air—choking our lungs wid coal dust— breaking our backs and hearts in the hell of the stokehole— feeding the bloody furnace—feeding our lives along wid the coal, I'm thinking—caged in by steel from a sight of the sky like bloody apes in the Zoo! (*With a harsh laugh*) Ho-ho, divil mend you! Is it to belong to that you're wishing? Is it a flesh and blood wheel of the engines you'd be?

YANK (*who has been listening with a contemptuous sneer, barks out the answer*) Sure ting! Dat's me. What about it?

PADDY (*as if to himself—with great sorrow*) Me time is past due. That a great wave wid sun in the heart of it may sweep me over the side sometime I'd be dreaming of the days that's gone!

YANK Aw, yuh crazy Mick! (*He springs to his feet and advances on* PADDY *threateningly—then stops, fighting some queer struggle within himself—lets his hands fall to his sides—contemptuously*) Aw, take it easy. Yuh're aw right, at dat. Yuh're bugs, dat's all— nutty as a cuckoo. All dat tripe yuh been pullin'—Aw, dat's all right. On'y it's dead, get me? Yuh don't belong no more, see. Yuh don't get de stuff. Yuh're too old. (*Disgustedly*) But aw say, come up for air onct in a while, can't yuh? See what's happened since yuh croaked. (*He suddenly bursts forth vehemently, growing more and more excited*) Say! Sure! Sure I meant it! What de hell—Say, lemme talk! Hey! Hey, you old Harp! Hey, youse guys! Say, listen to me—wait a moment—I gotter talk, see. I belong and he don't. He's dead but I'm livin'. Listen to me! Sure I'm part of de engines! Why de hell not! Dey move, don't dey? Dey're speed, ain't dey? Dey smash trou, don't dey? Twenty-five knots a hour! Dat's goin' some! Dat's new stuff! Dat belongs! But him, he's too old. He gets dizzy. Say, listen. All dat crazy tripe about nights and days; all dat crazy tripe about stars and moons; all dat crazy tripe about suns and winds, fresh air and de rest of it—Aw hell, dat's all a dope dream! Hittin' de pipe of de past, dat's what he's doin'. He's old and don't belong no more. But me, I'm young! I'm in de pink! I move wit it! It, get me! I mean de ting dat's de guts of all dis. It ploughs trou all de tripe he's been sayin'. It blows dat up! It knocks dat dead! It slams dat offen de face of de oith! It, get me! De engines and de coal and de smoke and all de rest of it! He can't breathe and swallow coal dust, but I kin, see? Dat's fresh air for me! Dat's food for me! I'm new, get me? Hell in de stokehole? Sure! It takes a man to work in hell. Hell, sure, dat's my fav'rite climate. I eat it up! I git fat on it! It's me makes it hot! It's me makes it roar! It's me makes it move! Sure, on'y for me everyting stops. It all goes dead, get me? De noise and smoke and all de engines movin' de woild, dey stop. Dere ain't nothin' no more! Dat's what I'm sayin'. Everyting else dat makes de woild move, somep'n makes it move. It can't move witout somep'n else, see? Den yuh get down to me. I'm at de bottom, get me! Dere ain't nothin' foither. I'm de end! I'm de start! I start somep'n and de woild moves! It—dat's me!—de new dat's moiderin' de old! I'm de ting in coal dat makes it boin; I'm steam and oil for de engines; I'm de ting in noise dat makes yuh hear it; I'm smoke and express trains and steamers and factory whistles; I'm de ting in gold dat makes it money! And I'm what makes iron into steel! Steel, dat stands for de whole ting! And I'm steel—steel—steel! I'm de muscles in steel, de punch behind it! (*As he says this he pounds with his fist against the steel bunks. All the men, roused to a pitch of frenzied self-glorification by his speech, do likewise. There is a deafening metallic roar, through which* YANK's *voice can be heard bellowing*) Slaves, hell! We run de whole woiks. All de rich guys dat tink dey're somep'n, dey ain't nothin'! Dey don't belong. But us guys, we're in de move, we're at de bottom, de whole ting is us! (PADDY *from the start of* YANK's *speech has been taking one gulp after another from his bottle, at first frightenedly, as if he were afraid to listen, then desperately, as if to drown his senses, but finally has achieved complete indifferent, even amused, drunkenness.* YANK *sees his lips moving. He quells the uproar with a shout*) Hey, youse guys, take it easy! Wait a moment! De nutty Harp is sayin' somep'n.

PADDY (*is heard now—throws his head back with a mocking burst of laughter*) Ho-ho-ho-ho-ho—

YANK (*drawing back his fist, with a snarl*) Aw! Look out who yuh're givin' the bark!

PADDY (*begins to sing the "Miller of Dee" with enormous good nature*).

"I care for nobody, no, not I,
And nobody cares for me."

YANK (*good-natured himself in a flash, interrupts* PADDY *with a slap on the bare back like a report*) Dat's de stuff! Now yuh're gettin' wise to somep'n. Care for nobody, dat's de dope! To hell wit 'em all! And nix on nobody else carin'. I kin care for myself, get me! (*Eight bells sound, muffled, vibrating through the steel walls as if some enormous brazen gong were imbedded in the heart of the ship. All the men jump up mechanically, file through the door silently close upon each other's heels in what is very like a prisoners' lockstep.* YANK *slaps* PADDY *on the back*) Our watch, yuh old Harp! (*Mockingly*) Come on down in hell. Eat up de coal dust. Drink in de heat. It's it, see! Act like yuh liked it, yuh better—or croak yuhself.

PADDY (*with jovial defiance*) To the divil wid it! I'll not report this watch. Let thim log me and be damned. I'm no slave the like of you. I'll be sittin' here at me ease, and drinking, and thinking, and dreaming dreams.

YANK (*contemptuously*) Tinkin' and dreamin', what'll that get yuh? What's tinkin' got to do wit it? We move, don't we? Speed, ain't it? Fog, dat's all you stand for. But we drive trou dat, don't

we? We split dat up and smash trou—twenty-five knots a hour!
(*Turns his back on* PADDY *scornfully*) Aw, yuh make me sick!
Yuh don't belong! (*He strides out the door in rear.* PADDY *hums
to himself, blinking drowsily*)

*Curtain*

# SCENE TWO

Two *days out. A section of the promenade deck.* MILDRED DOUGLAS
*and her aunt are discovered reclining in deck chairs. The former is
a girl of twenty, slender, delicate, with a pale, pretty face marred
by a self-conscious expression of disdainful superiority. She looks
fretful, nervous and discontented, bored by her own anemia. Her
aunt is a pompous and proud—and fat—old lady. She is a type even
to the point of a double chin and lorgnettes. She is dressed pre-
tentiously, as if afraid her face alone would never indicate her
position in life.* MILDRED *is dressed all in white.*

*The impression to be conveyed by this scene is one of the beauti-
ful, vivid life of the sea all about—sunshine on the deck in a great
flood, the fresh sea wind blowing across it. In the midst of this,
these two incongruous, artificial figures, inert and disharmonious,
the elder like a gray lump of dough touched up with rouge, the
younger looking as if the vitality of her stock had been sapped
before she was conceived, so that she is the expression not of its
life energy but merely of the artificialities that energy had won for
itself in the spending.*

MILDRED (*looking up with affected dreaminess*)  How the black
  smoke swirls back against the sky! Is it not beautiful?
AUNT (*without looking up*)  I dislike smoke of any kind.
MILDRED  My great-grandmother smoked a pipe—a clay pipe.
AUNT (*ruffling*)  Vulgar!
MILDRED  She was too distant a relative to be vulgar. Time mellows
  pipes.
AUNT (*pretending boredom but irritated*)  Did the sociology you
  took up at college teach you that—to play the ghoul on every
  possible occasion, excavating old bones? Why not let your great-
  grandmother rest in her grave?

MILDRED (*dreamily*) With her pipe beside her—puffing in Paradise.

AUNT (*with spite*) Yes, you are a natural born ghoul. You are even getting to look like one, my dear.

MILDRED (*in a passionless tone*) I detest you, Aunt. (*Looking at her critically*) Do you know what you remind me of? Of a cold pork pudding against a background of linoleum tablecloth in the kitchen of a—but the possibilities are wearisome. (*She closes her eyes*).

AUNT (*with a bitter laugh*) Merci for your candor. But since I am and must be your chaperon—in appearance, at least—let us patch up some sort of armed truce. For my part you are quite free to indulge any pose of eccentricity that beguiles you—as long as you observe the amenities—

MILDRED (*drawling*) The inanities?

AUNT (*going on as if she hadn't heard*) After exhausting the morbid thrills of social service work on New York's East Side—how they must have hated you, by the way, the poor that you made so much poorer in their own eyes!—you are now bent on making your slumming international. Well, I hope Whitechapel will provide the needed nerve tonic. Do not ask me to chaperon you there, however. I told your father I would not. I loathe deformity. We will hire an army of detectives and you may investigate everything—they allow you to see.

MILDRED (*protesting with a trace of genuine earnestness*) Please do not mock at my attempts to discover how the other half lives. Give me credit for some sort of groping sincerity in that at least. I would like to help them. I would like to be some use in the world. Is it my fault I don't know how? I would like to be sincere, to touch life somewhere. (*With weary bitterness*) But I'm afraid I have neither the vitality nor integrity. All that was burnt out in our stock before I was born. Grandfather's blast furnaces, flaming to the sky, melting steel, making millions—then father keeping those home fires burning, making more millions—and little me at the tail-end of it all. I'm a waste product in the Bessemer process—like the millions. Or rather, I inherit the acquired trait of the by-product, wealth, but none of the energy, none of the strength of the steel that made it. I am sired by gold and damned by it, as they say at the race track—damned in more ways than one. (*She laughs mirthlessly*).

AUNT (*unimpressed—superciliously*) You seem to be going in for sincerity today. It isn't becoming to you, really—except as an obvious pose. Be as artificial as you are, I advise. There's a sort of sincerity in that, you know. And, after all, you must confess you like that better.

MILDRED (*again affected and bored*) Yes, I suppose I do. Pardon me for my outburst. When a leopard complains of its spots, it must sound rather grotesque. (*In a mocking tone*) Purr, little leopard. Purr, scratch, tear, kill, gorge yourself and be happy—only stay in the jungle where your spots are camouflage. In a cage they make you conspicuous.

AUNT I don't know what you are talking about.

MILDRED It would be rude to talk about anything to you. Let's just talk. (*She looks at her wrist watch*) Well, thank goodness, it's about time for them to come for me. That ought to give me a new thrill, Aunt.

AUNT (*affectedly troubled*) You don't mean to say you're really going? The dirt—the heat must be frightful—

MILDRED Grandfather started as a puddler. I should have inherited an immunity to heat that would make a salamander shiver. It will be fun to put it to the test.

AUNT But don't you have to have the captain's—or someone's—permission to visit the stokehole?

MILDRED (*with a triumphant smile*) I have it—both his and the chief engineer's. Oh, they didn't want to at first, in spite of my social service credentials. They didn't seem a bit anxious that I should investigate how the other half lives and works on a ship. So I had to tell them that my father, the president of Nazareth Steel, chairman of the board of directors of this line, had told me it would be all right.

AUNT He didn't.

MILDRED How naïve age makes one! But I said he did, Aunt. I even said he had given me a letter to them—which I had lost. And they were afraid to take the chance that I might be lying. (*Excitedly*) So it's ho! for the stokehole. The second engineer is to escort me. (*Looking at her watch again*) It's time. And here he comes, I think. (*The* SECOND ENGINEER *enters. He is a husky, fine-looking man of thirty-five or so. He stops before the two and tips his cap, visibly embarrassed and ill-at-ease*).

SECOND ENGINEER Miss Douglas?

MILDRED Yes. (*Throwing off her rugs and getting to her feet*) Are we all ready to start?

SECOND ENGINEER  In just a second, ma'am. I'm waiting for the Fourth. He's coming along.

MILDRED (*with a scornful smile*)  You don't care to shoulder this responsibility alone, is that it?

SECOND ENGINEER (*forcing a smile*)  Two are better than one. (*Disturbed by her eyes, glances out to sea—blurts out*) A fine day we're having.

MILDRED  Is it?

SECOND ENGINEER  A nice warm breeze—

MILDRED  It feels cold to me.

SECOND ENGINEER  But it's hot enough in the sun—

MILDRED  Not hot enough for me. I don't like Nature. I was never athletic.

SECOND ENGINEER (*forcing a smile*)  Well, you'll find it hot enough where you're going.

MILDRED  Do you mean hell?

SECOND ENGINEER (*flabbergasted, decides to laugh*)  Ho-ho! No, I mean the stokehole.

MILDRED  My grandfather was a puddler. He played with boiling steel.

SECOND ENGINEER (*all at sea—uneasily*)  Is that so? Hum, you'll excuse me, ma'am, but are you intending to wear that dress?

MILDRED  Why not?

SECOND ENGINEER  You'll likely rub against oil and dirt. It can't be helped.

MILDRED  It doesn't matter. I have lots of white dresses.

SECOND ENGINEER  I have an old coat you might throw over—

MILDRED  I have fifty dresses like this. I will throw this one into the sea when I come back. That ought to wash it clean, don't you think?

SECOND ENGINEER (*doggedly*)  There's ladders to climb down that are none too clean—and dark alleyways—

MILDRED  I will wear this very dress and none other.

SECOND ENGINEER  No offense meant. It's none of my business. I was only warning you—

MILDRED  Warning? That sounds thrilling.

SECOND ENGINEER (*looking down the deck—with a sigh of relief*)  There's the Fourth now. He's waiting for us. If you'll come—

MILDRED  Go on. I'll follow you. (*He goes.* MILDRED *turns a mocking smile on her aunt*) An oaf—but a handsome, virile oaf.

AUNT (*scornfully*)  Poser!

MILDRED  Take care. He said there were dark alleyways—

AUNT  (*in the same tone*)  Poser!

MILDRED  (*biting her lips angrily*)  You are right. But would that my millions were not so anemically chaste!

AUNT  Yes, for a fresh pose I have no doubt you would drag the name of Douglas in the gutter!

MILDRED  From which it sprang. Good-by, Aunt. Don't pray too hard that I may fall into the fiery furnace.

AUNT  Poser!

MILDRED  (*viciously*)  Old hag! (*She slaps her aunt insultingly across the face and walks off, laughing gaily*).

AUNT  (*screams after her*)  I said poser!

*Curtain*

# SCENE THREE

THE *stokehole. In the rear, the dimly-outlined bulks of the furnaces and boilers. High overhead one hanging electric bulb sheds just enough light through the murky air laden with coal dust to pile up masses of shadows everywhere. A line of men, stripped to the waist, is before the furnace doors. They bend over, looking neither to right nor left, handling their shovels as if they were part of their bodies, with a strange, awkward, swinging rhythm. They use the shovels to throw open the furnace doors. Then from these fiery round holes in the black a flood of terrific light and heat pours full upon the men who are outlined in silhouette in the crouching, inhuman attitudes of chained gorillas. The men shovel with a rhythmic motion, swinging as on a pivot from the coal which lies in heaps on the floor behind to hurl it into the flaming mouths before them. There is a tumult of noise—the brazen clang of the furnace doors as they are flung open or slammed shut, the grating, teeth-gritting grind of steel against steel, of crunching coal. This clash of sounds stuns one's ears with its rending dissonance. But there is order in it, rhythm, a mechanical regulated recurrence, a tempo. And rising above all, making the air hum with the quiver of liberated energy, the roar of leaping flames in the furnaces, the monotonous throbbing beat of the engines.*

*As the curtain rises, the furnace doors are shut. The men are taking a breathing spell. One or two are arranging the coal behind them, pulling it into more accessible heaps. The others can be dimly made out leaning on their shovels in relaxed attitudes of exhaustion.*

PADDY (*from somewhere in the line—plaintively*) Yerra, will this divil's own watch nivir end? Me back is broke. I'm destroyed entirely.

YANK (*from the center of the line—with exuberant scorn*) Aw, yuh make me sick! Lie down and croak, why don't yuh? Always beefin', dat's you! Say, dis is a cinch! Dis was made for me! It's my meat, get me! (*A whistle is blown—a thin, shrill note from somewhere overhead in the darkness.* YANK *curses without resentment*) Dere's de damn engineer crackin' de whip. He tinks we're loafin'.

PADDY (*vindictively*) God stiffen him!

YANK (*in an exultant tone of command*) Come on, youse guys! Git into de game! She's gittin' hungry! Pile some grub in her. Trow it into her belly! Come on now, all of youse! Open her up! (*At this last all the men, who have followed his movements of getting into position, throw open their furnace doors with a deafening clang. The fiery light floods over their shoulders as they bend round for the coal. Rivulets of sooty sweat have traced maps on their backs. The enlarged muscle form bunches of high light and shadow*).

YANK (*chanting a count as he shovels without seeming effort*) One—two—tree— (*His voice rising exultantly in the joy of battle*) Dat's de stuff! Let her have it! All togedder now! Sling it into her! Let her ride! Shoot de piece now! Call de toin on her! Drive her into it! Feel her move! Watch her smoke! Speed, dat's her middle name! Give her coal, youse guys! Coal, dat's her booze! Drink it up, baby! Let's see yuh sprint! Dig in and gain a lap! Dere she go-o-es. (*This last in the chanting formula of the gallery gods at the six-day bike race. He slams his furnace door shut. The others do likewise with as much unison as their wearied bodies will permit. The effect is of one fiery eye after another being blotted out with a series of accompanying bangs*).

PADDY (*groaning*) Me back is broke. I'm bate out—bate— (*There is a pause. Then the inexorable whistle sounds again from the dim regions above the electric light. There is a growl of cursing rage from all sides*).

YANK (*shaking his fist upward—contemptuously*) Take it easy dere, you! Who d'yuh tink's runnin' dis game, me or you? When I git ready, we move. Not before! When I git ready, get me!

VOICES (*approvingly*) That's the stuff!
Yank tal him, py golly!
Yank ain't affeerd.
Goot poy, Yank!
Give him hell!
Tell 'im 'e's a bloody swine!
Bloody slave-driver!

YANK (*contemptuously*) He ain't got no noive. He's yellow, get me? All de engineers is yellow. Dey got streaks a mile wide. Aw, to hell wit him! Let's move, youse guys. We had a rest. Come on, she needs it! Give her pep! It ain't for him. Him and his whistle, dey don't belong. But we belong, see! We gotter feed de baby! Come on! (*He turns and flings his furnace door open. They all follow his lead. At this instant the* SECOND *and* FOURTH ENGINEERS *enter from the darkness on the left with* MILDRED *between them. She starts, turns paler, her pose is crumbling, she shivers with fright in spite of the blazing heat, but forces herself to leave the* ENGINEERS *and take a few steps nearer the men. She is right behind* YANK. *All this happens quickly while the men have their backs turned*).

YANK Come on, youse guys! (*He is turning to get coal when the whistle sounds again in a peremptory, irritating note. This drives* YANK *into a sudden fury. While the other men have turned full around and stopped dumfounded by the spectacle of* MILDRED *standing there in her white dress,* YANK *does not turn far enough to see her. Besides, his head is thrown back, he blinks upward through the murk trying to find the owner of the whistle, he brandishes his shovel murderously over his head in one hand, pounding on his chest, gorilla-like, with the other, shouting*) Toin off dat whistle! Come down outa dere, yuh yellow, brass-buttoned, Belfast bum, yuh! Come down and I'll knock yer brains out! Yuh lousy, stinkin', yellow mut of a Catholic-moiderin' bastard! Come down and I'll moider yuh! Pullin' dat whistle on me, huh? I'll show yuh! I'll crash yer skull in! I'll drive yer teet' down yer troat! I'll slam yer nose trou de back of yer head! I'll cut yer guts out for a nickel, yuh lousy boob, yuh dirty, crummy, muck-eatin' son of a— (*Suddenly he becomes conscious of all the other men staring at something directly behind his back. He whirls defensively with a snarling, murderous growl, crouching to spring, his lips drawn back over his teeth, his small eyes gleaming ferociously. He sees* MILDRED, *like a white apparition in the full light from the open furnace doors. He glares into her eyes, turned to stone. As for her, during his speech she has listened, paralyzed with horror, terror, her whole personality crushed, beaten in, collapsed, by the terrific impact of this unknown, abysmal brutality, naked and shameless. As she looks at his gorilla face, as his eyes bore into hers, she utters a low, choking cry and shrinks away from him, putting both hands up before her eyes to shut out the sight of his face, to protect her own. This startles* YANK *to a reaction. His mouth falls open, his eyes grow bewildered).*

MILDRED *(about to faint—to the* ENGINEERS, *who now have her one by each arm—whimperingly)* Take me away! Oh, the filthy beast! *(She faints. They carry her quickly back, disappearing in the darkness at the left, rear. An iron door clangs shut. Rage and bewildered fury rush back on* YANK. *He feels himself insulted in some unknown fashion in the very heart of his pride. He roars)* God damn yuh! *(And hurls his shovel after them at the door which has just closed. It hits the steel bulkhead with a clang and falls clattering on the steel floor. From overhead the whistle sounds again in a long, angry, insistent command).*

*Curtain*

# SCENE FOUR

THE *firemen's forecastle.* YANK'S *watch has just come off duty and had dinner. Their faces and bodies shine from a soap and water scrubbing but around their eyes, where a hasty dousing does not touch, the coal dust sticks like black make-up, giving them a queer, sinister expression.* YANK *has not washed either face or body. He stands out in contrast to them, a blackened, brooding figure. He is seated forward on a bench in the exact attitude of Rodin's "The Thinker." The others, most of them smoking pipes, are staring at* YANK *half-apprehensively, as if fearing an outburst; half-amusedly, as if they saw a joke somewhere that tickled them.*

VOICES  He ain't ate nothin'.
  Py golly, a fallar gat to gat grub in him.
  Divil a lie.
  Yank feeda da fire, no feeda da face.
  Ha-ha.
  He aint even washed hisself.
  He's forgot.
  Hey, Yank, you forgot to wash.
  YANK (*sullenly*)  Forgot nothin'! To hell wit washin'.
VOICES  It'll stick to you.
  It'll get under your skin.
  Give yer the bleedin' itch, that's wot.
  It makes spots on you—like a leopard.
  Like a piebald nigger, you mean.
  Better wash up, Yank.
  You sleep better.
  Wash up, Yank.
  Wash up! Wash up!
  YANK (*resentfully*)  Aw say, youse guys. Lemme alone. Can't youse see I'm tryin' to tink?

ALL (*repeating the word after him as one with cynical mockery*) Think! (*The word has a brazen, metallic quality as if their throats were phonograph horns. It is followed by a chorus of hard, barking laughter*).

YANK (*springing to his feet and glaring at them belligerently*) Yes, tink! Tink, dat's what I said! What about it? (*They are silent, puzzled by his sudden resentment at what used to be one of his jokes.* YANK *sits down again in the same attitude of "The Thinker"*).

VOICES Leave him alone.
He's got a grouch on.
Why wouldn't he?

PADDY (*with a wink at the others*) Sure I know what's the matther. 'Tis aisy to see. He's fallen in love, I'm telling you.

ALL (*repeating the word after him as one with cynical mockery*) Love! (*The word has a brazen, metallic quality as if their throats were phonograph horns. It is followed by a chorus of hard, barking laughter*).

YANK (*with a contemptuous snort*) Love, hell! Hate, dat's what. I've fallen in hate, get me?

PADDY (*philosophically*) 'Twould take a wise man to tell one from the other. (*With a bitter, ironical scorn, increasing as he goes on*) But I'm telling you it's love that's in it. Sure what else but love for us poor bastes in the stokehole would be bringing a fine lady, dressed like a white quane, down a mile of ladders and steps to be havin' a look at us? (*A growl of anger goes up from all sides*).

LONG (*jumping on a bench—hectically*) Hinsultin' us! Hinsultin' us, the bloody cow! And them bloody engineers! What right 'as they got to be exhibitin' us 's if we was bleedin' monkeys in a menagerie? Did we sign for hinsults to our dignity as 'onest workers? Is that in the ship's articles? You kin bloody well bet it ain't! But I knows why they done it. I arsked a deck steward 'o she was and 'e told me. 'Er old man's a bleedin' millionaire, a bloody Capitalist! 'E's got enuf bloody gold to sink this bleedin' ship! 'E makes arf the bloody steel in the world! 'E owns this bloody boat! And you and me, Comrades, we're 'is slaves! And the skipper and mates and engineers, they're 'is slaves! And she's 'is bloody daughter and we're all 'er slaves, too! And she gives 'er orders as 'ow she wants to see the bloody animals below decks and down they takes 'er! (*There is a roar of rage from all sides*).

YANK (*blinking at him bewilderedly*) Say! Wait a moment! Is all dat straight goods?

LONG Straight as string! The bleedin' steward as waits on 'em, 'e told me about 'er. And what're we goin' ter do, I arsks yer? 'Ave we got ter swaller 'er hinsults like dogs? It ain't in the ship's articles. I tell yer we got a case. We kin go to law—

YANK (*with abysmal contempt*) Hell! Law!

ALL (*repeating the word after him as one with cynical mockery*) Law! (*The word has a brazen metallic quality as if their throats were phonograph horns. It is followed by a chorus of hard, barking laughter*).

LONG (*feeling the ground slipping from under his feet—desperately*) As voters and citizens we kin force the bloody governments—

YANK (*with abysmal contempt*) Hell! Governments!

ALL (*repeating the word after him as one with cynical mockery*) Governments! (*The word has a brazen metallic quality as if their throats were phonograph horns. It is followed by a chorus of hard, barking laughter*).

LONG (*hysterically*) We're free and equal in the sight of God—

YANK (*with abysmal contempt*) Hell! God!

ALL (*repeating the word after him as one with cynical mockery*) God! (*The word has a brazen metallic quality as if their throats were phonograph horns. It is followed by a chorus of hard, barking laughter*).

YANK (*witheringly*) Aw, join de Salvation Army!

ALL Sit down! Shut up! Damn fool! Sea-lawyer! (LONG *slinks back out of sight*).

PADDY (*continuing the trend of his thoughts as if he had never been interrupted—bitterly*) And there she was standing behind us, and the Second pointing at us like a man you'd hear in a circus would be saying: In this cage is a queerer kind of baboon than ever you'd find in darkest Africy. We roast them in their own sweat—and be damned if you won't hear some of thim saying they like it! (*He glances scornfully at* YANK).

YANK (*with a bewildered uncertain growl*) Aw!

PADDY And there was Yank roarin' curses and turning round wid his shovel to brain her—and she looked at him, and him at her—

YANK (*slowly*) She was all white. I tought she was a ghost. Sure.

PADDY (*with heavy, biting sarcasm*) 'Twas love at first sight, divil a doubt of it! If you'd seen the endearin' look on her pale mug when she shriveled away with her hands over her eyes to shut out the sight of him! Sure, 'twas as if she'd seen a great hairy ape escaped from the Zoo!

YANK (*stung—with a growl of rage*) Aw!

PADDY And the loving way Yank heaved his shovel at the skull of her, only she was out the door! (*A grin breaking over his face*) 'Twas touching, I'm telling you! It put the touch of home, swate home in the stokehole. (*There is a roar of laughter from all*).

YANK (*glaring at* PADDY *menacingly*) Aw, choke dat off, see!

PADDY (*not heeding him—to the others*) And her grabbin' at the Second's arm for protection. (*With a grotesque imitation of a woman's voice*) Kiss me, Engineer dear, for it's dark down here and me old man's in Wall Street making money! Hug me tight, darlin', for I'm afeerd in the dark and me mother's on deck makin' eyes at the skipper! (*Another roar of laughter*).

YANK (*threateningly*) Say! What yuh tryin' to do, kid me, yuh old Harp?

PADDY Divil a bit! Ain't I wishin' myself you'd brained her?

YANK (*fiercely*) I'll brain her! I'll brain her yet, wait 'n' see! (*Coming over to* PADDY—*slowly*) Say, is dat what she called me—a hairy ape?

PADDY She looked it at you if she didn't say the word itself.

YANK (*grinning horribly*) Hairy ape, huh? Sure! Dat's de way she looked at me, aw right. Hairy ape! So dat's me, huh? (*Bursting into rage—as if she were still in front of him*) Yuh skinny tart! Yuh white-faced bum, yuh! I'll show yuh who's a ape! (*Turning to the others, bewilderment seizing him again*) Say, youse guys. I was bawlin' him out for pullin' de whistle on us. You heard me. And den I seen youse lookin' at somep'n and I tought he'd sneaked down to come up in back of me, and I hopped round to knock him dead wit de shovel. And dere she was wit de light on her! Christ, yuh coulda pushed me over with a finger! I was scared, get me? Sure! I tought she was a ghost, see? She was all in white like dey wrap around stiffs. You seen her. Kin yuh blame me? She didn't belong, dat's what. And den when I come to and seen it was a real skoit and seen de way she was lookin' at me—like Paddy said—Christ, I was sore, get me? I don't stand for dat stuff from nobody. And I flung de shovel —on'y she'd beat it. (*Furiously*) I wished it'd banged her! I wished it'd knocked her block off!

LONG  And be 'anged for murder or 'lectrocuted? She ain't bleedin'
well worth it.

YANK  I don't give a damn what! I'd be square wit her, wouldn't
I? Tink I wanter let her put somep'n over on me? Tink I'm
goin' to let her git away wit dat stuff? Yuh don't know me! No one
ain't never put nothin' over on me and got away wit it, see!—
not dat kind of stuff—no guy and no skoit neither! I'll fix her!
Maybe she'll come down again—

VOICE  No chance, Yank. You scared her out of a year's growth.

YANK  I scared her? Why de hell should I scare her? Who de hell
is she? Ain't she de same as me? Hairy ape, huh? (*With his old
confident bravado*) I'll show her I'm better'n her, if she on'y knew
it. I belong and she don't, see! I move and she's dead! Twenty-
five knots an hour, dat's me! Dat carries her but I make dat.
She's on'y baggage. Sure! (*Again bewilderedly*) But, Christ, she
was funny lookin'! Did yuh pipe her hands? White and skinny.
Yuh could see de bones through 'em. And her mush, dat was
dead white, too. And her eyes, dey was like dey'd seen a ghost.
Me, dat was! Sure! Hairy ape! Ghost, huh? Look at dat arm!
(*He extends his right arm, swelling out the great muscles*) I
coulda took her wit dat, wit just my little finger even, and broke
her in two. (*Again bewilderedly*) Say, who is dat skoit, huh?
What is she? What's she come from? Who made her? Who give
her de noive to look at me like dat? Dis ting's got my goat right.
I don't get her. She's new to me. What does a skoit like her mean,
huh? She don't belong, get me! I can't see her. (*With growing
anger*) But one ting I'm wise to, aw right, aw right! Youse all
kin bet your shoits I'll git even wit her. I'll show her if she tinks
she— She grinds de organ and I'm on de string, huh? I'll fix her!
Let her come down again and I'll fling her in de furnace! She'll
move den! She won't shiver at nothin', den! Speed, dat'll be
her! She'll belong den! (*He grins horribly*).

PADDY  She'll never come. She's had her belly-full, I'm telling you.
She'll be in bed now, I'm thinking, wid ten doctors and nurses
feedin' her salts to clean the fear out of her.

YANK  (*enraged*)  Yuh tink I made her sick, too, do yuh? Just
lookin' at me, huh? Hairy ape, huh? (*In a frenzy of rage*) I'll fix
her! I'll tell her where to git off! She'll git down on her knees
and take it back or I'll bust de face offen her! (*Shaking one fist
upward and beating on his chest with the other*) I'll find yuh! I'm

comin', d'yuh hear? I'll fix yuh, God damn yuh! (*He makes a rush for the door*).

VOICES Stop him!
He'll get shot!
He'll murder her!
Trip him up!
Hold him!
He's gone crazy!
Gott, he's strong!
Hold him down!
Look out for a kick!
Pin his arms!

(*They have all piled on him and, after a fierce struggle, by sheer weight of numbers have borne him to the floor just inside the door*).

PADDY (*who has remained detached*) Kape him down till he's cooled off. (*Scornfully*) Yerra, Yank, you're a great fool. Is it payin' attention at all you are to the like of that skinny sow widout one drop of rale blood in her?

YANK (*frenziedly, from the bottom of the heap*) She done me doit! She done me doit, didn't she? I'll git square wit her! I'll get her some way! Git offen me, youse guys! Lemme up! I'll show her who's a ape!

*Curtain*

# SCENE FIVE

THREE *weeks later. A corner of Fifth Avenue in the Fifties on a fine Sunday morning. A general atmosphere of clean, well-tidied, wide street; a flood of mellow, tempered sunshine; gentle, genteel breezes. In the rear, the show windows of two shops, a jewelry establishment on the corner, a furrier's next to it. Here the adornments of extreme wealth are tantalizingly displayed. The jeweler's window is gaudy with glittering diamonds, emeralds, rubies, pearls, etc., fashioned in ornate tiaras, crowns, necklaces, collars, etc. From each piece hangs an enormous tag from which a dollar sign and numerals in intermittent electric lights wink out the incredible prices. The same in the furrier's. Rich furs of all varieties hang there bathed in a downpour of artificial light. The general effect is of a background of magnificence cheapened and made grotesque by commercialism, a background in tawdry disharmony with the clear light and sunshine on the street itself.*

*Up the side street* YANK *and* LONG *come swaggering.* LONG *is dressed in shore clothes, wears a black Windsor tie, cloth cap.* YANK *is in his dirty dungarees. A fireman's cap with black peak is cocked defiantly on the side of his head. He has not shaved for days and around his fierce, resentful eyes—as around those of* LONG *to a lesser degree—the black smudge of coal dust still sticks like make-up. They hesitate and stand together at the corner, swaggering, looking about them with a forced, defiant contempt.*

LONG (*indicating it all with an oratorical gesture*) Well, 'ere we are. Fif' Avenoo. This 'ere's their bleedin' private lane, as yer might say. (*Bitterly*) We're trespassers 'ere. Proletarians keep orf the grass!

YANK (*dully*) I don't see no grass, yuh boob. (*Staring at the sidewalk*) Clean, ain't it? Yuh could eat a fried egg offen it. The white wings got some job sweepin' dis up. (*Looking up and down the avenue—surlily*) Where's all de white-collar stiffs yuh said was here—and de skoits—*her* kind?

LONG In church, blast 'em! Arskin' Jesus to give 'em more money.

YANK Choich, huh? I useter go to choich onct—sure—when I was a kid. Me old man and woman, dey made me. Dey never went demselves, dough. Always got too big a head on Sunday mornin', dat was dem. (*With a grin*) Dey was scrappers for fair, bot' of dem. On Satiday nights when dey bot' got a skinful dey could put up a bout oughter been staged at de Garden. When dey got trough dere wasn't a chair or table wit a leg under it. Or else dey bot' jumped on me for somep'n. Dat was where I loined to take punishment. (*With a grin and a swagger*) I'm a chip offen de old block, get me?

LONG Did yer old man follow the sea?

YANK Naw. Worked along shore. I runned away when me old lady croaked wit de tremens. I helped at truckin' and in de market. Den I shipped in de stokehole. Sure. Dat belongs. De rest was nothin'. (*Looking around him*) I ain't never seen dis before. De Brooklyn waterfront, dat was where I was dragged up. (*Taking a deep breath*) Dis ain't so bad at dat, huh?

LONG Not bad? Well, we pays for it wiv our bloody sweat, if yer wants to know!

YANK (*with sudden angry disgust*) Aw hell! I don't see no one, see—like her. All dis gives me a pain. It don't belong. Say, ain't dere a back room around dis dump? Let's go shoot a ball. All dis is too clean and quiet and dolled-up, get me! It gives me a pain.

LONG Wait and yer'll bloody well see—

YANK I don't wait for no one. I keep on de move. Say, what yuh drag me up here for, anyway? Tryin' to kid me, yuh simp, yuh?

LONG Yer wants to get back at 'er, don't yer? That's what yer been sayin' every bloomin' hour since she hinsulted yer.

YANK (*vehemently*) Sure ting I do! Didn't I try to get even wit her in Southampton? Didn't I sneak on de dock and wait for her by de gangplank? I was goin' to spit in her pale mug, see! Sure, right in her pop-eyes! Dat woulda made me even, see? But no chanct. Dere was a whole army of plainclothes bulls around. Dey spotted me and gimme de bum's rush. I never seen her. But I'll git square wit her yet, you watch! (*Furiously*) De lousy tart!

She tinks she kin get away wit moider—but not wit me! I'll fix her! I'll tink of a way!

LONG (*as disgusted as he dares to be*) Ain't that why I brought yer up 'ere—to show yer? Yer been lookin' at this 'ere 'ole affair wrong. Yer been actin' an' talkin' 's if it was all a bleedin' personal matter between yer and that bloody cow. I wants to convince yer she was on'y a representative of 'er clarss. I wants to awaken yer bloody clarss consciousness. Then yer'll see it's 'er clarss yer've got to fight, not 'er alone. There's a 'ole mob of 'em like 'er, Gawd blind 'em!

YANK (*spitting on his hands—belligerently*) De more de merrier when I gits started. Bring on de gang!

LONG Yer'll see 'em in arf a mo', when that church lets out. (*He turns and sees the window display in the two stores for the first time*) Blimey! Look at that, will yer? (*They both walk back and stand looking in the jeweler's.* LONG *flies into a fury*) Just look at this 'ere bloomin' mess! Just look at it! Look at the bleedin' prices on 'em—more'n our 'ole bloody stokehole makes in ten voyages sweatin' in 'ell! And they—'er and 'er bloody clarss—buys 'em for toys to dangle on 'em! One of these 'ere would buy scoff for a starvin' family for a year!

YANK Aw, cut de sob stuff! T' hell wit de starvin' family! Yuh'll be passin' de hat to me next. (*With naïve admiration*) Say, dem tings is pretty, huh? Bet yuh dey'd hock for a piece of change aw right. (*Then turning away, bored*) But, aw hell, what good are dey? Let her have 'em. Dey don't belong no more'n she does. (*With a gesture of sweeping the jewelers into oblivion*) All dat don't count, get me?

LONG (*who has moved to the furrier's—indignantly*) And I s'pose his 'ere don't count neither—skins of poor, 'armless animals slaughtered so as 'er and 'ers can keep their bleedin' noses warm!

YANK (*who has been staring at something inside—with queer excitement*) Take a slant at dat! Give it de once-over! Monkey fur —two t'ousand bucks! (*Bewilderedly*) Is dat straight goods— monkey fur? What de hell—?

LONG (*bitterly*) It's straight enuf. (*With grim humor*) They wouldn't bloody well pay that for a 'airy ape's skin—no, nor for the 'ole livin' ape with all 'is 'ead, and body, and soul thrown in!

YANK (*clenching his fists, his face growing pale with rage as if the skin in the window were a personal insult*) Trowin' it up in my face! Christ! I'll fix her!

LONG (*excitedly*)  Church is out. 'Ere they come, the bleedin' swine. (*After a glance at* YANK's *lowering face—uneasily*)  Easy goes, Comrade. Keep yer bloomin' temper. Remember force defeats itself. It ain't our weapon. We must impress our demands through peaceful means—the votes of the on-marching proletarians of the bloody world!

YANK (*with abysmal contempt*)  Votes, hell! Votes is a joke, see. Votes for women! Let dem do it!

LONG (*still more uneasily*)  Calm, now. Treat 'em wiv the proper contempt. Observe the bleedin' parasites but 'old yer 'orses.

YANK (*angrily*)  Get away from me! Yuh're yellow, dat's what. Force, dat's me! De punch, dat's me every time, see! (*The crowd from church enter from the right, sauntering slowly and affectedly, their heads held stiffly up, looking neither to right nor left, talking in toneless, simpering voices. The women are rouged, calcimined, dyed, overdressed to the nth degree. The men are in Prince Alberts, high hats, spats, canes, etc. A procession of gaudy marionettes, yet with something of the relentless horror of Frankensteins in their detached, mechanical unawareness*).

VOICES  Dear Doctor Caiaphas! He is so sincere!
What was the sermon? I dozed off.
About the radicals, my dear—and the false doctrines that are being preached.
We must organize a hundred per cent American bazaar.
And let everyone contribute one one-hundredth per cent of their income tax.
What an original idea!
We can devote the proceeds to rehabilitating the veil of the temple.
But that has been done so many times.

YANK (*glaring from one to the other of them—with an insulting snort of scorn*)  Huh! Huh! (*Without seeming to see him, they make wide detours to avoid the spot where he stands in the middle of the sidewalk*).

LONG (*frightenedly*)  Keep yer bloomin' mouth shut, I tells yer.

YANK (*viciously*)  G'wan! Tell it to Sweeney! (*He swaggers away and deliberately lurches into a top-hatted gentleman, then glares at him pugnaciously*)  Say, who d'yuh tink yuh're bumpin'? Tink yuh own de oith?

GENTLEMAN (*coldly and affectedly*)  I beg your pardon. (*He has *not looked at* YANK *and passes on without a glance, leaving him bewildered*).

LONG (*rushing up and grabbing* YANK's *arm*) 'Ere! Come away! This wasn't what I meant. Yer'll 'ave the bloody coppers down on us.

YANK (*savagely—giving him a push that sends him sprawling*) G'wan!

LONG (*picks himself up—hysterically*) I'll pop orf then. This ain't what I meant. And whatever 'appens, yer can't blame me. (*He slinks off left*).

YANK T' hell wit youse! (*He approaches a lady—with a vicious grin and a smirking wink*) Hello, Kiddo. How's every little ting? Got anyting on for tonight? I know an old boiler down to de docks we kin crawl into. (*The lady stalks by without a look, without a change of pace.* YANK *turns to others—insultingly*) Holy smokes, what a mug! Go hide yuhself before de horses shy at yuh. Gee, pipe de heine on dat one! Say, youse, yuh look like de stoin of a ferryboat. Paint and powder! All dolled up to kill! Yuh look like stiffs laid out for de boneyard! Aw, g'wan, de lot of youse! Yuh give me de eye-ache. Yuh don't belong, get me! Look at me, why don't youse dare? I belong, dat's me! (*Pointing to a skyscraper across the street which is in process of construction—with bravado*) See dat building goin' up dere? See de steel work? Steel, dat's me! Youse guys live on it and tink yuh're somep'n. But I'm *in* it, see! I'm de hoistin' engine dat makes it go up! I'm it—de inside and bottom of it! Sure! I'm steel and steam and smoke and de rest of it! It moves—speed—twenty-five stories up—and me at de top and bottom—movin'! Youse simps don't move. Yuh're on'y dolls I winds up to see 'm spin. Yuh're de garbage, get me—de leavins—de ashes we dump over de side! Now, what 'a' yuh gotta say? (*But as they seem neither to see nor hear him, he flies into a fury*) Bums! Pigs! Tarts! Bitches! (*He turns in a rage on the men, bumping viciously into them but not jarring them the least bit. Rather it is he who recoils after each collision. He keeps growling*) Git off de oith! G'wan, yuh bum! Look where yuh're goin', can't yuh? Git outa here! Fight, why don't yuh? Put up yer mits! Don't be a dog! Fight or I'll knock yuh dead! (*But, without seeming to see him, they all answer with mechanical affected politeness*) I beg your pardon. (*Then at a cry from one of the women, they all scurry to the furrier's window*).

THE WOMAN (*ecstatically, with a gasp of delight*) Monkey fur! (*The whole crowd of men and women chorus after her in the same tone of affected delight*) Monkey fur!

YANK (*with a jerk of his head back on his shoulders, as if he had received a punch full in the face—raging*) I see yuh, all in white! I see yuh, yuh white-faced tart, yuh! Hairy ape, huh? I'll hairy ape yuh! (*He bends down and grips at the street curbing as if to pick it out and hurl it. Foiled in this, snarling with passion, he leaps to the lamp-post on the corner and tries to pull it up for a club. Just at that moment a bus is heard rumbling up. A fat, high-hatted, spatted gentleman runs out from the side street. He calls out plaintively*) Bus! Bus! Stop there! (*and runs full tilt into the bending, straining* YANK, *who is bowled off his balance*).

YANK (*seeing a fight—with a roar of joy as he springs to his feet*) At last! Bus, huh? I'll bust yuh! (*He lets drive a terrific swing, his fist landing full on the fat gentleman's face. But the gentleman stands unmoved as if nothing had happened*).

GENTLEMAN I beg your pardon. (*Then irritably*) You have made me lose my bus. (*He claps his hands and begins to scream*) Officer! Officer! (*Many police whistles shrill out on the instant and a whole platoon of policemen rush in on* YANK *from all sides. He tries to fight but is clubbed to the pavement and fallen upon. The crowd at the window have not moved or noticed this disturbance. The clanging gong of the patrol wagon approaches with a clamoring din*).

*Curtain*

# SCENE SIX

NIGHT *of the following day. A row of cells in the prison on Blackwells Island. The cells extend back diagonally from right front to left rear. They do not stop, but disappear in the dark background as if they ran on, numberless, into infinity. One electric bulb from the low ceiling of the narrow corridor sheds its light through the heavy steel bars of the cell at the extreme front and reveals part of the interior.* YANK *can be seen within, crouched on the edge of his cot in the attitude of Rodin's "The Thinker." His face is spotted with black and blue bruises. A blood-stained bandage is wrapped around his head.*

YANK (*suddenly starting as if awakening from a dream, reaches out and shakes the bars—aloud to himself, wonderingly*) Steel. Dis is de Zoo, huh? (*A burst of hard, barking laughter comes from the unseen occupants of the cells, runs back down the tier, and abruptly ceases*).

VOICES (*mockingly*) The Zoo? That's a new name for this coop— a damn good name!

Steel, eh? You said a mouthful. This is the old iron house.

Who is that boob talkin'?

He's the bloke they brung in out of his head. The bulls had beat him up fierce.

YANK (*dully*) I musta been dreamin'. I tought I was in a cage at de Zoo—but de apes don't talk, do dey?

VOICES (*with mocking laughter*) You're in a cage aw right.

A coop!

A pen!

A sty!

A kennel! (*Hard laughter—a pause*).

Say, guy! Who are you? No, never mind lying. What are you? Yes, tell us your sad story. What's your game?

What did they jug yuh for?

YANK (*dully*) I was a fireman—stokin' on de liners. (*Then with sudden rage, rattling his cell bars*) I'm a hairy ape, get me? And I'll bust youse all in de jaw if yuh don't lay off kiddin' me.

VOICES Huh! You're a hard boiled duck, ain't you!

When you spit, it bounces! (*Laughter*).

Aw, can it. He's a regular guy. Ain't you?

What did he say he was—a ape?

YANK (*defiantly*) Sure ting! Ain't dat what youse all are—apes? (*A silence. Then a furious rattling of bars from down the corridor*).

A VOICE (*thick with rage*) I'll show yuh who's a ape, yuh bum!

VOICES Ssshh! Nix!

Can de noise!

Piano!

You'll have the guard down on us!

YANK (*scornfully*) De guard? Yuh mean de keeper, don't yuh? (*Angry exclamations from all the cells*).

VOICE (*placatingly*) Aw, don't pay no attention to him. He's off his nut from the beatin'-up he got. Say, you guy! We're waitin' to hear what they landed you for—or ain't yuh tellin'?

YANK Sure, I'll tell youse. Sure! Why de hell not? On'y—youse won't get me. Nobody gets me but me, see? I started to tell de Judge and all he says was: "Toity days to tink it over." Tink it over! Christ, dat's all I been doin' for weeks! (*After a pause*) I was tryin' to git even wit someone, see?—someone dat done me doit.

VOICES (*cynically*) De old stuff, I bet. Your goil, huh?

Give yuh the double-cross, huh?

That's them every time!

Did yuh beat up de odder guy?

YANK (*disgustedly*) Aw, yuh're all wrong! Sure dere was a skoit in it—but not what youse mean, not dat old tripe. Dis was a new kind of skoit. She was dolled up all in white—in de stokehole. I tought she was a ghost. Sure. (*A pause*).

VOICES (*whispering*) Gee, he's still nutty.

Let him rave. It's fun listenin'.

YANK (*unheeding—groping in his thoughts*) Her hands—dey was skinny and white like dey wasn't real but painted on somep'n. Dere was a million miles from me to her—twenty-five knots a hour. She was like some dead ting de cat brung in. Sure, dat's what. She didn't belong. She belonged in de window of a toy store, or on de top of a garbage can, see! Sure! (*He breaks out angrily*) But would yuh believe it, she had de noive to do me doit. She lamped me like she was seein' somep'n broke loose from de menagerie. Christ, yuh'd oughter seen her eyes! (*He rattles the bars of his cell furiously*) But I'll get back at her yet, you watch! And if I can't find her I'll take it out on de gang she runs wit. I'm wise to where dey hangs out now. I'll show her who belongs! I'll show her who's in de move and who ain't. You watch my smoke!

VOICES (*serious and joking*)    Dat's de talkin'!
Take her for all she's got!
What was this dame, anyway? Who was she, eh?

YANK    I dunno. First cabin stiff. Her old man's a millionaire, dey says—name of Douglas.

VOICES    Douglas? That's the president of the Steel Trust, I bet. Sure. I seen his mug in de papers.
He's filthy with dough.

VOICE    Hey, feller, take a tip from me. If you want to get back at that dame, you better join the Wobblies. You'll get some action then.

YANK    Wobblies? What de hell's dat?

VOICE    Ain't you ever heard of the I.W.W.?

YANK    Naw. What is it?

VOICE    A gang of blokes—a tough gang. I been readin' about 'em today in the paper. The guard give me the *Sunday Times*. There's a long spiel about 'em. It's from a speech made in the Senate by a guy named Senator Queen. (*He is in the cell next to* YANK's. *There is a rustling of paper*) Wait'll I see if I got light enough and I'll read you. Listen. (*He reads*) "There is a menace existing in this country today which threatens the vitals of our fair Republic—as foul a menace against the very life-blood of the American Eagle as was the foul conspiracy of Catiline against the eagles of ancient Rome!"

VOICE (*disgustedly*)    Aw, hell! Tell him to salt de tail of dat eagle!

VOICE (*reading*)    "I refer to that devil's brew of rascals, jailbirds, murderers and cutthroats who libel all honest working men by calling themselves the Industrial Workers of the World; but in the light of their nefarious plots, I call them the Industrious *Wreckers* of the World!"

YANK (*with vengeful satisfaction*)  Wreckers, dat's de right dope! Dat belongs! Me for dem!

VOICE  Ssshh! (*reading*) "This fiendish organization is a foul ulcer on the fair body of our Democracy—"

VOICE  Democracy, hell! Give him the boid, fellers—the raspberry! (*They do*).

VOICE  Ssshh! (*reading*) "Like Cato I say to this Senate, the I.W.W. must be destroyed! For they represent an ever-present dagger pointed at the heart of the greatest nation the world has ever known, where all men are born free and equal, with equal opportunities to all, where the Founding Fathers have guaranteed to each one happiness, where Truth, Honor, Liberty, Justice, and the Brotherhood of Man are a religion absorbed with one's mother's milk, taught at our father's knee, sealed, signed, and stamped upon in the glorious Constitution of these United States!" (*A perfect storm of hisses, catcalls, boos, and hard laughter*).

VOICES (*scornfully*)  Hurrah for de Fort' of July!
Pass de hat!
Liberty!
Justice!
Honor!
Opportunity!
Brotherhood!

ALL (*with abysmal scorn*)  Aw, hell!

VOICE  Give that Queen Senator guy the bark! All togedder now—one—two—tree—(*A terrific chorus of barking and yapping*).

GUARD (*from a distance*)  Quiet there, youse—or I'll git the hose. (*The noise subsides*).

YANK (*with growling rage*)  I'd like to catch dat senator guy alone for a second. I'd loin him some trute!

VOICE  Ssshh! Here's where he gits down to cases on the Wobblies. (*Reads*) "They plot with fire in one hand and dynamite in the other. They stop not before murder to gain their ends, nor at the outraging of defenseless womanhood. They would tear down society, put the lowest scum in the seats of the mighty, turn Almighty God's revealed plan for the world topsy-turvy, and make of our sweet and lovely civilization a shambles, a desolation where man, God's masterpiece, would soon degenerate back to the ape!"

VOICE (*to* YANK)  Hey, you guy. There's your ape stuff again.

YANK (*with a growl of fury*) I got him. So dey blow up tings, do dey? Dey turn tings round, do dey? Hey, lend me dat paper, will yuh?

VOICE Sure. Give it to him. On'y keep it to yourself, see. We don't wanter listen to no more of that slop.

VOICE Here you are. Hide it under your mattress.

YANK (*reaching out*) Tanks. I can't read much but I kin manage. (*He sits, the paper in the hand at his side, in the attitude of Rodin's "The Thinker." A pause. Several snores from down the corridor. Suddenly* YANK *jumps to his feet with a furious groan as if some appalling thought had crashed on him—bewilderedly*) Sure—her old man—president of de Steel Trust—makes half de steel in de world—steel—where I tought I belonged—drivin' trou —movin'—in dat—to make *her*—and cage me in for her to spit on! Christ! (*He shakes the bars of his cell door till the whole tier trembles. Irritated, protesting exclamations from those awakened or trying to get to sleep*) He made dis—dis cage! Steel! It don't belong, dat's what! Cages, cells, locks, bolts, bars—dat's what it means!—holdin' me down wit him at de top! But I'll drive trou! Fire, dat melts it! I'll be fire—under de heap—fire dat never goes out—hot as hell—breakin' out in de night—(*While he has been saying this last he has shaken his cell door to a clanging accompaniment. As he comes to the "breakin' out" he seizes one bar with both hands and, putting his two feet up against the others so that his position is parallel to the floor like a monkey's, he gives a great wrench backwards. The bar bends like a licorice stick under his tremendous strength. Just at this moment the* PRISON GUARD *rushes in, dragging a hose behind him*).

GUARD (*angrily*) I'll loin youse bums to wake me up! (*Sees* YANK) Hello, it's you, huh? Got the D.T.'s, hey? Well, I'll cure 'em. I'll drown your snakes for yuh! (*Noticing the bar*) Hell, look at dat bar bended! On'y a bug is strong enough for dat!

YANK (*glaring at him*) Or a hairy ape, yuh big yellow bum! Look out! Here I come! (*He grabs another bar*).

GUARD (*scared now—yelling off left*) Toin de hose on, Ben!—full pressure! And call de others—and a straitjacket! (*The curtain is falling. As it hides* YANK *from view, there is a splattering smash as the stream of water hits the steel of* YANK's *cell*).

*Curtain*

# SCENE SEVEN

NEARLY *a month later. An I.W.W. local near the waterfront, show-ing the interior of a front room on the ground floor, and the street outside. Moonlight on the narrow street, buildings massed in black shadow. The interior of the room, which is general assembly room, office, and reading room, resembles some dingy settlement boys' club. A desk and high stool are in one corner. A table with papers, stacks of pamphlets, chairs about it, is at center. The whole is decidedly cheap, banal, commonplace and unmysterious as a room could well be. The secretary is perched on the stool making entries in a large ledger. An eye shade casts his face into shadows. Eight or ten men, longshoremen, iron workers, and the like, are grouped about the table. Two are playing checkers. One is writing a letter. Most of them are smoking pipes. A big signboard is on the wall at the rear, "Industrial Workers of the World—Local No. 57."*

YANK (*comes down the street outside. He is dressed as in Scene Five. He moves cautiously, mysteriously. He comes to a point opposite the door; tiptoes softly up to it, listens, is impressed by the silence within, knocks carefully, as if he were guessing at the password to some secret rite. Listens. No answer. Knocks again a bit louder. No answer. Knocks impatiently, much louder*).

SECRETARY (*turning around on his stool*) What the hell is that—someone knocking? (*Shouts*) Come in, why don't you? (*All the men in the room look up.* YANK *opens the door slowly, gingerly, as if afraid of an ambush. He looks around for secret doors, mystery, is taken aback by the commonplaceness of the room and the men in it, thinks he may have gotten in the wrong place, then sees the signboard on the wall and is reassured*).

YANK (*blurts out*) Hello.

MEN (*reservedly*) Hello.

YANK (*more easily*) I thought I'd bumped into de wrong dump.

SECRETARY (*scrutinizing him carefully*) Maybe you have. Are you a member?

YANK Naw, not yet. Dat's what I came for—to join.

SECRETARY That's easy. What's your job—longshore?

YANK Naw. Fireman—stoker on de liners.

SECRETARY (*with satisfaction*) Welcome to our city. Glad to know you people are waking up at last. We haven't got many members in your line.

YANK Naw. Dey're all dead to de woild.

SECRETARY Well, you can help to wake 'em. What's your name? I'll make out your card.

YANK (*confused*) Name? Lemme tink.

SECRETARY (*sharply*) Don't you know your own name?

YANK Sure; but I been just Yank for so long—Bob, dat's it—Bob Smith.

SECRETARY (*writing*) Robert Smith. (*Fills out the rest of card*) Here you are. Cost you half a dollar.

YANK Is dat all—four bits? Dat's easy. (*Gives the Secretary the money*).

SECRETARY (*throwing it in drawer*) Thanks. Well, make yourself at home. No introductions needed. There's literature on the table. Take some of those pamphlets with you to distribute aboard ship. They may bring results. Sow the seed, only go about it right. Don't get caught and fired. We got plenty out of work. What we need is men who can hold their jobs—and work for us at the same time.

YANK Sure. (*But he still stands, embarrassed and uneasy*).

SECRETARY (*looking at him—curiously*) What did you knock for? Think we had a coon in uniform to open doors?

YANK Naw. I tought it was locked—and dat yuh'd wanter give me the once-over trou a peep-hole or somep'n to see if I was right.

SECRETARY (*alert and suspicious but with an easy laugh*) Think we were running a crap game? That door is never locked. What put that in your nut?

YANK (*with a knowing grin, convinced that this is all camouflage, a part of the secrecy*) Dis burg is full of bulls, ain't it?

SECRETARY (*sharply*) What have the cops got to do with us? We're breaking no laws.

YANK (*with a knowing wink*) Sure. Youse wouldn't for woilds. Sure. I'm wise to dat.

SECRETARY  You seem to be wise to a lot of stuff none of us knows about.

YANK  (*with another wink*)  Aw, dat's aw right, see. (*Then made a bit resentful by the suspicious glances from all sides*) Aw, can it! Youse needn't put me trou de toid degree. Can't youse see I belong? Sure! I'm reg'lar. I'll stick, get me? I'll shoot de woiks for youse. Dat's why I wanted to join in.

SECRETARY  (*breezily, feeling him out*)  That's the right spirit. Only are you sure you understand what you've joined? It's all plain and above board; still, some guys get a wrong slant on us. (*Sharply*) What's your notion of the purpose of the I.W.W.?

YANK  Aw, I know all about it.

SECRETARY  (*sarcastically*)  Well, give us some of your valuable information.

YANK  (*cunningly*)  I know enough not to speak outa my toin (*Then resentfully again*) Aw, say! I'm reg'lar. I'm wise to de game. I know yuh got to watch your step wit a stranger. For all youse know, I might be a plain-clothes dick, or somep'n, dat's what yuh're tinkin', huh? Aw, forget it! I belong, see? Ask any guy down to de docks if I don't.

SECRETARY  Who said you didn't?

YANK  After I'm 'nitiated, I'll show yuh.

SECRETARY  (*astounded*)  Initiated? There's no initiation.

YANK  (*disappointed*)  Ain't there no password—no grip nor nothin'?

SECRETARY  What'd you think this is—the Elks—or the Black Hand?

YANK  De Elks, hell! De Black Hand, dey're a lot of yellow back-stickin' Ginees. Naw. Dis is a man's gang, ain't it?

SECRETARY  You said it! That's why we stand on our two feet in the open. We got no secrets.

YANK  (*surprised but admiringly*)  Yuh mean to say yuh always run wide open—like dis?

SECRETARY  Exactly.

YANK  Den yuh sure got your noive wit youse!

SECRETARY  (*sharply*)  Just what was it made you want to join us? Come out with that straight.

YANK  Yuh call me? Well, I got noive, too! Here's my hand. Yuh wanter blow tings up, don't yuh? Well, dat's me! I belong!

SECRETARY  (*with pretended carelessness*)  You mean change the unequal conditions of society by legitimate direct action—or with dynamite?

YANK  Dynamite! Blow it offen de oith—steel—all de cages—all de factories, steamers, buildings, jails—de Steel Trust and all dat makes it go.

SECRETARY So—that's your idea, eh? And did you have any special job in that line you wanted to propose to us? (*He makes a sign to the men, who get up cautiously one by one and group behind* YANK).

YANK (*boldly*) Sure, I'll come out wit it. I'll show youse I'm one of de gang. Dere's dat millionaire guy, Douglas—

SECRETARY President of the Steel Trust, you mean? Do you want to assassinate him?

YANK Naw, dat don't get yuh nothin'. I mean blow up de factory, de woiks, where he makes de steel. Dat's what I'm after—to blow up de steel, knock all de steel in de woild up to de moon. Dat'll fix tings! (*Eagerly, with a touch of bravado*) I'll do it by me lonesome! I'll show yuh! Tell me where his woiks is, how to git there, all de dope. Gimme de stuff, de old butter—and watch me do de rest! Watch de smoke and see it move! I don't give a damn if dey nab me—long as it's done! I'll soive life for it—and give 'em de laugh! (*Half to himself*) And I'll write her a letter and tell her de hairy ape done it. Dat'll square tings.

SECRETARY (*stepping away from* YANK) Very interesting. (*He gives a signal. The men, huskies all, throw themselves on* YANK *and before he knows it they have his legs and arms pinioned. But he is too flabbergasted to make a struggle, anyway. They feel him over for weapons*).

MAN No gat, no knife. Shall we give him what's what and put the boots to him?

SECRETARY No. He isn't worth the trouble we'd get into. He's too stupid. (*He comes closer and laughs mockingly in* YANK's *face*) Ho-ho! By God, this is the biggest joke they've put up on us yet. Hey, you Joke! Who sent you—Burns or Pinkerton? No, by God, you're such a bonehead I'll bet you're in the Secret Service! Well, you dirty spy, you rotten agent provocator, you can go back and tell whatever skunk is paying you blood-money for betraying your brothers that he's wasting his coin. You couldn't catch a cold. And tell him that all he'll ever get on us, or ever has got, is just his own sneaking plots that he's framed up to put us in jail. We are what our manifesto says we are, neither more nor less—and we'll give him a copy of that any time he calls. And as for you—(*He glares scornfully at* YANK, *who is sunk in an obvious stupor*) Oh, hell, what's the use of talking? You're a brainless ape.

YANK (*aroused by the word to fierce but futile struggles*) What's dat, yuh Sheeny bum, yuh!

SECRETARY Throw him out, boys. (*In spite of his struggles, this is done with gusto and éclat. Propelled by several parting kicks,* YANK *lands sprawling in the middle of the narrow cobbled street. With a growl he starts to get up and storm the closed door, but stops bewildered by the confusion in his brain, pathetically impotent. He sits there, brooding, in as near to the attitude of Rodin's "Thinker" as he can get in his position*).

YANK (*bitterly*) So dem boids don't tink I belong, neider. Aw, to hell wit 'em! Dey're in de wrong pew—de same old bull—soap-boxes and Salvation Army—no guts! Cut out an hour offen de job a day and make me happy! Gimme a dollar more a day and make me happy! Tree square a day, and cauliflowers in de front yard—ekal rights—a woman and kids—a lousy vote—and I'm all fixed for Jesus, huh? Aw, hell! What does dat get yuh? Dis ting's in your inside, but it ain't your belly. Feedin' your face—sinkers and coffee—dat don't touch it. It's way down—at de bottom. Yuh can't grab it, and yuh can't stop it. It moves, and everything moves. It stops and de whole woild stops. Dat's me now—I don't tick, see?—I'm a busted Ingersoll, dat's what. Steel was me, and I owned de woild. Now I ain't steel, and de woild owns me. Aw, hell! I can't see—it's all dark, get me? It's all wrong! (*He turns a bitter mocking face up like an ape gibbering at the moon*) Say, youse up dere, Man in de Moon, yuh look so wise, gimme de answer, huh? Slip me de inside dope, de information right from de stable—where do I get off at, huh?

A POLICEMAN (*who has come up the street in time to hear this last—with grim humor*) You'll get off at the station, you boob, if you don't get up out of that and keep movin'.

YANK (*looking up at him—with a hard, bitter laugh*) Sure! Lock me up! Put me in a cage! Dat's de on'y answer yuh know. G'wan, lock me up!

POLICEMAN What you been doin'?

YANK Enuf to gimme life for! I was born, see? Sure, dat's de charge. Write it in de blotter. I was born, get me!

POLICEMAN (*jocosely*) God pity your old woman! (*Then matter-of-fact*) But I've no time for kidding. You're soused. I'd run you in but it's too long a walk to the station. Come on now, get up, or I'll fan your ears with this club. Beat it now! (*He hauls* YANK *to his feet*).

YANK (*in vague mocking tone*) Say, where do I go from here?

POLICEMAN (*giving him a push—with a grin, indifferently*) Go to hell.

*Curtain*

# SCENE EIGHT

TWILIGHT *of the next day. The monkey house at the Zoo. One spot of clear gray light falls on the front of one cage so that the interior can be seen. The other cages are vague, shrouded in shadow from which chatterings pitched in a conversational tone can be heard. On the one cage a sign from which the word "gorilla" stands out. The gigantic animal himself is seen squatting on his haunches on a bench in much the same attitude as Rodin's "Thinker."* YANK *enters from the left. Immediately a chorus of angry chattering and screeching breaks out. The gorilla turns his eyes but makes no sound or move.*

YANK (*with a hard, bitter laugh*) Welcome to your city, huh? Hail, hail, de gang's all here! (*At the sound of his voice the chattering dies away into an attentive silence.* YANK *walks up to the gorilla's cage and, leaning over the railing, stares in at its occupant, who stares back at him, silent and motionless. There is a pause of dead stillness. Then* YANK *begins to talk in a friendly confidential tone, half-mockingly, but with a deep undercurrent of sympathy*) Say, yuh're some hard-lookin' guy, ain't yuh? I seen lots of tough nuts dat de gang called gorillas, but yuh're de foist real one I ever seen. Some chest yuh got, and shoulders, and dem arms and mits! I bet yuh got a punch in eider fist dat'd knock 'em all silly! (*This with genuine admiration. The gorilla, as if he understood, stands upright, swelling out his chest and pounding on it with his fist.* YANK *grins sympathetically*) Sure, I get yuh. Yuh challenge de whole woild, huh? Yuh got what I was sayin' even if yuh muffed de woids. (*Then bitterness creeping in*) And why wouldn't yuh get me? Ain't we both members of de same club—de Hairy Apes? (*They stare at each other —a pause—then* YANK *goes on slowly and bitterly*) So yuh're what she seen when she looked at me, de white-faced tart! I was you to her, get me? On'y outa de cage—broke out—free to moider her, see? Sure! Dat's what she tought. She wasn't wise dat I was in a cage, too—worser'n yours—sure—a damn sight—'cause you got some chanct to bust loose—but me—(*He grows confused*) Aw, hell! It's all wrong, ain't it? (*A pause*) I s'pose yuh wanter know what I'm doin' here, huh? I been warmin' a bench down to de Battery—ever since last night. Sure. I seen de sun come up. Dat was pretty, too—all red and pink and green. I was lookin' at de skyscrapers—steel—and all de ships comin' in, sailin' out, all over de oith—and dey was steel, too. De sun was warm, dey wasn't no clouds, and dere was a breeze blowin'. Sure, it was great stuff, I got it aw right—what Paddy said about dat bein' de right dope—on'y I couldn't get *in* it, see? I couldn't belong in dat. It was over my head. And I kept tinkin'—and den I beat it up here to see what youse was like. And I waited till dey was all gone to git yuh alone. Say, how d'yuh feel sittin' in dat pen all de time, havin' to stand for 'em comin' and starin' at yuh—de white-faced, skinny tarts and de boobs what marry 'em —makin' fun of yuh, laughin' at yuh, gittin' scared of yuh—damn 'em! (*He pounds on the rail with his fist. The gorilla rattles the bars of his cage and snarls. All the other monkeys set up an angry chattering in the darkness.* YANK *goes on excitedly*) Sure! Dat's de way it hits me, too. On'y yuh're lucky, see? Yuh don't belong wit 'em and yuh know it. But me, I belong wit 'em—but I don't, see? Dey don't belong wit me, dat's what. Get me? Tinkin' is hard—(*He passes one hand across his forehead with a painful gesture. The gorilla growls impatiently.* YANK *goes on gropingly*) It's dis way, what I'm drivin' at. Youse can sit and dope dream in de past, green woods, de jungle and de rest of it. Den yuh belong and dey don't. Den yuh kin laugh at 'em, see? Yuh're de champ of de woild. But me—I ain't got no past to tink in, nor nothin' dat's comin', on'y what's now—and dat don't belong. Sure, you're de best off! Yuh can't tink, can yuh? Yuh can't talk neider. But I kin make a bluff at talkin' and tinkin' —a'most git away wit it—a'most!—and dat's where de joker comes in. (*He laughs*) I ain't on oith and I ain't in heaven, get me? I'm in de middle tryin' to separate 'em, takin' all de woist punches from bot' of 'em. Maybe dat's what dey call hell, huh? But you, yuh're at de bottom. You belong! Sure! Yuh're de on'y one in de woild dat does, yuh lucky stiff! (*The gorilla growls proudly*) And dat's why dey gotter put yuh in a cage,

see? (*The gorilla roars angrily*) Sure! Yuh get me. It beats it
when you try to tink it or talk it—it's way down—deep—behind
—you 'n' me we feel it. Sure! Bot' members of dis club! (*He
laughs—then in a savage tone*) What de hell! T' hell with it!
A little action, dat's our meat! Dat belongs! Knock 'em down
and keep bustin' 'em till dey croaks yuh with a gat—wit steel!
Sure! Are yuh game? Dey've looked at youse, ain't dey—in a
cage? Wanter git even? Wanter wind up like a sport 'stead of
croakin' slow in dere? (*The gorilla roars an emphatic affirmative.*
YANK *goes on with a sort of furious exaltation*) Sure! Yuh're
reg'lar! Yuh'll stick to de finish! Me 'n' you, huh?—bot' members
of this club! We'll put up one last star bout dat'll knock 'em
offen deir seats! Dey'll have to make de cages stronger after
we're trou! (*The gorilla is straining at his bars, growling, hopping
from one foot to the other.* YANK *takes a jimmy from under his
coat and forces the lock on the cage door. He throws this open*)
Pardon from de governor! Step out and shake hands. I'll take
yuh for a walk down Fif' Avenoo. We'll knock 'em offen de oith
and croak wit de band playin'. Come on, Brother. (*The gorilla
scrambles gingerly out of his cage. Goes to* YANK *and stands
looking at him.* YANK *keeps his mocking tone—holds out his hand*)
Shake—de secret grip of our order. (*Something, the tone of mock
cry, perhaps, suddenly enrages the animal. With a spring he
wraps his huge arms around* YANK *in a murderous hug. There is a
crackling snap of crushed ribs—a gasping cry, still mocking, from*
YANK) Hey, I didn't say kiss me! (*The gorilla lets the crushed
body slip to the floor; stands over it uncertainly, considering;
then picks it up, throws it in the cage, shuts the door, and shuffles
off menacingly into the darkness at left. A great uproar of frightened chattering and whimpering comes from the other cages.
Then* YANK *moves, groaning, opening his eyes, and there is silence. He mutters painfully*) Say—dey oughter match him—wit
Zybszko. He got me, aw right. I'm trou. Even him didn't tink I
belonged. (*Then, with sudden passionate despair*) Christ, where
do I get off at? Where do I fit in? (*Checking himself as suddenly*) Aw, what de hell! No squawkin', see! No quittin', get me!
Croak wit your boots on! (*He grabs hold of the bars of the cage
and hauls himself painfully to his feet—looks around him bewilderedly—forces a mocking laugh*) In de cage, huh? (*In the strident tones of a circus barker*) Ladies and gents, step forward and

take a slant at de one and only—(*His voice weakening*)—one and original—Hairy Ape from de wilds of—(*He slips in a heap on the floor and dies. The monkeys set up a chattering, whimpering wail. And, perhaps, the Hairy Ape at last belongs*).

*Curtain*

# Desire
# Under the Elms

# Characters

EPHRAIM CABOT

SIMEON

PETER

EBEN

ABBIE PUTNAM

*Young Girl, Two Farmers, The Fiddler, A Sheriff, and other folk from the neighboring farms.*

# Scene

The action of the entire play takes place in, and immediately outside of, the Cabot farmhouse in New England, in the year 1850. The south end of the house faces front to a stone wall with a wooden gate at center opening on a country road. The house is in good condition but in need of paint. Its walls are a sickly grayish, the green of the shutters faded. Two enormous elms are on each side of the house. They bend their trailing branches down over the roof. They appear to protect and at the same time subdue. There is a sinister maternity in their aspect, a crushing, jealous absorption. They have developed from their intimate contact with the life of man in the house an appalling humaneness. They brood oppressively over the house. They are like exhausted women resting their sagging breasts and hands and hair on its roof, and when it rains their tears trickle down monotonously and rot on the shingles.

There is a path running from the gate around the right corner of the house to the front door. A narrow porch is on this side. The end wall facing us has two windows in its upper story, two larger ones on the floor below. The two upper are those of the father's bedroom and that of the brothers. On the left, ground floor, is the kitchen—on the right, the parlor, the shades of which are always drawn down.

# PART ONE

## SCENE ONE

EXTERIOR *of the Farmhouse. It is sunset of a day at the beginning of summer in the year 1850. There is no wind and everything is still. The sky above the roof is suffused with deep colors, the green of the elms glows, but the house is in shadow, seeming pale and washed out by contrast.*

*A door opens and* EBEN CABOT *comes to the end of the porch and stands looking down the road to the right. He has a large bell in his hand and this he swings mechanically, awakening a deafening clangor. Then he puts his hands on his hips and stares up at the sky. He sighs with a puzzled awe and blurts out with halting appreciation.*

EBEN   God! Purty! (*His eyes fall and he stares about him frowningly. He is twenty-five, tall and sinewy. His face is well-formed, good-looking, but its expression is resentful and defensive. His defiant, dark eyes remind one of a wild animal's in captivity. Each day is a cage in which he finds himself trapped but inwardly unsubdued. There is a fierce repressed vitality about him. He has black hair, mustache, a thin curly trace of beard. He is dressed in rough farm clothes.*

*He spits on the ground with intense disgust, turns and goes back into the house.*

SIMEON *and* PETER *come in from their work in the fields. They are tall men, much older than their half-brother [*SIMEON *is thirty-nine and* PETER *thirty-seven], built on a squarer, simpler model, fleshier in body, more bovine and homelier in face, shrewder and more practical. Their shoulders stoop a bit from* *years of farm work. They clump heavily along in their clumsy thick-soled boots caked with earth. Their clothes, their faces, hands, bare arms and throats are earth-stained. They smell of earth. They stand together for a moment in front of the house and, as if with the one impulse, stare dumbly up at the sky, leaning on their hoes. Their faces have a compressed, unresigned expression. As they look upward, this softens).*

SIMEON (*grudgingly*) Purty.

PETER Ay-eh.

SIMEON (*suddenly*) Eighteen year ago.

PETER What?

SIMEON Jenn. My woman. She died.

PETER I'd fergot.

SIMEON I rec'lect—now an' agin. Makes it lonesome. She'd hair long's a hoss' tail—an' yaller like gold!

PETER Waal—she's gone. (*This with indifferent finality—then after a pause*) They's gold in the West, Sim.

SIMEON (*still under the influence of sunset—vaguely*) In the sky?

PETER Waal—in a manner o' speakin'—thar's the promise. (*Growing excited*) Gold in the sky—in the West—Golden Gate—California!—Goldest West!—fields o' gold!

SIMEON (*excited in his turn*) Fortunes layin' just atop o' the ground waitin' t' be picked! Solomon's mines, they says! (*For a moment they continue looking up at the sky—then their eyes drop*).

PETER (*with sardonic bitterness*) Here—it's stones atop o' the ground—stones atop o' stones—makin' stone walls—year atop o' year—him 'n' yew 'n' me 'n' then Eben—makin' stone walls fur him to fence us in!

SIMEON We've wuked. Give our strength. Give our years. Plowed 'em under in the ground—(*he stamps rebelliously*)—rottin'—makin' soil for his crops! (*A pause*) Waal—the farm pays good for hereabouts.

PETER If we plowed in Californi-a, they'd be lumps o' gold in the furrow!

SIMEON Californi-a's t'other side o' earth, a'most. We got t' calc'late—

PETER (*after a pause*) 'Twould be hard fur me, too, to give up what we've 'arned here by our sweat. (*A pause. EBEN sticks his head out of the dining-room window, listening*).

SIMEON Ay-eh. (*A pause*) Mebbe—he'll die soon.

PETER (*doubtfully*) Mebbe.

SIMEON  Mebbe—fur all we knows—he's dead now.

PETER  Ye'd need proof.

SIMEON  He's been gone two months—with no word.

PETER  Left us in the fields an evenin' like this. Hitched up an druv off into the West. That's plum onnateral. He hain't never been off this farm 'ceptin' t' the village in thirty year or more, not since he married Eben's maw. (*A pause. Shrewdly*) I calc'late we might git him declared crazy by the court.

SIMEON  He skinned 'em too slick. He got the best o' all on 'em. They'd never b'lieve him crazy. (*A pause*) We got t' wait—till he's under ground.

EBEN  (*with a sardonic chuckle*)  Honor thy father! (*They turn, startled, and stare at him. He grins, then scowls*) I pray he's died. (*They stare at him. He continues matter-of-factly*) Supper's ready.

SIMEON *and* PETER (*together*)  Ay-eh.

EBEN  (*gazing up at the sky*)  Sun's downin' purty.

SIMEON *and* PETER (*together*)  Ay-eh. They's gold in the West.

EBEN  Ay-eh. (*Pointing*) Yonder atop o' the hill pasture, ye mean?

SIMEON *and* PETER (*together*)  In Californi-a!

EBEN  Hunh? (*Stares at them indifferently for a second, then drawls*) Waal—supper's gittin' cold. (*He turns back into kitchen*).

SIMEON  (*startled—smacks his lips*)  I air hungry!

PETER  (*sniffing*)  I smells bacon!

SIMEON  (*with hungry appreciation*)  Bacon's good!

PETER  (*in same tone*)  Bacon's bacon! (*They turn, shouldering each other, their bodies bumping and rubbing together as they hurry clumsily to their food, like two friendly oxen toward their evening meal. They disappear around the right corner of house and can be heard entering the door*).

*Curtain*


SCENE TWO

THE *color fades from the sky. Twilight begins. The interior of the kitchen is now visible. A pine table is at center, a cookstove in the right rear corner, four rough wooden chairs, a tallow candle on the table. In the middle of the rear wall is fastened a big advertizing poster with a ship in full sail and the word "California" in big letters. Kitchen utensils hang from nails. Everything is neat and in order but the atmosphere is of a men's camp kitchen rather than that of a home.*

*Places for three are laid.* EBEN *takes boiled potatoes and bacon from the stove and puts them on the table, also a loaf of bread and a crock of water.* SIMEON *and* PETER *shoulder in, slump down in their chairs without a word.* EBEN *joins them. The three eat in silence for a moment, the two elder as naturally unrestrained as beasts of the field,* EBEN *picking at his food without appetite, glancing at them with a tolerant dislike.*

SIMEON (*suddenly turns to* EBEN) Looky here! Ye'd oughtn't t' said that, Eben.

PETER 'Twa'n't righteous.

EBEN What?

SIMEON Ye prayed he'd died.

EBEN Waal—don't yew pray it? (*A pause*).

PETER He's our Paw.

EBEN (*violently*) Not mine!

SIMEON (*dryly*) Ye'd not let no one else say that about yer Maw! Ha! (*He gives one abrupt sardonic guffaw.* PETER *grins*).

EBEN (*very pale*) I meant—I hain't his'n—I hain't like him—he hain't me!

PETER (*dryly*) Wait till ye've growed his age!

EBEN (*intensely*) I'm Maw—every drop o' blood! (*A pause. They stare at him with indifferent curiosity*).

PETER (*reminiscently*) She was good t' Sim 'n' me. A good Stepmaw's scurse.

SIMEON She was good t' everyone.

EBEN (*greatly moved, gets to his feet and makes an awkward bow to each of them—stammering*) I be thankful t' ye. I'm her—her heir. (*He sits down in confusion*).

PETER (*after a pause—judicially*) She was good even t' him.

EBEN (*fiercely*) An' fur thanks he killed her!

SIMEON (*after a pause*) No one never kills nobody. It's allus somethin'. That's the murderer.

EBEN Didn't he slave Maw t' death?

PETER   He's slaved himself t' death. He's slaved Sim 'n' me 'n' yew t' death—on'y none o' us hain't died—yit.

SIMEON   It's somethin'—drivin' him—t' drive us!

EBEN   (*vengefully*)   Waal—I hold him t' jedgment! (*Then scornfully*) Somethin'! What's somethin'?

SIMEON   Dunno.

EBEN   (*sardonically*)   What's drivin' yew to Californi-a, mebbe? (*They look at him in surprise*) Oh, I've heerd ye! (*Then, after a pause*) But ye'll never go t' the gold fields!

PETER   (*assertively*)   Mebbe!

EBEN   Whar'll ye git the money?

PETER   We kin walk. It's an a'mighty ways—Californi-a—but if yew was t' put all the steps we've walked on this farm end t' end we'd be in the moon!

EBEN   The Injuns'll skulp ye on the plains.

SIMEON   (*with grim humor*)   We'll mebbe make 'em pay a hair fur a hair!

EBEN   (*decisively*)   But t'aint that. Ye won't never go because ye'll wait here fur yer share o' the farm, thinkin' allus he'll die soon.

SIMEON   (*after a pause*)   We've a right.

PETER   Two-thirds belongs t'us.

EBEN   (*jumping to his feet*)   Ye've no right! She wa'n't yewr Maw! It was her farm! Didn't he steal it from her? She's dead. It's my farm.

SIMEON   (*sardonically*)   Tell that t' Paw—when he comes! I'll bet ye a dollar he'll laugh—fur once in his life. Ha! (*He laughs himself in one single mirthless bark*).

PETER   (*amused in turn, echoes his brother*)   Ha!

SIMEON   (*after a pause*)   What've ye got held agin us, Eben? Year after year it's skulked in yer eye—somethin'.

PETER   Ay-eh.

EBEN   Ay-eh. They's somethin'. (*Suddenly exploding*) Why didn't ye never stand between him 'n' my Maw when he was slavin' her to her grave—t' pay her back fur the kindness she done t' yew? (*There is a long pause. They stare at him in surprise*).

SIMEON   Waal—the stock'd got t' be watered.

PETER   'R they was woodin' t' do.

SIMEON   'R plowin'.

PETER   'R hayin'.

SIMEON   'R spreadin' manure.

PETER   'R weedin'.

SIMEON  'R prunin'.

PETER  'R milkin'.

EBEN (*breaking in harshly*)  An' makin' walls—stone atop o' stone
—makin' walls till yer heart's a stone ye heft up out o' the way
o' growth onto a stone wall t' wall in yer heart!

SIMEON (*matter-of-factly*)  We never had no time t' meddle.

PETER (*to* EBEN)  Yew was fifteen afore yer Maw died—an' big
fur yer age. Why didn't ye never do nothin'?

EBEN (*harshly*)  They was chores t' do, wa'n't they? (*A pause—
then slowly*)  It was on'y arter she died I come to think o' it.
Me cookin'—doin' her work—that made me know her, suffer her
sufferin'—she'd come back t' help—come back t' bile potatoes—
come back t' fry bacon—come back t' bake biscuits—come back
all cramped up t' shake the fire, an' carry ashes, her eyes weepin'
an' bloody with smoke an' cinders same's they used t' be. She
still comes back—stands by the stove thar in the evenin'—she
can't find it nateral sleepin' an' restin' in peace. She can't git
used t' bein' free—even in her grave.

SIMEON  She never complained none.

EBEN  She'd got too tired. She'd got too used t' bein' too tired.
That was what he done. (*With vengeful passion*)  An' sooner'r
later, I'll meddle. I'll say the thin's I didn't say then t' him! I'll
yell 'em at the top o' my lungs. I'll see t' it my Maw gits some
rest an' sleep in her grave! (*He sits down again, relapsing into
a brooding silence. They look at him with a queer indifferent
curiosity*).

PETER (*after a pause*)  Whar in tarnation d'ye s'pose he went,
Sim?

SIMEON  Dunno. He druv off in the buggy, all spick an' span, with
the mare all breshed an' shiny, druv off clackin' his tongue an'
wavin' his whip. I remember it right well. I was finishin' plowin',
it was spring an' May an' sunset, an' gold in the West, an' he
druv off into it. I yells "Whar ye goin', Paw?" an' he hauls up
by the stone wall a jiffy. His old snake's eyes was glitterin' in
the sun like he'd been drinkin' a jugful an' he says with a mule's
grin: "Don't ye run away till I come back!"

PETER  Wonder if he knowed we was wantin' fur Californi-a?

SIMEON  Mebbe. I didn't say nothin' and he says, lookin' kinder
queer an' sick: "I been hearin' the hens cluckin' an' the roosters
crowin' all the durn day. I been listenin' t' the cows lowin' an'
everythin' else kickin' up till I can't stand it no more. It's spring

an' I'm feelin' damned," he says. "Damned like an old hickory tree fit on'y fur burnin'," he says. An' then I calc'late I must've looked a mite hopeful, fur he adds real spry and vicious: "But don't git no fool idee I'm dead. I've sworn t' live a hundred an' I'll do it, if on'y t' spite yer sinful greed! An' now I'm ridin' out t' learn God's message t' me in the spring, like the prophets done. An' yew git back t' yer plowin'," he says. An' he druv off singin' a hymn. I thought he was drunk—'r I'd stopped him goin'.

EBEN (*scornfully*) No, ye wouldn't! Ye're scared o' him. He's stronger—inside—than both o' ye put together!

PETER (*sardonically*) An' yew—be yew Samson?

EBEN I'm gittin' stronger. I kin feel it growin' in me—growin' an' growin'—till it'll bust out—! (*He gets up and puts on his coat and a hat. They watch him, gradually breaking into grins.* EBEN *avoids their eyes sheepishly*) I'm goin' out fur a spell—up the road.

PETER T' the village?

SIMEON T' see Minnie?

EBEN (*defiantly*) Ay-eh!

PETER (*jeeringly*) The Scarlet Woman!

SIMEON Lust—that's what's growin' in ye!

EBEN Waal—she's purty!

PETER She's been purty fur twenty year!

SIMEON A new coat o' paint'll make a heifer out of forty.

EBEN She hain't forty!

PETER If she hain't, she's teeterin' on the edge.

EBEN (*desperately*) What d'yew know—

PETER All they is . . . Sim knew her—an' then me arter—

SIMEON An' Paw kin tell yew somethin' too! He was fust!

EBEN D'ye mean t' say he . . . ?

SIMEON (*with a grin*) Ay-eh! We air his heirs in everythin'!

EBEN (*intensely*) That's more to it! That grows on it! It'll bust soon! (*Then violently*) I'll go smash my fist in her face! (*He pulls open the door in rear violently*).

SIMEON (*with a wink at* PETER—*drawlingly*) Mebbe—but the night's wa'm—purty—by the time ye git thar mebbe ye'll kiss her instead!

PETER Sart'n he will! (*They both roar with coarse laughter.* EBEN *rushes out and slams the door—then the outside front door— comes around the corner of the house and stands still by the gate, staring up at the sky*).

SIMEON (*looking after him*)  Like his Paw.

PETER  Dead spit an' image!

SIMEON  Dog'll eat dog!

PETER  Ay-eh. (*Pause. With yearning*) Mebbe a year from now we'll be in Californi-a.

SIMEON  Ay-eh. (*A pause. Both yawn*) Let's git t'bed. (*He blows out the candle. They go out door in rear.* EBEN *stretches his arms up to the sky—rebelliously*)

EBEN  Waal—thar's a star, an' somewhar's they's him, an' here's me, an' thar's Min up the road—in the same night. What if I does kiss her? She's like t'night, she's soft 'n' wa'm, her eyes kin wink like a star, her mouth's wa'm, her arms're wa'm, she smells like a wa'm plowed field, she's purty . . . Ay-eh! By God A'mighty she's purty, an' I don't give a damn how many sins she's sinned afore mine or who she's sinned 'em with, my sin's as purty as any one or 'em! (*He strides off down the road to the left*).

### SCENE THREE

IT IS *the pitch darkness just before dawn.* EBEN *comes in from the left and goes around to the porch, feeling his way, chuckling bitterly and cursing half-aloud to himself.*

EBEN  The cussed old miser! (*He can be heard going in the front door. There is a pause as he goes upstairs, then a loud knock on the bedroom door of the brothers*) Wake up!

SIMEON (*startedly*)  Who's thar?

EBEN (*pushing open the door and coming in, a lighted candle in his hand. The bedroom of the brothers is revealed. Its ceiling is the sloping roof. They can stand upright only close to the center dividing wall of the upstairs.* SIMEON *and* PETER *are in a double bed, front.* EBEN's *cot is to the rear.* EBEN *has a mixture of silly grin and vicious scowl on his face*)  I be!

PETER (*angrily*)  What in hell's-fire . . . ?

EBEN  I got news fur ye! Ha! (*He gives one abrupt sardonic guffaw*).

SIMEON (*angrily*)  Couldn't ye hold it 'til we'd got our sleep?

EBEN It's nigh sunup. (*Then explosively*) He's gone an' married agen!

SIMEON *and* PETER (*explosively*) Paw?

EBEN Got himself hitched to a female 'bout thirty-five—an' purty, they says . . .

SIMEON (*aghast*) It's a durn lie!

PETER Who says?

SIMEON They been stringin' ye!

EBEN Think I'm a dunce, do ye? The hull village says. The preacher from New Dover, he brung the news—told it t'our preacher—New Dover, that's whar the old loon got himself hitched—that's whar the woman lived—

PETER (*no longer doubting—stunned*) Waal . . . !

SIMEON (*the same*) Waal . . . !

EBEN (*sitting down on a bed—with vicious hatred*) Ain't he a devil out o' hell? It's jest t' spite us—the damned old mule!

PETER (*after a pause*) Everythin'll go t' her now.

SIMEON Ay-eh. (*A pause—dully*) Waal—if it's done—

PETER It's done us. (*Pause—then persuasively*) They's gold in the fields o' Californi-a, Sim. No good a-stayin' here now.

SIMEON Jest what I was a-thinkin'. (*Then with decision*) S'well fust's last! Let's light out and git this mornin'.

PETER Suits me.

EBEN Ye must like walkin'.

SIMEON (*sardonically*) If ye'd grow wings on us we'd fly thar!

EBEN Ye'd like ridin' better—on a boat, wouldn't ye? (*Fumbles in his pocket and takes out a crumpled sheet of foolscap*) Waal, if ye sign this ye kin ride on a boat. I've had it writ out an' ready in case ye'd ever go. It says fur three hundred dollars t' each ye agree yewr shares o' the farm is sold t' me. (*They look suspiciously at the paper. A pause*).

SIMEON (*wonderingly*) But if he's hitched agen—

PETER An' whar'd yew git that sum o' money, anyways?

EBEN (*cunningly*) I know whar it's hid. I been waitin'—Maw told me. She knew whar it lay fur years, but she was waitin' . . . It's her'n—the money he hoarded from her farm an' hid from Maw. It's my money by rights now.

PETER Whar's it hid?

EBEN (*Cunningly*) Whar yew won't never find it without me. Maw spied on him—'r she'd never knowed. (*A pause. They look at him suspiciously, and he at them*) Waal, is it fa'r trade?

SIMEON   Dunno.

PETER   Dunno.

SIMEON   (*looking at window*)   Sky's grayin'.

PETER   Ye better start the fire, Eben.

SIMEON   An' fix some vittles.

EBEN   Ay-eh. (*Then with a forced jocular heartiness*) I'll git ye a good one. If ye're startin' t' hoof it t' Californi-a ye'll need somethin' that'll stick t' yer ribs. (*He turns to the door, adding meaningly*) But ye kin ride on a boat if ye'll swap. (*He stops at the door and pauses. They stare at him*).

SIMEON   (*suspiciously*)   Whar was ye all night?

EBEN   (*defiantly*) Up t' Min's. (*Then slowly*) Walkin' thar, fust I felt 's if I'd kiss her; then I got a-thinkin' o' what ye'd said o' him an' her an' I says, I'll bust her nose fur that! Then I got t' the village an' heerd the news an' I got madder'n hell an' run all the way t' Min's not knowin' what I'd do— (*He pauses—then sheepishly but more defiantly*) Waal—when I seen her, I didn't hit her —nor I didn't kiss her nuther—I begun t' beller like a calf an' cuss at the same time, I was so durn mad—an' she got scared— an' I jest grabbed holt an' tuk her! (*Proudly*) Yes, sirree! I tuk her. She may've been his'n—an' your'n, too—but she's mine now!

SIMEON   (*dryly*)   In love, air yew?

EBEN   (*with lofty scorn*)   Love! I don't take no stock in sech slop!

PETER   (*winking at* SIMEON)   Mebbe Eben's aimin' t' marry, too.

SIMEON   Min'd make a true faithful he'pmeet! (*They snicker*).

EBEN   What do I care fur her—'ceptin' she's round an' wa'm? The p'int is she was his'n—an' now she b'longs t' me! (*He goes to the door—then turns—rebelliously*) An' Min hain't sech a bad un. They's worse'n Min in the world, I'll bet ye! Wait'll we see this cow the Old Man's hitched t'! She'll beat Min, I got a notion! (*He starts to go out*).

SIMEON   (*suddenly*)   Mebbe ye'll try t' make her your'n, too?

PETER   Ha! (*He gives a sardonic laugh of relish at this idea*).

EBEN   (*spitting with disgust*) Her—here—sleepin' with him— stealin' my Maw's farm! I'd as soon pet a skunk 'r kiss a snake! (*He goes out. The two stare after him suspiciously. A pause. They listen to his steps receding*).

PETER   He's startin' the fire.

SIMEON   I'd like t' ride t' Californi-a—but—

PETER   Min might o' put some scheme in his head.

SIMEON   Mebbe it's all a lie 'bout Paw marryin'. We'd best wait an' see the bride.

PETER   An' don't sign nothin' till we does!

SIMEON   Nor till we've tested it's good money! (*Then with a grin*) But if Paw's hitched we'd be sellin' Eben somethin' we'd never git nohow!

PETER   We'll wait an' see. (*Then with sudden vindictive anger*) An' till he comes, let's yew 'n' me not wuk a lick, let Eben tend to thin's if he's a mind t', let's us jest sleep an' eat an' drink likker, an' let the hull damned farm go t' blazes!

SIMEON   (*excitedly*)   By God, we've 'arned a rest! We'll play rich fur a change. I hain't a-going to stir outa bed till breakfast's ready.

PETER   An' on the table!

SIMEON   (*after a pause—thoughtfully*)   What d'ye calc'late she'll be like—our new Maw? Like Eben thinks?

PETER   More 'n' likely.

SIMEON   (*vindictively*)   Waal—I hope she's a she-devil that'll make him wish he was dead an' livin' in the pit o' hell fur comfort!

PETER   (*fervently*)   Amen!

SIMEON   (*imitating his father's voice*)   "I'm ridin' out t' learn God's message t' me in the spring like the prophets done," he says. I'll bet right then an' thar he knew plumb well he was goin' whorin', the stinkin' old hypocrite!

## SCENE FOUR

SAME *as Scene Two—shows the interior of the kitchen with a lighted candle on table. It is gray dawn outside,* SIMEON *and* PETER *are just finishing their breakfast.* EBEN *sits before his plate of untouched food, brooding frowningly.*

PETER   (*glancing at him rather irritably*)   Lookin' glum don't help none.

SIMEON   (*sarcastically*)   Sorrowin' over his lust o' the flesh!

PETER   (*with a grin*)   Was she yer fust?

EBEN   (*angrily*)   None o' yer business. (*A pause*) I was thinkin' o' him. I got a notion he's gittin' near—I kin feel him comin' on like yew kin feel malaria chill afore it takes ye.

PETER   It's too early yet.

SIMEON   Dunno. He'd like t' catch us nappin'—jest t' have somethin' t' hoss us 'round over.

PETER (*mechanically gets to his feet.* SIMEON *does the same*) Waal —let's git t' wuk. (*They both plod mechanically toward the door before they realize. Then they stop short*).

SIMEON (*grinning*) Ye're a cussed fool, Pete—and I be wuss! Let him see we hain't wukin'! We don't give a durn!

PETER (*as they go back to the table*) Not a damned durn! It'll serve t' show him we're done with him. (*They sit down again.* EBEN *stares from one to the other with surprise*).

SIMEON (*grins at him*) We're aimin' t' start bein' lilies o' the field.

PETER   Nary a toil 'r spin 'r lick o' wuk do we put in!

SIMEON   Ye're sole owner—till he comes—that's what ye wanted. Waal, ye got t' be sole hand, too.

PETER   The cows are bellerin'. Ye better hustle at the milkin'.

EBEN (*with excited joy*) Ye mean ye'll sign the paper?

SIMEON (*dryly*) Mebbe.

PETER   Mebbe.

SIMEON   We're considerin'. (*Peremptorily*) Ye better git t' wuk.

EBEN (*with queer excitement*) It's Maw's farm agen! It's my farm! Them's my cows! I'll milk my durn fingers off fur cows o' mine! (*He goes out door in rear, they stare after him indifferently*).

SIMEON   Like his Paw.

PETER   Dead spit 'n' image!

SIMEON   Waal—let dog eat dog! (EBEN *comes out of front door and around the corner of the house. The sky is beginning to grow flushed with sunrise.* EBEN *stops by the gate and stares around him with glowing, possessive eyes. He takes in the whole farm with his embracing glance of desire*).

EBEN   It's purty! It's damned purty! It's mine! (*He suddenly throws his head back boldly and glares with hard, defiant eyes at the sky*) Mine, d'ye hear? Mine! (*He turns and walks quickly off left, rear, toward the barn. The two brothers light their pipes*).

SIMEON (*putting his muddy boots up on the table, tilting back his chair, and puffing defiantly*) Waal—this air solid comfort—fur once.

PETER Ay-eh. (*He follows suit. A pause. Unconsciously they both sigh*).

SIMEON (*suddenly*) He never was much o' a hand at milkin', Eben wa'n't.

PETER (*with a snort*) His hands air like hoofs! (*A pause*).

SIMEON Reach down the jug thar! Let's take a swaller. I'm feelin' kind o' low.

PETER Good idee! (*He does so—gets two glasses—they pour out drinks of whisky*) Here's t' the gold in Califomi-a!

SIMEON An' luck t' find it! (*They drink—puff resolutely—sigh—take their feet down from the table*).

PETER Likker don't pear t' sot right.

SIMEON We hain't used t' it this early. (*A pause. They become very restless*).

PETER Gittin' close in this kitchen.

SIMEON (*with immense relief*) Let's git a breath o' air. (*They arise briskly and go out rear—appear around house and stop by the gate. They stare up at the sky with a numbed appreciation*).

PETER Purty!

SIMEON Ay-eh. Gold's t' the East now.

PETER Sun's startin' with us fur the Golden West.

SIMEON (*staring around the farm, his compressed face tightened, unable to conceal his emotion*) Waal—it's our last mornin'—mebbe.

PETER (*the same*) Ay-eh.

SIMEON (*stamps his foot on the earth and addresses it desperately*) Waal—ye've thirty year o' me buried in ye—spread out over ye—blood an' bone an' sweat—rotted away—fertilizin' ye—richin' yer soul—prime manure, by God, that's what I been t' ye!

PETER Ay-eh! An' me!

SIMEON An' yew, Peter. (*He sighs—then spits*) Waal—no use'n cryin' over spilt milk.

PETER They's gold in the West—an' freedom, mebbe. We been slaves t' stone walls here.

SIMEON (*defiantly*) We hain't nobody's slaves from this out—nor no thin's slaves nuther. (*A pause—restlessly*) Speakin' o' milk, wonder how Eben's managin'?

PETER I s'pose he's managin'.

SIMEON Mebbe we'd ought t' help—this once.

PETER Mebbe. The cows knows us.

SIMEON An' likes us. They don't know him much.

PETER  An' the hosses, an' pigs, an' chickens. They don't know him much.

SIMEON  They knows us like brothers—an' likes us! (*Proudly*). Hain't we raised 'em t' be fust-rate, number one prize stock?

PETER  We hain't—not no more.

SIMEON (*dully*)  I was fergittin'. (*Then resignedly*) Waal, let's go help Eben a spell an' git waked up.

PETER  Suits me. (*They are starting off down left, rear, for the barn when* EBEN *appears from there hurrying toward them, his face excited*).

EBEN (*breathlessly*)  Waal—har they be! The old mule an' the bride! I seen 'em from the barn down below at the turnin'.

PETER  How could ye tell that far?

EBEN  Hain't I as far-sight as he's near-sight? Don't I know the mare 'n' buggy, an' two people settin' in it? Who else . . . ? An' I tell ye I kin feel 'em a-comin', too! (*He squirms as if he had the itch*).

PETER (*beginning to be angry*)  Waal—let him do his own un-hitchin'!

SIMEON (*angry in his turn*)  Let's hustle in an' git our bundles an' be a-goin' as he's a-comin'. I don't want never t' step inside the door agen arter he's back. (*They both start back around the corner of the house.* EBEN *follows them*).

EBEN (*anxiously*)  Will ye sign it afore ye go?

PETER  Let's see the color o' the old skinflint's money an' we'll sign. (*They disappear left. The two brothers clump upstairs to get their bundles.* EBEN *appears in the kitchen, runs to window, peers out, comes back and pulls up a strip of flooring in under stove, takes out a canvas bag and puts it on table, then sets the floorboard back in place. The two brothers appear a moment after. They carry old carpet bags*).

EBEN (*puts his hand on bag guardingly*)  Have ye signed?

SIMEON (*shows paper in his hand*)  Ay-eh. (*Greedily*) Be that the money?

EBEN (*opens bag and pours out pile of twenty-dollar gold pieces*)  Twenty-dollar pieces—thirty on 'em. Count 'em. (PETER *does so, arranging them in stacks of five, biting one or two to test them*).

PETER  Six hundred. (*He puts them in the bag and puts it inside his shirt carefully*).

SIMEON (*handing paper to* EBEN)  Har ye be.

EBEN (*after a glance, folds it carefully and hides it under his shirt —gratefully*) Thank yew.

PETER Thank yew fur the ride.

SIMEON We'll send ye a lump o' gold fur Christmas. (*A pause. EBEN stares at them and they at him*).

PETER (*awkwardly*) Waal—we're a-goin'.

SIMEON Comin' out t' the yard?

EBEN No. I'm waitin' in here a spell. (*Another silence. The brothers edge awkwardly to door in rear—then turn and stand*).

SIMEON Waal—good-by.

PETER Good-by.

EBEN Good-by. (*They go out. He sits down at the table, faces the stove and pulls out the paper. He looks from it to the stove. His face, lighted up by the shaft of sunlight from the window, has an expression of trance. His lips move. The two brothers come out to the gate*).

PETER (*looking off toward barn*) Thar he be—unhitchin'.

SIMEON (*with a chuckle*) I'll bet ye he's riled!

PETER An' thar she be.

SIMEON Let's wait 'n' see what our new Maw looks like.

PETER (*with a grin*) An' give him our partin' cuss!

SIMEON (*grinning*) I feel like raisin' fun. I feel light in my head an' feet.

PETER Me, too. I feel like laffin' till I'd split up the middle.

SIMEON Reckon it's the likker?

PETER No. My feet feel itchin' t' walk an' walk—an' jump high over thin's—an'. . . .

SIMEON Dance? (*A pause*).

PETER (*puzzled*) It's plumb onnateral.

SIMEON (*a light coming over his face*) I calc'late it's 'cause school's out. It's holiday. Fur once we're free!

PETER (*dazedly*) Free?

SIMEON The halter's broke—the harness is busted—the fence bars is down—the stone walls air crumblin' an' tumblin'! We'll be kickin' up an' tearin' away down the road!

PETER (*drawing a deep breath—oratorically*) Anybody that wants this stinkin' old rock-pile of a farm kin hev it. T'ain't our'n, no sirree!

SIMEON (*takes the gate off its hinges and puts it under his arm*) We harby 'bolishes shet gates, an' open gates, an' all gates, by thunder!

PETER   We'll take it with us fur luck an' let 'er sail free down some river.

SIMEON   (*as a sound of voices comes from left, rear*)   Har they comes! (*The two brothers congeal into two stiff, grim-visaged statues.* EPHRAIM CABOT *and* ABBIE PUTNAM *come in.* CABOT *is seventy-five, tall and gaunt, with great, wiry, concentrated power, but stoop-shouldered from toil. His face is as hard as if it were hewn out of a boulder, yet there is a weakness in it, a petty pride in its own narrow strength. His eyes are small, close together, and extremely near-sighted, blinking continually in the effort to focus on objects, their stare having a straining, ingrowing quality. He is dressed in his dismal black Sunday suit.* ABBIE *is thirty-five, buxom, full of vitality. Her round face is pretty but marred by its rather gross sensuality. There is strength and obstinacy in her jaw, a hard determination in her eyes, and about her whole personality the same unsettled, untamed, desperate quality which is so apparent in* EBEN).

CABOT   (*as they enter—a queer strangled emotion in his dry cracking voice*)   Har we be t' hum, Abbie.

ABBIE   (*with lust for the word*)   Hum! (*Her eyes gloating on the house without seeming to see the two stiff figures at the gate*) It's purty—purty! I can't b'lieve it's r'ally mine.

CABOT   (*sharply*)   Yewr'n? Mine! (*He stares at her penetratingly. She stares back. He adds relentingly*) Our'n—mebbe! It was lonesome too long. I was growin' old in the spring. A hum's got t' hev a woman.

ABBIE   (*her voice taking possession*)   A woman's got t' hev a hum!

CABOT   (*nodding uncertainly*)   Ay-eh. (*Then irritably*) Whar be they? Ain't thar nobody about—'r wukin'—'r nothin'?

ABBIE   (*sees the brothers. She returns their stare of cold appraising contempt with interest—slowly*)   Thar's two men loafin' at the gate an' starin' at me like a couple o' strayed hogs.

CABOT   (*straining his eyes*)   I kin see 'em—but I can't make out. . . .

SIMEON   It's Simeon.

PETER   It's Peter.

CABOT   (*exploding*)   Why hain't ye wukin'?

SIMEON   (*dryly*)   We're waitin' t' welcome ye hum—yew an' the bride!

CABOT   (*confusedly*)   Huh? Waal—this be yer new Maw, boys. (*She stares at them and they at her*).

SIMEON (*turns away and spits contemptuously*)  I see her!

PETER (*spits also*)  An' I see her!

ABBIE (*with the conqueror's conscious superiority*)  I'll go in an' look at *my* house. (*She goes slowly around to porch*).

SIMEON (*with a snort*)  Her house!

PETER (*calls after her*)  Ye'll find Eben inside. Ye better not tell him it's *yewr* house.

ABBIE (*mouthing the name*)  Eben. (*Then quietly*)  I'll tell Eben.

CABOT (*with a contemptuous sneer*)  Ye needn't heed Eben. Eben's a dumb fool—like his Maw—soft an' simple!

SIMEON (*with his sardonic burst of laughter*)  Ha! Eben's a chip o' yew—spit 'n' image—hard 'n' bitter's a hickory tree! Dog'll eat dog. He'll eat ye yet, old man!

CABOT (*commandingly*)  Ye git t' wuk!'

SIMEON (*as ABBIE disappears in house—winks at PETER and says tauntingly*)  So that thar's our new Maw, be it? Whar in hell did ye dig her up? (*He and PETER laugh*).

PETER  Ha! Ye'd better turn her in the pen with the other sows. (*They laugh uproariously, slapping their thighs*).

CABOT (*so amazed at their effrontery that he stutters in confusion*)  Simeon! Peter! What's come over ye? Air ye drunk?

SIMEON  We're free, old man—free o' yew an' the hull damned farm! (*They grow more and more hilarious and excited*).

PETER  An' we're startin' out fur the gold fields o' Californi-a!

SIMEON  Ye kin take this place an' burn it!

PETER  An' bury it—fur all we cares!

SIMEON  We're free, old man! (*He cuts a caper*).

PETER  Free! (*He gives a kick in the air*).

SIMEON (*in a frenzy*)  Whoop!

PETER  Whoop! (*They do an absurd Indian war dance about the old man who is petrified between rage and the fear that they are insane*).

SIMEON  We're free as Injuns! Lucky we don't skulp ye!

PETER  An' burn yer barn an' kill the stock!

SIMEON  An' rape yer new woman! Whoop! (*He and PETER stop their dance, holding their sides, rocking with wild laughter*).

CABOT (*edging away*)  Lust fur gold—fur the sinful, easy gold o' Californi-a! It's made ye mad!

SIMEON (*tauntingly*)  Wouldn't ye like us to send ye back some sinful gold, ye old sinner?

PETER  They's gold besides what's in Californi-a! (*He retreats back *beyond the vision of the old man and takes the bag of money and flaunts it in the air above his head, laughing).*

SIMEON  And sinfuller, too!

PETER  We'll be voyagin' on the sea! Whoop! (*He leaps up and down*).

SIMEON  Livin' free! Whoop! (*He leaps in turn*).

CABOT (*suddenly roaring with rage*)  My cuss on ye!

SIMEON  Take our'n in trade fur it! Whoop!

CABOT  I'll hev ye both chained up in the asylum!

PETER  Ye old skinflint! Good-by!

SIMEON  Ye old blood sucker! Good-by!

CABOT  Go afore I . . . !

PETER  Whoop! (*He picks a stone from the road.* SIMEON *does the same*).

SIMEON  Maw'll be in the parlor.

PETER  Ay-eh! One! Two!

CABOT (*frightened*)  What air ye . . . ?

PETER  Three! (*They both throw, the stones hitting the parlor window with a crash of glass, tearing the shade*).

SIMEON  Whoop!

PETER  Whoop!

CABOT (*in a fury now, rushing toward them*)  If I kin lay hands on ye—I'll break yer bones fur ye! (*But they beat a capering retreat before him,* SIMEON *with the gate still under his arm.* CABOT *comes back, panting with impotent rage. Their voices as they go off take up the song of the gold-seekers to the old tune of "Oh, Susannah!"*)

> "I jumped aboard the Liza ship,
> And traveled on the sea,
> And every time I thought of home
> I wished it wasn't me!
> Oh! Californi-a,
> That's the land fur me!
> I'm off to Californi-a!
> With my wash bowl on my knee."

(*In the meantime, the window of the upper bedroom on right is raised and* ABBIE *sticks her head out. She looks down at* CABOT *—with a sigh of relief*).

ABBIE  Waal—that's the last o' them two, hain't it? (*He doesn't answer. Then in possessive tones)* This here's a nice bedroom, Ephraim. It's a r'al nice bed. Is it my room, Ephraim?

CABOT (*grimly—without looking up*) Our'n! (*She cannot control a grimace of aversion and pulls back her head slowly and shuts the window. A sudden horrible thought seems to enter* CABOT's *head*) They been up to somethin'! Mebbe—mebbe they've pizened the stock—'r somethin'! (*He almost runs off down toward the barn. A moment later the kitchen door is slowly pushed open and* ABBIE *enters. For a moment she stands looking at* EBEN. *He does not notice her at first. Her eyes take him in penetratingly with a calculating appraisal of his strength as against hers. But under this her desire is dimly awakened by his youth and good looks. Suddenly he becomes conscious of her presence and looks up. Their eyes meet. He leaps to his feet, glowering at her speechlessly*).

ABBIE (*in her most seductive tones which she uses all through this scene*) Be you—Eben? I'm Abbie— (*She laughs*) I mean, I'm yer new Maw.

EBEN (*viciously*) No, damn ye!

ABBIE (*as if she hadn't heard—with a queer smile*) Yer Paw's spoke a lot o' yew. . . .

EBEN Ha!

ABBIE Ye mustn't mind him. He's an old man. (*A long pause. They stare at each other*) I don't want t' pretend playin' Maw t' ye, Eben. (*Admiringly*) Ye're too big an' too strong fur that. I want t' be frens with ye. Mebbe with me fur a fren ye'd find ye'd like livin' here better. I kin make it easy fur ye with him, mebbe. (*With a scornful sense of power*) I calc'late I kin git him t' do most anythin' fur me.

EBEN (*with bitter scorn*) Ha! (*They stare again,* EBEN *obscurely moved, physically attracted to her—in forced stilted tones*) Yew kin go t' the devil!

ABBIE (*calmly*) If cussin' me does ye good, cuss all ye've a mind t'. I'm all prepared t' have ye agin me—at fust. I don't blame ye nuther. I'd feel the same at any stranger comin' t' take my Maw's place. (*He shudders. She is watching him carefully*) Yew must've cared a lot fur yewr Maw, didn't ye? My Maw died afore I'd growed. I don't remember her none. (*A pause*) But yew won't hate me long, Eben. I'm not the wust in the world—an' yew an' me've got a lot in common. I kin tell that by lookin' at ye. Waal—I've had a hard life, too—oceans o' trouble an' nuthin' but wuk fur reward. I was a orphan early an' had t' wuk fur others in other folks' hums. Then I married an' he turned out a drunken spreer an' so he had to wuk fur others an' me too agen in other folks' hums, an' the baby died, an' my husband got sick an' died too, an' I was glad sayin' now I'm free fur once, on'y I diskivered right away all I was free fur was t' wuk agen in other folks' hums, doin' other folks' wuk till I'd most give up hope o' ever doin' my own wuk in my own hum, an' then your Paw come. . . . (CABOT *appears returning from the barn. He comes to the gate and looks down the road the brothers have gone. A faint strain of their retreating voices is heard: "Oh, Californi-a! That's the place for me." He stands glowering, his fist clenched, his face grim with rage*).

EBEN (*fighting against his growing attraction and sympathy— harshly*) An' bought yew—like a harlot! (*She is stung and flushes angrily. She has been sincerely moved by the recital of her troubles. He adds furiously*) An' the price he's payin' ye—this farm—was my Maw's, damn ye!—an' mine now!

ABBIE (*with a cool laugh of confidence*) Yewr'n? We'll see 'bout that! (*Then strongly*) Waal—what if I did need a hum? What else'd I marry an old man like him fur?

EBEN (*maliciously*) I'll tell him ye said that!

ABBIE (*smiling*) I'll say ye're lyin' a-purpose—an' he'll drive ye off the place!

EBEN Ye devil!

ABBIE (*defying him*) This be my farm—this be my hum—this be my kitchen—!

EBEN (*furiously, as if he were going to attack her*) Shut up, damn ye!

ABBIE (*walks up to him—a queer coarse expression of desire in her face and body—slowly*) An' upstairs—that be my bedroom—an' my bed! (*He stares into her eyes, terribly confused and torn. She adds softly*) I hain't bad nor mean—'ceptin' fur an enemy— but I got t' fight fur what's due me out o' life, if I ever 'spect t' git it. (*Then putting her hand on his arm—seductively*) Let's yew 'n' me be frens, Eben.

EBEN (*stupidly—as if hypnotized*) Ay-eh. (*Then furiously flinging off her arm*) No, ye durned old witch! I hate ye! (*He rushes out the door*).

ABBIE (*looks after him smiling satisfiedly—then half to herself, mouthing the word*) Eben's nice. (*She looks at the table, proudly*) I'll wash up *my* dishes now. (EBEN *appears outside, slamming the door behind him. He comes around corner, stops on seeing his father, and stands staring at him with hate*).

CABOT (*raising his arms to heaven in the fury he can no longer control*) Lord God o' Hosts, smite the undutiful sons with Thy wust cuss!

EBEN (*breaking in violently*) Yew 'n' yewr God! Allus cussin' folks—allus naggin' 'em!

CABOT (*oblivious to him—summoningly*) God o' the old! God o' the lonesome!

EBEN (*mockingly*) Naggin' His sheep t' sin! T' hell with yewr God! (CABOT *turns. He and* EBEN *glower at each other*).

CABOT (*harshly*) So it's yew. I might've knowed it. (*Shaking his finger threateningly at him*) Blasphemin' fool! (*Then quickly*) Why hain't ye t' wuk?

EBEN Why hain't yew? They've went. I can't wuk it all alone.

CABOT (*contemptuously*) Nor noways! I'm wuth ten o' ye yit, old's I be! Ye'll never be more'n half a man! (*Then, matter-of-factly*) Waal—let's git t' the barn. (*They go. A last faint note of the "Californi-a" song is heard from the distance.* ABBIE *is washing her dishes*).

*Curtain*

# PART TWO

## SCENE ONE

THE *exterior of the farmhouse, as in Part One—a hot Sunday afternoon two months later.* ABBIE, *dressed in her best, is discovered sitting in a rocker at the end of the porch. She rocks listlessly, enervated by the heat, staring in front of her with bored, half-closed eyes.*

EBEN *sticks his head out of his bedroom window. He looks around furtively and tries to see—or hear—if anyone is on the porch, but although he has been careful to make no noise,* ABBIE *has sensed his movement. She stops rocking, her face grows animated and eager, she waits attentively.* EBEN *seems to feel her presence, he scowls back his thoughts of her and spits with exaggerated disdain—then withdraws back into the room.* ABBIE *waits, holding her breath as she listens with passionate eagerness for every sound within the house.*

EBEN *comes out. Their eyes meet. His falter, he is confused, he turns away and slams the door resentfully. At this gesture,* ABBIE *laughs tantalizingly, amused but at the same time piqued and irritated. He scowls, strides off the porch to the path and starts to walk past her to the road with a grand swagger of ignoring her existence. He is dressed in his store suit, spruced up, his face shines from soap and water.* ABBIE *leans forward on her chair, her eyes hard and angry now, and, as he passes her, gives a sneering, taunting chuckle.*

EBEN (*stung—turns on her furiously*)  What air yew cacklin' 'bout?
ABBIE (*triumphant*)  Yew!
EBEN  What about me?
ABBIE  Ye look all slicked up like a prize bull.

EBEN (*with a sneer*)  Waal—ye hain't so durned purty yerself, be ye? (*They stare into each other's eyes, his held by hers in spite of himself, hers glowingly possessive. Their physical attraction becomes a palpable force quivering in the hot air*).

ABBIE (*softly*)  Ye don't mean that, Eben. Ye may think ye mean it, mebbe, but ye don't. Ye can't. It's agin nature, Eben. Ye been fightin' yer nature ever since the day I come—tryin' t' tell yerself I hain't purty t' ye. (*She laughs a low humid laugh without taking her eyes from his. A pause—her body squirms desirously—she murmurs languorously*)  Hain't the sun strong an' hot? Ye kin feel it burnin' into the earth—Nature—makin' thin's grow—bigger 'n' bigger—burnin' inside ye—makin' ye want t' grow—into somethin' else—till ye're jined with it—an' it's your'n—but it owns ye, too—an' makes ye grow bigger—like a tree—like them elums— (*She laughs again softly, holding his eyes. He takes a step toward her, compelled against his will*)  Nature'll beat ye, Eben. Ye might's well own up t' it fust 's last.

EBEN (*trying to break from her spell—confusedly*)  If Paw'd hear ye goin' on. . . . (*Resentfully*)  But ye've made such a damned idjit out o' the old devil . . . ! (ABBIE *laughs*).

ABBIE  Waal—hain't it easier fur yew with him changed softer?

EBEN (*defiantly*)  No. I'm fightin' him—fightin' yew—fightin' fur Maw's rights t' her hum! (*This breaks her spell for him. He glowers at her*)  An' I'm onto ye. Ye hain't foolin' me a mite. Ye're aimin' t' swaller up everythin' an' make it your'n. Waal, you'll find I'm a heap sight bigger hunk nor yew kin chew! (*He turns from her with a sneer*).

ABBIE (*trying to regain her ascendancy—seductively*)  Eben!

EBEN  Leave me be! (*He starts to walk away*).

ABBIE (*more commandingly*)  Eben!

EBEN (*stops—resentfully*)  What d'ye want?

ABBIE (*trying to conceal a growing excitement*)  Whar air ye goin'?

EBEN (*with malicious nonchalance*)  Oh—up the road a spell.

ABBIE  T' the village?

EBEN (*airily*)  Mebbe.

ABBIE (*excitedly*)  T' see that Min, I s'pose?

EBEN  Mebbe.

ABBIE (*weakly*)  What d'ye want t' waste time on her fur?

EBEN (*revenging himself now—grinning at her*)  Ye can't beat

Nature, didn't ye say? (*He laughs and again starts to walk away*)

ABBIE (*bursting out*) An ugly old hake!

EBEN (*with a tantalizing sneer*) She's purtier'n yew be!

ABBIE That every wuthless drunk in the country has. . . .

EBEN (*tauntingly*) Mebbe—but she's better'n yew. She owns up fa'r 'n' squar' t' her doin's.

ABBIE (*furiously*) Don't ye dare compare. . . .

EBEN She don't go sneakin' an' stealin'—what's mine.

ABBIE (*savagely seizing on his weak point*) Your'n? Yew mean— my farm?

EBEN I mean the farm yew sold yerself fur like any other old whore—my farm!

ABBIE (*stung—fiercely*) Ye'll never live t' see the day when even a stinkin' weed on it 'll belong t' ye! (*Then in a scream*) Git out o' my sight! Go on t' yer slut—disgracin' yer Paw 'n' me! I'll git yer Paw t' horsewhip ye off the place if I want t'! Ye're only livin' here 'cause I tolerate ye! Git along! I hate the sight o' ye! (*She stops panting and glaring at him*).

EBEN (*returning her glance in kind*) An' I hate the sight o' yew! (*He turns and strides off up the road. She follows his retreating figure with concentrated hate. Old* CABOT *appears coming up from the barn. The hard, grim expression of his face has changed. He seems in some queer way softened, mellowed. His eyes have taken on a strange, incongruous dreamy quality. Yet there is no hint of physical weakness about him—rather he looks more robust and younger.* ABBIE *sees him and turns away quickly with unconcealed aversion. He comes slowly up to her*).

CABOT (*mildly*) War yew an' Eben quarrelin' agen?

ABBIE (*shortly*) No.

CABOT Ye was talkin' a'mighty loud. (*He sits down on the edge of porch*).

ABBIE (*snappishly*) If ye heerd us they hain't no need askin' questions.

CABOT I didn't hear what ye said.

ABBIE (*relieved*) Waal—it wa'n't nothin' t' speak on.

CABOT (*after a pause*) Eben's queer.

ABBIE (*bitterly*) He's the dead spit 'n' image o' yew!

CABOT (*queerly interested*) D'ye think so, Abbie? (*After a pause, ruminatingly*) Me 'n' Eben's allus fit 'n' fit. I never could b'ar him noways. He's so thunderin' soft—like his Maw.

ABBIE (*scornfully*) Ay-eh! 'Bout as soft as yew be!

CABOT (*as if he hadn't heard*) Mebbe I been too hard on him.

ABBIE (*jeeringly*) Waal—ye're gittin' soft now—soft as slop! That's what Eben was sayin'.

CABOT (*his face instantly grim and ominous*) Eben was sayin'? Waal, he'd best not do nothin' t' try me 'r he'll soon diskiver. . . . (*A pause. She keeps her face turned away. His gradually softens. He stares up at the sky*) Purty, hain't it?

ABBIE (*crossly*) I don't see nothin' purty.

CABOT The sky. Feels like a wa'm field up thar.

ABBIE (*sarcastically*) Air yew aimin' t' buy up over the farm too? (*She snickers contemptuously*).

CABOT (*strangely*) I'd like t' own my place up thar. (*A pause*) I'm gittin' old, Abbie. I'm gittin' ripe on the bough. (*A pause. She stares at him mystified. He goes on*) It's allus lonesome cold in the house—even when it's bilin' hot outside. Hain't yew noticed?

ABBIE No.

CABOT It's wa'm down t' the barn—nice smellin' an' warm—with the cows. (*A pause*) Cows is queer.

ABBIE Like yew?

CABOT Like Eben. (*A pause*) I'm gittin' t' feel resigned t' Eben—jest as I got t' feel 'bout his Maw. I'm gittin' t' learn to b'ar his softness—jest like her'n. I calc'late I c'd a'most take t' him—if he wa'n't sech a dumb fool! (*A pause*) I s'pose it's old age a-creepin' in my bones.

ABBIE (*indifferently*) Waal—ye hain't dead yet.

CABOT (*roused*) No, I hain't, yew bet—not by a hell of a sight—I'm sound 'n' tough as hickory! (*Then moodily*) But arter three score and ten the Lord warns ye t' prepare. (*A pause*) That's why Eben's come in my head. Now that his cussed sinful brothers is gone their path t' hell, they's no one left but Eben.

ABBIE (*resentfully*) They's me, hain't they? (*Agitatedly*) What's all this sudden likin' ye've tuk to Eben? Why don't ye say nothin' 'bout me? Hain't I yer lawful wife?

CABOT (*simply*) Ay-eh. Ye be. (*A pause—he stares at her desirously—his eyes grow avid—then with a sudden movement he seizes her hands and squeezes them, declaiming in a queer camp meeting preacher's tempo*) Yew air my Rose o' Sharon! Behold, yew air fair; yer eyes air doves; yer lips air like scarlet; yer two breasts air like two fawns; yer navel be like a round goblet; yer belly be like a heap o' wheat. . . . (*He covers her hand with kisses. She does not seem to notice. She stares before her with hard angry eyes*).

ABBIE (*jerking her hands away—harshly*) So ye're plannin' t' leave the farm t' Eben, air ye?

CABOT (*dazedly*) Leave . . . ? (*Then with resentful obstinacy*) I hain't a-givin' it t' no one!

ABBIE (*remorselessly*) Ye can't take it with ye.

CABOT (*thinks a moment—then reluctantly*) No, I calc'late not. (*After a pause—with a strange passion*) But if I could, I would, by the Etarnal! 'R if I could, in my dyin' hour, I'd set it afire an' watch it burn—this house an' every ear o' corn an' every tree down t' the last blade o' hay! I'd sit an' know it was all a-dying with me an' no one else'd ever own what was mine, what I'd made out o' nothin' with my own sweat 'n' blood! (*A pause—then he adds with a queer affection*) 'Ceptin' the cows. Them I'd turn free.

ABBIE (*harshly*) An' me?

CABOT (*with a queer smile*) Ye'd be turned free, too.

ABBIE (*furiously*) So that's the thanks I git fur marryin' ye—t' have ye change kind to Eben who hates ye, an' talk o' turnin' me out in the road.

CABOT (*hastily*) Abbie! Ye know I wa'n't. . . .

ABBIE (*vengefully*) Just let me tell ye a thing or two 'bout Eben! Whar's he gone? T' see that harlot, Min! I tried fur t' stop him. Disgracin' yew an' me—on the Sabbath, too!

CABOT (*rather guiltily*) He's a sinner—nateral-born. It's lust eatin' his heart.

ABBIE (*enraged beyond endurance—wildly vindictive*) An' his lust fur me! Kin ye find excuses fur that?

CABOT (*stares at her—after a dead pause*) Lust—fur yew?

ABBIE (*defiantly*) He was tryin' t' make love t' me—when ye heerd us quarrelin'.

CABOT (*stares at her—then a terrible expression of rage comes over his face—he springs to his feet shaking all over*) By the A'mighty God—I'll end him!

ABBIE (*frightened now for* EBEN) No! Don't ye!

CABOT (*violently*) I'll git the shotgun an' blow his soft brains t' the top o' them elums!

ABBIE (*throwing her arms around him*) No, Ephraim!

CABOT (*pushing her away violently*) I will, by God!

ABBIE (*in a quieting tone*) Listen, Ephraim. 'Twa'n't nothin' bad —on'y a boy's foolin'—'twa'n't meant serious—jest jokin' an' teasin'. . . .

CABOT Then why did ye say—lust?

ABBIE It must hev sounded wusser'n I meant. An' I was mad at thinkin'—ye'd leave him the farm.

CABOT (*quieter but still grim and cruel*) Waal then, I'll horsewhip him off the place if that much'll content ye.

ABBIE (*reaching out and taking his hand*) No. Don't think o' me! Ye mustn't drive him off. 'Tain't sensible. Who'll ye get to help ye on the farm? They's no one hereabouts.

CABOT (*considers this—then nodding his appreciation*) Ye got a head on ye. (*Then irritably*) Waal, let him stay. (*He sits down on the edge of the porch. She sits beside him. He murmurs contemptuously*) I oughtn't t' git riled so—at that 'ere fool calf. (*A pause*) But har's the p'int. What son o' mine'll keep on here t' the farm—when the Lord does call me? Simeon an' Peter air gone t' hell—an' Eben's follerin' 'em.

ABBIE They's me.

CABOT Ye're on'y a woman.

ABBIE I'm yewr wife.

CABOT That hain't me. A son is me—my blood—mine. Mine ought t' git mine. An' then it's still mine—even though I be six foot under. D'ye see?

ABBIE (*giving him a look of hatred*) Ay-eh. I see. (*She becomes very thoughtful, her face growing shrewd, her eyes studying* CABOT *craftily*).

CABOT I'm gittin' old—ripe on the bough. (*Then with a sudden forced reassurance*) Not but what I hain't a hard nut t' crack even yet—an' fur many a year t' come! By the Etarnal, I kin break most o' the young fellers' backs at any kind o' work any day o' the year!

ABBIE (*suddenly*) Mebbe the Lord'll give *us* a son.

CABOT (*turns and stares at her eagerly*) Ye mean—a son—t' me 'n' yew?

ABBIE (*with a cajoling smile*) Ye're a strong man yet, hain't ye? 'Tain't noways impossible, be it? We know that. Why d'ye stare so? Hain't ye never thought o' that afore? I been thinkin' o' it all along. Ay-eh—an' I been prayin' it'd happen, too.

CABOT (*his face growing full of joyous pride and a sort of religious ecstasy*) Ye been prayin', Abbie?—fur a son?—t' us?

ABBIE  Ay-eh. (*With a grim resolution*) I want a son now.

CABOT (*excitedly clutching both of her hands in his*) It'd be the blessin' o' God, Abbie—the blessin' o' God A'mighty on me— in my old age—in my lonesomeness! They hain't nothin' I wouldn't do fur ye then, Abbie. Ye'd hev on'y t' ask it—anythin' ye'd a mind t'!

ABBIE (*interrupting*) Would ye will the farm t' me then—t' me an' it . . . ?

CABOT (*vehemently*) I'd do anythin' ye axed, I tell ye! I swar it! May I be everlastin' damned t' hell if I wouldn't! (*He sinks to his knees pulling her down with him. He trembles all over with the fervor of his hopes*) Pray t' the Lord agen, Abbie. It's the Sabbath! I'll jine ye! Two prayers air better nor one. "An' God hearkened unto Rachel"! An' God hearkened unto Abbie! Pray, Abbie! Pray fur him to hearken! (*He bows his head, mumbling. She pretends to do likewise but gives him a side glance of scorn and triumph*).

## SCENE TWO

ABOUT *eight in the evening. The interior of the two bedrooms on the top floor is shown.* EBEN *is sitting on the side of his bed in the room on the left. On account of the heat he has taken off everything but his undershirt and pants. His feet are bare. He faces front, brooding moodily, his chin propped on his hands, a desperate expression on his face.*

*In the other room* CABOT *and* ABBIE *are sitting side by side on the edge of their bed, an old four-poster with feather mattress. He is in his night shirt, she in her nightdress. He is still in the queer, excited mood into which the notion of a son has thrown him. Both rooms are lighted dimly and flickeringly by tallow candles.*

CABOT  The farm needs a son.

ABBIE  I need a son.

CABOT  Ay-eh. Sometimes ye air the farm an' sometimes the farm be yew. That's why I clove t' ye in my lonesomeness. (*A pause. He pounds his knee with his fist*) Me an' the farm has got t' beget a son!

ABBIE. Ye'd best go t' sleep. Ye're gittin' thin's all mixed.

CABOT (*with an impatient gesture*) No, I hain't. My mind's clear's a bell. Ye don't know me, that's it. (*He stares hopelessly at the floor*).

ABBIE (*indifferently*) Mebbe. (*In the next room* EBEN *gets up and paces up and down distractedly.* ABBIE *hears him. Her eyes fasten on the intervening wall with concentrated attention.* EBEN *stops and stares. Their hot glances seem to meet through the wall. Unconsciously he stretches out his arms for her and she half rises. Then aware, he mutters a curse at himself and flings himself face downward on the bed, his clenched fists above his head, his face buried in the pillow.* ABBIE *relaxes with a faint sigh but her eyes remain fixed on the wall; she listens with all her attention for some movement from* EBEN).

CABOT (*suddenly raises his head and looks at her—scornfully*) Will ye ever know me—'r will any man 'r woman? (*Shaking his head*) No. I calc'late 't wa'n't t' be. (*He turns away.* ABBIE *looks at the wall. Then, evidently unable to keep silent about his thoughts, without looking at his wife, he puts out his hand and clutches her knee. She starts violently, looks at him, sees he is not watching her, concentrates again on the wall and pays no attention to what he says*) Listen, Abbie. When I come here fifty odd year ago—I was jest twenty an' the strongest an' hardest ye ever seen—ten times as strong an' fifty times as hard as Eben. Waal—this place was nothin' but fields o' stones. Folks laughed when I tuk it. They couldn't know what I knowed. When ye kin make corn sprout out o' stones, God's livin' in yew! They wa'n't strong enuf fur that! They reckoned God was easy. They laughed. They don't laugh no more. Some died hereabouts. Some went West an' died. They're all under ground— fur follerin' arter an easy God. God hain't easy. (*He shakes his heads slowly*) An' I growed hard. Folks kept allus sayin' he's a hard man like 'twas sinful t' be hard, so's at last I said back at 'em: Waal then, by thunder, ye'll git me hard an' see how ye like it! (*Then suddenly*) But I give in t' weakness once. 'Twas arter I'd been here two year. I got weak—despairful— they was so many stones. They was a party leavin', givin' up,

goin' West. I jined 'em. We tracked on 'n' on. We come t'
broad medders, plains, whar the soil was black an' rich as gold.
Nary a stone. Easy. Ye'd on'y to plow an' sow an' then set an'
smoke yer pipe an' watch thin's grow. I could o' been a rich man
—but somethin' in me fit me an' fit me—the voice o' God sayin':
"This hain't wuth nothin' t' Me. Git ye back t' hum!" I got
afeerd o' that voice an' I lit out back t' hum here, leavin' my
claim an' crops t' whoever'd a mind t' take 'em. Ay-eh. I actoolly
give up what was rightful mine! God's hard, not easy! God's
in the stones! Build my church on a rock—out o' stones an'
I'll be in them! That's what He meant t' Peter! (*He sighs
heavily—a pause*) Stones. I picked 'em up an' piled 'em into
walls. Ye kin read the years o' my life in them walls, every
day a hefted stone, climbin' over the hills up and down, fencin'
in the fields that was mine, whar I'd made thin's grow out o'
nothin'—like the will o' God, like the servant o' His hand. It
wa'n't easy. It was hard an' He made me hard fur it. (*He
pauses*) All the time I kept gittin' lonesomer. I tuk a wife. She
bore Simeon an' Peter. She was a good woman. She wuked
hard. We was married twenty year. She never knowed me.
She helped but she never knowed what she was helpin'. I was
allus lonesome. She died. After that it wa'n't so lonesome fur
a spell. (*A pause*) I lost count o' the years. I had no time
t' fool away countin' 'em. Sim an' Peter helped. The farm
growed. It was all mine! When I thought o' that I didn't feel
lonesome. (*A pause*) But ye can't hitch yer mind t' one thin'
day an' night. I tuk another wife—Eben's Maw. Her folks
was contestin' me at law over my deeds t' the farm—my farm!
That's why Eben keeps a-talkin' his fool talk o' this bein' his
Maw's farm. She bore Eben. She was purty—but soft. She tried
t' be hard. She couldn't. She never knowed me nor nothin'. It
was lonesomer 'n hell with her. After a matter o' sixteen odd
years, she died. (*A pause*) I lived with the boys. They hated
me 'cause I was hard. I hated them 'cause they was soft.
They coveted the farm without knowin' what it meant. It made
me bitter 'n wormwood. It aged me—them coveting what I'd
made fur mine. Then this spring the call come—the voice o'
God cryin' in my wilderness, in my lonesomeness—t' go out an'
seek an' find! (*Turning to her with strange passion*) I sought
ye an' I found ye! Yew air my Rose o' Sharon! Yer eyes air

like. . . . (*She has turned a blank face, resentful eyes to his. He stares at her for a moment—then harshly*) Air ye any wiser fur all I've told ye?

ABBIE (*confusedly*) Mebbe.

CABOT (*pushing her away from him—angrily*) Ye don't know nothin'—nor never will. If ye don't hev a son t' redeem ye. . . . (*This in a tone of cold threat*).

ABBIE (*resentfully*) I've prayed, hain't I?

CABOT (*bitterly*) Pray agen—fur understandin'!

ABBIE (*a veiled threat in her tone*) Ye'll have a son out o' me, I promise ye.

CABOT How kin ye promise?

ABBIE I got second-sight mebbe. I kin foretell. (*She gives a queer smile*).

CABOT I believe ye have. Ye give me the chills sometimes. (*He shivers*) It's cold in this house. It's oneasy. They's thin's pokin' about in the dark—in the corners. (*He pulls on his trousers, tucking in his night shirt, and pulls on his boots*).

ABBIE (*surprised*) Whar air ye goin'?

CABOT (*queerly*) Down whar it's restful—whar it's warm—down t' the barn. (*Bitterly*) I kin talk t' the cows. They know. They know the farm an' me. They'll give me peace. (*He turns to go out the door*).

ABBIE (*a bit frightenedly*) Air ye ailin' tonight, Ephraim?

CABOT Growin'. Growin' ripe on the bough. (*He turns and goes, his boots clumping down the stairs.* EBEN *sits up with a start, listening.* ABBIE *is conscious of his movement and stares at the wall.* CABOT *comes out of the house around the corner and stands by the gate, blinking at the sky. He stretches up his hands in a tortured gesture*) God A'mighty, call from the dark! (*He listens as if expecting an answer. Then his arms drop, he shakes his head and plods off toward the barn.* EBEN *and* ABBIE *stare at each other through the wall.* EBEN *sighs heavily and* ABBIE *echoes it. Both become terribly nervous, uneasy. Finally* ABBIE *gets up and listens, her ear to the wall. He acts as if he saw every move she was making, he becomes resolutely still. She seems driven into a decision—goes out the door in rear determinedly. His eyes follow her. Then as the door of his room is opened softly, he turns away, waits in an attitude of strained fixity.* ABBIE *stands for a second staring at him, her eyes burning with desire. Then with a little cry she runs over and throws her arms about his neck, she pulls his head back and covers his mouth with kisses. At first, he submits dumbly; then he puts his arms about her neck and returns her kisses, but finally, suddenly aware of his hatred, he hurls her away from him, springing to his feet. They stand speechless and breathless, panting like two animals).*

ABBIE (*at last—painfully*) Ye shouldn't, Eben—ye shouldn't—I'd make ye happy!

EBEN (*harshly*) I don't want t' be happy—from yew!

ABBIE (*helplessly*) Ye do, Eben! Ye do! Why d'ye lie?

EBEN (*viciously*) I don't take t'ye, I tell ye! I hate the sight o' ye!

ABBIE (*with an uncertain troubled laugh*) Waal, I kissed ye anyways—an' ye kissed back—yer lips was burnin'—ye can't lie 'bout that! (*Intensely*) If ye don't care, why did ye kiss me back—why was yer lips burnin'?

EBEN (*wiping his mouth*) It was like pizen on 'em. (*Then tauntingly*) When I kissed ye back, mebbe I thought 'twas someone else.

ABBIE (*wildly*) Min?

EBEN Mebbe.

ABBIE (*torturedly*) Did ye go t' see her? Did ye r'ally go? I thought ye mightn't. Is that why ye throwed me off jest now?

EBEN (*sneeringly*) What if it be?

ABBIE (*raging*) Then ye're a dog, Eben Cabot!

EBEN (*threateningly*) Ye can't talk that way t' me!

ABBIE (*with a shrill laugh*) Can't I? Did ye think I was in love with ye—a weak thin' like yew? Not much! I on'y wanted ye fur a purpose o' my own—an' I'll hev ye fur it yet 'cause I'm stronger'n yew be!

EBEN (*resentfully*) I knowed well it was on'y part o' yer plan t' swaller everythin'!

ABBIE (*tauntingly*) Mebbe!

EBEN (*furious*) Git out o' my room!

ABBIE This air my room an' ye're on'y hired help!

EBEN (*threateningly*) Git out afore I murder ye!

ABBIE (*quite confident now*) I hain't a mite afeerd. Ye want me, don't ye? Yes, ye do! An' yer Paw's son'll never kill what he wants! Look at yer eyes! They's lust fur me in 'em, burnin'

'em up! Look at yer lips now! They're tremblin' an' longin' t'
kiss me, an' yer teeth t' bite! (*He is watching her now with a
horrible fascination. She laughs a crazy triumphant laugh*) I'm
a-goin' t' make all o' this hum my hum! They's one room hain't
mine yet, but it's a-goin' t' be tonight. I'm a-goin' down now
an' light up! (*She makes him a mocking bow*) Won't ye come
courtin' me in the best parlor, Mister Cabot?

EBEN (*staring at her—horribly confused—dully*) Don't ye dare!
It hain't been opened since Maw died an' was laid out thar!
Don't ye . . . ! (*But her eyes are fixed on his so burningly that
his will seems to wither before hers. He stands swaying toward
her helplessly*).

ABBIE (*holding his eyes and putting all her will into her words
as she backs out the door*) I'll expect ye afore long, Eben.

EBEN (*stares after her for a while, walking toward the door. A
light appears in the parlor window. He murmurs*) In the parlor?
(*This seems to arouse connotations for he comes back and puts
on his white shirt, collar, half ties the tie mechanically, puts on
coat, takes his hat, stands barefooted looking about him in
bewilderment, mutters wonderingly*) Maw! Whar air yew? (*Then
goes slowly toward the door in rear*).

## SCENE THREE

A FEW *minutes later. The interior of the parlor is shown. A
grim, repressed room like a tomb in which the family has been
interred alive.* ABBIE *sits on the edge of the horsehair sofa. She
has lighted all the candles and the room is revealed in all its
preserved ugliness. A change has come over the woman. She looks
awed and frightened now, ready to run away.*

*The door is opened and* EBEN *appears. His face wears an expression of obsessed confusion. He stands staring at her, his arms
hanging disjointedly from his shoulders, his feet bare, his hat in
his hand.*

ABBIE (*after a pause—with a nervous, formal politeness*) Won't
ye set?

EBEN (*dully*) Ay-eh. (*Mechanically he places his hat carefully on the floor near the door and sits stiffly beside her on the edge of the sofa. A pause. They both remain rigid, looking straight ahead with eyes full of fear*).

ABBIE When I fust come in—in the dark—they seemed somethin' here.

EBEN (*simply*) Maw.

ABBIE I kin still feel—somethin'. . . .

EBEN It's Maw.

ABBIE At fust I was feered o' it. I wanted t' yell an' run. Now—since yew come—seems like it's growin' soft an' kind t' me. (*Addressing the air—queerly*) Thank yew.

EBEN Maw allus loved me.

ABBIE Mebbe it knows I love yew, too. Mebbe that makes it kind t' me.

EBEN (*dully*) I dunno. I should think she'd hate ye.

ABBIE (*with certainty*) No. I kin feel it don't—not no more.

EBEN Hate ye fur stealin' her place—here in her hum—settin' in her parlor whar she was laid— (*He suddenly stops, staring stupidly before him*).

ABBIE What is it, Eben?

EBEN (*in a whisper*) Seems like Maw didn't want me t' remind ye.

ABBIE (*excitedly*) I knowed, Eben! It's kind t' me! It don't b'ar me no grudges fur what I never knowed an' couldn't help!

EBEN Maw b'ars him a grudge.

ABBIE Waal, so does all o' us.

EBEN Ay-eh. (*With passion*) I does, by God!

ABBIE (*taking one of his hands in hers and patting it*) Thar! Don't git riled thinkin' o' him. Think o' yer Maw who's kind t' us. Tell me about yer Maw, Eben.

EBEN They hain't nothin' much. She was kind. She was good.

ABBIE (*putting one arm over his shoulder. He does not seem to notice—passionately*) I'll be kind an' good t' ye!

EBEN Sometimes she used t' sing fur me.

ABBIE I'll sing fur ye!

EBEN This was her hum. This was her farm.

ABBIE. This is my hum! This is my farm!

EBEN He married her t' steal 'em. She was soft an' easy. He couldn't 'preciate her.

ABBIE   He can't 'preciate me!

EBEN   He murdered her with his hardness.

ABBIE   He's murderin' me!

EBEN   She died. (*A pause*) Sometimes she used to sing fur me. (*He bursts into a fit of sobbing*).

ABBIE   (*both her arms around him—with wild passion*) I'll sing fur ye! I'll die fur ye! (*In spite of her overwhelming desire for him, there is a sincere maternal love in her manner and voice— a horribly frank mixture of lust and mother love*) Don't cry, Eben! I'll take yer Maw's place! I'll be everythin' she was t' ye! Let me kiss ye, Eben! (*She pulls his head around. He makes a bewildered pretense of resistance. She is tender*) Don't be afeered! I'll kiss ye pure, Eben—same's if I was a Maw t' ye— an' ye kin kiss me back 's if yew was my son—my boy—sayin' good-night t' me! Kiss me, Eben. (*They kiss in restrained fashion. Then suddenly wild passion overcomes her. She kisses him lustfully again and again and he flings his arms about her and returns her kisses. Suddenly, as in the bedroom, he frees himself from her violently and springs to his feet. He is trembling all over, in a strange state of terror.* ABBIE *strains her arms toward him with fierce pleading*) Don't ye leave me, Eben! Can't ye see it hain't enuf—lovin' ye like a Maw—can't ye see it's got t' be that an' more—much more—a hundred times more—fur me t' be happy—fur yew t' be happy?

EBEN   (*to the presence he feels in the room*)   Maw! Maw! What d'ye want? What air ye tellin' me?

ABBIE   She's tellin' ye t' love me. She knows I love ye an' I'll be good t' ye. Can't ye feel it? Don't ye know? She's tellin' ye t' love me, Eben!

EBEN   Ay-eh. I feel—mebbe she—but—I can't figger out—why— when ye've stole her place—here in her hum—in the parlor whar she was—

ABBIE   (*fiercely*)   She knows I love ye!

EBEN   (*his face suddenly lighting up with a fierce, triumphant grin*)   I see it! I sees why. It's her vengeance on him—so's she kin rest quiet in her grave!

ABBIE   (*wildly*)   Vengeance o' God on the hull o' us! What d' we give a durn? I love ye, Eben! God knows I love ye! (*She stretches out her arms for him*).

EBEN   (*throws himself on his knees beside the sofa and grabs her*

*in his arms—releasing all his pent-up passion)* An' I love yew,
Abbie!—now I kin say it! I been dyin' fur want o' ye—every
hour since ye come! I love ye! (*Their lips meet in a fierce,
bruising kiss*).

## SCENE FOUR

EXTERIOR *of the farmhouse. It is just dawn. The front door at
right is opened and* EBEN *comes out and walks around to the
gate. He is dressed in his working clothes. He seems changed.
His face wears a bold and confident expression, he is grinning to
himself with evident satisfaction. As he gets near the gate, the
window of the parlor is heard opening and the shutters are flung
back and* ABBIE *sticks her head out. Her hair tumbles over her
shoulders in disarray, her face is flushed, she looks at* EBEN *with
tender, languorous eyes and calls softly*).

ABBIE　Eben. (*As he turns—playfully*) Jest one more kiss afore ye
go. I'm goin' to miss ye fearful all day.

EBEN　An' me yew, ye kin bet! (*He goes to her. They kiss several
times. He draws away, laughingly*) Thar. That's enuf, hain't
it? Ye won't hev none left fur next time.

ABBIE　I got a million o' 'em left fur yew! (*Then a bit anxiously*)
D'ye r'ally love me, Eben?

EBEN　(*emphatically*)　I like ye better'n any gal I ever knowed!
That's gospel!

ABBIE　Likin' hain't lovin'.

EBEN　Waal then—I love ye. Now air yew satisfied?

ABBIE　Ay-eh, I be. (*She smiles at him adoringly*).

EBEN　I better git t' the barn. The old critter's liable t' suspicion
an' come sneakin' up.

ABBIE　(*with a confident laugh*) Let him! I kin allus pull the
wool over his eyes. I'm goin' t' leave the shutters open and let
in the sun 'n' air. This room's been dead long enuf. Now it's
goin' t' be my room!

EBEN　(*frowning*) Ay-eh.

ABBIE　(*hastily*)　I meant—our room.

EBEN  Ay-eh.

ABBIE  We made it our'n last night, didn't we? We give it life—our lovin' did. (*A pause*).

EBEN  (*with a strange look*)  Maw's gone back t' her grave. She kin sleep now.

ABBIE  May she rest in peace! (*Then tenderly rebuking*) Ye oughtn't t' talk o' sad thin's—this mornin'.

EBEN  It jest come up in my mind o' itself.

ABBIE  Don't let it. (*He doesn't answer. She yawns*) Waal, I'm a-goin' t' steal a wink o' sleep. I'll tell the Old Man I hain't feelin' pert. Let him git his own vittles.

EBEN  I see him comin' from the barn. Ye better look smart an git upstairs.

ABBIE  Ay-eh. Good-by. Don't ferget me. (*She throws him a kiss. He grins—then squares his shoulders and awaits his father confidently.* CABOT *walks slowly up from the left, staring up at the sky with a vague face*).

EBEN  (*jovially*)  Mornin', Paw. Star-gazin' in daylight?

CABOT  Purty, hain't it?

EBEN  (*looking around him possessively*)  It's a durned purty farm.

CABOT  I mean the sky.

EBEN  (*grinning*)  How d'ye know? Them eyes o' your'n can't see that fur. (*This tickles his humor and he slaps his thigh and laughs*) Ho-ho! That's a good un!

CABOT  (*grimly sarcastic*)  Ye're feelin' right chipper, hain't ye? Whar'd ye steal the likker?

EBEN  (*good-naturedly*)  'Tain't likker. Jest life. (*Suddenly holding out his hand—soberly*) Yew 'n' me is quits. Let's shake hands.

CABOT  (*suspiciously*)  What's come over ye?

EBEN  Then don't. Mebbe it's jest as well. (*A moment's pause*) What's come over me? (*Queerly*) Didn't ye feel her passin'—goin' back t' her grave?

CABOT  (*dully*)  Who?

EBEN  Maw. She kin rest now an' sleep content. She's quits with ye.

CABOT  (*confusedly*)  I rested. I slept good—down with the cows. They know how t' sleep. They're teachin' me.

EBEN  (*suddenly jovial again*)  Good fur the cows! Waal—ye better git t' work.

CABOT  (*grimly amused*)  Air yew bossin' me, ye calf?

EBEN (*beginning to laugh*) Ay-eh! I'm bossin' yew! Ha-ha-ha! See how ye like it! Ha-ha-ha! I'm the prize rooster o' this roost. Ha-ha-ha! (*He gos off toward the barn laughing*).

CABOT (*looks after him with scornful pity*) Soft-headed. Like his Maw. Dead spit 'n' image. No hope in him! (*He spits with contemptuous disgust*) A born fool! (*Then matter-of-factly*) Waal —I'm gittin' peckish. (*He goes toward door*).

*Curtain*

# PART THREE

## SCENE ONE

A NIGHT *in late spring the following year. The kitchen and the two bedrooms upstairs are shown. The two bedrooms are dimly lighted by a tallow candle in each.* EBEN *is sitting on the side of the bed in his room, his chin propped on his fists, his face a study of the struggle he is making to understand his conflicting emotions. The noisy laughter and music from below where a kitchen dance is in progress annoy and distract him. He scowls at the floor.*

*In the next room a cradle stands beside the double bed.*

*In the kitchen all is festivity. The stove has been taken down to give more room to the dancers. The chairs, with wooden benches added, have been pushed back against the walls. On these are seated, squeezed in tight against one another, farmers and their wives and their young folks of both sexes from the neighboring farms. They are all chattering and laughing loudly. They evidently have some secret joke in common. There is no end of winking, of nudging, of meaning nods of the head toward* CABOT *who, in a state of extreme hilarious excitement increased by the amount he has drunk, is standing near the rear door where there is a small keg of whisky and serving drinks to all the men. In the left corner, front, dividing the attention with her husband,* ABBIE *is sitting in a rocking chair, a shawl wrapped about her shoulders. She is very pale, her face is thin and drawn, her eyes are fixed anxiously on the open door in rear as if waiting for someone.*

*The musician is tuning up his fiddle, seated in the far right corner. He is a lanky young fellow with a long, weak face. His pale eyes blink incessantly and he grins about him slyly with a greedy malice.*

ABBIE (*suddenly turning to a young girl on her right*) Whar's Eben?

YOUNG GIRL (*eying her scornfully*) I dunno, Mrs. Cabot. I hain't seen Eben in ages. (*Meaningly*) Seems like he's spent most o' his time t' hum since yew come.

ABBIE (*vaguely*) I tuk his Maw's place.

YOUNG GIRL Ay-eh. So I've heerd. (*She turns away to retail this bit of gossip to her mother sitting next to her.* ABBIE *turns to her left to a big stoutish middle-aged man whose flushed face and starting eyes show the amount of "likker" he has consumed*).

ABBIE Ye hain't seen Eben, hev ye?

MAN No, I hain't. (*Then he adds with a wink*) If yew hain't, who would?

ABBIE He's the best dancer in the county. He'd ought t' come an' dance.

MAN (*with a wink*) Mebbe he's doin' the dutiful an' walkin' the kid t' sleep. It's a boy, hain't it?

ABBIE (*nodding vaguely*) Ay-eh—born two weeks back—purty's a picter.

MAN They all is—t' their Maws. (*Then in a whisper, with a nudge and a leer*) Listen, Abbie—if ye ever git tired o' Eben, remember me! Don't fergit now! (*He looks at her uncomprehending face for a second—then grunts disgustedly*) Waal—guess I'll likker agin. (*He goes over and joins* CABOT *who is arguing noisily with an old farmer over cows. They all drink*).

ABBIE (*this time appealing to nobody in particular*) Wonder what Eben's a-doin'? (*Her remark is repeated down the line with many a guffaw and titter until it reaches the fiddler. He fastens his blinking eyes on* ABBIE).

FIDDLER (*raising his voice*) Bet I kin tell ye, Abbie, what Eben's doin'! He's down t' the church offerin' up prayers o' thanksgivin'. (*They all titter expectantly*).

A MAN What fur? (*Another titter*).

FIDDLER 'Cause unto him a—(*He hesitates just long enough*) brother is born! (*A roar of laughter. They all look from* ABBIE *to* CABOT. *She is oblivious, staring at the door.* CABOT, *although he hasn't heard the words, is irritated by the laughter and steps forward, glaring about him. There is an immediate silence).*

CABOT What're ye all bleatin' about—like a flock o' goats? Why don't ye dance, damn ye? I axed ye here t' dance—t' eat, drink an' be merry—an' thar ye set cacklin' like a lot o' wet hens with the pip! Ye've swilled my likker an' guzzled my vittles like hogs, hain't ye? Then dance fur me, can't ye? That's fa'r an' squar', hain't it? (*A grumble of resentment goes around but they are all evidently in too much awe of him to express it openly*).

FIDDLER (*slyly*) We're waitin' fur Eben. (*A suppressed laugh*).

CABOT (*with a fierce exultation*) T' hell with Eben! Eben's done fur now! I got a new son! (*His mood switching with drunken suddenness*) But ye needn't t' laugh at Eben, none o' ye! He's my blood, if he be a dumb fool. He's better nor any o' yew! He kin do a day's work a'most up t' what I kin—an' that'd put any o' yew pore critters t' shame!

FIDDLER An' he kin do a good night's work, too! (*A roar of laughter*).

CABOT Laugh, ye damn fools! Ye're right jist the same, Fiddler. He kin work day an' night too, like I kin, if need be!

OLD FARMER (*from behind the keg where he is weaving drunkenly back and forth—with great simplicity*) They hain't many t' touch ye, Ephraim—a son at seventy-six. That's a hard man fur ye! I be on'y sixty-eight an' I couldn't do it. (*A roar of laughter in which* CABOT *joins uproariously*).

CABOT (*slapping him on the back*) I'm sorry fur ye, Hi. I'd never suspicion sech weakness from a boy like yew!

OLD FARMER An' I never reckoned yew had it in ye nuther, Ephraim. (*There is another laugh*).

CABOT (*suddenly grim*) I got a lot in me—a hell of a lot—folks don't know on. (*Turning to the fiddler*) Fiddle 'er up, durn ye! Give 'em somethin' t' dance t'! What air ye, an ornament? Hain't this a celebration? Then grease yer elbow an' go it!

FIDDLER (*seizes a drink which the* OLD FARMER *holds out to him and downs it*) Here goes! (*He starts to fiddle "Lady of the Lake." Four young fellows and four girls form in two lines and dance a square dance. The* FIDDLER *shouts directions for the different movements, keeping his words in the rhythm of the music and interspersing them with jocular personal remarks to the dancers themselves. The people seated along the walls stamp their feet and clap their hands in unison.* CABOT *is especially active in this respect. Only* ABBIE *remains apathetic, staring at the door as if she were alone in a silent room*).

FIDDLER  Swing your partner t' the right! That's it, Jim! Give her a b'ar hug! Her Maw hain't lookin'. (*Laughter*) Change partners! That suits ye, don't it, Essie, now ye got Reub afore ye? Look at her redden up, will ye? Waal, life is short an' so's love, as the feller says. (*Laughter*).

CABOT (*excitedly, stamping his foot*)  Go it, boys! Go it, gals!

FIDDLER (*with a wink at the others*)  Ye're the spryest seventy-six ever I sees, Ephraim! Now if ye'd on'y good eye-sight . . . ! (*Suppressed laughter. He gives* CABOT *no chance to retort but roars*) Promenade! Ye're walkin' like a bride down the aisle, Sarah! Waal, while they's life they's allus hope, I've heered tell. Swing your partner to the left! Gosh A'mighty, look at Johnny Cook high-steppin'! They hain't goin' t' be much strength left fur howin' in the corn lot t'morrow. (*Laughter*).

CABOT  Go it! Go it! (*Then suddenly, unable to restrain himself any longer, he prances into the midst of the dancers, scattering them, waving his arms about wildly*) Ye're all hoofs! Git out o' my road! Give me room! I'll show ye dancin'. Ye're all too soft! (*He pushes them roughly away. They crowd back toward the walls, muttering, looking at him resentfully*).

FIDDLE (*jeeringly*)  Go it, Ephraim! Go it! (*He starts "Pop Goes the Weasel," increasing the tempo with every verse until at the end he is fiddling crazily as fast as he can go*).

CABOT (*starts to dance, which he does very well and with tremendous vigor. Then he begins to improvise, cuts incredibly grotesque capers, leaping up and cracking his heels together, prancing around in a circle with body bent in an Indian war dance, then suddenly straightening up and kicking as high as he can with both legs. He is like a monkey on a string. And all the while he intersperses his antics with shouts and derisive comments*) Whoop! Here's dancin' fur ye! Whoop! See that! Seventy-six, if I'm a day! Hard as iron yet! Beatin' the young 'uns like I allus done! Look at me! I'd invite ye t' dance on my hundredth birthday on'y ye'll all be dead by then. Ye're a sickly generation! Yer hearts air pink, not red! Yer veins is full o' mud an' water! I be the on'y man in the county! Whoop! See that! I'm a Injun! I've killed Injuns in the West afore ye was born—an' skulped 'em too! They's a arrer wound on my backside I c'd show ye! The hull tribe chased me. I outrun 'em all—with the arrer stuck in me! An' I tuk vengeance on 'em. Ten eyes fur an eye, that was my motter! Whoop! Look at me! I kin kick the ceilin' off the room! Whoop!

FIDDLER (*stops playing—exhaustedly*) God A'mighty, I got enuf. Ye got the devil's strength in ye.

CABOT (*delightedly*) Did I beat yew, too? Wa'al, ye played smart. Hev a swig. (*He pours whisky for himself and* FIDDLER. *They drink. The others watch* CABOT *silently with cold, hostile eyes. There is a dead pause. The* FIDDLER *rests.* CABOT *leans against the keg, panting, glaring around him confusedly. In the room above,* EBEN *gets to his feet and tiptoes out the door in rear, appearing a moment later in the other bedroom. He moves silently, even frightenedly, toward the cradle and stands there looking down at the baby. His face is as vague as his reactions are confused, but there is a trace of tenderness, of interested discovery. At the same moment that he reaches the cradle,* ABBIE *seems to sense something. She gets up weakly and goes to* CABOT).

ABBIE I'm goin' up t' the baby.

CABOT (*with real solicitation*) Air ye able fur the stairs? D'ye want me t' help ye, Abbie?

ABBIE No. I'm able. I'll be down agen soon.

CABOT Don't ye git wore out! He needs ye, remember—our son does! (*He grins affectionately, patting her on the back. She shrinks from his touch*).

ABBIE (*dully*) Don't—tech me. I'm goin'—up. (*She goes.* CABOT *looks after her. A whisper goes around the room.* CABOT *turns. It ceases. He wipes his forehead streaming with sweat. He is breathing pantingly*).

CABOT I'm a-goin' out t' git fresh air. I'm feelin' a mite dizzy. Fiddle up thar! Dance, all o' ye! Here's likker fur them as wants it. Enjoy yerselves. I'll be back. (*He goes, closing the door behind him*).

FIDDLER (*sarcastically*) Don't hurry none on our account! (*A suppressed laugh. He imitates* ABBIE) Whar's Eben? (*More laughter*).

A WOMAN (*loudly*) What's happened in this house is plain as the nose on yer face! (ABBIE *appears in the doorway upstairs and stands looking in surprise and adoration at* EBEN *who does not see her*).

A MAN Ssshh! He's li'ble t' be listenin' at the door. That'd be like him. (*Their voices die to an intensive whispering. Their faces are concentrated on this gossip. A noise as of dead leaves in the wind comes from the room.* CABOT *has come out from the porch and stands by the gate, leaning on it, staring at the sky blinkingly.* ABBIE *comes across the room silently.* EBEN *does not notice her until quite near*).

EBEN (*starting*) Abbie!

ABBIE Ssshh! (*She throws her arms around him. They kiss—then bend over the cradle together*) Ain't he purty?—dead spit 'n' image o' yew!

EBEN (*pleased*) Air he? I can't tell none.

ABBIE E-zactly like!

EBEN (*frowningly*) I don't like this. I don't like lettin' on what's mine's his'n. I been doin' that all my life. I'm gittin' t' the end o' b'arin' it!

ABBIE (*putting her finger on his lips*) We're doin' the best we kin. We got t' wait. Somethin's bound t' happen. (*She puts her arms around him*) I got t' go back.

EBEN I'm goin' out. I can't b'ar it with the fiddle playin' an' the laughin'.

ABBIE Don't git feelin' low. I love ye, Eben. Kiss me. (*He kisses her. They remain in each other's arms*).

CABOT (*at the gate, confusedly*) Even the music can't drive it out—somethin'. Ye kin feel it droppin' off the elums, climbin' up the roof, sneakin' down the chimney, pokin' in the corners! They's no peace in houses, they's no rest livin' with folks. Somethin's always livin' with ye. (*With a deep sigh*) I'll go t' the barn an' rest a spell. (*He goes wearily toward the barn*).

FIDDLER (*tuning up*) Let's celebrate the old skunk gittin' fooled! We kin have some fun now he's went. (*He starts to fiddle "Turkey in the Straw." There is real merriment now. The young folks get up to dance*).

## SCENE TWO

A HALF *hour later—Exterior—*EBEN *is standing by the gate looking up at the sky, an expression of dumb pain bewildered by itself on his face.* CABOT *appears, returning from the barn, walking* *wearily, his eyes on the ground. He sees* EBEN *and his whole mood immediately changes. He becomes excited, a cruel, triumphant grin comes to his lips, he strides up and slaps* EBEN *on the back. From within comes the whining of the fiddle and the noise of stamping feet and laughing voices.*

CABOT  So har ye be!

EBEN (*startled, stares at him with hatred for a moment—then dully*) Ay-eh.

CABOT (*surveying him jeeringly*) Why hain't ye been in t' dance? They was all axin' fur ye.

EBEN  Let 'em ax!

CABOT  They's a hull passel o' purty gals.

EBEN  T' hell with 'em!

CABOT  Ye'd ought t' be marryin' one o' 'em soon.

EBEN  I hain't marryin' no one.

CABOT  Ye might 'arn a share o' a farm that way.

EBEN (*with a sneer*) Like yew did, ye mean? I hain't that kind.

CABOT (*stung*) Ye lie! 'Twas yer Maw's folks aimed t' steal my farm from me.

EBEN  Other folks don't say so. (*After a pause—defiantly*) An' I got a farm, anyways!

CABOT (*derisively*) Whar?

EBEN (*stamps a foot on the ground*) Har!

CABOT (*throws his head back and laughs coarsely*) Ho-ho! Ye hev, hev ye? Waal, that's a good un!

EBEN (*controlling himself—grimly*) Ye'll see!

CABOT (*stares at him suspiciously, trying to make him out—a pause—then with scornful confidence*) Ay-eh. I'll see. So'll ye. It's ye that's blind—blind as a mole underground. (EBEN *suddenly laughs, one short sardonic bark: "Ha." A pause.* CABOT *peers at him with renewed suspicion*) What air ye hawin' 'bout? (EBEN *turns away without answering.* CABOT *grows angry*) God A'mighty, yew air a dumb dunce! They's nothin' in that thick skull o' your'n but noise—like a empty keg it be! (EBEN *doesn't seem to hear.* CABOT's *rage grows*) Yewr farm! God A'mighty! If ye wa'n't a born donkey ye'd know ye'll never own stick nor stone on it, specially now arter him bein' born. It's his'n, I tell ye—his'n arter I die—but I'll live a hundred jest t' fool ye all— an' he'll be growed then—yewr age a'most! (EBEN *laughs again his sardonic "Ha." This drives* CABOT *into a fury*) Ha? Ye think

ye kin git 'round that someways, do ye? Waal, it'll be her'n, too—
Abbie's—ye won't git 'round her—she knows yer tricks—she'll be
too much fur ye—she wants the farm her'n—she was afeerd o'
ye—she told me ye was sneakin' 'round tryin' t' make love t' her
t' git her on yer side . . . ye . . . ye mad fool, ye! (*He raises
his clenched fists threateningly*).

EBEN (*is confronting him choking with rage*) Ye lie, ye old skunk!
Abbie never said no sech thing!

CABOT (*suddenly triumphant when he sees how shaken* EBEN *is*)
She did. An' I says, I'll blow his brains t' the top o' them elums—
an' she says no, that hain't sense, who'll ye git t' help ye on the
farm in his place—an' then she says yew'n me ought t' have a son
—I know we kin, she says—an' I says, if we do, ye kin have anythin' I've got ye've a mind t'. An' she says, I wants Eben cut off
so's this farm'll be mine when ye die! (*With terrible gloating*)
An' that's what's happened, hain't it? An' the farm's her'n! An'
the dust o' the road—that's your'n! Ha! Now who's hawin'?

EBEN (*has been listening, petrified with grief and rage—suddenly
laughs wildly and brokenly*) Ha-ha-ha! So that's her sneakin'
game—all along!—like I suspicioned at fust—t' swaller it all—an'
me, too . . . ! (*Madly*) I'll murder her! (*He springs toward the
porch but* CABOT *is quicker and gets in between*).

CABOT No, ye don't!

EBEN Git out o' my road! (*He tries to throw* CABOT *aside. They
grapple in what becomes immediately a murderous struggle.
The old man's concentrated strength is too much for* EBEN.
CABOT *gets one hand on his throat and presses him back across
the stone wall. At the same moment,* ABBIE *comes out on the
porch. With a stifled cry she runs toward them*).

ABBIE Eben! Ephraim! (*She tugs at the hand on* EBEN's *throat*)
Let go, Ephraim! Ye're chokin' him!

CABOT (*removes his hand and flings* EBEN *sideways full length
on the grass, gasping and choking. With a cry,* ABBIE *kneels beside him, trying to take his head on her lap, but he pushes her
away.* CABOT *stands looking down with fierce triumph*) Ye
needn't t've fret, Abbie, I wa'n't aimin' t' kill him. He hain't
wuth hangin' fur—not by a hell of a sight! (*More and more
triumphantly*) Seventy-six an' him not thirty yit—an' look whar
he be fur thinkin' his Paw was easy! No, by God, I hain't easy!
An' him upstairs, I'll raise him t' be like me! (*He turns to leave
them*) I'm goin' in an' dance!—sing an' celebrate! (*He walks to*

*the porch—then turns with a great grin*) I don't calc'late it's left in him, but if he gits pesky, Abbie, ye jest sing out. I'll come a-runnin' an' by the Etarnal, I'll put him across my knee an' birch him! Ha-ha-ha! (*He goes into the house laughing. A moment later his loud "whoop" is heard*).

ABBIE (*tenderly*)  Eben. Air ye hurt? (*She tries to kiss him but he pushes her violently away and struggles to a sitting position*).

EBEN (*gaspingly*)  T' hell—with ye!

ABBIE (*not believing her ears*)  It's me, Eben—Abbie—don't ye know me?

EBEN (*glowering at her with hatred*)  Ay-eh—I know ye—now! (*He suddenly breaks down, sobbing weakly*).

ABBIE (*fearfully*)  Eben—what's happened t' ye—why did ye look at me 's if ye hated me?

EBEN (*violently, between sobs and gasps*)  I do hate ye! Ye're a whore—a damn trickin' whore!

ABBIE (*shrinking back horrified*)  Eben! Ye don't know what ye're sayin'!

EBEN (*scrambling to his feet and following her—accusingly*) Ye're nothin' but a stinkin' passel o' lies! Ye've been lyin' t' me every word ye spoke, day an' night, since we fust—done it. Ye've kept sayin' ye loved me. . . .

ABBIE (*frantically*)  I do love ye! (*She takes his hand but he flings hers away*).

EBEN (*unheeding*)  Ye've made a fool o' me—a sick, dumb fool— a-purpose! Ye've been on'y playin' yer sneakin', stealin' game all along—gittin' me t' lie with ye so's ye'd hev a son he'd think was his'n, an' makin' him promise he'd give ye the farm and let me eat dust, if ye did git him a son! (*Staring at her with anguished, bewildered eyes*) They must be a devil livin' in ye! T'ain't human t' be as bad as that be!

ABBIE (*stunned—dully*)  He told yew . . . ?

EBEN  Hain't it true? It hain't no good in yew lyin'.

ABBIE (*pleadingly*)  Eben, listen—ye must listen—it was long ago —afore we done nothin'—yew was scornin' me—goin' t' see Min— when I was lovin' ye—an' I said it t' him t' git vengeance on ye!

EBEN (*unheedingly. With tortured passion*)  I wish ye was dead! I wish I was dead along with ye afore this come! (*Ragingly*) But I'll git my vengeance too! I'll pray Maw t' come back t' help me—t' put her cuss on yew an' him!

ABBIE (*brokenly*)  Don't ye, Eben! Don't ye! (*She throws herself *on her knees before him, weeping*) I didn't mean t' do bad t' ye! Fergive me, won't ye?

EBEN (*not seeming to hear her—fiercely*) I'll git squar' with the old skunk—an' yew! I'll tell him the truth 'bout the son he's so proud o'! Then I'll leave ye here t' pizen each other—with Maw comin' out o' her grave at nights—an' I'll go t' the gold fields o' Californi-a whar Sim an' Peter be!

ABBIE (*terrified*) Ye won't—leave me? Ye can't!

EBEN (*with fierce determination*) I'm a-goin', I tell ye! I'll git rich thar an' come back an' fight him fur the farm he stole—an' I'll kick ye both out in the road—t' beg an' sleep in the woods— an' yer son along with ye—t' starve an' die! (*He is hysterical at the end*).

ABBIE (*with a shudder—humbly*) He's yewr son, too, Eben.

EBEN (*torturedly*) I wish he never was born! I wish he'd die this minit! I wish I'd never sot eyes on him! It's him—yew havin' him—a-purpose t' steal—that's changed everythin'!

ABBIE (*gently*) Did ye believe I loved ye—afore he come?

EBEN Ay-eh—like a dumb ox!

ABBIE An' ye don't believe no more?

EBEN B'lieve a lyin' thief! Ha!

ABBIE (*shudders—then humbly*) An' did ye r'ally love me afore?

EBEN (*brokenly*) Ay-eh—an' ye was trickin' me!

ABIE An' ye don't love me now!

EBEN (*violently*) I hate ye, I tell ye!

ABBIE An' ye're truly goin' West—goin' t' leave me—all account o' him being born?

EBEN I'm a-goin' in the mornin'—or may God strike me t' hell!

ABBIE (*after a pause—with a dreadful cold intensity—slowly*) If that's what his comin's done t' me—killin' yewr love—takin' yew away—my on'y joy—the on'y joy I ever knowed—like heaven t' me—purtier'n heaven—then I hate him, too, even if I be his Maw!

EBEN (*bitterly*) Lies! Ye love him! He'll steal the farm fur ye! (*Brokenly*) But t'ain't the farm so much—not no more—it's yew foolin' me—gittin' me t' love ye—lyin' yew loved me—jest t' git a son t' steal!

ABBIE (*distractedly*) He won't steal! I'd kill him fust! I do love ye! I'll prove t' ye . . . !

EBEN (*harshly*) 'T'ain't no use lyin' no more. I'm deaf t' ye! (*He turns away*) I hain't seein' ye agen. Good-by!

ABBIE (*pale with anguish*) Hain't ye even goin' t' kiss me—not once—arter all we loved?

EBEN (*in a hard voice*) I hain't wantin' t' kiss ye never agen! I'm wantin' t' forgit I ever sot eyes on ye!

ABBIE Eben!—ye mustn't—wait a spell—I want t' tell ye. . . .

EBEN I'm a-goin' in t' git drunk. I'm a-goin' t' dance.

ABBIE (*clinging to his arm—with passionate earnestness*) If I could make it—'s if he'd never come up between us—if I could prove t' ye I wa'n't schemin' t' steal from ye—so's everythin' could be jest the same with us, lovin' each other jest the same, kissin' an' happy the same's we've been happy afore he come— if I could do it—ye'd love me agen, wouldn't ye? Ye'd kiss me agen? Ye wouldn't never leave me, would ye?

EBEN (*moved*) I calc'late not. (*Then shaking her hand off his arm—with a bitter smile*) But ye hain't God, be ye?

ABBIE (*exultantly*) Remember ye've promised! (*Then with strange intensity*) Mebbe I kin take back one thin' God does!

EBEN (*peering at her*) Ye're gittin' cracked, hain't ye? (*Then going towards door*) I'm a-goin' t' dance.

ABBIE (*calls after him intensely*) I'll prove t' ye! I'll prove I love ye better'n. . . . (*He goes in the door, not seeming to hear. She remains standing where she is, looking after him—then she finishes desperately*) Better'n everythin' else in the world!

## SCENE THREE

JUST *before dawn in the morning—shows the kitchen and* CABOT's *bedroom. In the kitchen, by the light of a tallow candle on the table,* EBEN *is sitting, his chin propped on his hands, his drawn face blank and expressionless. His carpetbag is on the floor beside him. In the bedroom, dimly lighted by a small whale-oil lamp,* CABOT *lies asleep.* ABBIE *is bending over the cradle, listening, her face full of terror yet with an undercurrent of desperate triumph. Suddenly, she breaks down and sobs, appears about to throw herself on her knees beside the cradle; but the old man turns restlessly, groaning in his sleep, and she controls herself, and, shrinking away from the cradle with a gesture of horror, backs swiftly toward the door in rear and goes out. A moment later she comes into the kitchen and, running to* EBEN, *flings her arms about his neck and kisses him wildly. He hardens himself, he remains unmoved and cold, he keeps his eyes straight ahead.*

ABBIE (*hysterically*) I done it, Eben! I told ye I'd do it! I've proved I love ye—better'n everythin'—so's ye can't never doubt me no more!

EBEN (*dully*) Whatever ye done, it hain't no good now.

ABBIE (*wildly*) Don't ye say that! Kiss me, Eben, won't ye? I need ye t' kiss me arter what I done! I need ye t' say ye love me!

EBEN (*kisses her without emotion—dully*) That's fur good-by. I'm a-goin' soon.

ABBIE No! No! Ye won't go—not now!

EBEN (*going on with his own thoughts*) I been a-thinkin'—an' I hain't goin' t' tell Paw nothin'. I'll leave Maw t' take vengeance on ye. If I told him, the old skunk'd jest be stinkin' mean enuf to take it out on that baby. (*His voice showing emotion in spite of him*) An' I don't want nothin' bad t' happen t' him. He hain't t' blame fur yew. (*He adds with a certain queer pride*) An' he looks like me! An' by God, he's mine! An' some day I'll be a-comin' back an' . . . !

ABBIE (*too absorbed in her own thoughts to listen to him—pleadingly*) They's no cause fur ye t' go now—they's no sense—it's all the same's it was—they's nothin' come b'tween us now—arter what I done!

EBEN (*something in her voice arouses him. He stares at her a bit frightenedly*) Ye look mad, Abbie. What did ye do?

ABBIE I—I killed him, Eben.

EBEN (*amazed*) Ye killed him?

ABBIE (*dully*) Ay-eh.

EBEN (*recovering from his astonishment—savagely*) An' serves him right! But we got t' do somethin' quick t' make it look 's if the old skunk'd killed himself when he was drunk. We kin prove by 'em all how drunk he got.

ABBIE (*wildly*) No! No! Not him! (*Laughing distractedly*) But that's what I ought t' done, hain't it? I oughter killed him instead! Why didn't ye tell me?

EBEN (*appalled*) Instead? What d'ye mean?

ABBIE Not him.

EBEN (*his face grown ghastly*) Not—not that baby!

ABBIE (*dully*) Ay-eh!

EBEN (*falls to his knees as if he'd been struck—his voice trembling with horror*) Oh, God A'mighty! A'mighty God! Maw, whar was ye, why didn't ye stop her?

ABBIE (*simply*) She went back t' her grave that night we fust done it, remember? I hain't felt her about since. (*A pause.* EBEN *hides his head in his hands, trembling all over as if he had the ague. She goes on dully*) I left the piller over his little face. Then he killed himself. He stopped breathin'. (*She begins to weep softly*).

EBEN (*rage beginning to mingle with grief*) He looked like me. He was mine, damn ye!

ABBIE (*slowly and brokenly*) I didn't want t' do it. I hated myself fur doin' it. I loved him. He was so purty—dead spit 'n' image o' yew. But I loved yew more—an' yew was goin' away—far off whar I'd never see ye agen, never kiss ye, never feel ye pressed agin me agen—an' ye said ye hated me fur havin' him—ye said ye hated him an' wished he was dead—ye said if it hadn't been fur him comin' it'd be the same's afore between us.

EBEN (*unable to endure this, springs to his feet in a fury, threatening her, his twitching fingers seeming to reach out for her throat*) Ye lie! I never said—I never dreamed ye'd—I'd cut off my head afore I'd hurt his finger!

ABBIE (*piteously, sinking on her knees*) Eben, don't ye look at me like that—hatin' me—not after what I done fur ye—fur us— so's we could be happy agen—

EBEN (*furiously now*) Shut up, or I'll kill ye! I see yer game now —the same old sneakin' trick—ye're aimin' t' blame me fur the murder ye done!

ABBIE (*moaning—putting her hands over her ears*) Don't ye, Eben! Don't ye! (*She grasps his legs*).

EBEN (*his mood suddenly changing to horror, shrinks away from her*) Don't ye tech me! Ye're pizen! How could ye—t' murder a pore little critter— Ye must've swapped yer soul t' hell! (*Suddenly raging*) Ha! I kin see why ye done it! Not the lies ye jest told—but 'cause ye wanted t' steal agen—steal the last thin' ye'd left me—my part o' him—no, the hull o' him—ye saw he looked like me—ye knowed he was all mine—an' ye couldn't b'ar it—I know ye! Ye killed him fur bein' mine! (*All this has driven him almost insane. He makes a rush past her for the door—then turns —shaking both fists at her, violently*) But I'll take vengeance

now! I'll git the Sheriff! I'll tell him everythin'! Then I'll sing
"I'm off to Californi-a!" an' go—gold—Golden Gate—gold sun—
fields o' gold in the West! (*This last he half shouts, half croons
incoherently, suddenly breaking off passionately*) I'm a-goin'
fur the Sheriff t' come an' git ye! I want ye tuk away, locked
up from me! I can't stand t' luk at ye! Murderer an' thief 'r
not, ye still tempt me! I'll give ye up t' the Sheriff! (*He turns
and runs out, around the corner of house, panting and sobbing,
and breaks into a swerving sprint down the road*).

ABBIE (*struggling to her feet, runs to the door, calling after him*)   I
love ye, Eben! I love ye! (*She stops at the door weakly, swaying,
about to fall*) I don't care what ye do—if ye'll on'y love me agen—
(*She falls limply to the floor in a faint*).


SCENE FOUR


ABOUT *an hour later. Same as Scene Three. Shows the kitchen and*
CABOT's *bedroom. It is after dawn. The sky is brilliant with the
sunrise. In the kitchen,* ABBIE *sits at the table, her body limp
and exhausted, her head bowed down over her arms, her face hidden. Upstairs,* CABOT *is still asleep but awakens with a start. He
looks toward the window and gives a snort of surprise and irritation—throws back the covers and begins hurriedly pulling on his
clothes. Without looking behind him, he begins talking to* ABBIE
*whom he supposes beside him.*


CABOT   Thunder 'n' lightin', Abbie! I hain't slept this late in fifty
year! Looks 's if the sun was full riz a'most. Must've been the
dancin' an' likker. Must be gittin' old. I hope Eben's t' wuk. Ye
might've tuk the trouble t' rouse me, Abbie. (*He turns—sees no
one there—surprised*) Waal—whar air she? Gittin' vittles, I calc'-
late. (*He tiptoes to the cradle and peers down—proudly*)
Mornin', sonny. Purty's a picter! Sleepin' sound. He don't beller
all night like most o' 'em. (*He goes quietly out the door in
rear—a few moments later enters kitchen—sees* ABBIE—*with satisfaction*) So thar ye be. Ye got any vittles cooked?

ABBIE (*without moving*)   No.

CABOT (*coming to her, almost sympathetically*) Ye feelin' sick?

ABBIE No.

CABOT (*pats her on shoulder. She shudders*) Ye'd best lie down a spell. (*Half jocularly*) Yer son'll be needin' ye soon. He'd ought t' wake up with a gnashin' appetite, the sound way he's sleepin'.

ABBIE (*shudders—then in a dead voice*) He hain't never goin' t' wake up.

CABOT (*jokingly*) Takes after me this mornin'. I hain't slept so late in . . .

ABBIE He's dead.

CABOT (*stares at her—bewilderedly*) What. . . .

ABBIE I killed him.

CABOT (*stepping back from her—aghast*) Air ye drunk—'r crazy—'r . . . !

ABBIE (*suddenly lifts her head and turns on him—wildly*) I killed him, I tell ye! I smothered him. Go up an' see if ye don't b'lieve me! (CABOT *stares at her a second, then bolts out the rear door, can be heard bounding up the stairs, and rushes into the bedroom and over to the cradle.* ABBIE *has sunk back lifelessly into her former position.* CABOT *puts his hand down on the body in the crib. An expression of fear and horror comes over his face*).

CABOT (*shrinking away—tremblingly*) God A'mighty! God A'mighty. (*He stumbles out the door—in a short while returns to the kitchen—comes to* ABBIE, *the stunned expression still on his face—hoarsely*) Why did ye do it? Why? (*As she doesn't answer, he grabs her violently by the shoulder and shakes her*) I ax ye why ye done it! Ye'd better tell me 'r . . . !

ABBIE (*gives him a furious push which sends him staggering back and springs to her feet—with wild rage and hatred*) Don't ye dare tech me! What right hev ye t' question me 'bout him? He wa'n't yewr son! Think I'd have a son by yew? I'd die fust! I hate the sight o' ye an' allus did! It's yew I should've murdered, if I'd had good sense! I hate ye! I love Eben. I did from the fust. An' he was Eben's son—mine an' Eben's—not your'n!

CABOT (*stands looking at her dazedly—a pause—finding his words with an effort—dully*) That was it—what I felt—pokin' round the corners—while ye lied—holdin' yerself from me—sayin' ye'd a'ready conceived— (*He lapses into crushed silence—then with a strange emotion*) He's dead, sart'n. I felt his heart. Pore little critter! (*He blinks back one tear, wiping his sleeve across his nose*).

ABBIE (*hysterically*) Don't ye! Don't ye! (*She sobs unrestrainedly*).

CABOT (*with a concentrated effort that stiffens his body into a rigid line and hardens his face into a stony mask—through his teeth to himself*) I got t' be—like a stone—a rock o' judgment! (*A pause. He gets complete control over himself—harshly*) If he was Eben's I be glad he air gone! An' mebbe I suspicioned it all along. I felt they was somethin' onnateral—somewhars—the house got so lonesome—an' cold—drivin' me down t' the barn—t' the beasts o' the field. . . . Ay-eh. I must've suspicioned—somethin'. Ye didn't fool me—not altogether, leastways—I'm too old a bird—growin' ripe on the bough. . . . (*He becomes aware he is wandering, straightens again, looks at* ABBIE *with a cruel grin*) So ye'd liked t' hev murdered me 'stead o' him, would ye? Waal, I'll live to a hundred! I'll live t' see ye hung! I'll deliver ye up t' the jedgment o' God an' the law! I'll git the Sheriff now. (*Starts for the door*).

ABBIE (*dully*) Ye needn't. Eben's gone fur him.

CABOT (*amazed*) Eben—gone fur the Sheriff?

ABBIE Ay-eh.

CABOT T' inform agen ye?

ABBIE Ay-eh.

CABOT (*considers this—a pause—then in a hard voice*) Waal, I'm thankful fur him savin' me the trouble. I'll git t' wuk. (*He goes to the door—then turns—in a voice full of strange emotion*) He'd ought t' been my son, Abbie. Ye'd ought t' loved me. I'm a man. If ye'd loved me, I'd never told no Sheriff on ye no matter what ye did, if they was t' brile me alive!

ABBIE (*defensively*) They's more to it nor yew know, makes him tell.

CABOT (*dryly*) Fur yewr sake, I hope they be. (*He goes out—comes around to the gate—stares up at the sky. His control relaxes. For a moment he is old and weary. He murmurs despairingly*) God A'mighty, I be lonesomer'n ever! (*He hears running footsteps from the left, immediately is himself again.* EBEN *runs in, panting exhaustedly, wild-eyed and mad looking. He lurches through the gate.* CABOT *grabs him by the shoulder.* EBEN *stares at him dumbly*) Did ye tell the Sheriff?

EBEN (*nodding stupidly*) Ay-eh.

CABOT (*gives him a push away that sends him sprawling—laughing with withering contempt*) Good fur ye! A prime chip o' yer

Maw ye be! (*He goes toward the barn, laughing harshly.*
EBEN *scrambles to his feet. Suddenly* CABOT *turns—grimly threatening*) Git off this farm when the Sheriff takes her—or, by God, he'll have t' come back an' git me fur murder, too! (*He stalks off.*
EBEN *does not appear to have heard him. He runs to the door and comes into the kitchen.* ABBIE *looks up with a cry of anguished joy.* EBEN *stumbles over and throws himself on his knees beside her—sobbing brokenly*).

EBEN Fergive me!

ABBIE (*happily*) Eben! (*She kisses him and pulls his head over against her breast*).

EBEN I love ye! Fergive me!

ABBIE (*ecstatically*) I'd fergive ye all the sins in hell fur sayin' that! (*She kisses his head, pressing it to her with a fierce passion of possession*).

EBEN (*Brokenly*) But I told the Sheriff. He's comin' fur ye!

ABBIE I kin b'ar what happens t' me—now!

EBEN I woke him up. I told him. He says, wait 'til I git dressed. I was waiting. I got to thinkin' o' yew. I got to thinkin' how I'd loved ye. It hurt like somethin' was bustin' in my chest an' head. I got t' cryin'. I knowed sudden I loved ye yet, an' allus would love ye!

ABBIE (*caressing his hair—tenderly*) My boy, hain't ye?

EBEN I begun t' run back. I cut across the fields an' through the woods. I thought ye might have time t' run away—with me—an' . . .

ABBIE (*shaking her head*) I got t' take my punishment—t' pay fur my sin.

EBEN Then I want t' share it with ye.

ABBIE Ye didn't do nothin'.

EBEN I put it in yer head. I wisht he was dead! I as much as urged ye t' do it!

ABBIE No. It was me alone!

EBEN I'm as guilty as yew be! He was the child o' our sin.

ABBIE (*lifting her head as if defying God*) I don't repent that sin! I hain't askin' God t' fergive that!

EBEN Nor me—but it led up t' the other—an' the murder ye did, ye did 'count o' me—an' it's my murder, too. I'll tell the Sheriff —an' if ye deny it, I'll say we planned it t'gether—an' they'll all b'lieve me, fur they suspicion everythin' we've done, an' it'll seem likely an' true to 'em. An' it is true—way down. I did help ye—somehow.

ABBIE (*laying her head on his—sobbing*) No! I don't want yew t' suffer!

EBEN I got t' pay fur my part o' the sin! An' I'd suffer wuss leavin' ye, goin' West, thinkin' o' ye day an' night, bein' out when yew was in— (*Lowering his voice*) 'r bein' alive when yew was dead. (*A pause*) I want t' share with ye, Abbie—prison 'r death 'r hell 'r anythin'! (*He looks into her eyes and forces a trembling smile*) If I'm sharin' with ye, I won't feel lonesome, leastways.

ABBIE (*weakly*) Eben! I won't let ye! I can't let ye!

EBEN (*kissing her—tenderly*) Ye can't he'p yerself. I got ye beat fur once!

ABBIE (*forcing a smile—adoringly*) I hain't beat—s'long's I got ye!

EBEN (*hears the sound of feet outside*) Ssshh! Listen! They've come t' take us!

ABBIE No, it's him. Don't give him no chance to fight ye, Eben. Don't say nothin'—no matter what he says. An' I won't neither. (*It is* CABOT. *He comes up from the barn in a great state of excitement and strides into the house and then into the kitchen.* EBEN *is kneeling beside* ABBIE, *his arm around her, hers around him. They stare straight ahead*).

CABOT (*stares at them, his face hard. A long pause—vindictively*) Ye make a slick pair o' murderin' turtle doves! Ye'd ought t' be both hung on the same limb an' left thar t' swing in the breeze an' rot—a warnin' t' old fools like me t' b'ar their lonesomeness alone—an' fur young fools like ye t' hobble their lust. (*A pause. The excitement returns to his face, his eyes snap, he looks a bit crazy*) I couldn't work today. I couldn't take no interest. T' hell with the farm! I'm leavin' it! I've turned the cows an' other stock loose! I've druv 'em into the woods whar they kin be free! By freein' 'em, I'm freein' myself! I'm quittin' here today! I'll set fire t' house an' barn an' watch 'em burn, an' I'll leave yer Maw t' haunt the ashes, an' I'll will the fields back t' God, so that nothin' human kin never touch 'em! I'll be a-goin' to Californi-a!—t' jine Simeon an' Peter—true sons o' mine if they be dumb fools—an' the Cabots'll find Solomon's Mines t'gether! (*He suddenly cuts a mad caper*) Whoop! What was the song they sung? "Oh, Californi-a! That's the land fur me." (*He sings this—then gets on his knees by the floor-board under which the money was hid*) An' I'll sail thar on one o' the finest clippers I kin find! I've got the money! Pity ye didn't know whar this was hidden so's ye could steal. . . . (*He has pulled up the board. He stares—feels —stares again. A pause of dead silence. He slowly turns, slumping into a sitting position on the floor, his eyes like those of a dead fish, his face the sickly green of an attack of nausea. He swallows painfully several times—forces a weak smile at last*) So—ye did steal it!

EBEN (*emotionlessly*) I swapped it t' Sim an' Peter fur their share o' the farm—t' pay their passage t' Californi-a.

CABOT (*with one sardonic*) Ha! (*He begins to recover. Gets slowly to his feet—strangely*) I calc'late God give it to 'em—not yew! God's hard, not easy! Mebbe they's easy gold in the West but it hain't God's gold. It hain't fur me. I kin hear His voice warnin' me agen t' be hard an' stay on my farm. I kin see his hand usin' Eben t' steal t' keep me from weakness. I kin feel I be in the palm o' His hand, His fingers guidin' me. (*A pause— then he mutters sadly*) It's a-goin' t' be lonesomer now than ever it war afore—an' I'm gittin' old, Lord—ripe on the bough. . . . (*Then stiffening*) Waal—what d'ye want? God's lonesome, hain't He? God's hard an' lonesome! (*A pause. The Sheriff with two men comes up the road from the left. They move cautiously to the door. The Sheriff knocks on it with the butt of his pistol*).

SHERIFF Open in the name o' the law! (*They start*).

CABOT They've come fur ye. (*He goes to the rear door*) Come in, Jim! (*The three men enter.* CABOT *meets them in doorway*) Jest a minit, Jim. I got 'em safe here. (*The Sheriff nods. He and his companions remain in the doorway*).

EBEN (*suddenly calls*) I lied this mornin', Jim. I helped her to do it. Ye kin take me, too.

ABBIE (*brokenly*) No!

CABOT Take 'em both. (*He comes forward—stares at* EBEN *with a trace of grudging admiration*) Purty good—fur yew! Waal, I got t' round up the stock. Good-by.

EBEN Good-by.

ABBIE Good-by. (CABOT *turns and strides past the men—comes out and around the corner of the house, his shoulders squared, his face stony, and stalks grimly toward the barn. In the meantime the Sheriff and men have come into the room*).

SHERIFF (*embarrassedly*) Waal—we'd best start.

ABBIE Wait. (*Turns to* EBEN) I love ye, Eben.

EBEN I love ye, Abbie. (*They kiss. The three men grin and*

*shuffle embarrassedly.* EBEN *takes* ABBIE's *hand. They go out the door in rear, the men following, and come from the house, walking hand in hand to the gate.* EBEN *stops there and points to the sunrise sky*) Sun's a-rizin'. Purty, hain't it?

ABBIE    Ay-eh. (*They both stand for a moment looking up raptly in attitudes strangely aloof and devout*).

SHERIFF (*looking around at the farm enviously—to his companion*) It's a jim-dandy farm, no denyin'. Wished I owned it!

*Curtain*

# The
# Great God
# Brown

# Characters

WILLIAM A. BROWN

HIS FATHER, *A Contractor*

HIS MOTHER

DION ANTHONY

HIS FATHER, *A Builder*

HIS MOTHER

MARGARET

HER THREE SONS

CYBEL

TWO DRAFTSMEN } *in Brown's*
A STENOGRAPHER } *Office*

# Scenes

*Prologue:* The Pier of the Casino. Moonlight in middle June.

## ACT ONE

*Scene* I: Sitting room, Margaret Anthony's apartment. Afternoon, seven years later.

*Scene* II: Billy Brown's office. The same afternoon.

*Scene* III: Cybel's parlor. That night.

## ACT TWO

*Scene* I: Cybel's parlor. Seven years later. Dusk.

*Scene* II: Drafting room, William A. Brown's office. That evening.

*Scene* III: Library, William A. Brown's home. That night.

## ACT THREE

*Scene* I: Brown's office, a month later. Morning.

*Scene* II: Library, Brown's home. That evening.

*Scene* III: Sitting room, Margaret's home. That night.

## ACT FOUR

*Scene* I: Brown's office, weeks later. Late afternoon.

*Scene* II: Library, Brown's house, hours later. The same night.

*Epilogue:* The Pier of the Casino. Four years later.

# PROLOGUE

SCENE. *A cross section of the Pier of the Casino. In the rear, built out beyond the edge, is a rectangular space with benches on the three sides. A rail encloses the entire wharf at the back.*

*It is a moonlight night in mid-June. From the Casino comes the sound of the school quartet rendering "Sweet Adeline" with many ultra-sentimental barber-shop quavers. There is a faint echo of the ensuing hand-clapping—then nothing but the lapping of ripples against the piles and their swishing on the beach—then footsteps on the boards and* BILLY BROWN *walks along from right with his* MOTHER *and* FATHER. *The* MOTHER *is a dumpy woman of forty-five overdressed in black lace and spangles. The* FATHER *is fifty or more, the type of bustling, genial, successful, provincial business man, stout and hearty in his evening dress.*

BILLY BROWN *is a handsome, tall and athletic boy of nearly eighteen. He is blond and blue-eyed, with a likeable smile and a frank good-humored face, its expression already indicating a disciplined restraint. His manner has the easy self-assurance of a normal intelligence. He is in evening dress.*

*They walk arm in arm, the* MOTHER *between.*

MOTHER (*always addressing the* FATHER) This Commencement dance is badly managed. Such singing! Such poor voices! Why doesn't Billy sing?

BILLY (*to her*) Mine is a regular fog horn! (*He laughs*).

MOTHER (*to the air*) I had a pretty voice, when I was a girl (*Then, to the* FATHER, *caustically*) Did you see young Anthony strutting around the ballroom in dirty flannel pants?

FATHER He's just showing off.

MOTHER Such impudence! He's as ignorant as his father.

FATHER The old man's all right. My only kick against him is he's been too damned conservative to let me branch out.

MOTHER (*bitterly*) He has kept you down to his level—out of pure jealousy.

FATHER But he took me into partnership, don't forget—

MOTHER (*sharply*) Because you were the brains! Because he was afraid of losing you! (*A pause*).

BILLY (*admiringly*) Dion came in his old clothes on a bet with me. He's a real sport. He wouldn't have been afraid to appear in his pajamas! (*He grins with appreciation*).

MOTHER Isn't the moonlight clear! (*She goes and sits on the center bench.* BILLY *stands at the left corner, forward, his hand on the rail, like a prisoner at the bar, facing the judge. His* FATHER *stands in front of the bench on right. The* MOTHER *announces, with finality*) After he's through college, Billy must study for a profession of some sort, I'm determined on that! (*She turns to her husband, defiantly, as if expecting opposition*).

FATHER (*eagerly and placatingly*) Just what I've been thinking, my dear. Architecture! How's that? Billy a first-rate, number-one architect! That's my proposition! What I've always wished I could have been myself! Only I never had the opportunity. But Billy—we'll make him a partner in the firm after. Anthony, Brown *and Son, architects* and builders—instead of *contractors* and builders!

MOTHER (*yearning for the realization of a dream*) And we won't lay sidewalks—or dig sewers—ever again?

FATHER (*a bit ruffled*) I and Anthony can build anything your pet can draw—even if it's a church! (*Then, selling his idea*) It's a great chance for him! He'll design—expand us—make the firm famous.

MOTHER (*to the air—musingly*) When you proposed, I thought your future promised success—my future—(*with a sigh*)—Well, I suppose we've been comfortable. Now, it's his future. How would Billy like to be an architect? (*She does not look at him*).

BILLY (*to her*) All right, Mother. (*Then sheepishly*) I guess I've never bothered much about what I'd like to do after college—but architecture sounds all right to me, I guess.

MOTHER (*to the air—proudly*) Billy used to draw houses when he was little.

FATHER (*jubilantly*) Billy's got the stuff in him to win, if he'll only work hard enough.

BILLY (*dutifully*) I'll work hard, Dad.

MOTHER Billy can do anything!

BILLY (*embarrassed*) I'll try, Mother. (*There is a pause*).

MOTHER (*with a sudden shiver*)  The nights are so much colder than they used to be! Think of it, I once went moonlight bathing in June when I was a girl—but the moonlight was so warm and beautiful in those days, do you remember, Father?

FATHER (*puts his arm around her affectionately*)  You bet I do, Mother. (*He kisses her. The orchestra at the Casino strikes up a waltz*) There's the music. Let's go back and watch the young folks dance. (*They start off, leaving* BILLY *standing there*).

MOTHER (*suddenly calls back over her shoulder*)  I want to watch Billy dance.

BILLY (*dutifully*)  Yes, Mother! (*He follows them. For a moment the faint sound of the music and the lapping of waves is heard. Then footsteps again and the three* ANTHONYS *come in. First come the* FATHER *and* MOTHER, *who are not masked. The* FATHER *is a tall lean man of fifty-five or sixty with a grim, defensive face, obstinate to the point of stupid weakness. The* MOTHER *is a thin frail faded woman, her manner perpetually nervous and distraught, but with a sweet and gentle face that had once been beautiful. The* FATHER *wears an ill-fitting black suit, like a mourner. The* MOTHER *wears a cheap, plain, black dress. Following them, as if he were a stranger, walking alone, is their son,* DION. *He is about the same height as young* BROWN *but lean and wiry, without repose, continually in restless nervous movement. His face is masked. The mask is a fixed forcing of his own face —dark, spiritual, poetic, passionately supersensitive, helplessly unprotected in its childlike, religious faith in life—into the expression of mocking, reckless, defiant, gayly scoffing and sensual young Pan. He is dressed in a gray flannel shirt, open at the neck, sneakers over bare feet, and soiled white flannel trousers. The* FATHER *strides to the center bench and sits down. The* MOTHER, *who has been holding to his arm, lets go and stands by the bench at the right. They both stare at* DION, *who, with a studied carelessness, takes his place at the rail, where young* BROWN *had stood. They watch him, with queer, puzzled eyes.*)

MOTHER (*suddenly—pleading*)  You simply must send him to college!

FATHER  I won't. I don't believe in it. Colleges turn out lazy loafers to sponge on their poor old fathers! Let him slave like I had to! That'll teach him the value of a dollar! College'll only make him a bigger fool than he is already! I never got above grammar school

but I've made money and established a sound business. Let him
make a man out of himself like I made of myself!

DION (*mockingly—to the air*)  This Mr. Anthony is my father, but
he only imagines he is God the Father. (*They both stare at him*).

FATHER (*with angry bewilderment*)  What—what—what's that?

MOTHER (*gently remonstrating to her son*)  Dion, dear! (*Then to
her husband—tauntingly*)  Brown takes all the credit! He tells
everyone the success is all due to his energy—that you're only
an old stick-in-the-mud!

FATHER (*stung, harshly*)  The damn fool! He knows better'n anyone if I hadn't held him down to common sense, with his crazy
wild-cat notions, he'd have had us ruined long ago!

MOTHER  He's sending Billy to college—Mrs. Brown just told me
—going to have him study architecture afterwards, too, so's he can
help expand your firm!

FATHER (*angrily*)  What's that? (*Suddenly turns on DION furiously*)
Then you can make up your mind to go, too! And you'll learn
to be a better architect than Brown's boy or I'll turn you out
in the gutter without a penny! You hear?

DION (*mockingly—to the air*)  It's difficult to choose—but architecture sounds less laborious.

MOTHER (*fondly*)  You ought to make a wonderful architect, Dion.
You've always painted pictures so well—

DION (*with a start—resentfully*)  Why must she lie? Is it my fault?
She knows I only try to paint. (*Passionately*)  But I will, some
day! (*Then quickly, mocking again*)  On to college! Well, it won't
be home, anyway, will it? (*He laughs queerly and approaches
them. His FATHER gets up defensively. DION bows to him*)  I thank
Mr. Anthony for this splendid opportunity to create myself—
(*He kisses his mother, who bows with a strange humility as if
she were a servant being saluted by the young master—then adds
lightly*)—in my mother's image, so she may feel her life com-
fortably concluded. (*He sits in his FATHER's place at center and
his mask stares with a frozen mockery before him. They stand
on each side, looking dumbly at him*).

MOTHER (*at last, with a shiver*)  It's cold. June didn't use to be
cold. I remember the June when I was carrying you, Dion—three
months before you were born. (*She stares up at the sky*)  The
moonlight was warm, then. I could feel the night wrapped around
me like a gray velvet gown lined with warm sky and trimmed
with silver leaves!

FATHER (*gruffly—but with a certain awe*)  My mother used to believe the full of the moon was the time to sow. She was terrible old-fashioned. (*With a grunt*) I can feel it's bringing on my rheumatism. Let's go back indoors.

DION (*with intense bitterness*)  Hide! Be ashamed! (*They both start and stare at him*).

FATHER (*with bitter hopelessness. To his wife—indicating their son*)  Who is he? You bore him!

MOTHER (*proudly*)  He's my boy! He's Dion!

DION (*bitterly resentful*)  What else, indeed! The identical son! (*Then mockingly*) Are Mr. Anthony and his wife going in to dance? The nights grow cold! The days are dimmer than they used to be! Let's play hide-and-seek! Seek the monkey in the moon! (*He suddenly cuts a grotesque caper, like a harlequin and darts off, laughing with forced abandon. They stare after him—then slowly follow. Again there is silence except for the sound of the lapping waves. Then* MARGARET *comes in, followed by the humbly worshiping* BILLY BROWN. *She is almost seventeen, pretty and vivacious, blonde, with big romantic eyes, her figure lithe and strong, her facial expression intelligent but youthfully dreamy, especially now in the moonlight. She is in a simple white dress. On her entrance, her face is masked with an exact, almost transparent reproduction of her own features, but giving her the abstract quality of a Girl instead of the individual,* MARGARET).

MARGARET (*looking upward at the moon and singing in low tone as they enter*)  "Ah, moon of my delight that knowest no wane!"

BILLY (*eagerly*)  I've got that record—John McCormack. It's a peach! Sing some more. (*She looks upward in silence. He keeps standing respectfully in back of her, glancing embarrassedly toward her averted face. He tries to make conversation*) I think the *Rubáiyát's* great stuff, don't you? I never could memorize poetry worth a darn. Dion can recite lots of Shelley's poems by heart.

MARGARET (*slowly takes off her mask—to the moon*)  Dion! (*A pause*).

BILLY (*fidgeting*)  Margaret!

MARGARET (*to the moon*)  Dion is so wonderful!

BILLY (*blunderingly*)  I asked you to come out here because I wanted to tell you something.

MARGARET (*to the moon*)  Why did Dion look at me like that? It made me feel so crazy!

BILLY  I wanted to ask you something, too.

MARGARET  That one time he kissed me—I can't forget it! He was only joking—but I felt—and he saw and just laughed!

BILLY  Because that's the uncertain part. My end of it is a sure thing, and has been for a long time, and I guess everybody in town knows it—they're always kidding me—so it's a cinch you must know—how I feel about you.

MARGARET  Dion's so different from all the others. He can paint beautifully and write poetry and he plays and sings and dances so marvelously. But he's sad and shy, too, just like a baby sometimes, and he understands what I'm really like inside—and—and I'd love to run my fingers through his hair—and I love him! Yes, I love him! (*She stretches out her arms to the moon*) Oh, Dion, I love you!

BILLY  I love you, Margaret.

MARGARET  I wonder if Dion—I saw him looking at me again tonight —Oh, I wonder. . . !

BILLY (*takes her hand and blurts out*)  Can't you love me? Won't you marry me—after college—

MARGARET  Where is Dion now, I wonder?

BILLY (*shaking her hand in an agony of uncertainty*)  Margaret! Please answer me!

MARGARET (*her dream broken, puts on her mask and turns to him —matter-of-factly*)  It's getting chilly. Let's go back and dance, Billy.

BILLY (*desperately*)  I love you! (*He tries clumsily to kiss her*).

MARGARET (*with an amused laugh*)  Like a brother! You can kiss me if you like. (*She kisses him*) A big-brother kiss. It doesn't count. (*He steps back crushed, with head bowed. She turns away and takes off her mask—to the moon*) I wish Dion would kiss me again!

BILLY (*painfully*)  I'm a poor boob. I ought to know better. I'll bet I know. You're in love with Dion. I've seen you look at him. Isn't that it?

MARGARET  Dion! I love the sound of it!

BILLY (*huskily*)  Well—he's always been my best friend—I'm glad it's him—and I guess I know how to lose—(*He takes her hand and shakes it*)—so here's wishing you all the success and happiness in the world, Margaret—and remember I'll always be your

best friend! (*He gives her hand a final shake—swallows hard—
then manfully*) Let's go back in!

MARGARET (*to the moon—faintly annoyed*) What is Billy Brown
doing here? I'll go down to the end of the dock and wait. Dion
is the moon and I'm the sea. I want to feel the moon kissing the
sea. I want Dion to leave the sky to me. I want the tides of my
blood to leave my heart and follow him! (*She whispers like a
little girl*) Dion! Margaret! Peggy! Peggy is Dion's girl—Peggy is
Dion's little girl—(*She sings laughingly, elfishly*) Dion is my
Daddy-O! (*She is walking toward the end of the dock, off left*).

BILLY (*who has turned away*) I'm going. I'll tell Dion you're here.

MARGARET (*more and more strongly and assertively, until at the
end she is a wife and a mother*) And I'll be Mrs. Dion—Dion's
wife—and he'll be my Dion—my own Dion—my little boy—my
baby! The moon is drowned in the tides of my heart, and peace
sinks deep through the sea! (*She disappears off left, her upturned
unmasked face like that of a rapturous visionary. There is silence
again, in which the dance music is heard. Then this stops and
DION comes in. He walks quickly to the bench at center and
throws himself on it, hiding his masked face in his hands. After a
moment, he lifts his head, peers about, listens huntedly, then
slowly takes off his mask. His real face is revealed in the bright
moonlight, shrinking, shy and gentle, full of a deep sadness*).

DION (*with a suffering bewilderment*) Why am I afraid to dance,
I who love music and rhythm and grace and song and laughter?
Why am I afraid to live, I who love life and beauty of flesh and
the living colors of earth and sky and sea? Why am I afraid of
love, I who love love? Why am I afraid, I who am not afraid?
Why must I pretend to scorn in order to pity? Why must I hide
myself in self-contempt in order to understand? Why must I be
so ashamed of my strength, so proud of my weakness? Why must
I live in a cage like a criminal, defying and hating, I who love
peace and friendship? (*Clasping his hands above in supplication*)
Why was I born without a skin, O God, that I must wear armor
in order to touch or to be touched? (*A second's pause of waiting
silence—then he suddenly claps his mask over his face again,
with a gesture of despair and his voice becomes bitter and sardonic*) Or rather, Old Graybeard, why the devil was I ever born
at all? (*Steps are heard from the right. DION stiffens and his mask
stares straight ahead. BILLY comes in from the right. He is shuffling
along disconsolately. When he sees DION, he stops abruptly and*

*glowers resentfully—but at once the "good loser" in him conquers this*).

BILLY (*embarrassedly*)  Hello, Dion. I've been looking all over for you. (*He sits down on the bench at right, forcing a joking tone*) What are you sitting here for, you nut—trying to get more moonstruck? (*A pause—awkwardly*) I just left Margaret—

DION (*gives a start—immediately defensively mocking*)  Bless you, my children!

BILLY (*gruffly and slangily*)  I'm out of it—she gave me the gate. You're the original white-haired boy. Go on in and win! We've been chums ever since we were kids, haven't we?—and—I'm glad it's you, Dion. (*This huskily—he fumbles for* DION's *hand and gives it a shake*).

DION (*letting his hand fall back—bitterly*)  Chums? Oh, no, Billy Brown would despise me!

BILLY  She's waiting for you now, down at the end of the dock.

DION  For me? Which? Who? Oh, no, girls only allow themselves to look at what is seen!

BILLY  She's in love with you.

DION (*moved—a pause—stammers*)  Miracle? I'm afraid! (*He chants flippantly*) I love, thou lovest, he loves, she loves! She loves, she loves—what?

BILLY  And I know damn well, underneath your nuttiness, you're gone on her.

DION (*moved*)  Underneath? I love love! I'd love to be loved! But I'm afraid! (*Then aggressively*) *Was* afraid! Not now! Now I can make love—to anyone! Yes, I love Peggy! Why not? Who is she? Who am I? We love, you love, they love, one loves! No one loves! All the world loves a lover, God loves us all and we love Him! Love is a word—a shameless ragged ghost of a word— begging at all doors for life at any price!

BILLY (*always as if he hadn't listened to what the other said*)  Say, let's you and me room together at college—

DION  Billy wants to remain by her side!

BILLY  It's a bet, then! (*Forcing a grin*) You can tell her I'll see that you behave! (*Turns away*) So long. Remember she's waiting. (*He goes*).

DION (*dazedly, to himself*)  Waiting—waiting for me! (*He slowly removes his mask. His face is torn and transfigured by joy. He stares at the sky raptly*) O God in the moon, did you hear? She loves me! I am not afraid! I am strong! I can love! She protects me! Her arms are softly around me! She is warmly around me! She is my skin! She is my armor! Now I am born—I—the I!—one and indivisible—I who love Margaret! (*He glances at his mask triumphantly—in tones of deliverance*) You are outgrown! I am beyond you! (*He stretches out his arms to the sky*) O God, now I believe! (*From the end of the wharf, her voice is heard*).

MARGARET  Dion!

DION (*raptly*)  Margaret!

MARGARET (*nearer*)  Dion!

DION  Margaret!

MARGARET  Dion! (*She comes running in, her mask in her hands. He springs toward her with outstretched arms but she shrinks away with a frightened shriek and hastily puts on her mask.* DION *starts back. She speaks coldly and angrily*) Who are you? Why are you calling me? I don't know you!

DION (*heart-brokenly*)  I love you!

MARGARET (*freezingly*)  Is this a joke—or are you drunk?

DION (*with a final pleading whisper*)  Margaret! (*But she only glares at him contemptuously. Then with a sudden gesture he claps his mask on and laughs wildly and bitterly*) Ha-ha-ha! That's one on you, Peg!

MARGARET (*with delight, pulling off her mask*)  Dion! How did you ever—Why, I never knew you!

DION (*puts his arm around her boldly*)  How? It's the moon—the crazy moon—the monkey in the moon—playing jokes on us! (*He kisses her with his masked face with a romantic actor's passion again and again*) You love me! You know you do! Say it! Tell me! I want to hear! I want to feel! I want to know! I want to want! To want you as you want me!

MARGARET (*in ecstasy*)  Oh, Dion, I do! I do love you!

DION (*with ironic mastery—rhetorically*)  And I love you! Oh, madly! Oh, forever and ever, amen! You are my evening star and all my Pleiades! Your eyes are blue pools in which gold dreams glide, your body is a young white birch leaning backward beneath the lips of spring. So! (*He has bent her back, his arms supporting her, his face above hers*) So! (*He kisses her*).

MARGARET (*with overpowering passionate languor*)  Oh, Dion! Dion! I love you!

DION (*with more and more mastery in his tone*)  I love, you love, we love! Come! Rest! Relax! Let go your clutch on the world!

Dim and dimmer! Fading out in the past behind! Gone! Death! Now! Be born! Awake! Live! Dissolve into dew—into silence—into night—into earth—into space—into peace—into meaning—into joy—into God—into the Great God Pan! (*While he has been speaking, the moon has passed gradually behind a black cloud, its light fading out. There is a moment of intense blackness and silence. Then the light gradually comes on again. Dion's voice, at first in a whisper, then increasing in volume with the light, is heard*) Wake up! Time to get up! Time to exist! Time for school! Time to learn! Learn to pretend! Cover your nakedness! Learn to lie! Learn to keep step! Join the procession! Great Pan is dead! Be ashamed!

MARGARET (*with a sob*) Oh, Dion, I am ashamed!

DION (*mockingly*) Sssshh! Watch the monkey in the moon! See him dance! His tail is a piece of string that was left when he broke loose from Jehovah and ran away to join Charley Darwin's circus!

MARGARET I know you must hate me now! (*She throws her arms around him and hides her head on his shoulder*).

DION (*deeply moved*) Don't cry! Don't—! (*He suddenly tears off his mask—in a passionate agony*) Hate you? I love you with all my soul! Love me! Why can't you love me, Margaret? (*He tries to kiss her but she jumps to her feet with a frightened cry holding up her mask before her face protectingly*).

MARGARET Don't! Please! I don't know you! You frighten me!

DION (*puts on his mask again—quietly and bitterly*) All's well. I'll never let you see again. (*He puts his arm around her—gently mocking*) By proxy, I love you. There! Don't cry! Don't be afraid! Dion Anthony will marry you some day. (*He kisses her*) "I take this woman—" (*Tenderly joking*) Hello, woman! Do you feel older by aeons? Mrs. Dion Anthony, shall we go in and may I have the next dance?

MARGARET (*tenderly*) You crazy child! (*Then, laughing with joy*) Mrs. Dion Anthony! It sounds wonderful, doesn't it? (*They go out as*

*Curtain*

# ACT ONE

## SCENE ONE

SCENE. *Seven years later.*

*The sitting room of* MRS. DION ANTHONY's *half of a two-family house in the homes section of the town—one of those one-design districts that daze the eye with multiplied ugliness. The four pieces of furniture shown are in keeping—an armchair at left, a table with a chair in back of it at center, a sofa at right. The same court-room effect of the arrangement of benches in Act One is held to here. The background is a backdrop on which the rear wall is painted with the intolerable lifeless realistic detail of the stereotyped paintings which usually adorn the sitting rooms of such houses. It is late afternoon of a gray day in winter.*

DION *is sitting behind the table, staring before him. The mask hangs on his breast below his neck, giving the effect of two faces. His real face has aged greatly, grown more strained and tortured, but at the same time, in some queer way, more selfless and ascetic, more fixed in its resolute withdrawal from life. The mask, too, has changed. It is older, more defiant and mocking, its sneer more forced and bitter, its Pan quality becoming Mephistophelean. It has already begun to show the ravages of dissipation.*

DION (*suddenly reaches out and takes up a copy of the New Testament which is on the table and, putting a finger in at random, opens and reads aloud the text at which it points*) "Come unto me all ye who are heavy laden and I will give you rest." (*He stares before him in a sort of trance, his face lighted up from within but painfully confused—in an uncertain whisper*) I will come—but where are you, Savior? (*The noise of the outer door shutting is heard.* DION *starts and claps the mocking mask on his face again. He tosses the Testament aside contemptuously*) Blah! Fixation on old Mama Christianity! You infant blubbering in the dark, you! (*He laughs, with a bitter self-contempt. Footsteps approach. He picks up a newspaper and hides behind it hurriedly.* MARGARET *enters. She is dressed in stylish, expensive clothes and a fur coat, which look as if they had been remodeled and seen service. She has grown mature and maternal, in spite of her youth. Her pretty face is still fresh and healthy but there is the beginning of a permanently worried, apprehensive expression about the nose and mouth—an uncomprehending hurt in her eyes.* DION *pretends to be engrossed in his paper. She bends down and kisses him*).

MARGARET (*with a forced gayety*)  Good morning—at four in the afternoon! You were snoring when I left!

DION (*puts his arms around her with a negligent, accustomed gesture—mockingly*)  The Ideal Husband!

MARGARET (*already preoccupied with another thought—comes and sits in chair on left*)  I was afraid the children would disturb you, so I took them over to Mrs. Young's to play. (*A pause. He picks up the paper again. She asks anxiously*) I suppose they'll be all right over there, don't you? (*He doesn't answer. She is more hurt than offended*) I wish you'd try to take more interest in the children, Dion.

DION (*mockingly*)  Become a father—before breakfast? I'm in too delicate a condition. (*She turns away, hurt. Penitently he pats her hand—vaguely*) All right. I'll try.

MARGARET (*squeezing his hand—with possessive tenderness*)  Play with them. You're a bigger kid than they are—underneath.

DION (*self-mockingly—flipping the Bible*)  Underneath—I'm becoming downright infantile! "Suffer these little ones!"

MARGARET (*keeping to her certainty*)  You're my oldest.

DION (*with mocking appreciation*)  She puts the Kingdom of Heaven in its place!

MARGARET (*withdrawing her hand*)  I was serious.

DION  So was I—about something or other. (*He laughs*) This domestic diplomacy! We communicate in code—when neither has the other's key!

MARGARET (*frowns confusedly—then forcing a playful tone*)  I want to have a serious talk with you, young man! In spite of your promises, you've kept up the hard drinking and gambling you started the last year abroad.

DION From the time I realized it wasn't in me to be an artist— except in living—and not even in that! (*He laughs bitterly*).

MARGARET (*with conviction*) But you *can* paint, Dion—beautifully!

DION (*with deep pain*) No! (*He suddenly takes her hand and kisses it gratefully*) I love Margaret! Her blindness surpasseth all understanding! (*Then bitterly*)—or is it pity?

MARGARET We've only got about one hundred dollars left in the bank.

DION (*with dazed surprise*) What! Is all the money from the sale of the house gone?

MARGARET (*wearily*) Every day or so you've been cashing checks. You've been drinking—you haven't counted—

DION (*irritably*) I know! (*A pause—soberly*) No more estate to fall back on, eh? Well, for five years it kept us living abroad in peace. It bought us a little happiness—of a kind—didn't it?—living and loving and having children—(*A slight pause—bitterly*)— thinking one was creating before one discovered one couldn't!

MARGARET (*this time with forced conviction*) But you *can* paint —beautifully!

DION (*angrily*) Shut up! (*A pause—then jeeringly*) So my wife thinks it behooves me to settle down and support my family in the meager style to which they'll have to become accustomed?

MARGARET (*shamefacedly*) I didn't say—still—something's got to be done.

DION (*harshly*) Will Mrs. Anthony helpfully suggest what?

MARGARET I met Billy Brown on the street. He said you'd have made a good architect, if you'd stuck to it.

DION Flatterer! Instead of leaving college when my Old Man died? Instead of marrying Peggy and going abroad and being happy?

MARGARET (*as if she hadn't heard*) He spoke of how well you used to draw.

DION Billy was in love with Margaret at one time.

MARGARET He wanted to know why you've never been in to see him.

DION He's bound heaven-bent for success. It's the will of Mammon! Anthony and Brown, contractors and builders—death subtracts Anthony and I sell out—Billy graduates—Brown and Son, architects and builders—old man Brown perishes of paternal pride —and now we have William A. Brown, architect! Why his career itself already has an architectural design! One of God's mud pies!

MARGARET  He particularly told me to ask you to drop in.

DION  (*springs to his feet—assertively*)  No! Pride! I have been alive!

MARGARET  Why don't you have a talk with him?

DION  Pride in my failure!

MARGARET  You were always such close friends.

DION  (*more and more desperately*)  The pride which came after man's fall—by which he laughs as a creator at his self-defeats!

MARGARET  Not for my sake—but for your own—and, above all, for the children's!

DION  (*with terrible despair*)  Pride! Pride without which the Gods are worms!

MARGARET  (*after a pause, meekly and humbly*)  You don't want to? It would hurt you? All right, dear. Never mind. We'll manage somehow—you mustn't worry—you must start your beautiful painting again—and I can get that position in the library—it would be such fun for me working there! . . . (*She reaches out and takes his hand—tenderly*)  I love you, dear. I understand.

DION  (*slumps down into his chair, crushed, his face averted from hers, as hers is from him, although their hands are still clasped—in a trembling, expiring voice*)  Pride is dying! (*As if he were suffocating, he pulls the mask from his resigned, pale, suffering face. He prays like a Saint in the desert, exorcizing a demon*)  Pride is dead! Blessed are the meek! Blessed are the poor in spirit!

MARGARET  (*without looking at him—in a comforting, motherly tone*)  My poor boy!

DION  (*resentfully—clapping on his mask again and springing to his feet—derisively*)  Blessed are the meek for they shall inherit graves! Blessed are the poor in spirit for they are blind! (*Then with tortured bitterness*)  All right! Then I ask my wife to go and ask Billy Brown—that's more deadly than if I went myself! (*With wild mockery*)  Ask him if he can't find an opening for a talented young man who is only honest when he isn't sober—implore him, beg him in the name of old love, old friendship—to be a generous hero and save the woman and her children! (*He laughs with a sort of diabolical, ironical glee now, and starts to go out*).

MARGARET  (*meekly*)  Are you going up street, Dion?

DION  Yes.

MARGARET  Will you stop at the butchers' and have them send two pounds of pork chops?

DION  Yes.

MARGARET  And stop at Mrs. Young's and ask the children to hurry right home?

DION  Yes.

MARGARET  Will you be back for dinner, Dion?

DION  No. (*He goes, the outer door slams.* MARGARET *sighs with a tired incomprehension and goes to the window and stares out*).

MARGARET  (*worriedly*)  I hope they'll watch out, crossing the street.

*Curtain*

## SCENE TWO

SCENE. BILLY BROWN'S *office, at five in the afternoon. At center, a fine mahogany desk with a swivel chair in back of it. To the left of desk, an office armchair. To the right of desk, an office lounge. The background is a backdrop of an office wall, treated similarly to that of Scene One in its over-meticulous representation of detail.*

BILLY BROWN *is seated at the desk looking over a blue print by the light of a desk lamp. He has grown into a fine-looking, well-dressed, capable, college-bred American business man, boyish still and with the same engaging personality.*

*The telephone rings.*

BROWN  (*answering it*)  Yes? Who? (*This in surprise—then with eager pleasure*)  Let her come right in. (*He gets up and goes to the door, expectant and curious.* MARGARET *enters. Her face is concealed behind the mask of the pretty young matron, still hardly a woman, who cultivates a naïvely innocent and bravely hopeful attitude toward things and acknowledges no wound to the world. She is dressed as in Scene One but with an added touch of effective primping here and there*).

MARGARET  (*very gayly*)  Hello, Billy Brown!

BROWN  (*awkward in her presence, shakes her hand*)  Come in.

Sit down. This is a pleasant surprise, Margaret. (*She sits down on the lounge. He sits in his chair behind the desk, as before*).

MARGARET (*looking around*) What lovely offices! My, but Billy Brown is getting grand!

BROWN (*pleased*) I've just moved in. The old place was too stuffy.

MARGARET It looks so prosperous—but then, Billy is doing so wonderfully well, everyone says.

BROWN (*modestly*) Well, to be frank, it's been mostly luck. Things have come my way without my doing much about it. (*Then, with an abashed pride*) Still—I have done a little something myself. (*He picks the plan from the desk*) See this? It's my design for the new Municipal Building. It's just been accepted—provisionally—by the Committee.

MARGARET (*taking it—vaguely*) Oh? (*She looks at it abstractedly. There is a pause. Suddenly*) You mentioned the other day how well Dion used to draw—

BROWN (*a bit stiffly*) Yes, he certainly did. (*He takes the drawing from her and at once becomes interested and squints at it frowningly*) Did you notice that anything seemed lacking in this?

MARGARET (*indifferently*) Not at all.

BROWN (*with a cheerful grin*) The Committee wants it made a little more American. It's too much of a conventional Greco-Roman tomb, they say. (*Laughs*) They want an original touch of modern novelty stuck in to liven it up and make it look different from other town halls. (*Putting the drawing back on his desk*) And I've been figuring out how to give it to them but my mind doesn't seem to run that way. Have you any suggestion?

MARGARET (*as if she hadn't heard*) Dion certainly draws well, Billy Brown was saying?

BROWN (*trying not to show his annoyance*) Why, yes—he did—and still can, I expect. (*A pause. He masters what he feels to be an unworthy pique and turns to her generously*) Dion would have made a cracking good architect.

MARGARET (*proudly*) I know. He could be anything he wanted to.

BROWN (*a pause—embarrassedly*) Is he working at anything these days?

MARGARET (*defensively*) Oh, yes! He's painting wonderfully! But he's just like a child, he's so impractical. He doesn't try to have an exhibition anywhere, or anything.

BROWN (*surprised*) The one time I ran into him, I thought he told me he'd destroyed all his pictures—that he'd gotten sick of painting and completely given it up.

MARGARET (*quickly*)  He always tells people that. He doesn't want anyone even to look at his things, imagine! He keeps saying they're rotten—when they're too beautiful! He's too modest for his own good, don't you think? But it is true he hasn't done so much lately since we've been back. You see the children take up such a lot of his time. He just worships them! I'm afraid he's becoming a hopeless family man, just the opposite of what anyone would expect who knew him in the old days.

BROWN (*painfully embarrassed by her loyalty and his knowledge of the facts*)  Yes, I know. (*He coughs self-consciously*).

MARGARET (*aroused by something in his manner*)  But I suppose the gossips are telling the same silly stories about him they always did. (*She forces a laugh*)  Poor Dion! Give a dog a bad name! (*Her voice breaks a little in spite of herself*).

BROWN (*hastily*)  I haven't heard any stories—(*he stops uncertainly, then decides to plunge in*)—except about money matters.

MARGARET (*forcing a laugh*)  Oh, perhaps they're true enough. Dion is such a generous fool with his money, like all artists.

BROWN (*with a certain doggedness*)  There's a rumor that you've applied for a position at the Library.

MARGARET (*forcing a gay tone*)  Yes, indeed! Won't it be fun! Maybe it'll improve my mind! And one of us has got to be practical, so why not me? (*She forces a gay, girlish laugh*).

BROWN (*impulsively reaches out and takes her hand—awkwardly*)  Listen, Margaret. Let's be perfectly frank, will you? I'm such an old friend, and I want like the deuce to. . . . You know darn well I'd do anything in the world to help you—or Dion.

MARGARET (*withdrawing her hand, coldly*)  I'm afraid I—don't understand, Billy Brown.

BROWN (*acutely embarrassed*)  Well, I—I just meant—you know, if you needed—(*A pause. He looks questioningly at her averted face—then ventures on another tack, matter-of-factly*)  I've got a proposition to make to Dion—if I could ever get hold of him. It's this way: business has been piling up on me—a run of luck—but I'm short-handed. I need a crack chief draftsman darn badly—or I'm liable to lose out. Do you think Dion would consider it—as a temporary stop-gap—until he felt in the painting mood again?

MARGARET (*striving to conceal her eagerness and relief—judicially*)

Yes—I really do. He's such a good sport and Billy and he were such pals once. I know he'd be only too tickled to help him out.

BROWN (*diffidently*)   I thought he might be sensitive about working for—I mean, with me—when, if he hadn't sold out to Dad he'd be my partner now—(*earnestly*)—and, by jingo, I wish he was! (*Then, abruptly*) Let's try to nail him down right away, Margaret. Is he home now? (*He reaches for the phone*).

MARGARET (*hurriedly*)   No, he—he went out for a long walk.

BROWN   Perhaps I can locate him later around town somewhere.

MARGARET (*with a note of pleading*)   Please don't trouble. It isn't necessary. I'm sure when I talk to him—he's coming home to dinner—(*Getting up*) Then it's all settled, isn't it? Dion will be so glad to be able to help an old friend—he's so terribly loyal, and he's always liked Billy Brown so much! (*Holding out her hand*) I really must go now!

BROWN (*shakes her hand*)   Good-by, Margaret. I hope you'll be dropping in on us a lot when Dion gets here.

MARGARET   Yes. (*She goes*).

BROWN (*sits at his desk again, looking ahead in a not unsatisfying melancholy reverie. He mutters admiringly but pityingly*)   Poor Margaret! She's a game sport, but it's pretty damn tough on her! (*Indignantly*) By God, I'm going to give Dion a good talking-to one of these days!

*Curtain*

## SCENE THREE

SCENE. *Cybel's parlor. An automatic, nickel-in-the-slot player-piano is at center, rear. On its right is a dirty gilt second-hand sofa. At the left is a bald-spotted crimson plush chair. The backdrop for the rear wall is cheap wall-paper of a dull yellow-brown, resembling a blurred impression of a fallow field in early spring. There is a cheap alarm clock on top of the piano. Beside it her mask is lying.*

DION *is sprawled on his back, fast asleep on the sofa. His mask has fallen down on his chest. His pale face is singularly pure, spiritual and sad.*

*The player-piano is groggily banging out a sentimental medley of "Mother—Mammy" tunes.*

CYBEL *is seated on the stool in front of the piano. She is a strong, calm, sensual, blonde girl of twenty or so, her complexion fresh and healthy, her figure full-breasted and wide-hipped, her movements slow and solidly languorous like an animal's, her large eyes dreamy with the reflected stirring of profound instincts. She chews gum like a sacred cow forgetting time with an eternal end. Her eyes are fixed, incuriously, on* DION's *pale face.*

CYBEL (*as the tune runs out, glances at the clock, which indicates midnight, then goes slowly over to* DION *and puts her hand gently on his forehead*) Wake up!

DION (*stirs, sighs and murmurs dreamily*) "And He laid his hands on them and healed them." (*Then with a start he opens his eyes and, half sitting up, stares at her bewilderedly*) What—where —who are you? (*He reaches for his mask and claps it on defensively*).

CYBEL (*placidly*) Only another female. You were camping on my steps, sound asleep. I didn't want to run any risk getting into more trouble with the cops pinching you there and blaming me, so I took you in to sleep it off.

DION (*mockingly*) Blessed are the pitiful, Sister! I'm broke—but you will be rewarded in Heaven!

CYBEL (*calmly*) I wasn't wasting my pity. Why should I? You were happy, weren't you?

DION (*approvingly*) Excellent! You're not a moralist, I see.

CYBEL (*going on*) And you look like a good boy, too—when you're asleep. Say, you better beat it home to bed or you'll be locked out.

DION (*mockingly*) Now you're becoming maternal, Miss Earth. Is that the only answer—to pin my soul into every vacant diaper? (*She stares down at his mask, her face growing hard. He laughs*) But please don't stop stroking my aching brow. Your hand is a cool mud poultice on the sting of thought!

CYBEL (*calmly*) Stop acting. I hate ham fats. (*She looks at him as if waiting for him to remove his mask—then turns her back indifferently and goes to the piano*) Well, if you simply got to be a regular devil like all the other visiting sports, I s'pose I got to play with you. (*She takes her mask and puts it on—then turns. The mask is the rouged and eye-blackened countenance of the hardened prostitute. In a coarse, harsh voice*) Kindly state your dishonorable intentions, if any! I can't sit up all night keeping company! Let's have some music! (*She puts a plug in the machine. The same sentimental medley begins to play. The two masks stare at each other. She laughs*) Shoot! I'm all set! It's your play, Kid Lucifer!

DION (*slowly removes his mask. She stops the music with a jerk. His face is gentle and sad—humbly*) I'm sorry. It has always been such agony for me to be touched!

CYBEL (*taking off her mask—sympathetically as she comes back and sits down on her stool*) Poor kid! I've never had one, but I can guess. They hug and kiss you and take you on their laps and pinch you and want to see you getting dressed and undressed— as if they owned you—I bet you I'd never let them treat one of mine that way!

DION (*turning to her*) You're lost in blind alleys, too. (*Suddenly holding out his hand to her*) But you're strong. Let's be friends.

CYBEL (*with a strange sternness, searches his face*) And never nothing more?

DION (*with a strange smile*) Let's say, never anything less! (*She takes his hand. There is a ring at the outside door bell. They stare at each other. There is another ring*).

CYBEL (*puts on her mask, DION does likewise. Mockingly*) When you got to love to live it's hard to love living. I better join the A.F. of L. and soap-box for the eight-hour night! Got a nickel, baby? Play a tune. (*She goes out. DION puts a nickel in. The same sentimental tune starts. CYBEL returns, followed by BILLY BROWN. His face is rigidly composed, but his superior disgust for DION can be seen. DION jerks off the music and he and BILLY look at each other for a moment, CYBEL watching them both—then, bored, she yawns*) He's hunting for you. Put out the lights when you go. I'm going to sleep. (*She starts to go—then, as if reminded of something—to DION*) Life's all right, if you let it alone. (*Then mechanically flashing a trade smile at BILLY*) Now you know the way, Handsome, call again! (*She goes*).

BROWN (*after an awkward pause*) Hello, Dion! I've been looking all over town for you. This place was the very last chance. . . . (*Another pause—embarrassedly*) Let's take a walk.

DION (*mockingly*)  I've given up exercise. They claim it lengthens your life.

BROWN (*persuasively*)  Come on, Dion, be a good fellow. You're certainly not staying here—

DION  Billy would like to think me taken in *flagrante delicto*, eh?

BROWN  Don't be a damn fool! Listen to me! I've been looking you up for purely selfish reasons. I need your help.

DION (*astonished*)  What?

BROWN  I've a proposition to make that I hope you'll consider favorably out of old friendship. To be frank, Dion, I need you to lend me a hand down at the office.

DION (*with a harsh laugh*)  So it's the job, is it? Then my poor wife did a-begging go!

BROWN (*repelled—sharply*)  On the contrary, I had to beg her to beg you to take it! (*More angrily*) Look here, Dion! I won't listen to you talk that way about Margaret! And you wouldn't if you weren't drunk! (*Suddenly shaking him*) What in hell has come over you, anyway! You didn't use to be like this! What the devil are you going to do with yourself—sink into the gutter and drag Margaret with you? If you'd heard her defend you, lie about you, tell me how hard you were working, what beautiful things you were painting, how you stayed at home and idolized the children!—when everyone knows you've been out every night sousing and gambling away the last of your estate. . . . (*He stops, ashamed, controlling himself*).

DION (*wearily*)  She was lying about her husband, not me, you fool! But it's no use explaining. (*Then, in a sudden, excitable passion*) What do you want? I agree to anything—except the humiliation of yelling secrets at the deaf!

BROWN (*trying a bullying tone—roughly*)  Bunk! Don't try to crawl out! There's no excuse and you know it. (*Then as* DION *doesn't reply—penitently*) But I know I shouldn't talk this way, old man! It's only because we're such old pals—and I hate to see you wasting yourself—you who had more brains than any of us! But, damn it, I suppose you're too much of a rotten cynic to believe I mean what I've just said!

DION (*touched*)  I know Billy was always Dion Anthony's friend.

BROWN  You're damn right I am—and I'd have proved it long ago if you'd only given me half a chance! After all, I couldn't keep chasing after you and be snubbed every time. A man has some pride!

DION (*bitterly mocking*) Dead wrong! Never more! None whatever! It's unmoral! Blessed are the poor in spirit, Brother! When
shall I report?

BROWN (*eagerly*) Then you'll take the—you'll help me?

DION (*wearily bitter*) I'll take the job. One must do something
to pass away the time, while one is waiting—for one's next incar-
nation.

BROWN (*jokingly*) I'd say it was a bit early to be worrying about
that. (*Trying to get* DION *started*) Come along, now. It's pretty
late.

DION (*shakes his hand off his shoulder and walks away from him—
after a pause*) Is my father's chair still there?

BROWN (*turns away—embarrassed*) I—I don't really remember,
Dion— I'll look it up.

DION (*taking off his mask—slowly*) I'd like to sit where he spun
what I have spent. What aliens we were to each other! When he
lay dead, his face looked so familiar that I wondered where I had
met that man before. Only at the second of my conception. After
that, we grew hostile with concealed shame. And my mother?
I remember a sweet, strange girl, with affectionate, bewildered
eyes as if God had locked her in a dark closet without any explanation. I was the sole doll our ogre, her husband, allowed her
and she played mother and child with me for many years in that
house until at last through two tears I watched her die with the
shy pride of one who has lengthened her dress and put up her
hair. And I felt like a forsaken toy and cried to be buried with
her, because her hands alone had caressed without clawing. She
lived long and aged greatly in the two days before they closed
her coffin. The last time I looked, her purity had forgotten me,
she was stainless and imperishable, and I knew my sobs were
ugly and meaningless to her virginity; so I shrank away, back into
life, with naked nerves jumping like fleas, and in due course of
nature another girl called me her boy in the moon and married
me and became three mothers in one person, while I got paint on
my paws in an endeavor to see God! (*He laughs wildly—claps
on his mask*) But that Ancient Humorist had given me weak
eyes, so now I'll have to foreswear my quest for Him and go in
for the Omnipresent Successful Serious One, the Great God Mr.
Brown, instead! (*He makes him a sweeping, mocking bow*).

BROWN (*repelled but cajolingly*) Shut up, you nut! You're still drunk. Come on! Let's start! (*He grabs* DION *by the arm and switches off the light*).

DION (*from the darkness—mockingly*)  I am thy shorn, bald, nude sheep! Lead on, Almighty Brown, thou Kindly Light!

*Curtain*

# ACT TWO

## SCENE ONE

SCENE. CYBEL's *parlor—about sunset in spring seven years later. The arrangement of furniture is the same but the chair and sofa are new, bright-colored, costly pieces. The old automatic piano at center looks exactly the same. The cheap alarm clock is still on top of it. On either side of the clock, the masks of* DION *and* CYBEL *are lying. The background backdrop is brilliant, stunning wallpaper, on which crimson and purple flowers and fruits tumble over one another in a riotously profane lack of any apparent design.*

DION *sits in the chair on left,* CYBEL *on the sofa. A cardtable is between them. Both are playing solitaire.* DION *is now prematurely gray. His face is that of an ascetic, a martyr, furrowed by pain and self-torture, yet lighted from within by a spiritual calm and human kindliness.*

CYBEL *has grown stouter and more voluptuous, but her face is still unmarked and fresh, her calm more profound. She is like an unmoved idol of Mother Earth.*

*The piano is whining out its same old sentimental medley. They play their cards intently and contentedly. The music stops.*

CYBEL (*musingly*) I love the rotten old sob tunes. They make me wise to people. That's what's inside them—what makes them love and murder their neighbor—crying jags set to music!

DION (*compassionately*) Every song is a hymn. They keep trying to find the Word in the Beginning.

CYBEL They try to know too much. It makes them weak. I never puzzled them with myself. I gave them a Tart. They understood her and knew their parts and acted naturally. And on both sides we were able to keep our real virtue, if you get me (*She plays her last card—indifferently*) I've made it again.

DION (*smiling*) Your luck is uncanny. It never comes out for me.

CYBEL You keep getting closer, but it knows you still want to win—a little bit—and it's wise all I care about is playing. (*She lays out another game*) Speaking of my canned music, our Mr. Brown hates that old box. (*At the mention of* BROWN, DION *trembles as if suddenly possessed, has a terrible struggle with himself, then while she continues to speak, gets up like an automaton and puts on his mask. The mask is now terribly ravaged. All of its Pan quality has changed into a diabolical Mephistophelean cruelty and irony*) He doesn't mind the music inside. That gets him somehow. But he thinks the case looks shabby and he wants it junked. But I told him that just because he's been keeping me so long, he needn't start bossing like a husband or I'll— (*She looks up and sees the masked* DION *standing by the piano—calmly*) Hello! Getting jealous again?

DION (*jeeringly*) Are you falling in love with your keeper, old Sacred Cow?

CYBEL (*without taking offense*) Cut it! You've been asking me that for years. Be yourself! He's healthy and handsome—but he's too guilty. What makes you pretend you think love is so important, anyway? It's just one of a lot of things you do to keep life living.

DION (*in same tone*) Then you've lied when you've said you loved me, have you, Old Filth?

CYBEL (*affectionately*) You'll never grow up! We've been friends, haven't we, for seven years? I've never let myself want you nor you me. Yes, I love you. It takes all kinds of love to make a world! Ours is the living cream, I say, living rich and high! (*A pause. Coaxingly*) Stop hiding. I know you.

DION (*taking off his mask, wearily comes and sits down at her feet and lays his head in her lap—with a grateful smile*) You're strong. You always give. You've given my weakness strength to live.

CYBEL (*tenderly, stroking his hair maternally*) You're not weak. You were born with ghosts in your eyes and you were brave enough to go looking into your own dark—and you got afraid. (*After a pause*) I don't blame your being jealous of Mr. Brown sometimes. I'm jealous of your wife, even though I know you do love her.

DION (*slowly*) I love Margaret. I don't know who my wife is.

CYBEL (*after a pause—with a queer broken laugh*) Oh, God, sometimes the truth hits me such a sock between the eyes I can see the stars!—and then I'm so damn sorry for the lot of you, every damn mother's son-of-a-gun of you, that I'd like to run out naked into the street and love the whole mob to death like I was bringing you all a new brand of dope that'd make you forget everything that ever was for good! (*Then, with a twisted smile*) But they wouldn't see me, any more than they see each other. And they keep right on moving along and dying without my help anyway.

DION (*sadly*) You've given me strength to die.

CYBEL You may be important but your life's not. There's millions of it born every second. Life can cost too much even for a sucker to afford it—like everything else. And it's not sacred—only the you inside is. The rest is earth.

DION (*gets to his knees and with clasped hands looks up raptly and prays with an ascetic fervor*) "Into thy hands, O Lord," . . . (*Then suddenly, with a look of horror*) Nothing! To feel one's life blown out like the flame of a cheap match . . . ! (*He claps on his mask and laughs harshly*) To fall asleep and know you'll never, never be called to get on the job of existence again! "Swift be thine approaching flight! Come soon—soon!" (*He quotes this last with a mocking longing*).

CYBEL (*pats his head maternally*) There, don't be scared. It's born in the blood. When the time comes, you'll find it's easy.

DION (*jumps to his feet and walks about excitedly*) It won't be long. My wife dragged in a doctor the day before yesterday. He says my heart is gone—booze— He warned me, never another drop or— (*Mockingly*) What say? Shall we have a drink?

CYBEL (*like an idol*) Suit yourself. It's in the pantry. (*Then, as he hesitates*) What set you off on this bat? You were raving on about some cathedral plans. . . .

DION (*wildly mocking*) They've been accepted—Mr. Brown's designs! My designs really! You don't need to be told that. He hands me one mathematically correct barn after another and I doctor them up with cute allurements so that fools will desire to buy, sell, breed, sleep, love, hate, curse and pray in them! I do this with devilish cleverness to their entire delight! Once I dreamed of painting wind on the sea and the skimming flight of cloud shadows over the tops of trees! Now . . . (*He laughs*) But pride is a sin—even in a memory of the long deceased! Blessed are the poor in spirit! (*He subsides weakly on his chair, his hand pressed to his heart*).

CYBEL (*like an idol*) Go home and sleep. Your wife'll be worried.

DION She knows—but she'll never admit to herself that her husband ever entered your door. (*Mocking*) Aren't women loyal—to their vanity and their other things!

CYBEL Brown is coming soon, don't forget.

DION He knows too and can't admit. Perhaps he needs me here —unknown. What first aroused his passion to possess you exclusively, do you think? Because he knew you loved me and he felt himself cheated. He wanted what he thought was my love of the flesh! He feels I have no right to love. He'd like to steal it as he steals my ideas—complacently—righteously. Oh, the good Brown!

CYBEL But you like him, too! You're brothers, I guess, somehow.

DION (*raises his head as if starting to remove the mask*) I know. Poor Billy! God forgive me the evil I've done him!

CYBEL (*reaches out and takes his hand*) Poor boy!

DION (*presses her convulsively—then with forced harshness*) Well, homeward Christian Soldier! I'm off! By-bye, Mother Earth! (*He starts to go off right. She seems about to let him go*).

CYBEL (*suddenly starts and calls with deep grief*) Dion! (*He looks at her. A pause. He comes slowly back. She speaks strangely in a deep, far-off voice—and yet like a mother talking to her little son*) You mustn't forget to kiss me before you go, Dion. (*She removes his mask*) Haven't I told you to take off your mask in the house? Look at me, Dion. I've—just—seen—something. I'm afraid you're going away a long, long ways. I'm afraid I won't see you again for a long, long time. So it's good-by, dear. (*She kisses him gently. He begins to sob. She hands him back his mask*) Here you are. Don't get hurt. Remember, it's all a game, and after you're asleep I'll tuck you in.

DION (*in a choking, heart-broken cry*) Mother! (*Then he claps on his mask with a terrible effort of will—mockingly*) Go to the devil, you sentimental old pig! See you tomorrow! (*He goes, whistling, slamming the door*).

CYBEL (*like an idol again*) What's the good of bearing children! What's the use of giving birth to death? (*She sighs wearily, turns,*

*puts a plug in the piano, which starts up its old sentimental
tune. At the same moment* BROWN *enters quietly from the left.
He is the ideal of the still youthful, good-looking, well-groomed,
successful provincial American of forty. Just now, he is plainly
perturbed. He is not able to see either* CYBEL's *face or her mask*).

BROWN    Cybel! (*She starts, jams off the music and reaches for
her mask but has no time to put it on*) Wasn't that Dion I just saw
going out—after all your promises never to see him! (*She turns
like an idol, holding her mask behind her. He stares, bewildered—stammers*) I—I beg your pardon—I thought—

CYBEL    (*in her strange voice*)    Cybel's gone out to dig in the earth
and pray.

BROWN    (*with more assurance*)    But—aren't those her clothes?

CYBEL    Cybel doesn't want people to see me naked. I'm her sister.
Dion came to see me.

BROWN    (*relieved*)    So that's what he's up to, is it? (*Then with a
pitying sigh*) Poor Margaret! (*Then with playful reproof*) You
really shouldn't encourage him. He's married and got three big
sons.

CYBEL    And you haven't.

BROWN    (*stung*)    No, I'm not married.

CYBEL    He and I were friends.

BROWN    (*with a playful wink*)    Yes, I can imagine how the platonic
must appeal to Dion's pure, innocent type! It's no good your kidding me about Dion. We've been friends since we were kids. I
know him in and out. I've always stood up for him whatever he's
done—so you can be perfectly frank. I only spoke as I did on
account of Margaret—his wife—it's pretty tough on her.

CYBEL    You love his wife.

BROWN    (*scandalized*)    What? What are you talking about? (*Then
uncertainly*) Don't be a fool! (*A pause—then as if impelled by an
intense curiosity*) So Dion is your lover, eh? That's very interesting. (*He pulls his chair closer to hers*) Sit down. Let's talk.
(*She continues to stand, the mask held behind her*) Tell me—
I've always been curious—what is it that makes Dion so attractive
to women—especially certain types of women, if you'll pardon
me? He always has been and yet I never could see exactly what
they saw in him. Is it his looks—or because he's such a violent
sensualist—or because he poses as artistic and temperamental—
or because he's so wild—or just what is it?

CYBEL    He's alive!

BROWN (*suddenly takes one of her hands and kisses it—insinuatingly*) Well, don't you think I'm alive, too? (*Eagerly*) Listen. Would you consider giving up Dion—and letting me take care of you under a smiliar arrangement to the one I've made with Cybel? I like you, you can see that. I won't bother you much—I'm much too busy—you can do what you like—lead your own life —except for seeing him. (*He stops. A pause. She stares ahead unmoved as if she hadn't heard. He pleads*) Well—what do you say? Please do!

CYBEL (*her voice very weary*) Cybel said to tell you she'd be back next week, Mr. Brown.

BROWN (*with queer agony*) You mean you won't? Don't be so cruel! I love you! (*She walks away. He clutches at her pleadingly*) At least—I'll give you anything you ask!—please promise me you won't see Dion Anthony again!

CYBEL (*with deep grief*) He will never see me again, I promise you. Good-by!

BROWN (*jubilantly, kissing her hand—politely*) Thank you! Thank you! I'm exceedingly grateful. (*Tactfully*) I won't disturb you any further. Please forgive my intrusion, and remember me to Cybel when you write. (*He bows, turns, and goes off left*).

*Curtain*

SCENE TWO

SCENE. *The drafting room in* BROWN's *office.* DION's *drafting table with a high stool in front is at center. Another stool is to the left of it. At the right is a bench. It is in the evening of the same day. The black wall drop has windows painted on it with a dim street-lighted view of black houses across the way.*

DION *is sitting on the stool in back of the table, reading aloud from the "Imitation of Christ" by Thomas à Kempis to his mask, which is on the table before him. His own face is gentler, more spiritual, more saintlike and ascetic than ever before.*

DION (*like a priest, offering up prayers for the dying*) "Quickly must thou be gone from hence, see then how matters stand with

thee. Ah, fool—learn now to die to the world that thou mayst begin to live with Christ! Do now, beloved, do now all thou canst
because thou knowst not when thou shalt die; nor dost thou know
what shall befall thee after death. Keep thyself as a pilgrim,
and a stranger upon earth, to whom the affairs of this world do
not—belong! Keep thy heart free and raised upwards to God
because thou hast not here a lasting abode. 'Because at what
hour you know not the Son of Man will come!'" Amen. (*He
raises his hand over the mask as if he were blessing it, closes
the book and puts it back in his pocket. He raises the mask in his
hands and stares at it with a pitying tenderness*) Peace, poor
tortured one, brave pitiful pride of man, the hour of our deliverance comes. Tomorrow we may be with Him in Paradise! (*He
kisses it on the lips and sets it down again. There is the noise
of footsteps climbing the stairs in the hallway. He grabs up the
mask in a sudden panic and, as a knock comes on the door, he
claps it on and calls mockingly*) Come in, Mrs. Anthony, come
in! (MARGARET *enters. In one hand behind her, hidden from
him, is the mask of the brave face she puts on before the world
to hide her suffering and disillusionment, and which she has just
taken off. Her own face is still sweet and pretty but lined, drawn
and careworn for its years, sad, resigned, but a bit querulous*).

MARGARET (*wearily reproving*) Thank goodness I've found you!
Why haven't you been home the last two days? It's bad enough
your drinking again without your staying away and worrying us
to death!

DION (*bitterly*) My ears knew her footsteps. One gets to recognize
everything—and to see nothing!

MARGARET I finally sent the boys out looking for you and came
myself. (*With tired solicitude*) I suppose you haven't eaten a
thing, as usual. Won't you come home and let me fry you a
chop?

DION (*wonderingly*) Can Margaret still love Dion Anthony? Is
it possible she does?

MARGARET (*forcing a tired smile*) I suppose so, Dion. I certainly
oughtn't to, had I?

DION (*in same tone*) And I love Margaret! What haunted, haunting ghosts we are! We dimly remember so much it will take us
so many million years to forget! (*He comes forward, putting one
arm around her bowed shoulders, and they kiss*).

MARGARET (*patting his hand affectionately*) No, you certainly don't deserve it. When I stop to think of all you've made me go through in the years since we settled down here . . . ! I really don't believe I could ever have stood it if it weren't for the boys! (*Forcing a smile*) But perhaps I would, I've always been such a big fool about you.

DION (*a bit mockingly*) The boys! Three strong sons! Margaret can afford to be magnanimous!

MARGARET If they didn't find you, they were coming to meet me here.

DION (*with sudden wildness—torturedly, sinking on his knees beside her*) Margaret! Margaret! I'm lonely! I'm frightened! I'm going away! I've got to say good-by!

MARGARET (*patting his hair*) Poor boy! Poor Dion! Come home and sleep.

DION (*springs up frantically*) No! I'm a man! I'm a lonely man! I can't go back! I have conceived myself! (*Then with desperate mockery*) Look at me, Mrs. Anthony! It's the last chance! Tomorrow I'll have moved on to the next hell! Behold your man—the sniveling, cringing, life-denying Christian slave you have so nobly ignored in the father of your sons! Look! (*He tears the mask from his face, which is radiant with a great pure love for her and a great sympathy and tenderness*) O woman—my love—that I have sinned against in my sick pride and cruelty—forgive my sins—forgive my solitude—forgive my sickness—forgive me! (*He kneels and kisses the hem of her dress*).

MARGARET (*who has been staring at him with terror, raising her mask to ward off his face*) Dion! Dion! I can't bear it! You're like a ghost! You're dead! Oh, my God! Help! Help! (*She falls back fainting on the bench. He looks at her—then takes her hand which holds her mask and looks at that face—gently*) And now I am permitted to understand and love you, too! (*He kisses the mask first—then kisses her face, murmuring*) And you, sweetheart! Blessed, thrice blessed are the meek! (*There is a sound of heavy, hurrying footsteps on the stairs. He puts on his mask in haste. The* THREE SONS *rush into the room. The Eldest is about fourteen, the two others thirteen and twelve. They look healthy, normal, likeable boys, with much the same quality as* BILLY BROWN's *in Act One, Scene One. They stop short and stiffen all in a row, staring from the woman on the bench to their father, accusingly*).

ELDEST We heard someone yell. It sounded like Mother.

DION (*defensively*) No. It was this lady—my wife.

ELDEST But hasn't Mother come yet?

DION (*going to* MARGARET) Yes. Your Mother is here. (*He stands between them and puts her mask over* MARGARET's *face—then steps back*) She has fainted. You'd better bring her to.

BOYS Mother! (*They run to her side, kneel and rub her wrists. The* ELDEST *smooths back her hair*).

DION (*watching them*) At least I am leaving her well provided for. (*He addresses them directly*) Tell your mother she'll get word from Mr. Brown's house. I must pay him a farewell call. I am going. Good-by. (*They stop, staring at him fixedly, with eyes a mixture of bewilderment, distrust and hurt*).

ELDEST (*awkwardly and shamefacedly*) Honest, I think you ought to have . . .

SECOND Yes, honest you ought . . .

YOUNGEST Yes, honest . . .

DION (*in a friendly tone*) I know. But I couldn't. That's for you who can. You must inherit the earth for her. Don't forget now, boys. Good-by.

BOYS (*in the same awkward, self-conscious tone, one after another*) Good-by—good-by—good-by. (DION *goes*).

*Curtain*

## SCENE THREE

SCENE. *The library of* WILLIAM BROWN's *home—night of the same day. A backdrop of carefully painted, prosperous, bourgeois culture bookcases filled with sets, etc. The heavy table at center is expensive. The leather armchair at left of it and the couch at right are opulently comfortable. The reading lamp on the table is the only light.*

BROWN *sits in the chair at left reading an architectural periodical. His expression is composed and gravely receptive. In outline, his face suggests a Roman consul on an old coin. There is an incongruous distinction about it, the quality of unquestioning faith in the finality of its achievement.*

*There is a sudden loud thumping on the front door and the ringing of the bell.* BROWN *frowns and listens as a servant answers.* DION's *voice can be heard, raised mockingly.*

DION   Tell him it's the devil come to conclude a bargain.

BROWN   (*suppressing annoyance, calls out with forced good nature*)   Come on in, Dion. (DION *enters. He is in a wild state. His clothes are disheveled, his masked face has a terrible death-like intensity, its mocking irony becomes so cruelly malignant as to give him the appearance of a real demon, tortured into torturing others*) Sit down.

DION   (*stands and sings*)   William Brown's soul lies moldering in the crib but his body goes marching on!

BROWN   (*maintaining the same indulgent, big-brotherly tone which he tries to hold throughout the scene*)   Not so loud, for Pete's sake! I don't mind—but I've got neighbors.

DION   Hate them! Fear thy neighbor as thyself! That's the leaden rule for the safe and sane. (*Then advancing to the table with a sort of deadly calm*) Listen! One day when I was four years old, a boy sneaked up behind when I was drawing a picture in the sand he couldn't draw and hit me on the head with a stick and kicked out my picture and laughed when I cried. It wasn't what he'd done that made me cry, but him! I had loved and trusted him and suddenly the good God was disproved in his person and the evil and injustice of Man was born! Everyone called me cry-baby, so I became silent for life and designed a mask of the Bad Boy Pan in which to live and rebel against that other boy's God and protect myself from His cruelty. And that other boy, secretly he felt ashamed but he couldn't acknowledge it; so from that day he instinctively developed into the good boy, the good friend, the good man, William Brown!

BROWN   (*shamefacedly*)   I remember now. It was a dirty trick. (*Then with a trace of resentment*) Sit down. You know where the booze is. Have a drink, if you like. But I guess you've had enough already.

DION   (*looks at him fixedly for a moment—then strangely*)   Thanks be to Brown for reminding me. I must drink. (*He goes and gets a bottle of whisky and a glass*).

BROWN   (*with a good-humored shrug*)   All right. It's your funeral.

DION   (*returning and pouring out a big drink in the tumbler*)   And William Brown's! When I die, he goes to hell! Shöal! (*He drinks and stares malevolently. In spite of himself,* BROWN *is uneasy. A pause* ).

BROWN ( *with forced casualness* ) You've been on this toot for a week now.

DION ( *tauntingly* ) I've been celebrating the acceptance of *my* design for the cathedral.

BROWN ( *humorously* ) You certainly helped me a lot on it.

DION ( *with a harsh laugh* ) O perfect Brown! Never mind! I'll make him look in my mirror yet—and drown in it! ( *He pours out another big drink* ).

BROWN ( *rather tauntingly* ) Go easy. I don't want your corpse on my hands.

DION But I do ( *He drinks* ) Brown will still need me—to reassure him he's alive! I've loved, lusted, won and lost, sang and wept. I've been life's lover! I've fulfilled her will and if she's through with me now it's only because I was too weak to dominate her in turn. It isn't enough to be her creature, you've got to create her or she requests you to destroy yourself.

BROWN ( *good naturedly* ) Nonsense. Go home and get some sleep.

DION ( *as if he hadn't heard—bitingly* ) But to be neither creature nor creator! To exist only in her indifference! To be unloved by life! ( BROWN *stirs uneasily* ) To be merely a successful freak, the result of some snide neutralizing of life forces—a spineless cactus —a wild boar of the mountains altered into a packer's hog eating to become food—a Don Juan inspired to romance by a monkey's glands—and to have Life not even think you funny enough to see!

BROWN ( *stung—angrily* ) Bosh!

DION Consider Mr. Brown. His parents bore him on earth as if they were thereby entering him in a baby parade with prizes for the fattest—and he's still being wheeled along in the procession, too fat now to learn to walk, let alone to dance or run, and he'll never live until his liberated dust quickens into earth!

BROWN ( *gruffly* ) Rave on! ( *Then with forced good-nature* ) Well, Dion, at any rate, I'm satisfied.

DION ( *quickly and malevolently* ) No! Brown isn't satisfied! He's piled on layers of protective fat, but vaguely, deeply he feels at his heart the gnawing of a doubt! And I'm interested in that germ which wriggles like a question mark of insecurity in his blood, because it's part of the creative life Brown's stolen from me!

BROWN (*forcing a sour grin*) Steal germs? I thought you caught them.

DION (*as if he hadn't heard*) It's mine—and I'm interested in seeing it thrive and breed and become multitudes and eat until Brown is consumed!

BROWN (*cannot restrain a shudder*) Sometimes when you're drunk, you're positively evil, do you know it?

DION (*somberly*) When Pan was forbidden the light and warmth of the sun he grew sensitive and self-conscious and proud and re-vengeful—and became Prince of Darkness.

BROWN (*jocularly*) You don't fit the rôle of Pan, Dion. It sounds to me like Bacchus, alias the Demon Rum, doing the talking. (DION *recovers from his spasm with a start and stares at* BROWN *with terrible hatred. There is a pause. In spite of himself,* BROWN *squirms and adopts a placating tone*) Go home. Be a good scout. It's all well enough celebrating our design being accepted but—

DION (*in a steely voice*) I've been the brains! I've been the de-sign! I've designed even his success—drunk and laughing at him—laughing at his career! Not proud! Sick! Sick of myself and him! Designing and getting drunk! Saving my woman and children! (*He laughs*) Ha! And this cathedral is my master-piece! It will make Brown the most eminent architect in this state of God's Country. I put a lot into it—what was left of my life! It's one vivid blasphemy from sidewalk to the tips of its spires!—but so concealed that the fools will never know. They'll kneel and worship the ironic Silenus who tells them the best good is never to be born! (*He laughs triumphantly*) Well, blas-phemy is faith, isn't it? In self-preservation the devil must believe! But Mr. Brown, the Great Brown, has no faith! He couldn't design a cathedral without it looking like the First Supernatural Bank! He only believes in the immortality of the moral belly! (*He laughs wildly—then sinks down in his chair, gasping, his hands pressed to his heart. Then suddenly becomes deadly calm and pronounces like a cruel malignant condemnation*) From now on, Brown will never deisgn anything. He will devote his life to renovating the house of my Cybel into a home for my Margaret!

BROWN (*springing to his feet, his face convulsed with strange agony*) I've stood enough! How dare you . . . !

DION (*his voice like a probe*) Why has no woman ever loved him? Why has he always been the Big Brother, the Friend? Isn't their trust—a contempt?

BROWN You lie!

DION Why has he never been able to love—since my Margaret? Why has he never married? Why has he tried to steal Cybel, as he once tried to steal Margaret? Isn't it out of revenge—and envy?

BROWN (*violently*) Rot! I wanted Cybel, and I bought her!

DION Brown bought her for me! She has loved me more than he will ever know!

BROWN You lie! (*Then furiously*) I'll throw her back on the street!

DION To me! To her fellow creature! Why hasn't Brown had children—he who loves children—he who loves *my* children—he who envies me *my* children?

BROWN (*brokenly*) I'm not ashamed to envy you them!

DION They like Brown, too—as a friend—as an equal—as Margaret has always liked him—

BROWN (*brokenly*) And as I've liked her!

DION How many million times Brown has thought how much better for her it would have been if she'd chosen him instead!

BROWN (*torturedly*) You lie! (*Then with sudden frenzied defiance*) All right. If you force me to say it, I do love Margaret! I always have loved her and you've always known I did!

DION (*with a terrible composure*) No! That is merely the appearance, not the truth! Brown loves me! He loves me because I have always possessed the power he needed for love, because I am love!

BROWN (*frenziedly*) You drunken bum! (*He leaps on* DION *and grabs him by the throat*)

DION (*triumphantly, staring into his eyes*) Ah! Now he looks into the mirror! Now he sees his face! (BROWN *lets go of him and staggers back to his chair, pale and trembling*).

BROWN (*humbly*) Stop, for God's sake! You're mad!

DION (*sinking in his chair, more and more weakly*) I'm done. My heart, not Brown— (*Mockingly*) My last will and testament! I leave Dion Anthony to William Brown—for him to love and obey—for him to become me—then my Margaret will love me—my children will love me—Mr. and Mrs. Brown and sons, happily ever after! (*Staggering to his full height and looking upward de-*

*fiantly*) Nothing more—but Man's last gesture—by which he conquers—to laugh! Ha— (*He begins, stops as if paralyzed, and
drops on his knees by* BROWN's *chair, his mask falling off, his
Christian Martyr's face at the point of death*) Forgive me, Billy.
Bury me, hide me, forget me for your own happiness! May
Margaret love you! May you design the Temple of Man's Soul!
Blessed are the meek and the poor in spirit! (*He kisses* BROWN's
*feet—then more and more weakly and childishly*) What was
the prayer, Billy? I'm getting so sleepy. . . .

BROWN (*in a trancelike tone*) "Our Father who art in Heaven."

DION (*Drowsily*) "Our Father." . . . (*He dies. A pause.* BROWN
*remains in a stupor for a moment—then stirs himself, puts his
hand on* DION's *breast*).

BROWN (*dully*) He's dead—at last. (*He says this mechanically but
the last two words awaken him—wonderingly*) At last? (*Then
with triumph*) At last! (*He stares at* DION's *real face contemptuously*) So that's the poor weakling you really were! No wonder
you hid! And I've always been afraid of you—yes, I'll confess it
now, in awe of you! Paugh! (*He picks up the mask from the
floor*) No, not of you! Of this! Say what you like, it's strong if it is
bad! And this is what Margaret loved, not you! Not you! This
man!—this man who willed himself to me! (*Struck by an idea,
he jumps to his feet*) By God! (*He slowly starts to put the mask
on. A knocking comes on the street door. He starts guiltily, laying
the mask on the table. Then he picks it up again quickly,
takes the dead body and carries it off left. He reappears immediately and goes to the front door as the knocking recom-
mences—gruffly*) Hello! Who's there?

MARGARET It's Margaret, Billy. I'm looking for Dion.

BROWN (*uncertainly*) Oh—all right— (*Unfastening door*) Come
in. Hello, Margaret. Hello, Boys! He's here. He's asleep. I—I was
just dozing off too. (MARGARET *enters. She is wearing her mask.
The* THREE SONS *are with her*).

MARGARET (*seeing the bottle, forcing a laugh*) Has he been
celebrating?

BROWN (*with strange glibness now*) No. I was. He wasn't. He
said he'd sworn off tonight—forever—for your sake—and the kids!

MARGARET (*with amazed joy*) Dion said that? (*Then hastily defensive*) But of course he never does drink much. Where is he?

BROWN Upstairs. I'll wake him. He felt bad. He took off his clothes
to take a bath before he lay down. You just wait here. (*She*

*sits in the chair where* DION *had sat and stares straight before her. The* SONS *group around her, as if for a family photo.* BROWN *hurries out left).*

MARGARET  It's late to keep you boys up. Aren't you sleepy?

BOYS  No, Mother.

MARGARET  (*proudly*)  I'm glad to have three such strong boys to protect me.

ELDEST  (*boastingly*)  We'd kill anyone that touched you, wouldn't we?

NEXT  You bet! We'd make him wish he hadn't!

YOUNGEST  You bet!

MARGARET  You're Mother's brave boys! (*She laughs fondly—then curiously*)  Do you like Mr. Brown?

ELDEST  Sure thing! He's a regular fellow.

NEXT  He's all right!

YOUNGEST  Sure thing!

MARGARET  (*half to herself*)  Your father claims he steals his ideas.

ELDEST  (*with a sheepish grin*)  I'll bet father said that when he was —just talking.

NEXT  Mr. Brown doesn't have to steal, does he?

YOUNGEST  I should say not! He's awful rich.

MARGARET  Do you love your father?

ELDEST  (*scuffling—embarrassed*)  Why—of course—

NEXT  (*ditto*)  Sure thing!

YOUNGEST  Sure I do.

MARGARET  (*with a sigh*)  I think you'd better start on before— right now—before your father comes— He'll be very sick and nervous and he'll want to be quiet. So run along!

BOYS  All right. (*They file out and close the front door as* BROWN, *dressed in* DION's *clothes and wearing his mask, appears at left).*

MARGARET  (*taking off her mask, gladly*)  Dion! (*She stares wonderingly at him and he at her; goes to him and puts an arm around him*)  Poor dear, do you feel sick? (*He nods*)  But you look—(*squeezing his arms*)—why, you actually feel stronger and better already! Is it true what Billy told me—about your swearing off forever? (*He nods. She exclaims intensely*)  Oh, if you'll only —and get well—we can still be happy! Give Mother a kiss. (*They kiss. A shudder passes through both of them. She breaks away laughing with aroused desire*)  Why, Dion? Aren't you ashamed? You haven't kissed me like that in ages!

BROWN (*his voice imitating* DION's *and muffled by the mask*)  I've wanted to, Margaret!

MARGARET (*gayly and coquettishly now*)  Were you afraid I'd spurn you? Why, Dion, something has happened. It's like a miracle! Even your voice is changed! It actually sounds younger, do you know it? (*Then, solicitously*) But you must be worn out. Let's go home. (*With an impulsive movement she flings her arms wide open, throwing her mask away from her as if suddenly no longer needing it*) Oh, I'm beginning to feel so happy, Dion— so happy!

BROWN (*stifledly*)  Let's go home. (*She puts her arm around him. They walk to the door*).

*Curtain*

# ACT THREE

## SCENE ONE

SCENE. *The drafting room and private office of* BROWN *are both shown. The former is at left, the latter at right of a dividing wall at center. The arrangement of furniture in each room is the same as in previous scenes. It is ten in the morning of a day about a month later. The backdrop for both rooms is of plain wall with a few tacked-up designs and blue prints painted on it.*

TWO DRAFTSMEN, *a middle-aged and a young man, both stoop-shouldered, are sitting on stools behind what was formerly* DION's *table. They are tracing plans. They talk as they work.*

OLDER DRAFTSMAN  W.B. is late again.

YOUNGER DRAFTSMAN  Wonder what's got into him the last month? (*A pause. They work silently*).

OLDER DRAFTSMAN  Yes, ever since he fired Dion. . . .

YOUNGER DRAFTSMAN  Funny his firing him all of a sudden like that. (*A pause. They work*).

OLDER DRAFTSMAN  I haven't seen Dion around town since then. Have you?

YOUNGER DRAFTSMAN  No, not since Brown told us he'd canned him. I suppose he's off drowning his sorrow!

OLDER DRAFTSMAN  I heard someone had seen him at home and he was sober and looking fine. (*A pause. They work*).

YOUNGER DRAFTSMAN  What got into Brown? They say he fired all his old servants that same day and only uses his house to sleep in.

OLDER DRAFTSMAN (*with a sneer*)  Artistic temperament, maybe—the real name of which is swelled head! (*There is a noise of footsteps from the hall. Warningly*) Ssstt! (*They bend over their table.* MARGARET *enters. She does not need to wear a mask now. Her face has regained the self-confident spirit of its youth, her eyes shine with happiness*).

MARGARET (*heartily*)  Good morning! What a lovely day!

BOTH (*perfunctorily*)  Good morning, Mrs. Anthony.

MARGARET (*looking around*)  You've been changing around in here, haven't you? Where is Dion? (*They stare at her*) I forgot to tell him something important this morning and our phone's out of order. So if you'll tell him I'm here— (*They don't move. A pause.* MARGARET *says stiffly*) Oh, I realize Mr. Brown has given strict orders Dion is not to be disturbed, but surely. . . . (*Sharply*) Where is my husband, please?

OLDER DRAFTSMAN  We don't know.

MARGARET  You don't know?

YOUNGER DRAFTSMAN  We haven't seen him.

MARGARET  Why, he left home at eight-thirty!

OLDER DRAFTSMAN  To come here?

YOUNGER DRAFTSMAN  This morning?

MARGARET (*provoked*)  Why, of course, to come here—as he does every day! (*They stare at her. A pause*).

OLDER DRAFTSMAN (*evasively*)  We haven't seen him.

MARGARET (*with asperity*)  Where is Mr. Brown?

YOUNGER DRAFTSMAN (*at a noise of footsteps from the hall—sulkily*)  Coming now. (BROWN *enters. He is now wearing a mask which is an exact likeness of his face as it was in the last scene —the self-assured success. When he sees* MARGARET, *he starts back apprehensively*).

BROWN (*immediately controlling himself—breezily*)  Hello, Margaret! This is a pleasant surprise! (*He holds out his hand*).

MARGARET (*hardly taking it—reservedly*)  Good morning.

BROWN (*turning quickly to the* DRAFTSMEN)  I hope you explained to Mrs. Anthony how busy Dion . . .

MARGARET (*interrupting him—stiffly*)  I certainly can't understand—

BROWN (*hastily*)  I'll explain. Come in here and be comfortable. (*He throws open the door and ushers her into his private office*).

OLDER DRAFTSMAN  Dion must be putting over some bluff on her.

YOUNGER DRAFTSMAN  Pretending he's still here—and Brown's helping him. . . .

OLDER DRAFTSMAN  But why should Brown, after he . . . ?

YOUNGER DRAFTSMAN  Well, I suppose— Search me. (*They work*).

BROWN   Have a chair, Margaret. (*She sits on the chair stiffly. He sits behind the desk*).

MARGARET (*coldly*)   I'd like some explanation. . . .

BROWN (*coaxingly*)   Now, don't get angry, Margaret! Dion is hard at work on his design for the new State Capitol, and I don't want him disturbed, not even by you! So be a good sport! It's for his own good, remember! I asked him to explain to you.

MARGARET (*relenting*)   He told me you'd agreed to ask me and the boys not to come here—but then, we hardly ever did.

BROWN   But you might! (*Then with confidential friendliness*) This is for his sake, Margaret. I know Dion. He's got to be able to work without distractions. He's not the ordinary man, you appreciate that. And this design means his whole future! He's to get full credit for it, and as soon as it's accepted, I take him into partnership. It's all agreed. And after that I'm going to take a long vacation—go to Europe for a couple of years—and leave everything here in Dion's hands! Hasn't he told you all this?

MARGARET (*jubilant now*)   Yes—but I could hardly believe . . . (*Proudly*) I'm sure he can do it. He's been like a new man lately, so full of ambition and energy! It's made me so happy! (*She stops in confusion*).

BROWN (*deeply moved, takes her hand impulsively*)   And it has made me happy, too!

MARGARET (*confused—with an amused laugh*)   Why, Billy Brown! For a moment, I thought it was Dion, your voice sounded so much . . . !

BROWN (*with sudden desperation*)   Margaret, I've got to tell you! I can't go on like this any longer! I've got to confess . . . ! There's something . . . !

MARGARET (*alarmed*)   Not—not about Dion?

BROWN (*harshly*)   To hell with Dion! To hell with Billy Brown! (*He tears off his mask and reveals a suffering face that is ravaged and haggard, his own face tortured and distorted by the demon of* DION's *mask*) Think of me! I love you, Margaret! Leave him! I've always loved you! Come away with me! I'll sell out here! We'll go abroad and be happy!

MARGARET (*amazed*)   Billy Brown, do you realize what you're saying? (*With a shudder*) Are you crazy? Your face—is terrible. You're sick! Shall I phone for a doctor?

BROWN (*turning away slowly and putting on his mask—dully*)   No. I've been on the verge—of a breakdown—for some time. I get spells. . . . I'm better now. (*He turns back to her*) Forgive me! Forget what I said! But, for all our sakes, don't come here again.

MARGARET (*coldly*)   After this—I assure you . . . ! (*Then looking at him with pained incredulity*) Why, Billy—I simply won't believe—after all these years . . . !

BROWN   It will never happen again. Good-by.

MARGARET   Good-by. (*Then, wishing to leave on a pleasant change of subject—forcing a smile*) Don't work Dion to death! He's never home for dinner any more. (*She goes out past the* DRAFTSMAN *and off right, rear.* BROWN *sits down at his desk, taking off the mask again. He stares at it with bitter, cynical amusement*)

BROWN   You're dead, William Brown, dead beyond hope of resurrection! It's the Dion you buried in your garden who killed you, not you him! It's Margaret's husband who . . . (*He laughs harshly*) Paradise by proxy! Love by mistaken identity! God! (*This is almost a prayer—then fiercely defiant*) But it *is* paradise! I *do* love! (*As he is speaking, a well-dressed, important, stout man enters the drafting room. He is carrying a rolled-up plan in his hand. He nods condescendingly and goes directly to* BROWN's *door, on which he raps sharply, and, without waiting for an answer, turns the knob.* BROWN *has just time to turn his head and get his mask on*).

MAN (*briskly*)   Ah, good morning! I came right in. Hope I didn't disturb . . . ?

BROWN (*the successful architect now—urbanely*)   Not at all, sir. How are you? (*They shake hands*) Sit down. Have a cigar. And now what can I do for you this morning?

MAN (*unrolling his plan*)   It's your plan. My wife and I have been going over it again. We like it—and we don't—and when a man plans to lay out half a million, why he wants everything exactly right, eh? (BROWN *nods*) It's too cold, too spare, too like a tomb, if you'll pardon me, for a liveable home. Can't you liven it up, put in some decorations, make it fancier and warmer—you know what I mean. (*Looks at him a bit doubtfully*) People tell me you had an assistant, Anthony, who was a real shark on these details but that you've fired him—

BROWN (*suavely*)   Gossip! He's still with me but, for reasons of his own, doesn't wish it known. Yes, I trained him and he's very ingenious. I'll turn this right over to him and instruct him to carry out your wishes. . . .

**Curtain**

## SCENE TWO

SCENE. *The same as Act Two, Scene Three—the library of* BROWN's *home about eight the same night. He can be heard feeling his way in through the dark. He switches on the reading lamp on the table. Directly under it on a sort of stand is the mask of* DION, *its empty eyes staring front.*

BROWN *takes off his own mask and lays it on the table before* DION's. *He flings himself down in the chair and stares without moving into the eyes of* DION's *mask. Finally, he begins to talk to it in a bitter, mocking tone.*

BROWN   Listen! Today was a narrow escape—for us! We can't avoid discovery much longer. We must get our plot to working! We've already made William Brown's will, leaving you his money and business. We must hustle off to Europe now—and murder him there! (*A bit tauntingly*) Then you—the I in you—*I* will live with Margaret happily ever after. (*More tauntingly*) She will have children by me! (*He seems to hear some mocking denial from the mask. He bends toward it*) What? (*Then with a sneer*) Anyway, that doesn't matter! Your children already love me more than they ever loved you! And Margaret loves me more! You think you've won do you—that I've got to vanish into you in order to live? Not yet, my friend! Never! Wait! Gradually Margaret will love what is beneath—me! Little by little I'll teach her to know me, and then finally I'll reveal myself to her, and confess that I stole your place out of love for her, and she'll understand and forgive and love me! And you'll be forgotten! Ha! (*Again he bends down to the mask as if listening—torturedly*) What's that? She'll never believe? She'll never see? She'll never understand? You lie, devil! (*He reaches out his hands as if to take the mask by the throat, then shrinks back with a shudder of hopeless despair*) God have mercy! Let me believe! Blessed are the merciful! Let me obtain mercy! (*He waits, his face upturned—pleadingly*) Not yet? (*Despairingly*) Never? (*A pause. Then, in a sudden panic of dread, he reaches out for the mask of* DION *like*

a dope fiend after a drug. As soon as he holds it, he seems to
gain strength and is able to force a sad laugh*) Now I am drinking your strength, Dion—strength to love in this world and die
and sleep and become fertile earth, as you are becoming now in
my garden—your weakness the strength of my flowers, your
failure as an artist painting their petals with life? (*Then, with
bravado*) Come with me while Margaret's bridegroom dresses in
your clothes, Mr. Anthony! I need the devil when I'm in the
dark! (*He goes off left, but can be heard talking*) Your clothes
begin to fit me better than my own!  Hurry, Brother! It's time
we were home. Our wife is waiting! (*He reappears, having
changed his coat and trousers*) Come with me and tell her again
I love her! Come and hear her tell me how she loves you! (*He
suddenly cannot help kissing the mask*) I love you because she
loves you! My kisses on your lips are for her! (*He puts the mask
over his face and stands for a moment, seeming to grow tall
and proud—then with a laugh of bold self-assurance*) Out by
the back way! I mustn't forget I'm a desperate criminal, pursued by God, and by myself! (*He goes out right, laughing with
amused satisfaction*).

*Curtain*

### SCENE THREE

SCENE. *Is the same as Scene One of Act One—the sitting-room of
*MARGARET's *home. It is about half an hour after the last scene.*
MARGARET *sits on the sofa, waiting with the anxious, impatient ex-
pectancy of one deeply in love. She is dressed with a careful,
subtle extra touch to attract the eye. She looks young and happy.
She is trying to read a book. The front door is heard opening and
closing. She leaps up and runs back to throw her arms around
*BROWN *as he enters from right, rear. She kisses him passionately.*

MARGARET (*as he recoils with a sort of guilt—laughingly*) Why,
you hateful old thing, you! I really believe you were trying to
avoid kissing me! Well, just for that, I'll never . . .

BROWN (*with fierce, defiant passion, kisses her again and again*) Margaret!

MARGARET  Call me Peggy again. You used to when you really loved me. (*Softly*) Remember the school commencement dance —you and I on the dock in the moonlight?

BROWN (*with pain*)  No. (*He takes his arms from around her*)

MARGARET (*still holding him—with a laugh*)  Well, I like that! You old bear, you! Why not?

BROWN (*sadly*)  It was so long ago.

MARGARET (*a bit melancholy*)  You mean you don't want to be reminded that we're getting old?

BROWN  Yes. (*He kisses her gently*) I'm tired. Let's sit down. (*They sit on the sofa, his arm about her, her head on his shoulder*).

MARGARET (*with a happy sigh*)  I don't mind remembering— now I'm happy. It's only when I'm unhappy that it hurts—and I've been so happy lately, dear—and so grateful to you! (*He stirs uneasily. She goes on joyfully*) Everything's changed! I'd gotten pretty resigned to—and sad and hopeless, too—and then all at once you turn right around and everything is the same as when we were first married—much better even, for I was never sure of you then. You were always so strange and aloof and alone, it seemed I was never really touching you. But now I feel you've become quite human—like me—and I'm so happy, dear! (*She kisses him*).

BROWN (*his voice trembling*)  Then I made you happy—happier than ever before—no matter what happens? (*She nods*) Then— that justifies everything! (*He forces a laugh*).

MARGARET  Of course it does! I've always known that. But you— you wouldn't be—or you couldn't be—and I could never help you —and all the time I knew you were so lonely! I could always hear you calling to me that you were lost, but I couldn't find the path to you because I was lost, too! That's an awful way for a wife to feel! (*She laughs—joyfully*) But now you're here! You're mine! You're my long-lost lover, and my husband, and my big boy, too!

BROWN (*with a trace of jealousy*)  Where are your other big boys tonight?

MARGARET  Out to a dance. They've all acquired girls, I'll have you know.

BROWN (*mockingly*)  Aren't you jealous?

MARGARET (*gayly*) Of course! Terribly! But I'm diplomatic. I don't let them see. (*Changing the subject*) Believe me, they've noticed the change in you! The eldest was saying to me today: "It's great not to have Father so nervous, any more. Why, he's a regular sport when he gets started!" And the other two said very solemnly: "You bet!" (*She laughs*)

BROWN (*brokenly*) I—I'm glad.

MARGARET Dion! You're crying!

BROWN (*stung by the name, gets up—harshly*) Nonsense! Did you ever know Dion to cry about anyone?

MARGARET (*sadly*) You couldn't—then. You were too lonely. You had no one to cry to.

BROWN (*goes and takes a rolled-up plan from the table drawer—dully*) I've got to do some work.

MARGARET (*disappointedly*) What, has that old Billy Brown got you to work at home again, too?

BROWN (*ironically*) It's for Dion's good, you know—and yours.

MARGARET (*making the best of it—cheerfully*) All right. I won't be selfish. It really makes me proud to have you so ambitious. Let me help. (*She brings his drawing-board, which he puts on the table and pins his plan upon. She sits on sofa and picks up her book*).

BROWN (*carefully casual*) I hear you were in to see me today?

MARGARET Yes, and Billy wouldn't hear of it! I was quite furious until he convinced me it was all for the best. When is he going to take you into partnership?

BROWN Very soon now.

MARGARET And will he really give you full charge when he goes abroad?

BROWN Yes.

MARGARET (*practically*) I'd pin him down if I could. Promises are all right, but— (*she hesitates*) I don't trust him.

BROWN (*with a start, sharply*) What makes you say that?

MARGARET Oh, something that happened today.

BROWN What?

MARGARET I don't mean I blame him, but—to be frank, I think the Great God Brown, as you call him, is getting a bit queer and it's time he took a vacation. Don't you?

BROWN (*his voice a bit excited—but guardedly*) But why? What did he do?

MARGARET (*hesitatingly*) Well—it's really too silly—he suddenly got awfully strange. His face scared me. It was like a corpse. Then he raved on some nonsense about he'd always loved me. He went on like a perfect fool! (*She looks at* BROWN, *who is staring at her. She becomes uneasy*) Maybe I shouldn't tell you this. He simply wasn't responsible. Then he came to himself and was all right and begged my pardon and seemed dreadfully sorry, and I felt sorry for him. (*Then with a shudder*) But honestly, Dion, it was just too disgusting for words to hear him! (*With kind, devastating contempt*) Poor Billy!

BROWN (*with a show of tortured derision*) Poor Billy! Poor Billy the Goat! (*With mocking frenzy*) I'll kill him for you! I'll serve you his heart for breakfast!

MARGARET (*jumping up—frightenedly*) Dion!

BROWN (*waving his pencil knife with grotesque flourishes*) I tell you I'll murder this God-damned disgusting Great God Brown who stands like a fatted calf in the way of our health and wealth and happiness!

MARGARET (*bewilderedly, not knowing how much is pretending, puts an arm about him*) Don't, dear! You're being horrid and strange again. It makes me afraid you haven't really changed after all.

BROWN (*unheeding*) And then my wife can be happy! Ha! (*He laughs. She begins to cry. He controls himself—pats her head—gently*) All right, dear. Mr. Brown is now safely in hell. Forget him!

MARGARET (*stops crying—but still worriedly*) I should never have told you—but I never imagined you'd take it seriously. I've never thought of Billy Brown except as a friend, and lately not even that! He's just a stupid old fool!

BROWN Ha-ha! Didn't I say he was in hell? They're torturing him! (*Then controlling himself again—exhaustedly*) Please leave me alone now. I've got to work.

MARGARET All right, dear. I'll go into the next room and anything you want, just call. (*She pats his face—cajolingly*) Is it all forgotten?

BROWN Will you be happy?

MARGARET Yes.

BROWN Then it's dead, I promise! (*She kisses him and goes out. He stares ahead, then shakes off his thoughts and concentrates on his work—mockingly*) Our beautiful new Capitol calls you, Mr. Dion! To work! We'll adroitly hide old Silenus on the cupola! Let him dance over their law-making with his eternal leer! (*He bends over his work*).

*Curtain*

# ACT FOUR

## SCENE ONE

SCENE. *Same as Scene One of Act Three—the drafting room and* BROWN's *office. It is dusk of a day about a month later. The* TWO DRAFTSMEN *are bent over their table, working.*

BROWN (*at his desk, is working feverishly over a plan. He is wearing the mask of* DION. *The mask of* WILLIAM BROWN *rests on the desk beside him. As he works, he chuckles with malicious glee—finally flings down his pencil with a flourish*).

BROWN Done! In the name of the Almighty Brown, amen, amen! Here's a wondrous fair capitol! The design would do just as well for a Home for Criminal Imbeciles! Yet to them, such is my art, it will appear to possess a pure common-sense, a fat-bellied finality, as dignified as the suspenders of an assemblyman! Only to me will that pompous façade reveal itself as the wearily ironic grin of Pan as, his ears drowsy with the crumbling hum of past and future civilizations, he half-listens to the laws passed by his fleas to enslave him! Ha-ha-ha! (*He leaps grotesquely from behind his desk and cuts a few goatish capers, laughing with lustful merriment*) Long live Chief of Police Brown! District Attorney Brown! Alderman Brown! Assemblyman Brown! Mayor Brown! Congressman Brown! Governor Brown! Senator Brown President Brown (*He chants*) Oh, how many persons in one God make up the good God Brown? Hahahaha! (*The* TWO DRAFTSMEN *in the next room have stopped work and are listening*).

YOUNGER DRAFTSMAN Drunk as a fool!

OLDER DRAFTSMAN At least Dion used to have the decency to stay away from the office—

YOUNGER DRAFTSMAN  Funny how it's got hold of Brown so quick!

OLDER DRAFTSMAN  He was probably hitting it up on the Q.T. all the time.

BROWN  (*has come back to his desk, laughing to himself and out of breath*)  Time to become respectable again! (*He takes off the* DION *mask and reaches out for the* WILLIAM BROWN *one—then stops, with a hand on each, staring down on the plan with fascinated loathing. His real face is now sick, ghastly, tortured, hollow-cheeked and feverish-eyed*)  Ugly! Hideous! Despicable! Why must the demon in me pander to cheapness—then punish me with self-loathing and life-hatred? Why am I not strong enough to perish—or blind enough to be content? (*To heaven, bitterly but pleadingly*)  Give me the strength to destroy this!—and myself!—and him!—and I will believe in Thee! (*While he has been speaking there has been a noise from the stairs. The* TWO DRAFTSMEN *have bent over their work.* MARGARET *enters, closing the door behind her. At this sound,* BROWN *starts. He immediately senses who it is—with alarm*)  Margaret! (*He grabs up both masks and goes into room off right*).

MARGARET  (*she looks healthy and happy, but her face wears a worried, solicitous expression—pleasantly to the staring* DRAFTSMEN)  Good morning. Oh, you needn't look worried, it's Mr. Brown I want to see, not my husband.

YOUNGER DRAFTSMAN  (*Hesitatingly*)  He's locked himself in—but maybe if you'll knock—

MARGARET  (*knocks—somewhat embarrassedly*)  Mr. Brown! (BROWN *enters his office, wearing the* WILLIAM BROWN *mask. He comes quickly to the other door and unlocks it*).

BROWN  (*with a hectic cordiality*)  Come on, Margaret! Enter! This is delightful! Sit down! What can I do for you?

MARGARET  (*taken aback—a bit stiffly*)  Nothing much.

BROWN  Something about Dion, of course. Well, your darling pet is all right—never better!

MARGARET  (*coldly*)  That's a matter of opinion. I think you're working him to death.

BROWN  Oh, no, not him. It's Brown who is to die. We've agreed on that.

MARGARET  (*giving him a queer look*)  I'm serious.

BROWN  So am I. Deadly serious! Hahaha!

MARGARET  (*checking her indignation*)  That's what I came to see you about. Really, Dion has acted so hectic and on edge lately

I'm sure he's on the verge of a breakdown.

BROWN   Well, it certainly isn't drink. He hasn't had a drop. He doesn't need it! Haha! And I haven't either, although the gossips are beginning to say I'm soused all the time! It's because I've started to laugh! Hahaha! They can't believe in joy in this town except by the bottle! What funny little people! Hahaha! When you're the Great God Brown, eh, Margaret? Hahaha!

MARGARET   (*getting up—uneasily*)   I'm afraid I—

BROWN   Don't be afraid, my dear! I won't make love to you again! Honor bright! I'm too near the grave for such folly! But it must have been funny for you when you came here the last time— watching a disgusting old fool like me, eh?—too funny for words! Hahaha! (*Then with a sudden movement he flourishes the design before her*) Look! We've finished it! Dion has finished it! His fame is made!

MARGARET (*tartly*)   Really, Billy, I believe you are drunk!

BROWN   Nobody kisses me—so you can all believe the worst! Hahaha!

MARGARET   (*chillingly*)   Then if Dion is through, why can't I see him?

BROWN   (*crazily*)   See Dion? See Dion? Well, why not? It's an age of miracles. The streets are full of Lazaruses. Pray! I mean— wait a moment, if you please.

(BROWN *disappears into the room off right. A moment later he reappears in the mask of* DION. *He holds out his arms and* MARGARET *rushes into them. They kiss passionately. Finally he sits with her on the lounge*).

MARGARET   So you've finished it.

BROWN   Yes. The Committee is coming to see it soon. I've made all the changes they'll like, the fools!

MARGARET   (*lovingly*)   And can we go on that second honeymoon, right away now?

BROWN   In a week or so, I hope—as soon as I've gotten Brown off to Europe.

MARGARET   Tell me—isn't he drinking hard?

BROWN   (*laughing as* BROWN *did*)   Haha! Soused to the ears all the time! Soused on life! He can't stand it! It's burning his insides out!

MARGARET   (*alarmed*)   Dear! I'm worried about you. You sound as crazy as he did—when you laugh! You must rest!

BROWN   (*controlling himself*)   I'll rest in peace—when he's gone!

MARGARET (*with a queer look*) Why, Dion, that isn't your suit. It's just like—

BROWN It's his! We're getting to be like twins. I'm inheriting his clothes already! (*Then calming himself as he sees how frightened she is*) Don't be worried, dear. I'm just a trifle elated, now the job's done. I guess I'm a bit soused on life, too! (*The* COMMITTEE, *three important-looking, average personages, come into the drafting room*).

MARGARET (*forcing a smile*) Well, don't let it burn *your* insides out!

BROWN No danger! Mine were tempered in hell! Hahaha!

MARGARET (*kissing him, coaxingly*) Come home, dear—please!

OLDER DRAFTSMAN (*knocks on the door*) The Committee is here, Mr. Brown.

BROWN (*hurriedly to* MARGARET) You receive them. Hand them the design. I'll get Brown. (*He raises his voice*) Come right in, gentlemen. (*He goes off right, as the* COMMITTEE *enter the office. When they see* MARGARET, *they stop in surprise*).

MARGARET (*embarrassedly*) Good afternoon. Mr. Brown will be right with you. (*They bow.* MARGARET *holds out the design to them*) This is my husband's design. He finished it today.

COMMITTEE Ah! (*They crowd around to look at it—with enthusiasm*) Perfect! Splendid! Couldn't be better! Exactly what we suggested!

MARGARET (*joyfully*) Then you accept it? Mr. Anthony will be so pleased!

MEMBER Mr. Anthony?

ANOTHER Is he working here again?

THIRD Did I understand you to say this was your husband's design?

MARGARET (*excitedly*) Yes! Entirely his! He's worked like a dog —(*Appalled*) You don't mean to say—Mr. Brown never told you? (*They shake their heads in solemn surprise*) Oh, the contemptible cad! I hate him!

BROWN (*appearing at right—mockingly*) Hate me, Margaret? Hate Brown? How superfluous! (*Oratorically*) Gentlemen, I have been keeping a secret from you in order that you might be the more impressed when I revealed it. That design is entirely the inspiration of Mr. Dion Anthony's genius. I had nothing to do with it.

MARGARET (*contritely*) Oh, Billy! I'm sorry! Forgive me!

BROWN (*ignoring her, takes the plan from the* COMMITTEE *and begins unpinning it from the board—mockingly*) I can see by your faces you have approved this. You are delighted, aren't you? And why not, my dear sirs? Look at it, and look at you! Hahaha! It'll immortalize you, my good men! You'll be as death-defying a joke as any in Joe Miller! (*Then with a sudden complete change of tone—angrily*) You damn fools! Can't you see this is an insult— a terrible, blasphemous insult!—that this embittered failure Anthony is hurling in the teeth of our success—an insult to you, to me, to you, Margaret—and to Almighty God! (*In a frenzy of fury*) And if you are weak and cowardly enough to stand for it, I'm not! (*He tears the plan into four pieces. The* COMMITTEE *stands aghast.* MARGARET *runs forward*).

MARGARET (*in a scream*) You coward! Dion! Dion! (*She picks up the plan and hugs it to her bosom*).

BROWN (*with a sudden goatish caper*) I'll tell him you're here. (*He disappears, but reappears almost immediately in the mask of* DION. *He is imposing a terrible discipline on himself to avoid dancing and laughing. He speaks suavely*) Everything is all right—all for the best—you mustn't get excited! A little paste, Margaret! A little paste, gentlemen! And all will be well! Life is imperfect, Brothers! Men have their faults, Sister! But with a few drops of glue much may be done! A little dab of pasty resignation here and there—and even broken hearts may be repaired to do yeoman service! (*He has edged toward the door. They are all staring at him with petrified bewilderment. He puts his fingers to his lips*) Ssssh! This is Daddy's bedtime secret for today: Man is born broken. He lives by mending. The grace of God is glue! (*With a quick prancing movement, he has opened the door, gone through, and closed it after him silently, shaking with suppressed laughter. He springs lightly to the side of the petrified* DRAFTSMEN—*in a whisper*) They will find him in the little room. Mr. William Brown is dead! (*With light leaps he vanishes, his head thrown back, shaking with silent laughter. The sound of his feet leaping down the stairs, five at a time, can be heard. Then a pause of silence. The people in the two rooms stare. The* YOUNGER DRAFTSMAN *is the first to recover*).

YOUNGER DRAFTSMAN (*rushing into the next room, shouts in terrified tones*) Mr. Brown is dead!

COMMITTEE He murdered him! (*They all run into the little room off right.* MARGARET *remains, stunned with horror. They return in a moment, carrying the mask of* WILLIAM BROWN, *two on each side, as if they were carrying a body by the legs and shoulders. They solemnly lay him down on the couch and stand looking down at him*).

FIRST COMMITTEEMAN (*with a frightened awe*) I can't believe he's gone.

SECOND COMMITTEEMAN (*in same tone*) I can almost hear him talking. (*As if impelled, he clears his throat and addresses the mask importantly*) Mr. Brown— (*Then stops short*).

THIRD COMMITTEEMAN (*shrinking back*) No. Dead, all right! (*Then suddenly, hysterically angry and terrified*) We must take steps at once to run Anthony to earth!

MARGARET (*with a heart-broken cry*) Dion's innocent!

YOUNGER DRAFTSMAN I'll phone for the police, sir! (*He rushes to the phone*).

*Curtain*

## SCENE TWO

SCENE. *The same as Scene Two of Act Three—the library of* WILLIAM BROWN's *home. The mask of* DION *stands on the table beneath the light, facing front. On his knees beside the table, facing front, stripped naked except for a white cloth around his loins, is* BROWN. *The clothes he has torn off in his agony are scattered on the floor. His eyes, his arms, his whole body strain upward, his muscles writhe with his lips as they pray silently in their agonized supplication. Finally a voice seems torn out of him.*

BROWN Mercy, Compassionate Savior of Man! Out of my depths I cry to you! Mercy on thy poor clod, thy clod of unhallowed earth, thy clay, the Great God Brown! Mercy, Savior! (*He seems to wait for an answer—then leaping to his feet he puts out one hand to touch the mask like a frightened child reaching out for its nurse's hand—then with immediate mocking despair*) Bah! I am sorry, little children, but your kingdom is empty. God has become disgusted and moved away to some far ecstatic star where life is a dancing flame! We must die without him. (*Then—addressing the mask—harshly*) Together, my friend! You, too! Let Margaret suffer! Let the whole world suffer as I am suffering! (*There is a sound of a door being pushed violently open, padding feet in slippers, and* CYBEL, *wearing her mask, runs into the room. She stops short on seeing* BROWN *and the mask, and stares from one to the other for a second in confusion. She is dressed in a black kimono robe and wears slippers over her bare feet. Her yellow hair hangs down in a great mane over her shoulders. She has grown stouter, has more of the deep objective calm of an idol*).

BROWN (*staring at her—fascinated—with great peace as if her presence comforted him*)   Cybel! I was coming to you! How did you know?

CYBEL (*takes off her mask and looks from* BROWN *to the* DION *mask, now with a great understanding*)   So that's why you never came to me again! You are Dion Brown!

BROWN (*bitterly*)   I am the remains of William Brown! (*He points to the mask of* DION)   I am his murderer and his murdered!

CYBEL (*with a laugh of exasperated pity*)   Oh, why can't you ever learn to leave yourselves alone and leave me alone!

BROWN (*boyishly and naïvely*)   I am Billy.

CYBEL (*immediately, with a motherly solicitude*)   Then run, Billy, run! They are hunting for someone! They came to my place, hunting for a murderer, Dion! They must find a victim! They've got to quiet their fears, to cast out their devils, or they'll never sleep soundly again! They've got to absolve themselves by finding a guilty one! They've got to kill someone now, to live! You're naked! You must be Satan! Run, Billy, run! They'll come here! I ran here to warn—someone! So run away if you want to live!

BROWN (*like a sulky child*)   I'm too tired. I don't want to.

CYBEL (*with motherly calm*)   All right, you needn't, Billy. Don't sulk. (*As a noise comes from outside*) Anyway, it's too late. I hear them in the garden now.

BROWN (*listening, puts out his hand and takes the mask of* DION— *as he gains strength, mockingly*)   Thanks for this one last favor, Dion! Listen! Your avengers! Standing on your grave in the garden! Hahaha! (*He puts on the mask and springs to the left and makes a gesture as if flinging French windows open. Gayly mocking*) Welcome, dumb worshippers! I am your Great God

Brown! I have been advised to run from you but it is my almighty whim to dance into escape over your prostrate souls!
(*Shouts from the garden and a volley of shots.* BROWN *staggers
back and falls on the floor by the couch, mortally wounded*).

CYBEL (*runs to his side, lifts him on to the couch and takes off the
mask of* DION) You can't take this to bed with you. You've got to
go to sleep alone. (*She places the mask of* DION *back on its stand
under the light and puts on her own, just as, after a banging of
doors, crashing of glass, trampling of feet, a Squad of Police with
drawn revolvers, led by a grizzly, brutal-faced Captain, run into
the room. They are followed by* MARGARET, *still distractedly
clutching the pieces of the plan to her breast*).

CAPTAIN (*pointing to the mask of* DION—*triumphantly*) Got him!
He's dead!

MARGARET (*throws herself on her knees, takes the mask and kisses
it—heart-brokenly*) Dion! Dion! (*Her face hidden in her arms,
the mask in her hands above her bowed head, she remains, sobbing with deep, silent grief*).

CAPTAIN (*noticing* CYBEL *and* BROWN—*startled*) Hey! Look at this!
What're you doin' here? Who's he?

CYBEL You ought to know. You croaked him!

CAPTAIN (*with a defensive snarl—hastily*) It was Anthony! I saw
his mug! This feller's an accomplice. I bet yuh! Serves him
right! Who is he? Friend o' yours! Crook! What's his name? Tell
me or I'll fix yuh!

CYBEL Billy.

CAPTAIN Billy what?

CYBEL I don't know. He's dying. (*Then suddenly*) Leave me
alone with him and maybe I'll get him to squeal it.

CAPTAIN Yuh better! I got to have a clean report. I'll give yuh a
couple o' minutes. (*He motions to the Policemen, who follow
him off left.* CYBEL *takes off her mask and sits down by* BROWN's
*head. He makes an effort to raise himself toward her and she
helps him, throwing her kimono over his bare body, drawing
his head on to her shoulder*).

BROWN (*snuggling against her—gratefully*) The earth is warm.

CYBEL (*soothingly, looking before her like an idol*) Ssshh! Go to
sleep, Billy.

BROWN Yes, Mother. (*Then explainingly*) It was dark and I
couldn't see where I was going and they all picked on me.

CYBEL I know. You're tired.

BROWN   And when I wake up . . . ?

CYBEL   The sun will be rising again.

BROWN   To judge the living and the dead! (*Frightenedly*) I don't want justice. I want love.

CYBEL   There is only love.

BROWN   Thank you, Mother. (*Then feebly*) I'm getting sleepy. What's the prayer you taught me— Our Father—?

CYBEL   (*with calm exultance*)   Our Father Who Art!

BROWN   (*taking her tone—exultantly*)   Who art! Who art! (*Suddenly—with ecstasy*) I know! I have found Him! I hear Him speak! "Blessed are they that weep, for they shall laugh!" Only he that has wept can laugh! The laughter of Heaven sows earth with a rain of tears, and out of Earth's transfigured birth-pain the laughter of Man returns to bless and play again in innumerable dancing gales of flame upon the knees of God! (*He dies*).

CYBEL   (*gets up and fixes his body on the couch. She bends down and kisses him gently—she straightens up and looks into space— with a profound pain*)   Always spring comes again bearing life! Always again! Always, always forever again!— Spring again!—life again!—summer and fall and death and peace again!—(*with agonized sorrow*)—but always, always, love and conception and birth and pain again—spring bearing the intolerable chalice of life again!—(*then with agonized exultance*)—bearing the glorious, blazing crown of life again! (*She stands like an idol of Earth, her eyes staring out over the world*).

MARGARET   (*lifting her head adoringly to the mask—triumphant tenderness mingled with her grief*)   My lover! My husband! My boy! (*She kisses the mask*) Good-by. Thank you for happiness! And you're not dead, sweetheart! You can never die till my heart dies! You will live forever! You will sleep under my heart! I will feel you stirring in your sleep, forever under my heart! (*She kisses the mask again. There is a pause*).

CAPTAIN   (*comes just into sight at left and speaks front without looking at them—gruffly*)   Well, what's his name?

CYBEL   Man!

CAPTAIN   (*taking a grimy notebook and an inch-long pencil from his pocket*)   How d'yuh spell it?

**CURTAIN**

# EPILOGUE

SCENE. *Four years later. The same spot on the same dock as in Prologue on another moonlight night in June. The sound of the waves and of distant dance music.*

*MARGARET and her THREE SONS appear from the right. The eldest is now eighteen. All are dressed in the height of correct Prep-school elegance. They are all tall, athletic, strong and handsome-looking. They loom up around the slight figure of their mother like protecting giants, giving her a strange aspect of lonely, detached, small femininity. She wears her mask of the proud, indulgent Mother. She has grown appreciably older. Her hair is now a beautiful gray. There is about her manner and voice the sad but contented feeling of one who knows her life-purpose well accomplished but is at the same time a bit empty and comfortless with the finality of it. She is wrapped in a gray cloak.*

ELDEST    Doesn't Bee look beautiful tonight, Mother?

NEXT    Don't you think Mabel's the best dancer in there, Mother?

YOUNGEST    Aw, Alice has them both beat, hasn't she, Mother?

MARGARET  (*with a sad little laugh*)  Each of you is right. (*Then, with strange finality*) Good-by, boys.

BOYS  (*surprised*)  Good-by.

MARGARET   It was here on a night just like this your father first—proposed to me. Did you ever know that?

BOYS  (*embarrassedly*)  No.

MARGARET  (*yearningly*)  But the nights now are so much colder than they used to be. Think of it, I went in moonlight bathing in June when I was a girl. It was so warm and beautiful in those days. I remember the Junes when I was carrying you boys—(*A pause. They fidget uneasily. She asks pleadingly*) Promise me faithfully never to forget your father!

BOYS  (*uncomfortably*)  Yes, Mother.

MARGARET (*forcing a joking tone*) But you mustn't waste June on an old woman like me! Go in and dance. (*As they hesitate dutifully*) Go on. I really want to be alone—with my Junes.

BOYS (*unable to conceal their eagerness*) Yes, Mother. (*They go away*).

MARGARET (*slowly removes her mask, laying it on the bench, and stares up at the moon with a wistful, resigned sweetness*) So long ago! And yet I'm still the same Margaret. It's only our lives that grow old. We *are* where centuries only count as seconds and after a thousand lives our eyes begin to open—(*She looks around her with a rapt smile*)—and the moon rests in the sea! I want to feel the moon at peace in the sea! I want Dion to leave the sky for me! I want him to sleep in the tides of my heart! (*She slowly takes from under her cloak, from her bosom, as if from her heart, the mask of* DION *as it was at the last and holds it before her face*) My lover! My husband! My boy! You can never die till my heart dies! You will live forever. You are sleeping under my heart! I feel you stirring in your sleep, forever under my heart. (*She kisses him on the lips with a timeless kiss*).

*Curtain*

# Strange

# Interlude

# Characters

CHARLES MARSDEN

PROFFESSOR HENRY LEEDS

NINA LEEDS, *his daughter*

EDMUND DARRELL

SAM EVANS

MRS. AMOS EVANS, *Sam's mother*

GORDON EVANS

MADELINE ARNOLD

# Part One

ACT ONE: Library, the Leeds' home in a small university town of New England—an afternoon in late summer.

ACT TWO: The same. Fall of the following year. Night.

ACT THREE: Dining room of the Evans' homestead in northern New York state—late spring of the next year. Morning.

ACT FOUR: The same as Acts One and Two. Fall of the same year. Evening.

ACT FIVE: Sitting room of small house Evans has rented in a seashore suburb near New York. The following April. Morning.

# Part Two

ACT SIX: The same. A little over a year later. Evening.

ACT SEVEN: Sitting room of the Evans' apartment on Park Avenue. Nearly eleven years later. Early afternoon.

ACT EIGHT: Section of afterdeck of the Evans' cruiser anchored near the finish line at Poughkeepsie. Ten years later. Afternoon.

ACT NINE: A terrace on the Evans' estate on Long Island. Several months later. Late afternoon.

# PART ONE

## ACT ONE

SCENE: *The library of* PROFESSOR LEEDS' *home in a small university town in New England. This room is at the front part of his house with windows opening on the strip of lawn between the house and the quiet residential street. It is a small room with a low ceiling. The furniture has been selected with a love for old New England pieces. The walls are lined almost to the ceiling with glassed-in bookshelves. These are packed with books, principally editions, many of them old and rare, of ancient classics in the original Greek and Latin, of the later classics in French and German and Italian, of all the English authors who wrote while s was still like an f and a few since then, the most modern probably being Thackeray. The atmosphere of the room is that of a cosy, cultured retreat, sedulously built as a sanctuary where, secure with the culture of the past at his back, a fugitive from reality can view the present safely from a distance, as a superior with condescending disdain, pity, and even amusement.*

*There is a fair-sized table, a heavy armchair, a rocker, and an old bench made comfortable with cushions. The table, with the Professor's armchair at its left, is arranged toward the left of the room, the rocker is at center, the bench at right.*

*There is one entrance, a door in the right wall, rear.*

*It is late afternoon of a day in August. Sunshine, cooled and dimmed in the shade of trees, fills the room with a soothing light.*

*The sound of a* MAID'S VOICE—*a middle-aged woman—explaining familiarly but respectfully from the right, and* MARSDEN *enters. He is a tall thin man of thirty-five, meticulously well-dressed in tweeds of distinctly English tailoring, his appearance that of an*

*Anglicized New England gentleman. His face is too long for its width, his nose is high and narrow, his forehead broad, his mild blue eyes those of a dreamy self-analyst, his thin lips ironical and a bit sad. There is an indefinable feminine quality about him, but it is nothing apparent in either appearance or act. His manner is cool and poised. He speaks with a careful ease as one who listens to his own conversation. He has long fragile hands, and the stoop to his shoulders of a man weak muscularly, who has never liked athletics and has always been regarded as of delicate constitution. The main point about his personality is a quiet charm, a quality of appealing, inquisitive friendliness, always willing to listen, eager to sympathize, to like and to be liked.*

MARSDEN (*standing just inside the door, his tall, stooped figure leaning back against the books—nodding back at the* MAID *and smiling kindly*) I'll wait in here, Mary. (*His eyes follow her for a second, then return to gaze around the room slowly with an appreciative relish for the familiar significance of the books. He smiles affectionately and his amused voice recites the words with a rhetorical resonance*) Sanctum Sanctorum! (*His voice takes on a monotonous musing quality, his eyes stare idly at his drifting thoughts*)

How perfectly the Professor's unique haven! . . .

(*He smiles*)

Primly classical . . . when New Englander meets Greek! . . .

(*Looking at the books now*)

He hasn't added one book in years . . . how old was I when I first came here? . . . six . . . with my father . . . father . . . how dim his face has grown! . . . he wanted to speak to me just before he died . . . the hospital . . . smell of iodoform in the cool halls . . . hot summer . . . I bent down . . . his voice had withdrawn so far away . . . I couldn't understand him . . . what son can ever understand? . . . always too near, too soon, too distant or too late! . . .

(*His face has become sad with a memory of the bewildered suffering of the adolescent boy he had been at the time of his father's death. Then he shakes his head, flinging off his thoughts, and makes himself walk about the room*)

What memories on such a smiling afternoon! . . . this pleasant old town after three months . . . I won't go to Europe again . . . couldn't write a line there . . . how answer the fierce ques-

tion of all those dead and maimed? . . . too big a job for
me! . . .

(*He sighs—then self-mockingly*)

But back here . . . it is the interlude that gently questions . . .
in this town dozing . . . decorous bodies moving with circum-
spection through the afternoons . . . their habits affectionately
chronicled . . . an excuse for weaving amusing words . . . my
novels . . . not of cosmic importance, hardly . . .

(*Then self-reassuringly*)

but there is a public to cherish them, evidently . . . and I can
write! . . . more than one can say of these modern sex-yahoos!
. . . I must start work tomorrow . . . I'd like to use the Professor in a novel sometime . . . and his wife . . . seems impossible she's been dead six years . . . so aggressively his wife!
. . . poor Professor! now it's Nina who bosses him . . . but
that's different . . . she has bossed me, too, ever since she was
a baby . . . she's a woman now . . . known love and death
. . . Gordon brought down in flames . . . two days before the
armistice . . . what fiendish irony! . . . his wonderful athlete's
body . . . her lover . . . charred bones in a cage of twisted
steel . . . no wonder she broke down . . . Mother said she's become quite queer lately . . . Mother seemed jealous of my concern . . . why have I never fallen in love with Nina? . . .
could I? . . . that way . . . used to dance her on my knee . . .
sit her on my lap . . . even now she'd never think anything
about it . . . but sometimes the scent of her hair and skin . . .
like a dreamy drug . . . dreamy! . . . there's the rub! . . . all
dreams with me! . . . my sex life among the phantoms! . . .

(*He grins torturedly*)

Why? . . . oh, this digging in gets nowhere . . . to the devil
with sex! . . . our impotent pose of today to beat the loud drum
on fornication! . . . boasters . . . eunuchs parading with the
phallus! . . . giving themselves away . . . whom do they fool?
. . . not even themselves! . . .

(*His face suddenly full of an intense pain and disgust*)

Ugh! . . . always that memory! . . . why can't I ever forget?
. . . . as sickeningly clear as if it were yesterday . . . prep school
. . . Easter vacation . . . Fatty Boggs and Jack Frazer . . . that
house of cheap vice . . . one dollar! . . . why did I go? . . .
Jack, the dead game sport . . . how I admired him! . . . afraid
of his taunts . . . he pointed to the Italian girl . . . "Take

her!" . . . daring me . . . I went . . . miserably frightened . . .
what a pig she was! . . . pretty vicious face under caked powder
and rouge . . . surly and contemptuous . . . lumpy body . . .
short legs and thick ankles . . . slums of Naples . . . "What
you gawkin' about? Git a move on, kid" . . . kid! . . . I *was*
only a kid! . . . sixteen . . . test of manhood . . . ashamed to
face Jack again unless . . . fool! . . . I might have lied to him!
. . . but I honestly thought that wench would feel humiliated
if I . . . oh, stupid kid! . . . back at the hotel I waited till they
were asleep . . . then sobbed . . . thinking of Mother . . . feeling I had defiled her . . . and myself . . . forever! . . .
(*Mocking bitterly*)
"Nothing half so sweet in life as love's young dream," what? . . .
(*He gets to his feet impatiently*)
Why does my mind always have to dwell on that? . . . too
silly . . . no importance really . . . an incident such as any boy
of my age . . .
(*He hears someone coming quickly from the right and turns expectantly.* PROFESSOR LEEDS *enters, a pleased relieved expression
fighting the flurried worry on his face. He is a small, slender man
of fifty-five, his hair gray, the top of his head bald. His face,
prepossessing in spite of its too-small, over-refined features, is that
of a retiring, studious nature. He has intelligent eyes and a smile
that can be ironical. Temperamentally timid, his defense is an
assumption of his complacent, superior manner of the classroom
toward the world at large. This defense is strengthened by a
natural tendency toward a prim provincialism where practical
present-day considerations are concerned (though he is most liberal—even radical—in his tolerant understanding of the manners
and morals of Greece and Imperial Rome!). This classroom poise
of his, however, he cannot quite carry off outside the classroom.
There is an unconvincing quality about it that leaves his larger
audience—and particularly the* PROFESSOR *himself—subtly embarrassed. As* MARSDEN *is one of his old students, whom, in addition,
he has known from childhood, he is perfectly at ease with him*).
MARSDEN (*holding out his hand—with unmistakable liking*) Here
I am again, Professor!
PROFESSOR LEEDS (*shaking his hand and patting him on the back
—with genuine affection*) So glad to see you, Charlie! A surprise, too! We didn't expect you back so soon! (*He sits in his
chair on the left of the table while* MARSDEN *sits in the rocker*).

(*Looking away from* MARSDEN *a moment, his face now full of selfish relief as he thinks*)

Fortunate, his coming back . . . always calming influence on Nina . . .

MARSDEN   And I never dreamed of returning so soon. But Europe, Professor, is the big casualty they were afraid to set down on the list.

PROFESSOR LEEDS (*his face clouding*)   Yes, I suppose you found everything completely changed since before the war. (*He thinks resentfully*)

The war . . . Gordon! . . .

MARSDEN   Europe has "gone west"—(*He smiles whimsically*) to America, let's hope! (*Then frowningly*) I couldn't stand it. There were millions sitting up with the corpse already, who had a family right to be there—(*Then matter-of-factly*) I was wasting my time too. I couldn't write a line. (*Then gaily*) But where's Nina? I must see Nina!

PROFESSOR LEEDS   She'll be right in. She said she wanted to finish thinking something out— You'll find Nina changed, Charlie, greatly changed! (*He sighs—thinking with a trace of guilty alarm*)

The first thing she said at breakfast . . . "I dreamed of Gordon" . . . as if she wanted to taunt me! . . . how absurd! . . . her eyes positively glared! . . .

(*Suddenly blurting out resentfully*) She dreams about Gordon.

MARSDEN (*looking at him with amused surprise*)   Well, I'd hardly call that a change, would you?

PROFESSOR LEEDS (*thinking, oblivious to this remark*)

But I must constantly bear in mind that she's not herself . . . that she's a sick girl . . .

MARSDEN (*thinking*)

The morning news of Gordon's death came . . . her face like gray putty . . . beauty gone . . . no face can afford intense grief . . . it's only later when sorrow . . .

(*With concern*) Just what do you mean by changed, Professor? Before I left she seemed to be coming out of that horrible numbed calm.

PROFESSOR LEEDS (*slowly and carefully*)   Yes, she has played a lot of golf and tennis this summer, motored around with her friends, and even danced a good deal. And she eats with a ravenous appetite. (*Thinking frightenedly*)

Breakfast . . . "dreamed of Gordon" . . . what a look of hate for me in her eyes! . . .

MARSDEN   But that sounds splendid! When I left she wouldn't see anyone or go anywhere. (*Thinking pityingly*) Wandering from room to room . . . her thin body and pale lost face . . . gutted, love-abandoned eyes! . . .

PROFESSOR LEEDS   Well, now she's gone to the opposite extreme! Sees everyone—bores, fools—as if she'd lost all discrimination or wish to discriminate. And she talks interminably, Charlie—intentional nonsense, one would say! Refuses to be serious! Jeers at everything!

MARSDEN (*consolingly*)   Oh, that's all undoubtedly part of the effort she's making to forget.

PROFESSOR LEEDS (*absent-mindedly*)   Yes. (*Arguing with himself*) Shall I tell him? . . . no . . . it might sound silly . . . but it's terrible to be so alone in this . . . if Nina's mother had lived . . . my wife . . . dead! . . . and for a time I actually felt released! . . . wife! . . . help-meet! . . . now I need help! . . . no use! . . . she's gone! . . .

MARSDEN (*watching him—thinking with a condescending affection*) Good little man . . . he looks worried . . . always fussing about something . . . he must get on Nina's nerves. . . . (*Reassuringly*) No girl could forget Gordon in a hurry, especially after the shock of his tragic death.

PROFESSOR LEEDS (*irritably*)   I realize that. (*Thinking resentfully*) Gordon . . . always Gordon with everyone! . . .

MARSDEN   By the way, I located the spot near Sedan where Gordon's machine fell. Nina asked me to, you know.

PROFESSOR LEEDS (*irritated—expostulatingly*)   For heaven's sake, don't remind her! Give her a chance to forget if you want to see her well again. After all, Charlie, life must be lived and Nina can't live with a corpse forever! (*Trying to control his irritation and talk in an objective tone*) You see, I'm trying to see things through clearly and unsentimentally. If you'll remember, I was as broken up as anyone over Gordon's death. I'd become so reconciled to Nina's love for him—although, as you know, I was opposed at first, and for fair reasons, I think, for the boy, for all his good looks and prowess in sport and his courses, really came of common people and had no money of his own except as he made a career for himself.

MARSDEN (*a trifle defensively*) I'm sure he would have had a brilliant career.

PROFESSOR LEEDS (*impatiently*) No doubt. Although you must acknowledge, Charlie, that college heroes rarely shine brilliantly in after life. Unfortunately, the tendency to spoil them in the university is a poor training—

MARSDEN But Gordon was absolutely unspoiled, I should say.

PROFESSOR LEEDS (*heatedly*) Don't misunderstand me, Charlie! I'd be the first to acknowledge— (*A bit pathetically*) It isn't Gordon, Charlie. It's his memory, his ghost, you might call it, haunting Nina, whose influence I have come to dread because of the terrible change in her attitude toward me. (*His face twitches as if he were on the verge of tears—he thinks desperately*) I've got to tell him . . . he will see that I acted for the best . . . that I was justified. . . .

(*He hesitates—then blurts out*) It may sound incredible, but Nina has begun to act as if she hated me!

MARSDEN (*startled*) Oh, come now!

PROFESSOR LEEDS (*insistently*) Absolutely! I haven't wanted to admit it. I've refused to believe it, until it's become too appallingly obvious in her whole attitude toward me! (*His voice trembles*).

MARSDEN (*moved—expostulating*) Oh, now you're becoming morbid! Why, Nina has always idolized you! What possible reason—?

PROFESSOR LEEDS (*quickly*) I can answer that, I think. She has a reason. But why she should blame me when she must know I acted for the best— You probably don't know, but just before he sailed for the front Gordon wanted their marriage to take place, and Nina consented. In fact, from the insinuations she lets drop now, she must have been most eager, but at the time— However, I felt it was ill-advised and I took Gordon aside and pointed out to him that such a precipitate marriage would be unfair to Nina, and scarcely honorable on his part.

MARSDEN (*staring at him wonderingly*) You said that to Gordon? (*Thinking cynically*)
A shrewd move! . . . Gordon's proud spot, fairness and honor! . . . but was it honorable of you? . . .

PROFESSOR LEEDS (*with a touch of asperity*) Yes, I said it, and I gave him my reason. There *was* the possibility he might be killed, in the flying service rather more than a possibility, which needless to say, I did not point out, but which Gordon undoubtedly realized, poor boy! If he were killed, he would be leaving Nina a

widow, perhaps with a baby, with no resources, since he was
penniless, except what pension she might get from the government; and all this while she was still at an age when a girl,
especially one of Nina's charm and beauty, should have all of life
before her. Decidedly, I told him, in justice to Nina, they must
wait until he had come back and begun to establish his position
in the world. That was the square thing. And Gordon was quick
to agree with me!

MARSDEN (*thinking*)

The square thing! . . . but we must all be crooks where happiness is concerned! . . . steal or starve! . . .

(*Then rather ironically*) And so Gordon told Nina he'd suddenly
realized it wouldn't be fair to her. But I gather he didn't tell
her it was your scruple originally?

PROFESSOR LEEDS   No, I asked him to keep what I said strictly
confidential.

MARSDEN (*thinking ironically*)

Trusted to his honor again! . . . old fox! . . . poor Gordon! . . .
But Nina suspects now that you—?

PROFESSOR LEEDS (*startled*)   Yes. That's exactly it. She knows in
some queer way. And she acts toward me exactly as if she
thought I had deliberately destroyed her happiness, that I had
hoped for Gordon's death and been secretly overjoyed when the
news came! (*His voice is shaking with emotion*) And there you
have it, Charlie—the whole absurd mess! (*Thinking with a strident accusation*)

And it's true, you contemptible . . . !

(*Then miserably defending himself*)

No! . . . I acted unselfishly . . . for her sake! . . .

MARSDEN (*wonderingly*)   You don't mean to tell me she has ac-
cused you of all this?

PROFESSOR LEEDS   Oh, no, Charlie! Only by hints—looks—innuendos.
She knows she has no real grounds, but in the present state of
her mind the real and the unreal become confused—

MARSDEN (*thinking cynically*)

As always in all minds . . . or how could men live? . . .

(*Soothingly*) That's just what you ought to bear in your mind—
the state of hers—and not get so worked up over what I should
say is a combination of imagination on both your parts. (*He gets
to his feet as he hears voices from the right*) Buck up! This

must be Nina coming. (*The* PROFESSOR *gets to his feet, hastily composing his features into his bland, cultured expression*).

MARSDEN (*thinking self-mockingly but a bit worried about himself*)
My heart pounding! . . . seeing Nina again! . . . how senti-mental . . . how she'd laugh if she knew! . . . and quite rightly . . . absurd for me to react as if I loved . . . that way . . . her dear old Charlie . . . ha! . . .
(*He smiles with bitter self-mockery*)

PROFESSOR LEEDS (*thinking worriedly*)
I hope she won't make a scene . . . she's seemed on the verge all day . . . thank God, Charlie's like one of the family . . . but what a life for me! . . . with the opening of the new term only a few weeks off! . . . I can't do it . . . I'll have to call in a nerve specialist . . . but the last one did her no good . . . his outrageous fee . . . he can take it to court . . . I absolutely refuse . . . but if he should bring suit? . . . what a scandal . . . no, I'll have to pay . . . somehow . . . borrow . . . he has me in a corner, the robber! . . .

NINA (*enters and stands just inside the doorway looking directly at her father with defiant eyes, her face set in an expression of stubborn resolve. She is twenty, tall with broad square shoulders, slim strong hips and long beautifully developed legs—a fine athletic girl of the swimmer, tennis player, golfer type. Her straw-blond hair, framing her sunburned face, is bobbed. Her face is striking, handsome rather than pretty, the bone structure prominent, the forehead high, the lips of her rather large mouth clearly modelled above the firm jaw. Her eyes are beautiful and bewildering, extraordinarily large and a deep greenish blue. Since* GORDON's *death they have a quality of continually shuddering before some terrible enigma, of being wounded to their depths and made defiant and resentful by their pain. Her whole manner, the charged atmosphere she gives off, is totally at variance with her healthy outdoor physique. It is strained, nerve-racked, hectic, a terrible tension of will alone maintaining self-possession. She is dressed in smart sport clothes. Too preoccupied with her resolve to remember or see* MARSDEN, *she speaks directly to her father in a voice tensely cold and calm*) I have made up my mind, Father.

PROFESSOR LEEDS (*thinking distractedly*)
What does she mean? . . . oh, God help me! . . .
(*Flustered—hastily*) Don't you see Charlie, Nina?

MARSDEN (*troubled—thinking*)

She has changed . . . what has happened? . . .

(*He comes forward toward her—a bit embarrassed but affectionately using his pet name for her*) Hello, Nina Cara Nina! Are you trying to cut me dead, young lady?

NINA (*turning her eyes to* MARSDEN, *holding out her hand for him to shake, in her cool, preoccupied voice*) Hello, Charlie. (*Her eyes immediately return to her father*) Listen, Father!

MARSDEN (*standing near her, concealing his chagrin*)

That hurts! . . . I mean nothing! . . . but she's a sick girl . . . I must make allowance . . .

PROFESSOR LEEDS (*thinking distractedly*)

That look in her eyes! . . . hate! . . .

(*With a silly giggle*) Really, Nina, you're absolutely rude! What has Charlie done?

NINA (*in her cool tone*) Why, nothing. Nothing at all. (*She goes to him with a detached, friendly manner*) Did I seem rude, Charlie? I didn't mean to be. (*She kisses him with a cool, friendly smile*) Welcome home. (*Thinking wearily*)

What has Charlie done? . . . nothing . . . and never will . . . Charlie sits beside the fierce river, immaculately timid, cool and clothed, watching the burning, frozen naked swimmers drown at last. . . .

MARSDEN (*thinking torturedly*)

Cold lips . . . the kiss of contempt! . . . for dear old Charlie! . . .

(*Forcing a good-natured laugh*) Rude? Not a bit! (*Banteringly*) As I've often reminded you, what can I expect when the first word you ever spoke in this world was an insult to me. "Dog" you said, looking right at me—at the age of one! (*He laughs. The* PROFESSOR *laughs nervously.* NINA *smiles perfunctorily*).

NINA (*thinking wearily*)

The fathers laugh at little daughter Nina . . . I must get away! nice Charlie doggy . . . faithful . . . fetch and carry . . . bark softly in books at the deep night. . . .

PROFESSOR LEEDS (*thinking*)

What is she thinking? . . . I can't stand living like this! . . . (*Giggle gone to a twitching grin*) You are a cool one, Nina! You'd think you'd just seen Charlie yesterday!

NINA (*slowly—coolly and reflectively*) Well, the war is over.

Coming back safe from Europe isn't such an unusual feat now,
is it?

MARSDEN (*thinking bitterly*)

A taunt . . . I didn't fight . . . physically unfit . . . not like
Gordon . . . Gordon in flames . . . how she must resent my
living! . . . thinking of me, scribbling in press bureau . . . louder
and louder lies . . . drown the guns and the screams . . . deafen
the world with lies . . . hired choir of liars! . . .

(*Forcing a joking tone*) Little you know the deadly risks I ran,
Nina! If you'd eaten some of the food they gave me on my
renovated transport, you'd shower me with congratulations!
(*The* PROFESSOR *forces a snicker*).

NINA (*coolly*) Well, you're here, and that's that. (*Then suddenly
expanding in a sweet, genuinely affectionate smile*) And I *am*
glad, Charlie, always glad you're here! You know that.

MARSDEN (*delighted and embarrassed*) I hope so, Nina!

NINA (*turning on her father—determinedly*) I must finish what I
started to say, Father. I've thought it all out and decided that I
simply must get away from here at once—or go crazy! And I'm
going on the nine-forty tonight. (*She turns to* MARSDEN *with a
quick smile*) You'll have to help me pack, Charlie! (*Thinking
with weary relief*)

Now that's said . . . I'm going . . . never come back . . . oh,
how I loathe this room! . . .

MARSDEN (*thinking with alarm*)

What's this? . . . going? . . . going to whom? . . .

PROFESSOR LEEDS (*thinking—terrified*)

Going? . . . never come back to me? . . . no! . . .

(*Desperately putting on his prim severe manner toward an un-
ruly pupil*) This is rather a sudden decision, isn't it? You haven't
mentioned before that you were considering—in fact, you've led
me to believe that you were quite contented here—that is, of
course I mean for the time being, and I really think—

MARSDEN (*looking at* NINA—*thinking with alarm*)

Going away to whom? . . .

(*Then watching the* PROFESSOR *with a pitying shudder*)

He's on the wrong tack with his professor's manner . . . her
eyes seeing cruelly through him . . . with what terrible recognition! . . . God, never bless me with children! . . .

NINA (*thinking with weary scorn*)

The Professor of Dead Languages is talking again . . . a dead man lectures on the past of living . . . since I was born I have been in his class, loving-attentive, pupil-daughter Nina . . . my ears numb with spiritless messages from the dead . . . dead words droning on . . . listening because he is my cultured father . . . a little more inclined to deafness than the rest (let me be just) because he is my father . . . father? . . . what is father? . . .

PROFESSOR LEEDS (*thinking—terrified*)

I must talk her out of it! . . . find the right words! . . . oh, I know she won't hear me! . . . oh, wife, why did you die, you would have talked to her, she would have listened to you! . . . (*Continued in his professor's superior manner*) —and I really think, in justice to yourself above all, you ought to consider this step with great care before you definitely commit yourself. First and foremost, there is your health to be taken into consideration. You've been very ill, Nina, how perilously so perhaps you're not completely aware, but I assure you, and Charlie can corroborate my statement, that six months ago the doctors thought it might be years before—and yet, by staying home and resting and finding healthy outdoor recreation among your old friends, and keeping your mind occupied with the routine of managing the house-hold— (*He forces a prim playful smile*) and managing me, I might add!—you have wonderfully improved and I think it most ill-advised in the hottest part of August, while you're really still a convalescent—

NINA (*thinking*)

Talking! . . . his voice like a fatiguing dying tune droned on a beggar's organ . . . his words arising from the tomb of a soul in puffs of ashes . . .

(*Torturedly*)

Ashes! . . . oh, Gordon, my dear one! . . . oh, lips on my lips, oh, strong arms around me, oh, spirit so brave and generous and gay! . . . ashes dissolving into mud! . . . mud and ashes! . . . that's all! . . . gone! . . . gone forever from me! . . .

PROFESSOR LEEDS (*thinking angrily*)

Her eyes . . . I know that look . . . tender, loving . . . not for me . . . damn Gordon! . . . I'm glad he's dead! . . .

(*A touch of asperity in his voice*) And at a couple of hours' notice to leave everything in the air, as it were— (*Then judicially*) No, Nina, frankly, I can't see it. You know I'd gladly consent to anything in the world to benefit you, but—surely, you can't have reflected!

NINA (*thinking torturedly*)

Gordon darling, I must go away where I can think of you in silence! . . .

(*She turns on her father, her voice trembling with the effort to keep it in control—icily*) It's no use talking, Father. I *have* reflected and I am going!

PROFESSOR LEEDS (*with asperity*)  But I tell you it's quite impossible! I don't like to bring up the money consideration but I couldn't possibly afford— And how will you support yourself, if I may ask? Two years in the University, I am sorry to say, won't be much use to you when applying for a job. And even if you had completely recovered from your nervous breakdown, which it's obvious to anyone you haven't, then I most decidedly think you should finish out your science course and take your degree before you attempt—

(*Thinking desperately*)

No use! . . . she doesn't hear . . . thinking of Gordon . . . she'll defy me . . .

NINA (*thinking desperately*)

I must keep calm . . . I mustn't let go or I'll tell him everything . . . and I mustn't tell him . . . he's my father . . .

(*With the same cold calculating finality*) I've already had six months' training for a nurse. I will finish my training. There's a doctor I know at a sanitarium for crippled soldiers—a friend of Gordon's. I wrote to him and he answered that he'll gladly arrange it.

PROFESSOR LEEDS (*thinking furiously*)

Gordon's friend . . . Gordon again! . . .

(*Severely*) You seriously mean to tell me you, in your condition, want to nurse in a soldiers' hospital! Absurd!

MARSDEN (*thinking with indignant revulsion*)

Quite right, Professor! . . . her beauty . . . all those men . . . in their beds . . . it's too revolting! . . .

(*With a persuasive quizzing tone*) Yes, I must say I can't see you as a peace-time Florence Nightingale, Nina!

NINA (*coolly, struggling to keep control, ignoring these remarks*)

So you see, Father, I've thought of everything and there's not the slightest reason to worry about me. And I've been teaching Mary how to take care of you. So you won't need me at all. You can go along as if nothing had happened—and really, nothing will have happened that hasn't already happened.

PROFESSOR LEEDS  Why, even the manner in which you address me—the tone you take—proves conclusively that you're not yourself!

NINA (*her voice becoming a bit uncanny, her thoughts breaking through*)  No, I'm not myself yet. That's just it. Not all myself. But I've been becoming myself. And I must finish!

PROFESSOR LEEDS (*with angry significance—to* MARSDEN)  You hear her, Charlie? She's a sick girl!

NINA (*slowly and strangely*)  I'm not sick. I'm too well. But they are sick and I must give my health to help them to live on, and to live on myself. (*With a sudden intensity in her tone*)  I must pay for my cowardly treachery to Gordon! You should understand this, Father, you who— (*She swallows hard, catching her breath*)

(*Thinking desperately*)

I'm beginning to tell him! . . . I mustn't! . . . he's my father! . . .

PROFESSOR LEEDS (*in a panic of guilty fear, but defiantly*)  What do you mean? I am afraid you're not responsible for what you're saying.

NINA (*again with the strange intensity*)  I must pay! It's my plain duty! Gordon is dead! What use is my life to me or anyone? But I must make it of use—by giving it! (*Fiercely*)  I must learn to give myself, do you hear—give and give until I can make that gift of myself for a man's happiness without scruple, without fear, without joy except in his joy! When I've accomplished this I'll have found myself, I'll know how to start in living my own life again! (*Appealing to them with a desperate impatience*)  Don't you see? In the name of the commonest decency and honor, I owe it to Gordon!

PROFESSOR LEEDS (*sharply*)  No, I can't see—nor anyone else!

(*Thinking savagely*)

I hope Gordon is in hell! . . .

MARSDEN (*thinking*)

Give herself? . . . can she mean her body? . . . beautiful body . . . to cripples? . . . for Gordon's sake? . . . damn Gordon! . . .

(*Coldly*)  What do you mean, you owe it to Gordon, Nina?

PROFESSOR LEEDS (*bitterly*)  Yes, how ridiculous! It seems to me when you gave him your love, he got more than he could ever have hoped—

NINA (*with fierce self-contempt*)  I gave him? What did I give him? It's what I didn't give! That last night before he sailed—

in his arms until my body ached—kisses until my lips were
numb—knowing all that night—something in me knowing he
would die, that he would never kiss me again—knowing this
so surely yet with my cowardly brain lying, no, he'll come back
and marry you, you'll be happy ever after and feel his children
at your breast looking up with eyes so much like his, possessing
eyes so happy in possessing you! (*Then violently*) But Gordon
never possessed me! I'm still Gordon's silly virgin! And Gordon
is muddy ashes! And I've lost my happiness forever! All that
last night I knew he wanted me. I knew it was only the
honorable code-bound Gordon, who kept commanding from his
brain, no, you mustn't, you must respect her, you must wait
til you have a marriage license! (*She gives a mocking laugh*).

PROFESSOR LEEDS (*shocked*) Nina! This is really going too far!

MARSDEN (*repelled—with a superior sneer*) Oh, come now, Nina!
You've been reading books. Those don't sound like your thoughts.

NINA (*without looking at him, her eyes on her father's—intensely*)
Gordon wanted me! I wanted Gordon! I should have made him
take me! I knew he would die and I would have no children, that
there would be no big Gordon or little Gordon left to me, that
happiness was calling me, never to call again if I refused! And
yet I did refuse! I didn't make him take me! I lost him forever!
And now I am lonely and not pregnant with anything at all,
but—but loathing! (*She hurls this last at her father—fiercely*)
Why did I refuse? What was that cowardly something in me
that cried, no, you mustn't, what would your father say?

PROFESSOR LEEDS (*thinking—furiously*)
What an animal! . . . and my daughter! . . . she doesn't get it
from me! . . . was her mother like that? . . .
(*Distractedly*) Nina! I really can't listen!

NINA (*savagely*) And that's exactly what my father did say! Wait,
he told Gordon! Wait for Nina till the war's over, and you've
got a good job and can afford a marriage license!

PROFESSOR LEEDS (*crumbling pitifully*) Nina! I—!

MARSDEN (*flurriedly—going to him*) Don't take her seriously,
Professor! (*Thinking with nervous repulsion*)
Nina has changed . . . all flesh now . . . lust . . . who would
dream she was so sensual? . . . I wish I were out of this! . . .
I wish I hadn't come here today! . . .

NINA (*coldly and deliberately*) Don't lie any more, Father! Today I've made up my mind to face things. I know now why

Gordon suddenly dropped all idea of marriage before he left, how unfair to me he suddenly decided it would be! Unfair to me! Oh, that's humorous! To think I might have had happiness, Gordon, and now Gordon's child— (*Then directly accusing him*) You told him it'd be unfair, you put him on his honor, didn't you?

PROFESSOR LEEDS (*collecting himself—woodenly*) Yes. I did it for your sake, Nina.

NINA (*in the same voice as before*) It's too late for lies!

PROFESSOR LEEDS (*woodenly*) Let us say then that I *persuaded* myself it was for your sake. That may be true. You are young. You think one can live with truth. Very well. It is also true I was jealous of Gordon. I was alone and I wanted to keep your love. I hated him as one hates a thief one may not accuse nor punish. I did my best to prevent your marriage. I was glad when he died. There. Is that what you wish me to say?

NINA Yes. Now I begin to forget I've hated you. You were braver than I, at least.

PROFESSOR LEEDS I wanted to live comforted by your love until the end. In short, I am a man who happens to be your father. (*He hides his face in his hands and weeps softly*) Forgive that man!

MARSDEN (*thinking timidly*)

In short, forgive us our possessing as we forgive those who possessed before us . . . Mother must be wondering what keeps me so long . . . it's time for tea . . . I must go home . . .

NINA (*sadly*) Oh, I forgive you. But do you understand now that I must somehow find a way to give myself to Gordon still, that I must pay my debt and learn to forgive myself?

PROFESSOR LEEDS Yes.

NINA Mary will look after you.

PROFESSOR LEEDS Mary will do very well, I'm sure.

MARSDEN (*thinking*)

Nina has changed . . . this is no place for me . . . Mother is waiting tea. . . .

(*Then venturing on an uncertain tone of pleasantry*) Quite so, you two. But isn't this all nonsense? Nina will be back with us in a month, Professor, what with the depressing heat and humidity, and the more depressing halt and the lame!

PROFESSOR LEEDS (*sharply*) She must stay away until he gets well. This time I do speak for her sake.

NINA I'll take the nine-forty. (*Turning to* MARSDEN—*with a sudden girlishness*) Come on upstairs, Charlie, and help me pack. (*She grabs him by the hand and starts to pull him away*).

MARSDEN (*shrugging his shoulders—confusedly*) Well—I don't understand this!

NINA (*with a strange smile*) But some day I'll read it all in one of your books, Charlie, and it'll be so simple and easy to understand that I won't be able to recognize it, Charlie, let alone understand it! (*She laughs teasingly*) Dear old Charlie!

MARSDEN (*thinking in agony*)

God damn in hell . . . dear old Charlie! . . .

(*Then with a genial grin*) I'll have to propose, Nina, if you continue to be my severest critic! I'm a stickler for these little literary conventions, you know!

NINA All right. Propose while we pack. (*She leads him off, right*).

PROFESSOR LEEDS (*blows his nose, wipes his eyes, sighs, clears his throat, squares his shoulders, pulls his coat down in front, sets his tie straight, and starts to take a brisk turn about the room. His face is washed blandly clean of all emotion*)

Three weeks now . . . new term . . . I will have to be looking over my notes. . . .

(*He looks out of window, front*)

Grass parched in the middle . . . Tom forgotten the sprinkler . . . careless . . . ah, there goes Mr. Davis of the bank . . . bank . . . my salary will go farther now . . . books I really need . . . all bosh two can live as cheaply as one . . . there are worse things than being a trained nurse . . . good background of discipline . . . she needs it . . . she may meet rich fellow there . . . mature . . . only students here for her . . . and their fathers never approve if they have anything. . . .

(*He sits down with a forced sigh of peace*)

I am glad we had it out . . . his ghost will be gone now . . . no more Gordon, Gordon, Gordon, love and praise and tears, all for Gordon! . . . Mary will do very well by me . . . I will have more leisure and peace of mind . . . and Nina will come back home . . . when she is well again . . . the old Nina! . . . my little Nina! . . . she knows and she forgave me . . . she said so . . . said! . . . but could she really? . . . don't you imagine? . . . deep in her heart? . . . She still must hate? . . . oh, God! . . . I feel cold! . . . alone! . . . this home is abandoned! . . .

the house is empty and full of death! . . . there is a pain about
my heart! . . .

(*He calls hoarsely, getting to his feet*) Nina!

NINA'S VOICE (*her voice, fresh and girlish, calls from upstairs*)
Yes, Father. Do you want me?

PROFESSOR LEEDS (*struggling with himself—goes to door and calls
with affectionate blandness*) No. Never mind. Just wanted to
remind you to call for a taxi in good time.

NINA'S VOICE I won't forget.

PROFESSOR LEEDS (*looks at his watch*)
Five-thirty just . . . nine-forty, the train . . . then . . . Nina no
more! . . . four hours more . . . she'll be packing . . . then
good-bye . . . a kiss . . . nothing more ever to say to each
other . . . and I'll die in here some day . . . alone . . . gasp,
cry out for help . . . the president will speak at the funeral . . .
Nina will be here again . . . Nina in black . . . too late! . . .
(*He calls hoarsely*) Nina! (*There is no answer*)
In other room . . . doesn't hear . . . just as well . . .
(*He turns to the bookcase and pulls out the first volume his
hands come on and opens it at random and begins to read aloud
sonorously like a child whistling to keep up his courage in the
dark*)
"Stetit unus in arcem
Erectus capitis victorque ad sidera mittit
Sidereos oculos propiusque adspectat Olympum
Inquiritque Iovem;" . . .

*Curtain*


ACT TWO

SCENE: *The same as Scene One,* PROFESSOR LEEDS' *study. It is
about nine o'clock of a night in early fall, over a year later. The appearance of the room is unchanged except that all the shades, of
the color of pale flesh, are drawn down, giving the windows a
suggestion of lifeless closed eyes and making the room seem more
withdrawn from life than before. The reading lamp on the table*

*is lit. Everything on the table, papers, pencils, pens, etc., is arranged in meticulous order.*

MARSDEN *is seated on the chair at center. He is dressed carefully in an English made suit of blue serge so dark as to seem black, and which, combined with the gloomy brooding expression of his face, strongly suggests one in mourning. His tall, thin body sags wearily in the chair, his head is sunk forward, the chin almost touching his chest, his eyes stare sadly at nothing.*

MARSDEN (*his thoughts at ebb, without emphasis, sluggish and melancholy*)
Prophetic Professor! . . . I remember he once said . . . shortly after Nina went away . . . "some day, in here, . . . you'll find me" . . . did he forsee? . . . no . . . everything in life is so contemptuously accidental! . . . God's sneer at our self-importance! . . .
(*Smiling grimly*)
Poor Professor! he was horribly lonely . . . tried to hide it . . . always telling you how beneficial the training at the hospital would be for her . . . poor old chap! . . .
(*His voice grows husky and uncertain—he controls it—straightens himself*)
What time is it? . . .
(*He takes out his watch mechanically and looks at it*)
Ten after nine. . . . Nina ought to be here. . . .
(*Then with sudden bitterness*)
Will she feel any real grief over his death, I wonder? . . . I doubt it! . . . but why am I so resentful? . . . the two times I've visited the hospital she's been pleasant enough . . . pleasantly evasive! . . . perhaps she thought her father had sent me to spy on her . . . poor Professor! . . . at least she answered his letters . . . he used to show them to me . . . pathetically overjoyed . . . newsy, loveless scripts, telling nothing whatever about herself . . . well, she won't have to compose them any more . . . she never answered mine . . . she might at least have acknowledged them. . . . Mother thinks she's behaved quite inexcusably . . .
(*Then jealously*)
I suppose every single damned inmate has fallen in love with her! . . . her eyes seemed cynical . . . sick with men . . . as though I'd looked into the eyes of a prostitute . . . not that I

ever have . . . except that once . . . the dollar house . . . hers
were like patent leather buttons in a saucer of blue milk! . . .
(*Getting up with a movement of impatience*)
The devil! . . . what beastly incidents our memories insist on
cherishing! . . . the ugly and disgusting . . . the beautiful things
we have to keep diaries to remember! . . .
(*He smiles with a wry amusement for a second—then bitterly*)
That last night Nina was here . . . she talked so brazenly about
giving herself . . . I wish I knew the truth of what she's been
doing in that house full of men . . . particularly that self-important young ass of a doctor! . . . Gordon's friend! . . .
(*He frowns at himself, determinedly puts an end to his train of
thought and comes and sits down again in the chair—in sneering,
conversational tones as if he were this time actually addressing
another person*)
Really, it's hardly a decent time, is it, for that kind of specula-
tion . . . with her father lying dead upstairs? . . .
(*A silence as if he had respectably squelched himself—then he
pulls out his watch mechanically and stares at it. As he does so
a noise of a car is heard approaching, stopping at the curb
beyond the garden. He jumps to his feet and starts to go to
door—then hesitates confusedly*)
No, let Mary go . . . I wouldn't know what to do . . . take her
in my arms? . . . kiss her? . . . right now? . . . or wait until
she? . . .
(*A bell rings insistently from the back of the house. From the
front voices are heard, first* NINA's, *then a man's.* MARSDEN *starts,
his face suddenly angry and dejected*)
Someone with her! . . . a man! . . . I thought she'd be alone! . . .
(MARY *is heard shuffling to the front door which is opened.
Immediately, as* MARY *sees* NINA, *she breaks down and there is
the sound of her uncontrolled sobbing and choking, incoherent
words drowning out* NINA's *voice, soothing her*).
NINA (*as* MARY's *grief subsides a trifle, her voice is heard, flat and
toneless*) Isn't Mr. Marsden here, Mary? (*She calls*) Charlie!
MARSDEN (*confused—huskily*) In here—I'm in the study, Nina.
(*He moves uncertainly toward the door*).
NINA (*comes in and stands just inside the doorway. She is dressed
in a nurse's uniform with cap, a raglan coat over it. She appears
older than in the previous scene, her face is pale and much thinner, her cheek bones stand out, her mouth is taut in hard lines*

of a cynical scorn. *Her eyes try to armor her wounded spirit with a defensive stare of disillusionment. Her training has also tended to coarsen her fiber a trifle, to make her insensitive to suffering, to give her the nurse's professionally callous attitude. In her fight to regain control of her nerves she has over-striven after the cool and efficient poise, but she is really in a more highly strung, disorganized state than ever, although she is now more capable of suppressing and concealing it. She remains strikingly handsome and her physical appeal is enhanced by her pallor and the mysterious suggestion about her of hidden experience. She stares at* MARSDEN *blankly and speaks in queer flat tones*) Hello, Charlie. He's dead, Mary says.

MARSDEN (*nodding his head several times—stupidly*) Yes.

NINA (*in same tones*) It's too bad. I brought Doctor Darrell. I thought there might be a chance. (*She pauses and looks about the room—thinking confusedly*)
His books . . . his chair . . . he always sat there . . . there's his table . . . little Nina was never allowed to touch anything . . . she used to sit on his lap . . . cuddle against him . . . dreaming into the dark beyond the windows . . . warm in his arms before the fireplace . . . dreams like sparks soaring up to die in the cold dark . . . warm in his love, safe-drifting into sleep . . . "Daddy's girl, aren't you?" . . .
(*She looks around and then up and down*)
His home . . . my home . . . he was my father . . . he's dead . . .
(*She shakes her head*)
Yes, I hear you, little Nina, but I don't understand one word of it. . . .
(*She smiles with a cynical self-contempt*)
I'm sorry, Father! . . . you see you've been dead for me a long time . . . when Gordon died, all men died . . . what did you feel for me then? . . . nothing . . . and now I feel nothing . . . it's too bad . . .

MARSDEN (*thinking woundedly*)
I hoped she would throw herself in my arms . . . weeping . . . hide her face on my shoulder . . . "Oh, Charlie, you're all I've got left in the world . . ."
(*Then angrily*)
Why did she have to bring that Darrell with her?

NINA (*flatly*) When I said good-bye that night I had a premonition I'd never see him again.

MARSDEN (*glad of this opening for moral indignation*) You've never tried to see him, Nina! (*Then overcome by disgust with himself—contritely*) Forgive me! It was rotten of me to say that!

NINA (*shaking her head—flatly*) I didn't want him to see what he would have thought was me. (*Ironically*) That's the other side of it you couldn't dissect into words from here, Charlie! (*Then suddenly asking a necessary question in her nurse's cool, efficient tones*) Is he upstairs? (*Marsden nods stupidly*) I'll take Ned up. I might as well. (*She turns and walks out briskly*).

MARSDEN (*staring after her—dully*)

That isn't Nina. . . .

(*Indignantly*)

They've killed her soul down there! . . .

(*Tears come to his eyes suddenly and he pulls out his handkerchief and wipes them, muttering huskily*)

Poor old Professor! . . .

(*Then suddenly jeering at himself*)

For God's sake, stop acting! . . . it isn't the Professor! . . . dear old Charlie is crying because she didn't weep on his shoulder . . . as he had hoped! . . .

(*He laughs harshly—then suddenly sees a man outside the doorway and stares—then calls sharply*) Who's that?

EVANS (*his voice embarrassed and hesitating comes from the hall*) It's all right. (*He appears in the doorway, grinning bashfully*) It's me—I, I mean—Miss Leeds told me to come in here. (*He stretches out his hand awkwardly*) Guess you don't remember me, Mr. Marsden. Miss Leeds introduced us one day at the hospital. You were leaving just as I came in. Evans is my name.

MARSDEN (*who has been regarding him with waning resentment, forces a cordial smile and shakes hands*) Oh, yes. At first I couldn't place you.

EVANS (*awkwardly*) I sort of feel I'm butting in.

MARSDEN (*beginning to be taken by his likable boyish quality*) Not at all. Sit down. (*He sits in the rocker at center as EVANS goes to the bench at right. EVANS sits uncomfortably hunched forward, twiddling his hat in his hands. He is above the medium height, very blond, with guileless, diffident blue eyes, his figure inclined to immature lumbering outlines. His face is fresh and red-cheeked, handsome in a boyish fashion. His manner is bashful with women or older men, coltishly playful with his friends. There is a lack of self-confidence, a lost and strayed appealing air about him, yet with a hint of some unawakened obstinate force beneath his apparent weakness. Although he is twenty-five and has been out of college three years, he still wears the latest in collegiate clothes and as he looks younger than he is, he is always mistaken for an undergraduate and likes to be. It keeps him placed in life for himself).*

MARSDEN (*studying him keenly—amused*)

This is certainly no giant intellect . . . overgrown boy . . . likable quality though . . .

EVANS (*uneasy under* MARSDEN's *eyes*)

Giving me the once-over . . . seems like good egg . . . Nina says he is . . . suppose I ought to say something about his books, but I can't even remember a title of one . . .

(*He suddenly blurts out*) You've known Nina—Miss Leeds—ever since she was a kid, haven't you?

MARSDEN (*a bit shortly*) Yes. How long have you known her?

EVANS Well—really only since she's been at the hospital, although I met her once years ago at a Prom with Gordon Shaw.

MARSDEN (*indifferently*) Oh, you knew Gordon?

EVANS (*proudly*) Sure thing! I was in his class! (*With admiration amounting to hero-worship*) He sure was a wonder, wasn't he?

MARSDEN (*cynically*)

Gordon über alles and forever! . . . I begin to appreciate the Professor's viewpoint . . .

(*Casually*) A fine boy! Did you know him well?

EVANS No. The crowd he went with were mostly fellows who were good at sports—and I always was a dud. (*Forcing a smile*) I was always one of the first to get bounced off the squad in any sport. (*Then with a flash of humble pride*) But I never quit trying, anyway!

MARSDEN (*consolingly*) Well, the sport hero usually doesn't star after college.

EVANS Gordon did! (*Eagerly—with intense admiration*) In the war! He was an ace! And he always fought just as cleanly as he'd played football! Even the Huns respected him!

MARSDEN (*thinking cynically*)

This Gordon worshipper must be the apple of Nina's eye!

(*Casually*) Were you in the army?

EVANS (*shamefacedly*) Yes—infantry—but I never got to the front —never saw anything exciting. (*Thinking glumly*)

Won't tell him I tried for flying service . . . wanted to get in Gordon's outfit . . . couldn't make the physical exam. . . . never made anything I wanted . . . suppose I'll lose out with Nina, too . . .

(*Then rallying himself*)

Hey, you! . . . what's the matter with you? . . . don't quit! . . .

MARSDEN (*who has been staring him inquisitively*) How did you happen to come out here tonight?

EVANS I was calling on Nina when your wire came. Ned thought I better come along, too—might be of some use.

MARSDEN (*frowning*) You mean Doctor Darrell? (EVANS *nods*) Is he a close friend of yours?

EVANS (*hesitatingly*) Well, sort of. Roomed in the same dorm with me at college. He was a senior when I was a freshman. Used to help me along in lots of ways. Took pity on me, I was so green. Then about a year ago when I went to the hospital to visit a fellow who'd been in my outfit I ran into him again. (*Then with a grin*) But I wouldn't say Ned was close to anyone. He's a dyed-in-the-wool doc. He's only close to whatever's the matter with you! (*He chuckles—then hastily*) But don't get me wrong about him. He's the best egg ever! You know him, don't you?

MARSDEN (*stiffly*) Barely. Nina introduced us once. (*Thinking bitterly*)

He's upstairs alone with her . . . I hoped it would be I who . . .

EVANS Don't want him to get the wrong idea of Ned . . . Ned's my best friend . . . doing all he can to help me with Nina . . . he thinks she'll marry me in the end . . . God, if she only would! . . . I wouldn't expect her to love me at first . . . be happy only to take care of her . . . cook her breakfast . . . bring it up to her in bed . . . tuck the pillows behind her . . . comb her hair for her . . . I'd be happy just to kiss her hair! . . .

MARSDEN (*agitated—thinking suspiciously*)

What are Darrell's relations with Nina? . . . close to what's the matter with her? . . . damned thoughts! . . . why should I care? . . . I'll ask this Evans . . . pump him while I have a chance . . .

(*With forced indifference*) Is your friend, the Doctor, "close" to Miss Leeds? She's had quite a lot the matter with her since her breakdown, if that's what interests him! (*He smiles casually*).

EVANS (*gives a start, awakening from his dream*) Oh—er—yes. He's always trying to bully her into taking better care of herself, but she only laughs at him. (*Soberly*) It'd be much better if she'd take his advice.

MARSDEN (*suspiciously*)  No doubt.

EVANS (*pronounces with boyish solemnity*)  She isn't herself, Mr. Marsden. And I think nursing all those poor guys keeps the war before her when she ought to forget it. She ought to give up nursing and be nursed for a change, that's my idea.

MARSDEN (*struck by this—eagerly*)  Exactly my opinion. (*Thinking*)

If she'd settle down here . . . I could come over every day . . . I'd nurse her . . . Mother home . . . Nina here . . . how I could work then! . . .

EVANS (*thinking*)

He certainly seems all for me . . . so far! . . .

(*Then in a sudden flurry*)

Shall I tell him? . . . he'll be like her guardian now . . . I've got to know how he stands . . .

(*He starts with a solemn earnestness*) Mr. Marsden, I—there's something I ought to tell you, I think. You see, Nina's talked a lot about you. I know how much she thinks of you. And now her old man— (*He hesitates in confusion*) I mean, her father's dead—

MARSDEN (*in a sort of panic—thinking*)

What's this? . . . proposal? . . . in form? . . . for her hand? . . . to me? . . . Father Charlie now, eh? . . . ha! . . . God, what a fool! . . . does he imagine she'd ever love him? . . . but she might . . . not bad looking . . . likable, innocent . . . something to mother . . .

EVANS (*blundering on regardless now*)  I know it's hardly the proper time—

MARSDEN (*interrupting—dryly*)  Perhaps I can anticipate. You want to tell me you're in love with Nina?

EVANS  Yes, sir, and I've asked her to marry me.

MARSDEN  What did she say?

EVANS (*sheepishly*)  Nothing. She just smiled.

MARSDEN (*with relief*)  Ah. (*Then harshly*) Well, what could you expect? Surely you must know she still loves Gordon?

EVANS (*manfully*)  Sure I know it—and I admire her for it! Most girls forget too easily. She ought to love Gordon for a long time yet. And I know I'm an awful wash-out compared to him—but I love her as much as he did, or anyone could! And I'll work my way up for her—I know I can!—so I can give her everything she wants. And I wouldn't ask for anything in return except the right to take care of her. (*Blurts out confusedly*) I never think of her—that way—she's too beautiful and wonderful—not that I don't hope she'd come to love me in time—

MARSDEN (*sharply*) And just what do you expect me to do about all this?

EVANS (*taken aback*) Why—er—nothing, sir. I just thought you ought to know. (*Sheepishly he glances up at ceiling, then down at floor, twiddling his hat*).

MARSDEN (*thinking—at first with a grudging appreciation and envy*) He thinks he means that . . . pure love! . . . it's easy to talk . . . he doesn't know life . . . but he might be good for Nina . . . if she were married to this simpleton would she be faithful? . . . and then I? . . . what a vile thought! . . . I don't mean that! . . .

(*Then forcing a kindly tone*) You see, there's really nothing I can do about it. (*With a smile*) If Nina will, she will—and if she won't, she won't. But I can wish you good luck.

EVANS (*immediately all boyish gratitude*) Thanks! That's darn fine of you, Mr. Marsden!

MARSDEN But I think we'd better let the subject drop, don't you? We're forgetting that her father—

EVANS (*guiltily embarrassed*) Yes—sure—I'm a damn fool! Excuse me! (*There is the noise of steps from the hall and* DOCTOR EDMUND DARRELL *enters. He is twenty-seven, short, dark, wiry, his movements rapid and sure, his manner cool and observant, his dark eyes analytical. His head is handsome and intelligent. There is a quality about him, provoking and disturbing to women, of intense passion which he has rigidly trained himself to control and set free only for the objective satisfaction of studying his own and their reactions; and so he has come to consider himself as immune to love through his scientific understanding of its real sexual nature. He sees* EVANS *and* MARSDEN, *nods at* MARSDEN *silently, who returns it coldly, goes to the table and taking a prescription pad from his pocket, hastily scratches on it*).

MARSDEN (*thinking sneeringly*)

Amusing, these young doctors! . . . perspire with the effort to appear cool! . . . writing a prescription . . . cough medicine for the corpse, perhaps! . . . good-looking? . . . more or less . . . attractive to women, I dare say. . . .

DARRELL (*tears it off—hands it to* EVANS) Here, Sam. Run along up the street and get this filled.

EVANS (*with relief*) Sure. Glad of the chance for a walk. (*He goes out, rear*).

DARRELL (*turning to* MARSDEN) It's for Nina. She's got to get some sleep tonight. (*He sits down abruptly in the chair at center.* MARSDEN *unconsciously takes the* PROFESSOR's *place behind the table. The two men stare at each other for a moment,* DARRELL *with a frank probing, examining look that ruffles* MARSDEN *and makes him all the more resentful toward him*)

This Marsden doesn't like me . . . that's evident . . . but he interests me . . . read his books . . . wanted to know his bearing on Nina's case . . . his novels just well-written surface . . . no depth, no digging underneath . . . why? . . . has the talent but doesn't dare . . . afraid he'll meet himself somewhere . . . one of those poor devils who spend their lives trying not to discover which sex they belong to! . . .

MARSDEN

Giving me the fishy, diagnosing eye they practice at medical school . . . like freshmen from Ioway cultivating broad A's at Harvard! . . . what is his specialty? . . . neurologist, I think . . . I hope not psychoanalyst . . . a lot to account for, Herr Freud! . . . punishment to fit his crimes, be forced to listen eternally during breakfast while innumerable plain ones tell him dreams about snakes . . . pah, what an easy cure-all! . . . sex the philosopher's stone . . . "O Oedipus, O my king! The world is adopting you!" . . .

DARRELL

Must pitch into him about Nina . . . have to have his help . . . damn little time to convince him . . . he's the kind you have to explode a bomb under to get them to move . . . but not too big a bomb . . . they blow to pieces easily . . .

(*Brusquely*) Nina's gone to pot again! Not that her father's death is a shock in the usual sense of grief. I wish to God it were! No, it's a shock because it's finally convinced her she can't feel anything any more. That's what she's doing upstairs now—trying to goad herself into feeling something!

MARSDEN (*resentfully*) I think you're mistaken. She loved her father—

DARRELL (*shortly and dryly*) We can't waste time being sentimental, Marsden! She'll be down any minute, and I've got a lot
to talk over with you. (*As* MARSDEN *seems again about to protest*)
Nina has a real affection for you and I imagine you have for her.
Then you'll want as much as I do to get her straightened out.
She's a corking girl. She ought to have every chance for a happy
life. (*Then sharply driving his words in*) But the way she's
conditioned now, there's no chance. She's piled on too many
destructive experiences. A few more and she'll dive for the
gutter just to get the security that comes from knowing she's
touched bottom and there's no farther to go!

MARSDEN (*revolted and angry, half-springs to his feet*) Look here,
Darrell, I'll be damned if I'll listen to such a ridiculous statement!

DARRELL (*curtly—with authority*) How do you know it's ridiculous? What do you know of Nina since she left home? But she
hadn't been nursing with us three days before I saw she really
ought to be a patient; and ever since then I've studied her case.
So I think it's up to you to listen.

MARSDEN (*freezingly*) I'm listening. (*With apprehensive terror*)
Gutter . . . has she . . . I wish he wouldn't tell me! . . .

DARRELL (*thinking*)
How much need I tell him? . . . can't tell him the raw truth
about her promiscuity . . . he isn't built to face reality . . . no
writer is outside of his books . . . have to tone it down for him
. . . but not too much! . . .
Nina has been giving way more and more to a morbid longing
for martyrdom. The reason for it is obvious. Gordon went away
without—well, let's say marrying her. The war killed him. She
was left suspended. Then she began to blame herself and to
want to sacrifice herself and at the same time give happiness to
various fellow war-victims by pretending to love them. It's a
pretty idea but it hasn't worked out. Nina's a bad actress. She
hasn't convinced the men of her love—or herself of her good
intentions. And each experience of this kind has only left her
more a prey to a guilty conscience than before and more determined to punish herself!

MARSDEN (*thinking*)
What does he mean? . . . how far did she? . . . how many? . . .
(*Coldly and sneeringly*) May I ask on what specific actions of
hers this theory of yours is based?

DARRELL (*coldly in turn*) On her evident craving to make an exhibition of kissing, necking, petting—whatever you call it—spooning in general—with any patient in the institution who got a case on her! (*Ironically—thinking*)
Spooning! . . . rather a mild word for her affairs . . . but strong enough for this lady-like soul. . . .

MARSDEN (*bitterly*)
He's lying! . . . what's he trying to hide? . . . was he one of them? . . . her lover? . . . I must get her away from him . . . get her to marry Evans! . . .
(*With authority*) Then she mustn't go back to your hospital, that's certain!

DARRELL (*quickly*) You're quite right. And that brings me to what I want you to urge to her to do.

MARSDEN (*thinking suspiciously*)
He doesn't want her back . . . I must have been wrong . . . but there might be many reasons why he'd wish to get rid of her . . .
(*Coldly*) I think you exaggerate my influence.

DARRELL (*eagerly*) Not a bit. You're the last link connecting her with the girl she used to be before Gordon's death. You're closely associated in her mind with that period of happy security, of health and peace of mind. I know that from the way she talks about you. You're the only person she still respects—and really loves. (*As* MARSDEN *starts guiltily and glances at him in confusion—with a laugh*) Oh, you needn't look frightened. I mean the sort of love she'd feel for an uncle.

MARSDEN (*thinking in agony*)
Frightened? . . . was I? . . . only person she loves . . . and then he said "love she'd feel for an uncle" . . . Uncle Charlie now! . . . God damn him! . . .

DARREL (*eyeing him*)
Looks damnably upset . . . wants to evade all responsibility for her, I suppose . . . he's that kind . . . all the better! . . . he'll be only too anxious to get her safely married. . . .
(*Bluntly*) And that's why I've done all this talking. You've got to help snap her out of this.

MARSDEN (*bitterly*) And how, if I may ask?

DARRELL There's only one way I can see. Get her to marry Sam Evans.

MARSDEN (*astonished*) Evans? (*He makes a silly gesture toward the door—thinking confusedly*)

Wrong again . . . why does he want her married to . . . it's
some trick . . .

DARRELL    Yes, Evans. He's in love with her. And it's one of those
unselfish loves you read about. And she is fond of him. In a maternal way, of course—but that's just what she needs now, someone she cares about to mother and boss and keep her occupied.
And still more important, this would give her a chance to have
children. She's got to find normal outlets for her craving for
sacrifice. She needs normal love objects for the emotional life
Gordon's death blocked up in her. Now marrying Sam ought to do
the trick. Ought to. Naturally, no one can say for certain. But
I think his unselfish love, combined with her real liking for him.
will gradually give her back a sense of security and a feeling of
being worth something to life again, and once she's got that,
she'll be saved! (*He has spoken with persuasive feeling. He asks
anxiously*) Doesn't that seem good sense to you?

MARSDEN    (*suspicious—dryly non-committal*)    I'm sorry but I'm in
no position to say. I don't know anything about Evans, for one
thing.

DARRELL    (*emphatically*)    Well, I do. He's a fine healthy boy, clean
and unspoiled. You can take my word for that. And I'm convinced
he's got the right stuff in him to succeed, once he grows up and
buckles down to work. He's only a big kid now, but all he needs
is a little self-confidence and a sense of responsibility. He's holding down a fair job, too, considering he's just started in the
advertising game—enough to keep them living. (*With a slight
smile*) I'm prescribing for Sam, too, when I boost this wedding.

MARSDEN    (*his snobbery coming out*)    Do you know his family—
what sort of people?—

DARRELL    (*bitingly*)    I'm not acquainted with their social qualifica-
tions, if that's what you mean! They're upstate country folks—
fruit growers and farmers, well off, I believe. Simply, healthy
people, I'm sure of that although I've never met them.

MARSDEN    (*a bit shamefacedly—changing the subject hastily*)    Have
you suggested this match to Nina?

DARRELL    Yes, a good many times lately in a half-joking way. If I
were serious she wouldn't listen, she'd say I was prescribing. But
I think what I've said has planted it in her mind as a possibility.

MARSDEN    (*thinking suspiciously*)

Is this Doctor her lover? . . . trying to pull the wool over my eyes? . . . use me to arrange a convenient triangle for him? . . . (*Harshly—but trying to force a joking tone*) Do you know what I'm inclined to suspect, Doctor? That you may be in love with Nina yourself!

DARRELL (*astonished*) The deuce you do! What in the devil makes you think that? Not that any man mightn't fall in love with Nina. Most of them do. But I didn't happen to. And what's more I never could. In my mind she always belongs to Gordon. It's probably a reflection of her own silly fixed idea about him. (*Suddenly, dryly and harshly*) And I couldn't share a woman— even with a ghost! (*Thinking cynically*)

Not to mention the living who have had her! . . . Sam doesn't know about them . . . and I'll bet he couldn't believe it of her even if she confessed! . . .

MARSDEN (*thinking bafledly*)

Wrong again! . . . he isn't lying . . . but I feel he's hiding some-thing . . . why does he speak so resentfully of Gordon's memory? . . . why do I sympathize? . . .

(*In a strange mocking ironic tone*) I can quite appreciate your feeling about Gordon. I wouldn't care to share with a ghost-lover myself. That species of dead is so invulnerably alive! Even a doctor couldn't kill one, eh? (*He forces a laugh—then in a friendly confidential tone*) Gordon is too egregious for a ghost. That was the way Nina's father felt about him, too. (*Suddenly reminded of the dead man—in penitently sad tones*) You didn't know her father, did you? A charming old fellow!

DARRELL (*hearing a noise from the hall—warningly*) Sstt! (NINA *enters slowly. She looks from one to the other with a queer, quick inquisitive stare, but her face is a pale expressionless mask drained of all emotional response to human contacts. It is as if her eyes were acting on their own account as restless, prying, recording instruments. The two men have risen and stare at her anxiously.* DARRELL *moves back and to one side until he is standing in relatively the same place as* MARSDEN *had occupied in the previous scene while* MARSDEN *is in her father's place and she stops where she had been. There is a pause. Then just as each of the men is about to speak, she answers as if they had asked a question*).

NINA (*in a queer flat voice*) Yes, he's dead—my father—whose passion created me—who began me—he is ended. There is only his end living—his death. It lives now to draw nearer me, to draw me nearer, to become my end! (*Then with a strange twisted smile*) How we poor monkeys hide from ourselves behind the sounds called words!

MARSDEN (*thinking frightenedly*)

How terrible she is! . . . who is she? . . . not my Nina! . . . (*As if to reassure himself—timidly*) Nina! (DARRELL *makes an impatient gesture for him to let her go on. What she is saying interests him and he feels talking it out will do her good. She looks at* MARSDEN *for a moment startledly as if she couldn't recognize him*).

NINA   What? (*Then placing him—with real affection that is like a galling goad to him*) Dear old Charlie!

MARSDEN

Dear damned Charlie! . . . She loves to torture! . . . (*Then forcing a smile—soothingly*) Yes, Nina Cara Nina! Right here!

NINA (*forcing a smile*)   You look frightened, Charlie. Do I seem queer? It's because I've suddenly seen the lies in the sounds called words. You know—grief, sorrow, love, father—those sounds our lips make and our hands write. You ought to know what I mean. You work with them. Have you written another novel lately? But, stop to think, you're just the one who couldn't know what I mean. With you the lies have become the only truthful things. And I suppose that's the logical conclusion to the whole evasive mess, isn't it? Do you understand me, Charlie? Say lie— (*She says it, drawing it out*) L-i-i-e! Now say life. L-i-i-f-e! You see! Life is just a long drawn out lie with a sniffling sigh at the end! (*She laughs*).

MARSDEN (*in strange agony*)

She's hard! . . . like a whore! . . . tearing your heart with dirty finger nails! . . . my Nina! . . . cruel bitch! . . . some day I won't bear it! . . . I'll scream out the truth about every woman! no kinder at heart than dollar tarts! . . .
(*Then in a passion of remorse*)
Forgive me, Mother! . . . I didn't mean all! . . .

DARRELL (*a bit worried himself now—persuasively*)   Why not sit down, Nina, and let us two gentlemen sit down?

NINA (*smiling at him swiftly and mechanically*)   Oh, all right, Ned. (*She sits at center. He comes and sits on the bench.* MARSDEN *sits by the table. She continues sarcastically*) Are you prescribing for me again, Ned? This is my pet doctor, Charlie. He couldn't be happy in heaven unless God called him in because He'd caught something! Did you ever know a young scientist, Charlie? He believes if you pick a lie to pieces, the pieces are the truth! I like him because he's so inhuman. But once he kissed me—in a moment of carnal weakness! I was as startled as if a mummy had done it! And then he looked so disgusted with himself! I had to laugh! (*She smiles at him with a pitying scorn*).

DARRELL (*good-naturedly smiling*) That's right! Rub it in! (*Ruffled but amused in spite of it*)
I'd forgotten about that kiss . . . I was sore at myself afterwards . . . she was so damned indifferent! . . .

NINA (*wanderingly*) Do you know what I was doing upstairs? I was trying to pray. I tried hard to pray to the modern science God. I thought of a million light years to a spiral nebula—one other universe among innumerable others. But how could that God care about our trifling misery of death-born-of-birth? I couldn't believe in Him, and I wouldn't if I could! I'd rather imitate His indifference and prove I had that one trait at least in common!

MARSDEN (*worriedly*) Nina, why don't you lie down?

NINA (*jeeringly*) Oh, let me talk, Charlie! They're only words, remember! So many many words have jammed up into thoughts in my poor head! You'd better let them overflow or they'll burst the dam! I wanted to believe in any God at any price—a heap of stones, a mud image, a drawing on a wall, a bird, a fish, a snake, a baboon—or even a good man preaching the simple platitudes of truth, those Gospel words we love the sound of but whose meaning we pass on to spooks to live by!

MARSDEN (*again—half-rising—frightenedly*) Nina! You ought to stop talking. You'll work yourself into— (*He glances angrily at DARRELL as if demanding that, as a doctor, he do something*).

NINA (*with bitter hopelessness*) Oh, all right!

DARRELL (*answering his look—thinking*)
You poor fool! . . . it'll do her good to talk this out of her system . . . and then it'll be up to you to bring her around to Sam . . .
(*Starts toward the door*) Think I'll go out and stretch my legs.

MARSDEN (*thinking—in a panic*)
I don't want to be alone with her! . . . I don't know her! . . . I'm afraid! . . .
(*Protestingly*) Well—but—hold on—I'm sure Nina would rather—

NINA (*dully*) Let him go. I've said everything I can ever say—to him. I want to talk to you, Charlie. (DARRELL *goes out noiselessly with a meaning look at* MARSDEN—*a pause*).

MARSDEN (*thinking tremblingly*)

Here . . . now . . . what I hoped . . . she and I alone . . . she will cry . . . I will comfort her . . . why am I so afraid? . . . whom do I fear? . . . is it she? . . . or I? . . .

NINA (*suddenly, with pity yet with scorn*) Why have you always been so timid, Charlie? Why are you always afraid? What are you afraid of?

MARSDEN (*thinking in a panic*)

She sneaked into my soul to spy! . . .

(*Then boldly*)

Well then, a little truth for once in a way! . . .

(*Timidly*) I'm afraid of—of life, Nina.

NINA (*nodding slowly*) I know. (*After a pause—queerly*) The mistake began when God was created in a male image. Of course, women would see Him that way, but men should have been gentlemen enough, remembering their mothers, to make God a woman! But the God of Gods—the Boss—has always been a man. That makes life so perverted, and death so unnatural. We should have imagined life as created in the birth-pain of God the Mother. Then we would understand why we, Her children, have inherited pain, for we would know that our life's rhythm beats from Her great heart, torn with the agony of love and birth. And we would feel that death meant reunion with Her, a passing back into Her substance, blood of Her blood again, peace of Her peace! (MARSDEN *has been listening to her fascinatedly. She gives a strange little laugh*) Now wouldn't that be more logical and satisfying than having God a male whose chest thunders with egotism and is too hard for tired heads and thoroughly comfortless? Wouldn't it, Charlie?

MARSDEN (*with a strange passionate eagerness*) Yes! It would, indeed! It would, Nina!

NINA (*suddenly jumping to her feet and going to him—with a horrible moaning desolation*) Oh, God, Charlie, I want to believe in something! I want to believe so I can feel! I want to feel that he is dead—my father! And I can't feel anything, Charlie! I can't feel anything at all! (*She throws herself on her knees beside him and hides her face in her hands on his knees and begins to sob—stifled torn sounds*).

MARSDEN (*bends down, pats her head with trembling hands, soothes her with uncertain trembling words*) There—there—don't—Nina, please—don't cry—you ll make yourself sick—come now—get up—do! (*His hands grasping her arms he half raises her to her feet, but, her face still hidden in her hands, sobbing, she slips on to his lap like a little girl and hides her face on his shoulder. His expression becomes transported with a great happiness—in an ecstatic whisper*)

As I dreamed . . . with a deeper sweetness! . . .

(*He kisses her hair with a great reverence*)

There . . . this is all my desire . . . I am this kind of lover . . . this is my love . . . she is my girl . . . not woman . . . my little girl . . . and I am brave because of her little girl's pure love . . . and I am proud . . . no more afraid . . . no more ashamed of being pure! . . .

(*He kisses her hair again tenderly and smiles at himself—then soothingly with a teasing incongruous gaiety*) This will never do, Nina Cara Nina—never, never do, you know—I can't permit it!

NINA (*in a muffled voice, her sobbing beginning to ebb away into sighs—in a young girl's voice*) Oh, Charlie, you're so kind and comforting! I've wanted you so!

MARSDEN (*immediately disturbed*)

Wanted? . . . wanted? . . . not that kind of wanted . . . can she mean? . . .

(*Questioning hesitatingly*) You've wanted me, Nina?

NINA Yes—awfully! I've been so homesick. I've wanted to run home and 'fess up, tell how bad I've been, and be punished! Oh, I've got to be punished, Charlie, out of mercy for me, so I can forgive myself! And now Father dead, there's only you. You will, won't you—or tell me how to punish myself? You've simply got to, if you love me!

MARSDEN (*thinking intensely*)

If I love her! . . . oh, I do love her! . . .

(*Eagerly*) Anything you wish, Nina—anything!

NINA (*with a comforted smile, closing her eyes and cuddling up against him*) I knew you would. Dear old Charlie! (*As he gives a wincing start*) What is it? (*She looks up into his face*).

MARSDEN (*forcing a smile—ironically*) Twinge—rheumatics—getting old, Nina. (*Thinking with wild agony*)

Dear old Charlie! . . . descended again into hell! . . .

(*Then in a flat voice*) What do you want to be punished for, Nina?

NINA (*in a strange, far-away tone, looking up not at him but at the ceiling*) For playing the silly slut, Charlie. For giving my cool clean body to men with hot hands and greedy eyes which they called love! Ugh! (*A shiver runs over her body*).

MARSDEN (*thinking with sudden agony*)

Then she did! . . . the little filth! . . .

(*In his flat voice*) You mean you— (*Then pleadingly*) But not— Darrell?

NINA (*with simple surprise*) Ned? No, how could I? The war hadn't maimed him. There would have been no point in that. But I did with others—oh, four or five or six or seven men, Charlie. I forget—and it doesn't matter. They were all the same. Count them all as one, and that one a ghost of nothing. That is, to me. They were important to themselves, if I remember rightly. But I forget.

MARSDEN (*thinking in agony*)

But why? . . . the dirty little trollop! . . . why? . . .

(*In his flat voice*) Why did you do this, Nina?

NINA (*with a sad little laugh*) God knows, Charlie! Perhaps I knew at the time but I've forgotten. It's all mixed up. There was a desire to be kind. But it's horribly hard to give anything, and frightful to receive! And to give love—oneself—not in this world! And men are difficult to please, Charlie. I seemed to feel Gordon standing against a wall with eyes bandaged and these men were a firing squad whose eyes were also bandaged—and only I could see! No, I was the blindest! I would not see! I knew it was a stupid, morbid business, that I was more maimed than they were, really, that the war had blown my heart and insides out! And I knew too that I was torturing these tortured men, morbidly super-sensitive already, that they loathed the cruel mockery of my gift! Yet I kept on, from one to one, like a stupid, driven animal until one night not long ago I had a dream of Gordon diving down out of the sky in flames and he looked at me with such sad burning eyes, and all my poor maimed men, too, seemed staring out of his eyes with a burning pain, and I woke up crying, my own eyes burning. Then I saw what a fool I'd been—a guilty fool! So be kind and punish me!

MARSDEN (*thinking with bitter confusion*)

I wish she hadn't told me this . . . it has upset me terribly! . . . I positively must run home at once . . . Mother is waiting up . . . oh, how I'd love to hate this little whore! . . . then I could

punish! . . . I wish her father were alive . . . "now he's dead there's only you," she said . . . "I've wanted you," . . .
(*With intense bitterness*)
Dear old Father Charlie now! . . . ha! . . . that's how she wants me! . . .
(*Then suddenly in a matter-of-fact tone that is mockingly like her father's*) Then, under the circumstances, having weighed the pros and cons, so to speak, I should say that decidedly the most desirable course—

NINA (*drowsily—her eyes shut*) You sound so like Father, Charlie.

MARSDEN (*in the tone like her father's*) —is for you to marry that young Evans. He is a splendid chap, clean and boyish, with real stuff in him, too, to make a career for himself if he finds a help-meet who will inspire him to his best efforts and bring his latent ability to the surface.

NINA (*drowsily*) Sam is a nice boy. Yes, it would be a career for me to bring a career to his surface. I would be busy—surface life —no more depths, please God! But I don't love him, Father.

MARSDEN (*blandly—in the tone like her father's*) But you like him, Nina. And he loves you devotedly. And it's time you were having children—and when children come, love comes, you know.

NINA (*drowsily*) I want children. I must become a mother so I can give myself. I am sick of sickness.

MARSDEN (*briskly*) Then it's all settled?

NINA (*drowsily*) Yes. (*Very sleepily*) Thank you, Father. You've been so kind. You've let me off too easily. I don't feel as if you'd punish me hardly at all. But I'll never, never do it again, I promise—never, never!— (*She falls asleep and gives a soft little snore*).

MARSDEN (*still in her father's tones—very paternally—looking down*) She's had a hard day of it, poor child! I'll carry her up to her room. (*He rises to his feet with* NINA *sleeping peacefully in his arms. At this moment* SAM EVANS *enters from the right with the package of medicine in his hand*).

EVANS (*grinning respectfully*) Here's the— (*As he sees* NINA) Oh! (*Then excitedly*) Did she faint?

MARSDEN (*smiling kindly at* EVANS—*still in her father's tones*) Sssh! She's asleep. She cried and then she fell asleep—like a little girl. (*Then benignantly*) But first we spoke a word about you, Evans, and I'm sure you have every reason to hope.

EVANS (*overcome, his eyes on his shuffling feet and twiddling cap*) Thanks—I—I really don't know how to thank—

MARSDEN (*going to door—in his own voice now*) I've got to go home. My mother is waiting up for me. I'll just carry Nina upstairs and put her on her bed and throw something over her.

EVANS Can't I help you, Mr. Marsden?

MARSDEN (*dully*) No. I cannot help myself. (*As* EVANS *looks puzzled and startled he adds with an ironical, self-mocking geniality*) You'd better call me just Charlie after this. (*He smiles bitterly to himself as he goes out*).

EVANS (*looks after him for a moment—then cannot restrain a joyful, coltish caper—gleefully*) Good egg! Good old Charlie! (*As if he had heard or guessed,* MARSDEN'S *bitter laugh comes back from the end of the hallway*).

*Curtain*

ACT THREE

SCENE: *Seven months or so later—the dining room of the* EVANS' *homestead in northern New York state—about nine o'clock in the morning of a day in late spring of the following year.*

*The room is one of those big, misproportioned dining rooms that are found in the large, jigsaw country houses scattered around the country as a result of the rural taste for grandeur in the eighties. There is a cumbersome hanging lamp suspended from chains over the exact center of the ugly table with its set of straightbacked chairs set back at spaced intervals against the walls. The wall paper, a repulsive brown, is stained at the ceiling line with damp blotches of mildew, and here and there has started to peel back where the strips join. The floor is carpeted in a smeary brown with a dark red design blurred into it. In the left wall is one window with starched white curtains looking out on a covered side porch, so that no sunlight ever gets to this room and the light from the window, although it is a beautiful warm day in the flower garden beyond the porch, is cheerless and sickly. There is a door in the rear, to left of center, that leads to a hall opening on the same porch. To the right of door a heavy sideboard, a part of the set, displaying some "company" china and glassware. In the right wall, a door leading to the kitchen.* NINA *is seated at the foot of the table, her back to the window, writing a letter. Her whole personality seems changed, her face has a contented expression, there is an inner calm about her. And her personal appearance has changed in kind, her face and figure have filled out, she is prettier in a conventional way and less striking and unusual; nothing remains of the strange fascination of her face except her unchangeably mysterious eyes.*

NINA (*reading what she has just written over to herself*)

It's a queer house, Ned. There is something wrong with its psyche, I'm sure. Therefore you'd simply adore it. It's a hideous old place, a faded gingerbread with orange fixin's and numerous lightning rods. Around it are acres and acres of apple trees in full bloom, all white and pinkish and beautiful, like brides just tripping out of church with the bridegroom, Spring, by the arm.

Which reminds me, Ned, that it's over six months since Sam and I were married and we haven't seen hide nor hair of you since the ceremony. Do you think that is any nice way to act? You might at least drop me a line. But I'm only joking. I know how busy you must be now that you've got the chance you've always wanted to do research work. Did you get our joint letter of congratulation written after we read of your appointment?

But to get back to this house. I feel it has lost its soul and grown resigned to doing without it. It isn't haunted by anything at all— and ghosts of some sort are the only normal life a house has— like our minds, you know. So although last evening when we got here at first I said "obviously haunted" to myself, now that I've spent one night in it I know that whatever spooks there may once have been have packed up their manifestations a long time ago and drifted away over the grass, wisps of mist between the apple trees, without one backward glance of regret or recollection. It's incredible to think Sam was born and spent his childhood here. I'm glad he doesn't show it! We slept last night in the room he was born in. Or rather he slept, I couldn't. I lay awake and found it difficult to breathe, as if all the life in the air had long since been exhausted in keeping the dying living a little longer. It was hard to believe anyone had ever been born alive there. I know you're saying crossly "She's still morbid" but I'm not. I've never been more normal. I feel contented and placid. (*Looking up from the letter, thinking embarrassedly*)

Should I have told him? . . . no . . . my own secret . . . tell

no one . . . not even Sam . . . why haven't I told Sam? . . .
it'd do him so much good . . . he'd feel so proud of himself,
poor dear . . . no . . . I want to keep it just my baby . . . only
mine . . . as long as I can . . . and it will be time enough to
let Ned know when I go to New York . . . he can suggest a
good obstetrician . . . how delighted he'll be when he hears!
. . . he always said it would be the best thing for me . . . well,
I do feel happy when I think . . . and I love Sam now . . . in
a way . . . it will be his baby too . . .
(*Then with a happy sigh, turns back to letter*)
But speaking of Sam's birth, you really must meet his mother
sometime. It's amazing how little she is like him, a strange
woman from the bit I saw of her last night. She has been writing
Sam regularly once a week ever since she's known we were
married, the most urgent invitations to visit her. They were
really more like commands, or prayers. I suspect she is terribly
lonely all by herself in this big house. Sam's feeling toward her
puzzles me. I don't believe he ever mentioned her until her letters
began coming or that he'd ever have come to see the poor woman
if I hadn't insisted. His attitude rather shocked me. It was just
as though he'd forgotten he had a mother. And yet as soon as
he saw her he was sweet enough. She seemed dreadfully upset
to see Charlie with us, until we'd explained it was thanks to his
kindness and in his car we were taking this deferred honeymoon. Charlie's like a fussy old woman about his car, he's afraid
to let Sam or me drive it—

MARSDEN (*enters from the rear. He is spruce, dressed immaculately,
his face a bit tired and resigned, but smiling kindly. He has
a letter in his hand*)  Good morning. (*She gives a start and instinctively covers the letter with her hand*).

NINA  Good morning. (*Thinking amusedly*)

If he knew what I'd just written . . . poor old Charlie! . . .
(*Then indicating the letter he carries*) I see you're an early correspondent, too.

MARSDEN (*with sudden jealous suspicion*)

Why did she cover it up like that? . . . whom is she writing
to? . . .
(*Coming toward her*) Just a line to Mother to let her know
we've not all been murdered by rum-bandits. You know how she
worries.

NINA (*thinking with a trace of pitying contempt*)

Apron strings . . . still his devotion to her is touching . . . I hope if mine is a boy he will love me as much . . . oh, I hope it is a boy . . . healthy and strong and beautiful . . . like Gordon! . . .

(*Then suddenly sensing* MARSDEN's *curiosity—perfunctorily*) I'm writing to Ned Darrell. I've owed him one for ages. (*She folds it up and puts it aside*).

MARSDEN (*thinking glumly*)

I thought she'd forgotten him . . . still I suppose it's just friendly . . . and it's none of my business now she's married. . . .

(*Perfunctorily*) How did you sleep?

NINA  Not a wink. I had the strangest feeling.

MARSDEN  Sleeping in a strange bed, I suppose. (*Jokingly*) Did you see any ghosts?

NINA (*with a sad smile*)  No, I got the feeling the ghosts had all deserted the house and left it without a soul—as the dead so often leave the living— (*She forces a little laugh*) if you get what I mean.

MARSDEN (*thinking worriedly*)

Slipping back into that morbid tone . . . first time in a long while . . .

(*Teasingly*) Hello! Do I hear graveyards yawning from their sleep—and yet I observe it's a gorgeous morning without, the flowers are flowering, the trees are treeing with one another, and you, if I mistake not, are on your honeymoon!

NINA (*immediately gaily mocking*)  Oh, very well, old thing! "God's in his heaven, all's right with the world!" And Pippa's cured of the pip! (*She dances up to him*).

MARSDEN (*gallantly*)  Pippa is certainly a pippin this morning!

NINA (*kisses him quickly*)  You deserve one for that! All I meant was that ghosts remind me of men's smart crack about women, you can't live with them and can't live without them. (*Stands still and looks at him teasingly*) But there you stand proving me a liar by every breath you draw! You're ghostless and womanless—and as sleek and satisfied as a pet seal! (*She sticks out her tongue at him and makes a face of superior scorn*) Bah! That for you, 'Fraid-cat Charlie, you slacker bachelor! (*She runs to the kitchen door*) I'm going to bum some more coffee! How about you?

MARSDEN (*with a forced smile*) No, thank you. (*She disappears into the kitchen—thinking with bitter pain*)

Ghostless! . . . if she only knew . . . that joking tone hides her real contempt! . . .

(*Self-mockingly*)

"But when the girls began to play 'Fraid-cat Charlie ran away!"

(*Then rallying himself*)

Bosh! . . . I haven't had such thoughts . . . not since their marriage . . . happy in her happiness . . . but is she happy? . . . in the first few months she was obviously playing a part . . . kissed him too much . . . as if she'd determined to make herself a loving wife . . . and then all of a sudden she became contented . . . her face filled out . . . her eyes lazily examined peace . . . pregnant . . . yes, she must be . . . I hope so. . . . Why? . . . for her sake . . . my own, too . . . when she has a child I know I can entirely accept . . . forget I have lost her . . . lost her? . . . silly ass! . . . how can you lose what you never possessed? . . . except in dreams! . . .

(*Shaking his head exasperatedly*)

Round and round . . . thoughts . . . damn pests! . . . mosquitoes of the soul . . . whine, sting, suck one's blood . . . why did I invite Nina and Sam on this tour . . . it's a business trip with me, really . . . I need a new setting for my next novel . . . "Mr. Marsden departs a bit from his familiar field" . . . well, there they were stuck in the Professor's house . . . couldn't afford a vacation . . . never had a honeymoon . . . I've pretended to be done up every night so they could . . . I've gone to bed right after dinner so they could be alone and . . . I wonder if she can really like him . . . that way? . . .

(*The sound of* EVANS' *voice and his mother's is heard from the garden.* MARSDEN *goes over and carefully peers out*)

Sam with his mother . . . peculiar woman . . . strong . . . good character for a novel . . . no, she's too somber . . . her eyes are the saddest . . . and, at the same time, the grimmest . . . they're coming in . . . I'll drive around the country a bit . . . give them a chance for a family conference . . . discuss Nina's pregnancy, I suppose . . . does Sam know? . . . he gives no indication . . . why do wives hide it from their husbands? . . . ancient shame . . . guilty of continuing life, of bringing fresh pain into the world . . .

(*He goes out, rear. The outside door in the hall is heard being opened and* EVANS *and his mother evidently meet* MARSDEN *as he is about to go out. Their voices, his voice explaining, are heard, then the outer door being opened and shut again as* MARSDEN *departs. A moment later* EVANS *and his mother enter the dining room.* SAM *looks timorously happy, as if he could not quite believe in his good fortune and had constantly to reassure himself about it, yet he is riding the crest of the wave, he radiates love and devotion and boyish adoration. He is a charming-looking fresh boy now. He wears a sweater and linen knickers, collegiate to the last degree. His mother is a tiny woman with a frail figure, her head and face, framed in iron-gray hair, seeming much too large for her body, so that at first glance she gives one the impression of a wonderfully made, lifelike doll. She is only about forty-five but she looks at least sixty. Her face with its delicate features must have once been of a romantic, tender, clinging-vine beauty, but what has happened to her has compressed its defenseless curves into planes, its mouth into the thin line around a locked door, its gentle chin has been forced out aggressively by a long reliance on clenched teeth. She is very pale. Her big dark eyes are grim with the prisoner-pain of a walled-in soul. Yet a sweet loving-kindness, the ghost of an old faith and trust in life's goodness, hovers girlishly, fleetingly, about the corners of her mouth and softens into deep sorrow the shadowy grimness of her eyes. Her voice jumps startlingly in tone from a caressing gentleness to a blunted flat assertiveness, as if what she said then was merely a voice on its own without human emotion to inspire it*).

EVANS (*as they come in—rattling on in the cocksure boastful way of a boy showing off his prowess before his mother, confident of thrilled adulation*) In a few years you won't have to worry one way or another about the darned old apple crop. I'll be able to take care of you then. Wait and see! Of course, I'm not making so much now. I couldn't expect to. I've only just started. But I'm making good, all right, all right—since I got married—and it's only a question of time when— Why, to show you, Cole—he's the manager and the best egg ever—called me into his office and told me he'd had his eye on me, that my stuff was exactly what they wanted, and he thought I had the makings of a real find. (*Proudly*) How's that? That's certainly fair enough, isn't it?

MRS. EVANS (*vaguely—she has evidently not heard much of what he said*) That's fine, Sammy. (*Thinking apprehensively*) I do hope I'm wrong! . . . but that old shiver of dread took me the minute she stepped in the door! . . . I don't think she's told Sammy but I got to make sure. . . .

EVANS (*seeing her preoccupation now—deeply hurt—testily*) I'll bet you didn't hear a word I said! Are you still worrying about how the darn old apples are going to turn out?

MRS. EVANS (*with a guilty start—protestingly*) Yes, I did hear you, Sammy—every word! That's just what I was thinking about—how proud I am you're doing so wonderful well!

EVANS (*mollified but still grumbling*) You'd never guess it from the gloomy way you looked! (*But encouraged to go on*) And Cole asked me if I was married—seemed to take a real personal interest—said he was glad to hear it because marriage was what put the right kind of ambition into a fellow—unselfish ambition—working for his wife and not just himself— (*Then embarrassedly*) He even asked me if we were expecting an addition to the family.

MRS. EVANS (*seeing this is her chance—quickly—forcing a smile*) I've been meaning to ask you that myself, Sammy. (*Blurts out apprehensively*) She—Nina—she isn't going to have a baby, is she?

EVANS (*with an indefinable guilty air—as if he were reluctant to admit it*) I—why—you mean, is she now? I don't think so, Mother. (*He strolls over to the window whistling with an exaggeratedly casual air, and looks out*).

MRS. EVANS (*thinking with grim relief*)
He don't know . . . there's that much to be thankful for, anyway. . . .

EVANS (*thinking with intense longing*)
If that'd only happen! . . . soon! . . . Nina's begun to love me . . . a little . . . I've felt it the last two months . . . God, it's made me happy! . . . before that she didn't . . . only liked me . . . that was all I asked . . . never dared hope she'd come to love me . . . even a little . . . so soon . . . sometimes I feel it's too good to be true . . . don't deserve it . . . and now . . . if that'd happen . . . then I'd feel sure . . . it'd be there . . . half Nina, half me . . . living proof! . . .
(*Then an apprehensive note creeping in*)
And I know she wants a baby so much . . . one reason why she married me . . . and I know she's felt right along that then she'd love me . . . really love me . . .
(*Gloomily*)

I wonder why . . . ought to have happened before this . . . hope it's nothing wrong . . . with me! . . .

(*He starts, flinging off his thought—then suddenly clutching at a straw, turns hopefully to his mother*) Why did you ask me that, Mother? D'you think—?

MRS. EVANS (*hastily*) No, indeed! I don't think she is! I wouldn't say so at all!

EVANS (*dejectedly*) Oh—I thought perhaps— (*Then changing the subject*) I suppose I ought to go up and say hello to Aunt Bessie.

MRS. EVANS (*her face becoming defensive—in blunted tones, a trifle pleadingly*) I wouldn't, Sammy. She hasn't seen you since you were eight. She wouldn't know you. And you're on your honeymoon, and old age is always sad to young folks. Be happy while you can! (*Then pushing him toward door*) Look here! You catch that friend, he's just getting his car out. You drive to town with him, give me a chance to get to know my daughter-in-law, and call her to account for how she's taking care of you! (*She laughs forcedly*).

EVANS (*bursting out passionately*) Better than I deserve! She's an angel, Mother! I know you'll love her!

MRS. EVANS (*gently*) I do already, Sammy! She's so pretty and sweet!

EVANS (*kisses her—joyously*) I'll tell her that. I'm going out this way and kiss her good-bye. (*He runs out through the kitchen door*).

MRS. EVANS (*looking after him—passionately*)
He loves her! . . . he's happy! . . . that's all that counts! . . . being happy! . . .
(*Thinking apprehensively*)
If only she isn't going to have a baby . . . if only she doesn't care so much about having one . . . I got to have it out with her . . . got to! . . . no other way . . . in mercy . . . in justice . . . this has got to end with my boy . . . and he's got to live happy! . . .
(*At the sound of steps from the kitchen she straightens up in her chair stiffly*).

NINA (*comes in from the kitchen, a cup of coffee in her hand, smiling happily*) Good morning— (*She hesitates—then shyly*) Mother. (*She comes over and kisses her—slips down and sits on the floor beside her*).

MRS. EVANS (*flusteredly—hurriedly*) Good morning! It's a real fine day, isn't it? I ought to have been here and got your breakfast, but I was out gallivanting round the place with Sammy. I hope you found everything you wanted.

NINA  Indeed I did! And I ate so much I'm ashamed of myself! (*She nods at the cup of coffee and laughs*) See. I'm still at it.

MRS. EVANS  Good for you!

NINA  I ought to apologize for coming down so late. Sam should have called me. But I wasn't able to get to sleep until after daylight somehow.

MRS. EVANS (*strangely*)  You couldn't sleep? Why? Did you feel anything funny—about this house?

NINA (*struck by her tone—looks up*)  No. Why? (*Thinking*) How her face changes! . . . what sad eyes! . . .

MRS. EVANS (*thinking in an agony of apprehension*) Got to start in to tell her . . . got to . . .

NINA (*apprehensive herself now*) That sick dead feeling . . . when something is going to happen . . . I felt it before I got the cable about Gordon . . . (*Then taking a sip of coffee, and trying to be pleasantly casual*) Sam said you wanted to talk to me.

MRS. EVANS (*dully*)  Yes. You love my boy, don't you?

NINA (*startled—forcing a smile, quickly*)  Why, of course! (*Reassuring herself*) No, it isn't a lie . . . I do love him . . . the father of my baby . . .

MRS. EVANS (*blurts out*)  Are you going to have a baby, Nina?

NINA (*she presses* MRS. EVANS' *hand—simply*)  Yes, Mother.

MRS. EVANS (*in her blunt flat tones—with a mechanical rapidity to her words*)  Don't you think it's too soon? Don't you think you better wait until Sammy's making more money? Don't you think it'll be a drag on him and you? Why don't you just go on being happy together, just you two?

NINA (*thinking frightenedly*) What is behind what she's saying? . . . that feeling of death again! . . . (*Moving away from her—repulsed*)  No, I don't think any of those things, Mrs. Evans. I want a baby—beyond everything! We both do!

MRS. EVANS (*hopelessly*)  I know. (*Then grimly*) But you can't! You've got to make up your mind you can't! (*Thinking fiercely —even with satisfaction*) Tell her! . . . make her suffer what I was made to suffer! . . . I've been too lonely! . . .

NINA (*thinking with terrified foreboding*)

I knew it! . . . Out of a blue sky . . . black! . . .

(*Springing to her feet—bewilderedly*) What do you mean? How can you say a thing like that?

MRS. EVANS (*reaching out her hand tenderly, trying to touch* NINA) It's because I want Sammy—and you, too, child—to be happy. (*Then as* NINA *shrinks away from her hand—in her blunted tones*) You just can't.

NINA (*defiantly*) But I can! I have already! I mean—I am, didn't you understand me?

MRS. EVANS (*gently*) I know it's hard. (*Then inexorably*) But you can't go on!

NINA (*violently*) I don't believe you know what you're saying! It's too terrible for you—Sam's own mother—how would you have felt if someone—when you were going to have Sam—came to you and said—?

MRS. EVANS (*thinking fiercely*)

Now's my chance! . . .

(*Tonelessly*) They did say it! Sam's own father did—my husband! And I said it to myself! And I did all I could, all my husband could think of, so's I wouldn't—but we didn't know enough. And right to the time the pains come on, I prayed Sammy'd be born dead, and Sammy's father prayed, but Sammy was born healthy and smiling, and we just had to love him, and live in fear. He doubled the torment of fear we lived in. And that's what you'd be in for. And Sammy, he'd go the way his father went. And your baby, you'd be bringing it into torment. (*A bit violently*) I tell you it'd be a crime—a crime worse than murder! (*Then recovering—commiseratingly*) So you just can't, Nina!

NINA (*who has been listening distractedly—thinking*)

Don't listen to her! . . . feeling of death! . . . what is it? . . . she's trying to kill my baby! . . . oh, I hate her! . . .

(*Hysterically resentful*) What do you mean? Why don't you speak plainly? (*Violently*) I think you're horrible! Praying your baby would be born dead! That's a lie! You couldn't!

MRS. EVANS (*thinking*)

I know what she's doing now . . . just what I did . . . trying not to believe . . .

(*Fiercely*)

But I'll make her! . . . she's got to suffer, too! . . . I been too

lonely! . . . she's got to share and help me save my Sammy! . . .
(*With an even more blunted flat relentless tonelessness*) I
thought I was plain, but I'll be plainer. Only remember it's a
family secret, and now you're one of the family. It's the curse
on the Evanses. My husband's mother—she was an only child—
died in an asylum and her father before her. I know that for a
fact. And my husband's sister, Sammy's aunt, she's out of her
mind. She lives on the top floor of this house, hasn't been out of
her room in years, I've taken care of her. She just sits, doesn't
say a word, but she's happy, she laughs to herself a lot, she
hasn't a care in the world. But I remember when she was all
right, she was always unhappy, she never got married, most people around here were afraid of the Evanses in spite of their being
rich for hereabouts. They knew about the craziness going back,
I guess, for heaven knows how long. I didn't know about the
Evanses until after I'd married my husband. He came to the
town I lived in, no one there knew about the Evanses. He didn't
tell me until after we were married. He asked me to forgive
him, he said he loved me so much he'd have gone mad without me, said I was his only hope of salvation. So I forgave
him. I loved him an awful lot. I said to myself, I'll be his salvation
—and maybe I could have been if we hadn't had Sammy born.
My husband kept real well up to then. We'd swore we'd never
have children, we never forgot to be careful for two whole years.
Then one night we'd both gone to a dance, we'd both had a little
punch to drink, just enough—to forget—driving home in the moonlight—that moonlight!—such little things at the back of big things!
NINA (*in a dull moan*) I don't believe you! I won't believe you!
MRS. EVANS (*drones on*) My husband, Sammy's father, in spite
    of all he and I fought against it, he finally gave in to it when
    Sammy was only eight, he couldn't keep up any more living in
    fear for Sammy, thinking any minute the curse might get him,
    every time he was sick, or had a headache, or bumped his head,
    or started crying, or had a nightmare and screamed, or said
    something queer like children do naturally. (*A bit stridently*)
    Living like that with that fear is awful torment! I know that!
    I went through it by his side! It nearly drove me crazy, too—
    but I didn't have it in my blood! And that's why I'm telling you!
    You got to see you can't, Nina!
NINA (*suddenly breaking out—frenziedly*) I don't believe you! I
    don't believe Sam would ever have married me if he knew—!

MRS. EVANS (*sharply*) Who said Sammy knew? He don't know a single thing about it! That's been the work of my life, keeping him from knowing. When his father gave up and went off into it I sent Sammy right off to boarding school. I told him his father was sick, and a little while after I sent word his father was dead, and from then on until his father did really die during Sammy's second year to college, I kept him away at school in winter and camp in summers and I went to see him, I never let him come home. (*With a sigh*) It was hard, giving up Sammy, knowing I was making him forget he had a mother. I was glad taking care of them two kept me so busy I didn't get much chance to think then. But here's what I've come to think since, Nina: I'm certain sure my husband might have kept his mind with the help of my love if I hadn't had Sammy. And if I'd never had Sammy I'd never have loved Sammy—or missed him, would I? —and I'd have kept my husband.

NINA (*not heeding this last—with wild mockery*) And I thought Sam was so normal—so healthy and sane—not like me! I thought he'd give me such healthy, happy children and I'd forget myself in them and learn to love him!

MRS. EVANS (*horrified, jumping to her feet*) Learn to? You told me you did love Sammy!

NINA No! Maybe I almost have—lately—but only when I thought of his baby! Now I hate him! (*She begins to weep hysterically.* MRS. EVANS *goes to her and puts her arms around her.* NINA *sobs out*) Don't touch me! I hate you, too! Why didn't you tell him he must never marry!

MRS. EVANS What reason could I give, without telling him everything? And I never heard about you till after you were married. Then I wanted to write to you but I was scared he might read it. And I couldn't leave her upstairs to come away to see you. I kept writing Sammy to bring you here right off, although having him come frightened me to death for fear he might get to suspect something. You got to get him right away from here, Nina! I just kept hoping you wouldn't want children right away—young folks don't nowadays—until I'd seen you and told you everything. And I thought you'd love him like I did his father, and be satisfied with him alone.

NINA (*lifting her head—wildly*) No! I don't! I won't! I'll leave him!

MRS. EVANS (*shaking her, fiercely*)  You can't! He'd go crazy sure then! You'd be a devil! Don't you see how he loves you?

NINA (*breaking away from her—harshly*)  Well, I don't love him! I only married him because he needed me—and I needed children! And now you tell me I've got to kill my—oh, yes, I see I've got to, you needn't argue any more! I love it too much to make it run that chance! And I hate it too, now, because it's sick, it's not my baby, it's his! (*With terrible ironic bitterness*) And still you can dare to tell me I can't even leave Sam!

MRS. EVANS (*very sadly and bitterly*)  You just said you married him because he needed you. Don't he need you now—more'n ever? But I can't tell you not to leave him, not if you don't love him. But you oughtn't to have married him when you didn't love him. And it'll be your fault, what'll happen.

NINA (*torturedly*)  What will happen?—what do you mean?—Sam will be all right—just as he was before—and it's not my fault anyway!—it's not my fault! (*Then thinking conscience-strickenly*) Poor Sam . . . she's right . . . it's not his fault . . . it's mine . . . I wanted to use him to save myself . . . I acted the coward again . . . as I did with Gordon . . .

MRS. EVANS (*grimly*)  You know what'll happen to him if you leave him—after all I've told you! (*Then breaking into intense pleading*) Oh, I'd get down on my knees to you, don't make my boy run that risk! You got to give one Evans, the last one, a chance to live in this world! And you'll learn to love him, if you give up enough for him! (*Then with a grim smile*) Why, I even love that idiot upstairs, I've taken care of her so many years, lived her life for her with my life, you might say. You give your life to Sammy, then you'll love him same as you love yourself. You'll have to! That's sure as death! (*She laughs a queer gentle laugh full of amused bitterness*).

NINA (*with a sort of dull stupid wonderment*)  And you've found peace?—

MRS. EVANS (*sardonically*)  There's peace in the green fields of Eden, they say! You got to die to find out! (*Then proudly*) But I can say I feel proud of having lived fair to them that gave me love and trusted in me!

NINA (*struck—confusedly*)  Yes—that's true, isn't it? (*Thinking strangely*) Lived fair . . . pride . . . trust . . . play the game! . . . who is speaking to me . . . Gordon! . . . oh, Gordon, do you mean I must give Sam the life I didn't give you? . . . Sam loved you too . . . he said, if we have a boy, we'll call him Gordon in Gordon's honor . . . Gordon's honor! . . . what must I do now in your honor, Gordon? . . . yes! . . . I know! . . .

(*Speaking mechanically in a dull voice*) All right, Mother. I'll stay with Sam. There's nothing else I can do, is there, when it isn't his fault, poor boy! (*Then suddenly snapping and bursting out in a despairing cry*) But I'll be so lonely! I'll have lost my baby! (*She sinks down on her knees at* MRS. EVANS' *feet—piteously*) Oh, Mother, how can I keep on living?

MRS. EVANS (*thinking miserably*)

Now she knows my suffering . . . now I got to help her . . . she's got a right to have a baby . . . another baby . . . sometime . . . somehow . . . she's giving her life to save my Sammy . . . I got to save her! . . .

(*Stammeringly*) Maybe, Nina—

NINA (*dully and resentfully again now*) And how about Sam? You want him to be happy, don't you? It's just as important for him as it is for me that I should have a baby! If you know anything at all about him, you ought to see that!

MRS. EVANS (*sadly*) I know that. I see that in him, Nina. (*Gropingly*) There must be a way—somehow. I remember when I was carrying Sam, sometimes I'd forget I was a wife, I'd only remember the child in me. And then I used to wish I'd gone out deliberate in our first year, without my husband knowing, and picked a man, a healthy male to breed by, same's we do with stock, to give the man I loved a healthy child. And if I didn't love that other man nor him me where would be the harm? Then God would whisper: "It'd be a sin, adultery, the worst sin!" But after He'd gone I'd argue back again to myself, then we'd have a healthy child, I needn't be afraid! And maybe my husband would feel without ever knowing how he felt it, that I wasn't afraid and that child wasn't cursed and so he needn't fear and I could save him. (*Then scornfully*) But I was too afraid of God then to have ever done it! (*Then very simply*) He loved children so, my poor husband did, and the way they took to him, you never saw anything like it, he was a natural born father. And Sammy's the same.

NINA (*as from a distance—strangely*) Yes, Sammy's the same. But

I'm not the same as you. (*Defiantly*) I don't believe in God the Father!

MRS. EVANS (*strangely*) Then it'd be easy for you. (*With a grim smile*) And I don't believe in Him, neither, not any more. I used to be a great one for worrying about what's God and what's devil, but I got richly over it living here with poor folks that was being punished for no sins of their own, and me being punished with them for no sin but loving much. (*With decision*) Being happy, that's the nearest we can ever come to knowing what's good! Being happy, that's good! The rest is just talk! (*She pauses—then with a strange austere sternness*) I love my boy, Sammy. I could see how much he wants you to have a baby. Sammy's got to feel sure you love him—to be happy. Whatever you can do to make him happy is good—is good, Nina! I don't care what! You've got to have a healthy baby—sometime—so's you can both be happy! It's your rightful duty!

NINA (*confusedly—in a half-whisper*) Yes, Mother. (*Thinking longingly*)

I want to be happy! . . . it's my right . . . and my duty! . . .

(*Then suddenly in guilty agony*)

Oh, my baby . . . my poor baby . . . I'm forgetting you . . . desiring another after you are dead! . . . I feel you beating against my heart for mercy . . . oh! . . .

(*She weeps with bitter anguish*).

MRS. EVANS (*gently and with deep sympathy*) I know what you're suffering. And I wouldn't say what I just said now only I know us two mustn't see each other ever again. You and Sammy have got to forget me. (*As* NINA *makes a motion of protest—grimly and inexorably*) Oh, yes, you will—easy. People forget everything. They got to, poor people! And I'm saying what I said about a healthy baby so's you will remember it when you need to, after you've forgotten—this one.

NINA (*sobbing pitifully*) Don't! Please, Mother!

MRS. EVANS (*with sudden tenderness—gathering* NINA *up in her arms, brokenly*) You poor child! You're like the daughter of my sorrow! You're closer to me now than ever Sammy could be! I want you to be happy! (*She begins to sob, too, kissing* NINA's *bowed head*).

*Curtain*

## ACT FOUR

SCENE: *An evening early in the following winter about seven months later. The* PROFESSOR's *study again. The books in the cases have never been touched, their austere array shows no gaps, but the glass separating them from the world is gray with dust, giving them a blurred ghostly quality. The table, although it is the same, is no longer the* PROFESSOR's *table, just as the other furniture in the room, by its disarrangement, betrays that the* PROFESSOR's *well-ordered mind no longer trims it to his personality. The table has become neurotic. Volumes of the Encyclopedia Britannica mixed up with popular treatises on Mind Training for Success, etc., looking startlingly modern and disturbing against the background of classics in the original, are slapped helter-skelter on top of each other on it. The titles of these books face in all directions, no one volume is placed with any relation to the one beneath it—the effect is that they have no connected meaning. The rest of the table is littered with an ink bottle, pens, pencils, erasers, a box of typewriting paper and a typewriter at the center before the chair, which is pushed back, setting the rug askew. On the floor beside the table are an overflowing wastepaper basket, a few sheets of paper and the rubber cover for the typewriter like a collapsed tent. The rocking chair is no longer at center but has been pulled nearer the table, directly faces it with its back to the bench. This bench in turn has been drawn much closer, but is now placed more to the rear and half-faces front, its back squarely to the door in the corner.*

EVANS *is seated in the* PROFESSOR's *old chair. He has evidently been typing, or is about to type, for a sheet of paper can be seen in the machine. He smokes a pipe, which he is always relighting whether it needs it or not, and which he bites and shifts about and pulls in and out and puffs at nervously. His expression is dispirited, his eyes shift about, his shoulders are collapsed submissively. He seems much thinner, his face drawn and sallow. The collegiate clothes are no longer natty, they need pressing and look too big for him.*

EVANS (*turns to his typewriter and pounds out a few words with a sort of aimless desperation—then tears the sheet out of the machine with an exclamation of disgust, crumples it up and throws it violently on the floor, pushing his chair back and jumping to his feet*) Hell! (*He begins pacing up and down the room, puffing at his pipe, thinking tormentedly*)

No use . . . can't think of a darn thing . . . well, who could dope out a novel ad on another powdered milk, anyway? . . . all the stuff been used already . . . Tartars conquering on dried mares' milk . . . Metchnikoff, eminent scientist . . . been done to death . . . but simply got to work out something or . . . Cole said, what's been the matter with you lately? . . . you started off so well . . . I thought you were a real find, but your work's fallen off to nothing . . .

(*He sits down on the edge of the bench nearby, his shoulders hunched—despondently*)

Couldn't deny it . . . been going stale ever since we came back from that trip home . . . no ideas . . . I'll get fired . . . sterile . . .

(*With a guilty terror*)

in more ways than one, I guess! . . .

(*He springs to his feet as if this idea were a pin stuck in him—lighting his already lighted pipe, walks up and down again, forcing his thoughts into other channels*)

Bet the old man turns over in his grave at my writing ads in his study . . . maybe that's why I can't . . . bum influence . . . try tomorrow in my bedroom . . . sleeping alone . . . since Nina got sick . . . some woman's sickness . . . wouldn't tell me . . . too modest . . . still, there are some things a husband has a right to know . . . especially when we haven't . . . in five months . . . doctor told her she mustn't, she said . . . what doctor? . . . she's never said . . . what the hell's the matter with you, do you think Nina's lying? . . . no . . . but . . .

(*Desperately*)

If I was only sure it was because she's really sick . . . not just sick of me! . . .

(*He sinks down in the rocking chair despondently*)

Certainly been a big change in her . . . since that visit home . . . what happened between Mother and her? . . . she says nothing . . . they seemed to like each other . . . both of them cried when we left . . . still, Nina insisted on going that same day and Mother seemed anxious to get rid of us . . . can't make it out . . . next few weeks Nina couldn't be loving enough . . . I never was so happy . . . then she crashed . . . strain of waiting and hoping she'd get pregnant . . . and nothing happening . . . that's what did it . . . my fault! . . . how d'you know? . . . you can't tell that! . . .

(*He jumps to his feet again—walks up and down again distractedly*)

God, if we'd only have a kid! . . . then I'd show them all what I could do! . . . Cole always used to say I had the stuff, and Ned certainly thought so. . . .

(*With sudden relieved excitement*)

By Gosh, I was forgetting! . . . Ned's coming out tonight . . . forget to tell Nina . . . mustn't let her get wise I got him to come to look her over . . . she'd hate me for swallowing my pride after he's never been to see us . . . but I had to . . . this has got my goat . . . I've got to know what's wrong . . . and Ned's the only one I can trust . . .

(*He flings himself on chair in front of desk and, picking up a fresh sheet of paper, jams it into the machine*)

Gosh, I ought to try and get a new start on this before it's time . . .

(*He types a sentence or two, a strained frown of concentration on his face.* NINA *comes silently through the door and stands just inside it looking at him. She has grown thin again, her face is pale and drawn, her movements are those of extreme nervous tension*).

NINA (*before she can stifle her immediate reaction of contempt and dislike*)

How weak he is! . . . he'll never do anything . . . never give me my desire . . . if he'd only fall in love with someone else . . . go away . . . not be here in my father's room . . . I even have to give him a home . . . if he'd disappear . . . leave me free . . . if he'd die . . .

(*Checking herself—remorsefully*)

I must stop such thoughts . . . I don't mean it . . . poor Sam! . . . trying so hard . . . loving me so much . . . I give so little in return . . . he feels I'm always watching him with scorn . . . I can't tell him it's with pity . . . how can I help watching him? . . . help worrying over his worry because of what it might lead to . . . after what his mother . . . how horrible life is! . . .

he's worried now . . . he doesn't sleep . . . I hear him tossing about . . . I must sleep with him again soon . . . he's only home two nights a week . . . it isn't fair of me . . . I must try . . . I must! . . . he suspects my revulsion . . . it's hurting him . . . oh, poor dead baby I dared not bear, how I might have loved your father for your sake! . . .

EVANS (*suddenly feeling her presence, jerks himself to his feet—with a diffident guilty air which is noticeable about him now whenever he is in her presence*) Hello, dear. I thought you were lying down. (*Guiltily*) Did the noise of my typing bother you? I'm terribly sorry!

NINA (*irritated in spite of herself*)

Why is he always cringing? . . .

(*She comes forward to the chair at center and sits down—forcing a smile*) But there's nothing to be terribly sorry about! (*As he stands awkward and confused, like a schoolboy who has been called on to recite and cannot and is being "bawled out" before the class, she forces a playful tone*) Goodness, Sam, how tragic you can get about nothing at all!

EVANS (*still forced to justify himself—contritely*) I know it isn't pleasant for you having me drag my work out here, trying to pound out rotten ads. (*With a short laugh*) Trying to is right! (*Blurts out*) I wouldn't do it except that Cole gave me a warning to buck up—or get out.

NINA (*stares at him, more annoyed, her eyes hardening, thinking*) Yes! . . . he'll always be losing one job, getting another, starting with a burst of confidence each time, then . . .

(*Cutting him with a careless sneering tone*) Well, it isn't a job to worry much about losing, is it?

EVANS (*wincing pitiably*) No, not much money. But I used to think there was a fine chance to rise there—but of course that's my fault, I haven't made good— (*He finishes miserably*) somehow.

NINA (*her antagonism giving way to remorseful pity*)

What makes me so cruel? . . . he's so defenseless . . . his mother's baby . . . poor sick baby! . . . poor Sam!

(*She jumps to her feet and goes over to him*).

EVANS (*as she comes—with a defensive, boastful bravery*) Oh, I can get another job just as good, all right—maybe a lot better.

NINA (*reassuringly*) Certainly, you can! And I'm sure you're not going to lose this one. You're always anticipating trouble. (*She kisses him and sits on the arm of his chair, putting an arm around his neck and pulling his head on to her breast*) And it isn't your fault, you big goose, you! It's mine. I know how hard it makes everything for you, being tied to a wife who's too sick to be a wife. You ought to have married a big strapping, motherly—

EVANS (*in the seventh heaven now—passionately*) Bunk! All the other women in the world aren't worth your little finger! It's you who ought to have married someone worth while, not a poor fish like me! But no one could love you more than I do, no matter what he was!

NINA (*presses his head on her breast, avoiding his eyes, kisses him on the forehead*) And I love you, Sam. (*Staring out over his head—with loving pity, thinking*)

I almost do . . . poor unfortunate boy! . . . at these moments . . . as his mother loves him . . . but that isn't enough for him . . . I can hear his mother saying, "Sammy's got to feel sure you love him . . . to be happy." . . . I must try to make him feel sure . . .

(*Speaking gently*) I want you to be happy, Sam.

EVANS (*his face transformed with happiness*) I am—a hundred times more than I deserve!

NINA (*presses his head down on her breast so he cannot see her eyes—gently*) Ssshh. (*Thinking sadly*)

I promised her . . . but I couldn't see how hard it would be to let him love me . . . after his baby . . . was gone . . . it was hard even to keep on living . . . after that operation . . . Gordon's spirit followed me from room to room . . . poor reproachful ghost! . . .

(*With bitter mockery*)

Oh, Gordon, I'm afraid this is a deeper point of honor than any that was ever shot down in flames! . . . what would your honor say now? . . . "Stick to him! . . . play the game!" . . . oh, yes, I know . . . I'm sticking . . . but he isn't happy . . . I'm trying to play the game . . . then why do I keep myself from him? . . . but I was really sick . . . for a time after . . . since then, I couldn't . . . but . . . oh, I'll try . . . I'll try soon . . .

(*Tenderly—but having to force herself to say it*) Doesn't my boy want to sleep with me again—sometime soon?

EVANS (*passionately—hardly able to believe his ears*) Oh, it'd be wonderful, Nina! But are you sure you really want me to—that you'll feel well enough?

NINA (*repeats his words as if she were memorizing a lesson*) Yes, I want you to. Yes, I'll feel well enough. (*He seizes her hand and kisses it in a passionately grateful silence—she thinks with resigned finality*)

There, Sammy's mother and Gordon . . . I'll play the game . . . it will make him happy for a while . . . as he was in those weeks after we'd left his mother . . . when I gave myself with a mad pleasure in torturing myself for his pleasure! . . .

(*Then with weary hopelessness*)

He'll be happy until he begins to feel guilty again because I'm not pregnant . . .

(*With a grim bitter smile*)

Poor Sam, if he only knew the precautions . . . as if I wouldn't die rather than take the slightest chance of that happening! . . . ever again . . . what a tragic joke it was on both of us! . . . I wanted my baby so! . . . oh, God! . . . his mother said . . . "You've got to have a healthy baby . . . sometime . . . it's your rightful duty" . . . that seemed right then . . . but now . . . it seems cowardly . . . to betray poor Sam . . . and vile to give myself . . . without love or desire . . . and yet I've given myself to men before without a thought just to give them a moment's happiness . . . can't I do that again? . . . when it's a case of Sam's happiness? . . . and my own? . . .

(*She gets up from beside him with a hunted movement*) It must be half past eight. Charlie's coming to bring his suggestions on my outline for Gordon's biography.

EVANS (*his bliss shattered—dejectedly*)

Always happens . . . just as we get close . . . something comes between . . .

(*Then confusedly*) Say, I forgot to tell you Ned's coming out tonight.

NINA (*astonished*) Ned Darrell?

EVANS Sure. I happened to run into him the other day and invited him and he said Saturday evening. He couldn't tell what train. Said never mind meeting him.

NINA (*excitedly*) Why didn't you tell me before, you big booby! (*She kisses him*) There, don't mind. But it's just like you. Now someone'll have to go down to the store. And I'll have to get the spare room ready. (*She hurries to the doorway. He follows her*).

EVANS I'll help you.

NINA You'll do nothing of the kind! You'll stay right downstairs and bring them in here and cover up my absence. Thank heavens, Charlie won't stay long if Ned is here. (*The doorbell rings—excitedly*) There's one of them now. I'll run upstairs. Come up and tell me if it's Ned—and get rid of Charlie. (*She kisses him playfully and hurries out*).

EVANS (*looking after her—thinks*)
She seems better tonight . . . happier . . . she seems to love me . . . if she'll only get all well again, then everything will . . . (*The bell rings again*)
I must give Ned a good chance to talk to her . . .
(*He goes out to the outer door—returns a moment later with* MARSDEN. *The latter's manner is preoccupied and nervous. His face has an expression of anxiety which he tries to conceal. He seems a prey to some inner fear he is trying to hide even from himself and is resolutely warding off from his consciousness. His tall, thin body stoops as if a part of its sustaining will had been removed*).

EVANS (*with a rather forced welcoming note*) Come on in, Charlie. Nina's upstairs lying down.

MARSDEN (*with marked relief*) Then by all means don't disturb her. I just dropped in to bring back her outline with the suggestions I've made. (*He has taken some papers out of his pocket and hands them to* EVANS) I couldn't have stayed but a minute in any event. Mother is a bit under the weather these days.

EVANS (*perfunctorily*) Too bad. (*Thinking vindictively*)
Serve her right, the old scandal-monger, after the way she's gossiped about Nina! . . .

MARSDEN (*with assumed carelessness*) Just a little indigestion. Nothing serious but it annoys her terribly. (*Thinking frightenedly*)
That dull pain she complains of . . . I don't like it . . . and she won't see anyone but old Doctor Tibbetts . . . she's sixty-eight . . . I can't help fearing . . . no! . . .

EVANS (*bored—vaguely*) Well, I suppose you've got to be careful of every little thing when you get to her age.

MARSDEN (*positively bristling*) Her age? Mother isn't so old!

EVANS (*surprised*) Over sixty-five, isn't she?

MARSDEN (*indignantly*) You're quite out there! She's still under sixty-five—and in health and spirits she isn't more than fifty! Everyone remarks that! (*Annoyed at himself*)

Why did I lie to him about her age? . . . I must be on edge
. . . Mother is rather difficult to live with these days, getting me
worried to death, when it's probably nothing . . .

EVANS (*annoyed in his turn—thinking*)

Why all the fuss? . . . as if I gave a damn if the old girl was a
million! . . .

(*Indicating the papers*) I'll give these to Nina first thing in the
morning.

MARSDEN (*mechanically*) Righto. Thank you. (*He starts to go
toward door—then turns—fussily*) But you'd better take a look
while I'm here and see if it's clear. I've written on the margins.
See if there's anything you can't make out. (EVANS *nods helplessly and begins reading the sheets, going back beneath the
lamp*).

MARSDEN (*looking around him with squeamish disapproval*)

What a mess they've made of this study . . . poor Professor!
. . . dead and forgotten . . . and his tomb desecrated . . . does
Sam write his ads here of a week-end now? . . . the last touch!
. . . and Nina labors with love at Gordon's biography . . .
whom the Professor hated! . . . "life is so full of a number of
things!" . . . why does everyone in the world think they can
write? . . . but I've only myself to blame . . . why in the devil
did I ever suggest it to her? . . . because I hoped my helping her
while Sam was in the city would bring us alone together? . . .
but I made the suggestion before she had that abortion performed! . . . how do you know she did? . . . because I know!
. . . there are psychic affinities . . . her body confessed . . . and
since then, I've felt an aversion . . . as if she were a criminal . . .
she is! . . . how could she? . . . why? . . . I thought she
wanted a child . . . but evidently I don't know her . . . I suppose, afraid it would spoil her figure . . . her flesh . . . her
power to enslave men's senses . . . mine . . . and I had hoped
. . . looked forward to her becoming a mother . . . for my peace
of mind . . .

(*Catching himself—violently*)

Shut up! . . . what a base creature I'm becoming! . . . to have
such thoughts when Mother is sick and I ought to be thinking
only of her! . . . and it's none of my damn business, anyway! . . .

(*Glaring at* EVANS *resentfully as if he were to blame*)

Look at him! . . . he'll never suspect anything! . . . what a simple-simon! . . . he adored Gordon as a newsboy does a champion pugilist! . . . and Nina writes of Gordon as if he had been a demi-god! . . . when actually he came from the commonest people! . . .

(*He suddenly speaks to* EVANS *with a really savage satisfaction*) Did I tell you I once looked up Gordon's family in Beachampton? A truly deplorable lot! When I remembered Gordon and looked at his father I had either to suspect a lover in the wood pile or to believe in an Immaculate Conception . . . that is, until I saw his mother! Then a stork became the only conceivable explanation!

EVANS (*who has only half-heard and hasn't understood, says vaguely*) I never saw his folks. (*Indicating the papers*) I can make this all out all right.

MARSDEN (*sarcastically*) I'm glad it's understandable!

EVANS (*blunderingly*) I'll give it to Nina—and I hope your mother is feeling better tomorrow.

MARSDEN (*piqued*) Oh, I'm going. Why didn't you tell me if I was interrupting—your writing!

EVANS (*immediately guilty*) Oh, come on, Charlie, don't get peevish, you know I didn't mean— (*The bell rings.* EVANS *stammers in confusion, trying at a nonchalant air*) Hello! That must be Ned. You remember Darrell. He's coming out for a little visit. Excuse me. (*He blunders out of the door*).

MARSDEN (*looking after him with anger mixed with alarmed suspicion and surprise*)
Darrell? . . . what's he doing here? . . . have they been meeting? . . . perhaps he was the one who performed the . . . no, his idea was she ought to have a child . . . but if she came and begged him? . . . but why should Nina beg not to have a baby? . . .
(*Distractedly*)
Oh, I don't know! . . . it's all a sordid mess! . . . I ought to be going home! . . . I don't want to see Darrell! . . .
(*He starts for the door—then struck by a sudden thought, stops*)
Wait . . . I could ask him about Mother . . . yes . . . good idea . . .
(*He comes back to the middle of the room, front, and is standing there when* DARRELL *enters, followed by* EVANS. DARRELL *has not changed in appearance except that his expression is graver and more thoughtful. His manner is more convincingly authoritative,*

*more mature. He takes in* MARSDEN *from head to foot with one comprehensive glance).*

EVANS (*awkwardly*) Ned, you remember Charlie Marsden?

MARSDEN (*holding out his hand, urbanely polite*) How are you, Doctor?

DARRELL (*shaking his hand—briefly*) Hello.

EVANS I'll go up and tell Nina you're here, Ned. (*He goes, casting a resentful glance at* MARSDEN).

MARSDEN (*awkwardly, as* DARRELL *sits down in the chair at center, goes over and stands by the table*) I was on the point of leaving when you rang. Then I decided to stop and renew our acquaintance. (*He stoops and picks up one sheet of paper, and puts it back carefully on the table*).

DARRELL (*watching him—thinking*)

Neat . . . suspiciously neat . . . he's an old maid who seduces himself in his novels . . . so I suspect . . . I'd like a chance to study him more closely . . .

MARSDEN (*thinking resentfully*)

What a boor! . . . he might say something! . . .

(*Forcing a smile*) And I wanted to ask a favor of you, a word of advice as to the best specialist, the very best, it would be possible to consult—

DARRELL (*sharply*) On what?

MARSDEN (*almost naïvely*) My mother has a pain in her stomach.

DARRELL (*amused—dryly*) Possibly she eats too much.

MARSDEN (*as he bends and carefully picks another sheet from the floor to place it as carefully on the table*) She doesn't eat enough to keep a canary alive. It's a dull, constant pain, she says. She's terribly worried. She's terrified by the idea of cancer. But, of course, that perfect rot, she's never been sick a day in her life and—

DARRELL (*sharply*) She's showing more intelligence about her pain than you are.

MARSDEN (*bending down for another sheet, his voice trembling with terror*) I don't understand—quite. Do you mean to say you think—?

DARRELL (*brutally*) It's possible.

(*He has pulled out his pen and a card and is writing. Thinking grimly*)

Explode a bomb under him, as I did once before . . . only way to get him started doing anything. . . .

MARSDEN (*angrily*) But—that's nonsense!

DARRELL (*with satisfaction—unruffledly*) People who are afraid to face unpleasant possibilities until it's too late commit more murders and suicides than— (*Holds out card*) Doctor Schultz is your man. Take her to see him—tomorrow!

MARSDEN (*bursting out in anger and misery*) Damn it, you're condemning her without—! (*He breaks down chokingly*) You've no damn right!— (*He bends down, trembling all over, to pick up another piece of paper*).

DARRELL (*genuinely astonished and contrite*)
And I thought he was so ingrown he didn't care a damn about anyone! . . . his mother . . . now I begin to see him . . .
(*He jumps from his chair and going to* MARSDEN *puts a hand on his shoulder—kindly*) I beg your pardon, Marsden. I only wanted to drive it in that all delay is dangerous. Your mother's pain may be due to any number of harmless causes, but you owe it to her to make sure. Here. (*He hands out the card*).

MARSDEN (*straightens up and takes it, his eyes grateful now—humbly*) Thank you. I'll take her to see him tomorrow. (EVANS *comes in*).

EVANS (*to* MARSDEN, *blunderingly*) Say, Charlie, I don't want to hurry you but Nina wants some things at the store before it closes, and if you'd give me a lift—

MARSDEN (*dully*) Of course. Come along. (*He shakes hands with* DARRELL) Good night, Doctor—and thank you.

DARRELL Good night. (MARSDEN *goes, followed by* EVANS).

EVANS (*turns in the doorway and says meaningly*) Nina'll be right down. For Pete's sake, have a good heart-to-heart talk with her, Ned!

DARRELL (*frowning—impatiently*) Oh—all right! Run along. (EVANS *goes.* DARRELL *remains standing near the table looking after them, thinking about* MARSDEN)
Queer fellow, Marsden . . . mother's boy still . . . if she dies what will he do? . . .
(*Then dismissing* MARSDEN *with a shrug of his shoulders*)
Oh, well, he can always escape life in a new book. . . .
(*He moves around the table examining its disorder critically, then sits down in armchair—amused*).
Evidences of authorship . . . Sam's ads? . . . isn't making good, he said . . . was I wrong in thinking he had stuff in him? . . . hope not . . . always liked Sam, don't know why exactly . . .

said Nina'd gotten into a bad state again . . . what's happened to their marriage? . . . I felt a bit sorry for myself at their wedding . . . not that I'd ever fallen . . . but I did envy him in a way . . . she always had strong physical attraction for me . . . that time I kissed her . . . one reason I've steered clear since . . . take no chances on emotional didos . . . need all my mind on my work . . . got rid of even that slight suspicion . . . I'd forgotten all about her . . . she's a strange girl . . . interesting case . . . I should have kept in touch on that account . . . hope she'll tell me about herself . . . can't understand her not having child . . . it's so obviously the sensible thing . . .

(*Cynically*)

Probably why . . . to expect common sense of people proves you're lacking in it yourself! . . .

NINA (*enters silently. She has fixed herself up, put on her best dress, arranged her hair, rouged, etc.—but it is principally her mood that has changed her, making her appear a younger, prettier person for the moment.* DARRELL *immediately senses her presence, and, looking up, gets to his feet with a smile of affectionate admiration. She comes quickly over to him saying with frank pleasure*)   Hello, Ned. I'm certainly glad to see you again—after all these years!

DARRELL (*as they shake hands—smiling*)   Not as long as all that, is it? (*Thinking admiringly*)

Wonderful-looking as ever . . . Sam is a lucky devil! . . .

NINA (*thinking*)

Strong hands like Gordon's . . . take hold of you . . . not like Sam's . . . yielding fingers that let you fall back into yourself . . . (*Teasingly*) I ought to cut you dead after the shameful way you've ignored us!

DARRELL (*a bit embarrassedly*)   I've really meant to write. (*His eyes examining her keenly*)

Been through a lot since I saw her . . . face shows it . . . nervous tension pronounced . . . hiding behind her smile . . .

NINA (*uneasy under his glance*)

I hate that professional look in his eyes . . . watching symptoms . . . without seeing me . . .

(*With resentful mockery*) Well, what do you suspect is wrong with the patient now, Doctor? (*She laughs nervously*) Sit down, Ned. I suppose you can't help your diagnosing stare. (*She turns from him and sits down in the rocker at center*).

DARRELL (*quickly averting his eyes—sits down—jokingly*) Same old unjust accusation! You were always reading diagnosis into me, when what I was really thinking was what fine eyes you had, or what a becoming gown, or—

NINA (*smiling*) Or what a becoming alibi you could cook up! Oh, I know you! (*With a sudden change of mood she laughs gaily and naturally*) But you're forgiven—that is, if you can explain why you've never been to see us.

DARRELL Honestly, Nina, I've been so rushed with work I haven't had a chance to go anywhere.

NINA Or an inclination!

DARRELL (*smiling*) Well—maybe.

NINA Do you like the Institute so much? (*He nods gravely*) Is it the big opportunity you wanted?

DARRELL (*simply*) I think it is.

NINA (*with a smile*) Well, you're the taking kind for whom opportunities are made!

DARRELL (*smiling*) I hope so.

NINA (*sighing*) I wish that could be said of more of us— (*Then quickly*) —meaning myself.

DARRELL (*thinking with a certain satisfaction*)
Meaning Sam . . . that doesn't look hopeful for future wedded bliss! . . .
(*Teasingly*) But I heard you were "taking an opportunity" to go in for literature—collaborating with Marsden.

NINA No, Charlie is only going to advise. He'd never deign to appear as co-author. And besides, he never appreciated the real Gordon. No one did except me.

DARRELL (*thinking caustically*)
Gordon myth strong as ever . . . root of her trouble still . . .
(*Keenly inquisitive*) Sam certainly appreciated him, didn't he?

NINA (*not remembering to hide her contempt*) Sam? Why, he's the exact opposite in every way!

DARRELL (*caustically thinking*)
These heroes die hard . . . but perhaps she can write him out of her system. . . .
(*Persuasively*) Well, you're going ahead with the biography, aren't you? I think you ought to.

NINA (*dryly*) For my soul, Doctor? (*Listlessly*) I suppose I will. I don't know. I haven't much time. The duties of a wife—

(*Teasingly*) By the way, if it isn't too rude to inquire, aren't you getting yourself engaged to some fair lady or other?

DARRELL (*smiling—but emphatically*) Not on your life! Not until after I'm thirty-five, at least!

NINA (*sarcastically*) Then you don't believe in taking your own medicine? Why, Doctor! Think of how much good it would do you!— (*Excitedly with a hectic sarcasm*) —if you had a nice girl to love—or was it learn to love?—and take care of—whose character you could shape and whose life you could guide and make what you pleased, in whose unselfish devotion you could find peace! (*More and more bitterly sarcastic*) And you ought to have a baby, Doctor! You will never know what life is, you'll never be really happy until you've had a baby, Doctor—a fine, healthy baby! (*She laughs a bitter, sneering laugh*).

DARRELL (*after a quick, keen glance, thinking*)

Good! . . . she's going to tell . . .

(*Meekly*) I recognize my arguments. Was I really wrong on every point, Nina?

NINA (*harshly*) On every single point, Doctor!

DARRELL (*glancing at her keenly*) But how? You haven't given the baby end of it a chance yet, have you?

NINA (*bitterly*) Oh, haven't I? (*Then bursts out with intense bitterness*) I'll have you know I'm not destined to bear babies, Doctor!

DARELL (*startledly*)

What's that? . . . why not? . . .

(*Again with a certain satisfaction*)

Can she mean Sam? . . . that he . . .

(*Soothingly—but plainly disturbed*) Why don't you begin at the beginning and tell me all about it? I feel responsible.

NINA (*fiercely*) You are! (*Then wearily*) And you're not. No one is. You didn't know. No one could know.

DARRELL (*in same tone*) Know what? (*Thinking with the same eagerness to believe something he hopes*)

She must mean no one could know that Sam wasn't . . . but I might have guessed it . . . from his general weakness . . . poor unlucky devil . . .

(*Then as she remains silent—urgingly*) Tell me. I want to help you, Nina.

NINA (*touched*) It's too late, Ned. (*Then suddenly*) I've just thought—Sam said he happened to run into you. That isn't so, is it? He went to see you and told you how worried he was about me and asked you out to see me, didn't he? (*As* DARRELL *nods*) Oh, I don't mind! It's even rather touching. (*Then mockingly*) Well, since you're out here professionally, and my husband wants me to consult you, I might as well give you the whole case history! (*Wearily*) I warn you it isn't pretty, Doctor! But then life doesn't seem to be pretty, does it? And, after all, you aided and abetted God the Father in making this mess. I hope it'll teach you not to be so cocksure in future. (*More and more bitterly*) I must say you proceeded very unscientifically, Doctor! (*Then suddenly starts her story in a dull monotonous tone recalling that of* EVANS' *mother in the previous Act*) When we went to visit Sam's mother I'd known for two months that I was going to have a baby.

DARRELL (*startled—unable to hide a trace of disappointment*) Oh, then you actually were? (*Thinking disappointedly and ashamed of himself for being disappointed*)

All wrong, what I thought . . . she was going to . . . then why didn't she? . . .

NINA (*with a strange happy intensity*) Oh, Ned, I loved it more than I've ever loved anything in my life—even Gordon! I loved it so it seemed at times that Gordon must be its real father, that Gordon must have come to me in a dream while I was lying asleep beside Sam! And I was happy! I almost loved Sam then! I felt he was a good husband!

DARRELL (*instantly repelled—thinking with scornful jealousy*) Ha! . . . the hero again! . . . comes to her bed! . . . puts horns on poor Sam! . . . becomes the father of his child! . . . I'll be damned if hers isn't the most idiotic obsession I ever . . .

NINA (*her voice suddenly becoming flat and lifeless*) And then Sam's mother told me I couldn't have my baby. You see, Doctor, Sam's great-grandfather was insane, and Sam's grandmother died in an asylum, and Sam's father had lost his mind for years before he died, and an aunt who is still alive is crazy. So of course I had to agree it would be wrong—and I had an operation.

DARRELL (*who has listened with amazed horror—profoundly shocked and stunned*) Good God! Are you crazy, Nina? I simply can't believe! It would be too hellish! Poor Sam, of all people! (*Bewilderedly*) Nina! Are you absolutely sure?

NINA (*immediately defensive and mocking*) Absolutely, Doctor! Why? Do you think it's I who am crazy? Sam looks so healthy and sane, doesn't he? He fooled you completely, didn't he? You thought he'd be an ideal husband for me! And poor Sam's fooling himself too because he doesn't know anything about all this—so you can't blame him, Doctor!

DARRELL (*thinking in a real panic of horror—and a flood of protective affection for her*)
God, this is too awful! . . . on top of all the rest! . . . how did she ever stand it! . . . she'll lose her mind too! . . . and it's my fault! . . .
(*Getting up, comes to her and puts his hands on her shoulders, standing behind her—tenderly*) Nina! I'm so damn sorry! There's only one possible thing to do now. You'll have to make Sam give you a divorce.

NINA (*bitterly*) Yes? Then what do you suppose would be his finish? No, I've enough guilt in my memory now, thank you! I've got to stick to Sam! (*Then with a strange monotonous insistence*) I've promised Sam's mother I'd make him happy! He's unhappy now because he thinks he isn't able to give me a child. And I'm unhappy because I've lost my child. So I must have another baby—somehow—don't you think, Doctor?—to make us both happy? (*She looks up at him pleadingly. For a moment they stare into each other's eyes—then both turn away in guilty confusion*).

DARRELL (*bewilderedly thinking*)
That look in her eyes . . . what does she want me to think? . . . why does she talk so much about being happy? . . . am I happy? . . . I don't know . . . what is happiness? . . .
(*Confusedly*) Nina, I don't know what to think.

NINA (*thinking strangely*)
That look in his eyes . . . what did he mean? . . .
(*With the same monotonous insistence*) You must know what to think. I can't think it out myself any more. I need your advice—your *scientific* advice this time, if you please, Doctor. I've thought and thought about it. I've told myself it's what I ought to do. Sam's own mother urged me to do it. It's sensible and kind and just and good. I've told myself this a thousand times and yet I can't quite convince something in me that's afraid of something. I need the courage of someone who can stand outside and reason it out as if Sam and I were no more than guinea pigs. You've got to help me, Doctor! You've got to show me what's the sane—the truly sane, you understand!—thing I must do for Sam's sake, and my own.

DARRELL (*thinking confusedly*)

What do I have to do? . . . this was all my fault . . . I owe her something in return . . . I owe Sam something . . . *I* owe them happiness! . . .

(*Irritably*)

Damn it, there's a humming in my ears! . . . I've caught some fever . . . I swore to live coolly . . . let me see. . . .

(*In cold, emotionless professional voice, his face like a mask of a doctor*) A doctor must be in full possession of the facts, if he is to advise. What is it precisely that Sam's wife has thought so much of doing?

NINA (*in the same insistent tone*) Of picking out a healthy male about whom she cared nothing and having a child by him that Sam would believe was his child, whose life would give him confidence in his own living, who would be for him a living proof that his wife loved him. (*Confusedly, strangely and purposefully*)

This doctor is healthy. . . .

DARRELL (*in his ultra-professional manner—like an automaton of a doctor*) I see. But this needs a lot of thinking over. It isn't easy to prescribe— (*Thinking*)

I have a friend who has a wife . . . I was envious at his wedding . . . but what has that to do with it? . . . damn it, my mind won't work! . . . it keeps running away to her . . . it wants to mate with her mind . . . in the interest of Science? . . . what damned rot I'm thinking! . . .

NINA (*thinking as before*)

This doctor is nothing to me but a healthy male . . . when he was Ned he once kissed me . . . but I cared nothing about him . . . so that's all right, isn't it, Sam's Mother?

DARRELL (*thinking*)

Let me see. . . . I am in the laboratory and they are guinea pigs . . . in fact, in the interest of science, I can be for the purpose of this experiment, a healthy guinea pig myself and still remain an observer . . . I observe my pulse is high, for example, and that's obviously because I am stricken with a recurrence of an old desire . . . desire is a natural male reaction to the beauty of the female . . . her husband is my friend. . . . I have always tried to help him . . .

(*Coldly*) I've been considering what Sam's wife told me and her reasoning is quite sound. The child can't be her husband's.

NINA   Then you agree with Sam's mother? She said: "Being happy is the nearest we can ever come to knowing what good is!"

DARRELL   I agree with her decidedly. Sam's wife should find a healthy father for Sam's child at once. It is her sane duty to her husband. (*Worriedly thinking*)

Have I ever been happy? . . . I have studied to cure the body's unhappiness . . . I have watched happy smiles form on the lips of the dying . . . I have experienced pleasure with a number of women I desired but never loved . . . I have known a bit of honor and a trifle of self-satisfaction . . . this talk of happiness seems to me extraneous . . .

NINA   (*beginning to adopt a timid, diffident, guilty tone*)   This will have to be hidden from Sam so he can never know! Oh, Doctor, Sam's wife is afraid!

DARRELL   (*sharply professional*)   Nonsense! This is no time for timidity! Happiness hates the timid! So does Science! Certainly Sam's wife must conceal her action! To let Sam know would be insanely cruel of her—and stupid, for then no one could be the happier for her act! (*Anxiously thinking*)

Am I right to advise this? . . . yes, it is clearly the rational thing to do . . . but this advice betrays my friend! . . . no, it saves him! . . . it saves his wife . . . and if a third party should know a little happiness . . . is he any poorer, am I any the less his friend because I saved him? . . . no, my duty to him is plain . . . and my duty as an experimental searcher after truth . . . to observe these three guinea pigs, of which I am one . . .

NINA   (*thinking determinedly*)

I must have my baby! . . .

(*Timidly—gets from her chair and half-turns toward him—pleadingly*) You must give his wife courage, Doctor. You must free her from her feeling of guilt.

DARRELL   There can only be guilt when one deliberately neglects one's manifest duty to life. Anything else is rot! This woman's duty is to save her husband and herself by begetting a healthy child! (*Thinking guiltily and instinctively moving away from her*)

I am healthy . . . but he is my friend . . . there is such a thing as honor! . . .

NINA   (*determinedly*)

I must take my happiness! . . .

(*Frightenedly—comes after him*) But she is ashamed. It's adultery. It's wrong.

DARRELL (*moving away again—with a cold sneering laugh of impatience*) Wrong! Would she rather see her husband wind up in an asylum? Would she rather face the prospect of going to pot mentally, morally, physically herself through year after year of deviling herself and him? Really, Madame, if you can't throw overboard all such irrelevant moral ideas, I'll have to give up this case here and now! (*Thinking frightenedly*)

Who is talking? . . . is he suggesting me? . . . but you know very well I can't be the one, Doctor! . . . why not, you're healthy and it's a friendly act for all concerned . . .

NINA (*thinking determinedly*)

I must have my baby! . . .

(*Going further toward him—she can now touch him with her hand*) Please, Doctor, you must give her strength to do this right thing that seems to her so right and then so wrong! (*She puts out her hand and takes one of his*).

DARRELL (*thinking frightenedly*)

Whose hand is this? . . . it burns me . . . I kissed her once . . . her lips were cold . . . now they would burn with happiness for me! . . .

NINA (*taking his other hand and slowly pulling him around to face her, although he does not look at her—pleadingly*) Now she feels your strength. It gives her the courage to ask you, Doctor, to suggest the father. She has changed, Doctor, since she became Sam's wife. She can't bear the thought now of giving herself to any man she could neither desire nor respect. So each time her thoughts come to the man she must select they are afraid to go on! She needs your courage to choose!

DARRELL (*as if listening to himself*)

Sam is my friend . . . well, and isn't she your friend? . . . her two hands are so warm! . . . I must not even hint at my desire! . . .

(*Judicially calm*) Well, the man must be someone who is not unattractive to her physically, of course.

NINA Ned always attracted her.

DARRELL (*thinking frightenedly*)

What's that she said? . . . Ned? . . . attracts? . . .

(*In same tone*) And the man should have a mind that can truly understand—a scientific mind superior to the moral scruples that cause so much human blundering and unhappiness.

NINA She always thought Ned had a superior mind.

DARRELL (*thinking frightenedly*)

Did she say Ned? . . . she thinks Ned . . . ?

(*In same tone*) The man should like and admire her, he should be her good friend and want to help her, but he should not love her—although he might, without harm to anyone, desire her.

NINA Ned does not love her—but he used to like her and, I think, desire her. Does he now, Doctor?

DARRELL (*thinking*)

Does he? . . . who is he? . . . he is Ned! . . . Ned is I! . . . I desire her! . . . I desire happiness! . . .

(*Trembling now—gently*) But, Madame, I must confess the Ned you are speaking of is I, and I am Ned.

NINA (*gently*) And I am Nina, who wants her baby. (*Then she reaches out and turns his head until his face faces hers but he keeps his eyes down—she bends her head meekly and submissively—softly*) I should be so grateful, Ned. (*He starts, looks up at her wildly, makes a motion as though to take her in his arms, then remains fixed for a moment in that attitude, staring at her bowed head as she repeats submissively*) I should be so humbly grateful.

DARRELL (*suddenly falling on his knees and taking her hand in both of his and kissing it humbly—with a sob*) Yes—yes, Nina —yes—for your happiness—in that spirit! (*Thinking—fiercely triumphant*)

I shall be happy for a while! . . .

NINA (*raising her head—thinking—proudly triumphant*) I shall be happy! . . . I shall make my husband happy! . . .

*Curtain*

ACT FIVE

SCENE: *The sitting room of a small house* EVANS *has rented in a seashore suburb near New York. It is a bright morning in the following April.*

*The room is a typical sitting room of the quantity-production bungalow type. Windows on the left look out on a broad porch. A double doorway in rear leads into the hall. A door on right, to the dining room.* NINA *has tried to take the curse of offensive, banal newness off the room with some of her own things from her old home but the attempt has been half-hearted in the face of such overpowering commonness, and the result is a room as disorganized in character as the* PROFESSOR's *study in the last Act.*

*The arrangement of the furniture follows the same pattern as in preceding scenes. There is a Morris chair and a round golden oak table at left of center, an upholstered chair, covered with bright chintz at center, a sofa covered with the same chintz at right.*

NINA *is sitting in the chair at center. She has been trying to read a book but has let this drop listlessly on her lap. A great change is noticeable in her face and bearing. She is again the pregnant woman of Act Three but this time there is a triumphant strength about her expression, a ruthless self-confidence in her eyes. She has grown stouter, her face has filled out. One gets no impression of neurotic strain from her now, she seems nerveless and deeply calm.*

NINA (*as if listening for something within her—joyfully*)
There! . . . that can't be my imagination . . . I felt it plainly . . . life . . . my baby . . . my only baby . . . the other never really lived . . . this is the child of my love! . . . I love Ned! . . . I've loved him ever since that first afternoon . . . when I went to him . . . so scientifically! . . .
(*She laughs at herself*)
Oh, what a goose I was! . . . then love came to me . . . in his arms . . . happiness! . . . I hid it from him . . . I saw he was frightened . . . his own joy frightened him . . . I could feel him fighting with himself . . . during all those afternoons . . . our wonderful afternoons of happiness! . . . and I said nothing . . . I made myself be calculating . . . so when he finally said . . . dreadfully disturbed . . . "Look here, Nina, we've done all that is necessary, playing with fire is dangerous" . . . I said, "You're quite right, Ned, of all things I don't want to fall in love with you!" . . .
(*She laughs*)
He didn't like that! . . . he looked angry . . . and afraid . . . then for weeks he never even phoned . . . I waited . . . it was prudent to wait . . . but every day I grew more terrified . . .

then just as my will was breaking, his broke . . . he suddenly appeared again . . . but I held him to his aloof doctor's pose and sent him away, proud of his will power . . . and sick of himself with desire for me! . . . every week since then he's been coming out here . . . as my doctor . . . we've talked about our child wisely, dispassionately . . . as if it were Sam's child . . . we've never given in to our desire . . . and I've watched love grow in him until I'm sure . . .

(*With sudden alarm*)

But am I? . . . he's never once mentioned love . . . perhaps I've been a fool to play the part I've played . . . it may have turned him against me . . .

(*Suddenly with calm confidence*)

No . . . he does . . . I feel it . . . it's only when I start thinking, I begin to doubt . . .

(*She settles back and stares dreamily before her—a pause*)

There . . . again . . . his child! . . . my child moving in my life . . . my life moving in my child . . . the world is whole and perfect . . . all things are each other's . . . life is . . . and the is is beyond reason . . . questions die in the silence of this peace . . . I am living a dream within the great dream of the tide . . . breathing in the tide I dream and breathe back my dream into the tide . . . suspended in the movement of the tide, I feel life move in me, suspended in me . . . no whys matter . . . there is no why . . . I am a mother . . . God is a Mother . . .

(*She sighs happily, closing her eyes. A pause.* EVANS *enters from the hallway in rear. He is dressed carefully but his clothes are old ones—shabby collegiate gentility—and he has forgotten to shave. His eyes look pitiably harried, his manner has become a distressingly obvious attempt to cover up a chronic state of nervous panic and guilty conscience. He stops inside the doorway and looks at her with a pitiable furtiveness, arguing with himself, trying to get up his courage*)

Tell her! . . . go on! . . . you made up your mind to, didn't you? . . . don't quit now! . . . tell her you've decided . . . for her sake . . . to face the truth . . . that she can't love you . . . she's tried . . . she's acted like a good sport . . . but she's beginning to hate you . . . and you can't blame her . . . she wanted children . . . and you haven't been able . . .

(*Protesting feebly*)

But I don't know for certain . . . that that's my fault . . .
(*Then bitterly*)
Aw, don't kid yourself, if she'd married someone else . . . if
Gordon had lived and married her . . . I'll be in the first month
she'd . . . you'd better resign from the whole game . . . with a
gun! . . .
(*He swallows hard as if he were choking back a sob—then sav-
agely*)
Stop whining! . . . go on and wake her up! . . . say you're will-
ing to give her a divorce so she can marry some real guy who can
give her what she ought to have! . . .
(*Then with sudden terror*)
And if she says yes? . . . I couldn't bear it! . . . I'd die without
her! . . .
(*Then with a somber alien forcefulness*)
All right . . . good riddance! . . . I'd have the guts to bump
off then, all right! . . . that'd set her free . . . come on now!
. . . ask her! . . .
(*But his voice begins to tremble uncertainly again as he calls*)
Nina.

NINA (*opens her eyes and gazes calmly, indifferently at him*)
Yes?

EVANS (*immediately terrified and beaten—thinking*)
I can't! . . . the way she looks at me! . . . she'd say yes! . . .
(*Stammering*) I hate to wake you up but—it's about time for
Ned to come, isn't it?

NINA (*calmly*) I wasn't asleep.
(*Thinking as if she found it hard to concentrate on him, to
realize his existence*)
This man is my husband . . . it's hard to remember that . . .
people will say he's the father of my child . . .
(*With revulsion*)
That's shameful! . . . and yet that's exactly what I wanted! . . .
wanted! . . . not now! . . . now I love Ned! . . . I won't lose
him! . . . Sam must give me a divorce . . . I've sacrificed
enough of my life . . . what has he given me? . . . not even a
home . . . I had to sell my father's home to get money so we
could move near his job . . . and then he lost his job! . . . now
he's depending on Ned to help him get another! . . . my
love! . . . how shameless! . . .
(*Then contritely*)

Oh, I'm unjust . . . poor Sam doesn't know about Ned . . . and it was I who wanted to sell the place . . . I was lonely there . . . I wanted to be near Ned. . . .

EVANS (*thinking in agony*)

What's she thinking? . . . probably lucky for me I don't know! . . .

(*Forcing a brisk air as he turns away from her*) I hope Ned brings that letter he promised me to the manager of the Globe company. I'm keen to get on the job again.

NINA (*with scornful pity*) Oh, I guess Ned will bring the letter. I asked him not to forget.

EVANS I hope they'll have an opening right off. We can use the money. (*Hanging his head*) I feel rotten, living on you when you've got so little.

NINA (*indifferently but with authority, like a governess to a small boy*) Now, now!

EVANS (*relieved*) Well, it's true. (*Then coming to her—humbly ingratiating*) You've felt a lot better lately, haven't you, Nina?

NINA (*with a start—sharply*) Why?

EVANS You look ever so much better. You're getting fat. (*He forces a grin*).

NINA (*curtly*) Don't be absurd, please! As a matter of fact, I don't feel a bit better.

EVANS (*thinking despondently*)

Lately, she jumps on me every chance she gets . . . as if everything I did disgusted her! . . .

(*He strays over to the window and looks out listlessly*) I thought we'd get some word from Charlie this morning saying if he was coming down or not. But I suppose he's still too broken up over his mother's death to write.

NINA (*indifferently*) He'll probably come without bothering to write. (*Vaguely—wonderingly*)

Charlie . . . dear old Charlie . . . I've forgotten him, too. . . .

EVANS I think that's Ned's car now. Yes. It's stopping. I'll go out and meet him. (*He starts for the door in rear*).

NINA (*sharply, before she can restrain the impulse*) Don't be such a fool!

EVANS (*stops—stammers confusedly*) What—what's the matter?

NINA (*controlling herself—but irritably*) Don't mind me. I'm nervous. (*Thinking guiltily*)

One minute I feel ashamed of him for making such a fool of

himself over my lover . . . the next minute something hateful
urges me to drive him into doing it! . . .

(*The maid has answered the ring and opened the outer door.*
NED DARRELL *comes in from the rear. His face looks older. There
is an expression of defensive bitterness and self-resentment about
his mouth and eyes. This vanishes into one of desire and joy as he
sees* NINA. *He starts toward her impulsively*) Nina! (*Then stops
short as he sees* EVANS).

NINA (*forgetting* EVANS, *gets to her feet as if to receive* DARRELL
*in her arms—with love*) Ned!

EVANS (*affectionately and gratefully*) Hello, Ned! (*He holds out
his hand which* DARRELL *takes mechanically*).

DARRELL (*trying to overcome his guilty embarrassment*) Hello,
Sam. Didn't see you. (*Hurriedly reaching in his coat pocket*)
Before I forget, here's that letter. I had a talk over the phone
with Appleby yesterday. He's pretty sure there's an opening—
(*With a condescension he can't help*) —but you'll have to get
your nose on the grindstone to make good with him.

EVANS (*flushing guiltily—forcing a confident tone*) You bet I
will! (*Then gratefully and humbly*) Gosh, Ned, I can't tell you
how grateful I am!

DARRELL (*brusquely, to hide his embarrassment*) Oh, shut up!
I'm only too glad.

NINA (*watching* EVANS *with a contempt that is almost gloating—
in a tone of curt dismissal*) You'd better go and shave, hadn't
you, if you're going to town?

EVANS (*guiltily, passing his hand over his face—forcing a brisk
purposeful air*) Yes, of course. I forgot I hadn't. Excuse me, will
you? (*This to* DARRELL. EVANS *hurries out, rear*).

DARRELL (*as soon as he is out of earshot—turning on* NINA *accusingly*) How can you treat him that way? It makes me feel—
like a swine!

NINA (*flushing guiltily—protestingly*) What way? (*Then inconsequentially*) He's always forgetting to shave lately.

DARRELL You know what I mean, Nina! (*turns away from her—
thinking bitterly*)
What a rotten liar I've become! . . . and he trusts me absolutely! . . .

NINA (*thinking frightenedly*)
Why doesn't he take me in his arms? . . . oh, I feel he doesn't
love me now! . . . he's so bitter! . . .

(*Trying to be matter-of-fact*) I'm sorry, Ned. I don't mean to be cross but Sam does get on my nerves.

DARRELL (*thinking bitterly*)

Sometimes I almost hate her! . . . if it wasn't for her I'd have kept my peace of mind . . . no good for anything lately, damn it! . . . but it's idiotic to feel guilty . . . if Sam only didn't trust me! . . .

(*Then impatiently*)

Bosh! . . . sentimental nonsense! . . . end justifies means! . . . this will have a good end for Sam, I swear to that! . . . why doesn't she tell him she's pregnant? . . . what's she waiting for? . . .

NINA (*thinking passionately, looking at him*)

Oh, my lover, why don't you kiss me? . . .

(*Imploringly*) Ned! Don't be cross with me, please!

DARRELL (*fighting to control himself—coldly*)   I'm not cross, Nina. Only you must admit these triangular scenes are, to say the least, humiliating. (*Resentfully*) I won't come out here again!

NINA (*with a cry of pain*)   Ned!

DARRELL (*thinking exultingly at first*)

She loves me! . . . she's forgotten Gordon! . . . I'm happy! . . . do I love her? . . . no! . . . I won't! . . . I can't! . . . think what it would mean to Sam! . . . to my career! . . . be objective about it! . . . you guinea pig! . . . I'm her doctor . . . and Sam's . . . I prescribed child for them . . . that's all there is to it! . . .

NINA (*torn between hope and fear*)

What is he thinking? . . . he's fighting his love . . . oh, my lover! . . .

(*Again with longing*) Ned!

DARRELL (*putting on his best professional air, going to her*)   How do you feel today? You look as if you might have a little fever. (*He takes her hand as if to feel her pulse. Her hand closes over his. She looks up into his face. He keeps his turned away*).

NINA (*straining up toward him—with intense longing—thinking*) I love you! . . . take me! . . . what do I care for anything in the world but you! . . . let Sam die! . . .

DARRELL (*fighting himself—thinking*)

Christ! . . . touch of her skin! . . . her nakedness! . . . those afternoons in her arms! happiness! . . . what do I care for anything else? . . . to hell with Sam! . . .

NINA (*breaking out passionately*) Ned! I love you! I can't hide it any more! I won't! I love you, Ned!

DARRELL (*suddenly taking her in his arms and kissing her frantically*) Nina! Beautiful!

NINA (*triumphantly—between kisses*) You love me, don't you? Say you do, Ned!

DARRELL (*passionately*) Yes! Yes!

NINA (*with a cry of triumph*) Thank God! At last you've told me! You've confessed it to yourself! Oh, Ned, you've made me so happy! (*There is a ring from the front door bell.* DARRELL *hears it. It acts like an electric shock on him. He tears himself away from her. Instinctively she gets up too and moves to the lounge at right*).

DARRELL (*stupidly*) Someone—at the door. (*He sinks down in the chair by the table at left. Thinking torturedly*)
I said I loved her! . . . she won! . . . she used my desire! . . . but I don't love her! . . . I won't! . . . she can't own my life! . . .
(*Violently—almost shouts at her*) I don't, Nina! I tell you I don't!

NINA (*the maid has just gone to the front door*) Sshh! (*Then in a triumphant whisper*) You do, Ned! You do!

DARRELL (*with dogged stupidity*) I don't! (*The front door has been opened.* MARSDEN *appears in the rear, walks slowly and woodenly like a man in a trance into the room. He is dressed immaculately in deep mourning. His face is pale, drawn, haggard with loneliness and grief. His eyes have a dazed look as if he were still too stunned to comprehend clearly what has happened to him. He does not seem conscious of* DARRELL'S *presence at first. His shoulders are bowed, his whole figure droops*).

NINA (*thinking—in a strange superstitious panic*)
Black . . . in the midst of happiness . . . black comes . . . again . . . death . . . my father . . . comes between me and happiness! . . .
(*Then recovering herself, scornfully*)
You silly coward! . . . it's only Charlie! . . .
(*Then with furious resentment*)
The old fool! . . . what does he mean coming in on us without warning? . . .

MARSDEN (*forcing a pitiful smile to his lips*) Hello, Nina. I know it's an imposition—but—I've been in such a terrible state since

Mother— (*He falters, his face becomes distorted into an ugly mask of grief, his eyes water*).

NINA (*immediately sympathetic, gets up and goes to him impulsively*) There's no question of imposition, Charlie. We were expecting you. (*She has come to him and put her arms around him. He gives way and sobs, his head against her shoulder*).

MARSDEN (*brokenly*) You don't know, Nina—how terrible—it's terrible!—

NINA (*leading him to the chair at center, soothingly*) I know, Charlie.

(*Thinking with helpless annoyance*)

Oh, dear, what can I say? . . . his mother hated me . . . I'm not glad she's dead . . . but neither am I sorry . . .

(*With a trace of contempt*)

Poor Charlie . . . he was so tied to her apron strings . . .

(*Then kindly but condescendingly, comforting him*) Poor old Charlie!

MARSDEN (*the words and the tone shock his pride to life. He raises his head and half-pushes her away—resentfully, thinking*) Poor old Charlie! . . . damn it, what am I to her? . . . her old dog who's lost his mother? . . . Mother hated her . . . no, poor dear Mother was so sweet, she never hated anyone . . . she simply disapproved . . .

(*Coldly*) I'm all right, Nina. Quite all right now, thank you. I apologize for making a scene.

DARRELL (*has gotten up from his chair—with relief—thinking*) Thank God for Marsden . . . I feel sane again . . .

(*He comes to* MARSDEN—*cordially*) How are you, Marsden? (*Then offering conventional consolation, pats* MARSDEN's *shoulder*) I'm sorry, Marsden.

MARSDEN (*startled, looks up at him in amazement*) Darrell! (*Then with instant hostility*) There's nothing to be sorry about that I can discover! (*Then as they both look at him in surprise he realizes what he has said—stammeringly*) I mean—sorry—is hardly the right word—hardly—is it?

NINA (*worriedly*) Sit down, Charlie. You look so tired. (*He slumps down in the chair at center mechanically.* NINA *and* DARRELL *return to their chairs.* NINA *looks across him at* DARRELL —*triumphantly—thinking*)

You do love me, Ned! . . .

DARRELL (*thinking—answering her look—defiantly*)
I don't love you! . . .

MARSDEN (*stares intensely before him. Thinking suspiciously—morbidly agitated*)
Darrell! . . . and Nina! . . . there's something in this room!
. . . something disgusting! . . . like a brutal, hairy hand, raw
and red, at my throat! . . . stench of human life! . . . heavy
and rank! . . . outside it's April . . . green buds on the slim
trees . . . the sadness of spring . . . my loss at peace in Nature
. . . her sorrow of birth consoling my sorrow of death . . . something human and unnatural in this room! . . . love and hate and
passion and possession! . . . cruelly indifferent to my loss! . . .
mocking my loneliness! . . . no longer any love for me in any
room! . . . lust in this room! . . . lust with a loathsome jeer
taunting my sensitive timidities! . . . my purity! . . . purity?
. . . ha! yes, if you say prurient purity! . . . lust ogling me for
a dollar with oily shoe button Italian eyes! . . .
(*In terror*)
What thoughts! . . . what a low scoundrel you are! . . . and
your mother dead only two weeks! . . . I hate Nina! . . . that
Darrell in this room! . . . I feel their desires! . . . where is
Sam? . . . I'll tell him! . . . no, he wouldn't believe . . . he's
such a trusting fool . . . I must punish her some other way . . .
(*Remorsefully*)
What? . . . punish Nina? . . . my little Nina? . . . why, I want
her to be happy! . . . even with Darrell? . . . it's all so confused! . . . I must stop thinking! . . . I must talk! . . . forget!
. . . say something! . . . forget everything! . . .
(*He suddenly bursts into a flood of garrulity*) Mother asked for
you, Nina—three days before the end. She said, "Where is Nina
Leeds now, Charlie? When is she going to marry Gordon
Shaw?" Her mind was wandering, poor woman! You remember
how fond she always was of Gordon. She used to love to watch
the football games when he was playing. He was so handsome
and graceful, she always thought. She always loved a strong,
healthy body. She took such strict care of her own, she walked
miles every day, she loved bathing and boating in the summer
even after she was sixty, she was never sick a day in her life
until— (*He turns on* DARRELL—*coldly*) You were right, Doctor
Darrell. It was cancer. (*Then angrily*) But the doctor you sent
me to, and the others he called in could do nothing for her—

absolutely nothing! I might just as well have imported some witch doctors from the Solomon Islands! They at least would have diverted her in her last hours with their singing and dancing, but your specialists were at total loss! (*Suddenly with an insulting, ugly sneer, raising his voice*) I think you doctors are a pack of God-damned ignorant liars and hypocrites!

NINA (*sharply*) Charlie!

MARSDEN (*coming to himself—with a groan—shamefacedly*) Don't mind me. I'm not myself, Nina. I've been through hell! (*He seems about to sob—then abruptly springs to his feet, wildly*) It's this room! I can't stand this room! There's something repulsive about it!

NINA (*soothingly*) I know it's ugly, Charlie. I haven't had a chance to fix it up yet. We've been too broke.

MARSDEN (*confusedly*) Oh, it's all right. I'm ugly, too! Where's Sam?

NINA (*eagerly*) Right upstairs. Go on up. He'll be delighted to see you.

MARSDEN (*vaguely*) Very well. (*He goes to the door, then stops mournfully*) But from what I saw on that visit to his home, he doesn't love his mother much. I don't think he'll understand, Nina. He never writes to her, does he?

NINA (*uneasily*) No—I don't know.

MARSDEN She seemed lonely. He'll be sorry for it some day after she— (*He gulps*) Well— (*He goes*).

NINA (*in a sudden panic—thinking*)

Sam's mother! . . . "Make my boy, Sammy, happy!" . . . I promised . . . oh, why did Charlie have to remember her? . . . (*Then resolutely*)

I can't remember her now! . . . I won't! . . . I've got to be happy! . . .

DARRELL (*uneasily trying to force a casual conversation*) Poor Marsden is completely knocked off balance, isn't he? (*A pause*) My mother died when I was away at school. I hadn't seen her in some time, so her death was never very real to me; but in Marsden's case—

NINA (*with a possessive smile of tolerance*) Never mind Charlie, Ned. What do I care about Charlie? I love you! And you love me!

DARRELL (*apprehensively, forcing a tone of annoyed rebuke*) But I don't! And you don't! You're simply letting your romantic imagination run away with you— (*Showing his jealous resentment in spite of himself*) —as you did once before with Gordon Shaw!

NINA (*thinking*)

He is jealous of Gordon! . . . how wonderful that is! . . . (*With provoking calm*) I loved Gordon.

DARRELL (*irritably ignoring this as if he didn't want to hear it*) Romantic imagination! It has ruined more lives than all the diseases! Other diseases, I should say! It's a form of insanity! (*He gets up forcefully and begins to pace about the room. Thinking uneasily*)

Mustn't look at her . . . find an excuse and get away . . . and this time never come back! . . .

(*Avoiding looking at her, trying to argue reasonably—coldly*) You're acting foolishly, Nina—and very unfairly. The agreement we made has no more to do with love than a contract for building a house. In fact, you know we agreed it was essential that love mustn't enter into it. And it hasn't in spite of what you say. (*A pause. He walks about. She watches him. Thinking*)

She's got to come back to earth! . . . I've got to break with her! . . . bad enough now! . . . but to go on with it! . . . what a mess it'd make of all our lives! . . .

NINA (*thinking tenderly*)

Let his pride put all the blame on me! . . . I'll accept it gladly! . . .

DARRELL (*irritably*) Of course, I realize I've been to blame, too. I haven't been able to be as impersonal as I thought I could be. The trouble is there's been a dangerous physical attraction. Since I first met you, I've always desired you physically. I admit that now.

NINA (*smiling tenderly—thinking*)

Oh, he admits that, does he? . . . poor darling! . . . (*Enticingly*) And you still do desire me, don't you, Ned?

DARRELL (*keeping his back turned to her—roughly*) No! That part of it is finished! (NINA *laughs softly, possessively. He whirls around to face her—angrily*) Look here! You're going to have the child you wanted, aren't you?

NINA (*implacably*) My child wants its father!

DARRELL (*coming a little toward her—desperately*) But you're crazy! You're forgetting Sam! It may be stupid but I've got a guilty conscience! I'm beginning to think we've wronged the very one we were trying to help!

NINA You were trying to help me, too, Ned!

DARRELL (*stammering*) Well—all right—let's say that part of it was all right then. But it's got to stop! It can't go on!

NINA (*implacably*) Only your love can make me happy now! Sam must give me a divorce so I can marry you.

DARRELL (*thinking suspiciously*)

Look out! . . . there it is! . . . marry! . . . own me! . . . ruin my career! . . .

(*Scornfully*) Marry? Do you think I'm a fool? Get that out of your head quick! I wouldn't marry anyone—no matter what! (*As she continues to look at him with unmoved determination—pleadingly*) Be sensible, for God's sake! We're absolutely unsuited to each other! I don't admire your character! I don't respect you! I know too much about your past! (*Then indignantly*) And how about Sam? Divorce him? Have you forgotten all his mother told you? Do you mean to say you'd deliberately—? And you expect me to—? What do you think I am?

NINA (*inflexibly*) You're my lover! Nothing else matters. Yes, I remember what Sam's mother said. She said, "being happy is the nearest we can come to knowing what good is." And I'm going to be happy! I've lost everything in life so far because I didn't have the courage to take it—and I've hurt everyone around me. There's no use trying to think of others. One human being can't think of another. It's impossible. (*Gently and caressingly*) But this time I'm going to think of my own happiness—and that means you—and our child! That's quite enough for one human being to think of, dear, isn't it? (*She reaches out and takes his hand. A pause. With her other hand she gently pulls him around until he is forced to look into her eyes*).

DARRELL (*thinking fascinatedly*)

I see my happiness in her eyes . . . the touch of her soft skin! . . . those afternoons! . . . God, I was happy! . . .

(*In a strange dazed voice—as if it were forced out of him by an impulse stronger than his will*) Yes, Nina.

NINA (*in a determined voice*) I've given Sam enough of my life! And it hasn't made him happy, not the least bit! So what's the good? And how can we really know that his thinking our child was his would do him any good? We can't! It's all guesswork. The only thing sure is that we love each other.

DARRELL (*dazedly*) Yes. (*A noise from the hall and* EVANS *comes in from the rear. He sees their two hands together but mistakes their meaning*).

EVANS (*genially—with a forced self-confident air*) Well, Doc, how's the patient? I think she's much better, don't you—although she won't admit it.

DARRELL (*at the first sound of* EVANS' *voice, pulls his hand from* NINA'S *as if it were a hot coal—avoiding* EVANS' *eyes, moving away from her jerkily and self-consciously*) Yes. Much better.

EVANS Good! (*He pats* NINA *on the back. She shrinks away. His confidence vanishes in a flash. Thinking miserably*)

Why does she shrink away . . . if I even touch her? . . .

NINA (*matter-of-factly*) I must see how lunch is coming on. You'll stay, of course, Ned?

DARRELL (*struggling—shakenly*) No, I think I'd better— (*Thinking desperately*)

Got to go! . . . can't go! . . . got to go! . . .

EVANS Oh, come on, old man!

NINA (*thinking*)

He must stay . . . and after lunch we'll tell Sam. . . .

(*With certainty*) He'll stay. (*Meaningly*) And we want to have a long talk with you after lunch, Sam—don't we, Ned? (DARRELL *does not answer. She goes out, right*).

EVANS (*vaguely making talk*) I got Charlie to lie down. He's all in, poor guy. (*Then trying to face* DARRELL *who keeps looking away from him*) What did Nina mean, you want a long talk with me? Or is it a secret, Ned?

DARRELL (*controlling an impulse toward hysterical laughter*) A secret? Yes, you bet it's a secret! (*He flings himself in the chair at left, keeping his face averted. His thoughts bitter and desperate like a cornered fugitive's*).

This is horrible! . . . Sam thinks I'm finest fellow in world . . . and I do this to him! . . . as if he hadn't enough! . . . born under a curse! . . . I finish him! . . . a doctor! . . . God damn it! . . . I can see his end! . . . never forgive myself! . . . never forget! . . . break me! . . . ruin my career! . . .

(*More desperately*)

Got to stop this! . . . while there's time! . . . she said . . . after lunch, talk . . . she meant, tell him . . . that means kill him . . . then she'll marry me! . . .

(*Beginning to be angry*)

By God, I won't! . . . she'll find out! . . . smiling! . . . got me
where she wants me! . . . then be as cruel to me as she is to
him! . . . love me? . . . liar! . . . still loves Gordon! . . . her
body is a trap! . . . I'm caught in it! . . . she touches my hand,
her eyes get in mine, I lose my will! . . .

(*Furiously*)

By God, she can't make a fool of me that way! . . . I'll go away
some place! . . . go to Europe! . . . study! . . . forget her in
work! . . . keep hidden until boat sails so she can't reach
me! . . .

(*He is in a state of strange elation by this time*)

Go now! . . . no! . . . got to spike her guns with Sam! . . . by
God, I see! . . . tell him about baby! . . . that'll stop her! . . .
when she knows I've told him that, she'll see it's hopeless! . . .
she'll stick to him! . . . poor Nina! . . . I'm sorry! . . . she does
love me! . . . hell! . . . she'll forget! . . . she'll have her child!
. . . she'll be happy! . . . and Sam'll be happy! . . .

(*He suddenly turns to* EVANS *who has been staring at him,
puzzledly—in a whisper*) Look here, Sam. I can't stay to lunch.
I haven't time, I've got a million things to do. I'm sailing for
Europe in a few days.

EVANS (*surprised*) You're sailing?

DARRELL (*very hurriedly*) Yes—going to study over there for a
year or so. I haven't told anyone. I came out today to say good-
bye. You won't be able to reach me again. I'll be out of town visiting. (*Then elatedly*) And now for your secret! It ought to
make you very happy, Sam. I know how much you've wished
for it, so I'm going to tell you although Nina'll be furious with
me. She was saving it to surprise you with at her own proper
time— (*Still more elatedly*) —but I'm selfish enough to want to
see you happy before I go!

EVANS (*not daring to believe what he hopes—stammering*) What
—what is it, Ned?

DARRELL (*clapping him on the back—with strange joviality*)
You're going to be a father, old scout, that's the secret! (*Then
as* EVANS *just stares at him dumbly in a blissful satisfaction, he
rattles on*) And now I've got to run. See you again in a year
or so. I've said good-bye to Nina. Good-bye, Sam. (*He takes his
hand and clasps it*) Good luck! Buckle down to work now! You've
got the stuff in you! When I get back I'll expect to hear you're on
the high road to success! And tell Nina I'll expect to find you both

happy in your child—both of you, tell her!—happy in your child!
Tell her that, Sam! (*He turns and goes to the door. Thinking as
he goes*)

That does it! . . . honorably! . . . I'm free! . . .

(*He goes out—then out the front door—a moment later his motor
is heard starting—dies away*).

EVANS (*stares after him dumbly in the same state of happy stupe-
faction—mumbles*) Thank you—Ned. (*Thinking disjointedly*)
Why did I doubt myself? . . . now she loves me . . . she's loved
me right along . . . I've been a fool . . .

(*He suddenly falls on his knees*)

Oh, God, I thank you!

(NINA *comes in from the kitchen. She stops in amazement when
she sees him on his knees. He jumps to his feet and takes her
in his arms with confident happiness and kisses her*) Oh,
Nina, I love you so! And now I know you love me! I'll never be
afraid of anything again!

NINA (*bewildered and terror-stricken, trying feebly to push him
away—thinking*)

Has he . . . has he gone crazy? . . .

(*Weakly*) Sam! What's come over you, Sam?

EVANS (*tenderly*) Ned told me—the secret—and I'm so happy,
dear! (*He kisses her again*).

NINA (*stammering*) Ned told you—what?

EVANS (*tenderly*) That we're going to have a child, dear. You
mustn't be sore at him. Why did you want to keep it a secret
from me? Didn't you know how happy it would make me,
Nina?

NINA He told you we—we—you, the father—? (*Then suddenly
breaking from him—wildly*) Ned! Where is Ned?

EVANS He left a moment ago.

NINA (*stupidly*) Left? Call him back. Lunch is ready.

EVANS He's gone. He couldn't stay. He's got so much to do getting ready to sail.

NINA Sail?

EVANS Didn't he tell you he was sailing for Europe? He's going
over for a year or so to study.

NINA A year or so! (*Wildly*) I've got to call him up! No, I'll go
in and see him right now! (*She takes a wavering step toward the
door. Thinking in anguish*)

Go! . . . go to him! . . . find him! . . . my lover! . . .

EVANS He won't be there, I'm afraid. He said we couldn't reach him, that he'd be visiting friends out of town until he sailed. (*Solicitously*) Why, do you have to see him about something important, Nina? Perhaps I could locate—

NINA (*stammering and swaying*) No. (*She stifles an hysterical laugh*) No, nothing—nothing important—nothing is important— ha—! (*She stifles another laugh—then on the verge of fainting, weakly*) Sam! Help me—

EVANS (*rushes to her, supports her to sofa at right*) Poor darling! Lie down and rest. (*She remains in a sitting position, staring blankly before her. He chafes her wrists*) Poor darling! (*Thinking jubilantly*)

Her condition . . . this weakness comes from her condition! . . .

NINA (*thinking in anguish*)

Ned doesn't love me! . . . he's gone! . . . gone forever! . . . like Gordon! . . . no, not like Gordon! . . . like a sneak, a coward! . . . a liar! . . . oh, I hate him! . . . O Mother God, please let me hate him! . . . he must have been planning this! . . . he must have known it today when he said he loved me! . . . (*Thinking frenziedly*)

I won't bear it! . . . he thinks he has palmed me off on Sam forever! . . . and his child! . . . he can't! . . . I'll tell Sam he was lying! . . . I'll make Sam hate him! . . . I'll make Sam kill him! . . . I'll promise to love Sam if he kills him! . . . (*Suddenly turns to* EVANS—*savagely*) He lied to you!

EVANS (*letting her wrists drop—appalled—stammers*) You mean —Ned lied about—?

NINA (*in same tone*) Ned lied to you!

EVANS (*stammers*) You're not—going to have a child—

NINA (*savagely*) Oh, yes! Oh, yes, I am! Nothing can keep me from that! But you're—you're—I mean, you . . . (*Thinking in anguish*)

I can't say that to him! . . . I can't tell him without Ned to help me! . . . I can't! . . . look at his face! . . . oh, poor Sammy! . . . poor little boy! . . . poor little boy! . . . (*She takes his head and presses it to her breast and begins to weep. Weeping.*) I mean, you weren't to know about it, Sammy.

EVANS (*immediately on the crest again—tenderly*) Why? Don't you want me to be happy, Nina?

NINA Yes—yes, I do, Sammy. (*Thinking strangely*)

Little boy! . . . little boy! . . . one gives birth to little boys! . . . one doesn't drive them mad and kill them! . . .

EVANS (*thinking*)

She's never called me Sammy before . . . someone used to . . . oh, yes, Mother. . . .

(*Tenderly and boyishly*) And I'm going to make you happy from now on, Nina. I tell you, the moment Ned told me, something happened to me! I can't explain it, but—I'll make good now, Nina! I know I've said that before but I was only boasting. I was only trying to make myself think so. But now I say it knowing I can do it! (*Softly*) It's because we're going to have a child, Nina. I knew that you'd never come to really love me without that. That's what I was down on my knees for when you came in. I was thanking God—for our baby!

NINA (*tremblingly*) Sammy! Poor boy!

EVANS Ned said when he came back he'd expect to find us both happy—in our baby. He said to tell you that. You will be happy now, won't you, Nina?

NINA (*brokenly and exhaustedly*) I'll try to make you happy, Sammy. (*He kisses her, then hides his head on her breast. She stares out over his head. She seems to grow older. Thinking as if she were repeating the words of some inner voice of life*)

Not Ned's child! . . . not Sam's child! . . . mine! . . . there! . . . again! . . . I feel my child live . . . moving in my life . . . my life moving in my child . . . breathing in the tide I dream and breathe my dream back into the tide . . . God is a Mother. . . .

(*Then with sudden anguish*)

Oh, afternoons . . . dear wonderful afternoons of love with you, my lover . . . you are lost . . . gone from me forever! . . .

**Curtain**

# PART TWO

## ACT SIX

SCENE: *The same—an evening a little over a year later. The room has undergone a significant change. There is a comfortable, homey atmosphere as though now it definitely belonged to the type of person it was built for. It has a proud air of modest prosperity.*

*It is soon after dinner—about eight o'clock.* EVANS *is sitting by the table at left, glancing through a newspaper at headlines and reading an article here and there.* NINA *is in the chair at center, knitting a tiny sweater.* MARSDEN *is sitting on the sofa at right, holding a book which he pretends to be looking through, but glancing wonderingly at* EVANS *and* NINA.

*There is a startling change in* EVANS. *He is stouter, the haggard look of worry and self-conscious inferiority has gone from his face, it is full and healthy and satisfied. There is also, what is more remarkable, a decided look of solidity about him, of a determination moving toward ends it is confident it can achieve. He has matured, found his place in the world.*

*The change in* NINA *is also perceptible. She looks noticeably older, the traces of former suffering are marked on her face, but there is also an expression of present contentment and calm.*

MARSDEN *has aged greatly. His hair is gray, his expression one of a deep grief that is dying out into a resignation resentful of itself. He is dressed immaculately in dark tweed.*

NINA (*thinking*)

I wonder if there's a draft in the baby's room? . . . maybe I'd better close the window? . . . oh, I guess it's all right . . . he needs lots of fresh air . . . little Gordon . . . he does remind me

of Gordon . . . something in his eyes . . . my romantic imagination? . . . Ned said that . . . why hasn't Ned ever written?
. . . it's better he hasn't . . . how he made me suffer! . . . but
I forgive him . . . he gave me my baby . . . the baby certainly
doesn't look like him . . . everyone says he looks like Sam . . .
how absurd! . . . but Sam makes a wonderful father . . . he's
become a new man in the past year . . . and I've helped him . . .
he asks me about everything . . . I have a genuine respect for
him now . . . I can give myself without repulsion . . . I am making him happy . . . I've written his mother I'm making him happy
. . . I was proud to be able to write her that . . . how queerly
things work out! . . . all for the best . . . and I don't feel wicked
. . . I feel good . . .

(*She smiles strangely*)

MARSDEN (*thinking*)

What a change! . . . the last time I was here the air was poisoned . . . Darrell . . . I was sure he was her lover . . . but I
was in a morbid state . . . why did Darrell run away? . . .
Nina could have got Sam to divorce her if she really loved Darrell . . . then it's evident she couldn't have loved him . . . and
she was going to have Sam's baby . . . Darrell's love must have
seemed like treachery . . . so she sent him away . . . that must
be it . . .

(*With satisfaction*)

Yes, I've got it straight now. . . .

(*With contemptuous pity*)

Poor Darrell . . . I have no use for him but I did pity him when
I ran across him in Munich . . . he was going the pace . . .
looked desperate . . .

(*Then gloomily*)

My running away was about as successful as his . . . as if one
could leave one's memory behind! . . . I couldn't forget Mother
. . . she haunted me through every city of Europe . . .

(*Then irritatedly*)

I must get back to work! . . . not a line written in over a year!
. . . my public will be forgetting me! . . . a plot came to me
yesterday . . . my mind is coming around again . . . I am beginning to forget, thank God! . . .

(*Then remorsefully*)

No, I don't want to forget you, Mother! . . . but let me remember . . . without pain! . . .

EVANS (*turning over a page of his paper*) There's going to be the biggest boom before long this country has ever known, or I miss my guess, Nina.

NINA (*with great seriousness*) Do you think so, Sammy?

EVANS (*decidedly*) I'm dead sure of it.

NINA (*with a maternal pride and amusement*)

Dear Sam . . . I can't quite believe in this self-confident business man yet . . . but I have to admit he's proved it . . . he asked for more money and they gave it without question . . . they're anxious to keep him . . . they ought to be . . . how he's slaved! . . . for me and my baby! . . .

EVANS (*has been looking at* MARSDEN *surreptitiously over his paper*)

Charlie's mother must have hoarded up a half million . . . he'll let it rot in government bonds . . . wonder what he'd say if I proposed that he back me? . . . he's always taken a friendly interest . . . well, it's worth a bet, anyway . . . he'd be an easy partner to handle . . .

MARSDEN (*staring at* EVANS *wonderingly*)

What a changed Sam! . . . I preferred him the old way . . . futile but he had a sensitive quality . . . now he's brash . . . a little success . . . oh, he'll succeed all right . . . his kind are inheriting the earth . . . hogging it, cramming it down their tasteless gullets! . . . and he's happy! . . . actually happy! . . . he has Nina . . . a beautiful baby . . . a comfortable home . . . no sorrow, no tragic memories . . . and I have nothing! . . . but utter loneliness! . . .

(*With grieving self-pity*)

If only Mother had lived! . . . how horribly I miss her! . . . my lonely home . . . who will keep house for me now? . . . it has got to be done sympathetically or I won't be able to work . . . I must write to Jane . . . she'll probably be only too glad . . . (*Turning to* NINA) I think I'll write to my sister in California and ask her to come on and live with me. She's alone now that her youngest daughter is married, and she has very little money. And my hands are tied as far as sharing the estate with her is concerned. According to Mother's will, I'm cut off too if I give her a penny. Mother never got over her bitter feeling about Jane's marriage. In a way, she was right. Jane's husband wasn't much— no family or position or ability—and I doubt if she was ever happy with him. (*Sarcastically*) It was one of those love matches!

NINA (*smiling—teasingly*) There's no danger of your ever making a love match, is there, Charlie?

MARSDEN (*wincing—thinking*)

She can't believe any woman could possibly love me! . . . (*Caustically*) I trust I'll never make that kind of a fool of myself, Nina!

NINA (*teasingly*) Pooh! Aren't you the superior bachelor! I don't see anything to be so proud of! You're simply shirking, Charlie!

MARSDEN (*wincing but forcing a teasing air*) You were my only true love, Nina. I made a vow of perpetual bachelorhood when you threw me over in Sam's favor!

EVANS (*has listened to this last—jokingly*) Hello! What's this? I never knew you were my hated rival, Charlie!

MARSDEN (*dryly*) Oh—didn't you really? (*But* EVANS *has turned back to his paper. Thinking savagely*)

That fool, too! . . . he jokes about it! . . . as if I were the last one in the world he could imagine . . .

NINA (*teasingly*) Well, if I'm responsible, Charlie, I feel I ought to do something about it. I'll pick out a wife for you—guaranteed to suit! She must be at least ten years older than you, large and matronly and placid, and a wonderful cook and housekeeper—

MARSDEN (*sharply*) Don't be stupid! (*Thinking angrily*)

She picks someone beyond the age! . . . she never imagines sex could enter into it! . . .

NINA (*placatingly—seeing he is really angry*) Why, I was only picking out a type I thought would be good for you, Charlie—and for your work.

MARSDEN (*sneeringly—with a meaning emphasis*) You didn't mention chaste. I couldn't respect a woman who hadn't respected herself!

NINA (*thinking—stung*)

He's thinking of those men in the hospital . . . what a fool I was ever to tell him! . . .

(*Cuttingly*) Oh, so you think you deserve an innocent virgin!

MARSDEN (*coldly—controlling his anger*) Let's drop me, if you please. (*With a look at her that is challenging and malicious*) Did I tell you I ran into Doctor Darrell in Munich?

NINA (*startled—thinking frightenedly and confusedly*)

Ned! . . . he saw Ned! . . . why hasn't he told me before? . . . why did he look at me like that? . . . does he suspect? . . . (*Trying to be calm but stammering*) You saw—Ned?

MARSDEN (*with savage satisfaction*)

That struck home! . . . look at her! . . . guilty! . . . then I was right that day! . . .

(*Casually*) Yes, I chanced to run into him.

NINA (*more calmly now*) Why on earth didn't you tell us before, Charlie?

MARSDEN (*coolly*) Why? Is it such important news? You knew he was there, didn't you? I supposed he'd written you.

EVANS (*looking up from his paper—affectionately*) How was the old scout?

MARSDEN (*maliciously*) He seemed in fine feather—said he was having a gay time. When I saw him he was with a startling looking female—quite beautiful, if you like that type. I gathered they were living together.

NINA (*cannot restrain herself—breaks out*) I don't believe it! (*Then immediately controlling herself and forcing a laugh*) I mean, Ned was always so serious-minded it's hard to imagine him messed up in that sort of thing. (*Thinking in a queer state of jealous confusion*)

Hard to imagine! . . . my lover! . . . oh, pain again! . . . why? . . . I don't love him now . . . be careful! . . . Charlie's staring at me. . . .

MARSDEN (*thinking—jealously*)

Then she did love him! . . . does she still? . . .

(*Hopefully*)

Or is it only pique? . . . no woman likes to lose a man even when she no longer loves him. . . .

(*With malicious insistence*) Why is that hard to imagine, Nina? Darrell never struck me as a Galahad. After all, why shouldn't he have a mistress? (*Meaningly*) He has no tie over here to remain faithful to, has he?

NINA (*struggling with herself—thinking pitiably*)

He's right . . . why shouldn't Ned? . . . is that why he's never written? . . .

(*Airily*) I don't know what ties he has or hasn't got. It's nothing to me if he has fifty mistresses. I suppose he's no better than the rest of you.

EVANS (*looking over at her—tenderly reproachful*) That isn't fair, Nina. (*Thinking—proudly*)

I'm proud of that . . . never anyone before her . . .

NINA (*looking at him—with real gratitude*) I didn't mean you, dear. (*Thinking—proudly*)

Thank God for Sammy! . . . I know he's mine . . . no jealousy . . . no fear . . . no pain . . . I've found peace . . .

(*Then distractedly*)

Oh, Ned, why haven't you written? . . . stop it! . . . what a fool I am! . . . Ned's dead for me! . . . oh, I hate Charlie! . . . why did he tell me? . . .

MARSDEN (*looking at* EVANS—*contemptuously thinking*)

What a poor simpleton Sam is! . . . boasting of his virtue! . . . as if women loved you for that! . . . they despise it! . . . I don't want Nina to think I've had no experiences with women. . . . (*Mockingly*) So then it's Sam who is the Galahad, eh? Really Nina, you should have him put in the Museum among the prehistoric mammals!

EVANS (*pleased—comes back kiddingly*) Well, I never had your chances, Charlie! I couldn't run over to Europe and get away with murder the way you have!

MARSDEN (*foolishly pleased—admitting while denying*) Oh, I wasn't quite as bad as all that, Sam! (*Scornfully ashamed of himself—thinking*)

Poor sick ass that I am! . . . I want them to think I've been a Don Juan! . . . how pitiful and disgusting! . . . I wouldn't have a mistress if I could! . . . if I could? . . . of course I could! . . . I've simply never cared to degrade myself! . . .

NINA (*thinking—tormentedly*)

The thoughts of that woman! . . . Ned forgetting our afternoons in nights with her! . . . stop these thoughts! . . . I won't give in to them! . . . why did Charlie want to hurt me? . . . is he jealous of Ned? . . . Charlie has always loved me in some queer way of his own . . . how ridiculous! . . . look at him! . . . he's so proud of being thought a Don Juan! . . . I'm sure he never even dared to kiss a woman except his mother! . . .

(*Mockingly*) Do tell us about all your various mistresses in foreign parts, Charlie!

MARSDEN (*in confusion now*) I—I really don't remember, Nina!

NINA Why, you're the most heartless person I've ever heard of, Charlie! Not remember even one! And I suppose there are little Marsdens—and you've forgotten all about them too! (*She laughs maliciously—*EVANS *laughs with her*).

MARSDEN (*still more confused—with a silly idiotic smirk*) I can't

say about that, Nina. It's a wise father who knows his own child,
you know!

NINA (*frightenedly—thinking*)

What does he mean? . . . does he suspect about the baby too?
. . . I must be terribly careful of Charlie! . . .

EVANS (*looking up from his paper again*)   Did Ned say anything
about coming back?

NINA (*thinking—longingly*)

Come back? . . . oh, Ned, how I wish! . . .

MARSDEN (*looking at her—meaningly*)   No, he didn't say. I gathered
he was staying over indefinitely.

EVANS   I'd sure like to see him again.

NINA (*thinking*)

He has forgotten me . . . if he did come, he'd probably avoid
me. . . .

MARSDEN   He spoke of you. He asked if I'd heard whether Nina
had had her baby yet or not. I told him I hadn't.

EVANS (*heartily*)   Too bad you didn't know. You could have told
him what a world-beater we've got! Eh, Nina?

NINA (*mechanically*) Yes. (*Joyfully—thinking*)

Ned asked about my baby! . . . then he hadn't forgotten! . . .
if he came back he'd come to see his baby! . . .

EVANS (*solicitously*)   Isn't it time to nurse him again?

NINA (*starts to her feet automatically*)   Yes, I'm going now. (*She
glances at* MARSDEN, *thinking calculatingly*)

I must win Charlie over again . . . I don't feel safe . . .

(*She stops by his chair and takes his hand and looks into his
eyes gently and reproachfully*).

MARSDEN (*thinking shamefacedly*)

Why have I been trying to hurt her? . . . my Nina! . . . I am
nearer to her than anyone! . . . I'd give my life to make her
happy! . . .

NINA (*triumphantly*)

How his hand trembles! . . . what a fool to be afraid of Charlie!
. . . I can always twist him round my finger! . . .

(*She runs her hand through his hair, and speaks as though she
were hiding a hurt reproach beneath a joking tone*)   I shouldn't
like you any more, do you know it, after you've practically admitted you've philandered all over Europe! And I thought you
were absolutely true to me, Charlie!

MARSDEN (*so pleased he can hardly believe his ears*)

Then she did believe me! . . . she's actually hurt! . . . but I can't let her think . . .

(*With passionate earnestness, clasping her hand in both of his, looking into her eyes*) No, Nina! I swear to you!

NINA (*thinking—cruelly*)

Pah! . . . how limp his hands are! . . . his eyes are so shrinking! . . . is it possible he loves me? . . . like that? . . . what a sickening idea! . . . it seems incestuous somehow! . . . no, it's too absurd! . . .

(*Smiling, gently releases her hand*) All right. I forgive you, Charlie. (*Then matter-of-factly*) Excuse me, please, while I go up and feed my infant, or we're due to hear some lusty howling in a moment. (*She turns away, then impulsively turns back and kisses* MARSDEN *with real affection*) You're an old dear, do you know it, Charlie? I don't know what I'd do without you! (*Thinking*)

It's true, too! . . . he's my only dependable friend . . . I must never lose him . . . never let him suspect about little Gordon . . .

(*She turns to go*).

EVANS (*jumping up, throwing his paper aside*) Wait a second. I'll come with you. I want to say good night to him. (*He comes, puts his arm about her waist, kisses her and they go out together*).

MARSDEN (*thinking excitedly*)

I almost confessed I loved her! . . . a queer expression came over her face . . . what was it? . . . was it satisfaction? . . . she didn't mind? . . . was it pleasure? . . . then I can hope? . . .

(*Then miserably*)

Hope for what? . . . what do I want? . . . If Nina were free, what would I do? . . . would I do anything? . . . would I wish to? . . . what would I offer her? . . . money? . . . she could get that from others . . . myself? . . .

(*Bitterly*)

What a prize! . . . my ugly body . . . there's nothing in me to attract her . . . my fame? . . . God, what a shoddy, pitiful! . . . but I might have done something big . . . I might still . . . if I had the courage to write the truth . . . but I was born afraid . . . afraid of myself . . . I've given my talent to making fools feel pleased with themselves in order that they feel pleased with

me . . . and like me . . . I'm neither hated nor loved . . . I'm
liked . . . women like me . . . Nina likes me! . . .
(*Resentfully*)
She can't help letting the truth escape her! . . . "You're an old
dear, do you know it, Charlie?" Oh, yes, I know it . . . too
damned well! . . . dear old Charlie! . . .
(*In anguish*)
Dear old Rover, nice old doggie, we've had him for years, he's
so affectionate and faithful but he's growing old, he's getting
cross, we'll have to get rid of him soon! . . .
(*In a strange rage, threateningly*)
But you won't get rid of me so easily, Nina! . . .
(*Then confusedly and shamefacedly*)
Good God, what's the matter with me! . . . since Mother's death
I've become a regular idiot! . . .

EVANS (*comes back from the right, a beaming look of proud parent-
hood on his face*)   He was sleeping so soundly an earthquake
wouldn't have made him peep! (*He goes back to his chair—earnestly*) He sure is healthy and husky, Charlie. That tickles me
more than anything else. I'm going to start in training him as soon
as he's old enough—so he'll be a crack athlete when he goes to
college—what I wanted to be and couldn't. I want him to justify
the name of Gordon and be a bigger star than Gordon ever was,
if that's possible.

MARSDEN (*with a sort of pity—thinking*)
His is an adolescent mind . . . he'll never grow up . . . well, in
this adolescent country, what greater blessing could he wish
for? . . .
(*Forcing a smile*) How about training his mind?

EVANS (*confidently*)   Oh, that'll take care of itself. Gordon was
always near the top in his studies, wasn't he? And with Nina for
a mother, his namesake ought to inherit a full set of brains.

MARSDEN (*amused*)   You're the only genuinely modest person I
know, Sam.

EVANS (*embarrassed*)   Oh—me—I'm the boob of the family. (*Then
hastily*) Except when it comes to business. I'll make the money.
(*Confidently*) And you can bet your sweet life I will make it!

MARSDEN   I'm quite sure of that.

EVANS (*very seriously—in a confidential tone*)   I couldn't have said
that two years ago—and believed it. I've changed a hell of a lot!
Since the baby was born, I've felt as if I had a shot of dynamite
in each arm. They can't pile on the work fast enough. (*He grins—*

*then seriously*) It was about time I got hold of myself. I wasn't much for Nina to feel proud about having around the house in those days. Now—well—at least I've improved. I'm not afraid of my own shadow any more.

MARSDEN (*thinking strangely*)

Not to be afraid of one's shadow! . . . that must be the highest happiness of heaven! . . .

(*Flatteringly*) Yes, you've done wonders in the past year.

EVANS   Oh, I haven't even started yet. Wait till I get my chance! (*Glances at* MARSDEN *sharply, makes up his mind and leans forward toward him confidentially*) And I see my real chance, Charlie—lying right ahead, waiting for me to grab it—an agency that's been allowed to run down and go to seed. Within a year or so they'll be willing to sell out cheap. One of their people who's become a good pal of mine told me that in confidence, put it up to me. He'd take it on himself but he's sick of the game. But I'm not! I love it! It's great sport! (*Then putting a brake on this exuberance—matter-of-factly*) But I'll need a hundred thousand—and where will I get it? (*Looking at* MARSDEN *keenly but putting on a joking tone*) Any suggestion you can make, Charlie, will be gratefully received.

MARSDEN (*thinking suspiciously*)

Does he actually imagine I . . . ? and a hundred thousand, no less! . . . over one-fifth of my entire . . . by Jove, I'll have to throw cold water on that fancy! . . .

(*Shortly*) No, Sam, I can't think of anyone. Sorry.

EVANS (*without losing any confidence—with a grin*)

Check! . . . That's that! . . . Charlie's out . . . till the next time! . . . but I'll keep after him! . . .

(*Contemplating himself with pride*)

Gee, I have changed all right! I can remember when a refusal like that would have ruined my confidence for six months!

(*Heartily*) Nothing to be sorry about, old man. I only mentioned it on the off chance you might know of someone. (*Trying a bold closing stroke—jokingly*) Why don't you be my partner, Charlie? Never mind the hundred thousand. We'll get that elsewhere. I'll bet you might have darn fine original ideas to contribute. (*Thinking—satisfied*)

There! . . . That'll keep my proposition pinned up in his mind! . . .

(*Then jumping to his feet—briskly*) What do you say to a little stroll down to the shore and back? Come on—do you good.

(*Taking his arm and hustling him genially toward the door*) What you need is exercise. You're soft as putty. Why don't you take up golf?

MARSDEN (*with sudden resistance pulls away—determinedly*) No, I won't go, Sam. I want to think out a new plot.

EVANS Oh, all right. If it's a case of work, go to it! See you later. (*He goes out. A moment later the front door is heard closing*).

MARSDEN (*looks after him with a mixture of annoyance and scornful amusement*)

What a fount of meaningless energy he's tapped! . . . always on the go . . . typical terrible child of the age . . . . universal slogan, keep moving . . . moving where? . . . never mind that . . . don't think of ends . . . the means are the end . . . keep moving! . . .

(*He laughs scornfully and sits down in* EVANS' *chair, picking up the paper and glancing at it sneeringly*)

It's in every headline of this daily newer testament . . . going . . . going . . . never mind the gone . . . we won't live to see it . . . and we'll be so rich, we can buy off the deluge anyway! . . . even our new God has His price! . . . must have! . . . aren't we made in His image? . . . or vice-versa? . . .

(*He laughs again, letting the paper drop disdainfully—then bitterly*)

But why am I so superior? . . . where am I going? . . . to the same nowhere! . . . worse! . . . I'm not even going! . . . I'm there! . . .

(*He laughs with bitter self-pity—then begins to think with amused curiosity*)

Become Sam's partner? . . . there's a grotesque notion! . . . it might revive my sense of humor about myself, at least . . . I'm the logical one to help him . . . I helped him to Nina . . . logical partner . . . partner in Nina? . . . what inane thoughts! . . .

(*With a sigh*)

No use trying to think out that plot tonight . . . I'll try to read. . . .

(*He sees the book he has been reading on the couch and gets up to get it. There is a ring from the front door.* MARSDEN *turns toward it uncertainly. A pause. Then* NINA's *voice calls down the stairs*).

NINA The maid's out. Will you go to the door, Charlie?

MARSDEN    Surely. (*He goes out and opens the front door. A pause. Then he can be heard saying resentfully*) Hello, Darrell. (*And someone answering "Hello, Marsden" and coming in and the door closing*).

NINA (*from upstairs, her voice strange and excited*)    Who is it, Charlie?

DARRELL (*comes into view in the hall, opposite the doorway, at the foot of the stairs—his voice trembling a little with suppressed emotion*)    It's I, Nina—Ned Darrell.

NINA (*with a glad cry*)    Ned! (*Then in a voice which shows she is trying to control herself, and is frightened now*) I—make yourself at home. I'll be down—in a minute or two. (*DARRELL remains standing looking up the stairs in a sort of joyous stupor.* MARSDEN *stares at him*).

MARSDEN (*sharply*)    Come on in and sit down. (*DARRELL starts, comes into the room, plainly getting a grip on himself.* MARSDEN *follows him, glaring at his back with enmity and suspicion.* DARRELL *moves as far away from him as possible, sitting down on the sofa at right.* MARSDEN *takes* EVANS' *chair by the table.* DARRELL *is pale, thin, nervous, unhealthy looking. There are lines of desperation in his face, puffy shadows of dissipation and sleeplessness under his restless, harried eyes. He is dressed carelessly, almost shabbily. His eyes wander about the room, greedily taking it in*).

DARRELL (*thinking disjointedly*)
Here again! . . . dreamed of this house . . . from here, ran away . . . I've come back . . . my turn to be happy! . . .

MARSDEN (*watching him—savagely*)
Now I know! . . . absolutely! . . . his face! . . . her voice! . . . they did love each other! . . . they do now! . . .
(*Sharply*) When did you get back from Europe?

DARRELL (*curtly*)    This morning on the Olympic. (*Thinking—cautiously*)
Look out for this fellow . . . always had it in for me . . . like a woman . . . smells out love . . . he suspected before . . .
(*Then boldly*)
Well, who gives a damn now? . . . all got to come out! . . . Nina wanted to tell Sam . . . now I'll tell him myself! . . .

MARSDEN (*righteously indignant*)
What has brought him back? . . . what a devilish, cowardly trick to play on poor unsuspecting Sam! . . .

(*Revengefully*)

But I'm not unsuspecting! . . . I'm not their fool! . . .

(*Coldly*) What brought you back so soon? When I saw you in Munich you weren't intending—

DARRELL (*shortly*) My father died three weeks ago. I've had to come back about his estate. (*Thinking*)

Lie . . . Father's death just gave me an excuse to myself . . . wouldn't have come back for that . . . came back because I love her! . . . damn his questions! . . . I want to think . . . before I see her . . . sound of her voice . . . seemed to burn inside my head . . . God, I'm licked! . . . no use fighting it . . . I've done my damnedest . . . work . . . booze . . . other women . . . no use . . . I love her! . . . always! . . . to hell with pride! . . .

MARSDEN (*thinking*)

He has two brothers . . . they'll probably all share equally . . . his father noted Philadelphia surgeon . . . rich, I've heard . . .

(*With a bitter grin*)

Wait till Sam hears that! . . . he'll ask Darrell to back him . . . and Darrell will jump at it . . . chance to avert suspicion . . . conscience money, too! . . . it's my duty to protect Sam . . .

(*As he hears* NINA *coming down the stairs*)

I must watch them . . . it's my duty to protect Nina from herself . . . Sam is a simpleton . . . I'm all she has . . .

DARRELL (*hearing her coming—in a panic—thinking*)

Coming! . . . in a second I'll see her! . . .

(*Terrified*)

Does she still love me? . . . she may have forgotten . . . no, it's my child . . . she can never forget that! . . .

(NINA *comes in from the rear. She has put on a fresh dress, her hair is arranged, her face newly rouged and powdered, she looks extremely pretty and this is heightened by the feverish state of mind she is in—a mixture of love, of triumphant egotism in knowing her lover has come back to her, and of fear and uncertainty in feeling her new peace, her certainties, her contented absorption in her child failing her. She hesitates just inside the door, staring into* DARRELL'S *eyes, thinking a fierce question*).

NINA

Does he still love me? . . .

(*Then triumphantly as she reads him*)

Yes! . . . he does! . . . he does! . . .

DARRELL (*who has jumped to his feet—with a cry of longing*) Nina! (*Thinking with alarm now*)

She's changed! . . . changed! . . . can't tell if she loves! . . . (*He has started to go to her. Now he hesitates. His voice taking on a pleading uncertain quality*) Nina!

NINA (*thinking triumphantly—with a certain cruelty*)

He loves me! . . . he's mine . . . now more than ever! . . . he'll never dare leave me again! . . .

(*Certain of herself now, she comes to him and speaks with confident pleasure*) Hello, Ned! This is a wonderful surprise! How are you? (*She takes his hand*).

DARRELL (*taken aback—confusedly*) Oh—all right, Nina. (*Thinking in a panic*)

That tone! . . . as if she didn't care! . . . can't believe that! . . . she's playing a game to fool Marsden! . . .

MARSDEN (*who is watching them keenly—thinking*)

She loves his love for her . . . she's cruelly confident . . . much as I hate this man I can't help feeling sorry . . . I know her cruelty . . . it's time I took a hand in this . . . what a plot for a novel! . . .

(*Almost mockingly*) Darrell's father died, Nina. He had to come home to see about the estate.

DARRELL (*with a glare at* MARSDEN—*protestingly*) I was coming home anyway. I only intended to stay a year, and it's over that since— (*Intensely*) I was coming back anyway, Nina!

NINA (*thinking with triumphant happiness*)

You dear, you! . . . as if I didn't know that! . . . oh, how I'd love to take you in my arms! . . .

(*Happily*) I'm awfully glad you've come, Ned. We've missed you terribly.

DARRELL (*thinking—more and more at sea*)

She looks glad . . . but she's changed . . . I don't understand her . . . "we've missed" . . . that means Sam . . . what does that mean? . . .

(*Intensely, pressing her hand*) And I've missed you—terribly!

MARSDEN (*sardonically*) Yes, indeed, Darrell, I can vouch for their missing you—Sam in particular. He was asking about you only a short while ago—how things were going with you when I saw you in Munich. (*Maliciously*) By the way, who was the lady you were with that day? She was certainly startling looking.

NINA (*thinking—triumphantly mocking*)

A miss, Charlie! . . . he loves me! . . . what do I care about that woman? . . .

(*Gaily*) Yes, who was the mysterious beauty, Ned? Do tell us! (*She moves away from him and sits down at center.* DARRELL *remains standing*)

DARRELL (*glaring at* MARSDEN, *sullenly*) Oh, I don't remember— (*Thinking apprehensively with a bitter resentment*)

She doesn't give a damn! . . . if she loved me she'd be jealous! . . . but she doesn't give a damn! . . .

(*He blurts out resentfully at* NINA) Well, she was my mistress— for a time—I was lonely. (*Then with sudden anger turning on* MARSDEN) But what's all this to you, Marsden?

MARSDEN (*coolly*) Absolutely nothing. Pardon me. It was a tactless question. (*Then with continued open malice*) But I was starting to say how Sam had missed you, Darrell. It's really remarkable. One doesn't encounter such friendship often in these slack days. Why, he'd trust you with anything!

NINA (*wincing—thinking*)

That hurts . . . hurts Ned . . . Charlie is being cruel! . . .

DARRELL (*wincing—in a forced tone*) And I'd trust Sam with anything.

MARSDEN Of course. He is a person one can trust. They are rare. You're going to be amazed at the change in Sam, Darrell. Isn't he, Nina? He's a new man. I never saw such energy. If ever a man was bound for success Sam is. In fact, I'm so confident he is that as soon as he thinks the time is ripe to start his own firm I'm going to furnish the capital and become his silent partner.

DARRELL (*puzzled and irritated—thinking confusedly*)

What's he driving at? . . . why doesn't he get the hell out and leave us alone? . . . but I'm glad Sam is on his feet . . . makes it easier to tell him the truth. . . .

NINA (*thinking—worriedly*)

What's Charlie talking about? . . . it's time I talked to Ned . . . Oh, Ned, I do love you! . . . you can be my lover! . . . we won't hurt Sam! . . . he'll never know! . . .

MARSDEN Yes, ever since the baby was born Sam's been another man—in fact, ever since he knew there was going to be a baby, isn't it, Nina?

NINA (*agreeing as if she had only half-heard him*) Yes. (*Thinking*)

Ned's baby! . . . I must talk to him about our baby. . . .

MARSDEN Sam is the proudest parent I've ever seen!

NINA (*as before*) Yes, Sam makes a wonderful father, Ned. (*Thinking*)

Ned doesn't care for children . . . I know what you're hoping, Ned . . . but if you think I'm going to take Sam's baby from him, you're mistaken! . . . or if you think I'll run away with you and leave my baby . . .

MARSDEN (*with the same strange driving insistence*) If anything happened to that child I actually leave Sam would lose his reason! Don't you think so, Nina?

NINA (*with emphasis*) I know I'd lose mine! Little Gordon has become my whole life.

DARRELL (*thinking—with a sad bitter irony*)

Sam . . . wonderful father . . . lose his reason . . . little Gordon! . . . Nina called my son after Gordon! . . . romantic imagination! . . . Gordon is still her lover! . . . Gordon, Sam and Nina! . . . and my son! . . . closed corporation! . . . I'm forced out! . . .

(*Then rebelling furiously*)

No! . . . not yet, by God! . . . I'll smash it up! . . . I'll tell Sam the truth no matter what! . . .

NINA (*thinking with a strange calculation*)

I couldn't find a better husband than Sam . . . and I couldn't find a better lover than Ned . . . I need them both to be happy . . .

MARSDEN (*with sudden despairing suspicion*)

Good God . . . after all, is it Sam's child? . . . mightn't it be Darrell's! . . . why have I never thought of that? . . . No! . . . Nina couldn't be so vile! . . . to go on living with Sam, pretending . . . and, after all, why should she, you fool? . . . there's no sense! . . . she could have gone off with Darrell, couldn't she? . . . Sam would have given her a divorce . . . there was no possible reason for her staying with Sam, when she loved Darrell, unless exactly because this was Sam's baby . . . for its sake . . .

(*Hectically relieved*)

Of course! . . . of course! . . . that's all right! . . . I love that poor baby now! . . . I'll fight for its sake against these two! . . .

(*Smilingly gets to his feet—thinking*)
I can leave them alone now . . . for they won't be alone,
thanks to me! . . . I leave Sam and his baby in this room
with them . . . and their honor . . .
(*Suddenly raging*)
Their honor! . . . what an obscene joke! . . . the honor of a
harlot and a pimp! . . . I hate them! . . . if only God would
strike them dead! . . . now! . . . and I could see them die!
. . . I would praise His justice! . . . His kindness and mercy to
me! . . .

NINA (*thinking—with horrified confusion*)
Why doesn't Charlie go? . . . What is he thinking? . . . I sud-
denly feel afraid of him! . . .
(*She gets to her feet with a confused pleading cry*) Charlie!

MARSDEN (*immediately urbane and smiling*) It's all right. I'm
going out to find Sam. When he knows you're here he'll come
on the run, Darrell. (*He goes to the door. They watch him
suspiciously*) And you two probably have a lot to talk over. (*He
chuckles pleasantly and goes into the hall—mockingly warning*)
We'll be back before long. (*The front door is heard slamming.
NINA and DARRELL turn and look at each other guiltily and
frightenedly. Then he comes to her and takes both of her hands
uncertainly*).

DARRELL (*stammeringly*) Nina—I—I've come back to you—do
you—do you still care—Nina?

NINA (*giving way to his love passionately, as if to drown her
fears*) I love you, Ned!

DARRELL (*kisses her awkwardly—stammering*) I—I didn't know—
you seemed so cold—damn Marsden—he suspects, doesn't he?—
but it makes no difference now, does it? (*Then in a flood of
words*) Oh, it's been hell, Nina! I couldn't forget you! Other
women—they only made me love you more! I hated them and
loved you even at the moment when—that's honest! It was
always you in my arms—as you used to be—those afternoons
—God, how I've thought of them—lying awake—recalling every
word you said, each movement, each expression on your face,
smelling your hair, feeling your soft body— (*Suddenly taking her
in his arms and kissing her again and again—passionately*) Nina!
I love you so!

NINA And I've longed for you so much! Do you think I've forgotten those afternoons? (*Then in anguish*) Oh, Ned, why did

you run away? I can never forgive that! I can never trust you again!

DARRELL (*violently*) I was a fool! I thought of Sam! And that wasn't all! Oh, I wasn't all noble, I'll confess! I thought of myself and my career! Damn my career! A lot of good that did it! I didn't study! I didn't live! I longed for you—and suffered! I paid in full, believe me, Nina! But I know better now! I've come back. The time for lying is past! You've got to come away with me! (*He kisses her*).

NINA (*letting herself go, kissing him passionately*) Yes! My lover! (*Then suddenly resisting and pushing him away*) No! You're forgetting Sam—and Sam's baby!

DARRELL (*staring at her wildly*) Sam's baby? Are you joking? Ours, you mean! We'll take him with us, of course!

NINA (*sadly*) And Sam?

DARRELL Damn Sam! He's got to give you a divorce! Let him be generous for a change!

NINA (*sadly but determinedly*) He would be. You must be just to Sam. He'd give his life for my happiness. And this would mean his life. Could we be happy then? You know we couldn't! And I've changed, Ned. You've got to realize that. I'm not your old mad Nina. I still love you. I will always love you. But now I love my baby too. His happiness comes first with me!

DARRELL But—he's mine, too!

NINA No! You gave him to Sam to save Sam!

DARRELL To hell with Sam! It was to make you happy!

NINA So I could make Sam happy! That was in it too! I was sincere in that, Ned! If I hadn't been, I could never have gone to you that first day—or if I had, I'd never have forgiven myself. But as it is I don't feel guilty or wicked. I have made Sam happy! And I'm proud! I love Sam's happiness! I love the devoted husband and father in him! And I feel it's his baby—that we've made it his baby!

DARRELL (*distractedly*) Nina! For God's sake! You haven't come to love Sam, have you? Then—I'll go—I'll go away again—I'll never come back—I tried not to this time—but I had to, Nina!

NINA (*taking him in her arms—with sudden alarm*) No, don't go away, Ned—ever again. I don't love Sam! I love you!

DARRELL (*miserably*) But I don't understand! Sam gets everything—and I have nothing!

NINA  You have my love. (*With a strange, self-assured smile at him*) It seems to me you're complaining unreasonably!

DARRELL  You mean—I can be—your lover again?

NINA  (*simply, even matter-of-factly*)  Isn't that the nearest we can come to making everyone happy? That's all that counts.

DARRELL  (*with a harsh laugh*)  And is that what you call playing fair to Sam?

NINA  (*simply*)  Sam will never know. The happiness I have given him has made him too sure of himself ever to suspect me now. And as long as we can love each other without danger to him, I feel he owes that to us for all we've done for him. (*With finality*) That's the only possible solution, Ned, for all our sakes, now you've come back to me.

DARRELL  (*repulsed*)  Nina! How can you be so inhuman and calculating!

NINA  (*stung—mockingly*)  It was you who taught me the scientific approach, Doctor!

DARRELL  (*shrinking back from her—threateningly*)  Then I'll leave again! I'll go back to Europe! I won't endure—! (*Then in a queer, futile rage*) You think I'll stay—to be your lover—watching Sam with my wife and my child—you think that's what I came back to you for? You can go to hell, Nina!

NINA  (*calmly—sure of him*)  But what else can I do, Ned? (*Then warningly*) I hear them coming, dear. It's Sam, you know.

DARRELL  (*in a frenzy*)  What else can you do? Liar! But I can do something else! I can smash your calculating game for you! I can tell Sam—and I will—right now—by God, I will!

NINA  (*quietly*)  No. You won't, Ned. You can't do that to Sam.

DARRELL  (*savagely*)  Like hell I can't! (*The front door is opened.* EVANS' *voice is immediately heard, even before he bounds into the room. He rushes up to* NED *hilariously, shakes his hand and pounds his back, oblivious to* DARRELL's *wild expression*).

EVANS  You old son of a gun! Why didn't you let a guy know you were coming? We'd have met you at the dock, and brought the baby. Let me have a look at you! You look thinner. We'll fatten you up, won't we, Nina? Let us do the prescribing this time! Why didn't you let us know where you were, you old bum? We wanted to write you about the baby. And I wanted to boast about how I was getting on! You're the only person in the world—except Nina and Charlie—I would boast about that to.

NINA (*affectionately*) Mercy, Sam, give Ned a chance to get a word in! (*Looking at* NED *pityingly but challengingly*) He wants to tell you something, Sam.

DARRELL (*crushed—stammers*) No—I mean, yes—I want to tell you how damn glad I am . . . (*He turns away, his face is screwed up in his effort to hold back his tears. Thinking miserably*) I can't tell him! . . . God damn him, I can't! . . .

NINA (*with a strange triumphant calm*)
There! . . . that's settled for all time! . . . poor Ned! . . . how crushed he looks! . . . I mustn't let Sam look at him! . . .
(*She steps between them protectingly*) Where's Charlie, Sam?

MARSDEN (*appearing from the hall*) Here, Nina. Always here! (*He comes to her, smiling with assurance*).

NINA (*suddenly with a strange unnatural elation—looking from one to the other with triumphant possession*) Yes, you're here, Charlie—always! And you, Sam—and Ned! (*With a strange gaiety*) Sit down, all of you! Make yourselves at home! You are my three men! This is your home with me! (*Then in a strange half-whisper*) Ssshh! I thought I heard the baby. You must all sit down and be very quiet. You must not wake our baby. (*Mechanically, the three sit down, careful to make no noise—* EVANS *in his old place by the table,* MARSDEN *at center,* DARRELL *on the sofa at right. They sit staring before them in silence.* NINA *remains standing, dominating them, a little behind and to the left of* MARSDEN).

DARRELL (*thinking abjectly*)
I couldn't! . . . there are things one may not do and live with oneself afterwards . . . there are things one may not say . . . memory is too full of echoes! . . . there are secrets one must not reveal . . . memory is lined with mirrors! . . . he was too happy! . . . to kill happiness is a worse murder than taking life! . . . I gave him that happiness! . . . Sam deserves my happiness! . . . God bless you, Sam! . . .
(*Then in a strange objective tone—thinking*)
My experiment with the guinea pigs has been a success . . . the ailing ones, Sam, and the female, Nina, have been restored to health and normal function . . . only the other male, Ned, seems to have suffered deterioration.
(*Then bitterly humble*)
Nothing left but to accept her terms . . . I love her . . . I can

help to make her happy . . . half a loaf is better . . . to a
starving man. . . .

(*Glancing over at* EVANS—*bitterly gloating*)

And your child is mine! . . . your wife is mine! . . . your happiness is mine! . . . may you enjoy my happiness, her husband! . . .

EVANS (*looking at* DARRELL *affectionately*)

Sure good to see Ned again . . . a real friend if there ever was
one . . . looks blue about something . . . oh, that's right,
Charlie said his old man had kicked in . . . his old man was
rich . . . that's an idea . . . I'll bet he'd put up that capital . . .

(*Then ashamed of himself*)

Aw hell, what's the matter with me? . . . he's no sooner here
than I start . . . he's done enough . . . forget it! . . . now anyway . . . he looks pretty dissipated . . . too many women . . .
ought to get married and settle down . . . tell him that if I
didn't think he'd laugh at me giving him advice . . . but he'll
soon realize I'm not the old Sam he knew . . . I suppose Nina's
been boasting about that already . . . she's proud . . . she's
helped me . . . she's a wonderful wife and mother . . .

(*Looking up at her—solicitously*)

She acted a bit nervous just now . . . queer . . . like she used
to . . . haven't noticed her that way in a long time . . . suppose
it's the excitement of Ned turning up . . . mustn't let her get
over-excited . . . bad for the baby's milk. . . .

MARSDEN (*glancing furtively over his shoulder at* NINA—*broodingly
thinking*)

She's the old queer Nina now . . . the Nina I could never
fathom . . . her three men! . . . and we are! . . . I? . . . yes,
more deeply than either of the others since I serve for nothing
. . . a queer kind of love, maybe . . . I am not ordinary! . . .
our child . . . what could she mean by that? . . . child of us
three? . . . on the surface, that's insane . . . but I felt when she
said it there was something in it . . . she has strange devious
intuitions that tap the hidden currents of life . . . dark intermin-
gling currents that become the one stream of desire . . . I feel,
with regard to Nina, my life queerly identified with Sam's and
Darrell's . . . her child is the child of our three loves for her
. . . I would like to believe that . . . I would like to be her
husband in a sense . . . and the father of a child, after my fash-

ion . . . I could forgive her everything . . . permit everything . . .

(*Determinedly*)

And I do forgive! . . . and I will not meddle hereafter more than
is necessary to guard her happiness, and Sam's and our baby's
. . . as for Darrell, I am no longer jealous of him . . . she is
only using his love for her own happiness . . . he can never take
her away from me! . . .

NINA (*more and more strangely triumphant*)

My three men! . . . I feel their desires converge in me! . . .
to form one complete beautiful male desire which I absorb . . .
and am whole . . . they dissolve in me, their life is my life
. . . I am pregnant with the three! . . . . husband! . . . lover! . . .
father! . . . and the fourth man! . . . little man! . . . little
Gordon! . . . he is mine too! . . . that makes it perfect! . . .

(*With an extravagant suppressed exultance*)

Why, I should be the proudest woman on earth! . . . I should
be the happiest woman in the world! . . .

(*Then suppressing an outbreak of hysterical triumphant laughter
only by a tremendous effort*)

Ha-ha . . . only I better knock wood . . .

(*She raps with both knuckles in a fierce tattoo on the table*)

before God the Father hears my happiness! . . .

EVANS (*as the three turn to her—anxiously*) Nina? What's the
matter?

NINA (*controlling herself with a great effort comes to him—forcing
a smile—puts her arms around him affectionately*) Nothing,
dear. Nerves, that's all. I've gotten over-tired, I guess.

EVANS (*bullying her—with loving authority*) Then you go right
to bed, young lady! We'll excuse you.

NINA (*quietly and calmly now*) All right, dear. I guess I do
need to rest. (*She kisses him as she might kiss a big brother she
loved—affectionately*) Good night, you bossy old thing, you!

EVANS (*with deep tenderness*) Good night, darling.

NINA (*she goes and kisses Charlie dutifully on the cheek as she
might her father—affectionately*) Good night, Charlie.

MARSDEN (*with a touch of her father's manner*) That's a good
girl! Good night, dear.

NINA (*she goes and kisses DARRELL lovingly on the lips as she
would kiss her lover*) Good night, Ned.

DARRELL (*looks at her with grateful humility*) Thank you. Good night. (*She turns and walks quietly out of the room. The eyes of the three men follow her*).

*Curtain*

ACT SEVEN

SCENE: *Nearly eleven years later. The sitting room of the* EVANS' *apartment on Park Avenue, New York City—a room that is a tribute to* NINA's *good taste. It is a large, sunny room, the furniture expensive but extremely simple. The arrangement of the furniture shown is as in previous scenes except there are more pieces. Two chairs are by the table at left. There is a smaller table at center, and a chaise longue. A large, magnificently comfortable sofa is at right.*

*It is about one in the afternoon of a day in early fall.* NINA *and* DARRELL *and their son,* GORDON, *are in the room.* NINA *is reclining on the chaise longue watching* GORDON *who is sitting on the floor near her, turning over the pages of a book.* DARRELL *is sitting by the table at left, watching* NINA.

NINA *is thirty-five, in the full bloom of her womanhood. She is slimmer than in the previous scene. Her skin still retains a trace of summer tan and she appears in the pink of physical condition. But as in the first act of the play, there is beneath this a sense of great mental strain. One notices the many lines in her face at second glance. Her eyes are tragically sad in repose and her expression is set and masklike.*

GORDON *is eleven—a fine boy with, even at this age, the figure of an athlete. He looks older than he is. There is a grave expression to his face. His eyes are full of a quick-tempered sensitiveness. He does not noticeably resemble his mother. He looks nothing at all like his father. He seems to have sprung from a line distinct from any of the people we have seen.*

DARRELL *has aged greatly. His hair is streaked with gray. He has grown stout. His face is a bit jowly and puffy under the eyes. The features have become blurred. He has the look of a man with no definite aim or ambition to which he can relate his living. His eyes are embittered and they hide his inner self-resentment behind a pose of cynical indifference.*

GORDON (*thinking as he plays—resentfully*)
I wish Darrell'd get out of here! . . . why couldn't Mother let me run my own birthday? . . . I'd never had him here, you bet! . . . what's he always hanging 'round for? . . . why don't he go off on one of his old trips again . . . last time he was gone more'n a year . . . I was hoping he'd died! . . . what makes Mother like him so much? . . . she makes me sick! . . . I'd think she'd get sick of the old fool and tell him to get out and never come back! . . . I'd kick him out if I was big enough! . . . it's good for him he didn't bring me any birthday present or or I'd smash it first chance I got! . . .

NINA (*watching him—brooding with loving tenderness—sadly*) No longer my baby . . . my little man . . . eleven . . . I can't believe it . . . I'm thirty-five . . . five years more . . . at forty a woman has finished living . . . life passes by her . . . she rots away in peace! . . .
(*Intensely*)
I want to rot away in peace! . . . I'm sick of the fight for happiness! . . .
(*Smiling with a wry amusement at herself*)
What ungraceful thoughts on my son's birthday! . . . my love for him has been happiness . . . how handsome he is! . . . not at all like Ned . . . when I was carrying him I was fighting to forget Ned . . . hoping he might be like Gordon . . . and he is . . . poor Ned, I've made him suffer a great deal . . . !
(*She looks over at* DARRELL—*self-mockingly*)
My lover! . . . so very rarely now, those interludes of passion . . . what has bound us together all these years? . . . love? . . . if he could only have been contented with what I was able to give him! . . . but he has always wanted more . . . yet never had the courage to insist on all or nothing . . . proud without being proud enough! . . . he has shared me for his comfort's sake with a little gratitude and a big bitterness . . . and sharing me has corrupted him! . . .
(*Then bitterly*)
No, I can't blame myself! . . . no woman can make a man happy who has no purpose in life! . . . why did he give up his career? . . . because I had made him weak? . . .

(*With respectful scorn*)

No, it was I who shamed him into taking up biology and starting the station at Antigua . . . if I hadn't he'd simply have hung
around me year after year, doing nothing . . .

(*Irritatedly*)

Why does he stay so long? . . . over six months . . . I can't
stand having him around me that long any more! . . . why
doesn't he go back to the West Indies? . . . I always get a terrible feeling after he's been back a while that he's waiting for
Sam to die! . . . or go insane! . . .

DARRELL (*thinking—with an apathetic bitterness*)

What is she thinking? . . . we sit together in silence, thinking
. . . thoughts that never know the other's thoughts . . . our love
has become the intimate thinking together of thoughts that are
strangers . . . our love! . . . well, whatever it is that has bound
us together, it's strong! . . . I've broken with her, run away, tried
to forget her . . . running away to come back each time more
abject! . . . or, if she saw there was some chance I might break
loose, she'd find some way to call me back . . . and I'd forget
my longing for freedom, I'd come wagging my tail . . . no,
guinea pigs have no tails . . . I hope my experiment has proved
something! . . . Sam . . . happy and wealthy . . . and healthy!
. . . I used to hope he'd break down . . . I'd watch him and
read symptoms of insanity into every move he made . . . despicable? . . . certainly, but love makes one either noble or despicable! . . . he only grew healthier . . . now I've given up watching him . . . almost entirely . . . now I watch him grow fat
and I laugh! . . . the huge joke has dawned on me! . . . Sam is
the normal one! . . . we lunatics! . . . Nina and I! . . . have
made a sane life for him out of our madness! . . .

(*Watching* NINA—*sadly*)

Always thinking of her son . . . well, I gave him to her . . .
Gordon . . . I hate that name . . . why do I continue hanging
around here? . . . each time after a few months my love changes
to bitterness . . . I blame Nina for the mess I've made of life . . .

NINA (*suddenly turning on him*) When are you going back to
the West Indies, Ned?

DARRELL (*determinedly*) Soon!

GORDON (*stops playing to listen—thinking*)

Gosh, I'm glad! . . . How soon, I wonder? . . .

NINA (*with a trace of a sneer*) I don't see how you can afford to leave your work for such long periods. Don't you grow rusty?

DARRELL (*looking at her meaningly*) My life work is to rust—
nicely and unobtrusively! (*He smiles mockingly*).

NINA (*sadly—thinking*)

To rot away in peace . . . that's all he wants now, too! . . . and
this is what love has done to us! . . .

DARRELL (*bitterly*) My work was finished twelve years ago. As I
believe you know, I ended it with an experiment which resulted
so successfully that any further meddling with human lives would
have been superfluous!

NINA (*pityingly*) Ned!

DARRELL (*indifferent and cynical*) But you meant my present
dabbling about. You know better than to call that work. It's
merely my hobby. Our backing Sam has made Marsden and me
so wealthy that we're forced to take up hobbies. Marsden goes in
for his old one of dashing off genteel novels, while I play at
biology. Sam argued that golf would be healthier and less non-
sensical for me, but you insisted on biology. And give it its due,
it has kept me out in the open air and been conducive to
traveling and broadening my mind. (*Then forcing a smile*) But
I'm exaggerating. I really am interested, or I'd never keep
financing the Station. And when I'm down there I do work hard,
helping Preston. He's doing remarkable work already, and he's
still in his twenties. He'll be a big man— (*His bitterness cropping
up again*) at least if he takes my advice and never carries his
experiments as far as human lives!

NINA (*in a low voice*) How can you be so bitter, Ned—on Gordon's birthday?

DARRELL (*thinking cynically*)

She expects me to love the child she deliberately took from
me and gave to another man! . . . no, thank you, Nina! . . . I've
been hurt enough! . . . I'll not leave myself open there! . . .
(*Regarding his son bitterly*) Every day he gets more like Sam,
doesn't he?

GORDON (*thinking*)

He's talking about me . . . he better look out! . . .

NINA (*resentfully*) I don't think Gordon resembles Sam at all.
He reminds me a great deal of his namesake.

DARRELL (*touched on a sore spot—with a nasty laugh—cuttingly*)
Gordon Shaw? Not the slightest bit in the world! And you ought

to thank God he doesn't! It's the last thing I'd want wished on a boy of mine—to be like that rah-rah hero!

GORDON (*thinking contemptuously*)

Boy of his! . . . He hasn't got a boy! . . .

NINA (*amused and pleased by his jealousy*)

Poor Ned! . . . isn't he silly? . . . at his age, after all we've been through, to still feel jealous . . .

DARRELL I'd much rather have him (*Pointing to* GORDON) grow up to be an exact duplicate of the esteemed Samuel!

GORDON (*thinking resentfully*)

He's always making fun of my father! . . . he better look out! . . .

DARRELL (*more and more mockingly*) And what could be fairer? The good Samuel is an A one success. He has a charming wife and a darling boy, and a Park Avenue apartment and a membership in an expensive golf club. And, above all, he rests so complacently on the proud assurance that he is self-made!

NINA (*sharply*) Ned! You ought to be ashamed! You know how grateful Sam has always been to you!

DARRELL (*bitingly*) Would he be grateful if he knew how much I'd really done for him?

NINA (*sternly*) Ned!

GORDON (*suddenly jumps up and confronts* DARRELL, *his fists clenched, trembling with rage, stammers*) You—shut up—making fun of my father!

NINA (*in dismay*) Gordon!

DARRELL (*mockingly*) My dear boy, I wouldn't make fun of your father for the world!

GORDON (*baffledly—his lips trembling*) You—you did, too! (*Then intensely*) I hate you!

NINA (*shocked and indignant*) Gordon! How dare you talk like that to your Uncle Ned!

GORDON (*rebelliously*) He's not my uncle! He's not my anything!

NINA Not another word or you'll be punished, whether it's your birthday or not! If you can't behave better than that, I'll have to phone to all your friends they mustn't come here this afternoon, that you've been so bad you can't have a party! (*Thinking remorsefully*)

Is this my fault? . . . I've done my best to get him to love Ned! . . . but it only makes him worse! . . . it makes him turn against me! . . . turn from me to Sam!

GORDON (*sullenly*) I don't care! I'll tell Dad!

NINA (*peremptorily*) Leave the room! And don't come near me again, do you hear, until you've apologized to Uncle Ned! (*Thinking angrily*)

Dad! . . . It's always Dad with him now! . . .

DARRELL (*boredly*) Oh, never mind, Nina!

GORDON (*going out—mutters*) I won't 'pologize—never! (*Thinking vindictively*)

I hate her too when she sides with him! . . . I don't care if she is my mother! . . . she has no right! . . .

(*He goes out, rear*).

DARRELL (*irritably*) What if he does hate me? I don't blame him! He suspects what I know—that I've acted like a coward and a weakling toward him! I should have claimed him no matter what happened to other people! Whose fault is it if he hates me, and I dislike him because he loves another father? Ours! You gave him to Sam and I consented! All right! Then don't blame him for acting like Sam's son!

NINA But he shouldn't say he hates you. (*Thinking bitterly*)

Sam's! . . . he's becoming all Sam's! . . . I'm getting to mean nothing! . . .

DARRELL (*sardonically*) Perhaps he realizes subconsciously that I am his father, his rival in your love; but I'm not his father ostensibly, there are no taboos, so he can come right out and hate me to his heart's content! (*Bitterly*) If he realized how little you love me any more, he wouldn't bother!

NINA (*exasperatedly*) Oh, Ned, do shut up! I can't stand hearing those same old reproaches I've heard a thousand times before! I can't bear to hear myself making the same old bitter counter-accusations. And then there'll be the same old terrible scene of hate and you'll run away—it used to be to drink and women, now it's to the Station. Or I'll send you away, and then after a time I'll call you back, because I'll have gotten so lonely again living this lonely lie of my life, with no one to speak to except Sam's business friends and their deadly wives. (*She laughs helplessly*) Or else you'll get lonely in your lie a little before I do and come back again of your own desire! And then we'll kiss and cry and love each other again!

DARRELL (*with an ironical grimace*) Or I might cheat myself into believing I'd fallen in love with some nice girl and get myself engaged to be married again as I did once before! And then you'd be jealous again and have to find some way of getting me to break it off!

NINA (*forlornly amused*) Yes—I suppose the thought of a wife taking you away from me would be too much—again! (*Then helplessly*) Oh, Ned, when are we ever going to learn something about each other? We act like such brainless fools—with our love. It's always so wonderful when you first come back, but you always stay too long—or I always keep you too long! You never leave before we've come to the ugly bitter stage when we blame each other! (*Then suddenly forlornly tender*) Is it possible you can still love me, Ned?

DARRELL (*mournfully smiling*) I must, or I'd never act this fool way, would I?

NINA (*smiling back*) And I must love you. (*Then seriously*) After all, I can never forget that Gordon is the child of your love, Ned.

DARRELL (*sadly*) You'd better forget that, for his sake and your own. Children have sure intuitions. He feels cheated of your love—by me. So he's concentrating his affections on Sam whose love he knows is secure, and withdrawing from you.

NINA (*frightened—angrily*) Don't be stupid, Ned! That isn't so at all! I hate you when you talk that way!

DARRELL (*cynically*) Hate me, exactly. As he does! That's what I'm advising you to do if you want to keep his love! (*He smiles grimly*).

NINA (*sharply*) If Gordon doesn't love you it's because you've never made the slightest attempt to be lovable to him! There's no earthly reason why he should like you, when you come right down to it, Ned! Take today, for instance. It's his birthday but you'd forgotten, or didn't care! You never even brought him a present.

DARRELL (*with bitter sadness*) I did bring him a present. It's out in the hall. I bought him a costly delicate one so he could get full satisfaction and yet not strain himself when he smashed it, as he's smashed every present of mine in the past! And I left it out in the hall, to be given to him after I've gone because, after all, he is my son and I'd prefer he didn't smash it before my eyes! (*Trying to mock his own emotion back—with savage bitterness*) I'm selfish, you see! I don't want my son to be too happy at my expense, even on his birthday!

NINA (*tormented by love and pity and remorse*) Ned! For God's

sake! How can you torture us like that! Oh, it's too dreadful—
what I have done to you! Forgive me, Ned!

DARRELL (*his expression changing to one of pity for her—goes to
her and puts his hand on her head—tenderly*) I'm sorry. (*With
remorseful tenderness*) Dreadful, what you've done, Nina? Why,
you've given me the only happiness I've ever known! And no
matter what I may say or do in bitterness, I'm proud—and grateful, Nina!

NINA (*looks up at him with deep tenderness and admiration*)
Dearest, it's wonderful of you to say that! (*She gets up and puts
her hands on his shoulders and looks into his eyes—tenderly in a
sort of pleading*) Can't we be brave enough—for you to go away
—now, on this note—sure of our love—with no ugly bitterness for
once?

DARRELL (*joyfully*) Yes! I'll go—this minute if you wish!

NINA (*playfully*) Oh, you needn't go this minute! Wait and say
good-bye to Sam. He'd be terribly hurt if you didn't. (*Then
seriously*) And will you promise to stay away two years—even if I
call you back before then—and work this time, really work?

DARRELL I'll try, Nina!

NINA And then—surely come back to me!

DARRELL (*smiling*) Surely—again!

NINA Then good-bye, dear! (*She kisses him*).

DARRELL Again! (*He smiles and she smiles and they kiss again.
GORDON appears in the doorway at rear and stands for a moment
in a passion of jealousy and rage and grief, watching them*).

GORDON (*thinking with a strange tortured shame*)
I mustn't see her! . . . pretend I didn't see her! . . . mustn't
never let her know I saw her! . . .
(*He vanishes as silently as he had come*).

NINA (*suddenly moving away from DARRELL, looking around her
uneasily*) Ned, did you see—? I had the queerest feeling just
then that someone—

GORDON (*his voice sounds from the hall with a strained casualness*)
Mother! Uncle Charlie's downstairs. Shall he come right up?

NINA (*startled, her own voice straining to be casual*) Yes, dear—
of course! (*Then worriedly*) His voice sounded funny. Did it
to you? Do you suppose he—?

DARRELL (*with a wry smile*) It's possible. To be on the safe side,
you'd better tell him you kissed me good-bye to get rid of me!
(*Then angrily*) So Marsden's here again! The damned old

woman! I simply can't go him any more, Nina! Why Gordon should take such a fancy to that old sissy is beyond me!

NINA (*suddenly struck—thinking*)

Why, he's jealous of Gordon liking Charlie! . . .

(*Immediately all affectionate pity*)

Then he must love Gordon a little! . . .

(*Letting her pity escape her*) Poor Ned! (*She makes a movement toward him*).

DARRELL (*startled and afraid she may have guessed something he doesn't acknowledge to himself*) What? Why do you say that? (*Then rudely defensive*) Don't be silly! (*Resentfully*) You know well enough what I've always held against him! I wanted to put up all the money to back Sam when he started. I wanted to do it for Sam's sake—but especially for my child's sake. Why did Marsden absolutely insist on Sam letting him in equally? It isn't that I begrudge him the money he's made, but I know there was something queer in his mind and that he did it intentionally to spite me! (*From the hallway comes the sound of* MARSDEN'S *voice and* GORDON'S *greeting him vociferously as he lets him into the apartment. As* DARRELL *listens his expression becomes furious again. He bursts out angrily*) You're letting that old ass spoil Gordon, you fool, you! (MARSDEN *comes in from the rear, smiling, immaculately dressed as usual. He looks hardly any older except that his hair is grayer and his tall figure more stooped. His expression and the general atmosphere he gives out are more nearly like those of Act One. If not happy, he is at least living in comparative peace with himself and his environment*).

MARSDEN (*comes straight to* NINA) Hello, Nina Cara Nina! Congratulations on your son's birthday! (*He kisses her*) He's grown so much bigger and stronger in the two months since I've seen him. (*He turns and shakes hands with* DARRELL *coldly—with a trace of a patronizing air*) Hello, Darrell. Last time I was here you were leaving for the West Indies in a week but I see you're still around.

DARRELL (*furious—with a mocking air*) And here you are around again yourself! You're looking comfortable these days, Marsden. I hope your sister is well. It must be a great comfort, having her to take your mother's place! (*Then with a harsh laugh*) Yes, we're two bad pennies, eh, Marsden?—counterfeits—fakes—Sam's silent partners!

NINA (*thinking irritably*)

Ned's getting hateful again! . . . Poor Charlie! . . . I won't have him insulted! . . . he's become such a comfort . . . he understands so much . . . without my having to tell him . . .

(*Looking rebukingly at* DARRELL) Ned is sailing this week, Charlie.

MARSDEN (*thinking triumphantly*)

He's trying to insult me . . . I know all he means . . . but what do I care what he says . . . she's sending him away! . . . intentionally before me! . . . it means he's finished! . . .

DARRELL (*thinking resentfully*)

Is she trying to humiliate me before him? . . . I'll teach her! . . .

(*Then struggling with himself—remorsefully*)

No . . . not this time . . . I promised . . . no quarrel . . . remember . . .

(*Acquiescing—with a pleasant nod to* MARSDEN) Yes, I'm going this week and I expect to be gone at least two years this time— two years of hard work.

MARSDEN (*thinking with scornful pity*)

His work! . . . what a pretense! . . . a scientific dilettante! . . . could anything be more pitiable? . . . poor chap! . . .

(*Perfunctorily*) Biology must be an interesting study. I wish I knew more about it.

DARRELL (*stung yet amused by the other's tone—ironically*) Yes, so do I wish you did, Marsden! Then you might write more about life and less about dear old ladies and devilish bachelors! Why don't you write a novel about life sometime, Marsden? (*He turns his back on* MARSDEN *with a glance of repulsion and walks to the window and stares out*).

MARSDEN (*confusedly*) Yes—decidedly—but hardly in my line—

(*Thinking in anguish—picking up a magazine and turning over the pages aimlessly*)

That . . . is . . . true! . . . he's full of poison! . . . I've never married the word to life! . . . I've been a timid bachelor of Arts, not an artist! . . . my poor pleasant books! . . . all is well! . . . is this well, the three of us? . . . Darrell has become less and less her lover . . . Nina has turned more and more to me . . . we have built up a secret life of subtle sympathies and confidences . . . she has known I have understood about her mere physical passion for Darrell . . . what woman could be expected to love Sam passionately? . . . some day she'll confide all about

Darrell to me . . . now that he's finished . . . she knows that I
love her without my telling . . . she even knows the sort of love
it is. . . .

(*Passionately—thinking*)

My love is finer than any she has known! . . . I do not lust for
her! . . . I would be content if our marriage should be purely
the placing of our ashes in the same tomb . . . our urn side by
side and touching one another . . . could the others say as much,
could they love so deeply? . . .

(*Then suddenly miserably self-contemptuous*)

What! . . . platonic heroic at my age! . . . do I believe a word
of that? . . . look at her beautiful eyes! . . . wouldn't I give anything in life to see them desire me? . . . and the intimacy I'm
boasting about, what more does it mean than that I've been playing the dear old Charlie of her girlhood again? . . .

(*Thinking in anguish*)

Damned coward and weakling! . . .

NINA (*looking at him—pityingly—thinking*)

What does he always want of me? . . . me? . . . I am the only
one who senses his deep hurt . . . I feel how life has wounded
him . . . is that partly my fault, too? . . . I have wounded everyone . . . poor Charlie, what can I do for you? . . . if giving
myself to you would bring you a moment's happiness, could
I? . . . the idea used to be revolting . . . now, nothing about
love seems important enough to be revolting . . . poor Charlie,
he only thinks he ought to desire me! . . . dear Charlie, what a
perfect lover he would make for one's old age! . . . what a perfect lover when one was past passion! . . .

(*Then with sudden scornful revulsion*)

These men make me sick! . . . I hate all three of them! . . .
they disgust me! . . . the wife and mistress in me has been
killed by them! . . . thank God, I am only a mother now! . . .
Gordon is my little man, my only man! . . .

(*Suddenly*) I've got a job for you, Charlie—make the salad
dressing for lunch. You know, the one I'm so crazy about.

MARSDEN (*springs to his feet*) Righto! (*He puts his arm about
her waist and they go out together laughingly, without a glance
at* DARRELL).

DARRELL (*thinking dully*)

I mustn't stay to lunch . . . ghost at my son's feast! . . . I
better go now . . . why wait for Sam? . . . what is there to say to

him I can say? . . . and there's nothing about him I want to see . . . he's as healthy as a pig . . . and as sane . . . I was afraid once his mother had lied to Nina . . . I went upstate and investigated . . . true, every word of it . . . his great-grandfather, his grandmother, his father, were all insane . . .
(*Moving uneasily*)
Stop it! . . . time to go when those thoughts come . . . 'sail on Saturday . . . not come here again . . . Nina will soon be fighting Sam for my son's love! . . . I'm better out of that! . . . O Christ, what a mess it all is! . . .

GORDON (*appears in the doorway in rear. He carries a small, expensive yacht's model of a sloop with the sails set. He is in a terrific state of conflicting emotions, on the verge of tears yet stubbornly determined*)
I got to do it! . . . Gosh, it's awful . . . this boat is so pretty . . . why did it have to come from him? . . . I can get Dad to buy me another boat . . . but now I love this one . . . but he kissed Mother . . . she kissed him . . .
(*He walks up defiantly and confronts* DARRELL *who turns to him in surprise*) Hey—Darrell—did you—? (*He stops chokingly*).

DARRELL (*immediately realizing what is coming—thinking with somber anguish*)
So this has to happen! . . . what I dreaded! . . . my fate is merciless, it seems! . . .
(*With strained kindliness*) Did what?

GORDON (*growing hard—stammers angrily*) I found this—out in the hall. It can't be from anybody else. Is this—your present?

DARRELL (*hard and defiant himself*) Yes.

GORDON (*in a rage—tremblingly*) Then—here's what—I think of you! (*Beginning to cry, he breaks off the mast, bowsprit, breaks the mast in two, tears the rigging off and throws the dismantled hull at* DARRELL's *feet*) There! You can keep it!

DARRELL (*his anger overcoming him for an instant*) You—you mean little devil, you! You don't get that from me— (*He has taken a threatening step forward.* GORDON *stands white-faced, defying him.* DARRELL *pulls himself up short—then in a trembling voice of deeply wounded affection*) You shouldn't have done that, son. What difference do I make? It was never my boat. But it was your boat. You should consider the boat, not me. Don't you like boats for themselves? It was a beautiful little boat, I thought. That's why I—

GORDON (*sobbing miserably*) It was awful pretty! I didn't want to do it! (*He kneels down and gathers up the boat into his arms again*) Honest I didn't. I love boats! But I hate you! (*This last with passionate intensity*).

DARRELL (*dryly*) So I've observed. (*Thinking with angry anguish*) He hurts, damn him! . . .

GORDON No, you don't know! More'n ever now! More'n ever! (*The secret escaping him*) I saw you kissing Mother! I saw Mother, too!

DARRELL (*startled, but immediately forcing a smile*) But I was saying good-bye. We're old friends. You know that.

GORDON You can't fool me! This was different! (*Explosively*) It would serve you good and right—and Mother, too—if I was to tell Dad on you!

DARRELL Why, I'm Sam's oldest friend. Don't make a little fool of yourself!

GORDON You are not his friend. You've always been hanging around cheating him—hanging around Mother!

DARRELL Keep still! What do you mean cheating him?

GORDON I don't know. But I know you aren't his friend. And sometime I'm going to tell him I saw you—

DARRELL (*with great seriousness now—deeply moved*) Listen! There are things a man of honor doesn't tell anyone—not even his mother or father. You want to be a man of honor, don't you? (*Intensely*) There are things we don't tell, you and I! (*He has put his hand around* GORDON's *shoulder impulsively*) This is my son! . . . I love him! . . .

GORDON (*thinking—terribly torn*)
Why do I like him now? . . . I like him awful! . . .
(*Crying*) We?—who d'you mean?—I've got honor!—more'n you!
—you don't have to tell me!—I wasn't going to tell Dad anyway, honest I wasn't! We?—what d'you mean, we?—I'm not like you! I don't want to be ever like you! (*There is the sound of a door being flung open and shut and* EVANS' *hearty voice*).

EVANS (*from the entrance hall*) Hello, everybody!

DARRELL (*slapping* GORDON *on the back*) Buck up, son! Here he is! Hide that boat or he'll ask questions. (GORDON *runs and hides the boat under the sofa. When* EVANS *enters,* GORDON *is entirely composed and runs to him joyfully.* EVANS *has grown stouter, his face is heavy now, he has grown executive and used to command, he automatically takes charge wherever he is. He does*

*not look his age except that his hair has grown scanty and
there is a perceptible bald spot on top. He is expensively
tailored*).

EVANS (*hugging* GORDON *to him—lovingly*) How's the old son?
How's the birthday coming along?

GORDON   Fine, Dad!

EVANS   Hello, Ned! Isn't this kid of mine a whopper for his age,
though!

DARRELL (*smiling strainedly*)  Yes. (*Writhing—thinking*)

It hurts now! . . . to see my son his son! . . . I've had enough!
. . . get out! . . . any excuse! . . . I can phone afterwards! . . .
I'll yell out the whole business if I stay! . . .

I was just going, Sam. I've got to step around and see a fellow
who lives near—biologist. (*He has gone to the door*).

EVANS (*disappointedly*)  Then you won't be here for lunch?

DARRELL (*thinking*)

I'll yell the truth into your ears if I stay a second longer . . .
you damned lunatic! . . .

Can't stay. Sorry. This is important. I'm sailing in a few days—
lots to do—see you later, Sam. So long—Gordon.

GORDON (*as he goes out with awkward haste*)  Good-bye—Uncle
Ned. (*Thinking confusedly*)

Why did I call him that when I said I never would? . . . I
know . . . must be because he said he's sailing and I'm glad . . .

EVANS   So long, Ned. (*Thinking—good-naturedly superior*)

Ned and his biology! . . . He takes his hobby pretty seriously! . . .

(*With satisfaction*)

Well, he can afford to have hobbies now! . . . his investment
with me has made him a pile. . . .

Where's Mother, son?

GORDON   Out in the kitchen with Uncle Charlie. (*Thinking*)

I hope he never comes back! . . . why did I like him then? . . .
it was only for a second . . . I didn't really . . . I never could!
. . . why does he always call me Gordon as if he hated to? . . .

EVANS (*sitting down at left*)  I hope lunch is ready soon. I'm
hungry as the devil, aren't you?

GORDON (*absent-mindedly*)  Yes, Dad.

EVANS   Come over here and tell me about your birthday. (GORDON
*comes over.* EVANS *pulls him up on his lap*) How'd you like your
presents? What'd you get from Uncle Ned?

GORDON (*evasively*)  They were all dandy. (*Suddenly*) Why was I named Gordon?

EVANS  Oh, you know all about that—all about Gordon Shaw. I've told you time and again.

GORDON  You told me once he was Mother's beau—when she was a girl.

EVANS (*teasingly*)  What do you know about beaus? You're growing up!

GORDON  Did Mother love him a lot?

EVANS (*embarrassedly*)  I guess so.

GORDON (*thinking keenly*)

That's why Darrell hates me being called Gordon . . . he knows Mother loved Gordon better'n she does him . . . now I know how to get back at him . . . I'll be just like Gordon was and Mother'll love me better'n him! . . .

And then that Gordon was killed, wasn't he? Am I anything like him?

EVANS  I hope you are. If when you go to college you can play football or row like Gordon did, I'll—I'll give you anything you ask for! I mean that!

GORDON (*dreamily*)  Tell me about him again, will you, Dad— about the time he was stroking the crew and the fellow who was Number Seven began to crack, and he couldn't see him but he felt him cracking somehow, and he began talking back to him all the time and sort of gave him his strength so that when the race was over and they'd won Gordon fainted and the other fellow didn't.

EVANS (*with a fond laugh*)  Why, you know it all by heart! What's the use of my telling you?

NINA (*comes in from the rear while they are talking. She comes forward slowly—thinking resentfully*)

Does he love Sam more than he does me? . . . oh, no, he can't! . . . but he trusts him more! . . . he confides in him more! . . .

GORDON  Did you ever used to fight fellows, Dad?

EVANS (*embarrassedly*)  Oh, a little—when I had to.

GORDON  Could you lick Darrell?

NINA (*thinking frightenedly*)

Why does he ask that? . . .

EVANS (*surprised*)  Your Uncle Ned? What for? We've always been friends.

GORDON  I mean, if you weren't friends, could you?

EVANS (*boastfully*) Oh, yes, I guess so. Ned was never as strong as I was.

NINA (*thinking contemptuously*)

Ned is weak. . . .

(*Then apprehensively*)

But you're getting too strong, Sam. . . .

GORDON But Gordon could have licked you, couldn't he?

EVANS You bet he could!

GORDON (*thinking*)

She must have loved Gordon better'n Dad even! . . .

NINA (*she comes forward to the chair at center, forcing a smile*) What's all this talk about fighting? That's not nice. For heaven's sake, Sam, don't encourage him—

EVANS (*grinning*) Never mind the women, Gordon. You've got to know how to fight to get on in this world.

NINA (*thinking pityingly*)

You poor booby! . . . how brave you are now! . . .

(*Softly*) Perhaps you're right, dear. (*Looking around*) Has Ned gone?

GORDON (*defiantly*) Yes—and he's not coming back—and he's sailing soon!

NINA (*with a shudder*)

Why does he challenge me that way? . . . and cling to Sam? . . . he must have seen Ned and me . . . he doesn't offer to come to my lap . . . he used to . . . Ned was right . . . I've got to lie to him . . . get him back . . . here . . . on my lap! . . .

(*With a sneer—to* EVANS) I'm glad Ned's gone. I was afraid he was going to be on our hands all day.

GORDON (*eagerly, half-getting down from his father's lap*) You're glad—? (*Then cautiously thinking*)

She's cheating . . . I saw her kiss him. . . .

NINA Ned's getting to be an awful bore. He's so weak. He can't get started on anything unless he's pushed.

GORDON (*moving a little nearer—searching her face—thinking*)

She doesn't seem to like him so much . . . but I saw her kiss him! . . .

EVANS (*surprised*) Oh, come now, Nina, aren't you being a little hard on Ned? It's true he's sort of lost his grip in a way but he's our best friend.

GORDON (*moving away from his father again—resentfully—thinking*)

What's Dad standing up for him to her for? . . .

NINA (*thinking triumphantly*)

That's right, Sam . . . just what I wanted you to say! . . . (*Boredly*) Oh, I know he is but he gets on my nerves hanging around all the time. Without being too rude, I urged him to get back to his work, and made him promise me he wouldn't return for two years. Finally he promised—and then he became silly and sentimental and asked me to kiss him good-bye for good luck! So I kissed him to get rid of him! The silly fool!

GORDON (*thinking—overjoyed*)

Then! . . . that's why! . . . that's why! . . . and he'll be gone two years! . . . oh, I'm so glad! . . .

(*He goes to her and looks up into her face with shining eyes*)
Mother!

NINA Dear! (*She takes him up on her lap and hugs him in her arms*).

GORDON (*kisses her*) There! (*Triumphantly thinking*)

That makes up for his kiss! . . . That takes it off her mouth. . . .

EVANS (*grinning*) Ned must be falling for you—in his old age! (*Then sentimentally*) Poor guy! He's never married, that's the trouble. He's lonely. I know how he feels. A fellow needs a little feminine encouragement to help him keep his head up.

NINA (*snuggling* GORDON's *head against hers—laughing teasingly*) I think your hard-headed Dad is getting mushy and silly! What do you think, Gordon?

GORDON (*laughing with her*) Yes, he's mushy, Mother! He's silly! (*He kisses her and whispers*) I'm going to be like Gordon Shaw, Mother! (*She hugs him fiercely to her triumphantly happy*).

EVANS (*grinning*) You two are getting too hard-boiled for me. (*He laughs. They all laugh happily together*).

NINA (*suddenly overcome by a wave of conscience-stricken remorse and pity*)

Oh, I am hard on Ned! . . . poor dear generous Ned! . . . you told me to lie to your son against you . . . for my sake . . . I'm not worthy of your love! . . . I'm low and selfish! . . . but I do love you! . . . this is the son of our love in my arms! . . . oh, Mother God, grant my prayer that some day we may tell our son the truth and he may love his father! . . .

GORDON (*sensing her thoughts, sits up in her lap and stares into her face, while she guiltily avoids his eyes—in fear and resentment. Thinking*)

She's thinking about that Darrell now! . . . I know! . . . she likes him too! . . . she can't fool me! . . . I saw her kissing! . . . she didn't think he was a silly fool then! . . . she was lying to Dad and me! . . .

(*He pushes off her lap and backs away from her*).

NINA (*thinking frightenedly*)

He read my thoughts! . . . I mustn't even think of Ned when he's around! . . . poor Ned! . . . no, don't think of him! . . . (*Leaning forward toward* GORDON *with her arms stretched out entreatingly but adopting a playful tone*) Why, Gordon, what's come over you? You jumped off my lap as though you'd sat on a tack! (*She forces a laugh*).

GORDON (*his eyes on the floor—evasively*) I'm hungry. I want to see if lunch is nearly ready. (*He turns abruptly and runs out*).

EVANS (*in a voice of superior manly understanding, kindly but laying down the law to womanly weakness*) He's sick of being babied, Nina. You forget he's getting to be a big boy. And we want him to grow up a real he-man and not an old lady like Charlie. (*Sagaciously*) That's what's made Charlie like he is, I'll bet. His mother never stopped babying him.

NINA (*submissively—but with a look of bitter scorn at him*) Perhaps you're right, Sam.

EVANS (*confidently*) I know I am!

NINA (*thinking with a look of intense hatred*)

Oh, Mother God, grant that I may some day tell this fool the truth! . . .

*Curtain*

## ACT EIGHT

SCENE: *Late afternoon in late June, ten years later—the afterdeck of the* EVANS' *motor cruiser anchored in the lane of yachts near the finish line at Poughkeepsie. The bow and amidship of the cruiser are off right, pointed upstream. The portside rail is in the rear, the curve of the stern at left, the rear of the cabin with broad windows and a door is at right. Two wicker chairs are at left and a chaise longue at right. A wicker table with another chair is at center. The afterdeck is in cool shade, contrasted with the soft golden haze of late afternoon sunlight that glows on the river.*

NINA *is sitting by the table at center,* DARRELL *in the chair farthest left,* MARSDEN *in the chaise longue at right.* EVANS *is leaning over the rail directly back of* NINA, *looking up the river through a pair of binoculars.* MADELINE ARNOLD *is standing by his side.*

NINA's *hair has turned completely white. She is desperately trying to conceal the obvious inroads of time by an over-emphasis on makeup that defeats its end by drawing attention to what it would conceal. Her face is thin, her cheeks taut, her mouth drawn with forced smiling. There is little left of her face's charm except her eyes which now seem larger and more deeply mysterious than ever. But she has kept her beautiful figure. It has the tragic effect of making her face seem older and more worn-out by contrast. Her general manner recalls instantly the* NINA *of Act Four, neurotic, passionately embittered and torn. She is dressed in a white yachting costume.*

DARRELL *seems to have "thrown back" to the young doctor we had seen at the house of* NINA's *father in Act Two. He has again the air of the cool, detached scientist regarding himself and the people around him as interesting phenomena. In appearance, he is once more sharply defined, his face and body have grown lean and well-conditioned, the puffiness and jowls of the precious Act are gone. His skin is tanned almost black by his years in the tropics. His thick hair is iron-gray. He wears flannel pants, a blue coat, white buckskin shoes. He looks his fifty-one years, perhaps, but not a day more.* MARSDEN *has aged greatly. The stoop of his tall figure is accentuated, his hair has grown whitish. He is an older image of the* MARSDEN *of Act Five, who was so prostrated by his mother's death. Now it is his sister's death two months before that has plunged him into despair. His present grief, however, is more resigned to its fate than the old. He is dressed immaculately in black, as in Act Five.*

EVANS *is simply* EVANS, *his type logically developed by ten years of continued success and accumulating wealth, jovial and simple and good-natured as ever, but increasingly stubborn and self-opinionated. He has grown very stout. His jowly broad face has a heavy, flushed, apoplectic look. His head has grown quite bald on* top. *He is wearing a yachting cap, blue yachting coat, white flannel pants, buckskin shoes.*

MADELINE ARNOLD *is a pretty girl of nineteen, with dark hair and eyes. Her skin is deeply tanned, her figure tall and athletic, reminding one of* NINA's *when we first saw her. Her personality is direct and frank. She gives the impression of a person who always knows exactly what she is after and generally gets it, but is also generous and a good loser, a good sport who is popular with her own sex as well as sought after by men. She is dressed in a bright-colored sport costume.*

EVANS (*nervous and excited—on pins and needles—lowering his binoculars impatiently*) Can't see anything up there! There's a damned haze on the river! (*Handing the binoculars to* MADELINE) Here, Madeline. You've got young eyes.

MADELINE (*eagerly*) Thank you. (*She looks up the river through the glasses*).

NINA (*thinking—bitterly*)

Young eyes! . . . they look into Gordon's eyes! . . . he sees love in her young eyes! . . . mine are old now! . . .

EVANS (*pulling out his watch*) Soon be time for the start. (*Comes forward—exasperated*) Of course, the damned radio has to pick out this time to go dead! Brand new one I had installed especially for this race, too! Just my luck! (*Coming to* NINA *and putting his hand on her shoulder*) Gosh, I'll bet Gordon's some keyed-up right at this moment, Nina!

MADELINE (*without lowering the glasses*) Poor kid! I'll bet he is!

NINA (*thinking with intense bitterness*)

That tone in her voice! . . . her love already possesses him! . . . my son! . . .

(*Vindictively*)

But she won't! . . . as long as I live! . . .

(*Flatly*) Yes, he must be nervous.

EVANS (*taking his hand away, sharply*) I didn't mean nervous. He doesn't know what it is to have nerves. Nothing's ever got him rattled yet. (*This last with a resentful look down at her as he moves back to the rail*).

MADELINE (*with the calm confidence of one who knows*) Yes, you can bank on Gordon never losing his nerve.

NINA (*coldly*) I'm quite aware my son isn't a weakling— (*Mean-*

*ingly, with a glance at* MADELINE) even though he does do weak things sometimes.

MADELINE (*without lowering the glasses from her eyes—thinking good-naturedly*)

Ouch! . . . that was meant for me! . . .

(*Then hurt*)

Why does she dislike me so? . . . I've done my best, for Gordon's sake, to be nice to her. . . .

EVANS (*looking back at* NINA *resentfully—thinking*)

Another nasty crack at Madeline! . . . Nina's certainly become the prize bum sport! . . . I thought once her change of life was over she'd be ashamed of her crazy jealousy . . . instead of that it's got worse . . . but I'm not going to let her come between Gordon and Madeline . . . he loves her and she loves him . . . and her folks have got money and position, too . . . and I like her a lot . . . and, by God, I'm going to see to it their marriage goes through on schedule, no matter how much Nina kicks up! . . .

DARRELL (*keenly observant—thinking*)

Nina hates this young lady . . . of course! . . . Gordon's girl . . . she'll smash their engagement if she can . . . as she did mine once . . . once! . . . thank God my slavery is over! . . . how did she know I was back in town? . . . I wasn't going to see her again . . . but her invitation was so imploring . . . my duty to Gordon, she wrote . . . what duty? . . . pretty late in the day! . . . that's better left dead, too! . . .

EVANS (*looking at his watch again*) They ought to be lined up at the start any minute now. (*Pounding his fist on the rail—letting his pent-up feelings explode*) Come on, Gordon!

NINA (*startled—with nervous irritation*) Sam! I told you I have a splitting headache! (*Thinking intensely*)

You vulgar boor! . . . Gordon's engagement to her is all your fault! . . .

EVANS (*Resentfully*) I'm sorry. Why don't you take some aspirin? (*Thinking irritably*)

Nina in the dumps! . . . Charlie in mourning! . . . what a pair of killjoys! . . . I wanted to bring Gordon and his friends on board to celebrate . . . no chance! . . . have to take Madeline . . . stage a party in New York . . . leave this outfit flat . . . Nina'll be sore as the devil but she'll have to like it . . .

DARRELL (*examining* NINA *critically—thinking*)

She's gotten into a fine neurotic state . . . reminds me of when I first knew her . . .

(*Then exultantly*)

Thank God, I can watch her objectively again . . . these last three years away have finally done it . . . complete cure! . . .

(*Then remorsefully*)

Poor Nina! . . . we're all deserting her . . .

(*Then glancing at* MARSDEN—*with a trace of a sneer*)

Even Marsden seems to have left her for the dead! . . .

MARSDEN (*vaguely irritated—thinking*)

What am I doing here? . . . what do I care about this stupid race? . . . why did I let Nina bully me into coming? . . . I ought to be alone . . . with my memories of dear Jane . . . it will be two months ago Saturday she died . . .

(*His lips tremble, tears come to his eyes*)

MADELINE (*with an impatient sigh, lowering the glasses*) It's no use, Mr. Evans, I can't see a thing.

EVANS (*with angry disgust*) If only that damned radio was working!

NINA (*exasperatedly*) For heaven's sake, stop swearing so much!

EVANS (*hurt—indignantly*) What about it if I am excited? Seems to me you could show a little more interest without it hurting you, when it's Gordon's last race, his last appearance on a varsity!

(*He turns away from her*).

MADELINE (*thinking*)

He's right . . . she's acting rotten . . . if I were Gordon's mother, I certainly wouldn't . . .

EVANS (*turning back to* NINA—*resentfully*) You used to cheer loud enough for Gordon Shaw! And our Gordon's got him beat a mile, as an oarsman, at least! (*Turning to* DARRELL) And that isn't rather stuff either, Ned! All the experts say so!

DARRELL (*cynically*) Oh, come on, Sam! Surely no one could ever touch Shaw in anything! (*He glances at* NINA *with a sneer. Immediately angry at himself*)

What an idiot! . . . that popped out of me! . . . old habit! . . . I haven't loved her in years! . . .

NINA (*thinking indifferently*)

Ned still feels jealous . . . that no longer pleases me . . . I don't feel anything . . . except that I must get him to help me. . . . (*She turns to* DARRELL *bitterly*) Sam said "our" Gordon. He means his. Gordon's become so like Sam, Ned, you won't recognize him!

MADELINE (*thinking indignantly*)

She's crazy! . . . he's nothing like his father! . . . he's so strong and handsome! . . .

EVANS (*good-naturedly, with a trace of pride*) You flatter me, Nina. I wish I thought that. But he isn't a bit like me, luckily for him. He's a dead ringer for Gordon Shaw at his best.

MADELINE (*thinking*)

Shaw . . . I've seen his picture in the gym . . . my Gordon is better looking . . . he once told me Shaw was an old beau of his mother's . . . they say she was beautiful once . . .

NINA (*shaking her head—scornfully*) Don't be modest, Sam. Gordon *is* you. He may be a fine athlete like Gordon Shaw, because you've held that out to him as your ideal, but there the resemblance ceases. He isn't really like him at all, not the slightest bit!

EVANS (*restraining his anger with difficulty—thinking*)

I'm getting sick of this! . . . she's carrying her jealous grouch too far! . . .

(*Suddenly exploding, pounds his fist on the rail*) Damn it, Nina, if you had any feeling you couldn't—right at the moment when he's probably getting into the shell— (*He stops, trying to control himself, panting, his face red*).

NINA (*staring at him with repulsion—with cool disdain*) I didn't say anything so dire, did I—merely that Gordon resembles you in character. (*With malice*) Don't get so excited. It's bad for your high blood pressure. Ask Ned if it isn't. (*Intensely—thinking*) If he'd only die! . . .

(*Thinking—immediately*)

Oh, I don't mean that . . . I mustn't . . .

DARRELL (*thinking keenly*)

There's a death wish . . . things have gone pretty far . . . Sam does look as if he might have a bad pressure . . . what hope that would have given me at one time! . . . no more, thank God! . . .

(*In a joking tone*) Oh, I guess Sam's all right, Nina.

EVANS (*gruffly*) I never felt better. (*He jerks out his watch again*) Time for the start. Come on in the cabin, Ned, and shoot a drink. We'll see if McCabe's getting the damned radio fixed. (*Passing by* MARSDEN *he claps him on the shoulder exasperatedly*) Come on, Charlie! Snap out of it!

MARSDEN (*startled out of his trance—bewilderedly*)  Eh?—what is it?—are they coming?

EVANS (*recovering his good nature—with a grin, taking his arm*) You're coming to shoot a drink. You need about ten, I think, to get you in the right spirit to see the finish! (*To* DARRELL *who has gotten up but is still standing by his chair*) Come on, Ned.

NINA (*quickly*)  No, leave Ned with me. I want to talk to him. Take Madeline—and Charlie.

MARSDEN (*looking at her appealingly*)  But I'm perfectly contented sitting— (*Then after a look in her eyes—thinking*)
She wants to be alone with Darrell . . . all right . . . doesn't matter now . . . their love is dead . . . but there's still some secret between them she's never told me . . . never mind . . . she'll tell me sometime . . . I'm all she will have left . . . soon. . . .
(*Then stricken with guilt*)
Poor dear Jane! . . . how can I think of anyone but you! . . . God, I'm contemptible! . . . I'll get drunk with that fool! . . . that's all I'm good for! . . .

MADELINE (*thinking resentfully*)
She takes a fine do-this-little-girl tone toward me! . . . I'll give in to her now . . . but once I'm married! . . .

EVANS  Come on then, Madeline. We'll give you a small one. (*Impatiently*) Charlie! Head up!

MARSDEN (*with hectic joviality*)  I hope it's strong poison!

EVANS (*laughing*)  That's the spirit! We'll make a sport out of you yet!

MADELINE (*laughing, goes and takes* MARSDEN's *arm*)  I'll see you get home safe, Mr. Marsden! (*They go into the cabin,* EVANS *following them.* NINA *and* DARRELL *turn and look at each other wonderingly, inquisitively, for a long moment.* DARRELL *remains standing and seems to be a little uneasy*).

DARRELL (*thinking with melancholy interest*)
And now? . . . what? . . . I can look into her eyes . . . strange eyes that will never grow old . . . without desire or jealousy or bitterness . . . was she ever my mistress? . . . can she be the mother of my child? . . . is there such a person as my son? . . . I can't think of these things as real any more . . . they must have happened in another life. . . .

NINA (*thinking sadly*)

My old lover . . . how well and young he looks . . . now we no longer love each other at all . . . our account with God the Father is settled . . . afternoons of happiness paid for with years of pain . . . love, passion, ecstasy . . . in what a far-off life were they alive! . . . the only living life is in the past and future . . . the present is an interlude . . . strange interlude in which we call on past and future to bear witness we are living! . . .

(*With a sad smile*) Sit down, Ned. When I heard you were back I wrote you because I need a friend. It has been so long since we loved each other we can now be friends again. Don't you feel that?

DARRELL (*gratefully*)   Yes. I do. (*He sits down in one of the chairs at left, drawing it up closer to her. Thinking cautiously*)

I want to be her friend . . . but I will never . . .

NINA (*thinking cautiously*)

I must keep very cool and sensible or he won't help me. . . . (*With a friendly smile*) I haven't seen you look so young and handsome since I first knew you. Tell me your secret. (*Bitterly*) I need it! I'm old! Look at me! And I was actually looking forward to being old! I thought it would mean peace. I've been sadly disillusioned! (*Then forcing a smile*) So tell me what fountain of youth you've found.

DARRELL (*proudly*)   That's easy. Work! I've become as interested in biology as I once was in medicine. And not selfishly interested, that's the difference. There's no chance of my becoming a famous biologist and I know it. I'm very much a worker in the ranks. But our Station is a "huge success," as Sam would say. We've made some damned important discoveries. I say "we." I really mean Preston. You may remember I used to write you about him with enthusiasm. He's justified it. He *is* making his name world-famous. He's what I might have been—I did have the brains, Nina!—if I'd had more guts and less vanity, if I'd hewn to the line! (*Then forcing a smile*) But I'm not lamenting. I've found myself in helping him. In that way I feel I've paid my debt—that his work is partly my work. And he acknowledges it. He possesses the rare virtue of gratitude. (*With proud affection*) He's a fine boy, Nina! I suppose I should say man now he's in his thirties.

NINA (*thinking with bitter sorrow*)

So, Ned . . . you remember our love . . . with bitterness! . . .

as a stupid mistake! . . . the proof of a gutless vanity that
ruined your career! . . . oh! . . .
(*Then controlling herself—thinking cynically*)
Well, after all, how do I remember our love? . . . with no
emotion at all, not even bitterness! . . .
(*Then with sudden alarm*)
He's forgotten Gordon for this Preston! . . .
(*Thinking desperately*)
I must make him remember Gordon is his child or I can never
persuade him to help me! . . .
(*Reproachfully*) So you have found a son while I was losing
mine—who is yours, too!

NINA (*struck by this—impersonally interested*)   That's never occurred to me but now I think of it— (*Smiling*) Yes, perhaps unconsciously Preston is a compensating substitute. Well, it's done
both of us good and hasn't harmed anyone.

NINA (*with bitter emphasis*)   Except your real son—and me—but
we don't count, I suppose!

DARRELL (*coolly*)   Harmed Gordon? How? He's all right, isn't he?
(*With a sneer*) I should say from all I've been hearing that he
was your ideal of college hero—like his never-to-be-forgotten
namesake!

NINA (*thinking resentfully*)
He's sneering at his own son! . . .
(*Then trying to be calculating*)
But I mustn't get angry . . . I must make him help me. . . .
(*Speaking with gentle reproach*) And am I the ideal of a happy
mother, Ned?

DARRELL (*immediately moved by pity and ashamed of himself*)
Forgive me, Nina. I haven't quite buried all my bitterness, I'm
afraid. (*Gently*) I'm sorry you're unhappy, Nina.

NINA (*thinking with satisfaction*)
He means that . . . he still does care a little . . . if only it's
enough to . . . !
(*Speaking sadly*) I've lost my son, Ned! Sam has made him all
his. And it was done so gradually that, although I realized what
was happening, there was never any way I could interfere. What
Sam advised seemed always the best thing for Gordon's future.
And it was always what Gordon himself wanted, to escape from
me to boarding school and then to college, to become Sam's
athletic hero—

DARRELL (*impatiently*)  Oh, come now, Nina, you know you've always longed for him to be like Gordon Shaw!

NINA (*bursting out in spite of herself—violently*)  He's not like Gordon! He's forgotten me for that—! (*Trying to be more reasonable*) What do I care whether he's an athlete or not? It's such nonsense, all this fuss! I'm not the slightest bit interested in this race today, for example! I wouldn't care if he came in last! (*Stopping herself—thinking frightenedly*)

Oh, if he should ever guess I said that! . . .

DARRELL (*thinking keenly*)

Hello! . . . she said that as if she'd like to see him come last! . . . why? . . .

(*Then vindictively*)

Well, so would I! . . . it's time these Gordons took a good licking from life! . . .

MADELINE (*suddenly appears in the door from the cabin, her face flushed with excitement*)  They're off! Mr. Evans is getting something—it's terribly faint but—Navy and Washington are leading—Gordon's third! (*She disappears back in the cabin*).

NINA (*looking after her with hatred*)

Her Gordon! . . . she is so sure! . . . how I've come to detest her pretty face! . . .

DARRELL (*thinking with a sneer*)

"Gordon's third"! . . . you might think there was no one else pulling the shell! . . . what idiots women make of themselves about these Gordons! . . . she's pretty, that Madeline! . . . she's got a figure like Nina's when I first loved her . . . those afternoons . . . age is beginning to tell on Nina's face . . . but she's kept her wonderful body! . . .

(*With a trace of malice—dryly*) There's a young lady who seems to care a lot whether Gordon comes in last or not!

NINA (*trying to be sorrowful and appealing*)  Yes. Gordon is hers now, Ned. (*But she cannot bear this thought—vindictively*) That is, they're engaged. But, of course, that doesn't necessarily mean— Can you imagine him throwing himself away on a little fool like that? I simply can't believe he really loves her! Why, she's hardly even pretty and she's deadly stupid. I thought he was only flirting with her—or merely indulging in a passing physical affair. (*She winces*) At his age, one has to expect—even a mother must face nature. But for Gordon to take her seriously, and propose marriage—it's too idiotic for words!

DARRELL (*thinking cynically*)

Oh, so you'll compromise on his sleeping with her . . . if you have to . . . but she must have no real claim to dispute your ownership, eh? . . . you'd like to make her the same sort of convenient slave for him that I was for you! . . .

(*Resentfully*) I can't agree with you. I find her quite charming. It seems to me if I were in Gordon's shoes I'd do exactly what he has done. (*In confusion—thinking bitterly*)

In Gordon's shoes! . . . I always was in Gordon Shaw's shoes! . . . and why am I taking this young Gordon's part? . . . what is he to me, for God's sake? . . .

NINA (*unheedingly*) If he marries her, it means he'll forget me! He'll forget me as completely as Sam forgot his mother! She'll keep him away from me! Oh, I know what wives can do! She'll use her body until she persuades him to forget me! My son, Ned! And your son, too! (*She suddenly gets up and goes to him and takes one of his hands in both of hers*) The son of our old love, Ned!

DARRELL (*thinking with a strange shudder of mingled attraction and fear as she touches him*)

Our love . . . old love . . . old touch of her flesh . . . we're old . . . it's silly and indecent . . . does she think she still can own me? . . .

NINA (*in the tone a mother takes in speaking to her husband about their boy*) You'll have to give Gordon a good talking to, Ned.

DARRELL (*still more disturbed—thinking*)

Old . . . but she's kept her wonderful body . . . how many years since? . . . she has the same strange influence over me . . . touch of her flesh . . . it's dangerous . . . bosh, I'm only humoring her as a friend . . . as her doctor . . . and why shouldn't I have a talk with Gordon? . . . a father owes something to his son . . . he ought to advise him. . . .

(*Then alarmed*)

But I was never going to meddle again . . .

(*Sternly*) I swore I'd never again meddle with human lives, Nina!

NINA (*unheedingly*) You must keep him from ruining his life.

DARRELL (*doggedly—struggling with himself*) I won't touch a life that has more than one cell! (*Harshly*) And I wouldn't help you in this, anyway! You've got to give up owning people, meddling in their lives as if you were God and had created them!

NINA (*strangely forlorn*) I don't know what you mean, Ned. Gordon is my son, isn't he?

DARRELL (*with a sudden strange violence*) And mine! Mine, too! (*He stops himself. Thinking*)

Shut up, you fool! . . . is that the way to humor her? . . .

NINA (*with strange quiet*) I think I still love you a little, Ned.

DARRELL (*in her tone*) And I still love you a little, Nina. (*Then sternly*) But I will not meddle in your life again! (*With a harsh laugh*) And you've meddled enough with human love, old lady! Your time for that is over! I'll send you a couple of million cells you can torture without harming yourself! (*Regaining control—shamefacedly*) Nina! Please forgive me!

NINA (*starts as if out of a dream—anxiously*) What were you saying, Ned? (*She lets go of his hand and goes back to her chair*)

DARRELL (*dully*) Nothing.

NINA (*strangely*) We were talking about Sam, weren't we? How do you think he looks?

DARRELL (*confusedly casual*) Fine. A bit too fat, of course. He looks as though his blood pressure might be higher than it ought to be. But that's not unusual in persons of his build and age. It's nothing to hope—I meant, to worry over! (*Then violently*) God damn it, why did you make me say hope?

NINA (*calmly*) It may have been in your mind, too, mayn't it?

DARRELL No! I've nothing against Sam. I've always been his best friend. He owes his happiness to me.

NINA (*strangely*) There are so many curious reasons we dare not think about for thinking things!

DARRELL (*rudely*) Thinking doesn't matter a damn! Life is something in one cell that doesn't need to think!

NINA (*strangely*) I know! God the Mother!

DARRELL (*excitedly*) And all the rest is gutless egotism! But to hell with it! What I started to say was, what possible reason could I have for hoping for Sam's death?

NINA (*strangely*) We're always desiring death for ourselves or others, aren't we—while we while away our lives with the old surface ritual of coveting our neighbor's ass?

DARRELL (*frightenedly*) You're talking like the old Nina now—when I first loved you. Please don't! It isn't decent—at our age! (*thinking in terror*)

The old Nina! . . . am I the old Ned? . . . then that means? . . . but we must not meddle in each other's lives again! . . .

NINA (*strangely*) I am the old Nina! And this time I will not let my Gordon go from me forever!

EVANS (*appears in the doorway of the cabin—excited and irritated*) Madeline's listening in now. It went dead on me. (*Raising the binoculars as he goes to the rail, he looks up the river*) Last I got, Gordon third, Navy and Washington leading. They're the ones to fear, he said—Navy especially. (*Putting down the glasses—with a groan*) Damned haze! My eyes are getting old. (*Then suddenly with a grin*) You ought to see Charlie! He started throwing Scotch into him as if he were drinking against time. I had to take the bottle away from him. It's hit him an awful wallop. (*Then looking from one to the other—resentfully*) What's the matter with you two? There's a race going on, don't you know it? And you sit like dead clams!

DARRELL (*placatingly*) I thought someone'd better stay out here and let you know when they get in sight.

EVANS (*relieved*) Oh, sure, that's right! Here, take the glasses. You always had good eyes. (DARRELL *gets up and takes the glasses and goes to the rail and begins adjusting them*).

DARRELL Which crew was it you said Gordon feared the most?

EVANS (*has gone back to the cabin doorway*) Navy. (*Then proudly*) Oh, he'll beat them! But it'll be damn close. I'll see if Madeline's getting— (*He goes back to the cabin*).

DARRELL (*looking up the river—with vindictive bitterness—thinking*) Come on, Navy! . . .

NINA (*thinking bitterly*)
Madeline's Gordon! . . . Sam's Gordon! . . . the thanks I get for saving Sam at the sacrifice of my own happiness! . . . I won't have it! . . . what do I care what happens to Sam now? . . . I hate him! . . . I'll tell him Gordon isn't his child! . . . and threaten to tell Gordon too, unless! . . . he'll be in deadly fear of that! . . . he'll soon find some excuse to break their engagement! . . . he can! . . . he has the strangest influence over Gordon! . . . but Ned must back me up or Sam won't believe me! . . . Ned must tell him too! . . . but will Ned? . . . he'll be afraid of the insanity! . . . I must make him believe Sam's in no danger . . .

(*Intensely*) Listen, Ned, I'm absolutely sure, from things she wrote me before she died, that Sam's mother must have been deliberately lying to me about the insanity that time. She was jealous because Sam loved me and she simply wanted to be revenged, I'm sure.

DARRELL (*without lowering glasses—dryly*)  No. She told you the truth. I never mentioned it, but I went up there once and made a thorough investigation of his family.

NINA (*with resentful disappointment*)  Oh—I suppose you wanted to make sure so you could hope he'd go insane?

DARRELL (*simply*)  I needed to be able to hope that, then. I loved you horribly at that time, Nina—horribly!

NINA (*putting her hands on his arm*)  And you don't—any more, Ned? (*Thinking intensely*)
Oh, I must make him love me again . . . enough to make him tell Sam! . . .

DARRELL (*thinking strangely—struggling with himself*)
She'd like to own me again . . . I wish she wouldn't touch me . . . what is this tie of old happiness between our flesh? . . .
(*Harshly—weakly struggling to shake off her hands, without lowering the glasses*) I won't meddle again with human lives, I told you!

NINA (*unheeding, clinging to him*)  And I loved you horribly! I still do love you, Ned! I used to hope he'd go insane myself because I loved you so! But look at Sam! He's sane as a pig! There's absolutely no danger now!

DARRELL (*thinking—alarmed*)
What is she after now—what does she want me for?
(*Stiffly*) I'm no longer a doctor but I should say he's a healthy miss of Nature's. It's a thousand to one against it at this late day.

NINA (*with sudden fierce intensity*)  Then it's time to tell him the truth, isn't it? We've suffered all our lives for his sake! We've made him rich and happy! It's time he gave us back our son!

DARRELL (*thinking*)
Aha . . . so that's it! . . . tell Sam the truth? . . . at last! . . . by God, I'd like to tell him, at that! . . .
(*With a sneer*) Our son? You mean yours, my dear! Kindly count me out of any further meddling with—

NINA (*unruffledly—obsessed*)  But Sam won't believe me if I'm the only one to tell him! He'll think I'm lying for spite, that it's only my crazy jealousy! He'll ask you! You've got to tell him too, Ned!

DARRELL (*thinking*)

I'd like to see his face when I told him his famous oarsman isn't his son but mine! . . . that might pay me back a little for all he's taken from me! . . .

(*Harshly*) I've stopped meddling in Sam's life, I tell you!

NINA (*insistently*) Think of what Sam has made us go through, of how he's made us suffer! You've got to tell him! You still love me a little, don't you, Ned? You must when you remember the happiness we've known in each other's arms! You were the only happiness I've ever known in life!

DARRELL (*struggling weakly—thinking*)

She lies! . . . there was her old lover, Gordon! . . . he was always first! . . . then her son, Gordon! . . .

(*With desperate rancor—thinking*)

Come on, Navy! . . . beat her Gordons for me! . . .

NINA (*intensely*) Oh, if I'd only gone away with you that time when you came back from Europe! How happy we would have been, dear! How our boy would have loved you—if it hadn't been for Sam!

DARRELL (*thinking—weakly*)

Yes, if it hadn't been for Sam I would have been happy! . . . I would have been the world's greatest neurologist! . . . my boy would have loved me and I'd have loved him! . . .

NINA (*with a crowning intensity to break down his last resistance*) You must tell him, Ned! For my sake! Because I love you! Because you remember our afternoons—our mad happiness! Because you love me!

DARRELL (*beaten—dazedly*) Yes—what must I do?—meddle again? (*The noise of* MADELINE's *excited voice cheering and clapping her hands, of* MARSDEN's *voice yelling drunkenly, of* EVANS', *all shouting "Gordon! Gordon! Come on, Gordon!" comes from the cabin.* MARSDEN *appears swaying in the cabin doorway yelling "Gordon!" He is hectically tipsy.* DARRELL *gives a violent shudder as if he were coming out of a nightmare and pushes* NINA *away from him*).

DARRELL (*thinking—dazedly still, but in a tone of relief*)

Marsden again! . . . thank God! . . . he's saved me! . . . from her! . . . and her Gordons! . . .

(*Turning on her triumphantly*) No, Nina—sorry—but I can't help you. I told you I'd never meddle again with human lives! (*More and more confidently*) Besides, I'm quite sure Gordon isn't my son, if the real deep core of the truth were known! I was only a body to you. Your first Gordon used to come back to life. I was never more to you than a substitute for your dead lover! Gordon is really Gordon's son! So you see I'd be telling Sam a lie if I boasted that I— And I'm a man of honor! I've proved that, at least! (*He raises his glasses and looks up the river—thinking exultantly*)

I'm free! . . . I've beaten her at last! . . . now come on, Navy! . . . you've got to beat her Gordons for me! . . .

NINA (*after staring at him for a moment—walking away from him —thinking with a dull fatalism*)

I've lost him . . . he'll never tell Sam now . . . is what he said right? . . . is Gordon Gordon's? . . . oh, I hope so! . . . oh, dear, dead Gordon, help me to get back your son! . . . I must find some way. . . .

(*She sits down again*).

MARSDEN (*who has been staring at them with a foolish grin*) Hello, you two! Why do you look so guilty? You don't love each other any more! It's all nonsense! I don't feel the slightest twinge of jealousy. That's proof enough, isn't it? (*Then blandly apologetic*) Pardon me if I sound a bit pipped—a good bit! Sam said ten and then took the bottle away when I'd had only five! But it's enough! I've forgotten sorrow! There's nothing in life worth grieving about, I assure you, Nina! And I've gotten interested in this race now. (*He sings raucously*) Oh, we'll row, row, row, right down the river! And we'll row, row, row—" Remember that old tune—when you were a little girl, Nina? Oh, I'm forgetting Sam said to tell you Gordon was on even terms with the leaders! A gallant spurt did it! Nip and tuck now! I don't care who wins— as long as it isn't Gordon! I don't like him since he's grown up! He thinks I'm an old woman! (*Sings*) "Row, row, row." The field against Gordon!

DARRELL (*hectically*) Right! (*He looks through the glasses—excitedly*) I see a flashing in the water way up there! Must be their oars! They're coming! I'll tell Sam! (*He hurries into the cabin*).

NINA (*thinking dully*)

He'll tell Sam . . . no, he doesn't mean that . . . I must find some other way . . .

MARSDEN (*walks a bit uncertainly to NINA's chair*) Gordon really should get beaten today—for the good of his soul, Nina. That

Madeline is pretty, isn't she? These Gordons are too infernally lucky—while we others— (*He almost starts to blubber—angrily*) we others have got to beat him today! (*He slumps clumsily down to a sitting position on the deck by her chair and takes her hand and pats it*) There, there, Nina Cara Nina! Don't worry your pretty head! It will all come out all right! We'll only have a little while· longer to wait and then you and I'll be quietly married! (*Thinking frightenedly*)

The devil! . . . what am I saying? . . . I'm drunk! . . . all right, all the better! . . . I've wanted all my life to tell her! . . .

Of course, I realize you've got a husband at present but, never mind, I can wait. I've waited a lifetime already; but for a long while now I've had a keen psychic intuition that I wasn't born to die before— (EVANS *and* MADELINE *and* DARRELL *come rushing out of the cabin. They all have binoculars. They run to the rail and train their glasses up the river*).

MADELINE (*excitedly*) I see them! (*Grabbing his arm and pointing*) Look, Mr. Evans—there—don't you see?

EVANS (*excitedly*) No—not yet— Yes! Now I see them! (*Pounding on the rail*) Come on, Gordon boy!

MADELINE Come on, Gordon! (*The whistles and sirens from the yachts up the river begin to be heard. This grows momentarily louder as one after another other yachts join in the chorus as the crews approach nearer and nearer until toward the close of the scene there is a perfect pandemonium of sound*).

NINA (*with bitter hatred—thinking*)

How I hate her! . . .

(*Then suddenly with a deadly calculation—thinking*)

Why not tell her? . . . as Sam's mother told me? . . . of the insanity? . . . she thinks Gordon is Sam's son.

(*With a deadly smile of triumph*)

That will be poetic justice! . . . that will solve everything! . . . she won't marry him! . . . he will turn to me for comfort! . . . but I must plan it out carefully! . . .

MARSDEN (*driven on—extravagantly*) Listen, Nina! After we're married I'm going to write a novel—my first real novel! All the twenty odd books I've written have been long-winded fairy tales for grown-ups—about dear old ladies and witty, cynical bachelors and quaint characters with dialects, and married folk who always admire and respect each other, and lovers who avoid love in hushed whispers! That's what I've been, Nina—a hush-hush whisperer of lies! Now I'm going to give an honest healthy yell—turn on the sun into the shadows of lies—shout "This is life and this is sex, and here are passion and hatred and regret and joy and pain and ecstasy, and these are men and women and sons and daughters whose hearts are weak and strong, whose blood is blood and not a soothing syrup!" Oh, I can do it, Nina! I can write the truth! I've seen it in you, your father, my mother, sister, Gordon, Sam, Darrell and myself. I'll write the book of us! But here I am talking while my last chapters are in the making—right here and now— (*Hurriedly*) You'll excuse me, won't you, Nina? I must watch—my duty as an artist! (*He scrambles to his feet and peers about him with a hectic eagerness.* NINA *pays no attention to him*).

EVANS (*exasperatedly, taking down his glasses*) You can't tell a damn thing—which is which or who's ahead—I'm going to listen in again. (*He hurries into the cabin*).

NINA (*with a smile of cruel triumph—thinking*)
I can tell her . . . confidentially . . . I can pretend I'm forced to tell her . . . as Sam's mother did with me . . . because I feel it's due to her happiness and Gordon's . . . it will explain my objection to the engagement . . . oh, it can't help succeeding . . . my Gordon will come back! . . . I'll see he never gets away again! . . .
(*She calls*) Madeline!

MARSDEN (*thinking*)
Why is she calling Madeline? . . . I must watch all this carefully! . . .

EVANS (*comes rushing out in wild alarm*) Bad news! Navy has drawn ahead—half a length—looks like Navy's race, he said— (*Then violently*) But what does he know, that damn fool announcer—some poor boob—!

MADELINE (*excitedly*) He doesn't know Gordon! He's always best when he's pushed to the limit!

NINA (*she calls more sharply*) Madeline!

DARRELL (*turns around to stare at her—thinking*)
Why is she calling Madeline? . . . she's bound she'll meddle in their lives . . . I've got to watch her . . . well, let's see. . . .
(*He touches* MADELINE *on the shoulder*) Mrs. Evans is calling you, Miss Arnold.

MADELINE (*impatiently*) Yes, Mrs. Evans. But they're getting closer. Why don't you come and watch?

NINA (*not heeding—impressively*) There s something I must tell you.

MADELINE (*in hopeless irritation*) But— Oh, all right. (*She hurries over to her, glancing eagerly over her shoulder toward the river*) Yes, Mrs. Evans?

DARRELL (*moves from the rail toward them—thinking keenly*) I must watch this . . . she's in a desperate meddling mood! . . .

NINA (*impressively*) First, give me your word of honor that you'll never reveal a word of what I'm going to tell you to a living soul—above all not to Gordon!

MADELINE (*looking at her in amazement—soothingly*) Couldn't you tell me later, Mrs. Evans—after the race?

NINA (*sternly—grabbing her by the wrist*) No, now! Do you promise?

MADELINE (*with helpless annoyance*) Yes, Mrs. Evans.

NINA (*sternly*) For the sake of your future happiness and my son's I've got to speak! Your engagement forces me to! You've probably wondered why I objected. It's because the marriage is impossible. You can't marry Gordon! I speak as your friend! You must break your engagement with him at once!

MADELINE (*cannot believe her ears—suddenly panic-stricken*) But why—why?

DARRELL (*who has come closer—resentfully thinking*) She wants to ruin my son's life as she ruined mine! . . .

NINA (*relentlessly*) Why? Because—

DARRELL (*steps up suddenly beside them—sharply and sternly commanding*) No, Nina! (*He taps* MADELINE *on the shoulder and draws her aside.* NINA *lets go of her wrist and stares after them in a sort of stunned stupor*) Miss Arnold, as a doctor I feel it my duty to tell you that Mrs. Evans isn't herself. Pay no attention to anything she may say to you. She's just passed through a crucial period in a woman's life and she's morbidly jealous of you and subject to queer delusions! (*He smiles kindly at her*) So get back to the race! And God bless you! (*He grips her hand, strangely moved*).

MADELINE (*gratefully*) Thank you. I understand, I think. Poor Mrs. Evans! (*She hurries back to the rail, raising her glasses*).

NINA (*springing to her feet and finding her voice—with despairing accusation*) Ned!

DARRELL (*steps quickly to her side*) I'm sorry, Nina, but I warned you not to meddle. (*Then affectionately*) And Gordon is—well—

sort of my stepson, isn't he? I really want him to be happy. (*Then smiling good-naturedly*) All the same, I can't help hoping he'll be beaten in this race. As an oarsman he recalls his father, Gordon Shaw, to me. (*He turns away and raises his glasses, going back to the rail.* NINA *slumps down in her chair again*).

EVANS  Damn! They all look even from here! Can you tell which is which, Madeline?

MADELINE  No—not yet—oh, dear, this is awful! Gordon!

NINA  (*looking about her in the air—with a dazed question*) Gordon?

MARSDEN  (*thinking*)
Damn that Darrell! . . . if he hadn't interfered Nina would have told . . . something of infinite importance, I know! . . .
(*He comes and again sits on the deck by her chair and takes her hand*) Because what, Nina—my dear little Nina Cara Nina—because what? Let me help you!

NINA  (*staring before her as if she were in a trance—simply, like a young girl*) Yes, Charlie. Yes, Father. Because all of Sam's father's family have been insane. His mother told me that time so I wouldn't have his baby. I was going to tell Madeline that so she wouldn't marry Gordon. But it would have been a lie because Gordon isn't really Sam's child at all, he's Ned's. Ned gave him to me and I gave him to Sam so Sam could have a healthy child and be well and happy. And Sam is well and happy, don't you think? (*Childishly*) So I haven't been such an awfully wicked girl, have I, Father?

MARSDEN  (*horrified and completely sobered by what he has heard —stares at her with stunned eyes*)  Nina! Good God! Do you know what you're saying?

MADELINE  (*excitedly*)  There! The one on this side! I saw the color on their blades just now!

EVANS  (*anxiously*)  Are you sure? Then he's a little behind the other two!

DARRELL  (*excitedly*)  The one in the middle seems to be ahead! Is that the Navy? (*But the others pay no attention to him. All three are leaning over the rail, their glasses glued to their eyes, looking up the river. The noise from the whistles is now very loud. The cheering from the observation trains can be heard*).

MARSDEN  (*stares into her face with great pity now*)  Merciful God, Nina! Then you've lived all these years—with this horror! And you and Darrell deliberately—?

NINA (*without looking at him—to the air*) Sam's mother said I had a right to be happy too.

MARSDEN And you didn't love Darrell then—?

NINA (*as before*) I did afterwards. I don't now. Ned is dead, too. (*Softly*) Only you are alive now, Father—and Gordon.

MARSDEN (*gets up and bends over her paternally, stroking her hair with a strange, wild, joyous pity*) Oh, Nina—poor little Nina—my Nina—how you must have suffered! I forgive you! I forgive you everything! I forgive even your trying to tell Madeline—you wanted to keep Gordon—oh, I understand that—and I forgive you!

NINA (*as before—affectionately and strangely*) And I forgive you, Father. It was all your fault in the beginning, wasn't it? You mustn't ever meddle with human lives again!

EVANS (*wildly excited*) Gordon's sprinting, isn't he? He's drawing up on that middle one!

MADELINE Yes! Oh, come on, Gordon!

DARRELL (*exultantly*) Come on, Navy!

EVANS (*who is standing next to* NED, *whirls on him in a furious passion*) What's that? What the hell's the matter with you?

DARRELL (*facing him—with a strange friendliness slaps him on the back*) We've got to beat these Gordons, Sam! We've got to beat—

EVANS (*raging*) You—! (*He draws back his fist—then suddenly horrified at what he is doing but still angry, grabs* DARRELL *by both shoulders and shakes him*) Wake up! What the hell's got into you? Have you gone crazy?

DARRELL (*mockingly*) Probably! It runs in my family! All of my father's people were happy lunatics—not healthy, country folk like yours, Sam! Ha!

EVANS (*staring at him*) Ned, old man, what's the trouble? You said "Navy."

DARRELL (*ironically—with a bitter hopeless laugh*) Slip of the tongue! I meant Gordon! Meant Gordon, of course! Gordon is always meant—meant to win! Come on, Gordon! It's fate!

MADELINE Here they come! They're both spurting! I can see Gordon's back!

EVANS (*forgetting everything else, turns back to the race*) Come on, boy! Come on, son! (*The chorus of noise is now a bedlam as the crews near the finish line. The people have to yell and scream to make themselves heard*).

NINA (*getting up—thinking with a strange, strident, wild passion*)
I hear the Father laughing! . . . O Mother God, protect my
son! . . . let Gordon fly to you in heaven! . . . quick, Gordon!
. . . love is the Father's lightning! . . . Madeline will bring you
down in flames! . . . I hear His screaming laughter! . . . fly
back to me! . . .
(*She is looking desperately up into the sky as if some race of life
and death were happening there for her*).

EVANS (*holding on to a stanchion and leaning far out at the im-
minent risk of falling in*) One spurt more will do it! Come on,
boy, come on! It took death to beat Gordon Shaw! You can't be
beaten either, Gordon! Lift her out of the water, son! Stroke!
Stroke! He's gaining! Now! Over the line, boy! Over with her!
Stroke! That's done it! He's won! He's won!

MADELINE (*has been shrieking at the same time*) Gordon! Gordon! He's won! Oh, he's fainted! Poor dear darling! (*She remains standing on the rail, leaning out dangerously, holding on
with one hand, looking down longingly toward his shell*).

EVANS (*bounding back to the deck, his face congested and purple
with a frenzy of joy, dancing about*) He's won! By God, it was
close! Greatest race in the history of rowing! He's the greatest
oarsman God ever made! (*Embracing* NINA *and kissing her
frantically*) Aren't you happy, Nina? Our Gordon! The greatest
ever!

NINA (*torturedly—trying incoherently to force out a last despairing protest*) No!—not yours!—mine!—and Gordon's!—Gordon is
Gordon's!—he was my Gordon!—his Gordon is mine!

EVANS (*soothingly, humoring her—kissing her again*) Of course
he's yours, dear—and a dead ringer for Gordon Shaw, too! Gordon's body! Gordon's spirit! Your body and spirit, too, Nina! He's
not like me, lucky for him! I'm a poor boob! I never could row
worth a damn! (*He suddenly staggers as if he were very drunk,
leaning on* MARSDEN—*then gives a gasp and collapses inertly to
the deck, lying on his back*).

MARSDEN (*stares down at him stupidly—then thinking strangely*)
I knew it! . . . I saw the end beginning! . . .
(*He touches* NINA's *arm—in a low voice*) Nina—your husband!
(*Touching* DARRELL *who has stood staring straight before him with
a bitter ironical smile on his lips*) Ned—your friend! Doctor Dar-
rell—a patient!

NINA (*stares down at* EVANS—*slowly, as if trying to bring her mind back to him*) My husband? (*Suddenly with a cry of pain, sinks on her knees beside the body*) Sam!

DARRELL (*looking down at him—thinking yearningly*)
Is her husband dead . . . at last? . . .
(*Then with a shudder at his thoughts*)
No! . . . I don't hope! . . . I don't! . . .
(*He cries*) Sam! (*He kneels down, feels of his heart, pulse, looks into his face—with a change to a strictly professional manner*) He's not dead. Only a bad stroke.

NINA (*with a cry of grief*) Oh, Ned, did all our old secret hopes do this at last?

DARRELL (*professionally, staring at her coldly*) Bosh, Mrs. Evans! We're not in the Congo that we can believe in evil charms! (*Sternly*) In his condition, Mr. Evans must have absolute quiet and peace of mind or— And perfect care! You must tend him night and day! And I will! We've got to keep him happy!

NINA (*dully*) Again? (*Then sternly in her turn, as if swearing a pledge to herself*) I will never leave his side! I will never tell him anything that might disturb his peace!

MARSDEN (*standing above them—thinking exultantly*)
I will not have long to wait now! . . .
(*Then ashamed*)
How can I think such things . . . poor Sam! . . . he was . . . I mean he is my friend . . .
(*With assertive loyalty*) A rare spirit! A pure and simple soul! A good man—yes, a good man! God bless him! (*He makes a motion over the body like a priest blessing*).

DARRELL (*his voice suddenly breaking with a sincere human grief*)
Sam, old boy! I'm so damned sorry! I will give my life to save you!

NINA (*in dull anguish*) Save—again? (*Then lovingly, kissing* EVANS' *face*) Dear husband, you have tried to make me happy, I will give you my happiness again! I will give you Gordon to give to Madeline!

MADELINE (*still standing on the rail, staring after* GORDON's *shell*)
Gordon! . . . dear lover . . . how tired . . . but you'll rest in my arms . . . your head will lie on my breast . . . soon! . . .

**Curtain**

## ACT NINE

SCENE: *Several months later. A terrace on the* EVANS' *estate on Long Island. In the rear, the terrace overlooks a small harbor with the ocean beyond. On the right is a side entrance of the pretentious villa. On the left is a hedge with an arched gateway leading to a garden. The terrace is paved with rough stone. There is a stone bench at center, a recliner at right, a wicker table and armchair at left.*

*It is late afternoon of a day in early fall.* GORDON EVANS *is sitting on the stone bench, his chin propped on his hands,* MADELINE *standing behind him, her arm about his shoulders.* GORDON *is over six feet tall with the figure of a trained athlete. His sun-bronzed face is extremely handsome after the fashion of the magazine cover American collegian. It is a strong face but of a strength wholly material in quality. He has been too thoroughly trained to progress along a certain groove to success ever to question it or be dissatisfied with its rewards. At the same time, although entirely an unimaginative code-bound gentleman of his groove, he is boyish and likable, of an even, modest, sporting disposition. His expression is boyishly forlorn, but he is making a manly effort to conceal his grief.*

MADELINE *is much the same as in the previous Act except that there is now a distinct maternal older feeling in her attitude toward* GORDON *as she endeavors to console him.*

MADELINE (*tenderly, smoothing his hair*) There, dear! I know how horribly hard it is for you. I loved him, too. He was so wonderful and sweet to me.
GORDON (*his voice trembling*) I didn't really realize he was gone— until out at the cemetery— (*His voice breaks*).
MADELINE (*kissing his hair*) Darling! Please don't!
GORDON (*rebelliously*) Damn it, I don't see why he had to die! (*With a groan*) It was that constant grind at the office! I ought to have insisted on his taking better care of himself. But I wasn't

home enough, that's the trouble. I couldn't watch him. (*Then bitterly*) But I can't see why Mother didn't!

MADELINE (*reprovingly but showing she shares his feeling*) Now! You mustn't start feeling bitter toward her.

GORDON (*contritely*) I know I shouldn't. (*But returning to his bitter tone*) But I can't help remembering how unreasonably she's acted about our engagement.

MADELINE Not since your father was taken sick, she hasn't, dear. She's been wonderfully nice.

GORDON (*in the same tone*) Nice? Indifferent, you mean! She doesn't seem to care a damn one way or the other any more!

MADELINE You could hardly expect her to think of anyone but your father. She's been with him every minute. I never saw such devotion. (*Thinking*)
Will Gordon ever get old and sick like that? . . . oh, I hope we'll both die before! . . . but I'd nurse him just as she did his father . . . I'll always love him! . . .

GORDON (*consoled—proudly*) Yes, she sure was wonderful to him, all right! (*Then coming back to his old tone*) But—this may sound rotten of me—I always had a queer feeling she was doing it as a duty. And when he died, I felt her grief—not from love for him—at least, only the love of a friend, not a wife's love. (*As if under some urgent compulsion from within*) I've never told you, but I've always felt, ever since I was a little kid, that she didn't really love Dad. She liked him and respected him. She was a wonderful wife. But I'm sure she didn't love him. (*Blurting it out as if he couldn't help it*) I'll tell you, Madeline! I've always felt she cared a lot for—Darrell. (*Hastily*) Of course, I might be wrong. (*Then bursting out*) No, I'm not wrong! I've felt it too strongly, ever since I was a kid. And then when I was eleven—something happened. I've been sure of it since then.

MADELINE (*thinking in amazement, but not without a queer satisfaction*)
Does he mean that she was unfaithful to his father? . . . no, he'd never believe that . . . but what else could he mean? . . . (*Wonderingly*) Gordon! Do you mean you've been sure that your mother was—

GORDON (*outraged by something in her tone—jumping to his feet and flinging her hand off—roughly*) Was what? What do you mean, Madeline?

MADELINE (*frightened—placatingly puts her arms around him*)

I didn't mean anything, dear. I simply thought you meant—

GORDON (*still indignant*) All I meant was that she must have fallen in love with Darrell long after she was married—and then she sent him away for Dad's sake—and mine, too, I suppose. He kept coming back every couple of years. He didn't have guts enough to stay away for good! Oh, I suppose I'm unfair. I suppose it was damned hard on him. He fought it down, too, on account of his friendship for Dad. (*Then with a bitter laugh*) I suppose they'll be getting married now! And I'll have to wish them good luck. Dad would want me to. He was game. (*With a bitter gloomy air*) Life is damn queer, that's all I've got to say!

MADELINE (*thinking with a sort of tender, loving scorn for his boyish naïveté*)

How little he knows her! . . . Mr. Evans was a fine man but . . . Darrell must have been fascinating once . . . if she loved anyone she isn't the kind who would hesitate . . . any more than I have with Gordon . . . oh, I'll never be unfaithful to Gordon . . . I'll love him always! . . .

(*She runs her fingers through his hair caressingly—comfortingly*) You must never blame them, dear. No one can help love. We couldn't, could we? (*She sits beside him. He takes her in his arms. They kiss each other with rising passion.* MARSDEN *comes in noiselessly from the garden, a bunch of roses and a pair of shears in his hands. He looks younger, calm and contented. He is dressed in his all black, meticulous, perfectly tailored mourning costume. He stands looking at the two lovers, a queer agitation coming into his face*).

MARSDEN (*scandalized as an old maid—thinking*)

I must say! . . . his father hardly cold in his grave! . . . it's positively bestial! . . .

(*Then struggling with himself—with a defensive self-mockery*) Only it wasn't his father . . . what is Sam to Darrell's son? . . . and even if he were Sam's son, what have the living to do with the dead? . . . his duty is to love that life may keep on living . . . and what has their loving to do with me? . . . my life is cool green shade wherein comes no scorching zenith sun of passion and possession to wither the heart with bitter poisons . . . my life gathers roses, coolly crimson, in sheltered gardens, on late afternoons in love with evening . . . roses heavy with after-blooming of the long day, desiring evening . . . my life is an evening . . . Nina is a rose, my rose, exhausted by the long, hot day, leaning wearily toward peace. . . .

(*He kisses one of the roses with a simple sentimental smile— then still smiling, makes a gesture toward the two lovers*)

That is on another planet, called the world . . . Nina and I have moved on to the moon . . .

MADELINE (*passionately*)  Dear one! Sweetheart!

GORDON  Madeline! I love you!

MARSDEN (*looking at them—gaily mocking—thinking*)

Once I'd have felt jealous . . . cheated . . . swindled by God out of joy! . . . I would have thought bitterly, "The Gordons have all the luck!" . . . but now I know that dear old Charlie . . . yes, poor dear old Charlie!—passed beyond desire, has all the luck at last! . . .

(*Then matter-of-factly*)

But I'll have to interrupt their biological preparations . . . there are many things still to be done this evening . . . Age's terms of peace, after the long interlude of war with life, have still to be concluded . . . Youth must keep decently away . . . so many old wounds may have to be unbound, and old scars pointed to with pride, to prove to ourselves we have been brave and noble! . . .

(*He lets the shears drop to the ground. They jump startledly and turn around. He smiles quietly*) Sorry to disturb you. I've been picking some roses for your mother, Gordon. Flowers really have the power to soothe grief. I suppose it was that discovery that led to their general use at funerals—and weddings! (*He hands a rose to* MADELINE) Here, Madeline, here's a rose for you. Hail, Love, we who have died, salute you! (*He smiles strangely. She takes the rose automatically, staring at him uncomprehendingly*).

MADELINE (*thinking suspiciously*)

What a queer creature! . . . there's something uncanny! . . . oh, don't be silly! . . . it's only poor old Charlie! . . .

(*She makes him a mocking curtsey*) Thank you, Uncle Charlie!

GORDON (*thinking with sneering pity*)

Poor old guy! . . . he means well . . . Dad liked him. . . .

(*Pretending an interest in the roses*) They're pretty. (*Then suddenly*) Where's Mother—still in the house?

MARSDEN  She was trying to get rid of the last of the people. I'm going in. Shall I tell her you want to see her? It would give her an excuse to get away.

GORDON  Yes. Will you? (MARSDEN *goes into the house on right*).

MADELINE  You'd better see your mother alone. I'll go down to the plane and wait for you. You want to fly back before dark, don't you?

GORDON  Yes, and we ought to get started soon. (*Moodily*) Maybe it would be better if you weren't here. There are some things I feel I ought to say to her—and Darrell. I've got to do what I know Dad would have wanted. I've got to be fair. He always was to everyone all his life.

MADELINE  You dear, you! You couldn't be unfair to anyone if you tried! (*She kisses him*) Don't be too long.

GORDON  (*moodily*)  You bet I won't! It won't be so pleasant I'll want to drag it out!

MADELINE  Good-bye for a while then.

GORDON  So long. (*He looks after her lovingly as she goes out right, rear, around the corner of the house. Thinking*)
Madeline's wonderful! . . . I don't deserve my luck . . . but, God, I sure do love her! . . .
(*He sits down on the bench again, his chin on his hands*)
It seems rotten and selfish to be happy . . . when Dad . . . oh, he understands, he'd want me to be . . . it's funny how I got to care more for Dad than for Mother . . . I suppose it was finding out she loved Darrell . . . I can remember that day seeing her kiss him . . . it did something to me I never got over . . . but she made Dad happy . . . she gave up her own happiness for his sake . . . that was certainly damn fine . . . that was playing the game . . . I'm a hell of a one to criticize . . . my own mother! . . .
(*Changing the subject of his thoughts abruptly*)
Forget it! . . . think of Madeline . . . we'll be married . . . then two months' honeymoon in Europe . . . God, that'll be great! . . . then back and dive into the business . . . Dad relied on me to carry on where he left off . . . I'll have to start at the bottom but I'll get to the top in a hurry, I promise you that, Dad! . . .
(NINA *and* DARRELL *come out of the house on the right. He hears the sound of the door and looks around. Thinking resentfully*)
Funny! . . . I can't stand it even now! . . . when I see him with Mother! . . . I'd like to beat him up! . . .
(*He gets to his feet, his face unconsciously becoming older*

*and cold and severe. He stares accusingly at them as they come slowly toward him in silence.* NINA *looks much older than in the preceding Act. Resignation has come into her face, a resignation that uses no makeup, that has given up the struggle to be sexually attractive and look younger. She is dressed in deep black.* DAR-RELL's *deep sunburn of the tropics has faded, leaving his skin a Mongolian yellow. He, too, looks much older. His expression is sad and bitter*).

NINA (*glancing at* GORDON *searchingly—thinking sadly*)

He sent for me to say good-bye . . . really good-bye forever this time . . . he's not my son now, nor Gordon's son, nor Sam's, nor Ned's . . . he has become that stranger, another woman's lover. . . .

DARRELL (*also after a quick keen glance at* GORDON's *face—thinking*)

There's something up . . . some final accounting . . .

(*Thinking resignedly*)

Well, let's get it over . . . then I can go back to work. . . . I've stayed too long up here . . . Preston must be wondering if I've deserted him. . . .

(*Then with a wondering sadness*)

Is that my son? . . . my flesh and blood? . . . staring at me with such cold enmity? . . . how sad and idiotic this all is! . . .

NINA (*putting on a tone of joking annoyance*) Your message was a godsend, Gordon. Those stupid people with their social condolences were killing me. Perhaps I'm morbid but I always have the feeling that they're secretly glad someone is dead—that it flatters their vanity and makes them feel superior because they're living. (*She sits wearily on the bench.* DARRELL *sits on side of the recliner at right*).

GORDON (*repelled by this idea—stiffly*) They were all good friends of Dad's. Why shouldn't they be sincerely sorry? His death ought to be a loss to everyone who knew him. (*His voice trembles. He turns away and walks to the table. Thinking bitterly*)

She doesn't care a damn! . . . she's free to marry Darrell now! . . .

NINA (*thinking sadly, looking at his back*)

He's accusing me because I'm not weeping . . . well, I did weep . . . all I could . . . there aren't many tears left . . . it was too bad Sam had to die . . . living suited him . . . he was so con-

tented with himself . . . but I can't feel guilty . . . I helped him
to live . . . I made him believe I loved him . . . his mind was
perfectly sane to the end . . . and just before he died, he smiled
at me . . . so gratefully and forgivingly, I thought . . . closing
our life together with that smile . . . that life is dead . . . its
regrets are dead . . . I am sad but there's comfort in the thought
that now I am free at last to rot away in peace . . . I'll go and
live in Father's old home . . . Sam bought that back . . . I suppose he left it to me . . . Charlie will come in every day to
visit . . . he'll comfort and amuse me . . . we can talk together
of the old days . . . when I was a girl . . . when I was happy
. . . before I fell in love with Gordon Shaw and all this tangled
mess of love and hate and pain and birth began! . . .

DARRELL (*staring at* GORDON'S *back resentfully*)
It gets under my skin to see him act so unfeelingly toward his
mother! . . . if he only knew what she's suffered for his sake!
. . . the Gordon Shaw ideal passed on through Sam has certainly
made my son an insensitive clod! . . .
(*With disgust*)
Bah, what has that young man to do with me? . . . compared
to Preston he's only a well-muscled, handsome fool! . . .
(*With a trace of anger*)
But I'd like to jolt his stupid self-complacency! . . . if he knew
the facts about himself, he wouldn't be sobbing sentimentally
about Sam . . . he'd better change his tune or I'll certainly be
tempted to tell him . . . there's no reason for his not knowing
now . . .
(*His face is flushed. He has worked himself into a real anger*).

GORDON (*suddenly, having got back his control, turns to them—
coldly*) There are certain things connected with Dad's will I
thought I ought to— (*With a tinge of satisfied superiority*) I don't
believe Dad told you about his will, did he, Mother?

NINA (*indifferently*) No.

GORDON Well, the whole estate goes to you and me, of course.
I didn't mean that. (*With a resentful look at* DARRELL) But there
is one provision that is peculiar, to say the least. It concerns you,
Doctor Darrell—a half-million for your Station to be used in
biological research work.

DARRELL (*his face suddenly flushing with anger*) What's that?
That's a joke, isn't it? (*Thinking furiously*)

It's worse! . . . it's a deliberate insult! . . . a last sneer of ownership! . . . of my life! . . .

GORDON (*coldly sneering*) I thought it must be a joke myself—
but Dad insisted.

DARRELL (*angrily*) Well, I won't accept it—and that's final!

GORDON (*coldly*) It's not left to you but to the Station. Your
supervision is mentioned but I suppose if you won't carry on,
whoever is in real charge down there will be only too glad to
accept it.

DARRELL (*stupefied*) That means Preston! But Sam didn't even
know Preston—except from hearing me talk about him! What
had Sam to do with Preston? Preston is none of his business! I'll
advise Preston to refuse it! (*Thinking torturedly*)
But it's for science! . . . he has no right to refuse! . . . I have
no right to ask him to! . . . God damn Sam! . . . wasn't it
enough for him to own my wife, my son, in his lifetime? . . .
now in death he reaches out to steal Preston! . . . to steal my
work! . . .

NINA (*thinking bitterly*)
Even in death Sam makes people suffer . . .
(*Sympathetically*) It isn't for you—nor for Preston. It's for science,
Ned. You must look at it that way.

GORDON (*thinking resentfully*)
What a tender tone she takes toward him! . . . she's forgotten
Dad already! . . .
(*With a sneer*) You'd better accept. Half-millions aren't being
thrown away for nothing every day.

NINA (*in anguish—thinking*)
How can Gordon insult poor Ned like that! . . . his own father!
. . . Ned has suffered too much! . . .
(*Sharply*) I think you've said about enough, Gordon!

GORDON (*bitterly, but trying to control himself—meaningly*) I
haven't said all I'm going to say, Mother!

NINA (*thinking—at first frightenedly*)
What does he mean? . . . does he know about Ned being . . . ?
(*Then with a sort of defiant relief*)
Well, what does it matter what he thinks of me? . . . he's hers
now, anyway. . . .

DARRELL (*thinking vindictively*)
I hope he knows the truth, for if he doesn't, by God, I'll tell

him! . . . if only to get something back from Sam of all he's stolen from me! . . .

(*Authoritatively—as* GORDON *hesitates*) Well, what have you got to say? Your mother and I are waiting.

GORDON (*furiously, taking a threatening step toward him*) Shut up, you! Don't take that tone with me or I'll forget your age— (*Contemptuously*) and give you a spanking!

NINA (*thinking hysterically*)

Spanking! . . . the son spanks the father! . . .

(*Laughing hysterically*) Oh, Gordon, don't make me laugh! It's all so funny!

DARRELL (*jumps from his chair and goes to her—solicitously*) Nina! Don't mind him! He doesn't realize—

GORDON (*maddened, comes closer*) I realize a lot! I realize you've acted like a cur! (*He steps forward and slaps* DARRELL *across the face viciously.* DARRELL *staggers back from the force of the blow, his hands to his face.* NINA *screams and flings herself on* GORDON, *holding his arms*).

NINA (*piteously—hysterically*) For God's sake, Gordon! What would your father say? You don't know what you're doing! You're hitting your father!

DARRELL (*suddenly breaking down—chokingly*) No—it's all right, son—all right—you didn't know—

GORDON (*crushed, overcome by remorse for his blow*) I'm sorry—sorry—you're right, Mother—Dad would feel as if I'd hit him—just as bad as if I'd hit him!

DARRELL It's nothing, son—nothing!

GORDON (*brokenly*) That's damn fine, Darrell—damn fine and sporting of you! It was a rotten, dirty trick! Accept my apology, Darrell, won't you?

DARRELL (*staring at him stupidly—thinking*)

Darrell? . . . he calls me Darrell! . . . but doesn't he know? . . . I thought she told him. . . .

NINA (*laughing hysterically—thinking*)

I told him he hit his father . . . but he can't understand me! . . . why, of course he can't! . . . how could he? . . .

GORDON (*insistently holding out his hand*) I'm damned sorry! I didn't mean it! Shake hands, won't you?

DARRELL (*doing so mechanically—stupidly*) Only too glad—pleased to meet you—know you by reputation—the famous oarsman—great race you stroked last June—but I was hoping the Navy would give you a beating.

NINA (*thinking in desperate hysterical anguish*)

Oh, I wish Ned would go away and stay away forever! . . . I can't bear to watch him suffer any more! . . . it's too frightful! . . . yes, God the Father, I hear you laughing . . . you see the joke . . . I'm laughing too . . . it's all so crazy, isn't it? . . . (*Laughing hysterically*) Oh, Ned! Poor Ned! You were born unlucky!

GORDON (*making her sit down again—soothing her*) Mother! Stop laughing! Please! It's all right—all right between us! I've apologized! (*As she has grown calmer*) And now I want to say what I was going to say. It wasn't anything bad. It was just that I wanted you to know how fine I think you've both acted. I've known ever since I was a kid that you and Darrell were in love with each other. I hated the idea on Father's account—that's only natural, isn't it?—but I knew it was unfair, that people can't help loving each other any more than Madeline and I could have helped ourselves. And I saw how fair you both were to Dad— what a good wife you were, Mother—what a true friend you were, Darrell—and how damn much he loved you both! So all I wanted to say is, now he's dead, I hope you'll get married and I hope you'll be as happy as you both deserve— (*Here he breaks down, kissing her and then breaking away*) I've got to say goodbye—got to fly back before dark—Madeline's waiting. (*He takes* DARRELL's *hand and shakes it again. They have both been staring at him stupidly*) Good-bye Darrell! Good luck!

DARRELL (*thinking sufferingly*)

Why does he keep on calling me Darrell . . . he's my boy . . . I'm his father . . . I've got to make him realize I'm his father! . . .

(*Holding* GORDON's *hand*) Listen, son. It's my turn. I've got to tell you something—

NINA (*thinking torturedly*)

Oh, he mustn't! . . . I feel he mustn't! . . .

(*Sharply*) Ned! First, let me ask Gordon a question. (*Then looking her son in the eyes, slowly and impressively*) Do you think I was ever unfaithful to your father, Gordon?

GORDON (*startled, stares at her—shocked and horrified—then suddenly he blurts out indignantly*) Mother, what do you think I am—as rotten-minded as that! (*Pleadingly*) Please, Mother, I'm not as bad as that! I know you're the best woman that ever lived —the best of all! I don't even except Madeline!

NINA (*with a sobbing triumphant cry*) My dear Gordon! You do love me, don't you?

GORDON (*kneeling beside her and kissing her*) Of course!

NINA (*pushing him away—tenderly*) And now go! Hurry! Madeline is waiting! Give her my love! Come to see me once in a while in the years to come! Good-bye, dear! (*Turning to* DARRELL, *who is standing with a sad resigned expression—imploringly*) Did you still want to tell Gordon something, Ned?

DARRELL (*forcing a tortured smile*) Not for anything in the world! Good-bye, son.

GORDON Good-bye, sir. (*He hurries off around the corner of the house at left, rear, thinking troubledly*)
What does she think I am? . . . I've never thought that! . . . I couldn't! . . . my own mother! I'd kill myself if I ever even caught myself thinking . . . !
(*He is gone*).

NINA (*turns to* NED, *gratefully taking his hand and pressing it*) Poor dear Ned, you've always had to give! How can I ever thank you?

DARRELL (*with an ironical smile—forcing a joking tone*) By refusing me when I ask you to marry me! For I've got to ask you! Gordon expects it! And he'll be so pleased when he knows you turned me down. (MARSDEN *comes out of the house*) Hello, here comes Charlie. I must hurry. Will you marry me, Nina?

NINA (*with a sad smile*) No. Certainly not. Our ghosts would torture us to death! (*Then forlornly*) But I wish I did love you, Ned! Those were wonderful afternoons long ago! The Nina of those afternoons will always live in me, will always love her lover, Ned, the father of her baby!

DARRELL (*lifting her hand to his lips—tenderly*) Thank you for that! And that Ned will always adore his beautiful Nina! Remember him! Forget me! I'm going back to work. (*He laughs softly and sadly*) I leave you to Charlie. You'd better marry him, Nina—if you want peace. And after all, I think you owe it to him for his life-long devotion.

MARSDEN (*thinking uneasily*)
They're talking about me . . . why doesn't he go? . . . she doesn't

love him any more . . . even now he's all heat and energy and the tormenting drive of noon . . . can't he see she is in love with evening? . . .

(*Clearing his throat uneasily*) Do I hear my name taken in vain?

NINA (*looking at* MARSDEN *with a strange yearning*)

Peace! . . . yes . . . that is all I desire . . . I can no longer imagine happiness . . . Charlie has found peace . . . he will be tender . . . as my father was when I was a girl . . . when I could imagine happiness . . .

(*With a girlish coquettishness and embarrassment—making way for him on the bench beside her—strangely*) Ned's just proposed to me. I refused him, Charlie. I don't love him any more.

MARSDEN (*sitting down beside her*) I suspected as much. Then whom do you love, Nina Cara Nina?

NINA (*sadly smiling*) You, Charlie, I suppose. I have always loved your love for me. (*She kisses him—wistfully*) Will you let me rot away in peace?

MARSDEN (*strongly*) All my life I've waited to bring you peace.

NINA (*sadly teasing*) If you've waited that long. Charlie, we'd better get married tomorrow. But I forgot. You haven't asked me yet, have you? Do you want me to marry you, Charlie?

MARSDEN (*humbly*) Yes, Nina. (*Thinking with a strange ecstasy*) I knew the time would come at last when I would hear her ask that! . . . I could never have said it, never! . . . oh, russet-golden afternoon, you are a mellow fruit of happiness ripely falling! . . .

DARRELL (*amused—with a sad smile*) Bless you, my children! (*He turns to go*).

NINA I don't suppose we'll ever see you again, Ned.

DARRELL I hope not, Nina. A scientist shouldn't believe in ghosts. (*With a mocking smile*) But perhaps we'll become part of cosmic positive and negative electric charges and meet again.

NINA In our afternoons—again?

DARRELL (*smiling sadly*) Again. In our afternoons.

MARSDEN (*coming out of his day dream*) We'll be married in the afternoon, decidedly. I've already picked out the church, Nina—a gray ivied chapel, full of restful shadow, symbolical of the peace we have found. The crimsons and purples in the windows will stain our faces with faded passion. It must be in the hour before sunset when the earth dreams in afterthoughts and mystic premonitions of life's beauty. And then we'll go up to your old home to live. Mine wouldn't be suitable for us. Mother and Jane live there in memory. And I'll work in your father's old study. He won't mind me. (*From the bay below comes the roaring hum of an airplane motor.* NINA *and* DARRELL *jump startledly and go to the rear of the terrace to watch the plane ascend from the water, standing side by side.* MARSDEN *remains oblivious*).

NINA (*with anguish*) Gordon! Good-bye, dear! (*Pointing as the plane climbs higher moving away off to the left—bitterly*) See, Ned! He's leaving me without a backward look!

DARRELL (*joyfully*) No! He's circling. He's coming back! (*The roar of the engine grows steadily nearer now*) He's going to pass directly over us! (*Their eyes follow the plane as it comes swiftly nearer and passes directly over them*) See! He's waving to us!

NINA Oh, Gordon! My dear son! (*She waves frantically*).

DARRELL (*with a last tortured protest*) Nina! Are you forgetting? He's my son, too! (*He shouts up at the sky*) You're my son, Gordon! You're my— (*He controls himself abruptly—with a smile of cynical self-pity*) He can't hear! Well, at least I've done my duty! (*Then with a grim fatalism—with a final wave of his hand at the sky*) Good-bye, Gordon's son!

NINA (*with tortured exultance*) Fly up to heaven, Gordon! Fly with your love to heaven! Fly always! Never crash to earth like my old Gordon! Be happy, dear! You've got to be happy!

DARRELL (*sardonically*) I've heard that cry for happiness before, Nina! I remember hearing myself cry it—once—it must have been long ago! I'll get back to my cells—sensible unicellular life that floats in the sea and has never learned the cry for happiness! I'm going, Nina. (*As she remains oblivious, staring after the plane —thinking fatalistically*)

She doesn't hear, either. . . .

(*He laughs up at the sky*)

Oh, God, so deaf and dumb and blind! . . . teach me to be re-signed to be an atom! . . .

(*He walks off, right, and enters the house*).

NINA (*finally lowering her eyes—confusedly*) Gone. My eyes are growing dim. Where is Ned? Gone, too. And Sam is gone. They're all dead. Where are Father and Charlie? (*With a shiver of fear she hurries over and sits on the bench beside* MARSDEN, *huddling against him*) Gordon is dead, Father. I've just had a cable. What

I mean is, he flew away to another life—my son, Gordon, Charlie. So we're alone again—just as we used to be.

MARSDEN (*putting his arm around her—affectionately*) Just as we used to be, dear Nina Cara Nina, before Gordon came.

NINA (*looking up at the sky—strangely*) My having a son was a failure, wasn't it? He couldn't give me happiness. Sons are always their fathers. They pass through the mother to become their father again. The Sons of the Father have all been failures! Failing they died for us, they flew away to other lives, they could not stay with us, they could not give us happiness!

MARSDEN (*paternally—in her father's tone*) You had best forget the whole affair of your association with the Gordons. After all, dear Nina, there was something unreal in all that has happened since you first met Gordon Shaw, something extravagant and fantastic, the sort of thing that isn't done, really, in our afternoons. So let's you and me forget the whole distressing episode, regard it as an interlude, of trial and preparation, say, in which our souls have been scraped clean of impure flesh and made worthy to bleach in peace.

NINA (*with a strange smile*) Strange interlude! Yes, our lives are merely strange dark interludes in the electrical display of God the Father! (*Resting her head on his shoulder*) You're so restful, Charlie. I feel as if I were a girl again and you were my father and the Charlie of those days made into one. I wonder is our old garden the same? We'll pick flowers together in the aging afternoons of spring and summer, won't we? It will be a comfort to get home—to be old and to be home again at last—to be in love with peace together—to love each other's peace—to sleep with peace together—! (*She kisses him—then shuts her eyes with a deep sigh of requited weariness*) —to die in peace! I'm so contentedly weary with life!

MARSDEN (*with a serene peace*) Rest, dear Nina. (*Then tenderly*) It has been a long day. Why don't you sleep now—as you used to, remember?—for a little while?

NINA (*murmurs with drowsy gratitude*) Thank you, Father—have I been wicked?—you're so good—dear old Charlie!

MARSDEN (*reacting automatically and wincing with pain—thinking mechanically*)
God damn dear old . . . !
(*Then with a glance down at* NINA's *face, with a happy smile*)

No, God bless dear old Charlie . . . who, passed beyond desire, has all the luck at last! . . .

(NINA *has fallen asleep. He watches with contented eyes the evening shadows closing in around them*).

*Curtain*

# Mourning
# Becomes Electra

## *A Trilogy*

*To Carlotta, my wife*

*Part One*

# HOMECOMING

*A Play in Four Acts*


*Part Two*

# THE  HUNTED

*A Play in Five Acts*


*Part Three*

# THE  HAUNTED

*A Play in Four Acts*

# General Scene of the Trilogy

THE action of the trilogy, with the exception of an act of the second play, takes place in or immediately outside the Mannon residence, on the outskirts of one of the small New England seaport towns.

A special curtain shows the house as seen from the street. From this, in each play, one comes to the exterior of the house in the opening act and enters it in the following act.

This curtain reveals the extensive grounds—about thirty acres—which surround the house, a heavily wooded ridge in the background, orchards at the right and in the immediate rear, a large flower garden and a greenhouse to the left.

In the foreground, along the street, is a line of locust and elm trees. The property is enclosed by a white picket fence and a tall hedge. A driveway curves up to the house from two entrances with white gates. Between the house and the street is a lawn. By the right corner of the house is a grove of pine trees. Farther forward, along the driveway, maples and locusts. By the left corner of the house is a big clump of lilacs and syringas.

The house is placed back on a slight rise of ground about three hundred feet from the street. It is a large building of the Greek temple type that was the vogue in the first half of the nineteenth century. A white wooden portico with six tall columns contrasts with the wall of the house proper which is of gray cut stone. There are five windows on the upper floor and four on the ground floor, with the main entrance in the middle, a doorway with squared transom and sidelights flanked by intermediate columns. The window shutters are painted a dark green. Before the doorway a flight of four steps leads from the ground to the portico.

The three plays take place in either spring or summer of the years 1865–1866.

*Part One*

# HOMECOMING

*A Play in Four Acts*

# Characters

BRIGADIER-GENERAL EZRA MANNON

CHRISTINE, *his wife*

LAVINIA, *their daughter*

CAPTAIN ADAM BRANT, *of the clipper "Flying Trades"*

CAPTAIN PETER NILES, *U. S. Artillery*

HAZEL NILES, *his sister*

SETH BECKWITH

AMOS AMES

LOUISA, *his wife*

MINNIE, *her cousin*

# Scenes

# ACT ONE

SCENE—*Exterior of the Mannon house on a late afternoon in April,
1865. At front is the driveway which leads up to the house from
the two entrances on the street. Behind the driveway the white
Grecian temple portico with its six tall columns extends across the
stage. A big pine tree is on the lawn at the edge of the drive before
the right corner of the house. Its trunk is a black column in striking
contrast to the white columns of the portico. By the edge of the
drive, left front, is a thick clump of lilacs and syringas. A bench is
placed on the lawn at front of this shrubbery which partly screens
anyone sitting on it from the front of the house.*

*It is shortly before sunset and the soft light of the declining sun
shines directly on the front of the house, shimmering in a luminous
mist on the white portico and the gray stone wall behind, intensifying the whiteness of the columns, the somber grayness of the wall,
the green of the open shutters, the green of the lawn and shrubbery, the black and green of the pine tree. The white columns cast
black bars of shadow on the gray wall behind them. The windows
of the lower floor reflect the sun's rays in a resentful glare. The
temple portico is like an incongruous white mask fixed on the house
to hide its somber gray ugliness.*

*In the distance, from the town, a band is heard playing "John
Brown's Body." Borne on the light puffs of wind this music is at
times quite loud, then sinks into faintness as the wind dies.*

*From the left rear, a man's voice is heard singing the chanty
"Shenandoah"—a song that more than any other holds in it the
brooding rhythm of the sea. The voice grows quickly nearer. It is
thin and aged, the wraith of what must once have been a good
baritone.*

> "Oh, Shenandoah, I long to hear you
> A-way, my rolling river
> Oh, Shenandoah, I can't get near you

*Way-ay, I'm bound away*
*Across the wide Missouri."*

*The singer,* SETH BECKWITH, *finishes the last line as he enters from around the corner of the house. Closely following him are* AMOS AMES, *his wife* LOUISA, *and her cousin* MINNIE.

SETH BECKWITH, *the Mannons' gardener and man of all work, is an old man of seventy-five with white hair and beard, tall, raw-boned and stoop-shouldered, his joints stiffened by rheumatism, but still sound and hale. He has a gaunt face that in repose gives one the strange impression of a life-like mask. It is set in a grim expression, but his small, sharp eyes still peer at life with a shrewd prying avidity and his loose mouth has a strong suggestion of ribald humor. He wears his earth-stained working clothes.*

AMOS AMES, *carpenter by trade but now taking a holiday and dressed in his Sunday best, as are his wife and her cousin, is a fat man in his fifties. In character he is the townsfolk type of garrulous gossip-monger who is at the same time devoid of evil intent, scandal being for him merely the subject most popular with his audience.*

*His wife,* LOUISA, *is taller and stouter than he and about the same age. Of a similar scandal-bearing type, her tongue is sharpened by malice.*

*Her cousin,* MINNIE, *is a plump little woman of forty, of the meek, eager-listener type, with a small round face, round stupid eyes, and a round mouth pursed out to drink in gossip.*

*These last three are types of townsfolk rather than individuals, a chorus representing the town come to look and listen and spy on the rich and exclusive Mannons.*

*Led by* SETH, *they come forward as far as the lilac clump and stand staring at the house.* SETH, *in a mood of aged playfulness, is trying to make an impression on* MINNIE. *His singing has been for her benefit. He nudges her with his elbow, grinning.*

SETH   How's that fur singin' fur an old feller? I used to be noted fur my chanties. (*Seeing she is paying no attention to him but is staring with open-mouthed awe at the house, he turns to* AMES —*jubilantly*) By jingo, Amos, if that news is true, there won't be a sober man in town tonight! It's our patriotic duty to celebrate!

AMES (*with a grin*) We'd ought to, that's sartin!

LOUISA   You ain't goin' to git Amos drunk tonight, surrender or no surrender! An old reprobate, that's what you be!

SETH (*pleased*)  Old nothin'! On'y seventy-five! My old man lived to be ninety! Licker can't kill the Beckwiths! (*He and* AMES *laugh.* LOUISA *smiles in spite of herself.* MINNIE *is oblivious, still staring at the house*).

MINNIE  My sakes! What a purty house!

SETH  Wal, I promised Amos I'd help show ye the sights when you came to visit him. 'Taint everyone can git to see the Mannon place close to. They're strict about trespassin'.

MINNIE  My! They must be rich! How'd they make their money?

SETH  Ezra's made a pile, and before him, his father, Abe Mannon, he inherited some and made a pile more in shippin'. Started one of the fust Western Ocean packet lines.

MINNIE  Ezra's the General, ain't he?

SETH (*proudly*)  Ayeh. The best fighter in the hull of Grant's army!

MINNIE  What kind is he?

SETH (*boastfully expanding*)  He's able, Ezra is! Folks think he's cold-blooded and uppish, 'cause he's never got much to say to 'em But that's only the Mannons' way. They've been top dog around here for near on two hundred years and don't let folks fergit it.

MINNIE  How'd he come to jine the army if he's so rich?

SETH  Oh, he'd been a soldier afore this war. His paw made him go to West P'int. He went to the Mexican war and come out a major. Abe died that same year and Ezra give up the army and took holt of the shippin' business here. But he didn't stop there. He learned law on the side and got made a judge. Went in fur politics and got 'lected mayor. He was mayor when this war broke out but he resigned at once and jined the army again. And now he's riz to be General. Oh, he's able, Ezra is!

AMES  Ayeh. This town's real proud of Ezra.

LOUISA  Which is more'n you kin say fur his wife. Folks all hates her! She ain't the Mannon kind. French and Dutch descended, she is. Furrin lookin' and queer. Her father's a doctor in New York, but he can't be much of a one 'cause she didn't bring no money when Ezra married her.

SETH (*his face growing grim—sharply*)  Never mind her. We ain't talkin' 'bout her. (*Then abruptly changing the subject*) Wal, I've got to see Vinnie. I'm goin' round by the kitchen. You wait here. And if Ezra's wife starts to run you off fur trespassin', you tell her I got permission from Vinnie to show you round. (*He goes off around the corner of the house, left. The three stare about them gawkily, awed and uncomfortable. They talk in low voices).*

LOUISA   Seth is so proud of his durned old Mannons! I couldn't help givin' him a dig about Ezra's wife.

AMES   Wal, don't matter much. He's allus hated her.

LOUISA   Ssshh! Someone's comin' out. Let's get back here! (*They crowd to the rear of the bench by the lilac clump and peer through the leaves as the front door is opened and* CHRISTINE MANNON *comes out to the edge of the portico at the top of the steps.* LOUISA *prods her cousin and whispers excitedly*) That's her! (CHRISTINE MANNON *is a tall striking-looking woman of forty but she appears younger. She has a fine, voluptuous figure and she moves with a flowing animal grace. She wears a green satin dress, smartly cut and expensive, which brings out the peculiar color of her thick curly hair, partly a copper brown, partly a bronze gold, each shade distinct and yet blending with the other. Her face is unusual, handsome rather than beautiful. One is struck at once by the strange impression it gives in repose of being not living flesh but a wonderfully life-like pale mask, in which only the deep-set eyes, of a dark violet blue, are alive. Her black eyebrows meet in a pronounced straight line above her strong nose. Her chin is heavy, her mouth large and sensual, the lower lip full, the upper a thin bow, shadowed by a line of hair. She stands and listens defensively, as if the music held some meaning that threatened her. But at once she shrugs her shoulders with disdain and comes down the steps and walks off toward the flower garden, passing behind the lilac clump without having noticed* AMES *and the women).*

MINNIE   (*in an awed whisper*)   My! She's awful handsome, ain't she?

LOUISA   Too furrin lookin' fur my taste.

MINNIE   Ayeh. There's somethin' queer lookin' about her face.

AMES   Secret lookin'—'s if it was a mask she'd put on. That's the Mannon look. They all has it. They grow it on their wives. Seth's growed it on too, didn't you notice—from bein' with 'em all his life. They don't want folks to guess their secrets.

MINNIE   (*breathlessly eager*)   Secrets?

LOUISA   The Mannons got skeletons in their closets same as others! Worse ones. (*Lowering her voice almost to a whisper—to her husband*) Tell Minnie about old Abe Mannon's brother David marryin' that French Canuck nurse girl he'd got into trouble.

AMES Ssshh! Shet up, can't you? Here's Seth comin'. (*But he whispers quickly to* MINNIE) That happened way back when I was a youngster. I'll tell you later. (SETH *has appeared from around the left corner of the house and now joins them*).

SETH That durned nigger cook is allus askin' me to fetch wood fur her! You'd think I was her slave! That's what we get fur freein' 'em! (*Then briskly*) Wal, come along, folks. I'll show you the peach orchard and then we'll go to my greenhouse. I couldn't find Vinnie. (*They are about to start when the front door of the house is opened and* LAVINIA *comes out to the top of the steps where her mother had stood. She is twenty-three but looks considerably older. Tall like her mother, her body is thin, flat-breasted and angular, and its unattractiveness is accentuated by her plain black dress. Her movements are stiff and she carries herself with a wooden, square-shouldered, military bearing. She has a flat dry voice and a habit of snapping out her words like an officer giving orders. But in spite of these dissimilarities, one is immediately struck by her facial resemblance to her mother. She has the same peculiar shade of copper-gold hair, the same pallor and dark violet-blue eyes, the black eyebrows meeting in a straight line above her nose, the same sensual mouth, the same heavy jaw. Above all, one is struck by the same strange, life-like mask impression her face gives in repose. But it is evident* LA-VINIA *does all in her power to emphasize the dissimilarity rather than the resemblance to her parent. She wears her hair pulled tightly back, as if to conceal its natural curliness, and there is not a touch of feminine allurement to her severely plain get-up. Her head is the same size as her mother's, but on her thin body it looks too large and heavy*).

SETH (*seeing her*) There she be now. (*He starts for the steps— then sees she has not noticed their presence, and stops and stands waiting, struck by something in her manner. She is looking off right, watching her mother as she strolls through the garden to the greenhouse. Her eyes are bleak and hard with an intense, bitter enmity. Then her mother evidently disappears in the green-house, for* LAVINIA *turns her head, still oblivious to* SETH *and his friends, and looks off left, her attention caught by the band, the music of which, borne on a freshening breeze, has suddenly become louder. It is still playing "John Brown's Body."* LAVINIA *listens, as her mother had a moment before, but her reaction is the direct opposite to what her mother's had been. Her eyes light up with a grim satisfaction, and an expression of strange vindictive triumph comes into her face*).

LOUISA (*in a quick whisper to* MINNIE) That's Lavinia!

MINNIE She looks like her mother in face—queer lookin'—but she ain't purty like her.

SETH You git along to the orchard, folks. I'll jine you there. (*They walk back around the left of the house and disappear. He goes to* LAVINIA *eagerly*) Say, I got fine news fur you, Vinnie. The telegraph feller says Lee is a goner sure this time! They're only waitin' now fur the news to be made official. You can count on your paw comin' home!

LAVINIA (*grimly*) I hope so. It's time.

SETH (*with a keen glance at her—slowly*) Ayeh.

LAVINIA (*turning on him sharply*) What do you mean, Seth?

SETH (*avoiding her eyes—evasively*) Nothin'—'cept what you mean. (LAVINIA *stares at him. He avoids her eyes—then heavily casual*) Where was you gallivantin' night afore last and all yesterday?

LAVINIA (*starts*) Over to Hazel and Peter's house.

SETH Ayeh. There's where Hannah said you'd told her you was goin'. That's funny now—'cause I seen Peter upstreet yesterday and he asked me where you was keepin' yourself.

LAVINIA (*again starts—then slowly as if admitting a secret understanding between them*) I went to New York, Seth.

SETH Ayeh. That's where I thought you'd gone, mebbe. (*Then with deep sympathy*) It's durned hard on you, Vinnie. It's a durned shame.

LAVINIA (*stiffening—curtly*) I don't know what you're talking about.

SETH (*nods comprehendingly*) All right, Vinnie. Just as you say (*He pauses—then after hesitating frowningly for a moment, blurts out*) There's somethin' been on my mind lately I want to warn you about. It's got to do with what's worryin' you—that is, if there's anythin' in it.

LAVINIA (*stiffly*) There's nothing worrying me. (*Then sharply*) Warn me? About what?

SETH Mebbe it's nothin'—and then again mebbe I'm right, and if I'm right, then you'd ought t' be warned. It's to do with that Captain Brant.

LAVINIA (*starts again but keeps her tone cold and collected*) What about him?

SETH Somethin' I calc'late no one'd notice 'specially 'ceptin' me, because— (*Then hastily as he sees someone coming up the drive*) Here's Peter and Hazel comin'. I'll tell you later, Vinnie. I ain't got time now anyways. Those folks are waitin' for me.

LAVINIA I'll be sitting here. You come back afterwards. (*Then her cold disciplined mask breaking for a moment—tensely*) Oh, why do Peter and Hazel have to come now? I don't want to see anyone! (*She starts as if to go into the house*).

SETH You run in. I'll git rid of 'em fur you.

LAVINIA (*recovering herself—curtly*) No. I'll see them. (SETH *goes back around the corner of the house, left. A moment later* HAZEL *and* PETER NILES *enter along the drive from left, front.* HAZEL *is a pretty, healthy girl of nineteen, with dark hair and eyes. Her features are small but clearly modelled. She has a strong chin and a capable, smiling mouth. One gets a sure impression of her character at a glance—frank, innocent, amiable and good—not in a negative but in a positive, self-possessed way. Her brother,* PETER, *is very like her in character—straightforward, guileless and good-natured. He is a heavily built young fellow of twenty-two, awkward in movement and hesitating in speech. His face is broad, plain, with a snubby nose, curly brown hair, fine gray eyes and a big mouth. He wears the uniform of an artillery captain in the Union Army*).

LAVINIA (*with forced cordiality*) Good afternoon. How are you? (*She and* HAZEL *kiss and she shakes hands with* PETER).

HAZEL Oh, we're all right. But how are you, Vinnie, that's the question? Seems as if we hadn't seen you in ages! You haven't been sick, I hope!

LAVINA Well—if you call a pesky cold sick.

PETER Gosh, that's too bad! All over it now?

LAVINIA Yes—almost. Do sit down, won't you? (HAZEL *sits at left of bench,* LAVINIA *beside her in the middle.* PETER *sits gingerly on the right edge so that there is an open space between him and* LAVINIA).

HAZEL Peter can stay a while if you want him to, but I just dropped in for a second to find out if you'd had any more news from Orin.

LAVINIA Not since the letter I showed you.

HAZEL But that was ages ago! And I haven't had a letter in months, I guess he must have met another girl some place and given me the go by. (*She forces a smile but her tone is really hurt*).

PETER  Orin not writing doesn't mean anything. He never was much of a hand for letters.

HAZEL  I know that, but—you don't think he's been wounded, do you, Vinnie?

LAVINIA  Of course not. Father would have let us know.

PETER  Sure he would. Don't be foolish, Hazel! (*Then after a little pause*) Orin ought to be home before long now. You've heard the good news, of course, Vinnie?

HAZEL  Peter won't have to go back. Isn't that fine?

PETER  My wound is healed and I've got orders to leave tomorrow but they'll be cancelled, I guess. (*Grinning*) I won't pretend I'm the sort of hero that wants to go back, either! I've had enough!

HAZEL  (*impulsively*)  Oh, it will be so good to see Orin again. (*Then embarrassed, forces a self-conscious laugh and gets up and kisses* LAVINIA) Well, I must run. I've got to meet Emily. Good-bye, Vinnie. Do take care of yourself and come to see us soon. (*With a teasing glance at her brother*) And be kind to Peter. He's nice—when he's asleep. And he has something he's just dying to ask you!

PETER  (*horribly embarrassed*)  Darn you! (HAZEL *laughs and goes off down the drive, left front.* PETER *fidgets, his eyes on the ground.* LAVINIA *watches him. Since* HAZEL's *teasing statement, she has visibly withdrawn into herself and is on the defensive. Finally* PETER *looks up and blurts out awkwardly*) Hazel feels bad about Orin not writing. Do you think he really—loves her?

LAVINIA  (*stiffening—brusquely*)  I don't know anything about love! I don't want to know anything! (*Intensely*) I hate love!

PETER  (*crushed by this but trying bravely to joke*)  Gosh, then, if that's the mood you're in, I guess I better not ask—something I'd made up my mind to ask you today.

LAVINIA  It's what you asked me a year ago when you were home on leave, isn't it?

PETER  And you said wait till the war was over. Well, it's over now.

LAVINIA  (*slowly*)  I can't marry anyone, Peter. I've got to stay home. Father needs me.

PETER  He's got your mother.

LAVINIA  (*sharply*)  He needs me more! (*A pause. Then she turns pityingly and puts her hand on his shoulder*) I'm sorry, Peter.

PETER (*gruffly*) Oh, that's all right.

LAVINIA I know it's what girls always say in books, but I do love you as a brother, Peter. I wouldn't lose you as a brother for anything. We've been like that ever since we were little and started playing together—you and Orin and Hazel and I. So please don't let this come between us.

PETER 'Course it won't. What do you think I am? (*Doggedly*) Besides, I'm not giving up hope but what you'll change your mind in time. That is, unless it's because you love someone else—

LAVINIA (*snatching her hand back*) Don't be stupid, Peter!

PETER But how about this mysterious clipper captain that's been calling?

LAVINIA (*angrily*) Do you think I care anything about that—that—!

PETER Don't get mad. I only meant, folks say he's courting you.

LAVINIA Folks say more than their prayers!

PETER Then you don't—care for him?

LAVINIA (*intensely*) I hate the sight of him!

PETER Gosh! I'm glad to hear you say that, Vinnie. I was afraid—I imagined girls all liked him. He's such a darned romantic-looking cuss. Looks more like a gambler or a poet than a ship captain. I got a look as he was coming out of your gate—I guess it was the last time he was here. Funny, too. He reminded me of someone. But I couldn't place who it was.

LAVINIA (*startled, glances at him uneasily*) No one around here, that's sure. He comes from out West. Grandfather Hamel happened to meet him in New York and took a fancy to him, and Mother met him at Grandfather's house.

PETER Who is he, anyway, Vinnie?

LAVINIA I don't know much about him in spite of what you think. Oh, he did tell me the story of his life to make himself out romantic, but I didn't pay much attention. He went to sea when he was young and was in California for the Gold Rush. He's sailed all over the world—he lived on a South Sea island once, so he says.

PETER (*grumpily*) He seems to have had plenty of romantic experience, if you can believe him!

LAVINIA (*bitterly*) That's his trade—being romantic! (*Then agitatedly*) But I don't want to talk any more about him. (*She gets up and walks toward right to conceal her agitation, keeping her back turned to* PETER).

PETER (*with a grin*) Well, I don't either. I can think of more interesting subjects. (CHRISTINE MANNON *appears from left, between the clump of lilacs and the house. She is carrying a big bunch of flowers.* LAVINIA *senses her presence and whirls around. For a moment, mother and daughter stare into each other's eyes. In their whole tense attitudes is clearly revealed the bitter antagonism between them. But* CHRISTINE *quickly recovers herself and her air resumes its disdainful aloofness*).

CHRISTINE Ah, here you are at last! (*Then she sees* PETER, *who is visibly embarrassed by her presence*) Why, good afternoon, Peter, I didn't see you at first.

PETER Good afternoon, Mrs. Mannon. I was just passing and dropped in for a second. I guess I better run along now, Vinnie.

LAVINIA (*with an obvious eagerness to get him off—quickly*) All right. Good-bye, Peter.

PETER Good-bye. Good-bye, Mrs. Mannon.

CHRISTINE Good-bye, Peter. (*He disappears from the drive, left.* CHRISTINE *comes forward*) I must say you treat your one devoted swain pretty rudely. (LAVINIA *doesn't reply.* CHRISTINE *goes on coolly*) I was wondering when I was going to see you. When I returned from New York last night you seemed to have gone to bed.

LAVINIA I had gone to bed.

CHRISTINE You usually read long after that. I tried your door—but you had locked yourself in. When you kept yourself locked in all day I was sure you were intentionally avoiding me. But Annie said you had a headache. (*While she has been speaking she has come toward* LAVINIA *until she is now within arm's reach of her. The facial resemblance, as they stand there, is extraordinary.* CHRISTINE *stares at her coolly, but one senses an uneasy wariness beneath her pose*) Did you have a headache?

LAVINIA No. I wanted to be alone—to think over things.

CHRISTINE What things, if I may ask? (*Then, as if she were afraid of an answer to this question, she abruptly changes the subject*) Who are those people I saw wandering about the grounds?

LAVINIA Some friends of Seth's.

CHRISTINE Because they know that lazy old sot, does it give them the privilege of trespassing?

LAVINIA I gave Seth permission to show them around.

CHRISTINE And since when have you the right without consulting me?

LAVINIA I couldn't very well consult you when Seth asked me. You had gone to New York— (*She pauses a second—then adds slowly, staring fixedly at her mother*) to see Grandfather. Is he feeling any better? He seems to have been sick so much this past year.

CHRISTINE (*casually, avoiding her eyes*) Yes. He's much better now. He'll soon be going the rounds to his patients again, he hopes. (*As if anxious to change the subject, looking at the flowers she carries*) I've been to the greenhouse to pick these. I felt our tomb needed a little brightening. (*She nods scornfully toward the house*) Each time I come back after being away it appears more like a sepulchre! The "whited" one of the Bible—pagan temple front stuck like a mask on Puritan gray ugliness! It was just like old Abe Mannon to build such a monstrosity—as a temple for his hatred. (*Then with a little mocking laugh*) Forgive me, Vinnie. I forgot you liked it. And you ought to. It suits your temperament. (LAVINIA *stares at her but remains silent.* CHRISTINE *glances at her flowers again and turns toward the house*) I must put these in water. (*She moves a few steps toward the house—then turns again—with a studied casualness*) By the way, before I forget, I happened to run into Captain Brant on the street in New York. He said he was coming up here today to take over his ship and asked me if he might drop in to see you. I told him he could—and stay to supper with us. (*Without looking at* LAVINIA, *who is staring at her with a face grown grim and hard*) Doesn't that please you, Vinnie? Or do you remain true to your one and only beau, Peter?

LAVINIA Is that why you picked the flowers—because he is coming? (*Her mother does not answer. She goes on with a threatening undercurrent in her voice*) You have heard the news, I suppose? It means Father will be home soon!

CHRISTINE (*without looking at her—coolly*) We've had so many rumors lately. This report hasn't been confirmed yet, has it? I haven't heard the fort firing a salute.

LAVINIA You will before long!

CHRISTINE I'm sure I hope so as much as you.

LAVINIA You can say that!

CHRISTINE (*concealing her alarm—coldly*) What do you mean? You will kindly not take that tone with me, please! (*Cuttingly*) If you are determined to quarrel, let us go into the house. We might be overheard out here. (*She turns and sees* SETH *who has just come to the corner of the house, left, and is standing there watching them)* See. There is your old crony doing his best to listen now! *(Moving to the steps)* I am going in and rest a while. *(She walks up the steps).*

LAVINIA *(harshly)* I've got to have a talk with you, Mother— before long!

CHRISTINE *(turning defiantly)* Whenever you wish. Tonight after the Captain leaves you, if you like. But what is it you want to talk about?

LAVINIA You'll know soon enough!

CHRISTINE *(staring at her with a questioning dread—forcing a scornful smile)* You always make such a mystery of things, Vinnie. *(She goes into the house and closes the door behind her. SETH comes forward from where he had withdrawn around the corner of the house. LAVINIA makes a motion for him to follow her, and goes and sits on the bench at left. A pause. She stares straight ahead, her face frozen, her eyes hard. He regards her understandingly).*

LAVINIA *(abruptly)* Well? What is it about Captain Brant you want to warn me against? *(Then as if she felt she must defend her question from some suspicion that she knows is in his mind)* I want to know all I can about him because—he seems to be calling to court me.

SETH *(managing to convey his entire disbelief of this statement in one word)* Ayeh.

LAVINIA *(sharply)* You say that as if you didn't believe me.

SETH I believe anything you tell me to believe. I ain't been with the Mannons for sixty years without learning that. *(A pause. Then he asks slowly)* Ain't you noticed this Brant reminds you of someone in looks?

LAVINIA *(struck by this)* Yes. I have—ever since I first saw him— but I've never been able to place who— Who do you mean?

SETH Your Paw, ain't it, Vinnie?

LAVINIA *(startled—agitatedly)* Father? No! It can't be! *(Then as if the conviction were forcing itself on her in spite of herself)* Yes! He does—something about his face—that must be why I've had the strange feeling I've known him before—why I've felt— *(Then tensely as if she were about to break down)* Oh! I won't believe it! You must be mistaken, Seth! That would be too—!

SETH He ain't only like your Paw. He's like Orin, too—and all the Mannons I've known.

LAVINIA (*frightenedly*) But why—why should he—?

SETH More speshully he calls to my mind your Grandpaw's brother, David. How much do you know about David Mannon, Vinnie? I know his name's never been allowed to be spoke among Mannons since the day he left—but you've likely heard gossip, ain't you—even if it all happened before you was born.

LAVINIA I've heard that he loved the Canuck nurse girl who was taking care of Father's little sister who died, and had to marry her because she was going to have a baby; and that Grandfather put them both out of the house and then afterwards tore it down and built this one because he wouldn't live where his brother had disgraced the family. But what has that old scandal got to do with—

SETH Wait. Right after they was throwed out they married and went away. There was talk they'd gone out West, but no one knew nothin' about 'em afterwards—'ceptin' your Grandpaw let out to me one time she'd had the baby—a boy. He was cussin' it. (*Then impressively*) It's about her baby I've been thinkin', Vinnie.

LAVINIA (*a look of appalled comprehension growing on her face*) Oh!

SETH How old is that Brant, Vinnie?

LAVINIA Thirty-six, I think.

SETH Ayeh! That'd make it right. And here's another funny thing —his name. Brant's sort of queer for a name. I ain't never heard tell of it before. Sounds made up to me—like short fur somethin' else. Remember what that Canuck girl's name was, do you, Vinnie? Marie Brantôme! See what I'm drivin' at?

LAVINIA (*agitatedly, fighting against a growing conviction*) But— don't be stupid, Seth—his name would be Mannon and he'd be only too proud of it.

SETH He'd have good reason not to use the name of Mannon when he came callin' here, wouldn't he? If your Paw ever guessed—!

LAVINIA (*breaking out violently*) No! It can't be! God wouldn't let it! It would be too horrible—on top of—! I won't even think of it, do you hear? Why did you have to tell me?

SETH (*calmingly*) There now! Don't take on, Vinnie. No need gettin' riled at me. (*He waits—then goes on insistently*) All I'm drivin' at is that it's durned funny—his looks and the name— and you'd ought fur your Paw's sake to make sartin.

LAVINIA    How can I make certain?

SETH    Catch him off guard sometime and put it up to him strong
—as if you knowed it—and see if mebbe he don't give himself
away. (*He starts to go—looks down the drive at left*) Looks like
him comin' up the drive now, Vinnie. There's somethin' about
his walk calls back David Mannon, too. If I didn't know it was
him I'd think it was David's ghost comin' home. (*He turns away
abruptly*) Wal, calc'late I better git back to work. (*He walks
around the left corner of the house. A pause. Then* CAPTAIN
ADAM BRANT *enters from the drive, left, front. He starts on seeing*
LAVINIA *but immediately puts on his most polite, winning air.
One is struck at a glance by the peculiar quality his face in repose
has of being a life-like mask rather than living flesh. He has a
broad, low forehead, framed by coal-black straight hair which he
wears noticeably long, pushed back carelessly from his forehead
as a poet's might be. He has a big aquiline nose, bushy eyebrows, swarthy complexion, hazel eyes. His wide mouth is sensual
and moody—a mouth that can be strong and weak by turns. He
wears a mustache, but his heavy cleft chin is clean-shaven. In
figure he is tall, broad-shouldered and powerful. He gives the
impression of being always on the offensive or defensive, always
fighting life. He is dressed with an almost foppish extravagance,
with touches of studied carelessness, as if a romantic Byronic
appearance were the ideal in mind. There is little of the obvious
ship captain about him, except his big, strong hands and his
deep voice*).

BRANT    (*bowing with an exaggerated politeness*)    Good afternoon.
(*Coming and taking her hand which she forces herself to hold
out to him*) Hope you don't mind my walking in on you without
ceremony. Your mother told me—

LAVINIA    I know. She had to go out for a while and she said I
was to keep you company until she returned.

BRANT    (*gallantly*)    Well, I'm in good luck, then. I hope she doesn't
hurry back to stand watch over us. I haven't had a chance to be
alone with you since—that night we went walking in the moonlight, do you remember? (*He has kept her hand and he drops
his voice to a low, lover-like tone.* LAVINIA *cannot repress a start,
agitatedly snatching her hand from his and turning away from
him*).

LAVINIA    (*regaining command of herself—slowly*)    What do you
think of the news of Lee surrendering, Captain? We expect my

father home very soon now. (*At something in her tone he stares at her suspiciously, but she is looking straight before her*) Why don't you sit down?

BRANT Thank you. (*He sits on the bench at her right. He has become wary now, feeling something strange in her attitude but not able to make her out—casually*) Yes, you must be very happy at the prospect of seeing your father again. Your mother has told me how close you've always been to him.

LAVINIA Did she? (*Then with intensity*) I love Father better than anyone in the world. There is nothing I wouldn't do—to protect him from hurt!

BRANT (*watching her carefully—keeping his casual tone*) You care more for him than for your mother?

LAVINIA Yes.

BRANT Well, I suppose that's the usual way of it. A daughter feels closer to her father and a son to his mother. But I should think you ought to be a born exception to that rule.

LAVINIA Why?

BRANT You're so like your mother in some ways. Your face is the dead image of hers. And look at your hair. You won't meet hair like yours and hers again in a month of Sundays. I only know of one other woman who had it. You'll think it strange when I tell you. It was my mother.

LAVINIA (*with a start*) Ah!

BRANT (*dropping his voice to a reverent, hushed tone*) Yes, she had beautiful hair like your mother's, that hung down to her knees, and big, deep, sad eyes that were blue as the Caribbean Sea!

LAVINIA (*harshly*) What do looks amount to? I'm not a bit like her! Everybody knows I take after Father!

BRANT (*brought back with a shock, astonished at her tone*) But— you're not angry at me for saying that, are you? (*Then filled with uneasiness and resolving he must establish himself on an intimate footing with her again—with engaging bluntness*) You're puzzling today, Miss Lavinia. You'll excuse me if I come out with it bluntly. I've lived most of my life at sea and in camps and I'm used to straight speaking. What are you holding against me? If I've done anything to offend you, I swear it wasn't meant. (*She is silent, staring before her with hard eyes, rigidly upright. He appraises her with a calculating look, then goes on*) I wouldn't have bad feeling come between us for the world. I may

only be flattering myself, but I thought you liked me. Have you
forgotten that night walking along the shore?

LAVINIA (*in a cold, hard voice*)   I haven't forgotten. Did Mother
tell you you could kiss me?

BRANT   What—what do you mean? (*But he at once attributes the
question to her naïveté—laughingly*)  Oh! I see! But, come now,
Lavinia, you can't mean, can you, I should have asked her permission?

LAVINIA   Shouldn't you?

BRANT (*again uneasy—trying to joke it off*)   Well, I wasn't brought
up that strictly and, should or shouldn't, at any rate, I didn't—
and it wasn't the less sweet for that! (*Then at something in her
face he hurriedly goes off on another tack*)  I'm afraid I gabbed
too much that night. Maybe I bored you with my talk of clipper
ships and my love for them?

LAVINIA (*dryly*)   "Tall, white clippers," you called them. You said
they were like beautiful, pale women to you. You said you
loved them more than you'd ever loved a woman. Is that true,
Captain?

BRANT (*with forced gallantry*)   Aye. But I meant, before I met
you. (*Then thinking he has at last hit on the cause of her changed
attitude toward him—with a laugh*)  So that's what you're holding against me, is it? Well, I might have guessed. Women are
jealous of ships. They always suspect the sea. They know they're
three of a kind when it comes to a man! (*He laughs again but
less certainly this time, as he regards her grim, set expression*)
Yes, I might have seen you didn't appear much taken by my sea
gamming that night. I suppose clippers are too old a story to
the daughter of a ship builder. But unless I'm much mistaken,
you were interested when I told you of the islands in the South
Seas where I was shipwrecked my first voyage at sea.

LAVINIA (*in a dry, brittle tone*)   I remember your admiration for
the naked native women. You said they had found the secret of
happiness because they had never heard that love can be a sin.

BRANT (*surprised—sizing her up puzzledly*)   So you remember
that, do you? (*Then romantically*)  Aye! And they live in as near
the Garden of Paradise before sin was discovered as you'll find on
this earth! Unless you've seen it, you can't picture the green
beauty of their land set in the blue of the sea! The clouds like
down on the mountain tops, the sun drowsing in your blood, and
always the surf on the barrier reef singing a croon in your ears

like a lullaby! The Blessed Isles, I'd call them! You can forget there all men's dirty dreams of greed and power!

LAVINIA  And their dirty dreams—of love?

BRANT  (*startled again—staring at her uneasily*)  Why do you say that? What do you mean, Lavinia?

LAVINIA  Nothing. I was only thinking—of your Blessed Isles.

BRANT  (*uncertainly*)  Oh! But you said— (*Then with a confused, stupid persistence he comes closer to her, dropping his voice again to his love-making tone*)  Whenever I remember those islands now, I will always think of you, as you walked beside me that night with your hair blowing in the sea wind and the moonlight in your eyes! (*He tries to take her hand, but at his touch she pulls away and springs to her feet*).

LAVINIA  (*with cold fury*)  Don't you touch me! Don't you dare—! You liar! You—! (*Then as he starts back in confusion, she seizes this opportunity to follow* SETH's *advice—staring at him with deliberately insulting scorn*)  But I suppose it would be foolish to expect anything but cheap romantic lies from the son of a low Canuck nurse girl!

BRANT  (*stunned*)  What's that? (*Then rage at the insult to his mother overcoming all prudence—springs to his feet threateningly*)  Belay, damn you!—or I'll forget you're a woman—no Mannon can insult her while I—

LAVINIA  (*appalled now she knows the truth*)  So—it is true— You are her son! Oh!

BRANT  (*fighting to control himself—with harsh defiance*)  And what if I am? I'm proud to be! My only shame is my dirty Mannon blood! So that's why you couldn't stand my touching you just now, is it? You're too good for the son of a servant, eh? By God, you were glad enough before—!

LAVINIA  (*fiercely*)  It's not true! I was only leading you on to find out things!

BRANT  Oh, no! It's only since you suspected who I was! I suppose your father has stuffed you with his lies about my mother! But, by God, you'll hear the truth of it, now you know who I am— And you'll see if you or any Mannon has the right to look down on her!

LAVINIA  I don't want to hear— (*She starts to go toward the house*).

BRANT  (*grabbing her by the arm—tauntingly*)  You're a coward, are you, like all Mannons, when it comes to facing the truth about themselves? (*She turns on him defiantly. He drops her arm and goes on harshly*) I'll bet he never told you your grandfather, Abe Mannon, as well as his brother, loved my mother!

LAVINIA  It's a lie!

BRANT  It's the truth. It was his jealous revenge made him dis-own my father and cheat him out of his share of the business they'd inherited!

LAVINIA  He didn't cheat him! He bought him out!

BRANT  Forced him to sell for one-tenth its worth, you mean! He knew my father and mother were starving! But the money didn't last my father long! He'd taken to drink. He was a coward —like all Mannons—once he felt the world looked down on him. He skulked and avoided people. He grew ashamed of my mother —and me. He sank down and down and my mother worked and supported him. I can remember when men from the corner saloon would drag him home and he'd fall in the door, a sodden carcass. One night when I was seven he came home crazy drunk and hit my mother in the face. It was the first time he'd ever struck her. It made me blind mad. I hit at him with the poker and cut his head. My mother pulled me back and gave me a hiding. Then she cried over him. She'd never stopped loving him.

LAVINIA  Why do you tell me this? I told you once I don't want to hear—

BRANT  (*grimly*) You'll see the point of it damned soon! (*Un-heeding—as if the scene were still before his eyes*) For days after, he sat and stared at nothing. One time when we were alone he asked me to forgive him hitting her. But I hated him and I wouldn't forgive him. Then one night he went out and he didn't come back. The next morning they found him hanging in a barn!

LAVINIA  (*with a shudder*) Oh!

BRANT  (*savagely*) The only decent thing he ever did!

LAVINIA  You're lying! No Mannon would ever—

BRANT  Oh, wouldn't they? They are all fine, honorable gentle-men, you think! Then listen a bit and you'll hear something about another of them! (*Then going on bitterly with his story*) My mother sewed for a living and sent me to school. She was very strict with me. She blamed me for his killing him-self. But she was bound she'd make a gentleman of me—like he was!—if it took her last cent and her last strap! (*With a grim smile*) She didn't succeed, as you notice! At seventeen I ran away to sea—and forgot I had a mother, except I took part of her name—Brant was short and easy on ships—and I wouldn't wear the name of Mannon. I forgot her until two years ago when I came back from the East. Oh, I'd written to her now and then and sent her money when I happened to have any. But I'd forgotten her just the same—and when I got to New York I found her dying—of sickness and starvation! And I found out that when she'd been laid up, not able to work, not knowing where to reach me, she'd sunk her last shred of pride and written to your father asking for a loan. He never answered her. And I came too late. She died in my arms. (*With vindictive passion*) He could have saved her—and he deliberately let her die! He's as guilty of murder as anyone he ever sent to the rope when he was a judge!

LAVINIA (*springing to her feet—furiously*)  You dare say that about Father! If he were here—

BRANT  I wish to God he was! I'd tell him what I tell you now—that I swore on my mother's body I'd revenge her death on him.

LAVINIA (*with cold deadly intensity*)  And I suppose you boast that now you've done so, don't you?—in the vilest, most cowardly way—like the son of a servant you are!

BRANT (*again thrown off guard—furiously*)  Belay, I told you, with that kind of talk!

LAVINIA  She is only your means of revenge on Father, is that it?

BRANT (*stunned—stammers in guilty confusion*)  What?—She?—Who?—I don't know what you're talking about!

LAVINIA  Then you soon will know! And so will she! I've found out all I wanted to from you. I'm going in to talk to her now. You wait here until I call you!

BRANT (*furious at her tone*)  No! Be damned if you can order me about as if I was your servant!

LAVINIA (*icily*)  If you have any consideration for her, you'll do as I say and not force me to write my father. (*She turns her back on him and walks to the steps woodenly erect and square-shouldered*).

BRANT (*desperately now—with a grotesque catching at his lover's manner*)  I don't know what you mean, Lavinia. I swear before God it is only you I— (*She turns at the top of the steps at this and stares at him with such a passion of hatred that he is silenced. Her lips move as if she were going to speak, but she fights back the words, turns stiffly and goes into the house and closes the door behind her)*

*Curtain*

# ACT TWO

SCENE—In the house—EZRA MANNON's study. No time has elapsed. The study is a large room with a stiff, austere atmosphere. The furniture is old colonial. The walls are plain plastered surfaces tinted a dull gray with a flat white trim. At rear, right, is a door leading to the hall. On the right wall is a painting of George Washington in a gilt frame, flanked by smaller portraits of Alexander Hamilton and John Marshall. At rear, center, is an open fireplace. At left of fireplace, a bookcase filled with law books. Above the fireplace, in a plain frame, is a large portrait of EZRA MANNON himself, painted ten years previously. One is at once struck by the startling likeness between him and ADAM BRANT. He is a tall man in his early forties, with a spare, wiry frame, seated stiffly in an armchair, his hands on the arms, wearing his black judge's robe. His face is handsome in a stern, aloof fashion. It is cold and emotionless and has the same strange semblance of a life-like mask that we have already seen in the faces of his wife and daughter and BRANT.

On the left are two windows. Between them a desk. A large table with an armchair on either side, right and left, stands at left center, front. At right center is another chair. There are hooked rugs on the floor.

Outside the sun is beginning to set and its glow fills the room with a golden mist. As the action progresses this becomes brighter, then turns to crimson, which darkens to somberness at the end.

LAVINIA is discovered standing by the table. She is fighting to control herself, but her face is torn by a look of stricken anguish. She turns slowly to her father's portrait and for a moment stares at it fixedly. Then she goes to it and puts her hand over one of his hands with a loving, protecting gesture.

LAVINIA   Poor Father! (*She hears a noise in the hall and moves hastily away. The door from the hall is opened and* CHRISTINE *enters. She is uneasy underneath, but affects a scornful indignation).*

CHRISTINE  Really, this unconfirmed report must have turned your head—otherwise I'd find it difficult to understand your sending Annie to disturb me when you knew I was resting.

LAVINIA  I told you I had to talk to you.

CHRISTINE  (*looking around the room with aversion*)  But why in this musty room, of all places?

LAVINIA  (*indicating the portrait—quietly*)  Because it's Father's room.

CHRISTINE  (*starts, looks at the portrait and quickly drops her eyes.* LAVINIA *goes to the door and closes it.* CHRISTINE *says with forced scorn*)  More mystery?

LAVINIA  You better sit down. (CHRISTINE *sits in the chair at rear center.* LAVINIA *goes back to her father's chair at left of table*).

CHRISTINE  Well—if you're quite ready, perhaps you will explain.

LAVINIA  I suppose Annie told you I'd been to visit Hazel and Peter while you were away.

CHRISTINE  Yes. I thought it peculiar. You never visit anyone overnight. Why did you suddenly take that notion?

LAVINIA  I didn't.

CHRISTINE  You didn't visit them?

LAVINIA  No.

CHRISTINE  Then where did you go?

LAVINIA  (*accusingly*)  To New York! (CHRISTINE *starts.* LAVINIA *hurries on a bit incoherently*)  I've suspected something—lately—the excuse you've made for all your trips there the past year, that Grandfather was sick— (*As* CHRISTINE *is about to protest indignantly*)  Oh! I know he has been—and you've stayed at his house—but I've suspected lately that wasn't the real reason—and now I can prove it isn't! Because I waited outside Grandfather's house and followed you. I saw you meet Brant!

CHRISTINE  (*alarmed but concealing it—coolly*)  Well, what if you did? I told you myself I ran into him by accident—

LAVINIA  You went to his room!

CHRISTINE  (*shaken*)  He asked me to meet a friend of his—a lady. It was her house we went to.

LAVINIA  I asked the woman in the basement. He had hired the room under another name, but she recognized his description. And yours too. She said you had come there often in the past year.

CHRISTINE (*desperately*)  It was the first time I had ever been there. He insisted on my going. He said he had to talk to me about you. He wanted my help to approach your father—

LAVINIA (*furiously*)  How can you lie like that? How can you be so vile as to try to use me to hide your adultery?

CHRISTINE (*springing up—with weak indignation*)  Vinnie!

LAVINIA  Your adultery, I said!

CHRISTINE  No!

LAVINIA  Stop lying, I tell you! I went upstairs! I heard you telling him—"I love you, Adam"—and kissing him! (*with a cold bitter fury*)  You vile—! You're shameless and evil! Even if you are my mother, I say it! (CHRISTINE *stares at her, overwhelmed by this onslaught, her poise shattered for the moment. She tries to keep her voice indifferent but it trembles a little*).

CHRISTINE  I—I knew you hated me, Vinnie—but not as bitterly as that! (*Then with a return of her defiant coolness*)  Very well! I love Adam Brant. What are you going to do?

LAVINIA  How you say that—without any shame! You don't give one thought to Father—who is so good—who trusts you! Oh, how could you do this to Father? How could you?

CHRISTINE (*with strident intensity*)  You would understand if you were the wife of a man you hated!

LAVINIA (*horrified—with a glance at the portrait*)  Don't! Don't say that—before him! I won't listen!

CHRISTINE (*grabbing her by the arm*)  You will listen! I'm talking to you as a woman now, not as mother to daughter! That relationship has no meaning between us! You've called me vile and shameless! Well, I want you to know that's what I've felt about myself for over twenty years, giving my body to a man I—

LAVINIA (*trying to break away from her, half putting her hands up to her ears*)  Stop telling me such things! Let me go! (*She breaks away, shrinking from her mother with a look of sick repulsion. A pause. She stammers*)  You—then you've always hated Father?

CHRISTINE (*bitterly*)  No. I loved him once—before I married him —incredible as that seems now! He was handsome in his lieutenant's uniform! He was silent and mysterious and romantic! But marriage soon turned his romance into—disgust!

LAVINIA (*wincing again—stammers harshly*)  So I was born of your disgust! I've always guessed that, Mother—ever since I was little —when I used to come to you—with love—but you would always push me away! I've felt it ever since I can remember—your disgust! (*Then with a flare-up of bitter hatred*) Oh, I hate you! It's only right I should hate you!

CHRISTINE (*shaken—defensively*)  I tried to love you. I told myself it wasn't human not to love my own child, born of my body. But I never could make myself feel you were born of any body but his! You were always my wedding night to me—and my honeymoon!

LAVINIA  Stop saying that! How can you be so—! (*Then suddenly —with a strange jealous bitterness*) You've loved Orin! Why didn't you hate him, too?

CHRISTINE  Because by then I had forced myself to become resigned in order to live! And most of the time I was carrying him, your father was with the army in Mexico. I had forgotten him. And when Orin was born he seemed my child, only mine, and I loved him for that! (*Bitterly*) I loved him until he let you and your father nag him into the war, in spite of my begging him not to leave me alone. (*Staring at* LAVINIA *with hatred*) I know his leaving me was your doing principally, Vinnie!

LAVINIA (*sternly*)  It was his duty as a Mannon to go! He'd have been sorry the rest of his life if he hadn't! I love him better than you! I was thinking of him!

CHRISTINE  Well, I hope you realize I never would have fallen in love with Adam if I'd had Orin with me. When he had gone there was nothing left—but hate and a desire to be revenged— and a longing for love! And it was then I met Adam. I saw he loved me—

LAVINIA (*with taunting scorn*)  He doesn't love you! You're only his revenge on Father! Do you know who he really is? He's the son of that low nurse girl Grandfather put out of our house!

CHRISTINE (*concealing a start—coolly*)  So you've found that out? Were you hoping it would be a crushing surprise to me? I've known it all along. He told me when he said he loved me.

LAVINIA  Oh! And I suppose knowing who he was gave you all the more satisfaction—to add that disgrace!

CHRISTINE (*cuttingly*)  Will you kindly come to the point and tell me what you intend doing? I suppose you'll hardly let your father get in the door before you tell him!

LAVINIA (*suddenly becoming rigid and cold again—slowly*)  No. Not unless you force me to. (*Then as she sees her mother's astonishment—grimly*) I don't wonder you're surprised! You know you deserve the worst punishment you could get. And Father would disown you publicly, no matter how much the scandal cost him!

CHRISTINE  I realize that. I know him even better than you do!

LAVINIA  And I'd like to see you punished for your wickedness! So please understand this isn't for your sake. It's for Father's. He hasn't been well lately. I'm not going to have him hurt! It's my first duty to protect him from you!

CHRISTINE  I know better than to expect any generosity on my account.

LAVINIA  I won't tell him, provided you give up Brant and never see him again—and promise to be a dutiful wife to Father and make up for the wrong you've done him!

CHRISTINE  (*stares at her daughter—a pause—then she laughs dryly*) What a fraud you are, with your talk of your father and your duty! Oh, I'm not denying you want to save his pride—and I know how anxious you are to keep the family from more scandal! But all the same, that's not your real reason for sparing me!

LAVINIA  (*confused—guiltily*)  It is!

CHRISTINE  You wanted Adam Brant yourself!

LAVINIA  That's a lie!

CHRISTINE  And now you know you can't have him, you're determined that at least you'll take him from me!

LAVINIA  No!

CHRISTINE  But if you told your father, I'd have to go away with Adam. He'd be mine still. You can't bear that thought, even at the price of my disgrace, can you?

LAVINIA  It's your evil mind!

CHRISTINE  I know you, Vinnie! I've watched you ever since you were little, trying to do exactly what you're doing now! You've tried to become the wife of your father and the mother of Orin! You've always schemed to steal my place!

LAVINIA  (*wildly*)  No! It's you who have stolen all love from me since the time I was born! (*Then her manner becoming threatening*) But I don't want to listen to any more of your lies and excuses! I want to know right now whether you're going to do what I told you or not!

CHRISTINE  Suppose I refuse! Suppose I go off openly with Adam! Where will you and your father and the family name be after that scandal? And what if I were disgraced myself? I'd have the man I love, at least!

LAVINIA  (*grimly*)  Not for long! Father would use all his influence and get Brant blacklisted so he'd lose his command and never get another! You know how much the "Flying Trades" means to him. And Father would never divorce you. You could never marry. You'd be an anchor around his neck. Don't forget you're five years older than he is! He'll still be in his prime when you're an old woman with all your looks gone! He'd grow to hate the sight of you!

CHRISTINE (*stung beyond bearing—makes a threatening move as if to strike her daughter's face*) You devil! You mean little—! (*But* LAVINIA *stares back coldly into her eyes and she controls herself and drops her hand*).

LAVINIA I wouldn't call names if I were you! There is one you deserve!

CHRISTINE (*turning away—her voice still trembling*) I'm a fool to let you make me lose my temper—over your jealous spite! (*A pause.* LAVINIA *stares at her.* CHRISTINE *seems considering something. A sinister expression comes to her face. Then she turns back to* LAVINIA—*coldly*) But you wanted my answer, didn't you? Well, I agree to do as you said. I promise you I'll never see Adam again after he calls this evening. Are you satisfied?

LAVINIA (*stares at her with cold suspicion*) You seem to take giving him up pretty easily!

CHRISTINE (*hastily*) Do you think I'll ever give you the satisfaction of seeing me grieve? Oh, no, Vinnie! You'll never have a chance to gloat!

LAVINIA (*still suspiciously—with a touch of scorn*) If I loved anyone—!

CHRISTINE (*tauntingly*) If? I think you do love him—as much as you can love! (*With a sudden flurry of jealousy*) You little fool! Don't you know I made him flirt with you, so you wouldn't be suspicious?

LAVINIA (*gives a little shudder—then fiercely*) He didn't fool me! I saw what a liar he was! I just led him on—to find out things! I always hated him! (*CHRISTINE smiles mockingly and turns away, as if to go out of the room.* LAVINIA's *manner becomes threatening again*) Wait! I don't trust you! I know you're thinking already how you can fool me and break the promise you've just made! But you better not try it! I'll be watching you every minute! And I won't be the only one! I wrote to Father and Orin as soon as I got back from New York!

CHRISTINE (*startled*) About Adam?

LAVINIA   Only enough so they'd be suspicious and watch you too. I said a Captain Brant had been calling and folks had begun to gossip.

CHRISTINE   Ah! I see what it's going to mean—that you'll always have this to hold over me and I'll be under your thumb for the rest of my life! (*She cannot restrain her rage—threateningly*) Take care, Vinnie! You'll be responsible if—! (*She checks herself abruptly*).

LAVINIA (*suspiciously*)   If what?

CHRISTINE (*quickly*)   Nothing. I only meant if I went off with Adam. But of course you know I won't do that. You know there's nothing I can do now—but obey your orders!

LAVINIA (*continues to stare at her suspiciously—grimly*)   You ought to see it's your duty to Father, not my orders—if you had any honor or decency! (*Then brusquely*) Brant is waiting outside. You can tell him what you've got to do—and tell him if he ever dares come here again—! (*Forcing back her anger*) And see that you get rid of him right now! I'm going upstreet to get the latest news. I won't be gone more than a half-hour and I want him out of the house by the time I get back, do you hear? If he isn't, I'll write Father again. I won't even wait for him to come home! (*She turns her back on her mother and marches out the door, square-shouldered and stiff, without a backward glance.* CHRISTINE *looks after her, waiting until she hears the side door of the house close after her. Then she turns and stands in tense calculating thought. Her face has become like a sinister evil mask. Finally, as if making up her mind irrevocably, she comes to the table, tears off a slip of paper and writes two words on it. She tucks this paper in the sleeve of her dress and goes to the open window and calls*).

CHRISTINE   Adam! (*She moves toward the door to wait for him. Her eyes are caught by the eyes of her husband in the portrait over the fireplace. She stares at him with hatred and addresses him vindictively, half under her breath*) You can thank Vinnie, Ezra! (*She goes to the door and reaches it just as* BRANT *appears from the hall. She takes his hand and draws him into the room, closing the door behind him. One is immediately struck by the resemblance between his face and that of the portrait of* EZRA MANNON).

BRANT (*glancing uneasily at her, as they come to the center of the room*)   She knows—?

CHRISTINE   Yes. She followed me to New York. And she's found out who you are too, Adam.

BRANT (*with a grim smile*)   I know. She got that out of me— the proof of it, at any rate. Before I knew what was up I'd given myself away.

CHRISTINE   She must have noticed your resemblance to Orin. I was afraid that might start her thinking.

BRANT (*sees the portrait for the first time. Instantly his body shifts to a fighting tenseness. It is as if he were going to spring at the figure in the painting. He says slowly*)   That, I take it, is General Mannon?

CHRISTINE   Judge Mannon then. Don't forget he used to be a judge. He won't forget it.

BRANT (*his eyes still fixed on the portrait—comes and sits in* MAN-NON's *chair on the left of table. Unconsciously he takes the same attitude as* MANNON, *sitting erect, his hands on the arms of the chair—slowly*)   Does Orin by any chance resemble his father?

CHRISTINE (*stares at him—agitatedly*)   No! Of course not! What put such a stupid idea in your head?

BRANT   It would be damned queer if you fell in love with me because I recalled Ezra Mannon to you!

CHRISTINE (*going to him and putting an arm around his shoulder*)   No, no, I tell you! It was Orin you made me think of! It was Orin!

BRANT   I remember that night we were introduced and I heard the name Mrs. Ezra Mannon! By God, how I hated you then for being his! I thought, by God, I'll take her from him and that'll be part of my revenge! And out of that hatred my love came! It's damned queer, isn't it?

CHRISTINE (*hugging him to her*)   Are you going to let him take me from you now, Adam?

BRANT (*passionately*)   You ask that!

CHRISTINE   You swear you won't—no matter what you must do?

BRANT   By God, I swear it!

CHRISTINE (*kisses him*)   Remember that oath! (*She glances at the portrait—then turns back to* BRANT *with a little shiver—nervously*)   What made you sit there? It's his chair. I've so often seen him sitting there— (*Forcing a little laugh*) Your silly talk about resemblances— Don't sit there. Come. Bring that chair over here.

(*She moves to the chair at right center. He brings the chair at right of table close to hers*).

BRANT    We've got to decide what we must do. The time for skulking and lying is over—and by God I'm glad of it! It's a coward's game I have no stomach for! (*He has placed the chair beside hers. She is staring at the portrait*) Why don't you sit down, Christine?

CHRISTINE    (*slowly*)    I was thinking—perhaps we had better go to the sitting-room. (*Then defiantly*) No! I've been afraid of you long enough, Ezra! (*She sits down*).

BRANT    I felt there was something wrong the moment I saw her. I tried my damnedest to put her off the course by giving her some softsoap—as you'd told me to do to blind her. (*Frowning*) That was a mistake, Christine. It made her pay too much attention to me—and opened her eyes!

CHRISTINE    Oh, I know I've made one blunder after another. It's as if love drove me on to do everything I shouldn't. I never should have brought you to this house. Seeing you in New York should have been enough for me. But I loved you too much. I wanted you every possible moment we could steal! And I simply couldn't believe that he ever would come home. I prayed that he should be killed in the war so intensely that I finally believed it would surely happen! (*With savage intensity*) Oh, if he were only dead!

BRANT    That chance is finished now.

CHRISTINE    (*slowly—without looking at him*)    Yes—in that way.

BRANT    (*stares at her*)    What do you mean? (*She remains silent. He changes the subject uneasily*) There's only one thing to do! When he comes home I'll wait for him and not give Vinnie the satisfaction of telling him. I'll tell him myself. (*Vindictively*) By God! I'd give my soul to see his face when he knows you love Marie Brantôme's son! And then I'll take you away openly and laugh at him! And if he tries to stop me—! (*He stops and glances with savage hatred at the portrait*).

CHRISTINE    What would you do then?

BRANT    If ever I laid hands on him, I'd kill him!

CHRISTINE    And then? You would be hanged for murder! And where would I be? There would be nothing for me but to kill myself!

BRANT    If I could catch him alone, where no one would interfere, and let the best man come out alive—as I've often seen it done in the West!

CHRISTINE   This isn't the West.

BRANT   I could insult him on the street before everyone and make him fight me! I could let him shoot first and then kill him in self-defense.

CHRISTINE   (*scornfully*)   Do you imagine you could force him to fight a duel with you? Don't you know duelling is illegal? Oh, no! He'd simply feel bound to do his duty as a former judge and have you arrested! (*She adds calculatingly, seeing he is boiling inside*) It would be a poor revenge for your mother's death to let him make you a laughing stock!

BRANT   But when I take you off, the laugh will be on him! You can come on the "Flying Trades."

CHRISTINE   (*calculatingly reproachful*)   I don't think you'd propose that, Adam, if you stopped thinking of your revenge for a moment and thought of me! Don't you realize he would never divorce me, out of spite? What would I be in the world's eyes? My life would be ruined and I would ruin yours! You'd grow to hate me!

BRANT   (*passionately*)   Don't talk like that! It's a lie and you know it!

CHRISTINE   (*with bitter yearning*)   If I could only believe that, Adam! But I'll grow old so soon! And I'm afraid of time! (*Then abruptly changing tone*) As for my sailing on your ship, you'll find you won't have a ship! He'll see to it you lose this command and get you blacklisted so you'll have no chance of getting another.

BRANT   (*angrily*)   Aye! He can do that if he sets about it. There are twice as many skippers as ships these days.

CHRISTINE   (*calculatingly—without looking at him*)   If he had only been killed, we could be married now and I would bring you my share of the Mannon estate. That would only be justice. It's yours by right. It's what his father stole from yours.

BRANT   That's true enough, damn him!

CHRISTINE   You wouldn't have to worry about commands or owners' favors then. You could buy your own ship and be your own master!

BRANT   (*yearningly*)   That's always been my dream—some day to own my own clipper! And Clark and Dawson would be willing to sell the "Flying Trades." (*Then forgetting everything in his enthusiasm*) You've seen her, Christine. She's as beautiful a ship as you're a woman. Aye, the two of you are like sisters. If she was mine, I'd take you on a honeymoon then! To China—and on the voyage back, we'd stop at the South Pacific Islands I've told you about. By God, there's the right place for love and a honeymoon!

CHRISTINE (*slowly*) Yes—but Ezra is alive!

BRANT (*brought back to earth—gloomily*) I know it's only a dream.

CHRISTINE (*turning to stare at him—slowly*) You can have your dream—and I can have mine. There is a way. (*Then turning away again*) You remember my telling you he had written complaining of pains about his heart?

BRANT You're surely not hoping—

CHRISTINE No. He said it was nothing serious. But I've let it be known that he has heart trouble. I went to see our old family doctor and told him about Ezra's letter. I pretended to be dreadfully worried, until I got him worried too. He's the town's worst old gossip. I'm sure everyone knows about Ezra's weak heart by this time.

BRANT What are you driving at, Christine?

CHRISTINE Something I've been thinking of ever since I realized he might soon come home. And now that Vinnie—but even if we didn't have to consider her, it'd be the only way! I couldn't fool him long. He's a strange, hidden man. His silence always creeps into my thoughts. Even if he never spoke, I would feel what was in his mind and some night, lying beside him, it would drive me mad and I'd have to kill his silence by screaming out the truth! (*She has been staring before her—now she suddenly turns on* BRANT—*slowly*) If he died suddenly now, no one would think it was anything but heart failure. I've been reading a book in Father's medical library. I saw it there one day a few weeks ago—it was as if some fate in me forced me to see it! (*She reaches in the sleeve of her dress and takes out the slip of paper she had written on*) I've written something here. I want you to get it for me. (*His fingers close on it mechanically. He stares at it with a strange stupid dread. She hurries on so as not to give him time for reflection*) The work on the "Flying Trades" is all finished, isn't it? You sail to Boston tomorrow, to wait for cargo?

BRANT (*dully*) Aye.

CHRISTINE Get this at some druggist's down by the waterfront

the minute you reach there. You can make up some story about a
sick dog on your ship. As soon as you get it, mail it to me
here. I'll be on the lookout, so Vinnie will never know it came.
Then you must wait on the "Flying Trades" until you hear from
me or I come to you—afterward!

BRANT (*dully*) But how can you do it—so no one will suspect?

CHRISTINE He's taking medicine. I'll give him his medicine. Oh,
I've planned it carefully.

BRANT But—if he dies suddenly, won't Vinnie—

CHRISTINE There'll be no reason for her to suspect. She's worried
already about his heart. Besides, she may hate me, but she would
never think—

BRANT Orin will be coming home, too.

CHRISTINE Orin will believe anything I want him to. As for the
people here, they'd never dream of such a thing in the Mannon
house! And the sooner I do it, the less suspicion there'll be!
They will think the excitement of coming home and the reaction
were too much for his weak heart! Doctor Blake will think so.
I'll see that's what he thinks.

BRANT (*harshly*) Poison! It's a coward's trick!

CHRISTINE (*with fierce scorn now, seeing the necessity of goading
him*) Do you think you would be braver to give me up to
him and let him take away your ship?

BRANT No!

CHRISTINE Didn't you say you wanted to kill him?

BRANT Aye! But I'd give him his chance!

CHRISTINE Did he give your mother her chance?

BRANT (*aroused*) No, damn him!

CHRISTINE Then what makes you suddenly so scrupulous about
his death? (*With a sneer*) It must be the Mannon in you coming
out! Are you going to prove, the first time your love is put
to a real test, that you're a weak coward like your father?

BRANT Christine! If it was any man said that to me—!

CHRISTINE (*passionately*) Have you thought of this side of his
homecoming—that he's coming back to my bed? If you love me
as much as you claim, I should think that would rid you of
any scruples! If it was a question of some woman taking you
from me, I wouldn't have qualms about which was or wasn't
the way to kill her! (*More tauntingly*) But perhaps your love
has been only a lie you told me—to take the sneaking revenge
on him of being a backstairs lover! Perhaps—

BRANT (*stung, grabbing her by the shoulders—fiercely*) Stop it! I'll do anything you want! You know it! (*Then with a change to somber grimness—putting the paper in his pocket*) And you're right. I'm a damn fool to have any feeling about how Ezra Mannon dies!

CHRISTINE (*a look of exultant satisfaction comes to her face as she sees he is definitely won over now. She throws her arms around him and kisses him passionately*) Ah! Now you're the man I love again, not a hypocritical Mannon! Promise me, no more cowardly romantic scruples! Promise me!

BRANT I promise. (*The boom of a cannon sounds from the fort that guards the harbor. He and* CHRISTINE *start frightenedly and stand staring at each other. Another boom comes, reverberating, rattling the windows.* CHRISTINE *recovers herself*).

CHRISTINE You hear? That's the salute to his homecoming! (*She kisses him—with fierce insistence*) Remember your mother's death! Remember your dream of your own ship! Above all, remember you'll have me!—all your own—your wife! (*Then urgently*) And now you must go! She'll be coming back—and you're not good at hiding your thoughts. (*Urging him toward the door*) Hurry! I don't want you to meet her! (*The cannon at the fort keep booming at regular intervals until the end of the scene.* BRANT *goes out in the hall and a moment later the front door is heard closing after him.* CHRISTINE *hurries from the door to the window and watches him from behind the curtains as he goes down the drive. She is in a state of tense, exultant excitement. Then, as if an idea had suddenly come to her, she speaks to his retreating figure with a strange sinister air of elation*) You'll never dare leave me now, Adam—for your ships or your sea or your naked Island girls—when I grow old and ugly! (*She turns back from the window. Her eyes are caught by the eyes of her husband in the portrait and for a moment she stares back into them, as if fascinated. Then she jerks her glance away and, with a little shudder she cannot repress, turns and walks quickly from the room and closes the door behind her*).

*Curtain*

# ACT THREE

SCENE—*The same as Act One, Scene One—exterior of the Mannon house. It is around nine o'clock of a night a week later. The light of a half moon falls on the house, giving it an unreal, detached, eerie quality. The pure white temple front seems more than ever like an incongruous mask fixed on the somber, stone house. All the shutters are closed. The white columns of the portico cast black bars of shadow on the gray wall behind them. The trunk of the pine at right is an ebony pillar, its branches a mass of shade.*

*LAVINIA is sitting on the top of the steps to the portico. She is dressed, as before, severely in black. Her thin figure, seated stiffly upright, arms against her sides, the legs close together, the shoulders square, the head upright, is like that of an Egyptian statue. She is staring straight before her. The sound of SETH's thin, aged baritone mournfully singing the chanty "Shenandoah" is heard from down the drive, off right front. He is approaching the house and the song draws quickly nearer:*

> "Oh, Shenandoah, I long to hear you
> A-way, my rolling river.
> Oh, Shenandoah, I can't get near you
> Way-ay, I'm bound away
> Across the wide Missouri.
>
> "Oh, Shenandoah, I love your daughter
> A-way, my rolling river."

*He enters right front. He is a bit drunk but holding his liquor well. He walks up by the lilacs starting the next line "Oh, Shenandoah"—then suddenly sees LAVINIA on the steps and stops abruptly, a bit sheepish.*

LAVINIA (*disapprovingly*) This is the second time this week I've caught you coming home like this.

SETH (*unabashed, approaches the steps—with a grin*) I'm aimin' to do my patriotic duty, Vinnie. The first time was celebratin' Lee's surrender and this time is drownin' my sorrow for the President gittin' shot! And the third'll be when your Paw gits home!

LAVINIA Father might arrive tonight.

SETH Gosh, Vinnie, I never calc'lated he could git here so soon!

LAVINIA Evidently you didn't. He'd give you fits if he caught you drunk. Oh, I don't believe he'll come, but it's possible he might.

SETH (*is evidently trying to pull himself together. He suddenly leans over toward her and, lowering his voice, asks soberly*) Did you find out anything about that Brant?

LAVINIA (*sharply*) Yes. There's no connection. It was just a silly idea of yours.

SETH (*stares at her—then understandingly*) Wal, if you want it left that way, I'll leave it that way. (*A pause. He continues to stand looking at her, while she stares in front of her*).

LAVINIA (*in a low voice*) What was that Marie Brantôme like, Seth?

SETH Marie? She was always laughin' and singin'—frisky and full of life—with something free and wild about her like an animile. Purty she was, too! (*Then he adds*) Hair just the color of your Maw's and yourn she had.

LAVINIA I know.

SETH Oh, everyone took to Marie—couldn't help it. Even your Paw. He was only a boy then, but he was crazy about her, too, like a youngster would be. His mother was stern with him, while Marie, she made a fuss over him and petted him.

LAVINIA Father, too!

SETH Ayeh—but he hated her worse than anyone when it got found out she was his Uncle David's fancy woman.

LAVINIA (*in a low voice, as if to herself, staring at the house*) It's all so strange! It frightens me! (*She checks herself abruptly— turns to* SETH, *curtly*) I don't believe that about Father. You've had too much whiskey. Go to bed and sleep it off. (*She walks up the steps again*).

SETH (*gazes at her with understanding*) Ayeh. (*Then warningly, making a surreptitious signal as he sees the front door open-*

*ing behind her*) Ssstt! (CHRISTINE *appears outlined in the light from the hall. She is dressed in a gown of green velvet that sets off her hair. The light behind her glows along the edges of the dress and in the color of her hair. She closes the door and comes into the moonlight at the edge of the steps, standing above and a little to the right of* LAVINIA. *The moonlight, falling full on them, accentuates strangely the resemblance between their faces and at the same time the hostile dissimilarity in body and dress.* LAVINIA *does not turn or give any sign of knowing her mother is behind her. There is a second's uncomfortable silence.* SETH *moves off left*) Wal, I'll trot along! (*He disappears around the corner of the house. There is a pause. Then* CHRISTINE *speaks in a dry mocking tone*)

CHRISTINE     What are you moongazing at? Puritan maidens shouldn't peer too inquisitively into Spring! Isn't beauty an abomination and love a vile thing? (*She laughs with bitter mockery—then tauntingly*) Why don't you marry Peter? You don't want to be left an old maid, do you?

LAVINIA (*quietly*)     You needn't hope to get rid of me that way. I'm not marrying anyone. I've got my duty to Father.

CHRISTINE     Duty! How often I've heard that word in this house! Well, you can't say I didn't do mine all these years. But there comes an end.

LAVINIA (*grimly*)     And there comes another end—and you must do your duty again!

CHRISTINE (*starts as if to retort defiantly—then says calmly*)     Yes, I realize that.

LAVINIA (*after a pause—suspiciously*)     What's going on at the bottom of your mind? I know you're plotting something!

CHRISTINE (*controlling a start*)     Don't be stupid, please!

LAVINIA     Are you planning how you can see Adam again? You better not!

CHRISTINE (*calmly*)     I'm not so foolish. I said good-bye once. Do you think I want to make it harder for myself?

LAVINIA     Has it been hard for you? I'd never guess it—and I've been watching you.

CHRISTINE     I warned you you would have no change to gloat! (*After a pause*) When do you expect your father home? You want me to play my part well when he comes, don't you?— for his sake. I'd like to be forewarned.

LAVINIA     His letter said he wouldn't wait until his brigade was disbanded but would try to get leave at once. He might arrive tonight—or tomorrow—or the next day. I don't know.

CHRISTINE You think he might come tonight? (*Then with a mocking smile*) So he's the beau you're waiting for in the spring moonlight! (*Then after a pause*) But the night train got in long ago.

LAVINIA (*glances down the drive, left front—then starts to her feet excitedly*) Here's someone! (CHRISTINE *slowly rises. There is the sound of footsteps. A moment later* EZRA MANNON *enters from left, front. He stops short in the shadow for a second and stands, erect and stiff, as if at attention, staring at his house, his wife and daughter. He is a tall, spare, big-boned man of fifty, dressed in the uniform of a Brigadier-General. One is immediately struck by the mask-like look of his face in repose, more pronounced in him than in the others. He is exactly like the portrait in his study, which we have seen in Act Two, except that his face is more lined and lean and the hair and beard are grizzled. His movements are exact and wooden and he has a mannerism of standing and sitting in stiff, posed attitudes that suggest the statues of military heroes. When he speaks, his deep voice has a hollow repressed quality, as if he were continually withholding emotion from it. His air is brusque and authoritative*).

LAVINIA (*seeing the man's figure stop in the shadow—calls excitedly*) Who's that?

MANNON (*stepping forward into the moonlight*) It's I.

LAVINIA (*with a cry of joy*) Father! (*She runs to him and throws her arms around him and kisses him*) Oh, Father! (*She bursts into tears and hides her face against his shoulder*).

MANNON (*embarrassed—patting her head—gruffly*) Come! I thought I'd taught you never to cry.

LAVINIA (*obediently forcing back her tears*) I'm sorry, Father—but I'm so happy!

MANNON (*awkwardly moved*) Tears are queer tokens of happiness! But I appreciate your—your feeling.

CHRISTINE (*has slowly descended the steps, her eyes fixed on him —tensely*) Is it really you, Ezra? We had just given up hope of your coming tonight.

MANNON (*going stiffly to meet her*) Train was late. The railroad is jammed up. Everybody has got leave. (*He meets her at the foot of the steps and kisses her with a chill dignity—*

*formally*) I am glad to see you, Christine. You are looking well. (*He steps back and stares at her—then in a voice that betrays a deep undercurrent of suppressed feeling*) You have changed, somehow. You are prettier than ever— But you always were pretty.

CHRISTINE (*forcing a light tone*) Compliments from one's husband! How gallant you've become, Ezra! (*Then solicitously*) You must be terribly tired. Wouldn't you like to sit here on the steps for a while? The moonlight is so beautiful.

LAVINIA (*who has been hovering about jealously, now manages to worm herself between them—sharply*) No. It's too damp out here. And Father must be hungry. (*Taking his arm*) Come inside with me and I'll get you something to eat. You poor dear! You must be starved.

MANNON (*really revelling in his daughter's coddling but embarrassed before his wife—pulling his arm back—brusquely*) No, thanks! I would rather rest here for a spell. Sit down, Vinnie. (CHRISTINE *sits on the top step at center; he sits on the middle step at right;* LAVINIA *on the lowest step at left. While they are doing this he keeps on talking in his abrupt sentences, as if he were trying to cover up some hidden uneasiness*) I've got leave for a few days. Then I must go back and disband my brigade. Peace ought to be signed soon. The President's assassination is a frightful calamity. But it can't change the course of events.

LAVINIA Poor man! It's dreadful he should die just at his moment of victory.

MANNON Yes! (*Then after a pause—somberly*) All victory ends in the defeat of death. That's sure. But does defeat end in the victory of death? That's what I wonder! (*They both stare at him,* LAVINIA *in surprise,* CHRISTINE *in uneasy wonder. A pause*).

CHRISTINE Where is Orin? Couldn't you get leave for him too?

MANNON (*hesitates—then brusquely*) I've been keeping it from you. Orin was wounded.

LAVINIA Wounded! You don't mean—badly hurt?

CHRISTINE (*half starting to her feet impulsively—with more of angry bitterness than grief*) I knew it! I knew when you forced him into your horrible war—! (*Then sinking back—tensely*) You needn't trouble to break the news gradually, Ezra. Orin is dead, isn't he?

LAVINIA Don't say that! It isn't true, is it, Father?

MANNON (*curtly—a trace of jealousy in his tone*) Of course it isn't! If your mother would permit me to finish instead of jumping at conclusions about her baby—! (*With a grim, proud satisfaction*) He's no baby now. I've made a man of him. He did one of the bravest things I've seen in the war. He was wounded in the head—a close shave but it turned out only a scratch. But he got brain fever from the shock. He's all right now. He was in a rundown condition, they say at the hospital. I never guessed it. Nerves. I wouldn't notice nerves. He's always been restless. (*Half turning to* CHRISTINE) He gets that from you.

CHRISTINE    When will he be well enough to come home?

MANNON    Soon. The doctor advised a few more days' rest. He's still weak. He was out of his head for a long time. Acted as if he were a little boy again. Seemed to think you were with him. That is, he kept talking to "Mother."

CHRISTINE (*with a tense intake of breath*)    Ah!

LAVINIA (*pityingly—with a tinge of scorn in her voice*)    Poor Orin!

MANNON    I don't want you to baby him when he comes home, Christine. It would be bad for him to get tied to your apron strings again.

CHRISTINE    You needn't worry. That passed—when he left me. (*Another pause. Then* LAVINIA *speaks*).

LAVINIA    How is the trouble with your heart, Father? I've been so afraid you might be making it out less serious than it really was to keep us from worrying.

MANNON (*gruffly*)    If it was serious, I'd tell you, so you'd be prepared. If you'd seen as much of death as I have in the past four years, you wouldn't be afraid of it. (*Suddenly jumping to his feet—brusquely*) Let's change the subject! I've had my fill of death. What I want now is to forget it. (*He turns and paces up and down to the right of steps.* LAVINIA *watches him worriedly*) All I know is the pain is like a knife. It puts me out of commission while it lasts. The doctor gave me orders to avoid worry or any over-exertion or excitement.

CHRISTINE (*staring at him*)    You don't look well. But probably that's because you're so tired. You must go to bed soon, Ezra.

MANNON (*comes to a stop in his pacing directly before her and looks into her eyes—a pause—then he says in a voice that he tries to make ordinary*)    Yes, I want to—soon.

LAVINIA (*who has been watching him jealously—suddenly pulling him by the arm—with a childish volubility*)    No! Not yet! Please, Father! You've only just come! We've hardly talked at all!

(*Defiantly to her mother*) How can you tell him he looks tired? He looks as well as I've ever seen him. (*Then to her father with a vindictive look at* CHRISTINE) We've so much to tell you. All about Captain Brant. (*If she had expected her mother to flinch at this, she is disappointed.* CHRISTINE *is prepared and remains unmoved beneath the searching, suspicious glance* MANNON *now directs at her*).

MANNON   Vinnie wrote me you'd had company. I never heard of him. What business had he here?

CHRISTINE (*with an easy smile*)   You had better ask Vinnie! He's her latest beau! She even went walking in the moonlight with him!

LAVINIA (*with a gasp at being defied so brazenly*)   Oh!

MANNON (*now jealous and suspicious of his daughter*)   I notice you didn't mention that in your letter, young lady!

LAVINIA   I only went walking once with him—and that was be-fore— (*She checks herself abruptly*).

MANNON   Before what?

LAVINIA   Before I knew he's the kind who chases after every woman he sees.

MANNON (*angrily to* CHRISTINE)   A fine guest to receive in my absence!

LAVINIA   I believe he even thought Mother was flirting with him. That's why I felt it my duty to write you. You know how folks in town gossip, Father. I thought you ought to warn Mother she was foolish to allow him to come here.

MANNON   Foolish! It was downright—!

CHRISTINE (*coldly*)   I would prefer not to discuss this until we are alone, Ezra—if you don't mind! And I think Vinnie is ex-tremely inconsiderate the moment you're home—to annoy you with such ridiculous nonsense! (*She turns to* LAVINIA) I think you've done enough mischief. Will you kindly leave us?

LAVINIA   No.

MANNON (*sharply*)   Stop your squabbling, both of you! I hoped you had grown out of that nonsense! I won't have it in my house!

LAVINIA (*obediently*)   Yes, Father.

MANNON   It must be your bedtime, Vinnie.

LAVINIA   Yes, Father. (*She comes and kisses him—excitedly*) Oh, I'm so happy you're here! Don't let Mother make you believe I —You're the only man I'll ever love! I'm going to stay with you!

MANNON (*patting her hair—with gruff tenderness*)   I hope so. I want you to remain my little girl—for a while longer, at least. (*Then suddenly catching* CHRISTINE's *scornful glance—pushes* LAVINIA *away—brusquely*) March now!

LAVINIA  Yes, Father. (*She goes up the steps past her mother without a look. Behind her mother, in the portico, she stops and turns*) Don't let anything worry you, Father. I'll always take care of you. (*She goes in.* MANNON *looks at his wife who stares before her. He clears his throat as if about to say something—then starts pacing self-consciously up and down at the right of steps*).

CHRISTINE  (*forcing a gentle tone*)  Sit down, Ezra. You will only make yourself more tired, keeping on your feet. (*He sits awkwardly two steps below her, on her left, turned sideways to face her. She asks with disarming simplicity*) Now please tell me just what it is you suspect me of?

MANNON  (*taken aback*)  What makes you think I suspect you?

CHRISTINE  Everything! I've felt your distrust from the moment you came. Your eyes have been probing me, as if you were a judge again and I were the prisoner.

MANNON  (*guiltily*)  I—?

CHRISTINE  And all on account of a stupid letter Vinnie had no business to write. It seems to me a late day, when I am an old woman with grown-up children, to accuse me of flirting with a stupid ship captain!

MANNON  (*impressed and relieved—placatingly*)  There's no question of accusing you of that. I only think you've been foolish to give the gossips a chance to be malicious.

CHRISTINE  Are you sure that's all you have in your heart against me?

MANNON  Yes! Of course! What else? (*Patting her hand embarrassedly*) We'll say no more about it. (*Then he adds gruffly*) But I'd like you to explain how this Brant happened—

CHRISTINE  I'm only too glad to! I met him at Father's. Father has taken a fancy to him for some reason. So when he called here I couldn't be rude, could I? I hinted that his visits weren't welcome, but men of his type don't understand hints. But he's only been here four times in all, I think. And as for there having been gossip, that's nonsense! The only talk has been that he came to court Vinnie! You can ask anyone in town.

MANNON  Damn his impudence! It was your duty to tell him flatly he wasn't wanted!

CHRISTINE  (*forcing a contrite air*)  Well, I must confess I didn't mind his coming as much as I might have—for one reason. He always brought me news of Father. Father's been sick for the past year, as I wrote you. (*Then with a twitch of the lips, as if she were restraining a derisive smile*) You can't realize what a strain I've been under—worrying about Father and Orin and—you.

MANNON (*deeply moved, turns to her and takes her hand in both of his—awkwardly*) Christine—I deeply regret—having been unjust. (*He kisses her hand impulsively—then embarrassed by this show of emotion, adds in a gruff, joking tone*) Afraid old Johnny Reb would pick me off, were you?

CHRISTINE (*controlling a wild impulse to burst into derisive laughter*) Do you need to ask that? (*A pause. He stares at her, fascinated and stirred*).

MANNON (*finally blurts out*) I've dreamed of coming home to you, Christine! (*Leans toward her, his voice trembling with desire and a feeling of strangeness and awe—touching her hair with an awkward caress*) You're beautiful! You look more beautiful than ever—and strange to me. I don't know you. You're younger. I feel like an old man beside you. Only your hair is the same—your strange beautiful hair I always—

CHRISTINE (*with a start of repulsion, shrinking from his hand*) Don't! (*Then as he turns away, hurt and resentful at this rebuff—hastily*) I'm sorry, Ezra. I didn't mean—I—I'm nervous tonight. (MANNON *paces to the right and stands looking at the trees.* CHRISTINE *stares at his back with hatred. She sighs with affected weariness and leans back and closes her eyes*).

CHRISTINE I'm tired, Ezra.

MANNON (*blurts out*) I shouldn't have bothered you with that foolishness about Brant tonight. (*He forces a strained smile*) But I was jealous a mite, to tell you the truth. (*He forces himself to turn and, seeing her eyes are shut, suddenly comes and leans over her awkwardly, as if to kiss her, then is stopped by some strangeness he feels about her still face*).

CHRISTINE (*feeling his desire and instinctively shrinking—without opening her eyes*) Why do you look at me like that?

MANNON (*turns away guiltily*) Like what? (*Uneasily*) How do you know? Your eyes are shut. (*Then, as if some burden of depression were on him that he had to throw off, he blurts out heavily*) I can't get used to home yet. It's so lonely. I've got used to the feel of camps with thousands of men around me at night—a sense of protection, maybe! (*Suddenly uneasy again*)

Don't keep your eyes shut like that! Don't be so still! (*Then, as she opens her eyes—with an explosive appeal*) God, I want to talk to you, Christine! I've got to explain some things—inside me— to my wife—try to, anyway! (*He sits down beside her*) Shut your eyes again! I can talk better. It has always been hard for me to talk—about feelings. I never could when you looked at me. Your eyes were always so—so full of silence! That is, since we've been married. Not before, when I was courting you. They used to speak then. They made me talk—because they answered.

CHRISTINE (*her eyes closed—tensely*) Don't talk, Ezra.

MANNON (*as if he had determined, once started, to go on doggedly without heeding any interruption*) It was seeing death all the time in this war got me to thinking these things. Death was so common, it didn't mean anything. That freed me to think of life. Queer, isn't it? Death made me think of life. Before that life had only made me think of death!

CHRISTINE (*without opening her eyes*) Why are you talking of death?

MANNON That's always been the Mannons' way of thinking. They went to the white meeting-house on Sabbaths and meditated on death. Life was a dying. Being born was starting to die. Death was being born. (*Shaking his head with a dogged bewilderment*) How in hell people ever got such notions! That white meeting-house. It stuck in my mind—clean-scrubbed and white-washed—a temple of death! But in this war I've seen too many white walls splattered with blood that counted no more than dirty water. I've seen dead men scattered about, no more important than rubbish to be got rid of. That made the white meeting-house seem meaningless—making so much solemn fuss over death!

CHRISTINE (*opens her eyes and stares at him with a strange terror*) What has this talk of death to do with me?

MANNON (*avoiding her glance—insistently*) Shut your eyes again. Listen and you'll know. (*She shuts her eyes. He plods on with a note of desperation in his voice*) I thought about my life—lying awake nights—and about your life. In the middle of battle I'd think maybe in a minute I'll be dead. But my life as just me ending, that didn't appear worth a thought one way or another. But listen, me as your husband being killed that seemed queer and wrong—like something dying that had never lived. Then all the years we've been man and wife would rise up in my mind and I would try to look at them. But nothing was clear except that there'd always been some barrier between us—a wall hiding us from each other! I would try to make up my mind exactly what that wall was but I never could discover. (*With a clumsy appealing gesture*) Do you know?

CHRISTINE (*tensely*)   I don't know what you're talking about.

MANNON   But you've known it was there! Don't lie, Christine! (*He looks at her still face and closed eyes, imploring her to reassure him—then blunders on doggedly*) Maybe you've always known you didn't love me. I call to mind the Mexican War. I could see you wanted me to go. I had a feeling you'd grown to hate me. Did you? (*She doesn't answer*) That was why I went. I was hoping I might get killed. Maybe you were hoping that too. Were you?

CHRISTINE (*stammers*)   No, no, I— What makes you say such things?

MANNON   When I came back you had turned to your new baby, Orin. I was hardly alive for you any more. I saw that. I tried not to hate Orin. I turned to Vinnie, but a daughter's not a wife. Then I made up my mind I'd do my work in the world and leave you alone in your life and not care. That's why the shipping wasn't enough—why I became a judge and a mayor and such vain truck, and why folks in town look on me as so able! Ha! Able for what? Not for what I wanted most in life! Not for your love! No! Able only to keep my mind from thinking of what I'd lost! (*He stares at her—then asks pleadingly*) For you did love me before we were married. You won't deny that, will you?

CHRISTINE (*desperately*)   I don't deny anything!

MANNON (*drawing himself up with a stern pride and dignity and surrendering himself like a commander against hopeless odds*) All right, then. I came home to surrender to you—what's inside me. I love you. I loved you then, and all the years between, and I love you now.

CHRISTINE (*distractedly*)   Ezra! Please!

MANNON   I want that said! Maybe you have forgotten it. I wouldn't blame you. I guess I haven't said it or showed it much—ever. Something queer in me keeps me mum about the things I'd like most to say—keeps me hiding the things I'd like to show. Something keeps me sitting numb in my own heart—like a statue of a dead man in a town square. (*Suddenly he reaches over and takes her hand*) I want to find what that wall is marriage put between us! You've got to help me smash it down! We have twenty good years still before us! I've been thinking of what we could do to get back to each other. I've a notion if we'd leave the children and go off on a voyage together—to the other side of the world—find some island where we could be alone a while. You'll find I have changed, Christine. I'm sick of death! I want life! Maybe you could love me now! (*In a note of final desperate pleading*) I've got to make you love me!

CHRISTINE (*pulls her hand away from him and springs to her feet wildly*) For God's sake, stop talking. I don't know what you're saying. Leave me alone! What must be, must be! You make me weak! (*Then abruptly*) It's getting late.

MANNON (*terribly wounded, withdrawn into his stiff soldier armor —takes out his watch mechanically*) Yes—six past eleven. Time to turn in. (*He ascends two steps, his face toward the door. He says bitterly*) You tell me to stop talking! By God, that's funny!

CHRISTINE (*collected now and calculating—takes hold of his arm, seductively*) I meant—what is the good of words? There is no wall between us. I love you.

MANNON (*grabs her by the shoulders and stares into her face*) Christine! I'd give my soul to believe that—but—I'm afraid! (*She kisses him. He presses her fiercely in his arms—passionately*) Christine! (*The door behind him is opened and* LAVINIA *appears at the edge of the portico behind and above him. She wears slippers over her bare feet and has a dark dressing-gown over her night dress. She shrinks back from their embrace with aversion. They separate, startled*).

MANNON (*embarrassed—irritably*) Thought you'd gone to bed, young lady!

LAVINIA (*woodenly*) I didn't feel sleepy. I thought I'd walk a little. It's such a fine night.

CHRISTINE We are just going to bed. Your father is tired. (*She moves up, past her daughter, taking* MANNON's *hand, leading him after her to the door*).

MANNON No time for a walk, if you ask me. See you turn in soon.

LAVINIA Yes, Father.

MANNON Good night. (*The door closes behind them.* LAVINIA *stands staring before her—then walks stiffly down the steps and stands again. Light appears between the chinks of the shutters in the bedroom on the second floor to the left. She looks up*).

LAVINIA (*in an anguish of jealous hatred*)  I hate you! You steal even Father's love from me again! You stole all love from me when I was born! (*Then almost with a sob, hiding her face in her hands*) Oh, Mother! Why have you done this to me? What harm had I done you? (*Then looking up at the window again—with passionate disgust*) Father, how can you love that shameless harlot? (*Then frenziedly*) I can't bear it! I won't! Father! Father! (*The shutter of the bedroom is pushed open and* MANNON *leans out*).

MANNON (*sharply*)  What is it? Don't shout like that!

LAVINIA (*stammers lamely*)  I—I remembered I forgot to say good night, Father.

MANNON (*exasperated*)  Good heavens! What— (*Then gently*) Oh—all right—good night, Vinnie. Get to bed soon, like a good girl.

LAVINIA  Yes, Father. Good night. (*He goes back in the bedroom and pulls the shutter closed. She stands staring fascinatedly up at the window, wringing her hands in a pitiful desperation*).

*Curtain*

# ACT FOUR

SCENE—EZRA MANNON's *bedroom. A big four-poster bed is at rear, center, the foot front, the head against the rear wall. A small stand, with a candle on it, is by the head of the bed on the left. To the left of the stand is a door leading into* CHRISTINE's *room. The door is open. In the left wall are two windows. At left, front, is a table with a lamp on it and a chair beside it. In the right wall, front, is a door leading to the hall. Further back, against the wall, is a bureau.*

*None of these details can be discerned at first because the room is in darkness, except for what moonlight filters feebly through the shutters. It is around dawn of the following morning.*

CHRISTINE's *form can be made out, a pale ghost in the darkness, as she slips slowly and stealthily from the bed. She tiptoes to the table, left front, and picks up a light-colored dressing-gown that is flung over the chair and puts it on. She stands listening for some sound from the bed. A pause. Then* MANNON's *voice comes suddenly from the bed, dull and lifeless.*

MANNON  Christine.

CHRISTINE  (*starts violently—in a strained voice*)  Yes.

MANNON  Must be near daybreak, isn't it?

CHRISTINE  Yes. It is beginning to get gray.

MANNON  What made you jump when I spoke? Is my voice so strange to you?

CHRISTINE  I thought you were asleep.

MANNON  I haven't been able to sleep. I've been lying here thinking. What makes you so uneasy?

CHRISTINE  I haven't been able to sleep either.

MANNON  You slunk out of bed so quietly.

CHRISTINE  I didn't want to wake you.

MANNON  (*bitterly*)  Couldn't you bear it—lying close to me?

CHRISTINE  I didn't want to disturb you by tossing around.

MANNON  We'd better light the light and talk a while.

CHRISTINE  (*with dread*)  I don't want to talk! I prefer the dark.

MANNON  I want to see you. (*He takes matches from the stand by the bed and lights the candle on it.* CHRISTINE *hastily sits down in the chair by the table, pushing it so she sits facing left, front, with her face turned three-quarters away from him. He pushes his back up against the head of the bed in a half-sitting position. His face, with the flickering candle light on its side, has a grim, bitter expression*) You like the dark where you can't see your old man of a husband, is that it?

CHRISTINE  I wish you wouldn't talk like that, Ezra. If you are going to say stupid things, I'll go in my own room. (*She gets to her feet but keeps her face turned away from him*).

MANNON  Wait! (*Then a note of pleading in his voice*) Don't go. I don't want to be alone. (*She sits again in the same position as before. He goes on humbly*) I didn't mean to say those things. I guess there's bitterness inside me—my own cussedness, maybe— and sometimes it gets out before I can stop it.

CHRISTINE  You have always been bitter.

MANNON  Before we married?

CHRISTINE  I don't remember.

MANNON  You don't want to remember you ever loved me!

CHRISTINE  (*tensely*)  I don't want to talk of the past! (*Abruptly changing the subject*) Did you hear Vinnie the first part of the night? She was pacing up and down before the house like a sentry guarding you. She didn't go to bed until two. I heard the clock strike.

MANNON  There is one who loves me, at least! (*Then after a pause*) I feel strange, Christine.

CHRISTINE  You mean—your heart? You don't think you are going to be—taken ill, do you?

MANNON  (*harshly*)  No! (*A pause—then accusingly*) Is that what you're waiting for? Is that why you were so willing to give yourself tonight? Were you hoping—?

CHRISTINE  (*springing up*)  Ezra! Stop talking like that! I can't stand it! (*She moves as if to go into her own room*).

MANNON  Wait! I'm sorry I said that. (*Then, as she sits down again, he goes on gloomily*) It isn't my heart. It's something uneasy troubling my mind—as if something in me was listening, watching, waiting for something to happen.

CHRISTINE    Waiting for what to happen?

MANNON    I don't know. (*A pause—then he goes on somberly*) This house is not my house. This is not my room nor my bed. They are empty—waiting for someone to move in! And you are not my wife! You are waiting for something!

CHRISTINE    (*beginning to snap under the strain—jumps to her feet again*)    What would I be waiting for?

MANNON    For death—to set you free!

CHRISTINE    Leave me alone! Stop nagging at me with your crazy suspicions! (*Then anger and hatred come into her voice*) Not your wife! You acted as if I were your wife—your property—not so long ago!

MANNON    (*with bitter scorn*)    Your body? What are bodies to me? I've seen too many rotting in the sun to make grass greener! Ashes to ashes, dirt to dirt! Is that your notion of love? Do you think I married a body? (*Then, as if all the bitterness and hurt in him had suddenly burst its dam*) You were lying to me tonight as you've always lied! You were only pretending love! You let me take you as if you were a nigger slave I'd bought at auction! You made me appear a lustful beast in my own eyes!—as you've always done since our first marriage night! I would feel cleaner now if I had gone to a brothel! I would feel more honor between myself and life!

CHRISTINE    (*in a stifled voice*)    Look out, Ezra! I won't stand—

MANNON    (*with a harsh laugh*)    And I had hoped my homecoming would mark a new beginning—new love between us! I told you my secret feelings. I tore my insides out for you—thinking you'd understand! By God, I'm an old fool!

CHRISTINE    (*her voice grown strident*)    Did you think you could make me weak—make me forget all the years? Oh, no, Ezra! It's too late! (*Then her voice changes, as if she had suddenly resolved on a course of action, and becomes deliberately taunting*) You want the truth? You've guessed it! You've used me, you've given me children, but I've never once been yours! I never could be! And whose fault is it? I loved you when I married you! I wanted to give myself! But you made me so I couldn't give! You filled me with disgust!

MANNON    (*furiously*)    You say that to me! (*Then trying to calm himself—stammers*)    No! Be quiet! We mustn't fight! I mustn't lose my temper! It will bring on—!

CHRISTINE    (*goading him with calculating cruelty*)    Oh, no! You needn't adopt that pitiful tone! You wanted the truth and you're going to hear it now!

MANNON (*frightened—almost pleading*) Be quiet, Christine!

CHRISTINE I've lied about everything! I lied about Captain Brant! He is Marie Brantôme's son! And it was I he came to see, not Vinnie! I made him come!

MANNON (*seized with fury*) You dared—! You—! The son of that—!

CHRISTINE Yes, I dared! And all my trips to New York weren't to visit Father but to be with Adam! He's gentle and tender, he's everything you've never been. He's what I've longed for all these years with you—a lover! I love him! So now you know the truth!

MANNON (*in a frenzy—struggling to get out of bed*) You—you whore—I'll kill you! (*Suddenly he falls back, groaning, doubled up on his left side, with intense pain*).

CHRISTINE (*with savage satisfaction*) Ah! (*She hurries through the doorway into her room and immediately returns with a small box in her hand. He is facing away from her door, and, even if the intense pain left him any perception, he could not notice her departure and return, she moves so silently*).

MANNON (*gaspingly*) Quick—medicine!

CHRISTINE (*turned away from him, takes a pellet from the box, asking tensely as she does so*) Where is your medicine?

MANNON On the stand! Hurry!

CHRISTINE Wait. I have it now. (*She pretends to take something from the stand by the head of the bed—then holds out the pellet and a glass of water which is on the stand*) Here. (*He turns to her groaning and opens his mouth. She puts the pellet on his tongue and presses the glass of water to his lips*) Now drink.

MANNON (*takes a swallow of water—then suddenly a wild look of terror comes over his face. He gasps*) That's not—my medicine. (*She shrinks back to the table, the hand with the box held out behind her, as if seeking a hiding place. Her fingers release the box on the table top and she brings her hand in front of her as if instinctively impelled to prove to him she has nothing. His eyes are fixed on her in a terrible accusing glare. He tries to call for help but his voice fades to a wheezy whisper*) Help! Vinnie! (*He falls back in a coma, breathing stertorously. CHRISTINE stares at him fascinatedly—then starts with terror as she hears a noise from the hall and frantically snatches up the box from the table and holds it behind her back, turning to face the door as it *opens and* LAVINIA *appears in the doorway. She is dressed as at the end of Act Three, in nightgown, wrapper and slippers. She stands, dazed and frightened and hesitating, as if she had just awakened*).

LAVINIA   I had a horrible dream—I thought I heard Father calling me—it woke me up—

CHRISTINE (*trembling with guilty terror—stammers*)   He just had —an attack.

LAVINIA (*hurries to the bed*)   Father! (*She puts her arms around him*) He's fainted!

CHRISTINE   No. He's all right now. Let him sleep. (*At this moment* MANNON, *with a last dying effort, straightens up in a sitting position in* LAVINIA's *arms, his eyes glaring at his wife, and manages to raise his arm and point an accusing finger at her*).

MANNON (*gasps*)   She's guilty—not medicine! (*He falls back limply*).

LAVINIA   Father! (*Frightenedly she feels for his pulse, puts her ear against his chest to listen for a heartbeat*).

CHRISTINE   Let him alone. He's asleep.

LAVINIA   He's dead!

CHRISTINE (*repeats mechanically*)   Dead? (*Then in a strange flat tone*) I hope—he rests in peace.

LAVINIA (*turning on her with hatred*)   Don't you dare pretend—! You wanted him to die! You— (*She stops and stares at her mother with a horrified suspicion—then harshly accusing*) Why did he point at you like that? Why did he say you were guilty? Answer me!

CHRISTINE (*stammers*)   I told him—Adam was my lover.

LAVINIA (*aghast*)   You told him that—when you knew his heart —! Oh! You did it on purpose! You murdered him!

CHRISTINE   No—it was your fault—you made him suspicious—he kept talking of love and death—he forced me to tell him! (*Her voice becomes thick, as if she were drowsy and fighting off sleep. Her eyes half close*).

LAVINIA (*grabbing her by the shoulders—fiercely*)   Listen! Look at me! He said "not medicine!" What did he mean?

CHRISTINE (*keeping the hand with the poison pressed against her back*)   I—I don't know.

LAVINIA   You do know! What was it? Tell me!

CHRISTINE (*with a last effort of will manages to draw herself up and speak with a simulation of outraged feeling)*   Are you accusing your mother of—

LAVINIA   Yes! I—! (*Then distractedly*) No—you can't be that evil!

CHRISTINE   (*her strength gone—swaying weakly*)   I don't know what—you're talking about. (*She edges away from* LAVINIA *toward her bedroom door, the hand with the poison stretched out behind her—weakly*) I—feel faint. I must go—and lie down. I— (*She turns as if to run into the room, takes a tottering step —then her knees suddenly buckle under her and she falls in a dead faint at the foot of the bed. As her hand strikes the floor the fingers relax and the box slips out onto one of the hooked rugs*).

LAVINIA   (*does not notice this. Startled by* CHRISTINE'S *collapse, she automatically bends on one knee beside her and hastily feels for her pulse. Then satisfied she has only fainted, her anguished hatred immediately returns and she speaks with strident denunciation*)   You murdered him just the same—by telling him! I suppose you think you'll be free to marry Adam now! But you won't! Not while I'm alive! I'll make you pay for your crime! I'll find a way to punish you! (*She is starting to her feet when her eyes fall on the little box on the rug. Immediately she snatches it up and stares at it, the look of suspicion changing to a dreadful, horrified certainty. Then with a shuddering cry she shrinks back along the side of the bed, the box clutched in her hand, and sinks on her knees by the head of the bed, and flings her arms around the dead man. With anguished beseeching*) Father! Don't leave me alone! Come back to me! Tell me what to do!

*Curtain*

*Part Two*

# THE HUNTED

*A Play in Five Acts*

# Characters

CHRISTINE, *Ezra Mannon's widow*

LAVINIA (VINNIE), *her daughter*

ORIN, *her son, First Lieutenant of Infantry*

CAPTAIN ADAM BRANT

HAZEL NILES

PETER, *her brother, Captain of Artillery*

JOSIAH BORDEN, *manager of the shipping company*

EMMA, *his wife*

EVERETT HILLS, D.D., *of the First Congregational Church*

HIS WIFE

DOCTOR JOSEPH BLAKE

THE CHANTYMAN

# Scenes

ACT ONE: Exterior of the Mannon house—a moonlight night two days after the murder of EZRA MANNON.

ACT TWO: Sitting-room in the house—immediately follows Act One.

ACT THREE: EZRA MANNON's study—immediately follows Act Two.

ACT FOUR: The stern of the clipper ship "Flying Trades," at a wharf in East Boston—a night two days later.

ACT FIVE: Same as Act One—Exterior of the Mannon house the night of the following day.

# ACT ONE

SCENE—*The same as Acts One and Three of "Homecoming"—Exterior of the Mannon House.*

*It is a moonlight night two days after the murder of* EZRA MANNON. *The house has the same strange eerie appearance, its white portico like a mask in the moonlight, as it had on that night. All the shutters are closed. A funeral wreath is fixed to the column at the right of steps. Another wreath is on the door.*

*There is a sound of voices from inside the house, the front door is opened and* JOSIAH BORDEN *and his wife,* EVERETT HILLS, *the Congregational minister, and his wife, and* DOCTOR JOSEPH BLAKE, *the Mannons' family physician, come out.* CHRISTINE *can be seen in the hall just inside the door. There is a chorus of "Good night, Mrs. Mannon," and then turn to the steps and the door is closed.*

*These people—the* BORDENS, HILLS *and his wife and* DOCTOR BLAKE —*are, as were the Ames of Act one of "Homecoming," types of townsfolk, a chorus representing as those others had, but in a different stratum of society, the town as a human background for the drama of the Mannons.*

JOSIAH BORDEN, *the manager of the Mannon shipping company, is shrewd and competent. He is around sixty, small and wizened, white hair and beard, rasping nasal voice, and little sharp eyes. His wife, about ten years his junior, is a typical New England woman of pure English ancestry, with a horse face, buck teeth and big feet, her manner defensively sharp and assertive.* HILLS *is the type of well-fed minister of a prosperous small-town congregation— stout and unctuous, snobbish and ingratiating, conscious of godliness, but timid and always feeling his way. He is in the fifties, as is his wife, a sallow, flabby, self-effacing minister's wife.* DOCTOR BLAKE *is the old kindly best-family physician—a stout, self-important old man with a stubborn opinionated expression.*

*They come down the steps to the drive.* MRS. BORDEN *and* MRS.

HILLS *walk together toward left front until they are by the bench. There they stop to wait for the men who stand at the foot of the steps while* BORDEN *and* BLAKE *light cigars.*

MRS. BORDEN (*tartly*)   I can't abide that woman!

MRS. HILLS   No. There's something queer about her.

MRS. BORDEN (*grudgingly honest*)   Still and all, I come nearer to liking her now than I ever did before when I see how broken down she is over her husband's death.

MRS. HILLS   Yes. She looks terrible, doesn't she? Doctor Blake says she will have herself in bed sick if she doesn't look out.

MRS. BORDEN   I'd never have suspected she had that much feeling in her. Not but what she hasn't always been a dutiful wife, as far as anyone knows.

MRS. HILLS   Yes. She's seemed to be.

MRS. BORDEN   Well, it only goes to show how you can misjudge a person without meaning to—especially when that person is a Mannon. They're not easy to make head or tail of. Queer, the difference in her and Lavinia—the way they take his death. Lavinia is cold and calm as an icicle.

MRS. HILLS   Yes. She doesn't seem to feel as much sorrow as she ought.

MRS. BORDEN   That's where you're wrong. She feels it as much as her mother. Only she's too Mannon to let anyone see what she feels. But did you notice the look in her eyes?

MRS. HILLS   I noticed she never said a word to anyone. Where did she disappear to all of a sudden?

MRS. BORDEN   Went to the train with Peter Niles to meet Orin. I overheard her mother talking to Lavinia in the hall. She was insisting Peter should escort her to meet the train. Lavinia must have been starting to go alone. Her mother seemed real angry about it. (*Then glancing toward the men who have moved a little away from the steps and are standing talking in low tones*) Whatever are those men gossiping about? (*She calls*) Josiah! It's time we were getting home.

BORDEN   I'm coming, Emma. (*The three men join the women by the bench,* BORDEN *talking as they come*) It isn't for me to question the arrangements she's made, Joe, but it does seem as if Ezra should have been laid out in the town hall where the whole town could have paid their respects to him, and had a big public funeral tomorrow.

HILLS  That's my opinion. He was mayor of the town and a national war hero—

BLAKE  She says it was Ezra's wish he'd often expressed that everything should be private and quiet. That's just like Ezra. He never was one for show. He did the work and let others do the showing off.

HILLS  (*unctuously*)  He was a great man. His death is a real loss to everyone in this community. He was a power for good.

BORDEN  Yes. He got things done.

HILLS  What a tragedy to be taken his first night home after passing unharmed through the whole war!

BORDEN  I couldn't believe the news. Who'd ever suspect— It's queer. It's like fate.

MRS. HILLS  (*breaks in tactlessly*)  Maybe it is fate. You remember, Everett, you've always said about the Mannons that pride goeth before a fall and that some day God would humble them in their sinful pride. (*Everyone stares at her, shocked and irritated*).

HILLS  (*flusteredly*)  I don't remember ever saying—

BLAKE  (*huffily*)  If you'll excuse me, that's darn nonsense! I've known Ezra Mannon all my life, and to those he wanted to know he was as plain and simple—

HILLS  (*hastily*)  Of course, Doctor. My wife entirely misunderstood me. I was, perhaps wrongly, referring to Mrs. Mannon.

BLAKE  She's all right too—when you get to know her.

HILLS  (*dryly*)  I have no doubt.

BLAKE  And it's a poor time, when this household is afflicted by sudden death, to be—

HILLS  You are quite right, Doctor. My wife should have remembered—

MRS. HILLS  (*crushed*)  I didn't mean anything wrong, Doctor.

BLAKE  (*mollifiedly*)  Let's forget it then. (*Turning to* BORDEN—*with a self-satisfied, knowing air*)  As for your saying who'd ever expect it—well, you and Emma know I expected Ezra wouldn't last long.

BORDEN  Yes. I remember you said you were afraid his heart was bad.

MRS. BORDEN  I remember you did too.

BLAKE  From the symptoms Mrs. Mannon described from his letter to her, I was as certain as if I'd examined him he had angina. And I wasn't surprised neither. I'd often told Ezra he was

attempting more than one man could handle and if he didn't rest
he'd break down. The minute they sent for me I knew what'd
happened. And what she told me about waking up to find him
groaning and doubled with pain confirmed it. She'd given him
his medicine—it was what I would have prescribed myself—but
it was too late. And as for dying, his first night home—well,
the war was over, he was worn out, he'd had a long, hard
trip home—and angina is no respecter of time and place. It
strikes when it has a mind to.

BORDEN (*shaking his head*) Too bad. Too durned bad. The
town won't find another as able as Ezra in a hurry. (*They all
shake their heads and look sad. A pause*).

MRS. BORDEN Well, we aren't doing anyone any good standing
here. We ought to get home, Josiah.

MRS. HILLS Yes. We must, too, Everett. (*They begin moving slowly
off left,* HILLS *going with the two women.* DOCTOR BLAKE *nudges*
BORDEN *and motions him to stay behind. After the others disappear, he whispers with a meaning grin*).

BLAKE I'll tell you a secret, Josiah—strictly between you and me.

BORDEN (*sensing something from his manner—eagerly*) Of course.
What is it, Joe?

BLAKE I haven't asked Christine Mannon any embarrassing questions, but I have a strong suspicion it was love killed Ezra!

BORDEN Love?

BLAKE That's what! Leastways, love made angina kill him, if you
take my meaning. She's a damned handsome woman and he'd
been away a long time. Only natural between man and wife—
but not the treatment I'd recommend for angina. He should have
known better, but—well—he was human.

BORDEN (*with a salacious smirk*) Can't say as I blame him! She's
a looker! I don't like her and never did but I can imagine
worse ways of dying! (*They both chuckle*) Well, let's catch
up with the folks. (*They go off, left. They have hardly disappeared before the door of the house is opened and* CHRISTINE
MANNON *comes out and stands at the head of the steps a
moment, then descends to the drive. She is obviously in a terrible
state of strained nerves. Beneath the mask-like veneer of her face
there are deep lines about her mouth, and her eyes burn with a
feverish light. Feeling herself free from observation for a moment
she lets go, her mouth twitches, her eyes look desperately on
all sides, as if she longed to fly from something.* HAZEL NILES

*comes out of the house to the head of the steps. She is the same as in "Homecoming." CHRISTINE at once senses her presence behind her and regains her tense control of herself).*

HAZEL (*with a cheering, sympathetic air*) So here you are. I looked everywhere around the house and couldn't find you.

CHRISTINE (*tensely*) I couldn't stay in. I'm so nervous. It's been a little harrowing—all these people coming to stand around and stare at the dead—and at me.

HAZEL I know. But there won't be any more now. (*Then a tone of eagerness breaking through in spite of herself*) Peter and Vinnie ought to be back soon, if the train isn't late. Oh, I hope Orin will surely come!

CHRISTINE (*strangely*) The same train! It was late that night he came! Only two days ago! It seems a lifetime! I've grown old.

HAZEL (*gently*) Try not to think of it.

CHRISTINE (*tensely*) As if I hadn't tried! But my brain keeps on— over and over and over!

HAZEL I'm so afraid you will make yourself sick.

CHRISTINE (*rallying herself and forcing a smile*) There, I'm all right. I mustn't appear too old and haggard when Orin comes, must I? He always liked me to be pretty.

HAZEL It will be so good to see him again! (*Then quickly*) He ought to be such a comfort to you in your grief.

CHRISTINE Yes. (*Then strangely*) He used to be my baby, you know—before he left me. (*Suddenly staring at HAZEL, as if struck by an idea*) You love Orin, don't you?

HAZEL (*embarrassed—stammers shyly*) I—I—

CHRISTINE I am glad. I want you to. I want him to marry you. (*Putting an arm around her—in a strained tone*) We'll be secret conspirators, shall we, and I'll help you and you'll help me?

HAZEL I don't understand.

CHRISTINE You know how possessive Vinnie is with Orin. She's always been jealous of you. I warn you she'll do everything she can to keep him from marrying you.

HAZEL (*shocked*) Oh, Mrs. Mannon, I can't believe Vinnie—!

CHRISTINE (*unheeding*) So you must help me. We mustn't let Orin come under her influence again. Especially now in the morbid, crazy state of grief she's in! Haven't you noticed how queer she's become? She hasn't spoken a single word since her father's death! When I talk to her she won't answer me. And yet she follows me around everywhere—she hardly leaves me alone a minute. (*Forc-*

*ing a nervous laugh*) It gets on my nerves until I could scream!

HAZEL   Poor Vinnie! She was so fond of her father. I don't wonder she—

CHRISTINE (*staring at her—strangely*)   You are genuinely good and pure of heart, aren't you?

HAZEL (*embarrassed*)   Oh, no! I'm not at all—

CHRISTINE   I was like you once—long ago—before— (*Then with bitter longing*) If I could only have stayed as I was then! Why can't all of us remain innocent and loving and trusting? But God won't leave us alone. He twists and wrings and tortures our lives with others' lives until—we poison each other to death! (*Seeing* HAZEL's *look, catches herself—quickly*) Don't mind what I said! Let's go in, shall we? I would rather wait for Orin inside. I couldn't bear to wait and watch him coming up the drive—just like—he looks so much like his father at times—and like—but what nonsense I'm talking! Let's go in. I hate moonlight. It makes everything so haunted. (*She turns abruptly and goes into the house.* HAZEL *follows her and shuts the door. There is a pause. Then footsteps and voices are heard from off right front and a moment later* ORIN MANNON *enters with* PETER *and* LAVINIA. *One is at once struck by his startling family resemblance to* EZRA MANNON *and* ADAM BRANT [*whose likeness to each other we have seen in "Homecoming"*]. *There is the same life-like mask quality of his face in repose, the same aquiline nose, heavy eyebrows, swarthy complexion, thick straight black hair, light hazel eyes. His mouth and chin have the same general characteristics as his father's had, but the expression of his mouth gives an impression of tense oversensitiveness quite foreign to the General's, and his chin is a refined, weakened version of the dead man's. He is about the same height as* MANNON *and* BRANT, *but his body is thin and his swarthy complexion sallow. He wears a bandage around his head high up on his forehead. He carries himself by turns with a marked slouchiness or with a self-conscious square-shouldered stiffness that indicates a soldierly bearing is unnatural to him. When he speaks it is jerkily, with a strange, vague, preoccupied air. But when he smiles naturally his face has a gentle boyish charm which makes women immediately want to mother him. He wears a mustache similar to* BRANT's *which serves to increase their resemblance to each other. Although he is only twenty, he looks thirty. He is dressed in a baggy, ill-fitting uniform—that of a first lieutenant of infantry in the Union Army*).

ORIN (*as they enter looks eagerly toward the house—then with bitter, hurt disappointment in his tone*) Where's Mother? I thought she'd surely be waiting for me. (*He stands staring at the house*) God, how I've dreamed of coming home! I thought it would never end, that we'd go on murdering and being murdered until no one was left alive! Home at last! No, by God, I must be dreaming again! (*Then in an awed tone*) But the house looks strange. Or is it something in me? I was out of my head so long, everything has seemed queer since I came back to earth. Did the house always look so ghostly and dead?

PETER That's only the moonlight, you chump.

ORIN Like a tomb. That's what Mother used to say it reminded her of, I remember.

LAVINIA (*reproachfully*) It is a tomb—just now, Orin.

ORIN (*hurriedly—shamefacedly*) I—I'd forgotten. I simply can't realize he's dead yet. I suppose I'd come to expect he would live forever. (*A trace of resentment has crept into his tone*) Or, at least outlive me. I never thought his heart was weak. He told me the trouble he had wasn't serious.

LAVINIA (*quickly*) Father told you that, too? I was hoping he had. (*Then turning to* PETER) You go ahead in, Peter. Say we're coming a little behind. I want to speak to Orin a moment.

PETER Sure thing, Vinnie. (*He goes in the front door, closing it behind him*).

ORIN I'm glad you got rid of him. Peter is all right but—I want to talk to you alone. (*With a boyish brotherly air—putting an arm around her*) You certainly are a sight for sore eyes, Vinnie! How are you, anyway, you old bossy fuss-buzzer! Gosh, it seems natural to hear myself calling you that old nickname again. Aren't you glad to see me?

LAVINIA (*affectionately*) Of course I am!

ORIN I'd never guess it! You've hardly spoken a word since you met me. What's happened to you? (*Then, as she looks at him reproachfully, he takes away his arm—a bit impatiently*) I told you I can't get used to the idea of his being dead. Forgive me, Vinnie. I know what a shock it must be to you.

LAVINIA Isn't it a shock to you, Orin?

ORIN Certainly! What do you think I am? But—oh, I can't explain! You wouldn't understand, unless you'd been at the front. I hardened myself to expect my own death and everyone else's, and think nothing of it. I had to—to keep alive! It was part of my training as a soldier under him. He taught it to me, you might say! So when it's his turn he can hardly expect— (*He has talked with increasing bitterness.* LAVINIA *interrupts him sharply*).

LAVINIA  Orin! How can you be so unfeeling?

ORIN (*again shamefaced*)  I didn't mean that. My mind is still full of ghosts. I can't grasp anything but war, in which he was so alive. He was the war to me—the war that would never end until I died. I can't understand peace—his end! (*Then with exasperation*) God damn it, Vinnie, give me a chance to get used to things!

LAVINIA  Orin! ·

ORIN (*resentfully*)  I'm sorry! Oh, I know what you're thinking! I used to be such a nice gentlemanly cuss, didn't I?—and now— Well, you wanted me to be a hero in blue, so you better be resigned! Murdering doesn't improve one's manners! (*Abruptly changing the subject*) But what the devil are we talking about me for? Listen, Vinnie. There's something I want to ask you before I see Mother.

LAVINIA  Hurry, then! She'll be coming right out! I've got to tell you something too!

ORIN  What was that stuff you wrote about some Captain Brant coming to see Mother? Do you mean to tell me there's actually been gossip started about her? (*Then without waiting for a reply, bursting into jealous rage*) By God, if he dares come here again, I'll make him damned sorry he did!

LAVINIA (*grimly*)  I'm glad you feel that way about him. But there's no time to talk now. All I want to do is warn you to be on your guard. Don't let her baby you the way she used to and get you under her thumb again. Don't believe the lies she'll tell you! Wait until you've talked to me! Will you promise me?

ORIN (*staring at her bewilderedly*)  You mean—Mother? (*Then angrily*) What the hell are you talking about, anyway? Are you loony? Honestly, Vinnie, I call that carrying your everlasting squabble with Mother a bit too far! You ought to be ashamed of yourself! (*Then suspiciously*) What are you being so mysterious about? Is it Brant—?

LAVINIA (*at a sound from inside the house*)  Ssshh! (*The front door of the house is opened and* CHRISTINE *hurries out*).

CHRISTINE (*angrily to* PETER *who is in the hall*)  Why didn't you call me, Peter? You shouldn't have left him alone! (*She calls uncertainly*) Orin.

ORIN Mother! (*She runs down the steps and flings her arms around him*).

CHRISTINE My boy! My baby! (*She kisses him*).

ORIN (*melting, all his suspicion forgotten*) Mother! God, it's good to see you! (*Then almost roughly, pushing her back and staring at her*) But you're different! What's happened to you?

CHRISTINE (*forcing a smile*) I? Different? I don't think so, dear. Certainly I hope not—to you! (*Touching the bandage on his head—tenderly*) Your head! Does it pain dreadfully? You poor darling, how you must have suffered! (*She kisses him*) But it's all over now, thank God. I've got you back again! (*Keeping her arm around him, she leads him up the steps*) Let's go in. There's someone else waiting who will be so glad to see you.

LAVINIA (*who has come to the foot of the steps—harshly*) Remember, Orin! (CHRISTINE *turns around to look down at her. A look of hate flashes between mother and daughter.* ORIN *glances at his mother suspiciously and draws away from her*).

CHRISTINE (*immediately recovers her poise—to* ORIN, *as if* LAVINIA *hadn't spoken*) Come on in, dear. It's chilly. Your poor head— (*She takes his hand and leads him through the door and closes it behind them.* LAVINIA *remains by the foot of the steps, staring after them. Then the door is suddenly opened again and* CHRISTINE *comes out, closing it behind her, and walks to the head of the steps. For a moment mother and daughter stare into each other's eyes. Then* CHRISTINE *begins haltingly in a tone she vainly tries to make kindly and persuasive*) Vinnie, I—I must speak with you a moment—now Orin is here. I appreciate your grief has made you—not quite normal—and I make allowances. But I cannot understand your attitude toward me. Why do you keep following me everywhere—and stare at me like that? I had been a good wife to him for twenty-three years—until I met Adam. I was guilty then, I admit. But I repented and put him out of my life. I would have been a good wife again as long as your father had lived. After all, Vinnie, I am your mother. I brought you into the world. You ought to have some feeling for me. (*She pauses, waiting for some response but* LAVINIA *simply stares at her, frozen and silent. Fear creeps into* CHRISTINE's *tone*) Don't stare like that! What are you thinking? Surely you can't still have that insane suspicion

—that I— (*Then guiltily*) What did you do that night I fainted? I—I've missed something—some medicine I take to put me to sleep— (*Something like a grim smile of satisfaction forms on* LAVINIA's *lips.* CHRISTINE *exclaims frightenedly*) Oh, you did— you found—and I suppose you connect that—but don't you see how insane—to suspect—when Doctor Blake knows he died of—! (*Then angrily*) I know what you've been waiting for—to tell Orin your lies and get him to go to the police! You don't dare do that on your own responsibility—but if you can make Orin— Isn't that it? Isn't that what you've been planning the last two days? Tell me! (*Then, as* LAVINIA *remains silent,* CHRISTINE *gives way to fury and rushes down the steps and grabs her by the arm and shakes her*) Answer me when I speak to you! What are you plotting? What are you going to do? Tell me! (LAVINIA *keeps her body rigid, her eyes staring into her mother's.* CHRISTINE *lets go and steps away from her. Then* LAVINIA, *turning her back, walks slowly and woodenly off left between the lilac clump and the house.* CHRISTINE *stares after her, her strength seems to leave her, she trembles with dread. From inside the house comes the sound of* ORIN's *voice calling sharply "Mother! Where are you?"* CHRISTINE *starts and immediately by an effort of will regains control over herself. She hurries up the steps and opens the door. She speaks to* ORIN *and her voice is tensely quiet and normal*) Here I am, dear! (*She shuts the door behind her*).

*Curtain*

# ACT TWO

Scene—*The sitting-room of the Mannon house. Like the study, but much larger, it is an interior composed of straight severe lines with heavy detail. The walls are plain plastered surfaces, light gray with a white trim. It is a bleak room without intimacy, with an atmosphere of uncomfortable, stilted stateliness. The furniture is stationed about with exact precision. On the left, front, is a doorway leading to the dining-room. Further back, on the left, are a wall table and chair and a writing desk and chair. In the rear wall, center, is the doorway giving on the main hall and the stairs. At right is a fireplace with a chimneypiece of black marble, flanked by two windows. Portraits of ancestors hang on the walls. At the rear of the fireplace, on the right, is one of a grim-visaged minister of the witch-burning era. Between fireplace and front is another of* Ezra Mannon's *grandfather, in the uniform of an officer in Washington's army. Directly over the fireplace is the portrait of* Ezra's *father,* Abe Mannon, *done when he was sixty. Except for the difference in ages, his face looks exactly like* Ezra's *in the painting in the study.*

*Of the three portraits on the other walls, two are of women—* Abe Mannon's *wife and the wife of Washington's officer. The third has the appearance of a prosperous shipowner of Colonial days. All the faces in the portraits have the same mask quality of those of the living characters in the play.*

*At the left center of the room, front, is a table with two chairs. There is another chair at center, front, and a sofa at right, front, facing left.*

*The opening of this scene follows immediately the close of the preceding one.* Hazel *is discovered sitting on the chair at center, front.* Peter *is sitting on the sofa at right. From the hall* Orin *is heard calling "Mother! Where are you?" as at the close of the preceding act.*

HAZEL   Where can she have gone? She's worked herself into such a state of grief I don't think she knows what she's doing.

PETER   Vinnie's completely knocked out, too.

HAZEL   And poor Orin! What a terrible homecoming this is for him! How sick and changed he looks, doesn't he, Peter?

PETER   Head wounds are no joke. He's darned lucky to have come out alive. (*They stop talking self-consciously as* ORIN *and* CHRISTINE *enter from the rear.* ORIN *is questioning her suspiciously*).

ORIN   Why did you sneak away like that? What were you doing?

CHRISTINE   (*forcing a wan smile*)   The happiness of seeing you again was a little too much for me, I'm afraid, dear. I suddenly felt as if I were going to faint, so I rushed out in the fresh air.

ORIN   (*immediately ashamed of himself—tenderly, putting his arm around her*)   Poor Mother! I'm sorry— Look here, then. You sit down and rest. Or maybe you better go right to bed.

HAZEL   That's right, Orin, you make her. I've been trying to get her to but she won't listen to me.

CHRISTINE   Go to bed the minute he comes home! I should say not!

ORIN   (*worried and pleased at the same time*)   But you mustn't do anything to—

CHRISTINE   (*patting his cheek*)   Fiddlesticks! Having you again is just the medicine I need to give me strength—to bear things. (*She turns to* HAZEL)   Listen to him, Hazel! You'd think I was the invalid and not he.

HAZEL   Yes. You've got to take care of yourself, too, Orin.

ORIN   Oh, forget me. I'm all right.

CHRISTINE   We'll play nurses, Hazel and I, and have you your old self again before you know it. Won't we, Hazel?

HAZEL   (*smiling happily*)   Of course we will.

CHRISTINE   Don't stand, dear. You must be worn out. Wait. We'll make you comfortable. Hazel, will you bring me a cushion? (HAZEL *gets a cushion and helps to place it behind his back in the chair at right of table.* ORIN's *eyes light up and he grins boyishly, obviously revelling in being coddled*).

ORIN   How's this for the comforts of home, Peter? The front was never like this, eh?

PETER   Not so you'd notice it!

ORIN   (*with a wink at* HAZEL)   Peter will be getting jealous! You better call Vinnie in to put a pillow behind him!

HAZEL (*with a smile*) I can't picture Vinnie being that soft.

ORIN (*a jealous resentment creeping into his voice*) She can be soft—on occasion. She's always coddling Father and he likes it, although he pretends—

CHRISTINE (*turning away and restraining a shudder*) Orin! You're talking as if he were—alive! (*There is an uncomfortable silence.* HAZEL *goes quietly back to her chair at center.* CHRISTINE *goes around the table to the chair opposite* ORIN *and sits down*).

ORIN (*with a wry smile*) We'd all forgotten he's dead, hadn't we? Well, I can't believe it even yet. I feel him in this house— alive!

CHRISTINE Orin!

ORIN (*strangely*) Everything is changed—in some queer way— this house, Vinnie, you, I—everything but Father. He's the same and always will be—here—the same! Don't you feel that, Mother! (*She shivers, looking before her but doesn't answer*).

HAZEL (*gently*) You mustn't make your mother think of it, Orin.

ORIN (*staring at her—in a queer tone of gratitude*) You're the same, Hazel—sweet and good. (*He turns to his mother accusingly*) At least Hazel hasn't changed, thank God!

CHRISTINE (*rousing herself—turns to force a smile at him*) Hazel will never change, I hope. I am glad you appreciate her. (HAZEL *looks embarrassed.* CHRISTINE *goes on—with motherly solicitude*) Wasn't the long train trip terribly hard on you, dear?

ORIN Well, it wasn't a pleasure trip exactly. My head got aching till I thought it would explode.

CHRISTINE (*leans over and puts her hand on his forehead*) Poor boy! Does it pain now?

ORIN Not much. Not at all when your hand is there. (*Impulsively he takes her hand and kisses it—boyishly*) Gosh, Mother, it feels so darned good to be home with you! (*Then staring at her suspiciously again*) Let me have a good look at you. You're so different. I noticed it even outside. What is it?

CHRISTINE (*avoiding his eyes—forcing a smile*) It's just that I'm getting old, I'm afraid, dear.

ORIN No. You're more beautiful than ever! You're younger, too, somehow. But it isn't that. (*Almost pushing her hand away— bitterly*) Maybe I can guess!

CHRISTINE (*forces a laugh*) Younger and more beautiful! Do you hear him going on, Hazel? He has learned to be very gallant, I must say! (LAVINIA *appears in the doorway at rear. She enters but remains standing just inside the doorway and keeps her eyes fixed on her mother and* ORIN).

ORIN (*who is again looking at* HAZEL, *breaks out harshly*) Do you remember how you waved your handkerchief, Hazel, the day I set off to become a hero? I thought you would sprain your wrist! And all the mothers and wives and sisters and girls did the same! Sometime in some war they ought to make the women take the men's place for a month or so. Give them a taste of murder!

CHRISTINE Orin!

ORIN Let them batter each other's brains out with rifle butts and rip each other's guts with bayonets! After that, maybe they'd stop waving handkerchiefs and gabbing about heroes! (HAZEL *gives a shocked exclamation*)

CHRISTINE Please!

PETER (*gruffly*) Give it a rest, Orin! It's over. Give yourself a chance to forget it. None of us liked it any more than you did.

ORIN (*immediately shamefaced*) You're right, Peter. I'm a damned whining fool! I'm sorry, Hazel. That was rotten of me.

HAZEL It was nothing, Orin. I understand how you feel. Really I do.

ORIN I—I let off steam when I shouldn't. (*Then suddenly*) Do you still sing, Hazel? I used to hear you singing—down there. It made me feel life might still be alive somewhere—that, and my dreams of Mother, and the memory of Vinnie bossing me around like a drill sergeant. I used to hear you singing at the queerest times—so sweet and clear and pure! It would rise above the screams of the dying—

CHRISTINE (*tensely*) I wish you wouldn't talk of death!

LAVINIA (*from the doorway—in a brusque commanding tone like her father's*) Orin! Come and see Father.

ORIN (*starts up from his chair and makes an automatic motion as if to salute—mechanically*) Yes, sir. (*Then confusedly*) What the devil—? You sounded just like him. Don't do that again, for heaven's sake! (*He tries to force a laugh—then shamefacedly*) I meant to look at him the first thing—but I got talking—I'll go in right now.

CHRISTINE (*her voice tense and strained*) No! Wait! (*Angrily to* LAVINIA) Can't you let your brother have a minute to rest? You can see how worn out he is! (*Then to* ORIN) I've hardly had a

chance to say a word to you yet—and it has been so long!
Stay with me a little while, won't you?

ORIN (*touched, coming back to her*) Of course, Mother! You
come before everything!

LAVINIA (*starts to make a bitter retort, glances at* PETER *and*
HAZEL, *then remarks evenly*) Very well. Only remember what I
said, Orin. (*She turns her back and starts to go into the hall*).

CHRISTINE (*frightenedly*) Vinnie! Where are you going?

LAVINIA (*does not answer her but calls back to her brother over
her shoulder*) You'll come in a little while, won't you? (*She
disappears across the hall.* ORIN *gives his mother a sidelong
glance of uneasy suspicion.* CHRISTINE *is desperately trying to
appear calm.* PETER *and* HAZEL *stand up, feeling uncomfortable*).

HAZEL Peter, we really must be getting home.

PETER Yes.

CHRISTINE It was so kind of you to come.

HAZEL (*giving her hand to* ORIN) You must rest all you can now,
Orin—and try not to think about things.

ORIN You're darned kind, Hazel. It's fine to see you again—the
same as ever!

HAZEL (*delighted but pulling her hand away shyly*) I'm glad,
too. Good night, Orin.

PETER (*shakes his hand*) Good night. Rest up and take it easy.

ORIN Good night, Peter. Thanks for meeting me.

CHRISTINE (*goes with them to the hall*) I'm afraid this isn't a very
cheerful house to visit just now—but please come soon again.
You will do Orin more good than anyone, Hazel. (*The look of
suspicion again comes to* ORIN's *eyes. He sits down in the chair
at left of table and stares before him bitterly.* CHRISTINE *returns
from the hall, closing the sliding doors behind her silently. She
stands for a moment looking at* ORIN, *visibly bracing herself
for the ordeal of the coming interview, her eyes full of tense
calculating fear*).

ORIN (*without looking at her*) What's made you take such a
fancy to Hazel all of a sudden? You never used to think much
of her. You didn't want me going around with her.

CHRISTINE (*coming forward and sitting across the table from him—
in her gentle motherly tone*) I was selfish then. I was jealous,
too, I'll confess. But all I want now is your happiness, dear. I
know how much you used to like Hazel—

ORIN (*blurts out*) That was only to make you jealous! (*Then bitterly*) But now you're a widow. I'm not home an hour before you're trying to marry me off! You must be damned anxious to get rid of me again! Why?

CHRISTINE   You mustn't say that! If you knew how horribly lonely I've been without you—

ORIN   So lonely you've written me exactly two letters in the last six months!

CHRISTINE   But I wrote you much more! They must have been lost—

ORIN   I received all of Hazel's letters—and Vinnie's. It's darned funny yours should be the only ones to get lost! (*Unable to hold back any longer, he bursts forth*) Who is this Captain Brant who's been calling on you?

CHRISTINE   (*prepared for this—with well-feigned astonishment*) On me? You mean on Vinnie, don't you? (*Then as* ORIN *looks taken aback*) Wherever did you get that silly idea? Oh, of course, I know! Vinnie must have written you the same nonsense she did your father.

ORIN   She wrote him? What did he do?

CHRISTINE   Why, he laughed at it, naturally! Your father was very fond of Vinnie but he knew how jealous she's always been of me and he realized she'd tell any lie she could to—

ORIN   Oh, come on now, Mother! Just because you're always getting on each other's nerves it doesn't mean Vinnie would ever deliberately—

CHRISTINE   Oh, doesn't it, though? I think you'll discover before you're much older that there isn't anything your sister will stop at—that she will even accuse me of the vilest, most horrible things!

ORIN   Mother! Honestly now! You oughtn't to say that!

CHRISTINE   (*reaching out and taking his hand*) I mean it, Orin. I wouldn't say it to anyone but you. You know that. But we've always been so close, you and I. I feel you are really—my flesh and blood! She isn't! She is your father's! You're a part of me!

ORIN   (*with strange eagerness*) Yes! I feel that, too, Mother!

CHRISTINE   I know I can trust you to understand now as you always used to. (*With a tender smile*) We had a secret little world of our own in the old days, didn't we?—which no one but us knew about.

ORIN (*happily*) You bet we did! No Mannons allowed was our password, remember!

CHRISTINE And that's what your father and Vinnie could never forgive us! But we'll make that little world of our own again, won't we?

ORIN Yes!

CHRISTINE I want to make up to you for all the injustice you suffered at your father's hands. It may seem a hard thing to say about the dead, but he was jealous of you. He hated you because he knew I loved you better than anything in the world!

ORIN (*pressing her hand in both of his—intensely*) Do you, Mother? Do you honestly? (*Then he is struck by what she said about his father—woundedly*) I knew he had it in for me. But I never thought he went as far as to—hate me.

CHRISTINE He did, just the same!

ORIN (*with resentful bitterness*) All right, then! I'll tell you the truth, Mother! I won't pretend to you I'm sorry he's dead!

CHRISTINE (*lowering her voice to a whisper*) Yes. I am glad, too! —that he has left us alone! Oh, how happy we'll be together, you and I, if you only won't let Vinnie poison your mind against me with her disgusting lies!

ORIN (*immediately uneasy again*) What lies? (*He releases her hand and stares at her, morbidly suspicious*) You haven't told me about that Brant yet.

CHRISTINE There's nothing to tell—except in Vinnie's morbid revengeful mind! I tell you, Orin, you can't realize how she's changed while you've been away! She's always been a moody and strange girl, you know that, but since you've gone she has worried and brooded until I really believe she went a little out of her head. She got so she'd say the most terrible things about everyone. You simply wouldn't believe it, if I told you some of the things. And now, with the shock of your father's death on top of everything, I'm convinced she's actually insane. Haven't you noticed how queerly she acts? You must have!

ORIN I saw she'd changed a lot. She seemed strange. But—

CHRISTINE And her craziness all works out in hatred for me! Take this Captain Brant affair, for example—

ORIN Ah!

CHRISTINE A stupid ship captain I happened to meet at your grandfather's who took it into his silly head to call here a few times without being asked. Vinnie thought he was coming to court her. I honestly believe she fell in love with him, Orin. But she soon discovered that he wasn't after her at all!

ORIN   Who was he after—you?

CHRISTINE (*sharply*)   Orin! I'd be very angry with you if it weren't so ridiculous! (*She forces a laugh*) You don't seem to realize I'm an old married woman with two grown-up children! No, all he was after was to insinuate himself as a family friend and use your father when he came home to get him a better ship! I soon saw through his little scheme and he'll never call here again, I promise you that! (*She laughs—then with a teasing air*) And that's the whole of the great Captain Brant scandal! Are you satisfied now, you jealous goose, you?

ORIN (*penitent and happy*)   I'm a fool! The war has got me silly, I guess! If you knew all the hell I've been through!

CHRISTINE   It was Vinnie's fault you ever went to war! I'll never forgive her for that! It broke my heart, Orin! (*Then quickly*) But I was going to give you an example of her insane suspicions from the Captain Brant incident. Would you believe it that she has worked it all out that because his name is Brant, he must be the son of that nurse girl Marie Brantôme? Isn't that crazy? And to imagine for a moment, if he were, he'd ever come here to visit!

ORIN (*his face hardening*)   By God, I'd like to see him! His mother brought disgrace enough on our family without—

CHRISTINE (*frightened, shrinking from him*)   Orin! Don't look like that! You're so like your father! (*Then hurrying on*) But I haven't told you the worst yet. Vinnie actually accuses me—your mother —of being in love with that fool and of having met him in New York and gone to his room! I am no better than a prostitute in your sister's eyes!

ORIN (*stunned*)   I don't believe it! Vinnie couldn't!

CHRISTINE   I told you she'd gone crazy! She even followed me to New York, when I went to see your sick grandfather, to spy on me. She saw me meet a man—and immediately to her crazy brain the man was Brant. Oh, it's too revolting, Orin! You don't know what I've had to put up with from Vinnie, or you'd pity me!

ORIN   Good God! Did she tell Father that? No wonder he's dead! (*Then harshly*) Who was this man you met in New York?

CHRISTINE   It was Mr. Lamar, your grandfather's old friend who has known me ever since I was a baby! I happened to meet him and he asked me to go with him to call on his daughter. (*Then, seeing* ORIN *wavering, pitifully*) Oh, Orin! You pretend to love me! And yet you question me as if you suspected me, too! And you haven't Vinnie's excuse! You aren't out of your mind! (*She weeps hysterically*).

ORIN (*overcome at once by remorse and love*) No! I swear to you! (*He throws himself on his knees beside her and puts his arm around her*) Mother! Please! Don't cry! I do love you! I do!

CHRISTINE I haven't told you the most horrible thing of all! Vinnie suspects me of having poisoned your father!

ORIN (*horrified*) What! No, by God, that's too much! If that's true, she ought to be put in an asylum!

CHRISTINE She found some medicine I take to make me sleep, but she is so crazy I know she thinks— (*Then, with real terror, clinging to him*) Oh, Orin, I'm so afraid of her! God knows what she might do, in her state! She might even go to the police and— Don't let her turn you against me! Remember you're all I have to protect me! You are all I have in the world, dear!

ORIN (*tenderly soothing her*) Turn me against you? She can't be so crazy as to try that! But listen. I honestly think you— You're a little hysterical, you know. That—about Father—is all such damned nonsense! And as for her going to the police—do you suppose I wouldn't prevent that—for a hundred reasons— the family's sake—my own sake and Vinnie's, too, as well as yours—even if I knew—

CHRISTINE (*staring at him—in a whisper*) Knew? Orin, you don't believe—?

ORIN No! For God's sake! I only meant that no matter what you ever did, I love you better than anything in the world and—

CHRISTINE (*in an outburst of grateful joy—pressing him to her and kissing him*) Oh, Orin, you are my boy, my baby! I love you!

ORIN Mother! (*Then seizing her by the shoulders and staring into her eyes—with somber intensity*) I could forgive anything— anything!—in my mother—except that other—that about Brant!

CHRISTINE I swear to you—!

ORIN If I thought that damned—! (*With savage vengefulness*) By God, I'd show you then I hadn't been taught to kill for nothing!

CHRISTINE (*full of new terror now—for* BRANT'S *life—distractedly*) For God's sake, don't talk like that! You're not like my Orin! You're cruel and horrible! You frighten me!

ORIN (*immediately contrite and soothing, petting her*) There, there, Mother! We won't ever think about it again! We'll talk of something else. I want to tell you something. (*He sits on the floor at her feet and looks up into her face. A pause. Then he asks tenderly, taking her hand*) Did you really want me to come back, Mother?

CHRISTINE (*has calmed herself, but her eyes are still terrified and her voice trembles*) What a foolish question, dear.

ORIN But your letters got farther and farther between—and they seemed so cold! It drove me crazy! I wanted to desert and run home—or else get killed! If you only knew how I longed to be here with you—like this! (*He leans his head against her knee. His voice becomes dreamy and low and caressing*) I used to have the most wonderful dreams about you. Have you ever read a book called "Typee"—about the South Sea Islands?

CHRISTINE (*with a start—strangely*) Islands! Where there is peace?

ORIN Then you did read it?

CHRISTINE No.

ORIN Someone loaned me the book. I read it and reread it until finally those Islands came to mean everything that wasn't war, everything that was peace and warmth and security. I used to dream I was there. And later on all the time I was out of my head I seemed really to be there. There was no one there but you and me. And yet I never saw you, that's the funny part. I only felt you all around me. The breaking of the waves was your voice. The sky was the same color as your eyes. The warm sand was like your skin. The whole island was you. (*He smiles with a dreamy tenderness*) A strange notion, wasn't it? But you needn't be provoked at being an island because this was the most beautiful island in the world—as beautiful as you, Mother!

CHRISTINE (*has been staring over his head, listening fascinatedly, more and more deeply moved. As he stops, an agonizing tenderness for him wells up in her—with tortured longing*) Oh, if only you had never gone away! If you only hadn't let them take you from me!

ORIN (*uneasily*) But I've come back. Everything is all right now, isn't it?

CHRISTINE (*hastily*) Yes! I didn't mean that. It had to be.

ORIN And I'll never leave you again now. I don't want Hazel or anyone. (*With a tender grin*) You're my only girl!

CHRISTINE (*again with tenderness, stroking his hair—smiling*)

You're a big man now, aren't you? I can't believe it. It seems only yesterday when I used to find you in your nightshirt hiding in the hall upstairs on the chance that I'd come up and you'd get one more good-night kiss! Do you remember?

ORIN (*with a boyish grin*) You bet I remember! And what a row there was when Father caught me! And do you remember how you used to let me brush your hair and how I loved to? He hated me doing that, too. You've still got the same beautiful hair, Mother. That hasn't changed. (*He reaches up and touches her hair caressingly. She gives a little shudder of repulsion and draws away from him but he is too happy to notice*) Oh, Mother, it's going to be wonderful from now on! We'll get Vinnie to marry Peter and there will be just you and I! (*The sliding doors in rear are opened a little and* LAVINIA *slips silently in and stands looking at them*)

CHRISTINE (*immediately senses her presence—controlling a start, harshly*) What do you want? (ORIN *turns to look at his sister resentfully*).

LAVINIA (*in a flat, emotionless voice*) Aren't you coming in to see Father, Orin?

ORIN (*scrambling to his feet—irritably*) Oh, all right, I'll come now. (*He hurries out past* LAVINIA *with the air of one with a disagreeable duty he wants to get over quickly and closes the door with a bang behind him.* LAVINIA *stares at her mother a moment—then about-faces stiffly to follow him*).

CHRISTINE (*springs to her feet*) Vinnie! (*As* LAVINIA *turns to face her—sharply*) Come here—please. I don't want to shout across the room. (LAVINIA *comes slowly forward until she is at arm's length. Her eyes grow bleak and her mouth tightens to a thin line. The resemblance between mother and daughter as they stand confronting each other is strikingly brought out.* CHRISTINE *begins to speak in a low voice, coolly defiant, almost triumphant*) Well, you can go ahead now and tell Orin anything you wish! I've already told him—so you might as well save yourself the trouble. He said you must be insane! I told him how you lied about my trips to New York—for revenge!—because you loved Adam yourself! (LAVINIA *makes a movement like a faint shudder but is immediately stiff and frozen again.* CHRISTINE *smiles tauntingly*) So hadn't you better leave Orin out of it? You can't get him to go to the police for you. Even if you convinced him I poisoned your father, you couldn't! He doesn't want—any more than you do, or your father, or any of the Mannon dead—such a public disgrace as a murder trial would be! For it would all come out! Everything! Who Adam is and my adultery and your knowledge of it—and your love for Adam! Oh, believe me, I'll see to it that comes out if anything ever gets to a trial! I'll show you to the world as a daughter who desired her mother's lover and then tried to get her mother hanged out of hatred and jealousy! (*She laughs tauntingly.* LAVINIA *is trembling but her face remains hard and emotionless. Her lips open as if to speak but she closes them again.* CHRISTINE *seems drunk with her own defiant recklessness*) Go on! Try and convince Orin of my wickedness! He loves me! He hated his father! He's glad he's dead! Even if he knew I had killed him, he'd protect me! (*Then all her defiant attitude collapses and she pleads, seized by an hysterical terror, by some fear she has kept hidden*) For God's sake, keep Orin out of this! He's still sick! He's changed! He's grown hard and cruel! All he thinks of is death! Don't tell him about Adam! He would kill him! I couldn't live then! I would kill myself! (LAVINIA *starts and her eyes light up with a cruel hatred. Again her pale lips part as if she were about to say something but she controls the impulse and about-faces abruptly and walks with jerky steps from the room like some tragic mechanical doll.* CHRISTINE *stares after her—then as she disappears, collapses, catching at the table for support—terrifiedly*) I've got to see Adam! I've got to warn him! (*She sinks in the chair at right of table*).

*Curtain*

# ACT THREE

ORIN (*ashamed and guilty—bursts out angrily at himself*) Christ, I won't have such thoughts! I am a rotten swine to— Damn Vinnie! She must be crazy! (*Then, as if to distract his mind from these reflections, he turns to gaze down at his father. At the same moment* LAVINIA *appears silently in the doorway from the hall and stands looking at him. He does not notice her entrance. He stares at his father's mask-like face and addresses it with a strange friendly mockery*) Who are you? Another corpse! You and I have seen fields and hillsides sown with them—and they meant nothing!—nothing but a dirty joke life plays on life! (*Then with a dry smile*) Death sits so naturally on you! Death becomes the

Mannons! You were always like a statue of an eminent dead man—sitting on a chair in a park or straddling a horse in a town square—looking over the head of life without a sign of recognition—cutting it dead for the impropriety of living! (*He chuckles to himself with a queer affectionate amusement*) You never cared to know me in life—but I really think we might be friends now you are dead!

LAVINIA (*sternly*)  Orin!

ORIN (*turns to her startledly*)  Damn it, don't sneak around like that! What are you trying to do, anyway? I'm jumpy enough without— (*Then as she turns and locks the door behind her—suspiciously*) What are you locking the door for?

LAVINIA  I've got to talk to you—and I don't want to be interrupted. (*Then sternly*) What made you say such things just then? I wouldn't believe you could have grown so callous to all feeling of respect—

ORIN (*guilty and resentful*)  You folks at home take death so solemnly! You would have soon learned at the front that it's only a joke! You don't understand, Vinnie. You have to learn to mock or go crazy, can't you see? I didn't mean it in an unkind way. It simply struck me he looks so strangely familiar—the same familiar stranger I've never known. (*Then glancing at the dead man with a kindly amused smile*) Do you know his nickname in the army? Old Stick—short for Stick-in-the-Mud. Grant himself started it—said Father was no good on an offensive but he'd trust him to stick in the mud and hold a position until hell froze over!

LAVINIA  Orin! Don't you realize he was your father and he is dead?

ORIN (*irritably*)  What Grant said was a big compliment in a way.

LAVINIA  When I think of how proud of you he was when he came home! He boasted that you had done one of the bravest things he'd seen in the war!

ORIN (*astonished—then grins with bitter mockery*)  One of the bravest things he'd seen! Oh, that's too rich! I'll tell you the joke about that heroic deed. It really began the night before when I sneaked through their lines. I was always volunteering for extra danger. I was so scared anyone would guess I was afraid! There was a thick mist and it was so still you could hear the fog seeping into the ground. I met a Reb crawling toward our lines. His face drifted out of the mist toward mine. I shortened my sword and let him have the point under the ear. He stared at me with an idiotic look as if he'd sat on a tack —and his eyes dimmed and went out— (*His voice has sunk lower and lower, as if he were talking to himself. He pauses and stares over his father's body fascinatedly at nothing*).

LAVINIA (*with a shudder*) Don't think of that now!

ORIN (*goes on with the same air*) Before I'd gotten back I had to kill another in the same way. It was like murdering the same man twice. I had a queer feeling that war meant murdering the same man over and over, and that in the end I would discover the man was myself! Their faces keep coming back in dreams—and they change to Father's face—or to mine— What does that mean, Vinnie?

LAVINIA I don't know! I've got to talk to you! For heaven's sake, forget the war! It's over now!

ORIN Not inside us who killed! (*Then quickly—with a bitter, joking tone*) The rest is all a joke! The next morning I was in the trenches. This was at Petersburg. I hadn't slept. My head was queer. I thought what a joke it would be on the stupid Generals like Father if everyone on both sides suddenly saw the joke war was on them and laughed and shook hands! So I began to laugh and walked toward their lines with my hand out. Of course, the joke was on me and I got this wound in the head for my pains. I went mad, wanted to kill, and ran on, yelling. Then a lot of our fools went crazy, too, and followed me and we captured a part of their line we hadn't dared tackle before. I had acted without orders, of course—but Father decided it was better policy to overlook that and let me be a hero! So do you wonder I laugh!

LAVINIA (*soothingly, coming to him and taking his arm*) You were brave and you know it. I'm proud of you, too.

ORIN (*helplessly*) Oh, all right! Be proud, then! (*He leaves her and sprawls in the chair at left of table. She stands by the head of the bier and faces him. He says resentfully*) Well? Fire away and let's get this over! But you're wasting your breath. I know what you're going to say. Mother warned me. (*The whole memory of what his mother had said rushes over him*) My God, how can you think such things of Mother? What the hell's got into you? (*Then humoringly*) But I realize you're not yourself. I know how hard his death has hit you. Don't you think it would be better to postpone our talk until—

LAVINIA   No! (*Bitterly*) Has she succeeded in convincing you I'm out of my mind? Oh, Orin, how can you be so stupid? (*She goes to him and, grasping him by his shoulders, brings her face close to him—compellingly*) Look at me! You know in your heart I'm the same as I always was—your sister—who loves you, Orin!

ORIN (*moved*)   I didn't mean—I only think the shock of his death—

LAVINIA   I've never lied to you, have I? Even when we were little you always knew I told you the truth, didn't you?

ORIN   Yes—but—

LAVINIA   Then you must believe I wouldn't lie to you now!

ORIN   No one is saying you'd deliberately lie. It's a question of—

LAVINIA   And even if she's got you so under her thumb again that you doubt my word, you can't doubt the absolute proof!

ORIN (*roughly*)   Never mind what you call proofs! I know all about them already! (*Then excitedly*) Now, listen here, if you think you're going to tell me a lot of crazy stuff about Mother, I warn you I won't listen! So shut up before you start!

LAVINIA (*threateningly now*)   If you don't, I'll go to the police!

ORIN   Don't be a damn fool!

LAVINIA   As a last resort I will—if you force me to!

ORIN   By God, you must be crazy even to talk of—!

LAVINIA   They won't think so!

ORIN   Vinnie! Do you realize what it would mean—?

LAVINIA   I realize only too well! You and I, who are innocent, would suffer a worse punishment than the guilty—for we'd have to live on! It would mean that Father's memory and that of all the honorable Mannon dead would be dragged through the horror of a murder trial! But I'd rather suffer that than let the murder of our father go unpunished!

ORIN   Good God, do you actually believe—?

LAVINIA   Yes! I accuse her of murder! (*She takes the little box she has found in* CHRISTINE's *room right after the murder* [Act Four "Homecoming"] *from the bosom of her dress and holds it out to him*) You see this? I found it right after Father died!

ORIN   Don't be a damned lunatic! She told me all about that! It's only some stuff she takes to make her sleep!

LAVINIA (*goes on implacably, ignoring his interruptions*)   And Father knew she'd poisoned him! He said to me, "She's guilty!"

ORIN   That's all your crazy imagination! God, how can you think—? Do you realize you're deliberately accusing your own mother—

It's too horrible and mad! I'll have you declared insane by Doctor Blake and put away in an asylum!

LAVINIA   I swear by our dead father I am telling you the truth! (*She puts her hand on the dead man and addresses him*) Make Orin believe me, Father!

ORIN   (*harshly*) Don't drag him in! He always sided with you against Mother and me! (*He grabs her arm and forces the box from her hand*) Here! Give me that! (*He slips it into his coat pocket*).

LAVINIA   Ah! So you are afraid it's true!

ORIN   No! But I'm going to stop your damned— But I'm a fool to pay any attention to you! The whole thing is too insane! I won't talk to a crazy woman! But, by God, you look out, Vinnie! You leave Mother alone or—!

LAVINIA   (*regarding him bitterly*) Poor Father! He thought the war had made a man of you! But you're not! You're still the spoiled crybaby that she can make a fool of whenever she pleases!

ORIN   (*stung*) That's enough from you!

LAVINIA   Oh, she warned me just now what to expect! She boasted that you wouldn't believe me, and that even if you knew she'd murdered Father you would be glad because you hated him! (*Then a note of entreaty in her voice*) Orin! For God's sake— here, before him!—tell me that isn't true, at least!

ORIN   (*overcome by a sense of guilt—violently defensive*) Of course, I never said that—and I don't believe she did. But Mother means a thousand times more to me than he ever did! I say that before him now as I would if he could hear me!

LAVINIA   (*with a calculated scornful contempt now*) Then if I can't make you see your duty one way, I will another! If you won't help me punish her, I hope you're not such a coward that you're willing to let her lover escape!

ORIN   (*in a tone of awakening suspicion*) Lover? Who do you mean?

LAVINIA   I mean the man who plotted Father's murder with her, who must have got the poison for her! I mean the Captain Brant I wrote you about!

ORIN   (*thickly, trying to fight back his jealous suspicion*) You lie! She told me your rotten lies—about him—about following her to New York. That was Mr. Lamar she met.

LAVINIA   So that's what she told you! As if I could mistake Lamar for Adam Brant! What a fool you are, Orin! She kisses you and pretends she loves you—when she'd forgotten you were ever alive, when all she's thought of is this low lover of hers—!

ORIN (*wildly*) Stop! I won't stand—!

LAVINIA When all she is thinking of right now is how she can use you to keep me from doing anything, so she'll get a chance to run off and marry him!

ORIN You lie!

LAVINIA She pets you and plays the loving mother and you're so blind you can't see through her! I tell you she went to his room! I followed them upstairs. I heard her telling him, "I love you, Adam." She was kissing him!

ORIN (*grabs her by the shoulder and shakes her, forcing her to her knees—frenziedly*) Damn you! Tell me you're lying or—!

LAVINIA (*unafraid—looking up into his eyes—coldly*) You know I'm not lying! She's been going to New York on the excuse of visiting Grandfather Hamel, but really to give herself to—!

ORIN (*in anguish*) You lie, damn you! (*Threateningly*) You dare say that about Mother! Now you've got to prove it or else—! You're not insane! You know what you're saying! So you prove it—or by God, I'll—!

LAVINIA (*taking his hands off her shoulders and rising*) All I ask is a chance to prove it! (*Then intensely*) But when I do, will you help me punish Father's murderers?

ORIN (*in a burst of murderous rage*) I'll kill that bastard! (*In anguished uncertainty again*) But you haven't proved anything yet! It's only your word against hers! I don't believe you! You say Brant is her lover! If that's true, I'll hate her! I'll know she murdered Father then! I'll help you punish her! But you've got to prove it!

LAVINIA (*coldly*) I can do that very soon. She's frightened out of her wits! She'll go to see Brant the first chance she gets. We must give her that chance. Will you believe me when you find them together?

ORIN (*torturedly*) Yes. (*Then in a burst of rage*) God damn him, I'll—!

LAVINIA (*sharply*) Ssshh! Be quiet. There's someone in the hall! (*They wait, staring at the door. Then someone knocks loudly*).

CHRISTINE (*her voice comes through the door, frightened and strained*) Orin!

ORIN (*stammers*) God! I can't face her now!

LAVINIA (*in a quick whisper*) Don't let her know you suspect her. Pretend you think I'm out of my mind, as she wanted you to.

CHRISTINE Orin! Why don't you answer me? (*She tries the door-knob, and finding the door locked, her voice becomes terrified*) Why have you locked me out? Let me in! (*She pounds on the door violently*).

LAVINIA (*in a whisper*) Answer her. Let her in.

ORIN (*obeying mechanically—calls in a choked voice*) All right. I'm coming. (*He moves reluctantly toward the door*).

LAVINIA (*struck by a sudden idea—grasps his arm*) Wait! (*Before he can prevent it, she reaches in his pocket and gets possession of the box and puts it conspicuously on the body over the dead man's heart*) Watch her when she sees that—if you want proof!

CHRISTINE Open the door! (*He forces himself to open the door and steps aside.* CHRISTINE *almost falls in. She is in a state bordering on collapse. She throws her arms around* ORIN *as if seeking protection from him*) Orin! I got so afraid—when I found the door locked!

ORIN (*controls a furious jealous impulse to push her violently away from him—harshly*) What made you afraid, Mother?

CHRISTINE (*stammers*) Why do you look at me—like that? You look—so like—your father!

ORIN I am his son, too, remember that!

LAVINIA (*warningly*) Orin!

CHRISTINE (*turning on* LAVINIA *who stands by the head of the bier*) I suppose you've been telling him your vile lies, you—

ORIN (*remembering his instructions, forces himself to blurt out*) She—she's out of her head, Mother.

CHRISTINE Didn't I tell you! I knew you'd see that! (*Then anxiously, keeping her eyes on* LAVINIA) Did she tell you what she's going to do, Orin? I know she's plotting something—crazy! Did she threaten to go to the police? They might not believe she's crazy— (*Pleading desperately, her eyes still on* LAVINIA) You won't let her do anything dreadful like that, will you?

ORIN (*feeling her guilt, stammers*) No, Mother.

CHRISTINE (*her eyes, which have been avoiding the corpse, now fasten on the dead man's face with fascinated horror*) No— remember your father wouldn't want—any scandal—he mustn't be worried, he said—he needs rest and peace— (*She addresses the dead man directly in a strange tone of defiant scorn*) You seem the same to me in death, Ezra! You were always dead to me! I hate the sight of death! I hate the thought of it! (*Her eyes shift from his face and she sees the box of poison. She starts back with a stifled scream and stares at it with guilty fear*).

ORIN   Mother! For God's sake, be quiet! (*The strain snaps for him and he laughs with savage irony*) God! To think I hoped home would be an escape from death! I should never have come back to life—from my island of peace! (*Then staring at his mother strangely*) But that's lost now! You're my lost island, aren't you, Mother? (*He turns and stumbles blindly from the room.* LAVINIA *reaches out stealthily and snatches up the box. This breaks the spell for* CHRISTINE *whose eyes have been fixed on it hypnotically. She looks wildly at* LAVINIA's *frozen accusing face*).

LAVINIA (*in a cold, grim voice*)   It was Brant who got you this—medicine to make you sleep—wasn't it?

CHRISTINE (*distractedly*)   No! No! No!

LAVINIA   You're telling me it was. I knew it—but I wanted to make sure. (*She puts the box back in the bosom of her dress—turns, rigid and square-shouldered, and walks woodenly from the room*).

CHRISTINE (*stares after her wildly, then her eyes fasten again on the dead man's face. Suddenly she appeals to him distractedly*) Ezra! Don't let her harm Adam! I am the only guilty one! Don't let Orin—! (*Then, as if she read some answer in the dead man's face, she stops in terror and, her eyes still fixed on his face, backs to the door and rushes out*).

*Curtain*

# ACT FOUR

THE *stern section of a clipper ship moored alongside a wharf in East Boston, with the floor of the wharf in the foreground. The vessel lies with her bow and amidships off left and only the part aft of the mizzenmast is visible with the curve of the stern at right. The ship is unloaded and her black side rises nine or ten feet above the level of the wharf. On the poop deck above, at right, is the wheel. At left is the chart room and the entrance to the companionway stairs leading below to the cabin. At extreme left is the mizzenmast, the lowest yard just visible above, the boom of the spanker extending out above the deck to the right. Below the deck the portholes show a faint light from the interior of the cabin. On the wharf the end of a warehouse is at left front.*

*It is a night two days after Act Two—the day following* EZRA MANNON's *funeral. The moon is rising above the horizon off left rear, its light accentuating the black outlines of the ship.*

*Borne on the wind the melancholy refrain of the capstan chanty "Shenandoah," sung by a chantyman with the crew coming in on the chorus, drifts over the water from a ship that is weighing anchor in the harbor. Half in and half out of the shadow of the warehouse, the* CHANTYMAN *lies sprawled on his back, snoring in a drunken slumber. The sound of the singing seems to strike a responsive chord in his brain, for he stirs, grunts, and with difficulty raises himself to a sitting position in the moonlight beyond the shadow.*

*He is a thin, wiry man of sixty-five or so, with a tousled mop of black hair, unkempt black beard and mustache. His weather-beaten face is dissipated, he has a weak mouth, his big round blue eyes are bloodshot, dreamy and drunken. But there is something romantic, a queer troubadour-of-the-sea quality about him.*

CHANTYMAN (*listens to the singing with critical disapproval*)  A hell of a chantyman that feller be! Screech owls is op'ry singers compared to him! I'll give him a taste of how "Shenandoah" ought t' be sung! (*He begins to sing in a surprisingly good tenor voice, a bit blurry with booze now and sentimentally mournful to a degree, but still managing to get full value out of the chanty*)

"Oh, Shenandoah, I long to hear you—
A-way, my rolling river!
Oh, Shenandoah, I can't get near you—
Way—ay, I'm bound away
Across the wide Missouri!

"Oh, Shenandoah, I love your daughter
A-way, my rolling river!"

(*He stops abruptly, shaking his head—mournfully*) No good! Too drunk to do myself jestice! Pipe down, my John! Sleep it off! (*He sprawls back on his elbows—confusedly*) Where am I? What the hell difference is it? There's plenty o' fresh air and the moon fur a glim. Don't be so damn pertic'lar! What ye want anyways? Featherbed an' a grand piany? (*He sings with a maudlin zest*).

"A bottle o' wine and a bottle o' beer
And a bottle of Irish whiskey oh!
So early in the morning
The sailor likes his bottle oh!"

(*He stops and mutters*) Who'll buy a drink fur the slickest chantyman on the Western or any other damn ocean? Go to hell then! I kin buy it myself! (*He fumbles in his pants pocket*) I had it in this pocket—I remember I put it there pertic'lar—ten dollars in this pocket— (*He pulls the pocket inside out—with bewildered drunken anger*) By Christ, it's gone! I'm plucked clean! (*He struggles to a sitting position*) Where was I last? Aye, I remember! That yaller-haired pig with the pink dress on! Put her arm around me so lovin'! Told me how fine I could sing! (*He scrambles unsteadily to his feet*) By Christ, I'll go back an' give her a seaboot in her fat tail that'll learn her—! (*He takes a step but lurches into the shadow and leans against the warehouse*) Hard down! Heavy gales around Cape Stiff! All is sunk but honor, as the feller says, an' there's damn little o' that afloat! (*He stands against the warehouse, waiting for the sway-ing world to subside. The companionway door on the poop deck of the vessel is opened and* ADAM BRANT *comes cautiously out. He looks around him quickly with an uneasy suspicious air. He is dressed in a merchant captain's blue uniform. Satisfied that there is no one on the deck, he comes to the rail and stares expectantly up the wharf, off left. His attitude is tense and nervous and he keeps one hand in his coat pocket. The* CHANTY-MAN *loses his balance, lurches forward, then back against the warehouse with a thump.* BRANT *leaps back from the rail star-tledly, jerking a revolver from his coat pocket—then leans over the rail again and calls threateningly*).

BRANT Who's there? Come out and let me have a look at you or by God I'll shoot!

CHANTYMAN (*stares up, startled in his turn and momentarily so-bered—hastily*) Easy goes, shipmate! Stow that pistol! I'm doin' you no harm. (*He lurches out into the moonlight—suddenly pug-nacious*) Not that I'm skeered o' you or your shooter! Who the hell are you to be threatenin' the life of an honest chantyman? Tryin' to hold me up, air ye? I been robbed once tonight! I'll go to the police station and tell 'em there's a robber here—

BRANT (*hastily, with a placating air*) No harm meant. I'm skipper of this vessel and there have been a lot of waterfront thieves around here lately. I'm lacking a watchman and I've got to keep my weather eye open.

CHANTYMAN (*again momentarily sobered—touching his forehead*) Aye—aye, sir. Mind your eye. I heer'd tell robbers broke in the "Annie Lodge's" cabin two nights back. Smashed everything and stole two hundred dollars off her skipper. Murderous, too, they be! Near beat the watchman's brains out! (*Then drunken pugnaciousness comes over him again*) Think I'm one o' that gang, do ye? Come down out o' that and I'll show ye who's a thief! I don't give a damn if ye air a skipper! Ye could be Bully Watermann himself an' I'd not let you insult me! I ain't signed on your old hooker! You've got no rights over me! I'm on dry land, by Christ, and this is a free country and— (*His voice has risen to a shout.* BRANT *is alarmed that this uproar will attract someone. He puts the pistol back in his pocket hastily and peers anxiously down the wharf. Then he interrupts the* CHANTYMAN's *tirade by a sharp command*).

BRANT  Stow your damned jaw! Or, by the Eternal, I'll come down and pound some sense in your head!

CHANTYMAN  (*automatically reacts to the voice of authority—quietly*) Aye—aye, sir. (*Then inconsequentially*) You ain't needin' a chantyman fur your next vi'ge, are ye, sir?

BRANT  I'm not sailing for a month yet. If you're still out of a job then—

CHANTYMAN  (*proudly*) You don't know me, that's plain! I'm the finest damn chantyman that ever put a tune to his lip! I ain't lookin' fur berths—they're lookin' fur me! Aye! Skippers are on'y too glad to git me! Many's a time I've seed a skipper an' mates sweatin' blood to beat work out of a crew but nary a lick could they git into 'em till I raised a tune—and then there'd be full sail on her afore ye knowed it!

BRANT  (*impatiently*) I'm not doubting your ability. But I'd advise you to turn in and sleep it off.

CHANTYMAN  (*not heeding this—sadly*) Aye, but it ain't fur long, steam is comin' in, the sea is full o' smoky tea-kettles, the old days is dyin', an' where'll you an' me be then? (*Lugubriously drunken again*) Everything is dyin'! Abe Lincoln is dead. I used to ship on the Mannon packets an' I seed in the paper where Ezra Mannon was dead! (BRANT *starts guiltily. The* CHANTYMAN *goes on maudlinly*) Heart failure killed him, it said, but I know better! I've sailed on Mannon hookers an' been worked t' death and gotten swill fur grub, an' I know he didn't have no heart in him! Open him up an' you'd find a dried turnip! The old skin-flint must have left a pile o' money. Who gits it, I wonder? Leave a widder, did he?

BRANT  (*harshly*) How would I know? (*Changing the subject calculatingly*) What are you doing here, Chantyman? I'd expect a man with your voice would be in a saloon, singing and making merry!

CHANTYMAN  So I would! So I would! But I was robbed, sir—aye —an' I know who done it—a yaller-haired wench had her arm around me. Steer clear o' gals or they'll skin your hide off an' use it fur a carpet! I warn ye, skipper! They're not fur sailormen like you an' me, 'less we're lookin' fur sorrow! (*Then insinuatingly*) I ain't got the price of a drink, that's why I'm here, sir.

BRANT  (*reaches in his pocket and tosses him down a silver dollar*) Here!

CHANTYMAN  (*fumbles around and finds the dollar*) Thank ye sir.

(*Then flatteringly*) It's a fine ship you've got there, sir. Crack sail on her and she'll beat most of 'em—an' you're the kind to crack sail on, I kin tell by your cut.

BRANT (*pleased, glancing up at his ship's lofty rig*)  Aye! I'll make her go right enough!

CHANTYMAN  All you need is a good chantyman to help ye. Here's "Hanging Johnny" fur ye! (BRANT *starts at this. The* CHANTYMAN *suddenly begins to sing the chanty "Hanging Johnny" with sentimental mournfulness*)

"Oh, they call me Hanging Johnny
Away—ay—i—oh!
They says I hangs for money
Oh, hang, boys, hang!"

BRANT (*harshly*)  Stop that damned dirge! And get out of here! Look lively now!

CHANTYMAN (*starting to go*)  Aye—aye, sir. (*Then resentfully*) I see ye ain't got much ear fur music. Good night.

BRANT (*with exasperated relief*)  Good night. (*The* CHANTYMAN *goes unsteadily off left, between the warehouse and the ship. He bursts again into his mournful dirge, his voice receding*)

"They say I hanged my mother
Away—ay—i—oh!
They say I hanged my mother
Oh, hang, boys, hang!"

(BRANT, *standing by the rail looking after him, mutters a curse and starts pacing up and down the deck*) Damn that chanty! It's sad as death! I've a foreboding I'll never take this ship to sea. She doesn't want me now—a coward hiding behind a woman's skirts! The sea hates a coward! (*A woman's figure dressed in black, heavily veiled, moves stealthily out from the darkness between the ship and the warehouse, left. She sees the figure on the deck above her and shrinks back with a stifled gasp of fear.* BRANT *hears the noise. Immediately his revolver is in his hand and he peers down into the shadows of the warehouse*) Who's there?

CHRISTINE (*with a cry of relief*)  Adam!

BRANT  Christine! (*Then quickly*) Go back to the gangplank. I'll meet you there. (*She goes back. He hurries along the deck and disappears off left to meet her. Their voices are heard and a moment later they enter on the poop deck, from left. She leans against him weakly and he supports her with his arm around her*) I have to bring you this way. I bolted the door to the main deck.

CHRISTINE  I was so frightened! I wasn't sure which ship! Some drunken man came along singing—

BRANT  Aye. I just got rid of him. I fired the watchman this morning so I'd be alone at night. I was hoping you'd come soon. Did that drunk see you?

CHRISTINE  No. I hid behind some boxes. (*Then frightenedly*) Why have you got that pistol?

BRANT  (*grimly*)  I was going to give them a fight for it—if things went wrong.

CHRISTINE  Adam!

BRANT  By God, you don't think I'll ever let them take me alive, do you?

CHRISTINE  Please, please! Don't talk of that for a moment! Only hold me close to you! Tell me you love me!

BRANT  (*harshly*)  It's no time! I want to know what's happened! (*Then immediately repentant he kisses her—with rough tenderness*) Don't mind me! My nerves are gone from waiting alone here not knowing anything but what I read in the papers—that he was dead. These last days have been hell!

CHRISTINE  If you knew what they have been for me!

BRANT  There's something gone wrong! I can read that in your face! What is it, Christine?

CHRISTINE  (*falteringly*)  Vinnie knows—! She came into the room when he was dying! He told her—

BRANT  (*harshly*)  God! What is she going to do? (*Then, without giving her time to answer his question, he suddenly looks around uneasily*) Christine! How did you get away? She'd suspect you weren't going to your father's now. She followed you once before—

CHRISTINE  No. It's all right. This morning Orin said his cousins, the Bradfords, had invited him and Vinnie to visit them overnight at Blackridge and he was taking Vinnie with him because he thought a change would bring her back to her senses. I've made him think she's out of her head with grief—so he wouldn't listen to her—

BRANT (*eagerly*) And he believes that?

CHRISTINE (*weakly*) Yes—he does—now—but I don't know how long—

BRANT Ah!

CHRISTINE So I told him by all means to go. It gave me the chance I wanted to come to you. They went this morning. They don't know I've gone and even after they've found out they can't prove where I went. I can only stay a little while, Adam— we've got to plan—so many things have happened I couldn't foresee—I came to warn you—

BRANT Ssshh! Come below in the cabin! We're fools to be talking out here. (*He guides her with his arm around her through the door to the companionway stairs and closes it quietly behind them. A pause in which the singing of the crew on the ship in the harbor comes mournfully over the water. Then* ORIN *and* LAVINIA *come in stealthily along the deck from the left. She is dressed in black as before. He wears a long cloak over his uniform and has a slouch hat pulled down over his eyes. Her manner is cold and grim.* ORIN *is holding in a savage, revengeful rage. They approach the cabin skylight silently.* ORIN *bends down by it to listen. His face, in the light from the skylight, becomes distorted with jealous fury.* LAVINIA *puts a restraining hand on his arm.*

*The scene fades out into darkness. Several minutes are supposed to elapse. When the light comes on again, a section of the ship has been removed to reveal the interior of the cabin, a small compartment, the walls newly painted a light brown. The skylight giving on the deck above is in the middle of the ceiling. Suspended in the skylight is a ship's compass. Beneath it is a pine table with three chairs, one at rear, the other two at the table ends, left and right. On the table is a bottle of whiskey, half full, with a glass and a pitcher of water.*

*Built against the right wall of the cabin is a long narrow couch, like a bunk, with leather cushions. In the rear wall, at right, is a door leading into the captain's stateroom. A big sideboard stands against the left wall, center. Above it, a ship's clock. Farther back is a door opening on the alleyway leading to the main deck. The companionway stairs lead down to this alleyway.*

*There is a lighted lamp on the sideboard and a ship's lantern, also lighted, at the right end of the table.*

*In the cabin,* BRANT *is seated at the right of table,* CHRISTINE *to the rear of it. Her face looks haggard and ageing, the mouth pinched and drawn down at the corners, and her general appearance, the arrangement of her hair and clothes, has the dishevelled touch of the fugitive. She is just finishing her story of the murder and the events following it. He is listening tensely.*

    *On the deck above,* ORIN *and* LAVINIA *are discovered as before, with* ORIN *bending down by the transom, listening*).

CHRISTINE   When he was dying he pointed at me and told her I was guilty! And afterwards she found the poison—

BRANT (*springing to his feet*)   For God's sake, why didn't you—

CHRISTINE (*pitifully*)   I fainted before I could hide it! And I had planned it all so carefully. But how could I foresee that she would come in just at that moment? And how could I know he would talk to me the way he did? He drove me crazy! He kept talking of death! He was torturing me! I only wanted him to die and leave me alone!

BRANT (*his eyes lighting up with savage satisfaction*)   He knew before he died whose son I was, you said? By God, I'll bet that maddened him!

CHRISTINE (*repeats pitifully*)   I'd planned it so carefully—but something made things happen!

BRANT (*overcome by gloomy dejection, sinks down on his chair again*)   I knew it! I've had a feeling in my bones! It serves me right, what has happened and is to happen! It wasn't that kind of revenge I had sworn on my mother's body! I should have done as I wanted—fought with Ezra Mannon as two men fight for love of a woman! (*With bitter self-contempt*) I have my father's rotten coward blood in me, I think! Aye!

CHRISTINE   Adam! You make me feel so guilty!

BRANT (*rousing himself—shamefacedly*)   I didn't mean to blame you, Christine. (*Then harshly*) It's too late for regrets now, anyway. We've got to think what to do.

CHRISTINE   Yes! I'm so terrified of Vinnie! Oh, Adam, you must promise me to be on your guard every minute! If she convinces Orin you are my lover— Oh, why can't we go away, Adam? Once we're out of her reach, she can't do anything.

BRANT   The "Flying Trades" won't be sailing for a month or more. We can't get cargo as soon as the owners thought.

CHRISTINE   Can't we go on another ship—as passengers—to the East—we could be married out there—

BRANT (*gloomily*) But everyone in the town would know you were gone. It would start suspicion—

CHRISTINE No. Orin and Vinnie would lie to people. They'd have to for their own sakes. They'd say I was in New York with my father. Oh, Adam, it's the only thing we can do! If we don't get out of Vinnie's reach right away I know something horrible will happen!

BRANT (*dejectedly*) Aye. I suppose it's the only way out for us now. The "Atlantis" is sailing on Friday for China. I'll arrange with her skipper to give us passage—and keep his mouth shut. She sails at daybreak Friday. You'd better meet me here Thursday night. (*Then with an effort*) I'll write Clark and Dawson tonight they'll have to find another skipper for the "Flying Trades."

CHRISTINE (*noticing the hurt in his tone—miserably*) Poor Adam! I know how it hurts you to give up your ship.

BRANT (*rousing himself guiltily—pats her hand—with gruff tenderness*) There are plenty of ships—but there is only one you, Christine!

CHRISTINE I feel so guilty! I've brought you nothing but misfortune!

BRANT You've brought love—and the rest is only the price. It's worth it a million times! You're all mine now, anyway! (*He hugs her to him, staring over her head with sad blank eyes*).

CHRISTINE (*her voice trembling*) But I'm afraid I'm not much to boast about having—now. I've grown old in the past few days. I'm ugly. But I'll make myself beautiful again—for you—! I'll make up to you for everything! Try not to regret your ship too much, Adam!

BRANT (*gruffly*) Let's not talk of her any more. (*Then forcing a wry smile*) I'll give up the sea. I think it's through with me now anyway! The sea hates a coward.

CHRISTINE (*trying pitifully to cheer him*) Don't talk like that! You have me, Adam! You have me! And we will be happy—once we're safe on your Blessed Islands! (*Then suddenly, with a little shudder*) It's strange. Orin was telling me of an island— (*On the deck above,* ORIN, *who has bent closer to the transom, straightens up with a threatening movement.* LAVINIA *grips his arm, restraining him*).

BRANT (*with a bitter, hopeless yearning*) Aye—the Blessed Isles— Maybe we can still find happiness and forget! (*Then strangely, as if to himself*) I can see them now—so close—and a million miles away! The warm earth in the moonlight, the trade winds rustling the coco palms, the surf on the barrier reef singing a croon in your ears like a lullaby! Aye! There's peace, and forgetfulness for us there—if we can ever find those islands now!

CHRISTINE (*desperately*) We will find them! We will! (*She kisses him. A pause. Suddenly she glances frightenedly at the clock*) Look at the time! I've got to go, Adam!

BRANT For the love of God, watch out for Vinnie. If anything happened to you now—!

CHRISTINE Nothing will happen to me. But you must be on your guard in case Orin— Good-bye, my lover! I must go! I must! (*She tears herself from his arms but immediately throws herself in them again—terrifiedly*) Oh! I feel so strange—so sad—as if I'd never see you again! (*She begins to sob hysterically*) Oh, Adam, tell me you don't regret! Tell me we're going to be happy! I can't bear this horrible feeling of despair!

BRANT Of course we'll be happy! Come now! It's only a couple of days. (*They start for the door*) We'll go by the main deck. It's shorter. I'll walk to the end of the wharf with you. I won't go further. We might be seen.

CHRISTINE Then we don't have to say good-bye for a few minutes yet! Oh, thank God! (*They go out to the alleyway,* BRANT *closing the door behind him. A pause. On the deck above* ORIN *pulls a revolver from under his cloak and makes a move, as if to rush off left down to the main deck after them.* LAVINIA *has been dreading this and throws herself in his way, grasping his arm*).

ORIN (*in a furious whisper*) Let me go!

LAVINIA (*struggling with him*) No! Be quiet! Ssshh! I hear them on the main deck! Quick! Come to his cabin! (*She urges him to the companionway door, gets him inside and shuts the door behind them. A moment later the door on the left of the cabin below is opened and they enter*).

LAVINIA He's going to the end of the wharf. That gives us a few minutes. (*Grimly*) You wanted proof! Well, are you satisfied now?

ORIN Yes! God damn him! Death is too good for him! He ought to be—

LAVINIA (*sharply commanding*) Orin! Remember you promised not to lose your head. You've got to do everything exactly as we planned it, so there'll be no suspicion about us. There would be no justice if we let ourselves—

ORIN (*impatiently*) You've said all that before! Do you think I'm a fool? I'm not anxious to be hanged—for that skunk! (*Then with bitter anguish*) I heard her asking him to kiss her! I heard her warn him against me! (*He gives a horrible chuckle*) And my island I told her about—which was she and I—she wants to go there—with him! (*Then furiously*) Damn you! Why did you stop me? I'd have shot his guts out in front of her!

LAVINIA (*scornfully*) Outside on deck where the shot would be sure to be heard? We'd have been arrested—and then I'd have to tell the truth to save us. She'd be hanged, and even if we managed to get off, our lives would be ruined! The only person to come off lucky would be Brant! He could die happy, knowing he'd revenged himself on us more than he ever dared hope! Is that what you want?

ORIN (*sullenly*) No.

LAVINIA Then don't act like a fool again. (*Looks around the cabin calculatingly—then in a tone of command*) Go and hide outside. He won't see you when he passes along the alleyway in the dark. He'll come straight in here. That's the time for you—

ORIN (*grimly*) You needn't tell me what to do. I've had a thorough training at this game—thanks to you and Father.

LAVINIA Quick! Go out now! He won't be long!

ORIN (*goes to the door—then quickly*) I hear him coming. (*He slips out silently. She hurriedly hides herself by the sideboard at left, front. A moment later* BRANT *appears in the doorway and stands just inside it blinking in the light. He looks around the cabin sadly*).

BRANT (*huskily*) So it's good-bye to you, "Flying Trades"! And you're right! I wasn't man enough for you! (ORIN *steps through the door and with the pistol almost against* BRANT's *body fires twice.* BRANT *pitches forward to the floor by the table, rolls over, twitches a moment on his back and lies still.* ORIN *springs forward and stands over the body, his pistol aimed down at it, ready to fire again*).

LAVINIA (*stares fascinatedly at* BRANT's *still face*) Is he—dead?

ORIN Yes.

LAVINIA (*sharply*) Don't stand there! Where's the chisel you brought? Smash open everything in his stateroom. We must make it look as if thieves killed him, remember! Take anything valuable! We can sink it overboard afterwards! Hurry! (ORIN *puts his revolver on the table and takes a chisel that is stuck in his belt under his cloak and goes into the stateroom. A moment later there is the sound of splintering wood as he pries open a drawer*).

LAVINIA (*goes slowly to the body and stands looking down into* BRANT'S *face. Her own is frozen and expressionless. A pause.* ORIN *can be heard in the stateroom prying open* BRANT'S *desk and scattering the contents of drawers around. Finally* LAVINIA *speaks to the corpse in a grim bitter tone*) How could you love that vile old woman so? (*She throws off this thought—harshly*) But you're dead! It's ended! (*She turns away from him resolutely —then suddenly turns back and stands stiffly upright and grim beside the body and prays coldly, as if carrying out a duty*) May God find forgiveness for your sins! May the soul of our cousin, Adam Mannon, rest in peace! (ORIN *comes in from the stateroom and overhears the last of her prayer*).

ORIN (*harshly*) Rest in hell, you mean! (*He comes to her*) I've pried open everything I could find.

LAVINIA Then come along. Quick. There's your pistol. Don't forget that. (*She goes to the door*).

ORIN (*putting it in his pocket*) We've got to go through his pockets to make everything look like a burglary. (*He quickly turns* BRANT'S *pockets inside out and puts the revolver he finds, along with bills and coins, watch and chain, knife, etc., into his own*) I'll sink these overboard from the dock, along with what was in his stateroom. (*Having finished this, he still remains stooping over the body and stares into* BRANT'S *face, a queer fascinated expression in his eyes*).

LAVINIA (*uneasily*) Orin!

ORIN By God, he does look like Father!

LAVINIA No! Come along!

ORIN (*as if talking to himself*) This is like my dream. I've killed him before—over and over.

LAVINIA Orin!

ORIN Do you remember me telling you how the faces of the men I killed came back and changed to Father's face and finally became my own? (*He smiles grimly*) He looks like me, too! Maybe I've committed suicide!

LAVINIA (*frightenedly—grabbing his arm*) Hurry! Someone may come!

ORIN (*not heeding her, still staring at* BRANT—*strangely*) If I had been he I would have done what he did! I would have loved her as he loved her—and killed Father too—for her sake!

LAVINIA (*tensely—shaking him by the arm*)  Orin, for God's sake, will you stop talking crazy and come along? Do you want us to be found here? (*She pulls him away forcibly*).

ORIN (*with a last look at the dead man*)  It's queer! It's a rotten dirty joke on someone! (*He lets her hustle him out to the alleyway*).

*Curtain*

# ACT FIVE

SCENE—*The same as Act Three of "Homecoming"—exterior of the Mannon house. It is the following night. The moon has just risen. The right half of the house is in the black shadow cast by the pine trees but the moonlight falls full on the part to the left of the doorway. The door at center is open and there is a light in the hall behind. All the shutters of the windows are closed.*

*CHRISTINE is discovered walking back and forth on the drive before the portico, passing from moonlight into the shadow of the pines and back again. She is in a frightful state of tension, unable to keep still.*

*She sees someone she is evidently expecting approaching the house from up the drive, off left, and she hurries down as far as the bench to meet her.*

HAZEL (*enters from left—with a kindly smile*) Here I am! Seth brought your note and I hurried right over.

CHRISTINE (*kissing her—with unnatural effusiveness*) I'm so glad you've come! I know I shouldn't have bothered you.

HAZEL It's no bother at all, Mrs. Mannon. I'm only too happy to keep you company.

CHRISTINE I was feeling so terribly sad—and nervous here. I had let Hannah and Annie have the night off. I'm all alone. (*She sits on the bench*) Let's sit out here. I can't bear it in the house. (HAZEL *sits beside her*).

HAZEL (*pityingly*) I know. It must be terribly lonely for you. You must miss him so much.

CHRISTINE (*with a shudder*) Please don't talk about— He is buried! He is gone!

HAZEL (*gently*) He is at peace, Mrs. Mannon.

CHRISTINE (*with bitter mockery*) I was like you once! I believed in heaven! Now I know there is only hell!

HAZEL Ssshh! You mustn't say that.

CHRISTINE (*rousing herself—forcing a smile*) I'm not fit company for a young girl, I'm afraid. You should have youth and beauty and freedom around you. I'm old and ugly and haunted by death! (*Then, as if to herself—in a low desperate tone*) I can't let myself get ugly! I can't!

HAZEL You're only terribly worn out. You ought to try and sleep.

CHRISTINE I don't believe there's such a thing on this earth as sleep! It's only in the earth one sleeps! One must feel so at peace—at last—with all one's fears ended! (*Then forcing a laugh*) Good heavens, what a bore it must be for you, listening to my gloomy thoughts! I honestly didn't send for you to— I wanted to ask if you or Peter had heard anything from Orin and Vinnie.

HAZEL (*surprised*) Why, no. We haven't seen them since the funeral.

CHRISTINE (*forcing a smile*) They seem to have deserted me. (*Then quickly*) I mean they should have been home before this. I can't imagine what's keeping them. They went to Blackridge to stay overnight at the Bradfords'.

HAZEL Then there's nothing to worry about. But I don't see how they could leave you alone—just now.

CHRISTINE Oh, that part is all right. I urged them to go. They left soon after the funeral, and afterwards I thought it would be a good opportunity for me to go to New York and see my father. He's sick, you know, but I found him so much better I decided to come home again last night. I expected Vinnie and Orin back this noon, but here it's night and no sign of them. I—I must confess I'm worried—and frightened. You can't know the horror of being all night—alone in that house! (*She glances at the house behind her with a shudder*).

HAZEL Would it help you if I stayed with you tonight—I mean if they don't come?

CHRISTINE (*eagerly*) Oh, would you? (*Hysterical tears come to her eyes. She kisses* HAZEL *with impulsive gratitude*) I can't tell you how grateful I'd be! You're so good! (*Then forcing a laugh*) But it's an imposition to ask you to face such an ordeal. I can't stay still. I'm terrified at every sound. You would have to sit up.

HAZEL Losing a little sleep won't hurt me any.

CHRISTINE I mustn't sleep! If you see me falling asleep you must promise to wake me!

HAZEL But it's just what you need.

CHRISTINE  Yes—afterwards—but not now. I must keep awake. (*In tense desperation*) I wish Orin and Vinnie would come!

HAZEL  (*worriedly*) Perhaps Orin got so sick he wasn't able to. Oh, I hope that isn't it! (*Then getting up*) If I'm going to stay all night I'll have to run home and tell Mother, so she won't worry.

CHRISTINE  Yes—do. (*Then frightenedly*) You won't be long, will you? I'm afraid—to be alone.

HAZEL  (*kisses her—pityingly*) I'll be as quick as I possibly can. (*She walks down the drive, off left, waving her hand as she disappears.* CHRISTINE *stands by the bench—then begins to pace back and forth again*).

CHRISTINE  (*her eyes caught by something down the drive—in a tense whisper*) She's met someone by the gate! Oh, why am I so afraid! (*She turns, seized by panic, and runs to the house— then stops at the top of the steps and faces around, leaning against a column for support*) Oh, God, I'm afraid to know! (*A moment later* ORIN *and* LAVINIA *come up the drive from the left.* LAVINIA *is stiffly square-shouldered, her eyes hard, her mouth grim and set.* ORIN *is in a state of morbid excitement. He carries a newspaper in his hand*).

ORIN  (*speaking to* VINNIE *as they enter—harshly*) You let me do the talking! I want to be the one— (*He sees his mother— startledly*) Mother! (*Then with vindictive mockery*) Ah! So this time at least you are waiting to meet me when I come home!

CHRISTINE  (*stammers*) Orin! What kept you—?

ORIN  We just met Hazel. She said you were terribly frightened at being alone here. That is strange—when you have the memory of Father for company!

CHRISTINE  You—you stayed all this time—at the Bradfords'?

ORIN  We didn't go to the Bradfords'!

CHRISTINE  (*stupidly*) You didn't go—to Blackridge?

ORIN  We took the train there but we decided to stay right on and go to Boston instead.

CHRISTINE  (*terrifiedly*) To—Boston—?

ORIN  And in Boston we waited until the evening train got in. We met that train.

CHRISTINE  Ah!

ORIN  We had an idea you would take advantage of our being in Blackridge to be on it—and you were! And we followed you when you called on your lover in his cabin!

CHRISTINE (*with a pitiful effort at indignation*) Orin! How dare you talk—! (*Then brokenly*) Orin! Don't look at me like that! Tell me—

ORIN Your lover! Don't lie! You've lied enough, Mother! I was on deck, listening! What would you have done if you had discovered me? Would you have gotten your lover to murder me, Mother? I heard you warning him against me! But your warning was no use!

CHRISTINE (*chokingly*) What—? Tell me—!

ORIN I killed him!

CHRISTINE (*with a cry of terror*) Oh—oh! I knew! (*Then clutching at* ORIN) No—Orin! You—you're just telling me that—to punish me, aren't you? You said you loved me—you'd protect me—protect your mother—you couldn't murder—!

ORIN (*harshly, pushing her away*) You could murder Father, couldn't you? (*He thrusts the newspaper into her hands, pointing to the story*) Here! Read that, if you don't believe me! We got it in Boston to see whom the police would suspect. It's only a few lines. Brant wasn't important—except to you! (*She looks at the paper with fascinated horror. Then she lets it slip through her fingers, sinks down on the lowest step and begins to moan to herself, wringing her hands together in stricken anguish.* ORIN *turns from her and starts to pace up and down by the steps.* LAVINIA *stands at the left of the steps, rigid and erect, her face mask-like*).

ORIN (*harshly*) They think exactly what we planned they should think—that he was killed by waterfront thieves. There's nothing to connect us with his death! (*He stops by her. She stares before her, wringing her hands and moaning. He blurts out*) Mother! Don't moan like that! (*She gives no sign of having heard him. He starts to pace up and down again—with savage resentment*) Why do you grieve for that servant's bastard? I know he was the one who planned Father's murder! You couldn't have done that! He got you under his influence to revenge himself! He hypnotized you! I saw you weren't yourself the minute I got home, remember? How else could you ever have imagined you loved that low swine! How else could you ever have said the things— (*He stops before her*) I heard you planning to go with him to the island I had told you about—our island— that was you and I! (*He starts to pace up and down again distractedly. She remains as before except that her moaning has *begun to exhaust itself.* ORIN *stops before her again and grasps her by the shoulders, kneeling on the steps beside her desperately pleading now)* Mother! Don't moan like that! You're still under his influence! But you'll forget him! I'll make you forget him! I'll make you happy! We'll leave Vinnie here and go away on a long voyage—to the South Seas—

LAVINIA (*sharply*)　Orin!

ORIN (*not heeding her, stares into his mother's face. She has stopped moaning, the horror in her eyes is dying into blankness, the expression of her mouth congealing to one of numbed grief. She gives no sign of having heard him.* ORIN *shakes her— desperately*)　Mother! Don't you hear me? Why won't you speak to me? Will you always love him? Do you hate me now? (*He sinks on his knees before her*) Mother! Answer me! Say you forgive me!

LAVINIA (*with bitter scorn*)　Orin! After all that's happened, are you becoming her crybaby again? (ORIN *starts and gets to his feet, staring at her confusedly, as if he had forgotten her existence.* LAVINIA *speaks again in curt commanding tone that recalls her father*) Leave her alone! Go in the house! (*As he hesitates—more sharply*) Do you hear me? March!

ORIN (*automatically makes a confused motion of military salute —vaguely*)　Yes, sir. (*He walks mechanically up the steps—gazing up at the house—strangely*) Why are the shutters still closed? Father has gone. We ought to let in the moonlight. (*He goes into the house.* LAVINIA *comes and stands beside her mother.* CHRISTINE *continues to stare blankly in front of her. Her face has become a tragic death mask. She gives no sign of being aware of her daughter's presence.* LAVINIA *regards her with bleak, condemning eyes*).

LAVINIA (*finally speaks sternly*)　He paid the just penalty for his crime. You know it was justice. It was the only way true justice could be done. (*Her mother starts. The words shatter her merciful numbness and awaken her to agony again. She springs to her feet and stands glaring at her daughter with a terrible look in which a savage hatred fights with horror and fear. In spite of her frozen self-control,* LAVINIA *recoils before this. Keeping her eyes on her,* CHRISTINE *shrinks backward up the steps until she stands at the top between the two columns of the portico before the front door.* LAVINIA *suddenly makes a motion, as if to hold her back. She calls shakenly as if the words were wrung out of her against her will*) Mother! What are you going to do? You can live!

CHRISTINE (*glares at her as if this were the last insult—with strident mockery*) Live! (*She bursts into shrill laughter, stops it abruptly, raises her hands between her face and her daughter and pushes them out in a gesture of blotting* LAVINIA *forever from her sight. Then she turns and rushes into the house.* LAVINIA *again makes a movement to follow her. But she immediately fights down this impulse and turns her back on the house determinedly, standing square-shouldered and stiff like a grim sentinel in black*).

LAVINIA (*implacably to herself*) It is justice! (*From the street, away off right front,* SETH's *thin wraith of a baritone is raised in his favorite mournful "Shenandoah," as he nears the gateway to the drive, returning from his nightly visit to the saloon*).

"Oh, Shenandoah, I long to hear you
A-way, my rolling river!
Oh, Shenandoah, I can't get near you
Way—ay, I'm bound away
Across the wide—"

(*There is the sharp report of a pistol from the left ground floor of the house where* EZRA MANNON's *study is.* LAVINIA *gives a shuddering gasp, turns back to the steps, starts to go up them, stops again and stammers shakenly*) It is justice! It is your justice, Father! (ORIN's *voice is heard calling from the sitting-room at right "What's that"! A door slams. Then* ORIN's *horrified cry comes from the study as he finds his mother's body, and a moment later he rushes out frantically to* LAVINIA).

ORIN Vinnie! (*He grabs her arm and stammers distractedly*) Mother—shot herself—Father's pistol—get a doctor— (*Then with hopeless anguish*) No—it's too late—she's dead! (*Then wildly*) Why—why did she, Vinnie? (*With tortured self-accusation*) I drove her to it! I wanted to torture her! She couldn't forgive me! Why did I have to boast about killing him? Why—?

LAVINIA (*frightenedly, puts her hand over his mouth*) Be quiet!

ORIN (*tears her hand away—violently*) Why didn't I let her believe burglars killed him? She wouldn't have hated me then! She would have forgotten him! She would have turned to me! (*In a final frenzy of self-denunciation*) I murdered her!

LAVINIA (*grabbing him by the shoulders*)  For God's sake, will you be quiet?

ORIN (*frantically—trying to break away from her*)  Let me go! I've got to find her! I've got to make her forgive me! I—! (*He suddenly breaks down and weeps in hysterical anguish.* LAVINIA *puts her arm around him soothingly. He sobs despairingly*) But she's dead— She's gone—how can I ever get her to forgive me now?

LAVINIA (*soothingly*)  Ssshh! Ssshh! You have me, haven't you? I love you. I'll help you to forget. (*He turns to go back into the house, still sobbing helplessly.* SETH's *voice comes from the drive, right, close at hand:*

"She's far across the stormy water
Way-ay, I'm bound away—"

(*He enters right, front.* LAVINIA *turns to face him*).

SETH (*approaching*)  Say, Vinnie, did you hear a shot—?

LAVINIA (*sharply*)  I want you to go for Doctor Blake. Tell him Mother has killed herself in a fit of insane grief over Father's death. (*Then as he stares, dumbfounded and wondering, but keeping his face expressionless—more sharply*) Will you remember to tell him that?

SETH (*slowly*)  Ayeh. I'll tell him, Vinnie—anything you say. (*His face set grimly, he goes off, right front.* LAVINIA *turns and, stiffly erect, her face stern and mask-like, follows* ORIN *into the house*).

*Curtain*

*Part Three*

# THE HAUNTED

*A Play in Four Acts*

# Characters

LAVINIA MANNON

ORIN, *her brother*

PETER NILES

HAZEL, *his sister*

SETH

AMOS AMES

IRA MACKEL

JOE SILVA

ABNER SMALL

# Scenes

ACT ONE—*Scene* I: Exterior of the Mannon house—an evening in the summer of 1866.

ACT ONE—*Scene* II: Sitting-room in the house (immediately follows Scene One).

ACT TWO: The study—an evening a month later.

ACT THREE: The sitting-room (immediately follows Act Two).

ACT FOUR: Same as Act One, Scene One—Exterior of the Mannon house—a late afternoon three days later.

# ACT ONE

## SCENE ONE

EXTERIOR *of the Mannon house* (*as in the two preceding plays*) *on an evening of a clear day in summer a year later. It is shortly after sunset but the afterglow in the sky still bathes the white temple portico in a crimson light. The columns cast black bars of shadow on the wall behind them. All the shutters are closed and the front door is boarded up, showing that the house is unoccupied.*

*A group of five men is standing on the drive by the bench at left, front.* SETH BECKWITH *is there and* AMOS AMES, *who appeared in the first Act of* "Homecoming." *The others are* ABNER SMALL, JOE SILVA *and* IRA MACKEL.

*These four—*AMES, SMALL, SILVA *and* MACKEL—*are, as were the townsfolk of the first acts of* "Homecoming" *and* "The Hunted," *a chorus of types representing the town as a human background for the drama of the Mannons.*

SMALL *is a wiry little old man of sixty-five, a clerk in a hardware store. He has white hair and a wispy goat's beard, bright inquisitive eyes, ruddy complexion, and a shrill rasping voice.* SILVA *is a Portuguese fishing captain—a fat, boisterous man, with a hoarse bass voice. He has matted gray hair and a big grizzled mustache. He is sixty.* MACKEL, *who is a farmer, hobbles along with the aid of a cane. His shiny wrinkled face is oblong with a square white chin whisker. He is bald. His yellowish brown eyes are sly. He talks in a drawling wheezy cackle.*

*All five are drunk.* SETH *has a stone jug in his hand. There is a grotesque atmosphere of boys out on a forbidden lark about these old men.*

SMALL   God A'mighty, Seth, be you glued to that jug?

MACKEL   Gol durn him, he's gittin' stingy in his old age!

SILVA   (*bursts into song*)

"*A bottle of beer and a bottle of gin*
*And a bottle of Irish whiskey oh!*
*So early in the morning*
*A sailor likes his bottle oh!*"

AMES   (*derisively*)   You like your bottle 'ceptin' when your old woman's got her eye on ye!

SILVA   She's visitin' her folks to New Bedford. What the hell I care! (*Bursts into song again*)

"*Hurrah! Hurrah! I sing the jubilee*
*Hurrah! Hurrah! Her folks has set me free!*"

AMES   (*slapping him on the back*)   God damn you, Joe, you're gittin' to be a poet! (*They all laugh*).

SMALL   God A'mighty, Seth, ain't ye got no heart in ye? Watch me perishin' fur lack o' whiskey and ye keep froze to that jug! (*He reaches out for it*).

SETH   No, ye don't! I'm onto your game! (*With a wink at the others*) He's aimin' to git so full of Injun courage he wouldn't mind if a ghost sot on his lap! Purty slick you be, Abner! Swill my licker so's you kin skin me out o' my bet!

MACKEL   That's it, Seth! Don't let him play no skin games!

JOE   By God, if ghosts look like the livin', I'd let Ezra's woman's ghost set on my lap! M'm! (*He smacks his lips lasciviously*).

AMES   Me, too! She was a looker!

SMALL   (*with an uneasy glance at the house*)   It's her ghost folks is sayin' haunts the place, ain't it?

SETH   (*with a wink at the others*)   Oh, hers and a hull passel of others. The graveyard's full of Mannons and they all spend their nights to hum here. You needn't worry but you'll have plenty o' company, Abner! (*The others laugh, their mirth a bit forced, but* SMALL *looks rather sick*).

SMALL   It ain't in our bet for you to put sech notions in my head afore I go in, be it? (*Then forcing a perky bravado*) Think you kin scare me? There ain't no sech thing as ghosts!

SETH   An' I'm sayin' you're scared to prove there ain't! Let's git our bet set out plain afore witnesses. I'm lettin' you in the Mannon house and I'm bettin' you ten dollars and a gallon of licker you dasn't stay there till moonrise at ten o'clock. If you come out afore then, you lose. An' you're to stay in the dark and not even strike a match! Is that agreed?

SMALL (*trying to put a brave face on it*)  That's agreed—an' it's like stealin' ten dollars off you!

SETH  We'll see! (*Then with a grin*) An' you're supposed to go in sober! But I won't make it too dead sober! I ain't that hardhearted. I wouldn't face what you'll face with a gallon under my belt! (*Handing him the jug*) Here! Take a good swig! You're lookin' a mite pale about the gills a'ready!

SMALL  No sech thing! (*But he puts the jug to his lips and takes an enormous swallow*).

MACKEL  Whoa thar! Ye ain't drinkin' fur all on us! (SMALL *hands the jug to him and he drinks and passes it around until it finally reaches* SETH *again. In the meantime* SMALL *talks to* SETH).

SMALL  Be it all right fur me to go in afore dark? I'd like to know where I'm at while I kin see.

SETH  Wal, I calc'late you kin. Don't want you runnin' into furniture an' breakin' things when them ghosts git chasin' you! Vinnie an' Orin's liable to be back from Chiny afore long an' she'd give me hell if anythin' was broke. (*The jug reaches him. He takes a drink—then sets it down on the drive*) Come along! I've took the screws out o' that door. I kin let you right in. (*He goes toward the portico,* SMALL *following him, whistling with elaborate nonchalance*).

SMALL (*to the others who remain where they are*)  So long, fellers. We'll have a good spree on that ten dollars.

MACKEL (*with a malicious cackle*)  Mebbe! Would you like me fur one o' your pallbearers, Abner?

AMES  I'll comfort your old woman—providin' she'll want comfortin', which ain't likely!

SILVA  And I'll water your grave every Sunday after church! That's the kind of man I be, by God. I don't forget my friends when they're gone!

SETH (*from the portico*)  We'll all jine in, Joe! If he ain't dead, by God, we'll drown him! (*They all roar with laughter.* SMALL *looks bitter. The jest strikes him as being unfeeling— All glow has faded from the sky and it is getting dark*).

SMALL  To hell with ye! (SETH *pries off the board door and unlocks the inner door*).

SETH  Come on. I'll show you the handiest place to say your prayers. (*They go in. The group outside becomes serious*).

AMES (*voicing the opinion of all of them*)  Wal, all the same, I wouldn't be in Abner's boots. It don't do to monkey with them thin's.

MACKEL  You believe in ghosts, Amos?

AMES  Mebbe. Who knows there ain't?

MACKEL  Wal, I believe in 'em. Take the Nims' place out my way. Asa Nims killed his wife with a hatchet—she'd nagged him—then hung himself in the attic. I knew Ben Willett that bought the place. He couldn't live thar—had to move away. It's fallen to ruins now. Ben used to hear things clawin' at the walls an' winders and see the chairs move about. He wasn't a liar nor chicken-hearted neither.

SILVA  There is ghosts, by God! My cousin, Manuel, he seen one! Off on a whaler in the Injun Ocean, that was. A man got knifed and pushed overboard. After that, on moonlight nights, they'd see him a-settin' on the yards and hear him moanin' to himself. Yes, sir, my cousin Manuel, he ain't no liar neither—'ceptin' when he's drunk—and he seen him with his own eyes!

AMES (*with an uneasy glance around, reaching for the jug*)  Wal, let's have a drink. (*He takes a swig just as* SETH *comes out of the house, shutting the door behind him*).

MACKEL  That's Seth. He ain't anxious to stay in thar long, I notice! (SETH *hurries down to them, trying to appear to saunter*).

SETH (*with a forced note to his joking*)  God A'mighty, ye'd ought to see Abner! He's shyin' at the furniture covers an' his teeth are clickin' a'ready. He'll come runnin' out hell fur leather afore long. All I'm wonderin' is, has he got ten dollars.

MACKEL (*slyly*)  You seem a mite shaky.

SETH (*with a scowl*)  You're a liar. What're ye all lookin' glum as owls about?

MACKEL  Been talkin' of ghosts. Do you really believe that there house is haunted, Seth, or are ye only jokin' Abner?

SETH (*sharply*)  Don't be a durned fool! I'm on'y jokin' him, of course!

MACKEL (*insistently*)  Still, it'd be only natural if it was haunted. She shot herself there. Do you think she done it fur grief over Ezra's death, like the daughter let on to folks?

SETH 'Course she did!

MACKEL Ezra dyin' sudden his first night to hum—that was durned queer!

SETH (*angrily*) It's durned queer old fools like you with one foot in the grave can't mind their own business in the little time left to 'em. That's what's queer!

MACKEL (*angry in his turn*) Wal, all I say is if they hadn't been Mannons with the town lickin' their boots, there'd have been queer doin's come out! And as fur me bein' an old fool, you're older an' a worse fool! An' your foot's deeper in the grave than mine be!

SETH (*shaking his fist in* MACKEL'S *face*) It ain't so deep but what I kin whale the stuffin' out o' you any day in the week!

SILVA (*comes between them*) Here, you old roosters! No fightin' allowed!

MACKEL (*subsiding grumpily*) This is a free country, ain't it? I got a right to my opinions!

AMES (*suddenly looking off down left*) Ssshh! Look, Seth! There's someone comin' up the drive.

SETH (*peering*) Ayeh! Who the hell—? It's Peter'n Hazel. Hide that jug, durn ye! (*The jug is hidden under the lilacs. A moment later,* HAZEL *and* PETER *enter. They stop in surprise on seeing* SETH *and his friends.* SETH *greets them self-consciously*) Good evenin'. I was just showin' some friends around—

PETER Hello, Seth. Just the man we're looking for. We've just had a telegram. Vinnie and Orin have landed in New York and— (*He is interrupted by a muffled yell of terror from the house. As they all turn to look, the front door is flung open and* SMALL *comes tearing out and down the portico steps, his face chalky white and his eyes popping*).

SMALL (*as he reaches them—terrifiedly*) God A'mighty! I heard 'em comin' after me, and I run in the room opposite, an' I seed Ezra's ghost dressed like a judge comin' through the wall—and, by God, I run! (*He jerks a bill out of his pocket and thrusts it on* SETH) Here's your money, durn ye! I wouldn't stay in there fur a million! (*This breaks the tension, and the old men give way to an hysterical, boisterous, drunken mirth, roaring with laughter, pounding each other on the back*).

PETER (*sharply*) What's this all about? What was he doing in there?

SETH (*controlling his laughter—embarrassedly*) Only a joke,

Peter. (*Then turning on* SMALL—*scornfully*) That was Ezra's picture hangin' on the wall, not a ghost, ye durned idjut!

SMALL (*indignantly*) I know pictures when I see 'em an' I knowed him. This was him! Let's get out o' here. I've had enough of this durned place!

SETH You fellers trot along. I'll jine you later. (*They all mutter good evenings to* PETER *and* HAZEL *and go off, left front.* SMALL'S *excited voice can be heard receding as he begins to embroider on the horrors of his adventure.* SETH *turns to* PETER *apologetically*) Abner Small's always braggin' how brave he is—so I bet him he dasn't stay in there—

HAZEL (*indignantly*) Seth! What would Vinnie say if she knew you did such things?

SETH There ain't no harm done. I calc'late Abner didn't break nothin'. And Vinnie wouldn't mind when she knew why I done it. I was aimin' to stop the durned gabbin' that's been goin' round town about this house bein' haunted. You've heard it, ain't ye?

PETER I heard some silly talk but didn't pay any attenion—

SETH That durned idjut female I got in to clean a month after Vinnie and Orin sailed started it. Said she'd felt ghosts around. You know how them things grow. Seemed to me Abner's braggin' gave me a good chance to stop it by turnin' it all into a joke on him folks'd laugh at. An' when I git through tellin' my story of it round town tomorrow you'll find folks'll shet up and not take it serious no more.

PETER (*appreciatively*) You're right, Seth. That was a darned slick notion! Nothing like a joke to lay a ghost!

SETH Ayeh. But— (*He hesitates—then decides to say it*) Between you 'n' me 'n' the lamp-post, it ain't all sech a joke as it sounds—that about the hauntin', I mean.

PETER (*incredulously*) You aren't going to tell me you think the house is haunted too!

SETH (*grimly*) Mebbe, and mebbe not. All I know is I wouldn't stay in there all night if you was to give me the town!

HAZEL (*impressed but forcing a teasing tone*) Seth! I'm ashamed of you!

PETER First time I ever heard you say you were afraid of anything!

SETH There's times when a man's a darn fool not to be scared! Oh, don't git it in your heads I take stock in spirits trespassin'

round in windin' sheets or no sech lunactic doin's. But there
is sech a thing as evil spirit. An' I've felt it, goin' in there
daytimes to see to things—like somethin' rottin' in the walls!

PETER Bosh!

SETH (*quietly*) 'Tain't bosh, Peter. There's been evil in that house
since it was first built in hate—and it's kept growin' there ever
since, as what's happened there has proved. You understand I
ain't sayin' this to no one but you two. An' I'm only tellin' you fur
one reason—because you're closer to Vinnie and Orin than anyone and you'd ought to persuade them, now they're back, not
to live in it. (*He adds impressively*) Fur their own good! (*Then
with a change of tone*) An' now I've got that off my chest, tell
me about 'em. When are they comin'?

PETER Tomorrow. Vinnie asked us to open the house. So let's start
right in.

SETH (*with evident reluctance*) You want to do it tonight?

HAZEL We must, Seth. We've got so little time. We can at least
tidy up the rooms a little and get the furniture covers off.

SETH Wal, I'll go to the barn and git lanterns. There's candles
in the house. (*He turns abruptly and goes off left between
the lilacs and the house*).

HAZEL (*looking after him—uneasily*) I can't get over Seth acting
so strangely.

PETER Don't mind him. It's rum and old age.

HAZEL (*shaking her head—slowly*) No. There is something queer
about this house. I've always felt it, even before the General's
death and her suicide. (*She shudders*) I can still see her sitting
on that bench as she was that last night. She was so frightened
of being alone. But I thought when Vinnie and Orin came back
she would be all right. (*Then sadly*) Poor Orin! I'll never forget
to my dying day the way he looked when we saw him at the
funeral. I hardly recognized him, did you?

PETER No. He certainly was broken up.

HAZEL And the way he acted—like someone in a trance! I don't
believe when Vinnie rushed him off on this trip to the East he
knew what he was doing or where he was going or anything.

PETER A long voyage like that was the best thing to help them
both forget.

HAZEL (*without conviction*) Yes. I suppose it was—but— (*She
stops and sighs—then worriedly*) I wonder how Orin is. Vinnie's
letters haven't said much about him, or herself, for that matter—

only about the trip. (*She sees* SETH *approaching, whistling loudly, from left, rear, with two lighted lanterns*) Here's Seth. (*She walks up the steps to the portico.* PETER *follows her. She hesitates and stands looking at the house—in a low tone, almost of dread*) Seth was right. You feel something cold grip you the moment you set foot—

PETER  Oh, nonsense! He's got you going, too! (*Then with a chuckle*) Listen to him whistling to keep his courage up! (SETH *comes in from the left. He hands one of the lanterns to* PETER).

SETH  Here you be, Peter.

HAZEL  Well, let's go in. You better come out to the kitchen and help me first, Peter. We ought to start a fire. (*They go in. There is a pause in which* PETER *can be heard opening windows behind the shutters in the downstairs rooms. Then silence. Then* LAVINIA *enters, coming up the drive from left, front, and stands regarding the house. One is at once aware of an extraordinary change in her. Her body, formerly so thin and undeveloped, has filled out. Her movements have lost their square-shouldered stiffness. She now bears a striking resemblance to her mother in every respect, even to being dressed in the green her mother had affected. She walks to the clump of lilacs and stands there staring at the house*).

LAVINIA  (*turns back and calls coaxingly in the tone one would use to a child*) Don't stop there, Orin! What are you afraid of? Come on! (*He comes slowly and hesitantly in from left, front. He carries himself woodenly erect now like a soldier. His movements and attitudes have the statue-like quality that was so marked in his father. He now wears a close-cropped beard in addition to his mustache, and this accentuates his resemblance to his father. The Mannon semblance of his face in repose to a mask is more pronounced than ever. He has grown dreadfully thin and his black suit hangs loosely on his body. His haggard swarthy face is set in a blank lifeless expression*).

LAVINIA  (*glances at him uneasily—concealing her apprehension under a coaxing motherly tone*) You must be brave! This is the test! You have got to face it! (*Then anxiously as he makes no reply*) Do you feel you can—now we're here?

ORIN  (*dully*) I'll be all right—with you.

LAVINIA  (*takes his hand and pats it encouragingly*) That's all I wanted—to hear you say that. (*Turning to the house*) Look, I see a light through the shutters of the sitting-room. That must be

Peter and Hazel. (*Then as she sees he still keeps his eyes averted from the house*) Why don't you look at the house? Are you afraid? (*Then sharply commanding*) Orin! I want you to look now! Do you hear me?

ORIN (*dully obedient*) Yes, Vinnie. (*He jerks his head around and stares at the house and draws a deep shuddering breath*).

LAVINIA (*her eyes on his face—as if she were willing her strength into him*) Well? You don't see any ghosts, do you? Tell me!

ORIN (*obediently*) No.

LAVINIA Because there are none! Tell me you know there are none, Orin!

ORIN (*as before*) Yes.

LAVINIA (*searches his face uneasily—then is apparently satisfied*) Come. Let's go in. We'll find Hazel and Peter and surprise them— (*She takes his arm and leads him to the steps. He walks like an automaton. When they reach the spot where his mother had sat moaning, the last time he had seen her alive [Act Five of "The Hunted"] he stops with a shudder*).

ORIN (*stammers—pointing*) It was here—she—the last time I saw her alive—

LAVINIA (*quickly, urging him on commandingly*) That is all past and finished! The dead have forgotten us! We've forgotten them! Come! (*He obeys woodenly. She gets him up the steps and they pass into the house*).

*Curtain*


SCENE TWO

SAME *as Act Two of "The Hunted"—The sitting-room in the Mannon house.* PETER *has lighted two candles on the mantel and put the lantern on the table at front. In this dim, spotty light the room is full of shadows. It has the dead appearance of a room long shut up, and the covered furniture has a ghostly look. In the flickering candlelight the eyes of the Mannon portraits stare with a grim forbiddingness.*

LAVINIA *appears in the doorway at rear. In the lighted room, the change in her is strikingly apparent. At a first glance, one would mistake her for her mother as she appeared in the First Act of "Homecoming." She seems a mature woman, sure of her feminine attractiveness. Her brown-gold hair is arranged as her mother's had been. Her green dress is like a copy of her mother's in Act One of "Homecoming." She comes foward slowly. The movements of her body now have the feminine grace her mother's had possessed. Her eyes are caught by the eyes of the Mannons in the portraits and she approaches as if compelled in spite of herself until she stands directly under them in front of the fireplace. She suddenly addresses them in a harsh resentful voice).*

LAVINIA   Why do you look at me like that? I've done my duty by you! That's finished and forgotten! (*She tears her eyes from theirs and, turning away, becomes aware that* ORIN *has not followed her into the room, and is immediately frightened and uneasy and hurries toward the door, calling*) Orin!

ORIN (*his voice comes from the dark hall*)   I'm here.

LAVINIA   What are you doing out there? Come here! (ORIN *appears in the doorway. His face wears a dazed expression and his eyes have a wild, stricken look. He hurries to her as if seeking protection. She exclaims frightenedly*) Orin! What is it?

ORIN (*strangely*)   I've just been in the study. I was sure she'd be waiting for me in there, where— (*Torturedly*) But she wasn't! She isn't anywhere. It's only they— (*He points to the portraits*) They're everywhere! But she's gone forever. She'll never forgive me now!

LAVINIA (*harshly*)   Orin! Will you be quiet!

ORIN (*unheeding—with a sudden turn of bitter resentful defiance*) Well, let her go! What is she to me? I'm not her son any more! I'm Father's! I'm a Mannon! And they'll welcome me home!

LAVINIA (*angrily commanding*)   Stop it, do you hear me!

ORIN (*shocked back to awareness by her tone—pitifully confused*) I—I didn't—don't be angry, Vinnie!

LAVINIA (*soothing him now*)   I'm not angry, dear—only do get hold of yourself and be brave. (*Leading him to the sofa*) Here. Come. Let's sit down for a moment, shall we, and get used to being home? (*They sit down. She puts an arm around him reproachfully*) Don't you know how terribly you frighten me when you act so strangely? You don't mean to hurt me, do you?

ORIN (*deeply moved*)   God knows I don't, Vinnie! You're all I have in the world! (*He takes her hand and kisses it humbly*).

LAVINIA (*soothingly*) That's a good boy. (*Then with a cheerful matter-of-fact note*) Hazel and Peter must be back in the kitchen. Won't you be glad to see Hazel again?

ORIN (*dully now*) You've kept talking about them all the voyage home. Why? What can they have to do with us—now?

LAVINIA A lot. What we need most is to get back to simple normal things and begin a new life. And their friendship and love will help us more than anything to forget.

ORIN (*with sudden harshness*) Forget? I thought you'd forgotten long ago—if you ever remembered, which you never seemed to! (*Then with somber bitterness*) Love! What right have I—or you—to love?

LAVINIA (*defiantly*) Every right!

ORIN (*grimly*) Mother felt the same about— (*Then with a strange, searching glance at her*) You don't know how like Mother you've become, Vinnie. I don't mean only how pretty you've gotten—

LAVINIA (*with a strange shy eagerness*) Do you really think I'm as pretty now as she was, Orin?

ORIN (*as if she hadn't interrupted*) I mean the change in your soul, too. I've watched it ever since we sailed for the East. Little by little it grew like Mother's soul—as if you were stealing hers—as if her death had set you free—to become her!

LAVINIA (*uneasily*) Now don't begin talking nonsense again, please!

ORIN (*grimly*) Don't you believe in souls any more? I think you will after we've lived in this house awhile! The Mannon dead will convert you. (*He turns to the portraits mockingly*) Ask them if I'm not right!

LAVINIA (*sharply*) Orin! What's come over you? You haven't had one of these morbid spells since we left the Islands. You swore to me you were all over them, or I'd never have agreed to come home.

ORIN (*with a strange malicious air*) I had to get you away from the Islands. My brotherly duty! If you'd stayed there much longer— (*He chuckles disagreeably*).

LAVINIA (*with a trace of confusion*) I don't know what you're talking about. I only went there for your sake.

ORIN (*with another chuckle*) Yes—but afterwards—

LAVINIA (*sharply*) You promised you weren't going to talk any more morbid nonsense. (*He subsides meekly. She goes on reproachfully*) Remember all I've gone through on your account. For months after we sailed you didn't know what you were doing. I had to live in constant fear of what you might say. I wouldn't live through those horrible days again for anything on earth. And remember this homecoming is what you wanted. You told me that if you could come home and face your ghosts, you knew you could rid yourself forever of your silly guilt about the past.

ORIN (*dully*) I know, Vinnie.

LAVINIA And I believed you, you seemed so certain of yourself. But now you've suddenly become strange again. You frighten me. So much depends on how you start in, now we're home. (*Then sharply commanding*) Listen, Orin! I want you to start again—by facing all your ghosts right now! (*He turns and his eyes remain fixed on hers from now on. She asks sternly*) Who murdered Father?

ORIN (*falteringly*) Brant did—for revenge because—

LAVINIA (*more sternly*) Who murdered Father? Answer me!

ORIN (*with a shudder*) Mother was under his influence—

LAVINIA That's a lie! It was he who was under hers. You know the truth!

ORIN Yes.

LAVINIA She was an adulteress and a murderess, wasn't she?

ORIN Yes.

LAVINIA If we'd done our duty under the law, she would have been hanged, wouldn't she?

ORIN Yes.

LAVINIA But we protected her. She could have lived, couldn't she? But she chose to kill herself as a punishment for her crime— of her own free will! It was an act of justice! You had nothing to do with it! You see that now, don't you? (*As he hesitates, trembling violently, she grabs his arm fiercely*) Tell me!

ORIN (*hardly above a whisper*) Yes.

LAVINIA And your feeling of being responsible for her death was only your morbid imagination! You don't feel it now! You'll never feel it again!

ORIN No.

LAVINIA (*gratefully—and weakly because the strength she has willed into him has left her exhausted*) There! You see! You can do it when you will to! (*She kisses him. He breaks down,*

*sobbing weakly against her breast. She soothes him)* There!
Don't cry! You ought to feel proud. You've proven you can laugh
at your ghosts from now on. (*Then briskly, to distract his mind*)
Come now. Help me to take off these furniture covers. We might
as well start making ourselves useful. (*She starts to work. For a
moment he helps. Then he goes to one of the windows and
pushes back a shutter and stands staring out.* PETER *comes in the
door from rear. At the sight of* LAVINIA *he stops startledly, thinks
for a second it is her mother's ghost and gives an exclamation of
dread. At the same moment she sees him. She stares at him with
a strange eager possessiveness. She calls softly*).

LAVINIA  Peter! (*She goes toward him, smiling as her mother
might have smiled*) Don't you know me any more, Peter?

PETER  (*stammers*)  Vinnie! I—I thought you were—! I can't realize it's you! You've grown so like your— (*Checking himself awkwardly*) I mean you've changed so—and we weren't looking for
you until— (*He takes her hand automatically, staring at her stupidly*).

LAVINIA  I know. We had intended to stay in New York tonight
but we decided later we'd better come right home. (*Then
taking him in with a smiling appreciative possessiveness*) Let
me look at you, Peter. You haven't gone and changed, have
you? No, you're the same, thank goodness! I've been thinking
of you all the way home and wondering—I was so afraid you
might have.

PETER  (*plucking up his courage—blurts out*)  You—you ought to
know I'd never change—with you! (*Then, alarmed by his own
boldness, he hastily looks away from her*).

LAVINIA  (*teasingly*)  But you haven't said yet you're glad to see
me!

PETER  (*has turned back and is staring fascinatedly at her. A surge
of love and desire overcomes his timidity and he bursts out*)
I—you know how much I—! (*Then he turns away again in confusion and takes refuge in a burst of talk*) Gosh, Vinnie, you
ought to have given us more warning. We've only just started
to open the place up. I was with Hazel, in the kitchen, starting a
fire—

LAVINIA  (*laughing softly*)  Yes. You're the same old Peter! You're
still afraid of me. But you mustn't be now. I know I used to be
an awful old stick, but—

PETER  Who said so? You were not! (*Then with enthusiasm*) Gosh,

you look so darned pretty—and healthy. Your trip certainly
did you good! (*Staring at her again, drinking her in*) I can't get
over seeing you dressed in color. You always used to wear black.

LAVINIA (*with a strange smile*) I was dead then.

PETER You ought always to wear color.

LAVINIA (*immensely pleased*) Do you think so?

PETER Yes. It certainly is becoming. I— (*Then embarrassedly
changing the subject*) But where's Orin?

LAVINIA (*turning to look around*) Why, he was right here. (*She
sees him at the window*) Orin, what are you doing there? Here's
Peter. (ORIN *closes the shutter he has pushed open and turns
back from the window. He comes forward, his eyes fixed in a
strange preoccupation, as if he were unaware of their presence.*
LAVINIA *watches him uneasily and speaks sharply*) Don't you
see Peter! Why don't you speak to him? You mustn't be so rude.

PETER (*good-naturedly*) Give him a chance. Hello, Orin. Darned
glad to see you back. (*They shake hands.* PETER *has difficulty in
hiding his pained surprise at* ORIN's *sickly appearance*).

ORIN (*rousing himself, forces a smile and makes an effort at his
old friendly manner with* PETER) Hello, Peter. You know I'm
glad to see you without any polite palaver. Vinnie is the same
old bossy fuss-buzzer—you remember—always trying to teach me
manners!

PETER You bet I remember! But say, hasn't she changed, though?
I didn't know her, she's grown so fat! And I was just telling
her how well she looked in color. Don't you agree?

ORIN (*in a sudden strange tone of jeering malice*) Did you ask
her why she stole Mother's colors? I can't see why—yet—and I
don't think she knows herself. But it will prove a strange reason, I'm certain of that, when I do discover it!

LAVINIA (*making a warning sign to* PETER *not to take this seriously—forcing a smile*) Don't mind him, Peter.

ORIN (*his tone becoming sly, insinuating and mocking*) And
she's become romantic! Imagine that! Influence of the "dark and
deep blue ocean"—and of the Islands, eh, Vinnie?

PETER (*surprised*) You stopped at the Islands?

ORIN Yes. We took advantage of our being on a Mannon ship
to make the captain touch there on the way back. We stopped a
month. (*With resentful bitterness*) But they turned out to be
Vinnie's islands, not mine. They only made me sick—and the
naked women disgusted me. I guess I'm too much of a Mannon,

after all, to turn into a pagan. But you should have seen Vinnie
with the men—!

LAVINIA (*indignantly but with a certain guiltiness*) How can
you—!

ORIN (*jeeringly*) Handsome and romantic-looking, weren't they,
Vinnie?—with colored rags around their middles and flowers stuck
over their ears! Oh, she was a bit shocked at first by their
dances, but afterwards she fell in love with the Islanders. If
we'd stayed another month, I know I'd have found her some
moonlight night dancing under the palm trees—as naked as the
rest!

LAVINIA Orin! Don't be disgusting!

ORIN (*points to the portraits mockingly*) Picture, if you can, the
feelings of the God-fearing Mannon dead at that spectacle!

LAVINIA (*with an anxious glance at* PETER) How can you make
up such disgusting fibs?

ORIN (*with a malicious chuckle*) Oh, I wasn't as blind as I pretended to be! Do you remember Avahanni?

LAVINIA (*angrily*) Stop talking like a fool! (*He subsides meekly
again. She forces a smile and a motherly tone*) You're a
naughty boy, do you know it? What will Peter think? Of course,
he knows you're only teasing me—but you shouldn't go on like
that. It isn't nice. (*Then changing the subject abruptly*) Why
don't you go and find Hazel? Here. Let me look at you. I want
you to look your best when she sees you. (*She arranges him as a
mother would a boy, pulling down his coat, giving a touch to
his shirt and tie.* ORIN *straightens woodenly to a soldierly attention. She is vexed by this*) Don't stand like a ramrod! You'd
be so handsome if you'd only shave off that silly beard and
not carry yourself like a tin soldier!

ORIN (*with a sly cunning air*) Not look so much like Father, eh?
More like a romantic clipper captain, is that it? (*As she starts
and stares at him frightenedly, he smiles an ugly taunting smile*)
Don't look so frightened, Vinnie!

LAVINIA (*with an apprehensive glance at* PETER—*pleading and at
the same time warning*) Ssshh! You weren't to talk nonsense, remember! (*Giving him a final pat*) There! Now run along to
Hazel.

ORIN (*looks from her to* PETER *suspiciously*) You seem damned
anxious to get rid of me. (*He turns and stalks stiffly with hurt
dignity from the room.* LAVINIA *turns to* PETER. *The strain of*

ORIN's *conduct has told on her. She seems suddenly weak and frightened*)

PETER (*in shocked amazement*) What's come over him?

LAVINIA (*in a strained voice*) It's the same thing—what the war did to him—and on top of that Father's death—and the shock of Mother's suicide.

PETER (*puts his arm around her impulsively—comfortingly*) It'll be all right! Don't worry, Vinnie!

LAVINIA (*nestling against him gratefully*) Thank you, Peter. You're so good. (*Then looking into his eyes*) Do you still love me, Peter?

PETER Don't have to ask that, do you? (*He squeezes her awkwardly—then stammers*) But do you—think now—you maybe—can love me?

LAVINIA Yes!

PETER You really mean that!

LAVINIA Yes! I do! I've thought of you so much! Things were always reminding me of you—the ship and the sea—everything that was honest and clean! And the natives on the Islands reminded me of you too. They were so simple and fine— (*Then hastily*) You mustn't mind what Orin was saying about the Islands. He's become a regular bigoted Mannon.

PETER (*amazed*) But, Vinnie—!

LAVINIA Oh, I know it must sound funny hearing me talk like that. But remember I'm only half Mannon. (*She looks at the portraits defiantly*) And I've done my duty by them! They can't say I haven't!

PETER (*mystified but happy*) Gosh, you certainly have changed! But I'm darned glad!

LAVINIA Orin keeps teasing that I was flirting with that native he spoke about, simply because he used to smile at me and I smiled back.

PETER (*teasingly*) Now, I'm beginning to get jealous, too.

LAVINIA You mustn't. He made me think of you. He made me dream of marrying you—and everything.

PETER Oh, well then, I take it all back! I owe him a vote of thanks! (*He hugs her*).

LAVINIA (*dreamily*) I loved those Islands. They finished setting me free. There was something there mysterious and beautiful—a good spirit—of love—coming out of the land and sea. It made me forget death. There was no hereafter. There was only this

world—the warm earth in the moonlight—the trade wind in the
coco palms—the surf on the reef—the fires at night and the drum
throbbing in my heart—the natives dancing naked and innocent
—without knowledge of sin! (*She checks herself abruptly and
frightenedly*) But what in the world! I'm gabbing on like a
regular chatterbox. You must think I've become awfully scatter-
brained!

PETER (*with a chuckle*)  Gosh no! I'm glad you've grown that
way! You never used to say a word unless you had to!

LAVINIA (*suddenly filled with grateful love for him, lets herself
go and throws her arms around him*)  Oh, Peter, hold me close
to you! I want to feel love! Love is all beautiful! I never used to
know that! I was a fool! (*She kisses him passionately. He returns
it, aroused and at the same time a little shocked by her boldness. She goes on longingly*) We'll be married soon, won't we,
and settle out in the country away from folks and their evil talk.
We'll make an island for ourselves on land, and we'll have
children and love them and teach them to love life so that they
can never be possessed by hate and death! (*She gives a start—
in a whisper as if to herself*) But I'm forgetting Orin!

PETER  What's Orin got to do with us marrying?

LAVINIA  I can't leave him—until he's all well again. I'd be
afraid—

PETER  Let him live with us.

LAVINIA (*with sudden intensity*)  No! I want to be rid of the past.
(*Then after a quick look at him—in a confiding tone*) I want to
tell you what's wrong with Orin—so you and Hazel can help me.
He feels guilty about Mother killing herself. You see, he'd had a
quarrel with her that last night. He was jealous and mad and said
things he was sorry for after and it preyed on his mind until he
blames himself for her death.

PETER  But that's crazy!

LAVINIA  I know it is, Peter, but you can't do anything with him
when he gets his morbid spells. Oh, I don't mean he's the way
he is tonight most of the time. Usually he's like himself, only
quiet and sad—so sad it breaks my heart to see him—like a
little boy who's been punished for something he didn't do. Please
tell Hazel what I've told you, so she'll make allowances for any
crazy thing he might say.

PETER  I'll warn her. And now don't you worry any more about
him. We'll get him all right again one way or another.

LAVINIA (*again grateful for his simple goodness—lovingly*)  Bless you, Peter! (*She kisses him. As she does so,* HAZEL *and* ORIN *appear in the doorway at rear.* HAZEL *is a bit shocked, then smiles happily.* ORIN *starts as if he'd been struck. He glares at them with jealous rage and clenches his fists as if he were going to attack them*).

HAZEL (*with a teasing laugh*)  I'm afraid we're interrupting, Orin. (PETER *and* VINNIE *jump apart in confusion*).

ORIN (*threateningly*)  So that's it! By God—!

LAVINIA (*frightened but managing to be stern*)  Orin!

ORIN (*pulls himself up sharply—confusedly, forcing a sickly smile*)  Don't be so solemn—Fuss Buzzer! I was only trying to scare you—for a joke! (*Turning to* PETER *and holding out his hand, his smile becoming ghastly*)  I suppose congratulations are in order. I—I'm glad. (PETER *takes his hand awkwardly.* HAZEL *moves toward* LAVINIA *to greet her, her face full of an uneasy bewilderment.* LAVINIA *stares at* ORIN *with eyes full of dread*).

*Curtain*

# ACT TWO

SCENE—*Same as Act Three of "The Hunted"*—EZRA MANNON'S *study—on an evening a month later. The shutters of the windows are closed. Candles on the mantel above the fireplace light up the portrait of* EZRA MANNON *in his judge's robes.* ORIN *is sitting in his father's chair at left of table, writing by the light of a lamp. A small pile of manuscript is stacked by his right hand. He is intent on his work. He has aged in the intervening month. He looks almost as old now as his father in the portrait. He is dressed in black and the resemblance between the two is uncanny. A grim smile of satisfaction twitches his lips as he stops writing and reads over the paragraph he has just finished. Then he puts the sheet down and stares at the portrait, sitting back in his chair.*

ORIN (*sardonically, addressing the portrait*) The truth, the whole truth and nothing but the truth! Is that what you're demanding, Father? Are you sure you want the whole truth? What will the neighbors say if this whole truth is ever known? (*He chuckles grimly*) A ticklish decision for you, Your Honor! (*There is a knock on the door. He hastily grabs the script and puts it in the drawer of the desk*) Who's there?

LAVINIA It's I.

ORIN (*hastily locking the drawer and putting the key in his pocket*) What do you want?

LAVINIA (*sharply*) Please open the door!

ORIN All right. In a minute. (*He hurriedly straightens up the table and grabs a book at random from the bookcase and lays it open on the table as if he had been reading. Then he unlocks the door and comes back to his chair as* LAVINIA *enters. She wears a green velvet gown similar to that worn by* CHRISTINE *in Act Three of "Homecoming." It sets off her hair and eyes. She is obviously concealing beneath a surface calm a sense of dread and desperation).*

LAVINIA (*glances at him suspiciously, but forces a casual air*)  Why did you lock yourself in? (*She comes over to the table*) What are you doing?

ORIN  Reading.

LAVINIA (*picks up the book*)  Father's law books?

ORIN (*mockingly*)  Why not? I'm considering studying law. He wanted me to, if you remember.

LAVINIA  Do you expect me to believe that, Orin? What is it you're really doing?

ORIN  Curious, aren't you?

LAVINIA (*forcing a smile*)  Good gracious, why wouldn't I be? You've acted so funny lately, locking yourself in here with the blinds closed and the lamp burning even in the daytime. It isn't good for you staying in this stuffy room in this weather. You ought to get out in the fresh air.

ORIN (*harshly*)  I hate the daylight. It's like an accusing eye! No, we've renounced the day, in which normal people live— or rather it has renounced us. Perpetual night—darkness of death in life—that's the fitting habitat for guilt! You believe you can escape that, but I'm not so foolish!

LAVINIA  Now you're being stupid again!

ORIN  And I find artificial light more appropriate for my work— man's light, not God's—man's feeble striving to understand himself, to exist for himself in the darkness! It's a symbol of his life—a lamp burning out in a room of waiting shadows!

LAVINIA (*sharply*)  Your work? What work?

ORIN (*mockingly*)  Studying the law of crime and punishment as you saw.

LAVINIA (*forcing a smile again and turning away from him*)  All right, if you won't tell me. Go on being mysterious, if you like. (*In a tense voice*) It's so close in here! It's suffocating! It's bad for you! (*She goes to the window and throws the shutters open and looks out*) It's black as pitch tonight. There isn't a star.

ORIN (*somberly*)  Darkness without a star to guide us! Where are we going, Vinnie? (*Then with a mocking chuckle*) Oh, I know you think you know where you're going, but there's many a slip, remember!

LAVINIA (*her voice strident, as if her will were snapping*)  Be quiet! Can't you think of anything but— (*Then controlling her-*

*self, comes to him—gently*) I'm sorry. I'm terribly nervous tonight. It's the heat, I guess. And you get me so worried with your incessant brooding over the past. It's the worst thing for your health. (*She pats him on the arm—soothingly*) That's all I'm thinking about, dear.

ORIN  Thank you for your anxiety about my health! But I'm afraid there isn't much hope for you there! I happen to feel quite well!

LAVINIA (*whirling on him—distractedly*)  How can you insinuate such horrible—! (*Again controlling herself with a great effort, forcing a smile*) But you're only trying to rile me—and I'm not going to let you. I'm so glad you're feeling better. You ate a good supper tonight—for you. The long walk we took with Hazel did you good.

ORIN (*dully*)  Yes. (*He slumps down in his chair at left of table*) Why is it you never leave me alone with her more than a minute? You approved of my asking her to marry me—and now we're engaged you never leave us alone! (*Then with a bitter smile*) But I know the reason well enough. You're afraid I'll let something slip.

LAVINIA (*sits in the chair opposite him—wearily*)  Can you blame me, the way you've been acting?

ORIN (*somberly*)  No. I'm afraid myself of being too long alone with her—afraid of myself. I have no right in the same world with her. And yet I feel so drawn to her purity! Her love for me makes me appear less vile to myself! (*Then with a harsh laugh*) And, at the same time, a million times more vile, that's the hell of it! So I'm afraid you can't hope to get rid of me through Hazel. She's another lost island! It's wiser for you to keep Hazel away from me, I warn you. Because when I see love for a murderer in her eyes my guilt crowds up in my throat like poisonous vomit and I long to spit it out—and confess!

LAVINIA (*in a low voice*)  Yes, that is what I live in terror of— that in one of your fits you'll say something before someone—now after it's all past and forgotten—when there isn't the slightest suspicion—

ORIN (*harshly*)  Were you hoping you could escape retribution? You can't! Confess and atone to the full extent of the law! That's the only way to wash the guilt of our mother's blood from our souls!

LAVINIA (*distractedly*)  Ssshh! Will you stop!

ORIN  Ask our father, the Judge, if it isn't! He knows! He keeps telling me!

LAVINIA  Oh, God! Over and over and over! Will you never lose your stupid guilty conscience! Don't you see how you torture me? You're becoming my guilty conscience, too! (*With an instinctive flare-up of her old jealousy*) How can you still love that vile woman so—when you know all she wanted was to leave you without a thought and marry that—

ORIN  (*with fierce accusation*) Yes! Exactly as you're scheming now to leave me and marry Peter! But, by God, you won't! You'll damn soon stop your tricks when you know what I've been writing!

LAVINIA  (*tensely*) What have you written?

ORIN  (*his anger turned to gloating satisfaction*) Ah! That frightens you, does it? Well, you better be frightened!

LAVINIA  Tell me what you've written!

ORIN  None of your damned business.

LAVINIA  I've got to know!

ORIN  Well, as I've practically finished it—I suppose I might as well tell you. At his earnest solicitation— (*He waves a hand to the portrait mockingly*) as the last male Mannon—thank God for that, eh!—I've been writing the history of our family! (*He adds with a glance at the portrait and a malicious chuckle*) But I don't wish to convey that he approves of all I've set down—not by a damned sight!

LAVINIA  (*trying to keep calm—tensely*) What kind of history do you mean?

ORIN  A true history of all the family crimes, beginning with Grandfather Abe's—all of the crimes, including ours, do you understand?

LAVINIA  (*aghast*) Do you mean to tell me you've actually written—

ORIN  Yes! I've tried to trace to its secret hiding place in the Mannon past the evil destiny behind our lives! I thought if I could see it clearly in the past I might be able to foretell what fate is in store for us, Vinnie—but I haven't dared predict that— not yet—although I can guess— (*He gives a sinister chuckle*).

LAVINIA  Orin!

ORIN  Most of what I've written is about you! I found you the most interesting criminal of us all!

LAVINIA (*breaking*) How can you say such dreadful things to me, after all I—

ORIN (*as if he hadn't heard—inexorably*) So many strange hidden things out of the Mannon past combine in you! For one example, do you remember the first mate, Wilkins, on the voyage to Frisco? Oh, I know you thought I was in a stupor of grief—but I wasn't blind! I saw how you wanted him!

LAVINIA (*angrily, but with a trace of guilty confusion*) I never gave him a thought! He was an officer of the ship to me, and nothing more!

ORIN (*mockingly*) Adam Brant was a ship's officer, too, wasn't he? Wilkins reminded you of Brant—

LAVINIA No!

ORIN And that's why you suddenly discarded mourning in Frisco and bought new clothes—in Mother's colors!

LAVINIA (*furiously*) Stop talking about her! You'd think, to hear you, I had no life of my own!

ORIN You wanted Wilkins just as you'd wanted Brant!

LAVINIA That's a lie!

ORIN You're doing the lying! You know damned well that behind all your pretense about Mother's murder being an act of justice was your jealous hatred! She warned me of that and I see it clearly now! You wanted Brant for yourself!

LAVINIA (*fiercely*) It's a lie! I hated him!

ORIN Yes, after you knew he was her lover! (*He chuckles with a sinister mockery*) But we'll let that pass for the present—I know it's the last thing you could ever admit to yourself!—and come to what I've written about your adventures on my lost islands. Or should I say, Adam Brant's islands! He had been there too, if you'll remember! Probably he'd lived with one of the native women! He was that kind! Were you thinking of that when we were there?

LAVINIA (*chokingly*) Stop it! I—I warn you—I won't bear it much longer!

ORIN (*as if he hadn't heard—in the same sinister mocking tone*) What a paradise the Islands were for you, eh? All those handsome men staring at you and your strange beautiful hair! It was then you finally became pretty—like Mother! You knew they all desired you, didn't you? It filled you with pride! Especially Avahanni! You watched him stare at your body through your clothes, stripping you naked! And you wanted him!

LAVINIA No!

ORIN Don't lie! (*He accuses her with fierce jealousy*) What did you do with him the night I was sick and you went to watch their shameless dance? Something happened between you! I saw your face when you came back and stood with him in front of our hut!

LAVINIA (*quietly—with simple dignity now*) I had kissed him good night, that was all—in gratitude! He was innocent and good. He had made me feel for the first time in my life that everything about love could be sweet and natural.

ORIN So you kissed him, did you? And that was all?

LAVINIA (*with a sudden flare of deliberately evil taunting that recalls her mother in the last act of "Homecoming," when she was goading Ezra Mannon to fury just before his murder*) And what if it wasn't? I'm not your property! I have a right to love!

ORIN (*reacting as his father had—his face grown livid—with a hoarse cry of fury grabs her by the throat*) You—you whore! I'll kill you! (*Then suddenly he breaks down and becomes weak and pitiful*) No! You're lying about him, aren't you? For God's sake, tell me you're lying, Vinnie!

LAVINIA (*strangely shaken and trembling—stammers*) Yes—it was a lie—how could you believe I—Oh, Orin, something made me say that to you—against my will—something rose up in me—like an evil spirit!

ORIN (*laughs wildly*) Ghosts! You never seemed so much like Mother as you did just then!

LAVINIA (*pleading distractedly*) Don't talk about it! Let's forget it ever happened! Forgive me! Please forget it!

ORIN All right—if the ghosts will let us forget! (*He stares at her fixedly for a moment—then satisfied*) I believe you about Avahanni. I never really suspected, or I'd have killed him—and you, too! I hope you know that! (*Then with his old obsessed insistence*) But you were guilty in your mind just the same!

LAVINIA (*in a flash of distracted anger*) Stop harping on that! Stop torturing me or I—! I've warned you! I warn you again! I can't bear any more! I won't!

ORIN (*with a mocking diabolical sneer—quietly*) Then why don't you murder me? I'll help you plan it, as we planned Brant's, so there will be no suspicion on you! And I'll be grateful! I loathe my life!

LAVINIA (*speechless with horror—can only gasp*) Oh!

ORIN (*with a quiet mad insistence*) Can't you see I'm now in Father's place and you're Mother? That's the evil destiny out of the past I haven't dared predict! I'm the Mannon you're chained to! So isn't it plain—

LAVINIA (*putting her hands over her ears*) For God's sake, won't you be quiet! (*Then suddenly her horror turning into a violent rage—unconsciously repeating the exact threat she had goaded her mother to make to her in Act Two of "Homecoming"*) Take care, Orin! You'll be responsible if—! (*She stops abruptly, terrified by her own words*).

ORIN (*with a diabolical mockery*) If what? If I should die mysteriously of heart failure?

LAVINIA Leave me alone! Leave me alone! Don't keep saying that! How can you be so horrible? Don't you know I'm your sister, who loves you, who would give her life to bring you peace?

ORIN (*with a change to a harsh threatening tone*) I don't believe you! I know you're plotting something! But you look out! I'll be watching you! And I warn you I won't stand your leaving me for Peter! I'm going to put this confession I've written in safe hands —to be read in case you try to marry him—or if I should die—

LAVINIA (*frantically grabbing his arm and shaking him fiercely*) Stop having such thoughts! Stop making me have them! You're like a devil torturing me! I won't listen! (*She breaks down and sobs brokenly.* ORIN *stares at her dazedly—seems half to come back to his natural self and the wild look fades from his eyes leaving them glazed and lifeless*).

ORIN (*strangely*) Don't cry. The damned don't cry. (*He slumps down heavily in his father's chair and stares at the floor. Suddenly he says harshly again*) Go away, will you? I want to be alone— to finish my work. (*Still sobbing, her hand over her eyes,* LAVINIA *feels blindly for the door and goes out closing it after her.* ORIN *unlocks the table drawer, pulls out his manuscript, and takes up his pen*).

*Curtain*

# ACT THREE

SCENE—*Same as Act One, Scene Two—the sitting-room. The lamp on the table is lighted but turned low. Two candles are burning on the mantel over the fireplace at right, shedding their flickering light on the portrait of* ABE MANNON *above, and of the other Mannons on the walls on each side of him. The eyes of the portraits seem to possess an intense bitter life, with their frozen stare "looking over the head of life, cutting it dead for the impropriety of living," as* ORIN *had said of his father in Act Two of "The Hunted."*

*No time has elapsed since the preceding act.* LAVINIA *enters from the hall in the rear, having just come from the study. She comes to the table and turns up the lamp. She is in a terrific state of tension. The corners of her mouth twitch, she twines and untwines the fingers of her clasped hands with a slow wringing movement which recalls her mother in the last Act of "The Hunted."*

LAVINIA (*torturedly—begins to pace up and down, muttering her thoughts aloud*)  I can't bear it! Why does he keep putting his death in my head? He would be better off if— Why hasn't he the courage—? (*Then in a frenzy of remorseful anguish, her eyes unconsciously seeking the Mannon portraits on the right wall, as if they were the visible symbol of her God*) Oh, God, don't let me have such thoughts! You know I love Orin! Show me the way to save him! Don't let me think of death! I couldn't bear another death! Please! Please! (*At a noise from the hall she controls herself and pretends to be glancing through a book on the table.* SETH *appears in the doorway*).
SETH  Vinnie!
LAVINIA  What is it, Seth?
SETH  That durned idjut, Hannah, is throwin' fits agin. Went down cellar and says she felt ha'nts crawlin' behind her. You'd better

come and git her calmed down—or she'll be leavin'. (*Then he adds disgustedly*) That's what we git fur freein' 'em!

LAVINIA (*wearily*) All right. I'll talk to her. (*She goes out with* SETH. *A pause. Then a ring from the front door bell. A moment later* SETH *can be seen coming back along the hall. He opens the front door and is heard greeting* HAZEL *and* PETER *and follows them in as they enter the room*).

SETH Vinnie's back seein' to somethin'. You set down and she'll be here soon as she kin.

PETER All right, Seth. (SETH *goes out again. They come forward and sit down.* PETER *looks hearty and good-natured, the same as ever, but* HAZEL's *face wears a nervous, uneasy look although her air is determined*).

PETER I'll have to run along soon and drop in at the Council meeting. I can't get out of it. I'll be back in half an hour—maybe sooner.

HAZEL (*suddenly with a little shiver*) I hate this house now. I hate coming here. If it wasn't for Orin—He's getting worse, Keeping him shut up here is the worst thing Vinnie could do.

PETER He won't go out. You know very well she has to force him to walk with you.

HAZEL And comes along herself! Never leaves him alone hardly a second!

PETER (*with a grin*) Oh, that's what you've got against her, eh?

HAZEL (*sharply*) Don't be silly, Peter! I simply think, and I'd say it to her face, that she's a bad influence for Orin! I feel there's something awfully wrong—somehow. He scares me at times —and Vinnie—I've watched her looking at you. She's changed so. There's something bold about her.

PETER (*getting up*) If you're going to talk like that—! You ought to be ashamed, Hazel!

HAZEL Well, I'm not! I've got some right to say something about how he's cared for! And I'm going to from now on! I'm going to make her let him visit us for a spell. I've asked Mother and she'll be glad to have him.

PETER Say, I think that's a darned good notion for both of them. She needs a rest from him, too.

HAZEL Vinnie doesn't think it's a good notion! I mentioned it yesterday and she gave me such a look! (*Determinedly*) But I'm going to make him promise to come over tomorrow, no matter what she says!

PETER (*soothingly, patting her shoulder*) Don't get angry now—about nothing. I'll help you persuade her to let him come. (*Then with a grin*) I'll help you do anything to help Orin get well—if only for selfish reasons. As long as Vinnie's tied down to him we can't get married.

HAZEL (*stares at him—slowly*) Do you really want to marry her —now?

PETER Why do you ask such a fool question? What do you mean, do I want to now?

HAZEL (*her voice trembles and she seems about to burst into tears*) Oh, I don't know, Peter! I don't know!

PETER (*sympathetic and at the same time exasperated*) What in the dickens is the matter with you?

HAZEL (*hears a noise from the hall and collects herself—warningly*) Ssshh! (ORIN *appears in the doorway at rear. He glances at them, then quickly around the room to see if* LAVINIA *is there. They both greet him with "Hello, Orin"*).

ORIN Hello! (*Then in an excited whisper, coming to them*) Where's Vinnie?

HAZEL She's gone to see to something, Seth said.

PETER (*glancing at his watch*) Gosh, I've got to hurry to that darned Council meeting.

ORIN (*eagerly*) You're going?

PETER (*jokingly*) You needn't look so darned tickled about it! It isn't polite!

ORIN I've got to see Hazel alone!

PETER All right! You don't have to put me out! (*He grins, slapping* ORIN *on the back and goes out.* ORIN *follows him with his eyes until he hears the front door close behind him*).

ORIN (*turning to* HAZEL—*with queer furtive excitement*) Listen, Hazel! I want you to do something! But wait! I've got to get— (*He rushes out and can be heard going across the hall to the study.* HAZEL *looks after him worriedly. A moment later he hurries back with a big sealed envelope in his hand which he gives to* HAZEL, *talking breathlessly, with nervous jerks of his head, as he glances apprehensively at the door*) Here! Take this! Quick! Don't let her see it! I want you to keep it in a safe place and never let anyone know you have it! It will be stolen if I keep it here! I know her! Will you promise?

HAZEL But—what is it, Orin?

ORIN   I can't tell you. You mustn't ask me. And you must promise never to open it—unless something happens to me.

HAZEL  (*frightened by his tone*)  What do you mean?

ORIN   I mean if I should die—or—but this is the most important, if she tries to marry Peter—the day before the wedding—I want you to make Peter read what's inside.

HAZEL  You don't want her to marry Peter?

ORIN   No! She can't have happiness! She's got to be punished! (*Suddenly taking her hand—excitedly*) And listen, Hazel! You mustn't love me any more. The only love I can know now is the love of guilt for guilt which breeds more guilt—until you get so deep at the bottom of hell there is no lower you can sink and you rest there in peace! (*He laughs harshly and turns away from her*).

HAZEL  Orin! Don't talk like that! (*Then conquering her horror—resolutely tender and soothing*) Ssshh! Poor boy! Come here to me. (*He comes to her. She puts an arm around him*) Listen. I know something is worrying you—and I don't want to seem prying—but I've had such a strong feeling at times that it would relieve your mind if you could tell me what it is. Haven't you thought that, Orin?

ORIN   (*longingly*)  Yes! Yes! I want to confess to your purity! I want to be forgiven! (*Then checking himself abruptly as he is about to speak—dully*)  No. I can't. Don't ask me. I love her.

HAZEL  But, you silly boy, Vinnie told Peter herself what it is and told him to tell me.

ORIN   (*staring at her wildly*)  What did she tell?

HAZEL  About your having a quarrel with your poor mother that night before she—and how you've brooded over it until you blame yourself for her death.

ORIN   (*harshly*)  I see! So in case I did tell you—oh, she's cunning! But not cunning enough this time! (*Vindictively*) You remember what I've given you, Hazel, and you do exactly what I said with it. (*Then with desperate pleading*) For God's sake, Hazel, if you love me help me to get away from here—or something terrible will happen!

HAZEL  That's just what I want to do! You come over tomorrow and stay with us.

ORIN   (*bitterly*)  Do you suppose for a moment she'll ever let me go?

HAZEL  But haven't you a right to do as you want to?

ORIN (*furtively*)  I could sneak out when she wasn't looking—and then you could hide me and when she came for me tell her I wasn't there.

HAZEL (*indignantly*)  I won't do any such thing! I don't tell lies, Orin! (*Then scornfully*) How can you be so scared of Vinnie?

ORIN (*hearing a noise from the hall—hastily*)  Ssshh! She's coming! Don't let her see what I gave you. And go home right away and lock it up! (*He tiptoes away as if he were afraid of being found close to her and sits on the sofa at right, adopting a suspiciously careless attitude.* HAZEL *looks self-conscious and stiff.* LAVINIA *appears in the doorway and gives a start as she sees* HAZEL *and* ORIN *are alone. She quickly senses something in the atmosphere and glances sharply from one to the other as she comes into the room*).

LAVINIA (*to* HAZEL, *forcing a casual air*)  I'm sorry being so long.

HAZEL  I didn't mind waiting.

LAVINIA (*sitting down on the chair at center*)  Where's Peter?

HAZEL  He had to go to a Council meeting. He's coming back.

LAVINIA (*uneasiness creeping into her tone*)  Has he been gone long?

HAZEL  Not very long.

LAVINIA (*turning to* ORIN—*sharply*)  I thought you were in the study.

ORIN (*sensing her uneasiness—mockingly*)  I finished what I was working on.

LAVINIA  You finished—? (*She glances sharply at* HAZEL—*forcing a joking tone*) My, but you two look mysterious! What have you been up to?

HAZEL (*trying to force a laugh*)  Why, Vinnie? What makes you think—?

LAVINIA  You're hiding something. (HAZEL *gives a start and instinctively moves the hand with the envelope farther behind her back.* LAVINIA *notices this. So does* ORIN *who uneasily comes to* HAZEL's *rescue*).

ORIN  We're not hiding anything. Hazel has invited me over to their house to stay for a while—and I'm going.

HAZEL (*backing him up resolutely*)  Yes. Orin is coming tomorrow.

LAVINIA (*alarmed and resentful—coldly*)  It's kind of you. I know you mean it for the best. But he can't go.

HAZEL (*sharply*)  Why not?

LAVINIA  I don't care to discuss it, Hazel. You ought to know—

HAZEL (*angrily*) I don't know! Orin is of age and can go where he pleases!

ORIN Let her talk all she likes, Hazel. I'll have the upper hand for a change, from now on! (LAVINIA *looks at him, frightened by the triumphant satisfaction in his voice*).

HAZEL (*anxious to score her point and keep* ORIN's *mind on it*) I should think you'd be glad. It will be the best thing in the world for him.

LAVINIA (*turns on her—angrily*) I'll ask you to please mind your own business, Hazel!

HAZEL (*springs to her feet, in her anger forgetting to hide the envelope which she now holds openly in her hand*) It is my business! I love Orin better than you! I don't think you love him at all, the way you've been acting!

ORIN (*sees the envelope in plain sight and calls to her warningly*) Hazel! (*She catches his eye and hastily puts her hand behind her.* LAVINIA *sees the movement but doesn't for a moment realize the meaning of it.* ORIN *goes on warningly*) You said you had to go home early. I don't want to remind you but—

HAZEL (*hastily*) Yes, I really must. (*Starting to go, trying to keep the envelope hidden, aware that* LAVINIA *is watching her suspiciously—defiantly to* ORIN) We'll expect you tomorrow, and have your room ready. (*Then to* LAVINIA—*coldly*) After the way you've insulted me, Vinnie, I hope you realize there's no more question of any friendship between us. (*She tries awkwardly to sidle toward the door*).

LAVINIA (*suddenly gets between her and the door—with angry accusation*) What are you hiding behind your back? (HAZEL *flushes guiltily, but refusing to lie, says nothing.* LAVINIA *turns on* ORIN) Have you given her what you've written? (*As he hesitates —violently*) Answer me!

ORIN That's my business! What if I have?

LAVINIA You—you traitor! You coward! (*Fiercely to* HAZEL) Give it to me! Do you hear?

HAZEL Vinnie! How dare you talk that way to me! (*She tries to go but* LAVINIA *keeps directly between her and the door*).

LAVINIA You shan't leave here until—! (*Then breaking down and pleading*) Orin! Think what you're doing! Tell her to give it to me!

ORIN No!

LAVINIA (*goes and puts her arms around him—beseechingly as he avoids her eyes*) Think sanely for a moment! You can't do this! You're a Mannon!

ORIN (*harshly*) It's because I'm one!

LAVINIA For Mother's sake, you can't! You loved her!

ORIN A lot she cared! Don't call on her!

LAVINIA (*desperately*) For my sake, then! You know I love you! Make Hazel give that up and I'll do anything—anything you want me to!

ORIN (*stares into her eyes, bending his head until his face is close to hers—with morbid intensity*) You mean that?

LAVINIA (*shrinking back from him—falteringly*) Yes.

ORIN (*laughs with a crazy triumph—checks this abruptly—and goes to* HAZEL *who has been standing bewilderedly, not understanding what is behind their talk but sensing something sinister, and terribly frightened.* ORIN *speaks curtly, his eyes fixed on* LAVINIA) Let me have it, Hazel.

HAZEL (*hands him the envelope—in a trembling voice*) I'll go home. I suppose—we can't expect you tomorrow—now.

ORIN No. Forget me. The Orin you loved was killed in the war. (*With a twisted smile*) Remember only that dead hero and not his rotting ghost! Good-bye! (*Then harshly*) Please go! (HAZEL *begins to sob and hurries blindly from the room.* ORIN *comes back to* LAVINIA *who remains kneeling by the chair. He puts the envelope in her hand—harshly*) Here! You realize the promise you made means giving up Peter? And never seeing him again?

LAVINIA (*tensely*) Yes.

ORIN And I suppose you think that's all it means, that I'll be content with a promise I've forced out of you, which you'll always be plotting to break? Oh, no! I'm not such a fool! I've got to be sure— (*She doesn't reply or look at him. He stares at her and slowly a distorted look of desire comes over his face*) You said you would do anything for me. That's a large promise, Vinnie—anything!

LAVINIA (*shrinking from him*) What do you mean? What terrible thing have you been thinking lately—behind all your crazy talk? No, I don't want to know! Orin! Why do you look at me like that?

ORIN You don't seem to feel all you mean to me now—all you have made yourself mean—since we murdered Mother!

LAVINIA Orin!

ORIN I love you now with all the guilt in me—the guilt we share! Perhaps I love you too much, Vinnie!

LAVINIA You don't know what you're saying!

ORIN There are times now when you don't seem to be my sister, nor Mother, but some stranger with the same beautiful hair— (*He touches her hair caressingly. She pulls violently away. He laughs wildly*) Perhaps you're Marie Brantôme, eh? And you say there are no ghosts in this house?

LAVINIA (*staring at him with fascinated horror*) For God's sake—! No! You're insane! You can't mean—!

ORIN How else can I be sure you won't leave me? You would never dare leave me—then! You would feel as guilty then as I do! You would be as damned as I am! (*Then with sudden anger as he sees the growing horrified repulsion on her face*) Damn you, don't you see I must find some certainty some way or go mad? You don't want me to go mad, do you? I would talk too much! I would confess! (*Then as if the word stirred something within him his tone instantly changes to one of passionate pleading*) Vinnie! For the love of God, let's go now and confess and pay the penalty for Mother's murder, and find peace together!

LAVINIA (*tempted and tortured, in a longing whisper*) Peace! (*Then summoning her will, springs to her feet wildly*) No! You coward! There is nothing to confess! There was only justice!

ORIN (*turns and addresses the portraits on the wall with a crazy mockery*) You hear her? You'll find Lavinia Mannon harder to break than me! You'll have to haunt and hound her for a lifetime!

LAVINIA (*her control snapping—turning on him now in a burst of frantic hatred and rage*) I hate you! I wish you were dead! You're too vile to live! You'd kill yourself if you weren't a coward!

ORIN (*starts back as if he'd been struck, the tortured mad look on his face changing to a stricken terrified expression*) Vinnie!

LAVINIA I mean it! I mean it! (*She breaks down and sobs hysterically*).

ORIN (*in a pitiful pleading whisper*) Vinnie! (*He stares at her with the lost stricken expression for a moment more—then the obsessed wild look returns to his eyes—with harsh mockery*) Another act of justice, eh? You want to drive me to suicide as I drove Mother! An eye for an eye, is that it? But— (*He stops abruptly and stares before him, as if this idea were suddenly taking hold of his tortured imagination and speaks fascinatedly to himself*) Yes! That would be justice—now you are Mother! She is speaking now through you! (*More and more hypnotized by this train of thought*) Yes! It's the way to peace—to find her again —my lost island—Death is an Island of Peace, too—Mother will be waiting for me there— (*With excited eagerness now, speaking to the dead*) Mother! Do you know what I'll do then? I'll get on my knees and ask your forgiveness—and say— (*His mouth grows convulsed, as if he were retching up poison*) I'll say, I'm glad you found love, Mother! I'll wish you happiness—you and Adam! (*He laughs exultantly*) You've heard me! You're here in the house now! You're calling me! You're waiting to take me home! (*He turns and strides toward the door*).

LAVINIA (*who has raised her head and has been staring at him with dread during the latter part of his talk—torn by remorse, runs after him and throws her arms around him*) No, Orin! No!

ORIN (*pushes her away—with a rough brotherly irritation*) Get out of my way, can't you? Mother's waiting! (*He gets to the door. Then he turns back and says sharply*) Ssshh! Here's Peter! Shut up, now! (*He steps back in the room as* PETER *appears in the doorway*).

PETER   Excuse my coming right in. The door was open. Where's Hazel?

ORIN (*with unnatural casualness*) Gone home. (*Then with a quick, meaning, mocking glance at* LAVINIA) I'm just going in the study to clean my pistol. Darn thing's gotten so rusty. Glad you came now, Peter. You can keep Vinnie company. (*He turns and goes out the door.* PETER *stares after him puzzledly*).

LAVINIA (*with a stifled cry*) Orin! (*There is no answer but the sound of the study door being shut. She starts to run after him, stops herself, then throws herself into* PETER'S *arms, as if for protection against herself and begins to talk volubly to drown out thought*) Hold me close, Peter! Nothing matters but love, does it? That must come first! No price is too great, is it? Or for peace! One must have peace—one is too weak to forget—no one has the right to keep anyone from peace! (*She makes a motion to cover her ears with her hands*).

PETER (*alarmed by her hectic excitement*) He's a darned fool to monkey with a pistol—in his state. Shall I get it away from him?

LAVINIA (*holding him tighter—volubly*) Oh, won't it be wonderful, Peter—once we're married and have a home with a garden and trees! We'll be so happy! I love everything that grows simply —up toward the sun—everything that's straight and strong! I hate what's warped and twists and eats into itself and dies for a life-time in shadow. (*Then her voice rising as if it were about to break hysterically—again with the instinctive movement to cover her ears*) I can't bear waiting—waiting and waiting and wait-ing—! (*There is a muffled shot from the study across the hall*).

PETER (*breaking from her and running for the door*) Good God! What's that? (*He rushes into the hall*).

LAVINIA (*sags weakly and supports herself against the table—in a faint, trembling voice*) Orin! Forgive me! (*She controls herself with a terrible effort of will. Her mouth congeals into a frozen line. Mechanically she hides the sealed envelope in a drawer of the table and locks the drawer*) I've got to go in— (*She turns to go and her eyes catch the eyes of the* MANNONS *in the portraits fixed accusingly on her—defiantly*) Why do you look at me like that? Wasn't it the only way to keep your secret, too? But I'm through with you forever now, do you hear? I'm Mother's daugh-ter—not one of you! I'll live in spite of you! (*She squares her shoulders, with a return of abrupt military movement copied from her father which she had of old—as if by the very act of disowning the* MANNONS *she had returned to the fold—and marches stiffly from the room*).

*Curtain*

# ACT FOUR

Scene—*Same as Act One, Scene One—exterior of the house. It is in the late afternoon of a day three days later. The Mannon house has much the same appearance as it had in the first act of "Home-coming." Soft golden sunlight shimmers in a luminous mist on the Greek temple portico, intensifying the whiteness of the columns, the deep green of the shutters, the green of the shrubbery, the black and green of the pines. The columns cast black bars of shadow on the gray stone wall behind them. The shutters are all fastened back, the windows open. On the ground floor, the upper part of the windows, raised from the bottom, reflect the sun in a smouldering stare, as of brooding revengeful eyes.*

SETH *appears walking slowly up the drive from right, front. He has a pair of grass clippers and potters along pretending to trim the edge of the lawn along the drive. But in reality he is merely killing time, chewing tobacco, and singing mournfully to himself, in his aged, plaintive wraith of a once good baritone, the chanty "Shenandoah":*

SETH

"Oh, Shenandoah, I long to hear you
A-way, my rolling river,
Oh, Shenandoah, I can't get near you
Way-ay, I'm bound away
Across the wide Missouri.

"Oh, Shenandoah, I love your daughter
A-way, you rolling river."

SETH (*stops singing and stands peering off left toward the flower garden—shakes his head and mutters to himself*) There she be pickin' my flowers agin. Like her Maw used to—on'y wuss. She's got every room in the house full of 'em a'ready. Durn it, I hoped she'd stop that once the funeral was over. There won't be a one left in my garden! (*He looks away and begins pottering about again, and mutters grimly*) A durn queer thin' fur a sodger to kill himself cleanin' his gun, folks is sayin'. They'll fight purty shy of her now. A Mannon has come to mean sudden death to 'em. (*Then with a grim pride*). But Vinnie's able fur 'em. They'll never git her to show nothin'. Clean Mannon strain!

(LAVINIA *enters from the left. The three days that have intervened have effected a remarkable change in her. Her body, dressed in deep mourning, again appears flat-chested and thin. The* MANNON *mask-semblance of her face appears intensified now. It is deeply lined, haggard with sleeplessness and strain, congealed into a stony emotionless expression. Her lips are bloodless, drawn taut in a grim line. She is carrying a large bunch of flowers. She holds them out to* SETH *and speaks in a strange, empty voice*).

LAVINIA    Take these, Seth, and give them to Hannah. Tell her to set them around inside. I want the house to be full of flowers. Peter is coming, and I want everything to be pretty and cheerful. (*She goes and sits at the top of the steps, bolt upright, her arms held stiffly to her sides, her legs and feet pressed together, and stares back into the sun-glare with unblinking, frozen, defiant eyes*).

SETH    (*stands holding the flowers and regarding her worriedly*)    I seed you settin' out here on the steps when I got up at five this mornin'—and every mornin' since Orin— Ain't you been gittin' no sleep? (*She stares before her as if she had not heard him. He goes on coaxingly*) How'd you like if I hauled one of them sofas out fur you to lie on, Vinnie? Mebbe you could take a couple o' winks an' it'd do you good.

LAVINIA    No, thank you, Seth. I'm waiting for Peter. (*Then after a pause, curiously*) Why didn't you tell me to go in the house and lie down? (SETH *pretends not to hear the question, avoiding her eyes*) You understand, don't you? You've been with us Mannons so long! You know there's no rest in this house which Grandfather built as a temple of Hate and Death!

SETH    (*blurts out*)    Don't you try to live here, Vinnie! You marry Peter and git clear!

LAVINIA    I'm going to marry him! And I'm going away with him and forget this house and all that ever happened in it!

SETH   That's talkin', Vinnie!

LAVINIA   I'll close it up and leave it in the sun and rain to die. The portraits of the Mannons will rot on the walls and the ghosts will fade back into death. And the Mannons will be forgotten. I'm the last and I won't be one long. I'll be Mrs. Peter Niles. Then they're finished! Thank God! (*She leans back in the sunlight and closes her eyes.* SETH *stares at her worriedly, shakes his head and spits. Then he hears something and peers down the drive, off left*).

SETH   Vinnie. Here's Hazel comin'.

LAVINIA   (*jerks up stiffly with a look of alarm*)   Hazel? What does she want? (*She springs up as if she were going to run in the house, then stands her ground on the top of the steps, her voice hardening*)   Seth, you go work in back, please!

SETH   Ayeh. (*He moves slowly off behind the lilacs as* HAZEL *enters from left, front—calling back*)   Evenin', Hazel.

HAZEL   Good evening, Seth. (*She stops short and stares at* LAVINIA. LAVINIA's *eyes are hard and defiant as she stares back.* HAZEL *is dressed in mourning. Her face is sad and pale, her eyes show evidence of much weeping, but there is an air of stubborn resolution about her as she makes up her mind and walks to the foot of the steps*).

LAVINIA   What do you want? I've got a lot to attend to.

HAZEL   (*quietly*)   It won't take me long to say what I've come to say, Vinnie. (*Suddenly she bursts out*)   It's a lie about Orin killing himself by accident! I know it is! He meant to!

LAVINIA   You better be careful what you say. I can prove what happened. Peter was here—

HAZEL   I don't care what anyone says!

LAVINIA   I should think you'd be the last one to accuse Orin—

HAZEL   I'm not accusing him! Don't you dare say that! I'm accusing you! You drove him to it! Oh, I know I can't prove it—any more than I can prove a lot of things Orin hinted at! But I know terrible things must have happened—and that you're to blame for them, somehow!

LAVINIA   (*concealing a start of fear—changing to a forced reproachful tone*)   What would Orin think of you coming here the day of his funeral to accuse me of the sorrow that's afflicted our family?

HAZEL   (*feeling guilty and at the same time defiant and sure she is right*)   All right, Vinnie. I won't say anything more. But I know there's something—and so do you—something that was driving Orin crazy— (*She breaks down and sobs*) Poor Orin!

LAVINIA (*stares straight before her. Her lips twitch. In a stifled voice between her clenched teeth*) Don't—do that!

HAZEL (*controlling herself—after a pause*) I'm sorry. I didn't come to talk about Orin.

LAVINIA (*uneasily*) What did you come for?

HAZEL About Peter.

LAVINIA (*as if this were something she had been dreading—harshly*) You leave Peter and me alone!

HAZEL I won't! You're not going to marry Peter and ruin his life! (*Pleading now*) You can't! Don't you see he could never be happy with you, that you'll only drag him into this terrible thing—whatever it is—and make him share it?

LAVINIA There is no terrible thing!

HAZEL I know Peter can't believe evil of anyone, but living alone with you, married, you couldn't hide it, he'd get to feel what I feel. You could never be happy because it would come between you! (*Pleading again*) Oh, Vinnie, you've got to be fair to Peter! You've got to consider his happiness—if you really love him!

LAVINIA (*hoarsely*) I do love him!

HAZEL It has started already—his being made unhappy through you!

LAVINIA You're lying!

HAZEL He fought with Mother last night when she tried to talk to him—the first time he ever did such a thing! It isn't like Peter. You've changed him. He left home and went to the hotel to stay. He said he'd never speak to Mother or me again. He's always been such a wonderful son before—and brother. We three have been so happy. It's broken Mother's heart. All she does is sit and cry. (*Desperately*) Oh, Vinnie, you can't do it! You will be punished if you do! Peter would get to hate you in the end!

LAVINIA No!

HAZEL Do you want to take the risk of driving Peter to do what Orin did? He might—if he ever discovered the truth!

LAVINIA (*violently*) What truth, you little fool! Discover what?

HAZEL (*accusingly*) I don't know—but you know! Look in your heart and ask your conscience before God if you ought to marry Peter!

LAVINIA (*desperately—at the end of her tether*) Yes! Before God! Before anything! (*Then glaring at her—with a burst of rage*) You leave me alone—go away—or I'll get Orin's pistol and kill you! (*Her rage passes, leaving her weak and shaken. She goes to her chair and sinks on it*).

HAZEL (*recoiling*) Oh! You are wicked! I believe you would—! Vinnie! What's made you like this?

LAVINIA Go away!

HAZEL Vinnie! (LAVINIA *closes her eyes.* HAZEL *stands staring at her. After a pause—in a trembling voice*) All right. I'll go. All I can do is trust you. I know in your heart you can't be dead to all honor and justice—you, a Mannon! (LAVINIA *gives a little bitter laugh without opening her eyes*) At least you owe it to Peter to let him read what Orin had in that envelope. Orin asked me to make him read it before he married you. I've told Peter about that, Vinnie.

LAVINIA (*without opening her eyes—strangely, as if to herself*) The dead! Why can't the dead die!

HAZEL (*stares at her frightenedly, not knowing what to do—looks around her uncertainly and sees someone coming from off left, front—quickly*) Here he comes now. I'll go by the back. I don't want him to meet me. (*She starts to go but stops by the clump of lilacs—pityingly*) I know you're suffering, Vinnie—and I know your conscience will make you do what's right—and God will forgive you. (*She goes quickly behind the lilacs and around the house to the rear*).

LAVINIA (*looks after her and calls defiantly*) I'm not asking God or anybody for forgiveness. I forgive myself! (*She leans back and closes her eyes again—bitterly*) I hope there is a hell for the good somewhere! (PETER *enters from the left, front. He looks haggard and tormented. He walks slowly, his eyes on the ground—then sees* LAVINIA *and immediately makes an effort to pull himself together and appear cheerful*).

PETER Hello, Vinnie. (*He sits on the edge of the portico beside her. She still keeps her eyes closed, as if afraid to open them. He looks at her worriedly*) You look terribly worn out. Haven't you slept? (*He pats her hand with awkward tenderness. Her mouth twitches and draws down at the corners as she stifles a sob. He goes on comfortingly*) You've had an awfully hard time of it, but never mind, we'll be married soon.

LAVINIA (*without opening her eyes—longingly*) You'll love me and keep me from remembering?

PETER You bet I will! And the first thing is to get you away from this darned house! I may be a fool but I'm beginning to feel superstitious about it myself.

LAVINIA (*without opening her eyes—strangely*) Yes. Love can't live in it. We'll go away and leave it alone to die—and we'll forget the dead.

PETER (*a bitter resentful note coming into his voice*) We can't move too far away to suit me! I hate this damned town now and everyone in it!

LAVINIA (*opens her eyes and looks at him startledly*) I never heard you talk that way before, Peter—bitter!

PETER (*avoiding her eyes*) Some things would make anyone bitter!

LAVINIA You've quarreled with your mother and Hazel—on account of me—is that it?

PETER How did you know?

LAVINIA Hazel was just here.

PETER She told you? The darned fool! What did she do that for?

LAVINIA She doesn't want me to marry you.

PETER (*angrily*) The little sneak! What right has she—? (*Then a bit uneasily—forcing a smile*) Well, you won't pay any attention to her, I hope.

LAVINIA (*more as if she were answering some voice in herself than him—stiffening in her chair—defiantly*) No!

PETER She and Mother suddenly got a lot of crazy notions in their heads. But they'll get over them.

LAVINIA (*staring at him searchingly—uneasily*) Supposing they don't?

PETER They will after we are married—or I'm through with them!

LAVINIA (*a pause. Then she takes his face in her hands and turns it to hers*) Peter! Let me look at you! You're suffering! Your eyes have a hurt look! They've always been so trustful! They look suspicious and afraid of life now! Have I done this to you already, Peter? Are you beginning to suspect me? Are you wondering what it was Orin wrote?

PETER (*protesting violently*) No! Of course I'm not! Don't I know Orin was out of his mind? Why would I pay any attention—?

LAVINIA You swear you'll never suspect me—of anything?

PETER What do you think I am?

LAVINIA And you'll never let anyone come between us? Nothing can keep us from being happy, can it? You won't let anything, will you?

PETER  Of course I won't!

LAVINIA (*more and more desperately*)  I want to get married right away, Peter! I'm afraid! Would you marry me now—this evening? We can find a minister to do it. I can change my clothes in a second and put on the color you like? Marry me today, Peter! I'm afraid to wait!

PETER (*bewildered and a bit shocked*)  But—you don't mean that, do you? We couldn't. It wouldn't look right the day Orin—out of respect for him. (*Then suspicious in spite of himself*) I can't see why you're so afraid of waiting. Nothing can happen, can it? Was there anything in what Orin wrote that would stop us from—?

LAVINIA (*with a wild beaten laugh*)  The dead coming between! They always would, Peter! You trust me with your happiness! But that means trusting the Mannon dead—and they're not to be trusted with love! I know them too well! And I couldn't bear to watch your eyes grow bitter and hidden from me and wounded in their trust of life! I love you too much!

PETER (*made more uneasy and suspicious by this*)  What are you talking about, Vinnie? You make me think there was something—

LAVINIA (*desperately*)  No—nothing! (*Then suddenly throwing her arms around him*) No! Don't think of that—not yet! I want a little while of happiness—in spite of all the dead! I've earned it! I've done enough—! (*Growing more desperate—pleading wildly*) Listen, Peter! Why must we wait for marriage? I want a moment of joy—of love—to make up for what's coming! I want it now! Can't you be strong, Peter? Can't you be simple and pure? Can't you forget sin and see that all love is beautiful? (*She kisses him with desperate passion*) Kiss me! Hold me close! Want me! Want me so much you'd murder anyone to have me! I did that—for you! Take me in this house of the dead and love me! Our love will drive the dead away! It will shame them back into death! (*At the topmost pitch of desperate, frantic abandonment*) Want me! Take me, Adam! (*She is brought back to herself with a start by this name escaping her—bewilderedly, laughing idiotically*) Adam? Why did I call you Adam? I never even heard that name before—outside of the Bible! (*Then suddenly with a hopeless, dead finality*) Always the dead between! It's no good trying any more!

PETER (*convinced she is hysterical and yet shocked and repelled by her display of passion*) Vinnie! You're talking crazy! You don't know what you're saying! You're not—like that!

LAVINIA (*in a dead voice*) I can't marry you, Peter. You mustn't ever see me again. (*He stares at her, stunned and stupid*) Go home. Make it up with your mother and Hazel. Marry someone else. Love isn't permitted to me. The dead are too strong!

PETER (*his mind in a turmoil*) Vinnie! You can't—! You've gone crazy—! What's changed you like this? (*Then suspiciously*) Is it —what Orin wrote? What was it? I've got a right to know, haven't I? (*Then as she doesn't answer—more suspiciously*) He acted so queer about—what happened to you on the Islands. Was it something there—something to do with that native—?

LAVINIA (*her first instinctive reaction one of hurt insult*) Peter! Don't you dare—! (*Then suddenly seizing on this as a way out— with calculated coarseness*) All right! Yes, if you must know! I won't lie any more! Orin suspected I'd lusted with him! And I had!

PETER (*shrinking from her aghast—brokenly*) Vinnie! You've gone crazy! I don't believe— You—you couldn't!

LAVINIA (*stridently*) Why shouldn't I? I wanted him! I wanted to learn love from him—love that wasn't a sin! And I did, I tell you! He had me! I was his fancy woman!

PETER (*wincing as if she had struck him in the face, stares at her with a stricken look of horrified repulsion—with bitter, broken anger*) Then—Mother and Hazel were right about you—you are bad at heart—no wonder Orin killed himself—God, I—I hope you'll be punished—I—! (*He hurries blindly off down the drive to the left*).

LAVINIA (*watches him go—then with a little desperate cry starts after him*) Peter! It's a lie! I didn't—! (*She stops abruptly and stiffens into her old, square-shouldered attitude. She looks down the drive after him—then turns away, saying in a lost, empty tone*) Good-bye, Peter. (SETH *enters from the left rear, coming around the corner of the house. He stands for a moment watching her, grimly wondering. Then to call her attention to his presence, he begins singing half under his breath his melancholy "Shenandoah" chanty, at the same time looking at the ground around him as if searching for something*).

SETH

"Oh, Shenandoah, I can't get near you
Way-ay, I'm bound away—"

LAVINIA (*without looking at him, picking up the words of the chanty—with a grim writhen smile*) I'm not bound away—not now, Seth. I'm bound here—to the Mannon dead! (*She gives a dry little cackle of laughter and turns as if to enter the house*).

SETH (*frightened by the look on her face, grabs her by the arm*) Don't go in there, Vinnie!

LAVINIA (*grimly*) Don't be afraid. I'm not going the way Mother and Orin went. That's escaping punishment. And there's no one left to punish me. I'm the last Mannon. I've got to punish myself! Living alone here with the dead is a worse act of justice than death or prison! I'll never go out or see anyone! I'll have the shutters nailed closed so no sunlight can ever get in. I'll live alone with the dead, and keep their secrets, and let them hound me, until the curse is paid out and the last Mannon is let die! (*With a strange cruel smile of gloating over the years of self-torture*) I know they will see to it I live for a long time! It takes the Mannons to punish themselves for being born!

SETH (*with grim understanding*) Ayeh. And I ain't heard a word you've been sayin', Vinnie. (*Pretending to search the ground again*) Left my clippers around somewheres.

LAVINIA (*turns to him sharply*) You go now and close the shutters and nail them tight.

SETH   Ayeh.

LAVINIA   And tell Hannah to throw out all the flowers.

SETH   Ayeh. (*He goes past her up the steps and into the house. She ascends to the portico—and then turns and stands for a while, stiff and square-shouldered, staring into the sunlight with frozen eyes.* SETH *leans out of the window at the right of the door and pulls the shutters closed with a decisive bang. As if this were a word of command,* LAVINIA *pivots sharply on her heel and marches woodenly into the house, closing the door behind her*).

*Curtain*

# The Iceman
# Cometh

# Characters

HARRY HOPE, proprietor of a saloon and rooming house*

ED MOSHER, Hope's brother-in-law, one-time circus man*

PAT MCGLOIN, one-time Police Lieutenant*

WILLIE OBAN, a Harvard Law School alumnus*

JOE MOTT, one-time proprietor of a Negro gambling house

PIET WETJOEN ("THE GENERAL"), one-time leader of a Boer commando*

CECIL LEWIS ("THE CAPTAIN"), one-time Captain of British infantry*

JAMES CAMERON ("JIMMY TOMORROW"), one-time Boer War correspondent*

HUGO KALAMAR, one-time editor of Anarchist periodicals

LARRY SLADE, one-time Syndicalist-Anarchist*

ROCKY PIOGGI, night bartender*

DON PARRITT*

PEARL*

MARGIE*   } street walkers

CORA

CHUCK MORELLO, day bartender*

THEODORE HICKMAN (HICKEY), a hardware salesman

MORAN

LIEB

* Roomers at Harry Hope's

# Synopsis of Scenes

Harry Hope's is a Raines-Law hotel of the period, a cheap gin-mill of the five-cent whiskey, last-resort variety situated on the downtown West Side of New York. The building, owned by Hope, is a narrow five-story structure of the tenement type, the second floor a flat occupied by the proprietor. The renting of rooms on the upper floors, under the Raines-Law loopholes, makes the establishment legally a hotel and gives it the privilege of serving liquor in the back room of the bar after closing hours and on Sundays, provided a meal is served with the booze, thus making a back room legally a hotel restaurant. This food provision was generally circumvented by putting a property sandwich in the middle of each table, an old desiccated ruin of dust-laden bread and mummified ham or cheese which only the drunkest yokel from the sticks ever regarded as anything but a noisome table decoration. But at Harry Hope's, Hope being a former minor Tammanyite and still possessing friends, this food technicality is ignored as irrelevant, except during the fleeting alarms of reform agitation. Even Hope's back room is not a separate room, but simply the rear of the barroom divided from the bar by drawing a dirty black curtain across the room.

# ACT ONE

SCENE: *The back room and a section of the bar of* HARRY HOPE'S *saloon on an early morning in summer, 1912. The right wall of the back room is a dirty black curtain which separates it from the bar. At rear, this curtain is drawn back from the wall so the bartender can get in and out. The back room is crammed with round tables and chairs placed so close together that it is a difficult squeeze to pass between them. In the middle of the rear wall is a door opening on a hallway. In the left corner, built out into the room, is the toilet with a sign "This is it" on the door. Against the middle of the left wall is a nickel-in-the-slot phonograph. Two windows, so glazed with grime one cannot see through them, are in the left wall, looking out on a backyard. The walls and ceiling once were white, but it was a long time ago, and they are now so splotched, peeled, stained and dusty that their color can best be described as dirty. The floor, with iron spittoons placed here and there, is covered with sawdust. Lighting comes from single wall brackets, two at left and two at rear.*

*There are three rows of tables, from front to back. Three are in the front line. The one at left-front has four chairs; the one at center-front, four; the one at right-front, five. At rear of, and half between, front tables one and two is a table of the second row with five chairs. A table, similarly placed at rear of front tables two and three, also has five chairs. The third row of tables, four chairs to one and six to the other, is against the rear wall on either side of the door.*

*At right of this dividing curtain is a section of the barroom, with the end of the bar seen at rear, a door to the hall at left of it. At front is a table with four chairs. Light comes from the street windows off right, the gray subdued light of early morning in a narrow street. In the back room,* LARRY SLADE *and* HUGO KALAMAR *are at the table at left-front,* HUGO *in a chair facing right,* LARRY *at rear of table facing front, with an empty chair between them. A fourth chair is at right of table, facing left.* HUGO *is a small man in his late fifties. He has a head much too big for his body, a high forehead, crinkly long black hair streaked with gray, a square face with a pug nose, a walrus mustache, black eyes which peer near-sightedly from behind thick-lensed spectacles, tiny hands and feet. He is dressed in threadbare black clothes and his white shirt is frayed at collar and cuffs, but everything about him is fastidiously clean. Even his flowing Windsor tie is neatly tied. There is a foreign atmosphere about him, the stamp of an alien radical, a strong resemblance to the type Anarchist as portrayed, bomb in hand, in newspaper cartoons. He is asleep now, bent forward in his chair, his arms folded on the table, his head resting sideways on his arms.*

LARRY SLADE *is sixty. He is tall, raw-boned, with coarse straight white hair, worn long and raggedly cut. He has a gaunt Irish face with a big nose, high cheekbones, a lantern jaw with a week's stubble of beard, a mystic's meditative pale-blue eyes with a gleam of sharp sardonic humor in them. As slovenly as* HUGO *is neat, his clothes are dirty and much slept in. His gray flannel shirt, open at the neck, has the appearance of having never been washed. From the way he methodically scratches himself with his long-fingered, hairy hands, he is lousy and reconciled to being so. He is the only occupant of the room who is not asleep. He stares in front of him, an expression of tired tolerance giving his face the quality of a pitying but weary old priest's.*

*All four chairs at the middle table, front, are occupied.* JOE MOTT *sits at left-front of the table, facing front. Behind him, facing right-front, is* PIET WETJOEN *("The General"). At center of the table, rear,* JAMES CAMERON *("Jimmy Tomorrow") sits facing front. At right of table, opposite* JOE, *is* CECIL LEWIS *("The Captain").*

JOE MOTT *is a Negro, about fifty years old, brown-skinned, stocky, wearing a light suit that had once been flashily sporty but is now about to fall apart. His pointed tan buttoned shoes, faded pink shirt and bright tie belong to the same vintage. Still, he manages to preserve an atmosphere of nattiness and there is nothing dirty about his appearance. His face is only mildly negroid in type. The nose is thin and his lips are not noticeably thick. His hair is crinkly and he is beginning to get bald. A scar from a knife slash runs from his left cheekbone to jaw. His face would be hard and tough if it were not for its good nature and lazy humor. He is asleep, his nodding head supported by his left hand.*

PIET WETJOEN, *the Boer, is in his fifties, a huge man with a bald head and a long grizzled beard. He is slovenly dressed in a dirty shapeless patched suit, spotted by food. A Dutch farmer type, his once great muscular strength has been debauched into flaccid tallow. But despite his blubbery mouth and sodden bloodshot blue eyes, there is still a suggestion of old authority lurking in him like a memory of the drowned. He is hunched forward, both elbows on the table, his hand on each side of his head for support.*

JAMES CAMERON* ("Jimmy Tomorrow") is about the same size and age as* HUGO, *a small man. Like* HUGO, *he wears threadbare black, and everything about him is clean. But the resemblance ceases there.* JIMMY *has a face like an old well-bred, gentle bloodhound's, with folds of flesh hanging from each side of his mouth, and big brown friendly guileless eyes, more bloodshot than any bloodhound's ever were. He has mouse-colored thinning hair, a little bulbous nose, buck teeth in a small rabbit mouth. But his forehead is fine, his eyes are intelligent and there once was a competent ability in him. His speech is educated, with the ghost of a Scotch rhythm in it. His manners are those of a gentleman. There is a quality about him of a prim, Victorian old maid, and at the same time of a likable, affectionate boy who has never grown up. He sleeps, chin on chest, hands folded in his lap.*

CECIL LEWIS* ("The Captain") is as obviously English as Yorkshire pudding and just as obviously the former army officer. He is going on sixty. His hair and military mustache are white, his eyes bright blue, his complexion that of a turkey. His lean figure is still erect and square-shouldered. He is stripped to the waist, his coat, shirt, undershirt, collar and tie crushed up into a pillow on the table in front of him, his head sideways on this pillow, facing front, his arms dangling toward the floor. On his lower left shoulder is the big ragged scar of an old wound.*

*At the table at right, front,* HARRY HOPE, *the proprietor, sits in the middle, facing front, with* PAT MCGLOIN *on his right and* ED MOSHER *on his left, the other two chairs being unoccupied.*

*Both* MCGLOIN *and* MOSHER *are big paunchy men.* MCGLOIN *has his old occupation of policeman stamped all over him. He is in his fifties, sandy-haired, bullet-headed, jowly, with protruding ears and little round eyes. His face must once have been brutal and greedy, but time and whiskey have melted it down into a good-humored, parasite's characterlessness. He wears old clothes and is slovenly. He is slumped sideways on his chair, his head drooping jerkily toward one shoulder.*

ED MOSHER *is going on sixty. He has a round kewpie's face—a kewpie who is an unshaven habitual drunkard. He looks like an enlarged, elderly, bald edition of the village fat boy—a sly fat boy, congenitally indolent, a practical joker, a born grafter and con merchant. But amusing and essentially harmless, even in his most enterprising days, because always too lazy to carry crookedness beyond petty swindling. The influence of his old circus career is apparent in his get-up. His worn clothes are flashy; he wears phony rings and a heavy brass watch-chain (not connected to a watch). Like* MCGLOIN, *he is slovenly. His head is thrown back, his big mouth open.*

HARRY HOPE *is sixty, white-haired, so thin the description "bag of bones" was made for him. He has the face of an old family horse, prone to tantrums, with balkiness always smoldering in its wall eyes, waiting for any excuse to shy and pretend to take the bit in its teeth.* HOPE *is one of those men whom everyone likes on sight, a softhearted slob, without malice, feeling superior to no one, a sinner among sinners, a born easy mark for every appeal. He attempts to hide his defenselessness behind a testy truculent manner, but this has never fooled anyone. He is a little deaf, but not half as deaf as he sometimes pretends. His sight is failing but is not as bad as he complains it is. He wears five-and-ten-cent-store spectacles which are so out of alignment that one eye at times peers half over one glass while the other eye looks half under the other. He has badly fitting store teeth, which click like castanets when he begins to fume. He is dressed in an old coat from one suit and pants from another.*

*In a chair facing right at the table in the second line, between the first two tables, front, sits* WILLIE OBAN, *his head on his left arm outstretched along the table edge. He is in his late thirties, of average height, thin. His haggard, dissipated face has a small nose, a pointed chin, blue eyes with colorless lashes and brows. His blond hair, badly in need of a cut, clings in a limp part to his skull. His eyelids flutter continually as if any light were too strong for his eyes. The clothes he wears belong on a scarecrow. They seem constructed of an inferior grade of dirty blotting paper. His shoes are even more disreputable, wrecks of imitation leather, one laced with twine, the other with a bit of wire. He has no socks, and his bare feet show through holes in the soles, with his big toes sticking*

*out of the uppers. He keeps muttering and twitching in his sleep.
As the curtain rises,* ROCKY, *the night bartender, comes from the
bar through the curtain and stands looking over the back room. He
is a Neapolitan-American in his late twenties, squat and muscular,
with a flat, swarthy face and beady eyes. The sleeves of his collar-
less shirt are rolled up on his thick, powerful arms and he wears a
soiled apron. A tough guy but sentimental, in his way, and good-
natured. He signals to* LARRY *with a cautious "Sstt" and motions him
to see if* HOPE *is asleep.* LARRY *rises from his chair to look at* HOPE
*and nods to* ROCKY. ROCKY *goes back to the bar but immediately
returns with a bottle of bar whiskey and a glass. He squeezes
between the tables to* LARRY.

ROCKY (*In a low voice out of the side of his mouth*) Make it fast.
(LARRY *pours a drink and gulps it down.* ROCKY *takes the bottle
and puts it on the table where* WILLIE OBAN *is*) Don't want de
Boss to get wise when he's got one of his tightwad buns on.
(*He chuckles with an amused glance at* HOPE) Jees, ain't de old
bastard a riot when he starts dat bull about turnin' over a new
leaf? "Not a damned drink on de house," he tells me, "and all
dese bums got to pay up deir room rent. Beginnin' tomorrow,"
he says. Jees, yuh'd tink he meant it!
(*He sits down in the chair at* LARRY'S *left*)
LARRY (*Grinning*) I'll be glad to pay up—tomorrow. And I know
my fellow inmates will promise the same. They've all a touching
credulity concerning tomorrows. (*A half-drunken mockery in his
eyes*) It'll be a great day for them, tomorrow—the Feast of All
Fools, with brass bands playing! Their ships will come in, loaded
to the gunwales with cancelled regrets and promises fulfilled and
clean slates and new leases!
ROCKY (*Cynically*) Yeah, and a ton of hop!
LARRY (*Leans toward him, a comical intensity in his low voice*)
Don't mock the faith! Have you no respect for religion, you
unregenerate Wop? What's it matter if the truth is that their
favoring breeze has the stink of nickel whiskey on its breath, and
their sea is a growler of lager and ale, and their ships are long
since looted and scuttled and sunk on the bottom? To hell with
the truth! As the history of the world proves, the truth has no
bearing on anything. It's irrelevant and immaterial, as the
lawyers say. The lie of a pipe dream is what gives life to the
whole misbegotten mad lot of us, drunk or sober. And that's

enough philosophic wisdom to give you for one drink of rotgut.

ROCK (*Grins kiddingly*) De old Foolosopher, like Hickey calls yuh, ain't yuh? I s'pose you don't fall for no pipe dream?

LARRY (*A bit stiffly*) I don't, no. Mine are all dead and buried behind me. What's before me is the comforting fact that death is a fine long sleep, and I'm damned tired, and it can't come too soon for me.

ROCKY Yeah, just hangin' around hopin' you'll croak, ain't yuh? Well, I'm bettin' you'll have a good long wait. Jees, somebody'll have to take an axe to croak you!

LARRY (*Grins*) Yes, it's my bad luck to be cursed with an iron constitution that even Harry's booze can't corrode.

ROCKY De old anarchist wise guy dat knows all de answers! Dat's you, huh?

LARRY (*Frowns*) Forget the anarchist part of it. I'm through with the Movement long since. I saw men didn't want to be saved from themselves, for that would mean they'd have to give up greed, and they'll never pay that price for liberty. So I said to the world, God bless all here, and may the best man win and die of gluttony! And I took a seat in the grandstand of philosophical detachment to fall asleep observing the cannibals do their death dance. (*He chuckles at his own fancy—reaches over and shakes* HUGO's *shoulder*) Ain't I telling him the truth, Comrade Hugo?

ROCKY Aw, fer Chris' sake, don't get dat bughouse bum started!

HUGO (*Raises his head and peers at* ROCKY *blearily through his thick spectacles—in a guttural declamatory tone*) Capitalist swine! Bourgeois stool pigeons! Have the slaves no right to sleep even? (*Then he grins at* ROCKY *and his manner changes to a giggling, wheedling playfulness, as though he were talking to a child*) Hello, leedle Rocky! Leedle monkey-face! Vere is your leedle slave girls? (*With an abrupt change to a bullying tone*) Don't be a fool! Loan me a dollar! Damned bourgeois Wop! The great Malatesta is my good friend! Buy me a trink!

(*He seems to run down, and is overcome by drowsiness. His head sinks to the table again and he is at once fast asleep*)

ROCKY He's out again. (*More exasperated than angry*) He's lucky no one don't take his cracks serious or he'd wake up every mornin' in a hospital.

LARRY (*Regarding* HUGO *with pity*) No. No one takes him seriously. That's his epitaph. Not even the comrades any more. If I've been through with the Movement long since, it's been through with him, and, thanks to whiskey, he's the only one doesn't know it.

ROCKY   I've let him get by wid too much. He's goin' to pull dat slavegirl stuff on me once too often. (*His manner changes to defensive argument*) Hell, yuh'd tink I wuz a pimp or somethin'. Everybody knows me knows I ain't. A pimp don't hold no job. I'm a bartender. Dem tarts, Margie and Poil, dey're just a side line to pick up some extra dough. Strictly business, like dey was fighters and I was deir manager, see? I fix the cops fer dem so's dey can hustle widout gettin' pinched. Hell, dey'd be on de Island most of de time if it wasn't fer me. And I don't beat dem up like a pimp would. I treat dem fine. Dey like me. We're pals, see? What if I do take deir dough? Dey'd on'y trow it away. Tarts can't hang on to dough. But I'm a bartender and I work hard for my livin' in dis dump. You know dat, Larry.

LARRY   (*With inner sardonic amusement—flatteringly*) A shrewd business man, who doesn't miss any opportunity to get on in the world. That's what I'd call you.

ROCKY   (*Pleased*) Sure ting. Dat's me. Grab another ball, Larry. (LARRY *pours a drink from the bottle on* WILLIE's *table and gulps it down.* ROCKY *glances around the room*) Yuh'd never tink all dese bums had a good bed upstairs to go to. Scared if dey hit the hay dey wouldn't be here when Hickey showed up, and dey'd miss a coupla drinks. Dat's what kept you up too, ain't it?

LARRY   It is. But not so much the hope of booze, if you can believe that. I've got the blues and Hickey's a great one to make a joke of everything and cheer you up.

ROCKY   Yeah, some kidder! Remember how he woiks up dat gag about his wife, when he's cockeyed, cryin' over her picture and den springin' it on yuh all of a sudden dat he left her in de hay wid de iceman? (*He laughs*) I wonder what's happened to him. Yuh could set your watch by his periodicals before dis. Always got here a coupla days before Harry's birthday party, and now he's on'y got till tonight to make it. I hope he shows soon. Dis dump is like de morgue wid all dese bums passed out. (WILLIE OBAN *jerks and twitches in his sleep and begins to mumble. They watch him*).

WILLIE   (*Blurts from his dream*) It's a lie! (*Miserably*) Papa! Papa!

LARRY   Poor devil. (*Then angry with himself*) But to hell with pity! It does no good. I'm through with it!

ROCKY   Dreamin' about his old man. From what de old-timers say, de old gent sure made a pile of dough in de bucket-shop game before de cops got him. (*He considers* WILLIE *frowningly*) Jees, I've seen him bad before but never dis bad. Look at dat get-up. Been playin' de old reliever game. Sold his suit and shoes at Solly's two days ago. Solly give him two bucks and a bum outfit. Yesterday he sells de bum one back to Solly for four bits and gets dese rags to put on. Now he's through. Dat's Solly's final edition he wouldn't take back for nuttin'. Willie sure is on de bottom. I ain't never seen no one so bad, except Hickey on de end of a coupla his bats.

LARRY (*Sardonically*) It's a great game, the pursuit of happiness.

ROCKY Harry don't know what to do about him. He called up his old lady's lawyer like he always does when Willie gets licked. Yuh remember dey used to send down a private dick to give him the rush to a cure, but de lawyer tells Harry nix, de old lady's off of Willie for keeps dis time and he can go to hell.

LARRY (*Watches* WILLIE, *who is shaking in his sleep like an old dog*) There's the consolation that he hasn't far to go! (*As if replying to this,* WILLIE *comes to a crisis of jerks and moans.* LARRY *adds in a comically intense, crazy whisper*) Be God, he's knocking on the door right now!

WILLIE (*Suddenly yells in his nightmare*) It's a God-damned lie! (*He begins to sob*) Oh, Papa! Jesus!

(*All the occupants of the room stir on their chairs but none of them wakes up except* HOPE)

ROCKY (*Grabs his shoulder and shakes him*) Hey, you! Nix! Cut out de noise!

(WILLIE *opens his eyes to stare around him with a bewildered horror*)

HOPE (*Opens one eye to peer over his spectacles—drowsily*) Who's that yelling?

ROCKY Willie, Boss. De Brooklyn boys is after him.

HOPE (*Querulously*) Well, why don't you give the poor feller a drink and keep him quiet? Bejees, can't I get a wink of sleep in my own back room?

ROCKY (*Indignantly to* LARRY) Listen to that blind-eyed, deef old bastard, will yuh? He give me strict orders not to let Willie hang up no more drinks, no matter—

HOPE (*Mechanically puts a hand to his ear in the gesture of deafness*) What's that? I can't hear you. (*Then drowsily irascible*) You're a cockeyed liar. Never refused a drink to anyone needed it bad in my life! Told you to use your judgment. Ought to know better. You're too busy thinking up ways to cheat me. Oh, I ain't as blind as you think. I can still see a cash register, bejees!

ROCKY (*Grins at him affectionately now—flatteringly*) Sure, Boss. Swell chance of foolin' you!

HOPE I'm wise to you and your sidekick, Chuck. Bejees, you're burglars, not barkeeps! Blind-eyed, deef old bastard, am I? Oh, I heard you! Heard you often when you didn't think. You and Chuck laughing behind my back, telling people you throw the money up in the air and whatever sticks to the ceiling is my share! A fine couple of crooks! You'd steal the pennies off your dead mother's eyes!

ROCKY (*Winks at* LARRY) Aw, Harry, me and Chuck was on'y kiddin'.

HOPE (*More drowsily*) I'll fire both of you. Bejees, if you think you can play me for an easy mark, you've come to the wrong house. No one ever played Harry Hope for a sucker!

ROCKY (*To* LARRY) No one but everybody.

HOPE (*His eyes shut again—mutters*) Least you could do—keep things quiet—

(*He falls asleep*)

WILLIE (*Pleadingly*) Give me a drink, Rocky. Harry said it was all right. God, I need a drink.

ROCKY Den grab it. It's right under your nose.

WILLIE (*Avidly*) Thanks.

(*He takes the bottle with both twitching hands and tilts it to his lips and gulps down the whiskey in big swallows*)

ROCKY (*Sharply*) When! When! (*He grabs the bottle*) I didn't say, take a bath! (*Showing the bottle to* LARRY—*indignantly*) Jees, look! He's killed a half pint or more!

(*He turns on* WILLIE *angrily, but* WILLIE *has closed his eyes and is sitting quietly, shuddering, waiting for the effect*)

LARRY (*With a pitying glance*) Leave him be, the poor devil. A half pint of that dynamite in one swig will fix him for a while— if it doesn't kill him.

ROCKY (*Shrugs his shoulders and sits down again*) Aw right by me. It ain't my booze.

(*Behind him, in the chair at left of the middle table,* JOE MOTT, *the Negro, has been waking up*)

JOE (*His eyes blinking sleepily*) Whose booze? Gimme some. I don't care whose. Where's Hickey? Ain't he come yet? What time's it, Rocky?

ROCKY  Gettin' near time to open up. Time you begun to sweep up in de bar.

JOE (*Lazily*)  Never mind de time. If Hickey ain't come, it's time Joe goes to sleep again. I was dreamin' Hickey come in de door, crackin' one of dem drummer's jokes, wavin' a big bankroll and we was all goin' be drunk for two weeks. Wake up and no luck. (*Suddenly his eyes open wide*) Wait a minute, dough. I got idea. Say, Larry, how 'bout dat young guy, Parritt, come to look you up last night and rented a room? Where's he at?

LARRY  Up in his room, asleep. No hope in him, anyway, Joe. He's broke.

JOE  Dat what he told you? Me and Rocky knows different. Had a roll when he paid you his room rent, didn't he, Rocky? I seen it.

ROCKY  Yeah. He flashed it like he forgot and den tried to hide it quick.

LARRY (*Surprised and resentful*)  He did, did he?

ROCKY  Yeah, I figgered he don't belong, but he said he was a friend of yours.

LARRY  He's a liar. I wouldn't know him if he hadn't told me who he was. His mother and I were friends years ago on the Coast. (*He hesitates—then lowering his voice*) You've read in the papers about that bombing on the Coast when several people got killed? Well, the one woman they pinched, Rosa Parritt, is his mother. They'll be coming up for trial soon, and there's no chance for them. She'll get life, I think. I'm telling you this so you'll know why if Don acts a bit queer, and not jump on him. He must be hard hit. He's her only kid.

ROCKY (*Nods—then thoughtfully*)  Why ain't he out dere stickin' by her?

LARRY (*Frowns*)  Don't ask questions. Maybe there's a good reason.

ROCKY (*Stares at him—understandingly*)  Sure. I get it. (*Then wonderingly*) But den what kind of a sap is he to hang on to his right name?

LARRY (*Irritably*)  I'm telling you I don't know anything and I don't want to know. To hell with the Movement and all connected with it! I'm out of it, and everything else, and damned glad to be.

ROCKY (*Shrugs his shoulders—indifferently*) Well, don't tink I'm interested in dis Parritt guy. He's nuttin' to me.

JOE Me neider. If dere's one ting more'n anudder I cares nuttin' about, it's de sucker game you and Hugo call de Movement. (*He chuckles—reminiscently*) Reminds me of damn fool argument me and Mose Porter has de udder night. He's drunk and I'm drunker. He says, "Socialist and Anarchist, we ought to shoot dem dead. Dey's all no-good sons of bitches." I says, "Hold on, you talk's if Anarchists and Socialists was de same." "Dey is," he says. "Dey's both no-good bastards." "No, dey ain't," I says. "I'll explain the difference. De Anarchist he never works. He drinks but he never buys, and if he do ever get a nickel, he blows it in on bombs, and he wouldn't give you nothin'. So go ahead and shoot him. But de Socialist, sometimes, he's got a job, and if he gets ten bucks, he's bound by his religion to split fifty-fifty wid you. You say—how about my cut, Comrade? And you gets de five. So you don't shoot no Socialists while I'm around. Dat is, not if dey got anything. Of course, if dey's broke, den dey's no-good bastards, too." (*He laughs, immensely tickled*)

LARRY (*Grins with sardonic appreciation*) Be God, Joe, you've got all the beauty of human nature and the practical wisdom of the world in that little parable.

ROCKY (*Winks at* JOE) Sure, Larry ain't de on'y wise guy in dis dump, hey, Joe? (*At a sound from the hall he turns as* DON PARRITT *appears in the doorway.* ROCKY *speaks to* LARRY *out of the side of his mouth*) Here's your guy.

(PARRITT *comes forward. He is eighteen, tall and broad-shouldered but thin, gangling and awkward. His face is good-looking, with blond curly hair and large regular features, but his personality is unpleasant. There is a shifting defiance and ingratiation in his light-blue eyes and an irritating aggressiveness in his manner. His clothes and shoes are new, comparatively expensive, sporty in style. He looks as though he belonged in a pool room patronized by would-be sports. He glances around defensively, sees* LARRY *and comes forward*)

PARRITT Hello, Larry. (*He nods to* ROCKY *and* JOE) Hello.

(*They nod and size him up with expressionless eyes*)

LARRY (*Without cordiality*) What's up? I thought you'd be asleep.

PARRITT Couldn't make it. I got sick of lying awake. Thought I might as well see if you were around.

LARRY (*Indicates the chair on the right of table*) Sit down and join the bums then. (PARRITT *sits down.* LARRY *adds meaningfully*) The rules of the house are that drinks may be served at all hours.

PARRITT (*Forcing a smile*) I get you. But, hell, I'm just about broke. (*He catches* ROCKY's *and* JOE's *contemptuous glances—quickly*) Oh, I know you guys saw— You think I've got a roll. Well, you're all wrong. I'll show you. (*He takes a small wad of dollar bills from his pocket*) It's all ones. And I've got to live on it till I get a job. (*Then with defensive truculence*) You think I fixed up a phony, don't you? Why the hell would I? Where would I get a real roll? You don't get rich doing what I've been doing. Ask Larry. You're lucky in the Movement if you have enough to eat.

(LARRY *regards him puzzledly*)

ROCKY (*Coldly*) What's de song and dance about? We ain't said nuttin'.

PARRITT (*Lamely—placating them now*) Why, I was just putting you right. But I don't want you to think I'm a tightwad. I'll buy a drink if you want one.

JOE (*Cheering up*) If? Man, when I don't want a drink, you call de morgue, tell dem come take Joe's body away, 'cause he's sure enuf dead. Gimme de bottle quick, Rocky, before he changes his mind!

(ROCKY *passes him the bottle and glass. He pours a brimful drink and tosses it down his throat, and hands the bottle and glass to* LARRY)

ROCKY I'll take a cigar when I go in de bar. What're you havin'?

PARRITT Nothing. I'm on the wagon. What's the damage?

(*He holds out a dollar bill*)

ROCKY Fifteen cents.

(*He makes change from his pocket*)

PARRITT Must be some booze!

LARRY It's cyanide cut with carbolic acid to give it a mellow flavor. Here's luck!

(*He drinks*)

ROCKY Guess I'll get back in de bar and catch a coupla winks before opening-up time.

(*He squeezes through the tables and disappears, right-rear, behind the curtain. In the section of bar at right, he comes forward and sits at the table and slumps back, closing his eyes and yawning*)

JOE (*Stares calculatingly at* PARRITT *and then looks away—aloud to himself, philosophically*) One-drink guy. Dat well done run dry. No hope till Harry's birthday party. 'Less Hickey shows up. (*He turns to* LARRY) If Hickey comes, Larry, you wake me up if you has to bat me wid a chair.

(*He settles himself and immediately falls asleep*)

PARRITT Who's Hickey?

LARRY A hardware drummer. An old friend of Harry Hope's and all the gang. He's a grand guy. He comes here twice a year regularly on a periodical drunk and blows in all his money.

PARRITT (*With a disparaging glance around*) Must be hard up for a place to hang out.

LARRY It has its points for him. He never runs into anyone he knows in his business here.

PARRITT (*Lowering his voice*) Yes, that's what I want, too. I've got to stay under cover, Larry, like I told you last night.

LARRY You did a lot of hinting. You didn't tell me anything.

PARRITT You can guess, can't you? (*He changes the subject abruptly*) I've been in some dumps on the Coast, but this is the limit. What kind of joint is it, anyway?

LARRY (*With a sardonic grin*) What is it? It's the No Chance Saloon. It's Bedrock Bar, The End of the Line Café, The Bottom of the Sea Rathskeller! Don't you notice the beautiful calm in the atmosphere? That's because it's the last harbor. No one here has to worry about where they're going next, because there is no farther they can go. It's a great comfort to them. Although even here they keep up the appearances of life with a few harmless pipe dreams about their yesterdays and tomorrows, as you'll see for yourself if you're here long.

PARRITT (*Stares at him curiously*) What's your pipe dream, Larry?

LARRY (*Hiding resentment*) Oh, I'm the exception. I haven't any left, thank God. (*Shortly*) Don't complain about this place. You couldn't find a better for lying low.

PARRITT I'm glad of that, Larry. I don't feel any too damned good. I was knocked off my base by that business on the Coast, and since then it's been no fun dodging around the country, thinking every guy you see might be a dick.

LARRY (*Sympathetically now*) No, it wouldn't be. But you're safe here. The cops ignore this dump. They think it's as harmless as a graveyard. (*He grins sardonically*) And, be God, they're right.

PARRITT It's been lonely as hell. (*Impulsively*) Christ, Larry, I was glad to find you. I kept saying to myself, "If I can only find Larry. He's the one guy in the world who can understand—" (*He hesitates, staring at* LARRY *with a strange appeal*)

LARRY (*Watching him puzzledly*) Understand what?

PARRITT (*Hastily*) Why, all I've been through. (*Looking away*) Oh, I know you're thinking, This guy has a hell of a nerve. I haven't seen him since he was a kid. I'd forgotten he was alive. But I've never forgotten you, Larry. You were the only friend of Mother's who ever paid attention to me, or knew I was alive. All the others were too busy with the Movement. Even Mother. And I had no Old Man. You used to take me on your knee and tell me stories and crack jokes and make me laugh. You'd ask me questions and take what I said seriously. I guess I got to feel in the years you lived with us that you'd taken the place of my Old Man. (*Embarrassedly*) But, hell, that sounds like a lot of mush. I suppose you don't remember a damned thing about it.

LARRY (*Moved in spite of himself*) I remember well. You were a serious lonely little shaver. (*Then resenting being moved, changed the subject*) How is it they didn't pick you up when they got your mother and the rest?

PARRITT (*In a lowered voice but eagerly, as if he wanted this chance to tell about it*) I wasn't around, and as soon as I heard the news I went under cover. You've noticed my glad rags. I was staked to them—as a disguise, sort of. I hung around pool rooms and gambling joints and hooker shops, where they'd never look for a Wobblie, pretending I was a sport. Anyway, they'd grabbed everyone important, so I suppose they didn't think of me until afterward.

LARRY The papers say the cops got them all dead to rights, that the Burns dicks knew every move before it was made, and someone inside the Movement must have sold out and tipped them off.

PARRITT (*Turns to look* LARRY *in the eyes—slowly*) Yes, I guess that must be true, Larry. It hasn't come out who it was. It may never come out. I suppose whoever it was made a bargain with the Burns men to keep him out of it. They won't need his evidence.

LARRY (*Tensely*) By God, I hate to believe it of any of the crowd, if I am through long since with any connection with them. I know they've damned fools, most of them, as stupidly greedy for power as the worst capitalist they attack, but I'd swear there couldn't be a yellow stool pigeon among them.

PARRITT   Sure. I'd have sworn that, too, Larry.

LARRY   I hope his soul rots in hell, whoever it is!

PARRITT   Yes, so do I.

LARRY   (*After a pause—shortly*)  How did you locate me? I hoped I'd found a place of retirement here where no one in the Movement would ever come to disturb my peace.

PARRITT   I found out through Mother.

LARRY   I asked her not to tell anyone.

PARRITT   She didn't tell me, but she'd kept all your letters and I found where she'd hidden them in the flat. I sneaked up there one night after she was arrested.

LARRY   I'd never have thought she was a woman who'd keep letters.

PARRITT   No, I wouldn't, either. There's nothing soft or sentimental about Mother.

LARRY   I never answered her last letters. I haven't written her in a couple of years—or anyone else. I've gotten beyond the desire to communicate with the world—or, what's more to the point, to let it bother me any more with its greedy madness.

PARRITT   It's funny Mother kept in touch with you so long. When she's finished with anyone, she's finished. She's always been proud of that. And you know how she feels about the Movement. Like a revivalist preacher about religion. Anyone who loses faith in it is more than dead to her; he's a Judas who ought to be boiled in oil. Yet she seemed to forgive you.

LARRY   (*Sardonically*)  She didn't, don't worry. She wrote to denounce me and try to bring the sinner to repentance and a belief in the One True Faith again.

PARRITT   What made you leave the Movement, Larry? Was it on account of Mother?

LARRY   (*Starts*)  Don't be a damned fool! What the hell put that in your head?

PARRITT   Why, nothing—except I remember what a fight you had with her before you left.

LARRY   (*Resentfully*)  Well, if you do, I don't. That was eleven years ago. You were only seven. If we did quarrel, it was because I told her I'd become convinced the Movement was only a beautiful pipe dream.

PARRITT   (*With a strange smile*)  I don't remember it that way.

LARRY   Then you can blame your imagination—and forget it. (*He changes the subject abruptly*) You asked me why I quit the Movement. I had a lot of good reasons. One was myself, and another was my comrades, and the last was the breed of swine called men in general. For myself, I was forced to admit, at the end of thirty years' devotion to the Cause, that I was never made for it. I was born condemned to be one of those who has to see all sides of a question. When you're damned like that, the questions multiply for you until in the end it's all question and no answer. As history proves, to be a worldly success at anything, especially revolution, you have to wear blinders like a horse and see only straight in front of you. You have to see, too, that this is all black, and that is all white. As for my comrades in the Great Cause, I felt as Horace Walpole did about England, that he could love it if it weren't for the people in it. The material the ideal free society must be constructed from is men themselves and you can't build a marble temple out of a mixture of mud and manure. When man's soul isn't a sow's ear, it will be time enough to dream of silk purses. (*He chuckles sardonically—then irritably as if suddenly provoked at himself for talking so much*) Well, that's why I quit the Movement, if it leaves you any wiser. At any rate, you see it had nothing to do with your mother.

PARRITT   (*Smiles almost mockingly*)   Oh, sure, I see. But I'll bet Mother has always thought it was on her account. You know her, Larry. To hear her go on sometimes, you'd think she was the Movement.

LARRY   (*Stares at him, puzzled and repelled—sharply*)   That's a hell of a way for you to talk, after what happened to her!

PARRITT   (*At once confused and guilty*)   Don't get me wrong. I wasn't sneering, Larry. Only kidding. I've said the same thing to her lots of times to kid her. But you're right. I know I shouldn't now. I keep forgetting she's in jail. It doesn't seem real. I can't believe it about her. She's always been so free. I— But I don't want to think of it. (LARRY *is moved to a puzzled pity in spite of himself.* PARRITT *changes the subject*) What have you been doing all the years since you left—the Coast, Larry?

LARRY   (*Sardonically*)   Nothing I could help doing. If I don't believe in the Movement, I don't believe in anything else either, especially not the State. I've refused to become a useful member of its society. I've been a philosophical drunken bum, and proud of it. (*Abruptly his tone sharpens with resentful warning*) Lis-

ten to me. I hope you've deduced that I've my reason for answering the impertinent questions of a stranger, for that's all you
are to me. I have a strong hunch you've come here expecting
something of me. I'm warning you, at the start, so there'll be no
misunderstanding, that I've nothing left to give, and I want to
be left alone, and I'll thank you to keep your life to yourself. I
feel you're looking for some answer to something. I have no
answer to give anyone, not even myself. Unless you call what
Heine wrote in his poem to morphine an answer.
(*He quotes a translation of the closing couplet sardonically*)

"Lo, sleep is good; better is death; in sooth,
The best of all were never to be born."

PARRITT (*Shrinks a bit frightenedly*)  That's the hell of an answer.
(*Then with a forced grin of bravado*) Still, you never know when
it might come in handy.
(*He looks away.* LARRY *stares at him puzzledly, interested in
spite of himself and at the same time vaguely uneasy*)

LARRY (*Forcing a casual tone*)  I don't suppose you've had much
chance to hear news of your mother since she's been in jail?

PARRITT  No. No chance. (*He hesitates—then blurts out*) Anyway, I don't think she wants to hear from me. We had a fight just
before that business happened. She bawled me out because I was
going around with tarts. That got my goat, coming from her.
I told her, "You've always acted the free woman, you've never
let anything stop you from—" (*He checks himself—goes on hurriedly*) That made her sore. She said she wouldn't give a damn
what I did except she'd begun to suspect I was too interested in
outside things and losing interest in the Movement.

LARRY (*Stares at him*)  And were you?

PARRITT (*Hesitates—then with intensity*)  Sure I was! I'm no
damned fool! I couldn't go on believing forever that gang was
going to change the world by shooting off their loud traps on
soapboxes and sneaking around blowing up a lousy building or
a bridge! I got wise it was all a crazy pipe dream! (*Appealingly*)
The same as you did, Larry. That's why I came to you. I knew
you'd understand. What finished me was this last business of someone selling out. How can you believe anything after a thing like
that happens? It knocks you cold! You don't know what the hell is
what! You're through! (*Appealingly*) You know how I feel, don't
you, Larry? (LARRY *stares at him, moved by sympathy and pity in*

*spite of himself, disturbed, and resentful at being disturbed, and puzzled by something he feels about* PARRITT *that isn't right. But before he can reply,* HUGO *suddenly raises his head from his arms in a half-awake alcoholic daze and speaks)*

HUGO (*Quotes aloud to himself in a guttural declamatory style*) "The days grow hot, O Babylon! 'Tis cool beneath thy villow trees!" (PARRITT *turns startledly as* HUGO *peers muzzily without recognition at him.* HUGO *exclaims automatically in his tone of denunciation*) Gottammed stool pigeon!

PARRITT (*Shrinks away—stammers*) What? Who do you mean? (*Then furiously*) You lousy bum, you can't call me that! (*He draws back his fist*)

HUGO (*Ignores this—recognizing him now, bursts into his childish teasing giggle*) Hello, leedle Don! Leedle monkey-face. I did not recognize you. You have grown big boy. How is your mother? Where you come from? (*He breaks into his wheedling, bullying tone*) Don't be a fool! Loan me a dollar! Buy me a trink! (*As if this exhausted him, he abruptly forgets it and plumps his head down on his arms again and is asleep*)

PARRITT (*With eager relief*) Sure, I'll buy you a drink, Hugo. I'm broke, but I can afford one for you. I'm sorry I got sore. I ought to have remembered when you're soused you call everyone a stool pigeon. But it's no damned joke right at this time. (*He turns to* LARRY, *who is regarding him now fixedly with an uneasy expression as if he suddenly were afraid of his own thoughts—forcing a smile*) Gee, he's passed out again. (*He stiffens defensively*) What are you giving me the hard look for? Oh, I know. You thought I was going to hit him? What do you think I am? I've always had a lot of respect for Hugo. I've always stood up for him when people in the Movement panned him for an old drunken has-been. He had the guts to serve ten years in the can in his own country and get his eyes ruined in solitary. I'd like to see some of them here stick that. Well, they'll get a chance now to show— (*Hastily*) I don't mean— But let's forget that. Tell me some more about this dump. Who are are all these tanks? Who's that guy trying to catch pneumonia?

(*He indicates* LEWIS)

LARRY (*Stares at him almost frightenedly—then looks away and grasps eagerly this chance to change the subject. He begins to describe the sleepers with sardonic relish but at the same time showing his affection for them*) That's Captain Lewis, a one-time hero of the British Army. He strips to display that scar on his back he got from a native spear whenever he's completely plastered. The bewhiskered bloke opposite him is General Wetjoen, who led a commando in the War. The two of them met when they came here to work in the Boer War spectacle at the St. Louis Fair and they've been bosom pals ever since. They dream the hours away in happy dispute over the brave days in South Africa when they tried to murder each other. The little guy between them was in it, too, as correspondent for some English paper. His nickname here is Jimmy Tomorrow. He's the leader of our Tomorrow Movement.

PARRITT   What do they do for a living?

LARRY   As little as possible. Once in a while one of them makes a successful touch somewhere, and some of them get a few dollars a month from connections at home who pay it on condition they never come back. For the rest, they live on free lunch and their old friend, Harry Hope, who doesn't give a damn what anyone does or doesn't do, as long as he likes you.

PARRITT   It must be a tough life.

LARRY   It's not. Don't waste your pity. They wouldn't thank you for it. They manage to get drunk, by hook or crook, and keep their pipe dreams, and that's all they ask of life. I've never known more contented men. It isn't often that men attain the true goal of their heart's desire. The same applies to Harry himself and his two cronies at the far table. He's so satisfied with life he's never set foot out of this place since his wife died twenty years ago. He has no need of the outside world at all. This place has a fine trade from the Market people across the street and the waterfront workers, so in spite of Harry's thirst and his generous heart, he comes out even. He never worries in hard times because there's always old friends from the days when he was a jitney Tammany politician, and a friendly brewery to tide him over. Don't ask me what his two pals work at because they don't. Except at being his lifetime guests. The one facing this way is his brother-in-law, Ed Mosher, who once worked for a circus in the ticket wagon. Pat McGloin, the other one, was a police lieutenant back in the flush times of graft when everything went. But he got too greedy and when the usual reform investigation came he was caught red-handed and thrown off the Force. (*He nods at* JOE) Joe here has a yesterday in the same flush period. He ran a colored gambling house then and was a hell of

a sport, so they say. Well, that's our whole family circle of inmates, except the two barkeeps and their girls, three ladies of
the pavement that room on the third floor.

PARRITT (*Bitterly*) To hell with them! I never want to see a
whore again! (*As* LARRY *flashes him a puzzled glance, he adds
confusedly*) I mean, they always get you in dutch.

(*While he is speaking* WILLIE OBAN *has opened his eyes. He
leans toward them, drunk now from the effect of the huge drink
he took, and speaks with a mocking suavity*)

WILLIE Why omit me from your Who's Who in Dypsomania,
Larry? An unpardonable slight, especially as I am the only inmate of royal blood. (*To* PARRITT—*ramblingly*) Educated at
Harvard, too. You must have noticed the atmosphere of culture
here. My humble contribution. Yes, Generous Stranger—I trust
you're generous—I was born in the purple, the son, but unfortunately not the heir, of the late world-famous Bill Oban, King
of the Bucket Shops. A revolution deposed him, conducted by
the District Attorney. He was sent into exile. In fact, not to
mince matters, they locked him in the can and threw away
the key. Alas, his was an adventurous spirit that pined in con-
finement. And so he died. Forgive these reminiscences. Undoubtedly all this is well known to you. Everyone in the world
knows.

PARRITT (*Uncomfortably*) Tough luck. No, I never heard of him.

WILLIE (*Blinks at him incredulously*) Never heard? I thought
everyone in the world— Why, even at Harvard I discovered my
father was well known by reputation, although that was some
time before the District Attorney gave him so much unwelcome
publicity. Yes, even as a freshman I was notorious. I was accepted
socially with all the warm cordiality that Henry Wadsworth Long-
fellow would have shown a drunken Negress dancing the cancan
at high noon on Brattle Street. Harvard was my father's idea.
He was an ambitious man. Dictatorial, too. Always knowing what
was best for me. But I did make myself a brilliant student.
A dirty trick on my classmates, inspired by revenge, I fear. (*He
quotes*) "Dear college days, with pleasure rife! The grandest
gladdest days of life!" But, of course, that is a Yale hymn, and
they're given to rah-rah exaggeration at New Haven. I was a
brilliant student at Law School, too. My father wanted a lawyer
in the family. He was a calculating man. A thorough knowledge of the law close at hand in the house to help him find
fresh ways to evade it. But I discovered the loophole of whiskey

and escaped his jurisdiction. (*Abruptly to* PARRITT) Speaking of whiskey, sir, reminds me—and, I hope, reminds you—that when meeting a Prince the customary salutation is "What'll you have?"

PARRITT (*With defensive resentment*) Nix! All you guys seem to think I'm made of dough. Where would I get the coin to blow everyone?

WILLIE (*Sceptically*) Broke? You haven't the thirsty look of the impecunious. I'd judge you to be a plutocrat, your pockets stuffed with ill-gotten gains. Two or three dollars, at least. And don't think we will question how you got it. As Vespasian remarked, the smell of all whiskey is sweet.

PARRITT What do you mean, how I got it? (*To* LARRY, *forcing a laugh*) It's a laugh, calling me a plutocrat, isn't it, Larry, when I've been in the Movement all my life.

(LARRY *gives him an uneasy suspicious glance, then looks away, as if avoiding something he does not wish to see*)

WILLIE (*Disgustedly*) Ah, one of those, eh? I believe you now, all right! Go away and blow yourself up, that's a good lad. Hugo is the only licensed preacher of that gospel here. A dangerous terrorist, Hugo! He would as soon blow the collar off a schooner of beer as look at you! (*To* LARRY) Let us ignore this useless youth, Larry. Let us join in prayer that Hickey, the Great Salesman, will soon arrive bringing the blessed burgeois long green! Would that Hickey or Death would come! Meanwhile, I will sing a song. A beautiful old New England folk ballad which I picked up at Harvard amid the debris of education.

(*He sings in a boisterous baritone, rapping on the table with his knuckles at the indicated spots in the song:*)

"Jack, oh, Jack, was a sailor lad
And he came to a tavern for gin.
He rapped and he rapped with a (*Rap, rap, rap*)
But never a soul seemed in."

(*The drunks at the tables stir.* ROCKY *gets up from his chair in the bar and starts back for the entrance to the back room.* HOPE *cocks one irritable eye over his specs.* JOE MOTT *opens both of his and grins.* WILLIE *interposes some drunken whimsical exposition to* LARRY) The origin of this beautiful ditty is veiled in mystery, Larry. There was a legend bruited about in Cambridge lavatories that Waldo Emerson composed it during his uninformative period as a minister, while he was trying to write a

sermon. But my own opinion is, it goes back much further, and
Jonathan Edwards was the author of both words and music.
(*He sings:*)

"He rapped and rapped, and tapped and tapped
  Enough to wake the dead
Till he heard a damsel (*Rap, rap, rap*)
  On a window right over his head."

(*The drunks are blinking their eyes now, grumbling and cursing.*
ROCKY *appears from the bar at rear, right, yawning*)
HOPE (*With fuming irritation*)  Rocky! Bejees, can't you keep that
  crazy bastard quiet?
(ROCKY *starts for* WILLIE)
WILLIE  And now the influence of a good woman enters our mari-
  ner's life. Well, perhaps "good" isn't the word. But very, very
  kind.
(*He sings:*)

"Oh, come up," she cried, "my sailor lad,
  And you and I'll agree,
And I'll show you the prettiest (*Rap, rap, rap*)
  That ever you did see."

(*He speaks*) You see, Larry? The lewd Puritan touch, obviously, and it grows more marked as we go on.
(*He sings:*)

"Oh, he put his arm around her waist,
  He gazed in her bright blue eyes
And then he—"

(*But here* ROCKY *shakes him roughly by the shoulder*)
ROCKY  Piano! What d'yuh tink dis dump is, a dump?
HOPE  Give him the bum's rush upstairs! Lock him in his room!
ROCKY (*Yanks* WILLIE *by the arm*)  Come on, Bum.
WILLIE (*Dissolves into pitiable terror*)  No! Please, Rocky! I'll go
  crazy up in that room alone! It's haunted! I— (*He calls to* HOPE)
  Please, Harry! Let me stay here! I'll be quiet!
HOPE (*Immediately relents—indignantly*)  What the hell you do-
  ing to him, Rocky? I didn't tell you to beat up the poor guy.
  Leave him alone, long as he's quiet.
(ROCKY *lets go of* WILLIE *disgustedly and goes back to his
  chair in the bar*)

WILLIE *(Huskily)* Thanks, Harry. You're a good scout. *(He closes his eyes and sinks back in his chair exhaustedly, twitching and quivering again)*

HOPE *(Addressing* MCGLOIN *and* MOSHER, *who are sleepily awake—accusingly)* Always the way. Can't trust nobody. Leave it to that Dago to keep order and it's like bedlam in a cathouse, singing and everything. And you two big barflies are a hell of a help to me, ain't you? Eat and sleep and get drunk! All you're good for, bejees! Well, you can take that "I'll-have-the-same" look off your maps! There ain't going to be no more drinks on the house till hell freezes over! *(Neither of the two is impressed either by his insults or his threats. They grin hangover grins of tolerant affection at him and wink at each other.* HARRY *fumes)* Yeah, grin! Wink, bejees! Fine pair of sons of bitches to have glued on me for life!

*(But he can't get a rise out of them and he subsides into a fuming mumble. Meanwhile, at the middle table,* CAPTAIN LEWIS *and* GENERAL WETJOEN *are as wide awake as heavy hangovers permit.* JIMMY TOMORROW *nods, his eyes blinking.* LEWIS *is gazing across the table at* JOE MOTT, *who is still chuckling to himself over* WILLIE'S *song. The expression on* LEWIS'S *face is that of one who can't believe his eyes)*

LEWIS *(Aloud to himself, with a muzzy wonder)* Good God! Have I been drinking at the same table with a bloody Kaffir?

JOE *(Grinning)* Hello, Captain. You comin' up for air? Kaffir? Who's he?

WETJOEN *(Blurrily)* Kaffir, dot's a nigger, Joe. *(*JOE *stiffens and his eyes narrow.* WETJOEN *goes on with heavy jocosity)* Dot's joke on him, Joe. He don't know you. He's still plind drunk, the ploody Limey chentleman! A great mistake I missed him at the pattle of Modder River. Vit mine rifle I shoot damn fool Limey officers py the dozen, but him I miss. De pity of it! *(He chuckles and slaps* LEWIS *on his bare shoulder)* Hey, wake up, Cecil, you ploody fool! Don't you know your old friend, Joe? He's no damned Kaffir! He's white, Joe is!

LEWIS *(Light dawning—contritely)* My profound apologies, Joseph, old chum. Eyesight a trifle blurry, I'm afraid. Whitest colored man I ever knew. Proud to call you my friend. No hard feelings, what? *(He holds out his hand)*

JOE *(At once grins good-naturedly and shakes his hand)* No, Captain, I know it's mistake. Youse regular, if you is a Limey. (*Then his face hardening*) But I don't stand for "nigger" from nobody. Never did. In de old days, people calls me "nigger" wakes up in de hospital. I was de leader ob de Dirty Half-Dozen Gang. All six of us colored boys, we was tough and I was de toughest.

WETJOEN (*Inspired to boastful reminiscence*) Me, in old days in Transvaal, I vas so tough and strong I grab axle of ox wagon mit full load and lift like feather.

LEWIS (*Smiling amiably*) As for you, my balmy Boer that walks like a man, I say again it was a grave error in our foreign policy ever to set you free, once we nabbed you and your commando with Cronje. We should have taken you to the London zoo and incarcerated you in the baboons' cage. With a sign: "Spectators may distinguish the true baboon by his blue behind."

WETJOEN (*Grins*) Gott! to dink ten better Limey officers, at least, I shoot clean in the mittle of forehead at Spion Kopje, and you I miss! I neffer forgive myself!

(JIMMY TOMORROW *blinks benignantly from one to the other with a gentle dunken smile*)

JIMMY (*Sentimentally*) Now, come, Cecil, Piet! We must forget the War. Boer and Briton, each fought fairly and played the game till the better man won and then we shook hands. We are all brothers within the Empire united beneath the flag on which the sun never sets. (*Tears come to his eyes. He quotes with great sentiment, if with slight application*) "Ship me somewhere east of Suez—"

LARRY (*Breaks in sardonically*) Be God, you're there already, Jimmy. Worst is best here, and East is West, and tomorrow is yesterday. What more do you want?

JIMMY (*With bleary benevolence, shaking his head in mild rebuke*) No, Larry, old friend, you can't deceive me. You pretend a bitter, cynic philosophy, but in your heart you are the kindest man among us.

LARRY (*Disconcerted—irritably*) The hell you say!

PARRITT (*Leans toward him—confidentially*) What a bunch of cuckoos!

JIMMY (*As if reminded of something—with a pathetic attempt at a brisk, no-more-nonsense air*) Tomorrow, yes. It's high time I straightened out and got down to business again. (*He brushes*

*his sleeve fastidiously*) I must have this suit cleaned and pressed.
I can't look like a tramp when I—

JOE (*Who has been brooding—interrupts*) Yes, suh, white folks always said I was white. In de days when I was flush, Joe Mott's
de only colored man dey allows in de white gamblin' houses.
"You're all right, Joe, you're white," dey says. (*He chuckles*)
Wouldn't let me play craps, dough. Dey know I could make dem
dice behave. "Any odder game and any limit you like, Joe," dey
says. Man, de money I lost! (*He chuckles—then with an underlying defensiveness*) Look at de Big Chief in dem days. He
knew I was white. I'd saved my dough so I could start my own
gamblin' house. Folks in de know tells me, see de man at de
top, den you never has trouble. You git Harry Hope give you a
letter to de Chief. And Harry does. Don't you, Harry?

HOPE (*Preoccupied with his own thoughts*) Eh? Sure. Big Bill
was a good friend of mine. I had plenty of friends high up in
those days. Still could have if I wanted to go out and see them.
Sure, I gave you a letter. I said you was white. What the hell
of it?

JOE (*To* CAPTAIN LEWIS *who has relapsed into a sleepy daze and
is listening to him with an absurd strained attention without com-
prehending a word*) Dere. You see, Captain. I went to see de
Chief, shakin' in my boots, and dere he is sittin' behind a big
desk, lookin' as big as a freight train. He don't look up. He keeps
me waitin' and waitin', and after 'bout an hour, seems like to me,
he says slow and quiet like dere wasn't no harm in him, "You
want to open a gamblin' joint, does you, Joe?" But he don't give
me no time to answer. He jumps up, lookin' as big as two freight
trains, and he pounds his fist like a ham on de desk, and he
shouts, "You black son of a bitch, Harry says you're white and
you better be white or dere's a little iron room up de river waitin'
for you!" Den he sits down and says quiet again, "All right. You
can open. Git de hell outa here!" So I opens, and he finds out
I'se white, sure 'nuff, 'cause I run wide open for years and pays
my sugar on de dot, and de cops and I is friends. (*He chuckles
with pride*) Dem old days! Many's de night I come in here. Dis
was a first-class hangout for sports in dem days. Good
whiskey, fifteen cents, two for two bits. I t'rows down a fifty-
dollar bill like it was trash paper and says, "Drink it up, boys, I
don't want no change." Ain't dat right, Harry?

HOPE (*Caustically*) Yes, and bejees, if I ever seen you throw fifty cents on the bar now, I'd know I had delirium tremens! You've told that story ten million times and if I have to hear it again, that'll give me D.T.s anyway!

JOE (*Chuckling*) Gittin' drunk every day for twenty years ain't give you de Brooklyn boys. You needn't be scared of me!

LEWIS (*Suddenly turns and beams on* HOPE) Thank you, Harry, old chum. I will have a drink, now you mention it, seeing it's so near your birthday.

(*The others laugh*)

HOPE (*Puts his hand to his ear—angrily*) What's that? I can't hear you.

LEWIS (*Sadly*) No, I fancied you wouldn't.

HOPE I don't have to hear, bejees! Booze is the only thing you ever talk about!

LEWIS (*Sadly*) True. Yet there was a time when my conversation was more comprehensive. But as I became burdened with years, it seemed rather pointless to discuss my other subject.

HOPE You can't joke with me! How much room rent do you owe me, tell me that?

LEWIS Sorry. Adding has always baffled me. Subtraction is my forte.

HOPE (*Snarling*) Arrh! Think you're funny! Captain, bejees! Showing off your wounds! Put on your clothes, for Christ's sake! This ain't no Turkish bath! Lousy Limey army! Took 'em years to lick a gang of Dutch hayseeds!

WETJOEN Dot's right, Harry. Gif him hell!

HOPE No lip out of you, neither, you Dutch spinach! General, hell! Salvation Army, that's what you'd ought t'been General in! Bragging what a shot you were, and, bejees, you missed him! And he missed you, that's just as bad! And now the two of you bum on me! (*Threateningly*) But you've broke the camel's back this time, bejees! You pay up tomorrow or out you go!

LEWIS (*Earnestly*) My dear fellow, I give you my word of honor as an officer and a gentleman, you shall be paid tomorrow.

WETJOEN Ve swear it, Harry! Tomorrow vidout fail!

MCGLOIN (*A twinkle in his eye*) There you are, Harry. Sure, what could be fairer?

MOSHER (*With a wink at* MCGLOIN) Yes, you can't ask more than that, Harry. A promise is a promise—as I've often discovered.

HOPE (*Turns on them*) I mean the both of you, too! An old grafting flatfoot and a circus bunco steerer! Fine company for me,

bejees! Couple of con men living in my flat since Christ knows
when! Getting fat as hogs, too! And you ain't even got the
decency to get me upstairs where I got a good bed! Let me sleep
on a chair like a bum! Kept me down here waitin' for Hickey to
show up, hoping I'd blow you to more drinks!

MCGLOIN   Ed and I did our damnedest to get you up, didn't we,
Ed?

MOSHER   We did. But you said you couldn't bear the flat because
it was one of those nights when memory brought poor old Bessie
back to you.

HOPE   (*His face instantly becoming long and sad and sentimental—
mournfully*)   Yes, that's right, boys. I remember now. I could
almost see her in every room just as she used to be—and it's
twenty years since she—
(*His throat and eyes fill up. A suitable sentimental hush falls
on the room*)

LARRY   (*In a sardonic whisper to* PARRITT)   Isn't a pipe dream of
yesterday a touching thing? By all accounts, Bessie nagged the
hell out of him.

JIMMY   (*Who has been dreaming, a look of prim resolution on his
face, speaks aloud to himself*)   No more of this sitting around
and loafing. Time I took hold of myself. I must have my shoes
soled and heeled and shined first thing tomorrow morning. A general spruce-up. I want to have a well-groomed appearance when
I—
(*His voice fades out as he stares in front of him. No one pays
any attention to him except* LARRY *and* PARRITT)

LARRY   (*As before, in a sardonic aside to* PARRITT)   The tomorrow
movement is a sad and beautiful thing, too!

MCGLOIN   (*With a huge sentimental sigh—and a calculating look at*
HOPE)   Poor old Bessie! You don't find her like in these days. A
sweeter woman never drew breath.

MOSHER   (*In a similar calculating mood*)   Good old Bess. A man
couldn't want a better sister than she was to me.

HOPE   (*Mournfully*)   Twenty years, and I've never set foot out of
this house since the day I buried her. Didn't have the heart. Once
she'd gone, I didn't give a damn for anything. I lost all my ambition. Without her, nothing seemed worth the trouble. You remember, Ed, you, too, Mac—the boys was going to nominate me
for Alderman. It was all fixed. Bessie wanted it and she was so
proud. But when she was taken, I told them, "No, boys, I can't
do it. I simply haven't the heart. I'm through." I would have won

the election easy, too. (*He says this a bit defiantly*) Oh, I know there was jealous wise guys said the boys was giving me the nomination because they knew they couldn't win that year in this ward. But that's a damned lie! I knew every man, woman and child in the ward, almost. Bessie made me make friends with everyone, helped me remember all their names. I'd have been elected easy.

MCGLOIN  You would, Harry. It was a sure thing.

MOSHER  A dead cinch, Harry. Everyone knows that.

HOPE  Sure they do. But after Bessie died, I didn't have the heart. Still, I know while she'd appreciate my grief, she wouldn't want it to keep me cooped up in here all my life. So I've made up my mind I'll go out soon. Take a walk around the ward, see all the friends I used to know, get together with the boys and maybe tell 'em I'll let 'em deal me a hand in their game again. Yes, bejees, I'll do it. My birthday, tomorrow, that'd be the right time to turn over a new leaf. Sixty. That ain't too old.

MCGLOIN  (*Flatteringly*)  It's the prime of life, Harry.

MOSHER  Wonderful thing about you, Harry, you keep young as you ever was.

JIMMY  (*Dreaming aloud again*)  Get my things from the laundry. They must still have them. Clean collar and shirt. If I wash the ones I've got on any more, they'll fall apart. Socks, too. I want to make a good appearance. I met Dick Trumbull on the street a year or two ago. He said, "Jimmy, the publicity department's never been the same since you got—resigned. It's dead as hell." I said, "I know. I've heard rumors the management were at their wits' end and would be only too glad to have me run it for them again. I think all I'd have to do would be go and see them and they'd offer me the position. Don't you think so, Dick?" He said, "Sure, they would, Jimmy. Only take my advice and wait a while until business conditions are better. Then you can strike them for a bigger salary than you got before, do you see?" I said, "Yes, I do see, Dick, and many thanks for the tip." Well, conditions must be better by this time. All I have to do is get fixed up with a decent front tomorrow, and it's as good as done.

HOPE  (*Glances at* JIMMY *with a condescending affectionate pity— in a hushed voice*)  Poor Jimmy's off on his pipe dream again. Bejees, he takes the cake!

(*This is too much for* LARRY. *He cannot restrain a sardonic guffaw. But no one pays any attention to him*)

LEWIS (*Opens his eyes, which are drowsing again—dreamily to* WETJOEN) I'm sorry we had to postpone our trip again this April, Piet. I hoped the blasted old estate would be settled up by then. The damned lawyers can't hold up the settlement much longer. We'll make it next year, even if we have to work and earn our passage money, eh? You'll stay with me at the old place as long as you like, then you can take the *Union Castle* from Southampton to Cape Town. (*Sentimentally, with real yearning*) England in April. I want you to see that, Piet. The old veldt has its points, I'll admit, but it isn't home—especially home in April.

WETJOEN (*Blinks drowsily at him—dreamily*) Ja, Cecil, I know how beautiful it must be, from all you tell me many times. I vill enjoy it. But I shall enjoy more ven I am home, too. The veldt, ja! You could put England on it, and it would look like a farmer's small garden. Py Gott, there is space to be free, the air like vine is, you don't need booze to be drunk! My relations vill so surprised be. They vill not know me, it is so many years. Dey vill be so glad I haf come home at last.

JOE (*Dreamily*) I'll make my stake and get my new gamblin' house open before you boys leave. You got to come to de openin'. I'll treat you white. If you're broke, I'll stake you to buck any game you chooses. If you wins, dat's velvet for you. If you loses, it don't count. Can't treat you no whiter dan dat, can I?

HOPE (*Again with condescending pity*) Bejees, Jimmy's started them off smoking the same hop.

(*But the three are finished, their eyes closed again in sleep or a drowse*)

LARRY (*Aloud to himself—in his comically tense, crazy whisper*) Be God, this bughouse will drive me stark, raving loony yet!

HOPE (*Turns on him with fuming suspicion*) What? What d'you say?

LARRY (*Placatingly*) Nothing, Harry. I had a crazy thought in my head.

HOPE (*Irascibly*) Crazy is right! Yah! The old wise guy! Wise, hell! A damned old fool Anarchist I-Won't-Worker! I'm sick of you and Hugo, too. Bejees, you'll pay up tomorrow, or I'll start a Harry Hope Revolution! I'll tie a dispossess bomb to your tails that'll blow you out in the street! Bejees, I'll make your Movement move!

(*The witticism delights him and he bursts into a shrill cackle. At once* MCGLOIN *and* MOSHER *guffaw enthusiastically*)

MOSHER (*Flatteringly*) Harry, you sure say the funniest things! (*He reaches on the table as if he expected a glass to be there— then starts with well-acted surprise*) Hell, where's my drink? That Rocky is too damned fast cleaning tables. Why, I'd only taken one sip of it.

HOPE (*His smiling face congealing*) No, you don't! (*Acidly*) Any time you only take one sip of a drink, you'll have lockjaw and paralysis! Think you can kid me with those old circus con games? —me, that's known you since you was knee-high, and, bejees, you was a crook even then!

MCGLOIN (*Grinning*) It's not like you to be hard-hearted, Harry. Sure, it's hot, parching work laughing at your jokes so early in the morning on an empty stomach!

HOPE Yah! You, Mac! Another crook! Who asked you to laugh? We was talking about poor old Bessie, and you and her no-good brother start to laugh! A hell of a thing! Talking mush about her, too! "Good old Bess." Bejees, she'd never forgive me if she knew I had you two bums living in her flat, throwing ashes and cigar butts on her carpet. You know her opinion of you, Mac. "That Pat McGloin is the biggest drunken grafter that ever disgraced the police force," she used to say to me. "I hope they send him to Sing Sing for life."

MCGLOIN (*Unperturbed*) She didn't mean it. She was angry at me because you used to get me drunk. But Bess had a heart of gold underneath her sharpness. She knew I was innocent of all the charges.

WILLIE (*Jumps to his feet drunkenly and points a finger at* MCGLOIN —*imitating the manner of a cross-examiner—coldly*) One moment, please. Lieutenant McGloin! Are you aware you are under oath? Do you realize what the penalty for perjury is? (*Purringly*) Come now, Lieutenant, isn't it a fact that you're as guilty as hell? No, don't say, "How about your old man?" I am asking the questions. The fact that he was a crooked old bucket-shop bastard has no bearing on your case. (*With a change to maudlin joviality*) Gentlemen of the Jury, court will now recess while the D.A. sings out a little ditty he learned at Harvard. It was composed in a wanton moment by the Dean of the Divinity School on a moonlight night in July, 1776, while sobering up in a Turkish bath. (*He sings:*)

"Oh, come up," she cried, "my sailor lad,
And you and I'll agree.

And I'll show you the prettiest (*Rap, rap, rap on table*)
That ever you did see."

(*Suddenly he catches* HOPE'S *eyes fixed on him condemningly,
and sees* ROCKY *appearing from the bar. He collapses back on
his chair, pleading miserably*) Please, Harry! I'll be quiet! Don't
make Rocky bounce me upstairs! I'll go crazy alone! (*To* MC-
GLOIN) I apologize, Mac. Don't get sore. I was only kidding you.
(ROCKY, *at a relenting glance from* HOPE, *returns to the bar*)

MCGLOIN (*Good-naturedly*) Sure, kid all you like, Willie. I'm
hardened to it. (*He pauses—seriously*) But I'm telling you some
day before long I'm going to make them reopen my case. Everyone knows there was no real evidence against me, and I took the
fall for the ones higher up. I'll be found innocent this time
and reinstated. (*Wistfully*) I'd like to have my old job on the
Force back. The boys tell me there's fine pickings these days,
and I'm not getting rich here, sitting with a parched throat
waiting for Harry Hope to buy a drink.
(*He glances reproachfully at* HOPE)

WILLIE Of course, you'll be reinstated, Mac. All you need is a
brilliant young attorney to handle your case. I'll be straightened
out and on the wagon in a day or two. I've never practiced but
I was one of the most brilliant students in Law School, and your
case is just the opportunity I need to start. (*Darkly*) Don't
worry about my not forcing the D.A. to reopen your case. I went
through my father's papers before the cops destroyed them, and
I remember a lot of people, even if I can't prove— (*Coaxingly*)
You will let me take your case, won't you, Mac?

MCGLOIN (*Soothingly*) Sure I will and it'll make your reputation,
Willie.
(MOSHER *winks at* HOPE, *shaking his head, and* HOPE *answers
with identical pantomine, as though to say, "Poor dopes, they're
off again!"*)

LARRY (*Aloud to himself more than to* PARRITT—*with irritable
wonder*) Ah, be damned! Haven't I heard their visions a thousand times? Why should they get under my skin now? I've got
the blues, I guess. I wish to hell Hickey'd turn up.

MOSHER (*Calculatingly solicitous—whispering to* HOPE) Poor Willie needs a drink bad, Harry—and I think if we all joined him
it'd make him feel he was among friends and cheer him up.

HOPE More circus con tricks! (*Scathingly*) You talking of your
dear sister! Bessie had you sized up. She used to tell me, "I don't

know what you can see in that worthless, drunken, petty-larceny brother of mine. If I had my way," she'd say, "he'd get booted out in the gutter on his fat behind." Sometimes she didn't say behind, either.

MOSHER (*Grins genially*) Yes, dear old Bess had a quick temper, but there was no real harm in her. (*He chuckles reminiscently*) Remember the time she sent me down to the bar to change a ten-dollar bill for her?

HOPE (*Has to grin himself*) Bejees, do I! She coulda bit a piece out of a stove lid, after she found it out.

(*He cackles appreciatively*)

MOSHER I was sure surprised when she gave me the ten spot. Bess usually had better sense, but she was in a hurry to go to church. I didn't really mean to do it, but you know how habit gets you. Besides, I still worked then, and the circus season was going to begin soon, and I needed a little practice to keep my hand in. Or, you never can tell, the first rube that came to my wagon for a ticket might have left with the right change and I'd be disgraced. (*He chuckles*) I said, "I'm sorry, Bess, but I had to take it all in dimes. Here, hold out your hands and I'll count it out for you, so you won't kick afterwards I short-changed you." (*He begins a count which grows more rapid as he goes on*) Ten, twenty, thirty, forty, fifty, sixty, seventy, eighty, ninety, a dollar. Ten, twenty, thirty, forty, fifty, sixty— You're counting with me, Bess, aren't you? —eighty, ninety, two dollars. Ten, twenty— Those are pretty shoes you got on, Bess—forty, fifty, seventy, eighty, ninety, three dollars. Ten, twenty, thirty— What's on at the church tonight. Bess? —fifty, sixty, seventy, ninety, four dollars. Ten, twenty, thirty, fifty, seventy, eighty, ninety— That's a swell new hat, Bess, looks very becoming—six dollars. (*He chuckles*) And so on. I'm bum at it now for lack of practice, but in those days I could have short-changed the Keeper of the Mint.

HOPE (*Grinning*) Stung her for two dollars and a half, wasn't it, Ed?

MOSHER Yes. A fine percentage, if I do say so, when you're dealing to someone who's sober and can count. I'm sorry to say she discovered my mistakes in arithmetic just after I beat it around the corner. She counted it over herself. Bess somehow never had the confidence in me a sister should. (*He sighs tenderly*) Dear old Bess.

HOPE (*Indignant now*) You're a fine guy bragging how you short-changed your own sister! Bejees, if there was a war and you was in it, they'd have to padlock the pockets of the dead!

MOSHER (*A bit hurt at this*) That's going pretty strong, Harry. I always gave a sucker some chance. There wouldn't be no fun robbing the dead. (*He becomes reminiscently melancholy*) Gosh, thinking of the old ticket wagon brings those days back. The greatest life on earth with the greatest show on earth! The grandest crowd of regular guys ever gathered under one tent! I'd sure like to shake their hands again!

HOPE (*Acidly*) They'd have guns in theirs. They'd shoot you on sight. You've touched every damned one of them. Bejees, you've even borrowed fish from the trained seals and peanuts from every elephant that remembered you!

(*This fancy tickles him and he gives a cackling laugh*)

MOSHER (*Overlooking this—dreamily*) You know, Harry, I've made up my mind I'll see the boss in a couple of days and ask for my old job. I can get back my magic touch with change easy, and I can throw him a line of bull that'll kid him I won't be so un-reasonable about sharing the profits next time. (*With insinuating complaint*) There's no percentage in hanging around this dive, taking care of you and shooing away your snakes, when I don't even get an eye-opener for my trouble.

HOPE (*Implacably*) No! (MOSHER *sighs and gives up and closes his eyes. The others, except* LARRY *and* PARRITT, *are all dozing again now.* HOPE *goes on grumbling*) Go to hell or the circus, for all I care. Good riddance, bejees! I'm sick of you! (*Then worriedly*) Say, Ed, what the hell you think's happened to Hickey? I hope he'll turn up. Always got a million funny stories. You and the other bums have begun to give me the graveyard fantods. I'd like a good laugh with old Hickey. (*He chuckles at a memory*) Re-member that gag he always pulls about his wife and the iceman? He'd make a cat laugh!

ROCKY *appears from the bar. He comes front, behind* MOSHER'S *chair, and begins pushing the black curtain along the rod to the rear wall*)

ROCKY Openin' time, Boss. (*He presses a button at rear which switches off the lights. The back room becomes drabber and dingier than ever in the gray daylight that comes from the street windows, off right, and what light can penetrate the grime of the two backyard windows at left.* ROCKY *turns back to* HOPE—*grump-*

*ily*) Why don't you go up to bed, Boss? Hickey'd never turn up dis time of de mornin'!

HOPE (*Starts and listens*)  Someone's coming now.

ROCKY (*Listens*)  Aw, dat's on'y my two pigs. It's about time dey showed.

(*He goes back toward the door at left of the bar*)

HOPE (*Sourly disappointed*)  You keep them dumb broads quiet. I don't want to go to bed. I'm going to catch a couple more winks here and I don't want no damn-fool laughing and screeching. (*He settles himself in his chair, grumbling*) Never thought I'd see the day when Harry Hope's would have tarts rooming in it. What'd Bessie think? But I don't let 'em use my rooms for business. And they're good kids. Good as anyone else. They got to make a living. Pay their rent, too, which is more than I can say for— (*He cocks an eye over his specs at* MOSHER *and grins with satisfaction*) Bejees, Ed, I'll bet Bessie is doing somersaults in her grave!

(*He chuckles. But* MOSHER'S *eyes are closed, his head nodding, and he doesn't reply, so* HOPE *closes his eyes.* ROCKY *has opened the barroom door at rear and is standing in the hall beyond it, facing right. A girl's laugh is heard*)

ROCKY (*Warningly*)  Nix! Piano!

(*He comes in, beckoning them to follow. He goes behind the bar and gets a whiskey bottle and glasses and chairs.* MARGIE *and* PEARL *follow him, casting a glance around. Everyone except* LARRY *and* PARRITT *is asleep or dozing. Even* PARRITT *has his eyes closed. The two girls, neither much over twenty, are typical dollar street walkers, dressed in the usual tawdry get-up.* PEARL *is obviously Italian with black hair and eyes.* MARGIE *has brown hair and hazel eyes, a slum New Yorker of mixed blood. Both are plump and have a certain prettiness that shows even through their blobby make-up. Each retains a vestige of youthful freshness, although the game is beginning to get them and give them hard, worn expressions. Both are sentimental, feather-brained, giggly, lazy, good-natured and reasonably contented with life. Their attitude toward* ROCKY *is much that of two maternal, affectionate sisters toward a bullying brother whom they like to tease and spoil. His attitude toward them is that of the owner of two performing pets he has trained to do a profitable act under his management. He feels a proud proprietor's affection for them, and is tolerantly lax in his discipline*)

MARGIE (*Glancing around*)  Jees, Poil, it's de Morgue wid all de stiffs on deck. (*She catches* LARRY's *eye and smiles affectionately*) Hello, Old Wise Guy, ain't you died yet?

LARRY (*Grinning*)  Not yet, Margie. But I'm waiting impatiently for the end.

(PARRITT *opens his eyes to look at the two girls, but as soon as they glance at him he closes them again and turns his head away*)

MARGIE (*As she and* PEARL *come to the table at right, front, followed by* ROCKY)  Who's de new guy? Friend of yours, Larry? (*Automatically she smiles seductively at* PARRITT *and addresses him in a professional chant*) Wanta have a good time, kid?

PEARL  Aw, he's passed out. Hell wid him!

HOPE (*Cocks an eye over his specs at them—with drowsy irritation*) You dumb broads cut the loud talk.

(*He shuts his eye again*)

ROCKY (*Admonishing them good-naturedly*)  Sit down before I knock yuh down. (MARGIE *and* PEARL *sit at left, and rear, of table,* ROCKY *at right of it. The girls pour drinks.* ROCKY *begins in a brisk, business-like manner but in a lowered voice with an eye on* HOPE)  Well, how'd you tramps do?

MARGIE  Pretty good. Didn't we, Poil?

PEARL  Sure. We nailed a coupla all-night guys.

MARGIE  On Sixth Avenoo. Boobs from de sticks.

PEARL  Stinko, de bot' of 'em.

MARGIE  We thought we was in luck. We steered dem to a real hotel. We figgered dey was too stinko to bother us much and we could cop a good sleep in beds that ain't got cobble stones in de mattress like de ones in dis dump.

PEARL  But we was outa luck. Dey didn't bother us much dat way, but dey wouldn't go to sleep either, see? Jees, I never hoid such gabby guys.

MARGIE  Dey got onta politics, drinkin' outa de bottle. Dey forgot we was around. "De Bull Moosers is de on'y reg'lar guys," one guy says. And de other guy says, "You're a God-damned liar! And I'm a Republican!" Den dey'd laugh.

PEARL  Den dey'd get mad and make a bluff dey was goin' to scrap, and den dey'd make up and cry and sing "School Days." Jees, imagine tryin' to sleep wid dat on de phonograph!

MARGIE  Maybe you tink we wasn't glad when de house dick come up and told us all to git dressed and take de air!

PEARL  We told de guys we'd wait for dem 'round de corner.

MARGIE  So here we are.

ROCKY  (*Sententiously*)  Yeah. I see you. But I don't see no dough yet.

PEARL  (*With a wink at* MARGE—*teasingly*)  Right on de job, ain't he, Margie?

MARGIE  Yeah, our little business man! Dat's him!

ROCKY  Come on! Dig!

(*They both pull up their skirts to get the money from their stockings.* ROCKY *watches this move carefully*)

PEARL  (*Amused*)  Pipe him keepin' cases, Margie.

MARGIE  (*Amused*)  Scared we're holdin' out on him.

PEARL  Way he grabs, yuh'd tink it was him done de woik. (*She holds out a little roll of bills to* ROCKY) Here y'are, Grafter!

MARGIE  (*Holding hers out*)  We hope it chokes yuh.

(ROCKY *counts the money quickly and shoves it in his pocket*)

ROCKY  (*Genially*)  You dumb baby dolls gimme a pain. What would you do wid money if I wasn't around? Give it all to some pimp.

PEARL  (*Teasingly*)  Jees, what's the difference—? (*Hastily*) Aw, I don't mean dat, Rocky.

ROCKY  (*His eyes growing hard—slowly*)  A lotta difference, get me?

PEARL  Don't get sore. Jees, can't yuh take a little kiddin'?

MARGIE  Sure, Rocky, Poil was on'y kiddin'.

(*Soothingly*) We know yuh got a reg'lar job. Dat's why we like yuh, see? Yuh don't live offa us. Yuh're a bartender.

ROCKY  (*Genially again*)  Sure, I'm a bartender. Everyone knows me knows dat. And I treat you goils right, don't I? Jees, I'm wise yuh hold out on me, but I know it ain't much, so what the hell, I let yuh get away wid it. I tink yuh're a coupla good kids. Yuh're aces wid me, see?

PEARL  You're aces wid us, too. Ain't he, Margie?

MARGIE  Sure, he's aces. (ROCKY *beams complacently and takes the glasses back to the bar.* MARGIE *whispers*) Yuh sap, don't yuh know enough not to kid him on dat? Serve yuh right if he beat yuh up!

PEARL  (*Admiringly*)  Jees, I'll bet he'd give yuh an awful beatin,' too, once he started. Ginnies got awful tempers.

MARGIE  Anyway, we wouldn't keep no pimp, like we was reg'lar old whores. We ain't dat bad.

PEARL  No. We're tarts, but dat's all.

ROCKY  (*Rinsing glasses behind the bar*)  Cora got back around three o'clock. She woke up Chuck and dragged him outa de hay to go to a chop suey joint. (*Disgustedly*) Imagine him standin' for dat stuff!

MARGIE  (*Disgustedly*)  I'll bet dey been sittin' around kiddin' demselves wid dat old pipe dream about gettin' married and settlin' down on a farm. Jees, when Chuck's on de wagon, dey never lay off dat dope! Dey give yuh an earful everytime yuh talk to 'em!

PEARL  Yeah. Chuck wid a silly grin on his ugly map, de big boob, and Cora gigglin' like she was in grammar school and some tough guy'd just told her babies wasn't brung down de chimney by a boid!

MARGIE  And her on de turf long before me and you was! And bot' of 'em arguin' all de time, Cora sayin' she's scared to marry him because he'll go on drunks again. Just as dough any drunk could scare Cora!

PEARL  And him swearin', de big liar, he'll never go on no more periodicals! An' den her pretendin'— But it gives me a pain to talk about it. We ought to phone de booby hatch to send round de wagon for 'em.

ROCKY  (*Comes back to the table—disgustedly*)  Yeah, of all de pipe dreams in dis dump, dey got de nuttiest! And nuttin' stops dem. Dey been dreamin' it for years, every time Chuck goes on de wagon. I never could figger it. What would gettin' married get dem? But de farm stuff is de sappiest part. When bot' of 'em was dragged up in dis ward and ain't never been nearer a farm dan Coney Island! Jees, dey'd tink dey'd gone deef if dey didn't hear de El rattle! Dey'd get D.T.s if dey ever hoid a cricket choip! I hoid crickets once on my cousin's place in Joisey. I couldn't sleep a wink. Dey give me de heebie-jeebies. (*With deeper disgust*) Jees, can yuh picture a good barkeep like Chuck diggin' spuds? And imagine a whore hustlin' de cows home! For Christ sake! Ain't dat a sweet picture!

MARGIE  (*Rebukingly*)  Yuh oughtn't to call Cora dat, Rocky. She's a good kid. She may be a tart, but—

ROCKY  (*Considerately*)  Sure, dat's all I meant, a tart.

PEARL  (*Giggling*)  But he's right about de damned cows, Margie. Jees, I bet Cora don't know which end of de cow has de horns! I'm goin' to ask her.

(*There is the noise of a door opening in the hall and the sound of a man's and woman's arguing voices*)

ROCKY  Here's your chance. Dat's dem two nuts now.

(CORA *and* CHUCK *look in from the hallway and then come in.* CORA *is a thin peroxide blonde, a few years older than* PEARL *and* MARGIE, *dressed in similar style, her round face showing more of the wear and tear of her trade than theirs, but still with traces of a doll-like prettiness.* CHUCK *is a tough, thick-necked, barrel-chested Italian-American, with a fat, amiable, swarthy face. He has on a straw hat with a vivid band, a loud suit, tie and shirt, and yellow shoes. His eyes are clear and he looks healthy and strong as an ox*)

CORA  (*Gaily*)  Hello, bums. (*She looks around*) Jees, de Morgue on a rainy Sunday night! (*She waves to* LARRY—*affectionately*) Hello, Old Wise Guy! Ain't you croaked yet?

LARRY  (*Grins*)  Not yet, Cora. It's damned tiring, this waiting for the end.

CORA  Aw, gwan, you'll never die! Yuh'll have to hire someone to croak yuh wid an axe.

HOPE  (*Cocks one sleepy eye at her—irritably*)  You dumb hookers, cut the loud noise! This ain't a cathouse!

CORA  (*Teasingly*)  My, Harry! Such language!

HOPE  (*Closes his eyes—to himself with a gratified chuckle*)  Bejees, I'll bet Bessie's turning over in her grave!

(CORA *sits down between* MARGIE *and* PEARL. CHUCK *takes an empty chair from* HOPES's *table and puts it by hers and sits down. At* LARRY's *table,* PARRITT *is glaring resentfully toward the girls*)

PARRITT  If I'd known this dump was a hooker hangout, I'd never have come here.

LARRY  (*Watching him*)  You seem down on the ladies.

PARRITT  (*Vindictively*)  I hate every bitch that ever lived! They're all alike! (*Catching himself guiltily*) You can understand how I feel, can't you, when it was getting mixed up with a tart that made me have that fight with Mother? (*Then with a resentful sneer*) But what the hell does it matter to you? You're in the grandstand. You're through with life.

LARRY  (*Sharply*)  I'm glad you remember it. I don't want to know a damned thing about your business.

(*He closes his eyes and settles on his chair as if preparing for sleep.* PARRITT *stares at him sneeringly. Then he looks away and his expression becomes furtive and frightened*)

CORA  Who's de guy wid Larry?

ROCKY  A tightwad. To hell wid him.

PEARL  Say, Cora, wise me up. Which end of a cow is de horns on?

CORA  (*Embarrassed*)  Aw, don't bring dat up. I'm sick of hearin' about dat farm.

ROCKY  You got nuttin' on us!

CORA  (*Ignoring this*)  Me and dis overgrown tramp has been scrappin' it. He says Joisey's de best place, and I says Long Island because we'll be near Coney. And I tells him, "How do I know yuh're off of periodicals for life? I don't give a damn how drunk yuh get, the way we are, but I don't wanta be married to no soak."

CHUCK  And I tells her I'm off de stuff for life. Den she beefs we won't be married a month before I'll trow it in her face she was a tart. "Jees, Baby," I tells her. "Why should I? What de hell yuh tink I tink I'm marryin', a voigin? Why should I kick as long as yuh lay off it and don't do no cheatin' wid de iceman or nobody?" (*He gives her a rough hug*)  Dat's on de level, Baby. (*He kisses her*)

CORA  (*Kissing him*)  Aw, yuh big tramp!

ROCKY  (*Shakes his head with profound disgust*)  Can yuh tie it? I'll buy a drink. I'll do anything. (*He gets up*)

CORA  No, dis round's on me. I run into luck. Dat's why I dragged Chuck outa bed to celebrate. It was a sailor. I rolled him. (*She giggles*)  Listen, it was a scream. I've run into some nutty souses, but dis guy was de nuttiest. De booze dey dish out around de Brooklyn Navy Yard must be as turrible bug-juice as Harry's. My dogs was givin' out when I seen dis guy holdin' up a lamppost, so I hurried to get him before a cop did. I says, "Hello, Handsome, wanta have a good time?" Jees, he was paralyzed! One of dem polite jags. He tries to bow to me, imagine, and I had to prop him up or he'd fell on his nose. And what d'yuh tink he said? "Lady," he says, "can yuh kindly tell me de nearest way to de Museum of Natural History?" (*They all laugh*)  Can yuh imagine! At two A.M. As if I'd know where de dump was anyway. But I says, "Sure ting, Honey Boy, I'll be only too glad." So I steered him into a side street where it was dark and propped him against a wall and give him a frisk. (*She giggles*)  And what d'yuh tink he does? Jees, I ain't lyin', he begins to laugh, de big sap! He says, "Quit ticklin' me." While I was friskin' him for his roll! I near died! Den I toined him 'round and give him a push to start him. "Just keep goin'," I told him. "It's a big white building on your right. You can't miss it." He must be swimmin' in de North River yet!

(*They all laugh*)

CHUCK Ain't Uncle Sam de sap to trust guys like dat wid dough!

CORA (*With a business-like air*) I picked twelve bucks offa him. Come on, Rocky. Set 'em up. (ROCKY *goes back to the bar.* CORA *looks around the room*) Say, Chuck's kiddin' about de iceman a minute ago reminds me. Where de hell's Hickey?

ROCKY Dat's what we're all wonderin'.

CORA He oughta be here. Me and Chuck seen him.

ROCKY (*Excited, comes back from the bar, forgetting the drinks*) You seen Hickey? (*He nudges* HOPE) Hey, Boss, come to! Cora's seen Hickey.

(HOPE *is instantly wide awake and everyone in the place, except* HUGO *and* PARRITT, *begins to rouse up hopefully, as if a mysterious wireless message had gone round*)

HOPE Where'd you see him, Cora?

CORA Right on de next corner. He was standin' dere. We said, "Welcome to our city. De gang is expectin' yuh wid deir tongues hangin' out a yard long." And I kidded him, "How's de iceman, Hickey? How's he doin' at your house?" He laughs and says, "Fine." And he says, "Tell de gang I'll be along in a minute. I'm just finishin' figurin' out de best way to save dem and bring dem peace."

HOPE (*Chuckles*) Bejees, he's thought up a new gag! It's a wonder he didn't borry a Salvation Army uniform and show up in that! Go out and get him, Rocky. Tell him we're waitin' to be saved! (ROCKY *goes out, grinning*)

CORA Yeah, Harry, he was only kiddin'. But he was funny, too, somehow. He was different, or somethin'.

CHUCK Sure, he was sober, Baby. Dat's what made him different. We ain't never seen him when he wasn't on a drunk, or had de willies gettin' over it.

CORA Sure! Gee, ain't I dumb?

HOPE (*With conviction*) The dumbest broad I ever seen! (*Then puzzledly*) Sober? That's funny. He's always lapped up a good starter on his way here. Well, bejees, he won't be sober long! He'll be good and ripe for my birthday party tonight at twelve. (*He chuckles with excited anticipation—addressing all of them*) Listen! He's fixed some new gag to pull on us. We'll pretend to let him kid us, see? And we'll kid the pants off him.

(*They all say laughingly,* "Sure, Harry," "Righto," "That's the stuff," "We'll fix him," *etc., etc., their faces excited with the same eager anticipation.* ROCKY *appears in the doorway at the end of the bar with* HICKEY, *his arm around* HICKEY's *shoulders*)

ROCKY (*With an affectionate grin*)   Here's the old son of a bitch! (*They all stand up and greet him with affectionate acclaim,* "Hello, Hickey!" *etc. Even* HUGO *comes out of his coma to raise his head and blink through his thick spectacles with a welcoming giggle*)

HICKEY (*Jovially*)   Hello, Gang! (*He stands a moment, beaming around at all of them affectionately. He is about fifty, a little under medium height, with a stout, roly-poly figure. His face is round and smooth and big-boyish with bright blue eyes, a button nose, a small, pursed mouth. His head is bald except for a fringe of hair around his temples and the back of his head. His expression is fixed in a salesman's winning smile of self-confident affability and hearty good fellowship. His eyes have the twinkle of a humor which delights in kidding others but can also enjoy equally a joke on himself. He exudes a friendly, generous personality that makes everyone like him on sight. You get the impression, too, that he must have real ability in his line. There is an efficient, business-like approach in his manner, and his eyes can take you in shrewdly at a glance. He has the salesman's mannerisms of speech, an easy flow of glib, persuasive convincingness. His clothes are those of a successful drummer whose territory consists of minor cities and small towns—not flashy but conspicuously spic and span. He immediately puts on an entrance act, places a hand affectedly on his chest, throws back his head, and sings in a falsetto tenor*) "It's always fair weather, when good fellows get together!" (*Changing to a comic bass and another tune*) "And another little drink won't do us any harm!" (*They all roar with laughter at this burlesque which his personality makes really funny. He waves his hand in a lordly manner to* ROCKY) Do your duty, Brother Rocky. Bring on the rat poison! (ROCKY *grins and goes behind the bar to get drinks amid an approving cheer from the crowd.* HICKEY *comes forward to shake hands with* HOPE—*with affectionate heartiness*) How goes it, Governor?

HOPE (*Enthusiastically*)   Bejees, Hickey, you old bastard, it's good to see you! (HICKEY *shakes hands with* MOSHER *and* MCGLOIN; *leans right to shake hands with* MARGIE *and* PEARL; *moves to the*

*middle table to shake hands with* LEWIS, JOE MOTT, WETJOEN *and*
JIMMY; *waves to* WILLIE, LARRY *and* HUGO. *He greets each by
name with the same affectionate heartiness and there is an inter-
change of* "How's the kid?" "How's the old scout?" "How's the
boy?" "How's everything?" *etc., etc.* ROCKY *begins setting out
drinks, whiskey glasses with chasers, and a bottle for each table,
starting with* LARRY's *table.* HOPE *says:*) Sit down, Hickey. Sit
down. (HICKEY *takes the chair, facing front, at the front of the
table in the second row which is half between* HOPE's *table and
the one where* JIMMY TOMORROW *is.* HOPE *goes on with excited pleasure*) Bejees, Hickey, it seems natural to see your ugly,
grinning map. (*With a scornful nod to* CORA) This dumb broad
was tryin' to tell us you'd changed, but you ain't a damned bit.
Tell us about yourself. How've you been doin'? Bejees, you look
like a million dollars.

ROCKY (*Coming to* HICKEY's *table, puts a bottle of whiskey, a glass
and a chaser on it—then hands* HICKEY *a key*) Here's your key,
Hickey. Same old room.

HICKEY (*Shoves the key in his pocket*) Thanks, Rocky. I'm going
up in a little while and grab a snooze. Haven't been able to
sleep lately and I'm tired as hell. A couple of hours good kip
will fix me.

HOPE (*As* ROCKY *puts drinks on his table*) First time I ever heard
you worry about sleep. Bejees, you never would go to bed. (*He
raises his glass, and all the others except* PARRITT *do likewise*)
Get a few slugs under your belt and you'll forget sleeping. Here's
mud in your eye, Hickey.

(*They all join in with the usual humorous toasts*)

HICKEY (*Heartily*) Drink hearty, boys and girls! (*They all drink,
but* HICKEY *drinks only his chaser*)

HOPE Bejees, is that a new stunt, drinking your chaser first?

HICKEY No, I forgot to tell Rocky— You'll have to excuse me, boys
and girls, but I'm off the stuff. For keeps.

(*They stare at him in amazed incredulity*)

HOPE What the hell— (*Then with a wink at the others, kiddingly*)
Sure! Joined the Salvation Army, ain't you? Been elected Presi-
dent of the W.C.T.U? Take that bottle away from him, Rocky.
We don't want to tempt him into sin.

(*He chuckles and the others laugh*)

HICKEY (*Earnestly*) No, honest, Harry. I know it's hard to believe
but— (*He pauses—then adds simply*) Cora was right, Harry. I

have changed. I mean, about booze. I don't need it any more. (*They all stare, hoping it's a gag, but impressed and disappointed and made vaguely uneasy by the change they now sense in him*)

HOPE (*His kidding a bit forced*) Yeah, go ahead, kid the pants off us! Bejees, Cora said you was coming to save us! Well, go on. Get this joke off your chest! Start the service! Sing a God-damned hymn if you like. We'll all join in the chorus. "No drunkard can enter this beautiful home." That's a good one. (*He forces a cackle*)

HICKEY (*Grinning*) Oh, hell, Governor! You don't think I'd come around here peddling some brand of temperance bunk, do you? You know me better than that! Just because I'm through with the stuff don't mean I'm going Prohibition. Hell, I'm not that ungrateful! It's given me too many good times. I feel exactly the same as I always did. If anyone wants to get drunk, if that's the only way they can be happy, and feel at peace with themselves, why the hell shouldn't they? They have my full and entire sympathy. I know all about that game from soup to nuts. I'm the guy that wrote the book. The only reason I've quit is— Well, I finally had the guts to face myself and throw overboard the damned lying pipe dream that'd been making me miserable, and do what I had to do for the happiness of all concerned—and then all at once I found I was at peace with myself and I didn't need booze any more. That's all there was to it. (*He pauses. They are staring at him, uneasy and beginning to feel defensive.* HICKEY *looks round and grins affectionately—apologetically*) But what the hell! Don't let me be a wet blanket, making fool speeches about myself. Set 'em up again, Rocky. Here. (*He pulls a big roll from his pocket and peels off a ten-dollar bill. The faces of all brighten*) Keep the balls coming until this is killed. Then ask for more.

ROCKY Jees, a roll dat'd choke a hippopotamus! Fill up, youse guys. (*They all pour out drinks*)

HOPE That sounds more like you, Hickey. That water-wagon bull —Cut out the act and have a drink, for Christ's sake.

HICKEY It's no act, Governor. But don't get me wrong. That don't mean I'm a teetotal grouch and can't be in the party. Hell, why d'you suppose I'm here except to have a party, same as I've always done, and help celebrate your birthday tonight? You've all been good pals to me, the best friends I've ever had. I've been thinking about you ever since I left the house—all the time I was walking over here—

HOPE  Walking? Bejees, do you mean to say you walked?

HICKEY  I sure did. All the way from the wilds of darkest Astoria. Didn't mind it a bit, either. I seemed to get here before I knew it. I'm a bit tired and sleepy but otherwise I feel great. (*Kiddingly*) That ought to encourage you, Governor—show you a little walk around the ward is nothing to be so scared about. (*He winks at the others.* HOPE *stiffens resentfully for a second.* HICKEY *goes on*) I didn't make such bad time either for a fat guy, considering it's a hell of a ways, and I sat in the park a while thinking. It was going on twelve when I went in the bedroom to tell Evelyn I was leaving. Six hours, say. No, less than that. I'd been standing on the corner some time before Cora and Chuck came along, thinking about all of you. Of course, I was only kidding Cora with that stuff about saving you. (*Then seriously*) No, I wasn't either. But I didn't mean booze. I meant save you from pipe dreams. I know now, from my experience, they're the things that really poison and ruin a guy's life and keep him from finding any peace. If you knew how free and contented I feel now. I'm like a new man. And the cure for them is so damned simple, once you have the nerve. Just the old dope of honesty is the best policy—honesty with yourself, I mean. Just stop lying about yourself and kidding yourself about tomorrows. (*He is staring ahead of him now as if he were talking aloud to himself as much as to them. Their eyes are fixed on him with uneasy resentment. His manner becomes apologetic again*) Hell, this begins to sound like a damned sermon on the way to lead the good life. Forget that part of it. It's in my blood, I guess. My old man used to whale salvation into my heinie with a birch rod. He was a preacher in the sticks of Indiana, like I've told you. I got my knack of sales gab from him, too. He was the boy who could sell those Hoosier hayseeds building lots along the Golden Street! (*Taking on a salesman's persuasiveness*) Now listen, boys and girls, don't look at me as if I was trying to sell you a gold-brick. Nothing up my sleeve, honest. Let's take an example. Any one of you. Take you, Governor. That walk around the ward you never take—

HOPE (*Defensively sharp*)  What about it?

HICKEY (*Grinning affectionately*)  Why, you know as well as I do, Harry. Everything about it.

HOPE (*Defiantly*)  Bejees, I'm going to take it!

HICKEY  Sure, you're going to—this time. Because I'm going to help you. I know it's the thing you've got to do before you'll ever know what real peace means. (*He looks at* JIMMY TOMORROW) Same thing with you, Jimmy. You've got to try and get your old job back. And no tomorrow about it! (*As* JIMMY *stiffens with a pathetic attempt at dignity—placatingly*) No, don't tell me, Jimmy. I know all about tomorrow. I'm the guy that wrote the book.

JIMMY   I don't understand you. I admit I've foolishly delayed, but as it happens, I'd just made up my mind that as soon as I could get straightened out—

HICKEY   Fine! That's the spirit! And I'm going to help you. You've been damned kind to me, Jimmy, and I want to prove how grateful I am. When it's all over and you don't have to nag at yourself any more, you'll be grateful to me, too! (*He looks around at the others*) And all the rest of you, ladies included, are in the same boat, one way or another.

LARRY   (*Who has been listening with sardonic appreciation—in his comically intense, crazy whisper*)   Be God, you've hit the nail on the head, Hickey! This dump is the Palace of Pipe Dreams!

HICKEY   (*Grins at him with affectionate kidding*)   Well, well! The Old Grandstand Foolosopher speaks! You think you're the big exception, eh? Life doesn't mean a damn to you any more, does it? You're retired from the circus. You're just waiting impatiently for the end—the good old Long Sleep! (*He chuckles*) Well, I think a lot of you, Larry, you old bastard. I'll try and make an honest man of you, too!

LARRY   (*Stung*)   What the devil are you hinting at, anyway?

HICKEY   You don't have to ask me, do you, a wise old guy like you? Just ask yourself. I'll bet you know.

PARRITT   (*Is watching* LARRY'S *face with a curious sneering satisfaction*)   He's got your number all right, Larry! (*He turns to* HICKEY) That's the stuff, Hickey. Show the old faker up! He's got no right to sneak out of everything.

HICKEY   (*Regards him with surprise at first, then with a puzzled interest*)   Hello. A stranger in our midst. I didn't notice you before, Brother.

PARRITT   (*Embarrassed, his eyes shifting away*)   My name's Parritt. I'm an old friend of Larry's. (*His eyes come back to* HICKEY *to find him still sizing him up—defensively*)   Well? What are you staring at?

HICKEY (*Continuing to stare—puzzledly*) No offense, Brother. I was trying to figure— Haven't we met before some place?

PARRITT (*Reassured*) No. First time I've ever been East.

HICKEY No, you're right. I know that's not it. In my game, to be a shark at it, you teach yourself never to forget a name or a face. But still I know damned well I recognized something about you. We're members of the same lodge—in some way.

PARRITT (*Uneasy again*) What are you talking about? You're nuts.

HICKEY (*Dryly*) Don't try to kid me, Little Boy. I'm a good sales-man—so damned good the firm was glad to take me back after every drunk—and what made me good was I could size up any-one. (*Frowningly puzzled again*) But I don't see— (*Suddenly breezily good-natured*) Never mind. I can tell you're having trouble with yourself and I'll be glad to do anything I can to help a friend of Larry's.

LARRY Mind your own business, Hickey. He's nothing to you—or to me, either. (HICKEY *gives him a keen inquisitive glance.* LARRY *looks away and goes on sarcastically*) You're keeping us all in suspense. Tell us more about how you're going to save us.

HICKEY (*Good-naturedly but seeming a little hurt*) Hell, don't get sore, Larry. Not at me. We've always been good pals, haven't we? I know I've always liked you a lot.

LARRY (*A bit shamefaced*) Well, so have I liked you. Forget it, Hickey.

HICKEY (*Beaming*) Fine! That's the spirit! (*Looking around at the others, who have forgotten their drinks*) What's the matter, everybody? What is this, a funeral? Come on and drink up! A little action! (*They all drink*) Have another. Hell, this is a celebration! Forget it, if anything I've said sounds too serious. I don't want to be a pain in the neck. Any time you think I'm talking out of turn, just tell me to go chase myself! (*He yawns with growing drowsiness and his voice grows a bit muffled*) No, boys and girls, I'm not trying to put anything over on you. It's just that I know now from experience what a lying pipe dream can do to you—and how damned relieved and contented with yourself you feel when you're rid of it. (*He yawns again*) God, I'm sleepy all of a sudden. That long walk is beginning to get me. I better go upstairs. Hell of a trick to go dead on you like this. (*He starts to get up but relaxes again. His eyes blink as he tries to keep them open*) No, boys and girls, I've never known what real peace was until now. It's a grand feeling,

like when you're sick and suffering like hell and the Doc gives you
a shot in the arm, and the pain goes, and you drift off. (*His
eyes close*) You can let go of yourself at last. Let yourself sink
down to the bottom of the sea. Rest in peace. There's no farther
you have to go. Not a single damned hope or dream left to
nag you. You'll all know what I mean after you— (*He pauses—
mumbles*) Excuse—all in—got to grab forty winks— Drink up,
everybody—on me—

(*The sleep of complete exhaustion overpowers him. His chin sags
to his chest. They stare at him with puzzled uneasy fascination*)

HOPE (*Forcing a tone of irritation*)     Bejees, that's a fine stunt, to
go to sleep on us! (*Then fumingly to the crowd*) Well, what the
hell's the matter with you bums? Why don't you drink up?
You're always crying for booze, and now you've got it under your
nose, you sit like dummies! (*They start and gulp down their
whiskies and pour another.* HOPE *stares at* HICKEY) Bejees, I
can't figure Hickey. I still say he's kidding us. Kid his own
grandmother, Hickey would. What d'you think, Jimmy?

JIMMY (*Unconvincingly*)     It must be another of his jokes, Harry,
although— Well, he does appear changed. But he'll probably be
his natural self again tomorrow— (*Hastily*) I mean, when he
wakes up.

LARRY (*Staring at* HICKEY *frowningly—more aloud to himself
than to them*)     You'll make a mistake if you think he's only
kidding.

PARRITT (*In a low confidential voice*)     I don't like that guy, Larry.
He's too damned nosy. I'm going to steer clear of him.

(LARRY *gives him a suspicious glance, then looks hastily away*)

JIMMY (*With an attempt at open-minded reasonableness*)     Still,
Harry, I have to admit there was some sense in his nonsense.
It is time I got my job back—although I hardly need him to
remind me.

HOPE (*With an air of frankness*)     Yes, and I ought to take a walk
around the ward. But I don't need no Hickey to tell me, seeing
I got it all set for my birthday tomorrow.

LARRY (*Sardonically*)     Ha! (*Then in his comically intense, crazy
whisper*) Be God, it looks like he's going to make two sales of his
peace at least! But you'd better make sure first it's the real
McCoy and not poison.

HOPE (*Disturbed—angrily*)     You bughouse I-Won't-Work harp,
who asked you to shove in an oar? What the hell d'you mean,

poison? Just because he has your number— (*He immediately feels ashamed of this taunt and adds apologetically*) Bejees, Larry, you're always croaking about something to do with death. It gets my nanny. Come on, fellers, let's drink up. (*They drink.* HOPE's *eyes are fixed on* HICKEY *again*) Stone cold sober and dead to the world! Spilling that business about pipe dreams! Bejees, I don't get it. (*He bursts out again in angry complaint*) He ain't like the old Hickey! He'll be a fine wet blanket to have around at my birthday party! I wish to hell he'd never turned up!

MOSHER (*Who has been the least impressed by* HICKEY's *talk and is the first to recover and feel the effect of the drinks on top of his hangover—genially*) Give him time, Harry, and he'll come out of it. I've watched many cases of almost fatal teetotalism, but they all came out of it completely cured and as drunk as ever. My opinion is the poor sap is temporarily bughouse from overwork. (*Musingly*) You can't be too careful about work. It's the deadliest habit known to science, a great physician once told me. He practiced on street corners under a torchlight. He was positively the only doctor in the world who claimed that rattlesnake oil, rubbed on the prat, would cure heart failure in three days. I remember well his saying to me, "You are naturally delicate, Ed, but if you drink a pint of bad whiskey before breakfast every evening, and never work if you can help it, you may live to a ripe old age. It's staying sober and working that cuts men off in their prime."

(*While he is talking, they turn to him with eager grins. They are longing to laugh, and as he finishes they roar. Even* PARRITT *laughs.* HICKEY *sleeps on like a dead man, but* HUGO, *who had passed into his customary coma again, head on table, looks up through his thick spectacles and giggles foolishly*)

HUGO (*Blinking around at them. As the laughter dies he speaks in his giggling, wheedling manner, as if he were playfully teasing children*) Laugh, leedle bourgeois monkey-faces! Laugh like fools, leedle stupid peoples! (*His tone suddenly changes to one of guttural soapbox denunciation and he pounds on the table with a small fist*) I vill laugh, too! But I vill laugh last! I vill laugh at you! (*He declaims his favorite quotation*) "The days grow hot, O Babylon! 'Tis cool beneath thy villow trees!"

(*They all hoot him down in a chorus of amused jeering.* HUGO *is not offended. This is evidently their customary reaction. He giggles good-naturedly.* HICKEY *sleeps on. They have all forgotten their uneasiness about him now and ignore him*)

LEWIS (*Tipsily*)  Well, now that our little Robespierre has got the daily bit of guillotining off his chest, tell me more about your doctor friend, Ed. He strikes me as the only bloody sensible medico I ever heard of. I think we should appoint him house physician here without a moment's delay.

(*They all laughingly assent*)

MOSHER (*Warming to his subject, shakes his head sadly*)  Too late! The old Doc has passed on to his Maker. A victim of overwork, too. He didn't follow his own advice. Kept his nose to the grindstone and sold one bottle of snake oil too many. Only eighty years old when he was taken. The saddest part was that he knew he was doomed. The last time we got paralyzed together he told me: "This game will get me yet, Ed. You see before you a broken man, a martyr to medical science. If I had any nerves I'd have a nervous breakdown. You won't believe me, but this last year there was actually one night I had so many patients, I didn't even have time to get drunk. The shock to my system brought on a stroke which, as a doctor, I recognized was the beginning of the end." Poor old Doc! When he said this he started crying. "I hate to go before my task is completed, Ed," he sobbed. "I'd hoped I'd live to see the day when, thanks to my miraculous cure, there wouldn't be a single vacant cemetery lot left in this glorious country." (*There is a roar of laughter. He waits for it to die and then goes on sadly*)  I miss Doc. He was a gentleman of the old school. I'll bet he's standing on a street corner in hell right now, making suckers of the damned, telling them there's nothing like snake oil for a bad burn.

(*There is another roar of laughter. This time it penetrates* HICKEY's *exhausted slumber. He stirs on his chair, trying to wake up, managing to raise his head a little and force his eyes half open. He speaks with a drowsy, affectionately encouraging smile. At once the laughter stops abruptly and they turn to him startledly*)

HICKEY  That's the spirit—don't let me be a wet blanket—all I want is to see you happy—

(*He slips back into heavy sleep again. They all stare at him, their faces again puzzled, resentful and uneasy*)

*Curtain*

# ACT TWO

Scene: *The back room only. The black curtain dividing it from the bar is the right wall of the scene. It is getting on toward midnight of the same day.*

*The back room has been prepared for a festivity. At center, front, four of the circular tables are pushed together to form one long table with an uneven line of chairs behind it, and chairs at each end. This improvised banquet table is covered with old table cloths, borrowed from a neighboring beanery, and is laid with glasses, plates and cutlery before each of the seventeen chairs. Bottles of bar whiskey are placed at intervals within reach of any sitter. An old upright piano and stool have been moved in and stand against the wall at left, front. At right, front, is a table without chairs. The other tables and chairs that had been in the room have been moved out, leaving a clear floor space at rear for dancing. The floor has been swept clean of sawdust and scrubbed. Even the walls show evidence of having been washed, although the result is only to heighten their splotchy leprous look. The electric light brackets are adorned with festoons of red ribbon. In the middle of the separate table at right, front, is a birthday cake with six candles. Several packages, tied with ribbon, are also on the table. There are two necktie boxes, two cigar boxes, a fifth containing a half dozen handkerchiefs, the sixth is a square jeweler's watch box.*

*As the curtain rises, CORA, CHUCK, HUGO, LARRY, MARGIE, PEARL and ROCKY are discovered. CHUCK, ROCKY and the three girls have dressed up for the occasion. CORA is arranging a bouquet of flowers in a vase, the vase being a big schooner glass from the bar, on top of the piano. CHUCK sits in a chair at the foot (left) of the banquet table. He has turned it so he can watch her. Near the middle of the row of chairs behind the table, LARRY sits, facing front, a drink of whiskey before him. He is staring before him in frown-*

*ing, disturbed meditation. Next to him, on his left,* HUGO *is in his habitual position, passed out, arms on table, head on arms, a full whiskey glass by his head. By the separate table at right, front,* MARGIE *and* PEARL *are arranging the cake and presents, and* ROCKY *stands by them. All of them, with the exception of* CHUCK *and* ROCKY, *have had plenty to drink and show it, but no one, except* HUGO, *seems to be drunk. They are trying to act up in the spirit of the occasion but there is something forced about their manner, an undercurrent of nervous irritation and preoccupation.*

CORA (*Standing back from the piano to regard the flower effect*) How's dat, Kid?

CHUCK (*Grumpily*)   What de hell do I know about flowers?

CORA   Yuh can see dey're pretty, can't yuh, yuh big dummy?

CHUCK (*Mollifying*)   Yeah, Baby, sure. If yuh like 'em, dey're aw right wid me.

(CORA *goes back to give the schooner of flowers a few more touches*)

MARGIE (*Admiring the cake*)   Some cake, huh, Poil? Lookit! Six candles. Each for ten years.

PEARL   When do we light de candles, Rocky?

ROCKY (*Grumpily*)   Ask dat bughouse Hickey. He's elected himself boss of dis boithday racket. Just before Harry comes down, he says. Den Harry blows dem out wid one breath, for luck. Hickey was goin' to have sixty candles, but I says, Jees, if de old guy took dat big a breath, he'd croak himself.

MARGIE (*Challengingly*)   Well, anyways, it's some cake, ain't it?

ROCKY (*Without enthusiasm*)   Sure, it's aw right by me. But what de hell is Harry goin' to do wid a cake? If he ever et a hunk, it'd croak him.

PEARL   Jees, yuh're a dope! Ain't he, Margie?

MARGIE   A dope is right!

ROCKY (*Stung*)   You broads better watch your step or—

PEARL (*Defiantly*)   Or what?

MARGIE   Yeah! Or what?

(*They glare at him truculently*)

ROCKY   Say, what de hell's got into youse? It'll be twelve o'clock and Harry's boithday before long. I ain't lookin' for no trouble.

PEARL (*Ashamed*)   Aw, we ain't neider, Rocky.

(*For the moment this argument subsides*)

CORA (*Over her shoulder to* CHUCK—*acidly*) A guy what can't see flowers is pretty must be some dumbbell.

CHUCK Yeah? Well, if I was as dumb as you— (*Then mollifyingly*) Jees, yuh got your scrappin' pants on, ain't yuh? (*Grins good-naturedly*) Hell, Baby, what's eatin' yuh? All I'm tinkin' is, flowers is dat louse Hickey's stunt. We never had no flowers for Harry's boithday before. What de hell can Harry do wid flowers? He don't know a cauliflower from a geranium.

ROCKY Yeah, Chuck, it's like I'm tellin' dese broads about de cake. Dat's Hickey's wrinkle, too. (*Bitterly*) Jees, ever since he woke up, yuh can't hold him. He's taken on de party like it was his boithday.

MARGIE Well, he's payin' for everything, ain't he?

ROCKY Aw, I don't mind de boithday stuff so much. What gets my goat is de way he's tryin' to run de whole dump and everyone in it. He's buttin' in all over de place, tellin' everybody where dey get off. On'y he don't really tell yuh. He just keeps hintin' around.

PEARL Yeah. He was hintin' to me and Margie.

MARGIE Yeah, de lousy drummer.

ROCKY He just gives yuh an earful of dat line of bull about yuh got to be honest wid yourself and not kid yourself, and have de guts to be what yuh are. I got sore. I told him dat's aw right for de bums in dis dump. I hope he makes dem wake up. I'm sick of listenin' to dem hop demselves up. But it don't go wid me, see? I don't kid myself wid no pipe dream. (PEARL *and* MARGIE *exchange a derisive look. He catches it and his eyes narrow*) What are yuh grinnin' at?

PEARL (*Her face hard—scornfully*) Nuttin'.

MARGIE Nuttin'.

ROCKY It better be nuttin'! Don't let Hickey put no ideas in your nuts if you wanta stay healthy! (*Then angrily*) I wish de louse never showed up! I hope he don't come back from de delicatessen. He's gettin' everyone nuts. He's ridin' someone every minute. He's got Harry and Jimmy Tomorrow run ragged, and de rest is hidin' in deir rooms so dey won't have to listen to him. Dey're all actin' cagey wid de booze, too, like dey was scared if dey get too drunk, dey might spill deir guts, or somethin'. And everybody's gettin' a prize grouch on.

CORA Yeah, he's been hintin' round to me and Chuck, too. Yuh'd tink he suspected me and Chuck hadn't no real intention of gettin' married. Yuh'd tink he suspected Chuck wasn't goin' to lay off periodicals—or maybe even didn't want to.

CHUCK  He didn't say it right out or I'da socked him one. I told him, "I'm on de wagon for keeps and Cora knows it."

CORA  I told him, "Sure, I know it. And Chuck ain't never goin' to trow it in my face dat I was a tart, neider. And if yuh tink we're just kiddin' ourselves, we'll show yuh!"

CHUCK  We're goin' to show him!

CORA  We got it all fixed. We've decided Joisey is where we want de farm, and we'll get married dere, too, because yuh don't need no license. We're goin' to get married tomorrow. Ain't we, Honey?

CHUCK  You bet, Baby.

ROCKY  (*Disgusted*)  Christ, Chuck, are yuh lettin' dat bughouse louse Hickey kid yuh into—

CORA  (*Turns on him angrily*)  Nobody's kiddin' him into it, nor me neider! And Hickey's right. If dis big tramp's goin' to marry me, he ought to do it, and not just shoot off his old bazoo about it.

ROCKY  (*Ignoring her*)  Yuh can't be dat dumb, Chuck.

CORA  You keep outa dis! And don't start beefin' about crickets on de farm drivin' us nuts. You and your crickets! Yuh'd tink dey was elephants!

MARGIE  (*Coming to* ROCKY's *defense—sneeringly*)  Don't notice dat broad, Rocky. Yuh heard her say "tomorrow," didn't yuh? It's de same old crap.

CORA  (*Glares at her*)  Is dat so?

PEARL  (*Lines up with* MARGIE—*sneeringly*)  Imagine Cora a bride! Dat's a hot one! Jees, Cora, if all de guys you've stayed wid was side by side, yuh could walk on 'em from here to Texas!

CORA  (*Starts moving toward her threateningly*)  Yuh can't talk like dat to me, yuh fat Dago hooker! I may be a tart, but I ain't a cheap old whore like you!

PEARL  (*Furiously*)  I'll show yuh who's a whore!

(*They start to fly at each other, but* CHUCK *and* ROCKY *grab them from behind*)

CHUCK  (*Forcing* CORA *onto a chair*)  Sit down and cool off, Baby.

ROCKY  (*Doing the same to* PEARL)  Nix on de rough stuff, Poil.

MARGIE  (*Glaring at* CORA)  Why don't you leave Poil alone, Rocky? She'll fix dat blonde's clock! Or if she don't, I will!

ROCKY  Shut up, you!  (*Disgustedly*)  Jees, what dames! D'yuh wanta gum Harry's party?

PEARL (*A bit shamefaced—sulkily*) Who wants to? But nobody
  can't call me a —.

ROCKY (*Exasperatedly*) Aw, bury it! What are you, a voigin?
  (PEARL *stares at him, her face growing hard and bitter. So does*
  MARGIE)

PEARL Yuh mean you tink I'm a whore, too, huh?

MARGIE Yeah, and me?

ROCKY Now don't start nuttin'!

PEARL I suppose it'd tickle you if me and Margie did what dat
  louse, Hickey, was hintin' and come right out and admitted we
  was whores.

ROCKY Aw right! What of it? It's de truth, ain't it?

CORA (*Lining up with* PEARL *and* MARGIE—*indignantly*) Jees,
  Rocky, dat's a fine hell of a ting to say to two goils dat's been as
  good to yuh as Poil and Margie! (*To* PEARL) I didn't mean to
  call yuh dat, Poil. I was on'y mad.

PEARL (*Accepts the apology gratefully*) Sure, I was mad, too,
  Cora. No hard feelin's.

ROCKY (*Relieved*) Dere. Dat fixes everyting, don't it?

PEARL (*Turns on him—hard and bitter*) Aw right, Rocky. We're
  whores. You know what dat makes you, don't you?

ROCKY (*Angrily*) Look out, now!

MARGIE A lousy little pimp, dat's what!

ROCKY I'll loin yuh!
  (*He gives her a slap on the side of the face*)

PEARL A dirty little Ginny pimp, dat's what!

ROCKY (*Gives her a slap, too*) And dat'll loin you!
  (*But they only stare at him with hard sneering eyes*)

MARGIE He's provin' it to us, Poil.

PEARL Yeah! Hickey's convoited him. He's give up his pipe dream!

ROCKY (*Furious and at the same time bewildered by their defiance*)
  Lay off me or I'll beat de hell—

CHUCK (*Growls*) Aw, lay off dem. Harry's party ain't no time to
  beat up your stable.

ROCKY (*Turns to him*) Whose stable? Who d'yuh tink yuh're
  talkin' to? I ain't never beat dem up! What d'yuh tink I am? I just
  give dem a slap, like any guy would his wife, if she got too
  gabby. Why don't yuh tell dem to lay off me? I don't want no
  trouble on Harry's boithday party.

MARGIE (*A victorious gleam in her eye—tauntingly*) Aw right, den, yuh poor little Ginny. I'll lay off yuh till de party's over if Poil will.

PEARL (*Tauntingly*) Sure, I will. For Harry's sake, not yours, yuh little Wop!

ROCKY (*Stung*) Say, listen, youse! Don't get no wrong idea— (*But an interruption comes from* LARRY *who bursts into a sardonic laugh. They all jump startledly and look at him with unanimous hostility.* ROCKY *transfers his anger to him*) Who de hell yuh laughin' at, yuh half-dead old stew bum?

CORA (*Sneeringly*) At himself, he ought to be! Jees, Hickey's sure got his number!

LARRY (*Ignoring them, turns to* HUGO *and shakes him by the shoulder—in his comically intense, crazy whisper*) Wake up, Comrade! Here's the Revolution starting on all sides of you and you're sleeping through it! Be God, it's not to Bakunin's ghost you ought to pray in your dreams, but to the great Nihilist, Hickey! He's started a movement that'll blow up the world!

HUGO (*Blinks at him through his thick spectacles—with guttural denunciation*) You, Larry! Renegade! Traitor! I vill have you shot! (*He giggles*) Don't be a fool! Buy me a trink! (*He sees the drink in front of him, and gulps it down. He begins to sing the Carmagnole in a guttural basso, pounding on the table with his glass*) "Dansons la Carmagnole! Vive le son! Vive le son! Dansons la Carmagnole! Vive le son des canons!"

ROCKY Can dat noise!

HUGO (*Ignores this—to* LARRY, *in a low tone of hatred*) That bourgeois svine, Hickey! He laughs like good fellow, he makes jokes, he dares make hints to me so I see what he dares to think. He thinks I am finish, it is too late, and so I do not vish the Day come because it vill not be my Day. Oh, I see what he thinks! He thinks lies even vorse, dat I— (*He stops abruptly with a guilty look, as if afraid he was letting something slip—then revengefully*) I vill have him hanged the first one of all on de first lamppost! (*He changes his mood abruptly and peers around at* ROCKY *and the others—giggling again*) Vhy you so serious, leedle monkey-faces? It's all great joke, no? So ve get drunk, and ve laugh like hell, and den ve die, and de pipe dream vanish! (*A bitter mocking contempt creeps into his tone*) But be of good cheer, leedle stupid peoples! "The days grow hot, O Babylon!" Soon, leedle proletarians, ve vill have free picnic in the cool shade, ve vill eat hot dogs and trink free beer beneath the villow trees! Like hogs, yes! Like beautiful leedle hogs! (*He stops startledly, as if confused and amazed at what he has heard himself say. He mutters with hatred*) Dot Gottamned liar, Hickey. It is he who makes me sneer. I want to sleep.

(*He lets his head fall forward on his folded arms again and closes his eyes.* LARRY *gives him a pitying look, then quickly drinks his drink*)

CORA (*Uneasily*) Hickey ain't overlookin' no bets, is he? He's even give Hugo de woiks.

LARRY I warned you this morning he wasn't kidding.

MARGIE (*Sneering*) De old wise guy!

PEARL Yeah, still pretendin' he's de one exception, like Hickey told him. He don't do no pipe dreamin'! Oh, no!

LARRY (*Sharply resentful*) I—! (*Then abruptly he is drunkenly good-natured, and you feel this drunken manner is an evasive exaggeration*) All right, take it out on me, if it makes you more content. Sure, I love every hair of your heads, my great big beautiful baby dolls, and there's nothing I wouldn't do for you!

PEARL (*Stiffly*) De old Irish bunk, huh? We ain't big. And we ain't your baby dolls! (*Suddenly she is mollified and smiles*) But we admit we're beautiful. Huh, Margie?

MARGIE (*Smiling*) Sure ting! But what would he do wid beautiful dolls, even if he had de price, de old goat? (*She laughs teasingly—then pats* LARRY *on the shoulder affectionately*) Aw, yuh're aw right at dat, Larry, if yuh are full of bull!

PEARL Sure. Yuh're aces wid us. We're noivous, dat's all. Dat lousy drummer—why can't he be like he's always been? I never seen a guy change so. You pretend to be such a fox, Larry. What d'yuh tink's happened to him?

LARRY I don't know. With all his gab I notice he's kept that to himself so far. Maybe he's saving the great revelation for Harry's party. (*Then irritably*) To hell with him! I don't want to know. Let him mind his own business and I'll mind mine.

CHUCK Yeah, dat's what I say.

CORA Say, Larry, where's dat young friend of yours disappeared to?

LARRY I don't care where he is, except I wish it was a thousand miles away! (*Then, as he sees they are surprised at his vehemence, he adds hastily*) He's a pest.

ROCKY (*Breaks in with his own preoccupation*) I don't give a damn what happened to Hickey, but I know what's gonna happen if he don't watch his step. I told him, "I'll take a lot from you, Hickey, like everyone else in dis dump, because yuh've always been a grand guy. But dere's tings I don't take from you nor nobody, see? Remember dat, or you'll wake up in a hospital—or maybe worse, wid your wife and de iceman walkin' slow behind yuh."

CORA   Aw, yuh shouldn't make dat iceman crack, Rocky. It's aw right for him to kid about it but—I notice Hickey ain't pulled dat old iceman gag dis time. (*Excitedly*) D'yuh suppose dat he did catch his wife cheatin'? I don't mean wid no iceman, but wid some guy.

ROCKY   Aw, dat's de bunk. He ain't pulled dat gag or showed her photo around because he ain't drunk. And if he'd caught her cheatin' he'd be drunk, wouldn't he? He'd have beat her up and den gone on de woist drunk he'd ever staged. Like any other guy'd do.

(*The girls nod, convinced by this reasoning*)

CHUCK   Sure! Rocky's got de right dope, Baby. He'd be paralyzed. (*While he is speaking, the Negro,* JOE, *comes in from the hallway. There is a noticeable change in him. He walks with a tough, truculent swagger and his good-natured face is set in sullen suspicion*)

JOE   (*To* ROCKY—*defiantly*) I's stood tellin' people dis dump is closed for de night all I's goin' to. Let Harry hire a doorman. pay him wages, if he wants one.

ROCKY   (*Scowling*)   Yeah? Harry's pretty damned good to you.

JOE   (*Shamefaced*)   Sure he is. I don't mean dat. Anyways, it's all right. I told Schwartz, de cop, we's closed for de party. He'll keep folks away. (*Aggressively again*) I want a big drink, dat's what!

CHUCK   Who's stoppin' yuh? Yuh can have all yuh want on Hickey.

JOE   (*Has taken a glass from the table and has his hand on a bottle when* HICKEY's *name is mentioned. He draws his hand back as if he were going to refuse—then grabs it defiantly and pours a big drink*)   All right, I's earned all de drinks on him I could drink in a year for listenin' to his crazy bull. And here's hopin' he gets de lockjaw! (*He drinks and pours out another*) I drinks on him but I don't drink wid him. No, suh, never no more!

ROCKY   Aw, bull! Hickey's aw right. What's he done to you?

JOE (*Sullenly*) Dat's my business. I ain't buttin' in yours, is I? (*Bitterly*) Sure, you think he's all right. He's a white man, ain't he? (*His tone becomes aggressive*) Listen to me, you white boys! Don't you get it in your heads I's pretendin' to be what I ain't, or dat I ain't proud to be what I is, get me? Or you and me's goin' to have trouble!

(*He picks up his drink and walks left as far away from them as he can get and slumps down on the piano stool*)

MARGIE (*In a low angry tone*) What a noive! Just because we act nice to him, he gets a swelled nut! If dat ain't a coon all over!

CHUCK Talkin' fight talk, huh? I'll moider de nigger!

(*He takes a threatening step toward* JOE, *who is staring before him guiltily now*)

JOE (*Speaks up shamefacedly*) Listen, boys, I's sorry. I didn't mean dat. You been good friends to me. I's nuts, I guess. Dat Hickey, he gets my head all mixed up wit' craziness.

(*Their faces at once clear of resentment against him*)

CORA Aw, dat's aw right, Joe. De boys wasn't takin' yuh serious. (*Then to the others, forcing a laugh*) Jees, what'd I say, Hickey ain't overlookin' no bets. Even Joe. (*She pauses—then adds puzzledly*) De funny ting is, yuh can't stay sore at de bum when he's around. When he forgets de bughouse preachin', and quits tellin' yuh where yuh get off, he's de same old Hickey. Yuh can't help likin' de louse. And yuh got to admit he's got de right dope— (*She adds hastily*) I mean, on some of de bums here.

MARGIE (*With a sneering look at* ROCKY) Yeah, he's coitinly got one guy I know sized up right! Huh, Poil?

PEARL He coitinly has!

ROCKY Cut it out, I told yuh!

LARRY (*Is staring before him broodingly. He speaks more aloud to himself than to them*) It's nothing to me what happened to him. But I have a feeling he's dying to tell us, inside him, and yet he's afraid. He's like that damned kid. It's strange the queer way he seemed to recognize him. If he's afraid, it explains why he's off booze. Like that damned kid again. Afraid if he got drunk, he'd tell—

(*While he is speaking,* HICKEY *comes in the doorway at rear. He looks the same as in the previous act, except that now his face beams with the excited expectation of a boy going to a party. His arms are piled with packages*)

HICKEY (*Booms in imitation of a familiar Polo Grounds bleacherite cry—with rising volume*) Well! Well!! Well!!! (*They all jump startledly. He comes forward, grinning*) Here I am in the nick of time. Give me a hand with these bundles, somebody.

(MARGIE *and* PEARL *start taking them from his arms and putting them on the table. Now that he is present, all their attitudes show the reaction* CORA *has expressed. They can't help liking him and forgiving him*)

MARGIE Jees, Hickey, yuh scared me outa a year's growth, sneakin' in like dat.

HICKEY Sneaking? Why, me and the taxi man made enough noise getting my big surprise in the hall to wake the dead. You were all so busy drinking in words of wisdom from the Old Wise Guy here, you couldn't hear anything else. (*He grins at* LARRY) From what I heard, Larry, you're not so good when you start playing Sherlock Holmes. You've got me all wrong. I'm not afraid of anything now—not even myself. You better stick to the part of Old Cemetery, the Barker for the Big Sleep—that is, if you can still let yourself get away with it!

(*He chuckles and gives* LARRY *a friendly slap on the back.* LARRY *gives him a bitter angry look*)

CORA (*Giggles*) Old Cemetery! That's him, Hickey. We'll have to call him dat.

HICKEY (*Watching* LARRY *quizzically*) Beginning to do a lot of puzzling about me, aren't you, Larry? But that won't help you. You've got to think of yourself. I couldn't give you my peace. You've got to find your own. All I can do is help you, and the rest of the gang, by showing you the way to find it.

(*He has said this with a simple persuasive earnestness. He pauses, and for a second they stare at him with fascinated resentful uneasiness*)

ROCKY (*Breaks the spell*) Aw, hire a church!

HICKEY (*Placatingly*) All right! All right! Don't get sore, boys and girls. I guess that did sound too much like a lousy preacher. Let's forget it and get busy on the party.

(*They look relieved*)

CHUCK Is dose bundles grub, Hickey? You bought enough already to feed an army.

HICKEY (*With boyish excitement again*) Can't be too much! I want this to be the biggest birthday Harry's ever had. You and Rocky go in the hall and get the big surprise. My arms are busted lugging it.

(*They catch his excitement.* CHUCK *and* ROCKY *go out, grinning expectantly. The three girls gather around* HICKEY, *full of thrilled curiosity*)

PEARL  Jees, yuh got us all het up! What is it, Hickey?

HICKEY  Wait and see. I got it as a treat for the three of you more than anyone. I thought to myself, I'll bet this is what will please those whores more than anything. (*They wince as if he had slapped them, but before they have a chance to be angry, he goes on affectionately*) I said to myself, I don't care how much it costs, they're worth it. They're the best little scouts in the world, and they've been damned kind to me when I was down and out! Nothing is too good for them. (*Earnestly*) I mean every word of that, too—and then some! (*Then, as if he noticed the expression on their faces for the first time*) What's the matter? You look sore. What—? (*Then he chuckles*) Oh, I see. But you know how I feel about that. You know I didn't say it to offend you. So don't be silly now.

MARGIE  (*Lets out a tense breath*)  Aw right, Hickey. Let it slide.

HICKEY  (*Jubilantly, as* CHUCK *and* ROCKY *enter carrying a big wicker basket*)  Look! There it comes! Unveil it, boys.

(*They pull off a covering burlap bag. The basket is piled with quarts of champagne*)

PEARL  (*With childish excitement*)  It's champagne! Jees, Hickey, if you ain't a sport!

(*She gives him a hug, forgetting all animosity, as do the other girls*)

MARGIE  I never been soused on champagne. Let's get stinko, Poil.

PEARL  You betcha my life! De bot' of us!

(*A holiday spirit of gay festivity has seized them all. Even* JOE MOTT *is standing up to look at the wine with an admiring grin, and* HUGO *raises his head to blink at it*)

JOE  You sure is hittin' de high spots, Hickey. (*Boastfully*) Man, when I runs my gamblin' house, I drinks dat old bubbly water in steins! (*He stops guiltily and gives* HICKEY *a look of defiance*) I's goin' to drink it dat way again, too, soon's I make my stake! And dat ain't no pipe dream, neider!

(*He sits down where he was, his back turned to them*)

ROCKY  What'll we drink it outa, Hickey? Dere ain't no wine glasses.

HICKEY (*Enthusiastically*) Joe has the right idea! Schooners! That's the spirit for Harry's birthday!

(ROCKY and CHUCK *carry the basket of wine into the bar. The three girls go back and stand around the entrance to the bar, chatting excitedly among themselves and to* CHUCK *and* ROCKY *in the bar*)

HUGO (*With his silly giggle*) Ve vill trink vine beneath the villow trees!

HICKEY (*Grins at him*) That's the spirit, Brother—and let the lousy slaves drink vinegar!

(HUGO *blinks at him startledly, then looks away*)

HUGO (*Mutters*) Gottamned liar!

(*He puts his head back on his arms and closes his eyes, but this time his habitual pass-out has a quality of hiding*)

LARRY (*Gives* HUGO *a pitying glance—in a low tone of anger*) Leave Hugo be! He rotted ten years in prison for his faith! He's earned his dream! Have you no decency or pity?

HICKEY (*Quizzically*) Hello, what's this? I thought you were in the grandstand. (*Then with a simple earnestness, taking a chair by* LARRY, *and putting a hand on his shoulder*) Listen, Larry, you're getting me all wrong. Hell, you ought to know me better. I've always been the best-natured slob in the world. Of course, I have pity. But now I've seen the light, it isn't my old kind of pity—the kind yours is. It isn't the kind that lets itself off easy by encouraging some poor guy to go on kidding himself with a lie—the kind that leaves the poor slob worse off because it makes him feel guiltier than ever—the kind that makes his lying hopes nag at him and reproach him until he's a rotten skunk in his own eyes. I know all about that kind of pity. I've had a bellyful of it in my time, and it's all wrong! (*With a salesman's persuasiveness*) No, sir. The kind of pity I feel now is after final results that will really save the poor guy, and make him contented with what he is, and quit battling himself, and find peace for the rest of his life. Oh, I know how you resent the way I have to show you up to yourself. I don't blame you. I know from my own experience it's bitter medicine, facing yourself in the mirror with the old false whiskers off. But you forget that, once you're cured. You'll be grateful to me when all at once you find you're able to admit, without feeling ashamed, that all the grandstand foolosopher bunk and the waiting for the Big Sleep stuff is a pipe dream. You'll say to yourself, I'm just an old man who is scared of life, but even more scared of dying. So I'm keeping drunk and hanging on to life at any price, and what of it? Then you'll know what real peace means, Larry, because you won't be scared of either life or death any more. You simply won't give a damn! Any more than I do!

LARRY (*Has been staring into his eyes with a fascinated wondering dread*) Be God, if I'm not beginning to think you've gone mad! (*With a rush of anger*) You're a liar!

HICKEY (*Injuredly*) Now, listen, that's no way to talk to an old pal who's trying to help you. Hell, if you really wanted to die, you'd just take a hop off your fire escape, wouldn't you? And if you really were in the grandstand, you wouldn't be pitying everyone. Oh, I know the truth is tough at first. It was for me. All I ask is for you to suspend judgment and give it a chance. I'll absolutely guarantee— Hell, Larry, I'm no fool. Do you suppose I'd deliberately set out to get under everyone's skin and put myself in dutch with all my old pals, if I wasn't certain, from my own experience, that is means contentment in the end for all of you? (LARRY *again is staring at him fascinatedly.* HICKEY *grins*) As for my being bughouse, you can't crawl out of it that way. Hell, I'm too damned sane. I can size up guys, and turn 'em inside out, better than I ever could. Even where they're strangers like that Parritt kid. He's licked, Larry. I think there is only one possible way out you can help him to take. That is, if you have the right kind of pity for him.

LARRY (*Uneasily*) What do you mean? (*Attempting indifference*) I'm not advising him, except to leave me out of his troubles. He's nothing to me.

HICKEY (*Shakes his head*) You'll find he won't agree to that. He'll keep after you until he makes you help him. Because he has to be punished, so he can forgive himself. He's lost all his guts. He can't manage it alone, and you're the only one he can turn to.

LARRY For the love of God, mind your own business! (*With forced scorn*) A lot you know about him! He's hardly spoken to you!

HICKEY No, that's right. But I do know a lot about him just the same. I've had hell inside me. I can spot it in others. (*Frowning*) Maybe that's what gives me the feeling there's something familiar about him, something between us. (*He shakes his head*) No, it's more than that. I can't figure it. Tell me about him. For instance, I don't imagine he's married, is he?

LARRY No.

HICKEY   Hasn't he been mixed up with some woman? I don't mean trollops. I mean the old real love stuff that crucifies you.

LARRY   (*With a calculating relieved look at him—encouraging him along this line*) Maybe you're right. I wouldn't be surprised.

HICKEY   (*Grins at him quizzically*) I see. You think I'm on the wrong track and you're glad I am. Because then I won't suspect whatever he did about the Great Cause. That's another lie you tell yourself, Larry, that the good old Cause means nothing to you any more. (LARRY *is about to burst out in denial but* HICKEY *goes on*) But you're all wrong about Parritt. That isn't what's got him stopped. It's what's behind that. And it's a woman. I recognize the symptoms.

LARRY   (*Sneeringly*) And you're the boy who's never wrong! Don't be a damned fool. His trouble is he was brought up a devout believer in the Movement and now he's lost his faith. It's a shock, but he's young and he'll soon find another dream just as good. (*He adds sardonically*) Or as bad.

HICKEY   All right. I'll let it go at that, Larry. He's nothing to me except I'm glad he's here because he'll help me make you wake up to yourself. I don't even like the guy, or the feeling there's anything between us. But you'll find I'm right just the same, when you get to the final showdown with him.

LARRY   There'll be no showdown! I don't give a tinker's damn—

HICKEY   Sticking to the old grandstand, eh? Well, I knew you'd be the toughest to convince of all the gang, Larry. And, along with Harry and Jimmy Tomorrow, you're the one I want most to help. (*He puts an arm around* LARRY's *shoulder and gives him an affectionate hug*) I've always liked you a lot, you old bastard! (*He gets up and his manner changes to his bustling party excitement—glancing at his watch*) Well, well, not much time before twelve. Let's get busy, boys and girls. (*He looks over the table where the cake is*) Cake all set. Good. And my presents, and yours, girls, and Chuck's, and Rocky's. Fine. Harry'll certainly be touched by your thought of him. (*He goes back to the girls*) You go in the bar, Pearl and Margie, and get the grub ready so it can be brought right in. There'll be some drinking and toasts first, of course. My idea is to use the wine for that, so get it all set. I'll go upstairs now and root everyone out. Harry the last. I'll come back with him. Somebody light the candles on the cake when you hear us coming, and you start playing Harry's favorite tune, Cora. Hustle now, everybody. We want this to come off in style.

(*He bustles into the hall.* MARGIE *and* PEARL *disappear in the bar.* CORA *goes to the piano.* JOE *gets off the stool sullenly to let her sit down*)

CORA    I got to practice. I ain't laid my mits on a box in Gawd knows when. (*With the soft pedal down, she begins gropingly to pick out "The Sunshine of Paradise Alley"*) Is dat right, Joe? I've forgotten dat has-been tune. (*She picks out a few more notes*) Come on, Joe, hum de tune so I can follow.

(JOE *begins to hum and sing in a low voice and correct her. He forgets his sullenness and becomes his old self again*)

LARRY    (*Suddenly gives a laugh—in his comically intense, crazy tone*)    Be God, it's a second feast of Belshazzar, with Hickey to do the writing on the wall!

CORA    Aw, shut up. Old Cemetery! Always beefin'! (WILLIE *comes in from the hall. He is in a pitiable state, his face pasty, haggard with sleeplessness and nerves, his eyes sick and haunted. He is sober.* CORA *greets him over her shoulder kiddingly*) If it ain't Prince Willie! (*Then kindly*) Gee, kid, yuh look sick. Git a coupla shots in yuh.

WILLIE    (*Tensely*)    No, thanks. Not now. I'm tapering off.

(*He sits down weakly on* LARRY's *right*)

CORA    (*Astonished*)    What d'yuh know? He means it!

WILLIE    (*Leaning toward* LARRY *confidentially—in a low shaken voice*)    It's been hell up in that damned room, Larry! The things I've imagined! (*He shudders*) I thought I'd go crazy. (*With pathetic boastful pride*) But I've got it beat now. By tomorrow morning I'll be on the wagon. I'll get back my clothes the first thing. Hickey's loaning me the money. I'm going to do what I've always said—go to the D.A.'s office. He was a good friend of my Old Man's. He was only assistant, then. He was in on the graft, but my Old Man never squealed on him. So he certainly owes it to me to give me a chance. And he knows that I really was a brilliant law student. (*Self-reassuringly*) Oh, I know I can make good, now I'm getting off the booze forever. (*Moved*) I owe a lot to Hickey. He's made me wake up to myself—see what a fool— It wasn't nice to face but— (*With bitter resentment*) It isn't what he says. It's what you feel behind—what he hints— Christ, you'd think all I really wanted to do with my life was sit here and stay drunk. (*With hatred*) I'll show him!

LARRY (*Masking pity behind a sardonic tone*) If you want my advice, you'll put the nearest bottle to your mouth until you don't give a damn for Hickey!

WILLIE (*Stares at a bottle greedily, tempted for a moment—then bitterly*) That's fine advice! I thought you were my friend!
(*He gets up with a hurt glance at* LARRY, *and moves away to take a chair in back of the left end of the table, where he sits in dejected, shaking misery, his chin on his chest*)

JOE (*To* CORA) No, like dis. (*He beats time with his finger and sings in a low voice*) "She is the sunshine of Paradise Alley."
(*She plays*) Dat's more like it. Try it again.
(*She begins to play through the chorus again.* DON PARRITT *enters from the hall. There is a frightened look on his face. He slinks in furtively, as if he were escaping from someone. He looks relieved when he sees* LARRY *and comes and slips into the chair on his right.* LARRY *pretends not to notice his coming, but he instinctively shrinks with repulsion.* PARRITT *leans toward him and speaks ingratiatingly in a low secretive tone*)

PARRITT Gee, I'm glad you're here, Larry. That damned fool, Hickey, knocked on my door. I opened up because I thought it must be you, and he came busting in and made me come downstairs. I don't know what for. I don't belong in this birthday celebration. I don't know this gang and I don't want to be mixed up with them. All I came here for was to find you.

LARRY (*Tensely*) I've warned you—

PARRITT (*Goes on as if he hadn't heard*) Can't you make Hickey mind his own business? I don't like that guy, Larry. The way he acts, you'd think he had something on me. Why, just now he pats me on the shoulder, like he was sympathizing with me, and says, "I know how it is, Son, but you can't hide from yourself, not even here on the bottom of the sea. You've got to face the truth and then do what must be done for your own peace and the happiness of all concerned." What did he mean by that, Larry?

LARRY How the hell would I know?

PARRITT Then he grins and says, "Never mind, Larry's getting wise to himself. I think you can rely on his help in the end. He'll have to choose between living and dying, and he'll never choose to die while there is a breath left in the old bastard!" And then he laughs like it was a joke on you. (*He pauses.* LARRY *is rigid on his chair, staring before him.* PARRITT *asks him with a sudden taunt in his voice*) Well, what do you say to that, Larry?

LARRY I've nothing to say. Except you're a bigger fool than he is to listen to him.

PARRITT (*With a sneer*) Is that so? He's no fool where you're concerned. He's got your number, all right! (LARRY's *face tightens but he keeps silent.* PARRITT *changes to a contrite, appealing air*) I don't mean that. But you keep acting as if you were sore at me, and that gets my goat. You know what I want most is to be friends with you, Larry. I haven't a single friend left in the world. I hoped you— (*Bitterly*) And you could be, too, without it hurting you. You ought to, for Mother's sake. She really loved you. You loved her, too, didn't you?

LARRY (*Tensely*) Leave what's dead in its grave.

PARRITT I suppose, because I was only a kid, you didn't think I was wise about you and her. Well, I was. I've been wise, ever since I can remember, to all the guys she's had, although she'd tried to kid me along it wasn't so. That was a silly stunt for a free Anarchist woman, wasn't it, being ashamed of being free?

LARRY Shut your damned trap!

PARRITT (*Guiltily but with a strange undertone of satisfaction*) Yes, I know I shouldn't say that now. I keep forgetting she isn't free any more. (*He pauses*) Do you know, Larry, you're the one of them all she cared most about? Anyone else who left the Movement would have been dead to her, but she couldn't forget you. She'd always make excuses for you. I used to try and get her goat about you. I'd say, "Larry's got brains and yet he thinks the Movement is just a crazy pipe dream." She'd blame it on booze getting you. She'd kid herself that you'd give up booze and come back to the Movement—tomorrow! She'd say, "Larry can't kill in himself a faith he's given his life to, not without killing himself." (*He grins sneeringly*) How about it, Larry? Was she right? (LARRY *remains silent. He goes on insistently*) I suppose what she really meant was, come back to her. She was always getting the Movement mixed up with herself. But I'm sure she really must have loved you, Larry. As much as she could love anyone besides herself. But she wasn't faithful to you, even at that, was she? That's why you finally walked out on her, isn't it? I remember that last fight you had with her. I was listening. I was on your side, even if she was my mother, because I liked you so much; you'd been so good to me—like a father. I remember her putting on her high-and-mighty free-woman stuff, saying you were still a slave to bourgeois morality and jealousy and you thought a woman you loved was a piece of private property you owned. I remember that you got mad and you told her, "I don't like living with a whore, if that's what you mean!"

LARRY (*Bursts out*) You lie! I never called her that!

PARRITT (*Goes on as if* LARRY *hadn't spoken*) I think that's why she still respects you, because it was you who left her. You were the only one to beat her to it. She got sick of the others before they did of her. I don't think she ever cared much about them, anyway. She just had to keep on having lovers to prove to herself how free she was (*He pauses—then with a bitter repulsion*) It made home a lousy place. I felt like you did about it. I'd get feeling it was like living in a whorehouse—only worse, because she didn't have to make her living—

LARRY You bastard! She's your mother! Have you no shame?

PARRITT (*Bitterly*) No! She brought me up to believe that family-respect stuff is all bourgeois, property-owning crap. Why should I be ashamed?

LARRY (*Making a move to get up*) I've had enough!

PARRITT (*Catches his arm—pleadingly*) No! Don't leave me! Please! I promise I won't mention her again! (LARRY *sinks back in his chair*) I only did it to make you understand better. I know this isn't the place to— Why didn't you come up to my room, like I asked you? I kept waiting. We could talk everything over there.

LARRY There's nothing to talk over!

PARRITT But I've got to talk to you. Or I'll talk to Hickey. He won't let me alone! I feel he knows, anyway! And I know he'd understand, all right—in his way. But I hate his guts! I don't want anything to do with him! I'm scared of him, honest. There's something not human behind his damned grinning and kidding.

LARRY (*Starts*) Ah! You feel that, too?

PARRITT (*Pleadingly*) But I can't go on like this. I've got to decide what I've got to do. I've got to tell you, Larry!

LARRY (*Again starts up*) I won't listen!

PARRITT (*Again holds him by the arm*) All right! I won't. Don't go! (LARRY *lets himself be pulled down on his chair.* PARRITT *examines his face and becomes insultingly scornful*) Who do you think you're kidding? I know damned well you've guessed—

LARRY I've guessed nothing!

PARRITT But I want you to guess now! I'm glad you have! I know now, since Hickey's been after me, that I meant you to guess right from the start. That's why I came to you. (*Hurrying on with an attempt at a plausible frank air that makes what he says seem doubly false*) I want you to understand the reason. You see, I began studying American history. I got admiring Washington and Jefferson and Jackson and Lincoln. I began to feel patriotic and love this country. I saw it was the best government in the world, where everybody was equal and had a chance. I saw that all the ideas behind the Movement came from a lot of Russians like Bakunin and Kropotkin and were meant for Europe, but we didn't need them here in a democracy where we were free already. I didn't want this country to be destroyed for a damned foreign pipe dream. After all, I'm from old American pioneer stock. I began to feel I was a traitor for helping a lot of cranks and bums and free women plot to overthrow our government. And then I saw it was my duty to my country—

LARRY (*Nauseated—turns on him*) You stinking rotten liar! Do you think you can fool me with such hypocrite's cant! (*Then turning away*) I don't give a damn what you did! It's on your head—whatever it was! I don't want to know—and I won't know!

PARRITT (*As if* LARRY *had never spoken—falteringly*) But I never thought Mother would be caught. Please believe that, Larry. You know I never would have—

LARRY (*His face haggard, drawing a deep breath and closing his eyes—as if he were trying to hammer something into his own brain*) All I know is I'm sick of life! I'm through! I've forgotten myself! I'm drowned and contented on the bottom of a bottle. Honor or dishonor, faith or treachery are nothing to me but the opposites of the same stupidity which is ruler and king of life, and in the end they rot into dust in the same grave. All things are the same meaningless joke to me, for they grin at me from the one skull of death. So go away. You're wasting breath. I've forgotten your mother.

PARRITT (*Jeers angrily*) The old foolosopher, eh? (*He spits out contemptuously*) You lousy old faker!

LARRY (*So distracted he pleads weakly*) For the love of God, leave me in peace the little time that's left to me!

PARRITT Aw, don't pull that pitiful old-man junk on me! You old bastard, you'll never die as long as there's a free drink of whiskey left!

LARRY (*Stung—furiously*) Look out how you try to taunt me back into life, I warn you! I might remember the thing they call justice there, and the punishment for— (*He checks himself with an ef-fort—then with a real indifference that comes from exhaustion*) I'm old and tired. To hell with you! You're as mad as Hickey, and as big a liar. I'd never let myself believe a word you told me.

PARRITT (*Threateningly*) The hell you won't! Wait till Hickey gets through with you!

(PEARL *and* MARGIE *come in from the bar. At the sight of them,* PARRITT *instantly subsides and becomes self-conscious and defensive, scowling at them and then quickly looking away*)

MARGIE (*Eyes him jeeringly*) Why, hello, Tightwad Kid. Come to join de party? Gee, don't he act bashful, Poil?

PEARL Yeah. Especially wid his dough. (PARRITT *slinks to a chair at the left end of the table, pretending he hasn't heard them. Suddenly there is a noise of angry, cursing voices and a scuffle from the hall.* PEARL *yells*) Hey, Rocky! Fight in de hall!

(ROCKY *and* CHUCK *run from behind the bar curtain and rush into the hall.* ROCKY'S *voice is heard in irritated astonishment,* "What de hell?" *and then the scuffle stops and* ROCKY *appears holding* CAPTAIN LEWIS *by the arm, followed by* CHUCK *with a similar hold on* GENERAL WETJOEN. *Although these two have been drinking they both are sober, for them. Their faces are sullenly angry, their clothes disarranged from the tussle*)

ROCKY (*Leading* LEWIS *forward—astonished, amused and irritated*) Can yuh beat it? I've heard youse two call each odder every name yuh could think of but I never seen you— (*Indignantly*) A swell time to stage your first bout, on Harry's boithday party! What started de scrap?

LEWIS (*Forcing a casual tone*) Nothing, old chap. Our business, you know. That bloody ass, Hickey, made some insinuation about me, and the boorish Boer had the impertinence to agree with him.

WETJOEN Dot's a lie! Hickey made joke about me, and this Limey said yes, it was true!

ROCKY Well, sit down, de bot' of yuh, and cut out de rough stuff. (*He and* CHUCK *dump them down in adjoining chairs toward the left end of the table, where, like two sulky boys, they turn their backs on each other as far as possible in chairs which both face front*)

MARGIE (*Laughs*) Jees, lookit de two bums! Like a coupla kids! Kiss and make up, for Gawd's sakes!

ROCKY   Yeah. Harry's party begins in a minute and we don't want no soreheads around.

LEWIS   (*Stiffly*) Very well. In deference to the occasion, I apologize, General Wetjoen—provided that you do also.

WETJOEN   (*Sulkily*) I apologize, Captain Lewis—because Harry is my good friend.

ROCKY   Aw, hell! If yuh can't do better'n dat—!

(MOSHER *and* MCGLOIN *enter together from the hall. Both have been drinking but are not drunk*)

PEARL   Here's de star boarders.

(*They advance, their heads together, so interested in a discussion they are oblivious to everyone*)

MCGLOIN   I'm telling you, Ed, it's serious this time. That bastard, Hickey, has got Harry on the hip. (*As he talks,* MARGIE, PEARL, ROCKY *and* CHUCK *prick up their ears and gather round.* CORA, *at the piano, keeps running through the tune, with soft pedal, and singing the chorus half under her breath, with* JOE *still correcting her mistakes. At the table,* LARRY, PARRITT, WILLIE, WETJOEN *and* LEWIS *sit motionless, staring in front of them.* HUGO *seems asleep in his habitual position*) And you know it isn't going to do us no good if he gets him to take that walk tomorrow.

MOSHER   You're damned right. Harry'll mosey around the ward, dropping in on everyone who knew him when. (*Indignantly*) And they'll all give him a phony glad hand and a ton of good advice about what a sucker he is to stand for us.

MCGLOIN   He's sure to call on Bessie's relations to do a little cryin' over dear Bessie. And you know what that bitch and all her family thought of me.

MOSHER   (*With a flash of his usual humor—rebukingly*) Remember, Lieutenant, you are speaking of my sister! Dear Bessie wasn't a bitch. She was a God-damned bitch! But if you think my loving relatives will have time to discuss you, you don't know them. They'll be too busy telling Harry what a drunken crook I am and saying he ought to have me put in Sing Sing!

MCGLOIN   (*Dejectedly*) Yes, once Bessie's relations get their hooks in him, it'll be as tough for us as if she wasn't gone.

MOSHER   (*Dejectedly*) Yes, Harry has always been weak and easily influenced, and now he's getting old he'll be an easy mark for those grafters. (*Then with forced reassurance*) Oh, hell, Mac, we're saps to worry. We've heard Harry pull that bluff about taking a walk every birthday he's had for twenty years.

MCGLOIN (*Doubtfully*) But Hickey wasn't sicking him on those times. Just the opposite. He was asking Harry what he wanted to go out for when there was plenty of whiskey here.

MOSHER (*With a change to forced carelessness*) Well, after all, I don't care whether he goes out or not. I'm clearing out tomorrow morning anyway. I'm just sorry for you, Mac.

MCGLOIN (*Resentfully*) You needn't be, then. Ain't I going myself? I was only feeling sorry for you.

MOSHER Yes, my mind is made up. Hickey may be a lousy, interfering pest, now he's gone teetotal on us, but there's a lot of truth in some of his bull. Hanging around here getting plastered with you, Mac, is pleasant, I won't deny, but the old booze gets you in the end, if you keep lapping it up. It's time I quit for a while. (*With forced enthusiasm*) Besides, I feel the call of the old carefree circus life in my blood again. I'll see the boss tomorrow. It's late in the season but he'll be glad to take me on. And won't all the old gang be tickled to death when I show up on the lot!

MCGLOIN Maybe—if they've got a rope handy!

MOSHER (*Turns on him—angrily*) Listen! I'm damned sick of that kidding!

MCGLOIN You are, are you? Well, I'm sicker of your kidding me about getting reinstated on the Force. And whatever you'd like, I can't spend my life sitting here with you, ruining my stomach with rotgut. I'm tapering off, and in the morning I'll be fresh as a daisy. I'll go and have a private chin with the Commissioner. (*With forced enthusiasm*) Man alive, from what the boys tell me, there's sugar galore these days, and I'll soon be ridin' around in a big red automobile—

MOSHER (*Derisively—beckoning an imaginary Chinese*) Here, One Lung Hop! Put fresh peanut oil in the lamp and cook the Lieutenant another dozen pills! It's his gowed-up night!

MCGLOIN (*Stung—pulls back a fist threateningly*) One more crack like that and I'll—!

MOSHER (*Putting up his fists*) Yes? Just start—!

(CHUCK *and* ROCKY *jump between them*)

ROCKY Hey! Are you guys nuts? Jees, it's Harry's boithday party! (*They both look guilty*) Sit down and behave.

MOSHER (*Grumpily*) All right. Only tell him to lay off me. (*He lets* ROCKY *push him in a chair, at the right end of the table, rear*)

MCGLOIN (*Grumpily*) Tell him to lay off me.

(*He lets* CHUCK *push him into the chair on* MOSHER's *left. At this moment* HICKEY *bursts in from the hall, bustling and excited*)

HICKEY Everything all set? Fine! (*He glances at his watch*) Half a minute to go. Harry's starting down with Jimmy. I had a hard time getting them to move! They'd rather stay hiding up there, kidding each other along. (*He chuckles*) Harry don't even want to remember it's his birthday now! (*He hears a noise from the stairs*) Here they come! (*Urgently*) Light the candles! Get ready to play, Cora! Stand up, everybody! Get that wine ready, Chuck and Rocky! (MARGIE *and* PEARL *light the candles on the cake.* CORA *gets her hands set over the piano keys, watching over her shoulder.* ROCKY *and* CHUCK *go in the bar. Everybody at the table stands up mechanically.* HUGO *is the last, suddenly coming to and scrambling to his feet.* HARRY HOPE *and* JIMMY TOMORROW *appear in the hall outside the door.* HICKEY *looks up from his watch*) On the dot! It's twelve! (*Like a cheer leader*) Come on now, everybody, with a Happy Birthday, Harry!

(*With his voice leading they all shout "Happy Birthday, Harry!" in a spiritless chorus.* HICKEY *signals to* CORA, *who starts playing and singing in a whiskey soprano "She's the Sunshine of Paradise Alley."* HOPE *and* JIMMY *stand in the doorway. Both have been drinking heavily. In* HOPE *the effect is apparent only in a bristling, touchy, pugnacious attitude. It is entirely different from the usual irascible beefing he delights in and which no one takes seriously. Now he really has a chip on his shoulder.* JIMMY, *on the other hand, is plainly drunk, but it has not had the desired effect, for beneath a pathetic assumption of gentlemanly poise, he is obviously frightened and shrinking back within himself.* HICKEY *grabs* HOPE's *hand and pumps it up and down. For a moment* HOPE *appears unconscious of this handshake. Then he jerks his hand away angrily*)

HOPE Cut out the glad hand, Hickey. D'you think I'm a sucker? I know you, bejees, you sneaking, lying drummer! (*With rising anger, to the others*) And all you bums! What the hell you trying to do, yelling and raising the roof? Want the cops to close the joint and get my license taken away? (*He yells at* CORA *who has stopped singing but continues to play mechanically with many mistakes*) Hey, you dumb tart, quit banging that box! Bejees, the least you could do is learn the tune!

CORA (*Stops—deeply hurt*)    Aw, Harry! Jees, ain't I—
(*Her eyes begin to fill*)

HOPE (*Glaring at the other girls*)    And you two hookers, screaming
at the top of your lungs! What d'you think this is, a dollar cathouse? Bejees, that's where you belong!

PEARL (*Miserably*)    Aw, Harry—
(*She begins to cry*)

MARGIE    Jees, Harry, I never thought you'd say that—like yuh
meant it. (*She puts her arm around* PEARL—*on the verge of tears
herself*) Aw, don't bawl, Poil. He don't mean it.

HICKEY (*Reproachfully*)    Now, Harry! Don't take it out on the gang
because you're upset about yourself. Anyway, I've promised you
you'll come through all right, haven't I? So quit worrying. (*He
slaps* HOPE *on the back encouragingly.* HOPE *flashes him a glance
of hate*) Be yourself, Governor. You don't want to bawl out the
old gang just when they're congratulating you on your birthday,
do you? Hell, that's no way!

HOPE (*Looking guilty and shamefaced now—forcing an unconvincing attempt at his natural tone*)    Bejees, they ain't as dumb as
you. They know I was only kidding them. They know I appreciate their congratulations. Don't you, fellers? (*There is a listless
chorus of "Sure, Harry," "Yes," "Of course we do," etc. He comes
forward to the two girls, with* JIMMY *and* HICKEY *following him,
and pats them clumsily*) Bejees, I like you broads. You know I
was only kidding.
(*Instantly they forgive him and smile affectionately*)

MARGIE    Sure we know, Harry.

PEARL    Sure.

HICKEY (*Grinning*)    Sure. Harry's the greatest kidder in this dump
and that's saying something! Look how he's kidded himself for
twenty years! (*As* HOPE *gives him a bitter, angry glance, he digs
him in the ribs with his elbow playfully*) Unless I'm wrong, Governor, and I'm betting I'm not. We'll soon know, eh? Tomorrow
morning. No, by God, it's *this* morning now!

JIMMY (*With a dazed dread*)    This morning?

HICKEY    Yes, it's today at last, Jimmy. (*He pats him on the back*)
Don't be so scared! I've promised I'll help you.

JIMMY (*Trying to hide his dread behind an offended, drunken
dignity*)    I don't understand you. Kindly remember I'm fully
capable of settling my own affairs!

HICKEY (*Earnestly*)    Well, isn't that exactly what I want you to do, settle with yourself once and for all? (*He speaks in his ear in confidential warning*) Only watch out on the booze, Jimmy. You know, not too much from now on. You've had a lot already, and you don't want to let yourself duck out of it by being too drunk to move—not this time!

(JIMMY *gives him a guilty, stricken look and turns away and slumps into the chair on* MOSHER's *right*)

HOPE (*To* MARGIE—*still guiltily*) Bejees, Margie, you know I didn't mean it. It's that lousy drummer riding me that's got my goat.

MARGIE I know. (*She puts a protecting arm around* HOPE *and turns him to face the table with the cake and presents*) Come on. You ain't noticed your cake yet. Ain't it grand?

HOPE (*Trying to brighten up*) Say, that's pretty. Ain't ever had a cake since Bessie— Six candles. Each for ten years, eh? Bejees, that's thoughtful of you.

PEARL It was Hickey got it.

HOPE (*His tone forced*) Well, it was thoughtful of him. He means well, I guess. (*His eyes, fixed on the cake, harden angrily*) To hell with his cake.

(*He starts to turn away.* PEARL *grabs his arm*)

PEARL Wait, Harry. Yuh ain't seen de presents from Margie and me and Cora and Chuck and Rocky. And dere's a watch all engraved wid your name and de date from Hickey.

HOPE To hell with it! Bejees, he can keep it!

(*This time he does turn away*)

PEARL Jees, he ain't even goin' to look at our presents.

MARGIE (*Bitterly*) Dis is all wrong. We gotta put some life in dis party or I'll go nuts! Hey, Cora, what's de matter wid dat box? Can't yuh play for Harry? Yuh don't have to stop just because he kidded yuh!

HOPE (*Rouses himself—with forced heartiness*) Yes, come on, Cora. You was playing it fine. (CORA *begins to play half-heartedly.* HOPE *suddenly becomes almost tearfully sentimental*) It was Bessie's favorite tune. She was always singing it. It brings her back. I wish—

(*He chokes up*)

HICKEY (*Grins at him—amusedly*) Yes, we've all heard you tell us you thought the world of her, Governor.

HOPE (*Looks at him with frightened suspicion*) Well, so I did, bejees! Everyone knows I did! (*Threateningly*) Bejees, if you say I didn't—

HICKEY (*Soothingly*) Now, Governor. I didn't say anything. You're the only one knows the truth about that.

(HOPE *stares at him confusedly.* CORA *continues to play. For a moment there is a pause, broken by* JIMMY TOMORROW *who speaks with muzzy, self-pitying melancholy out of a sentimental dream*)

JIMMY Marjorie's favorite song was "Loch Lomond." She was beautiful and she played the piano beautifully and she had a beautiful voice. (*With gentle sorrow*) You were lucky, Harry. Bessie died. But there are more bitter sorrows than losing the woman one loves by the hand of death—

HICKEY (*With an amused wink at* HOPE) Now, listen, Jimmy, you needn't go on. We've all heard that story about how you came back to Cape Town and found her in the hay with a staff officer. We know you like to believe that was what started you on the booze and ruined your life.

JIMMY (*Stammers*) I—I'm talking to Harry. Will you kindly keep out of— (*With a pitiful defiance*) My life is not ruined!

HICKEY (*Ignoring this—with a kidding grin*) But I'll bet when you admit the truth to yourself, you'll confess you were pretty sick of her hating you for getting drunk. I'll bet you were really damned relieved when she gave you such a good excuse. (JIMMY *stares at him strickenly.* HICKEY *pats him on the back again—with sincere sympathy*) I know how it is, Jimmy. I—

(*He stops abruptly and for a second he seems to lose his self-assurance and become confused*)

LARRY (*Seizing on this with vindictive relish*) Ha! So that's what happened to you, is it? Your iceman joke finally came home to roost, did it? (*He grins tauntingly*) You should have remembered there's truth in the old superstition that you'd better look out what you call because in the end it comes to you!

HICKEY (*Himself again—grins to* LARRY *kiddingly*) Is that a fact, Larry? Well, well! Then you'd better watch out how you keep calling for that old Big Sleep! (LARRY *starts and for a second looks superstitiously frightened. Abruptly* HICKEY *changes to his jovial, bustling, master-of-ceremonies manner*) But what are we waiting for, boys and girls? Let's start the party rolling! (*He shouts to the bar*) Hey, Chuck and Rocky! Bring on the big surprise! Governor, you sit at the head of the table here. (*He makes* HARRY *sit down on the chair at the end of the table, right. To* MARGIE *and* PEARL) Come on, girls, sit down. (*They sit side*

*by side on* JIMMY's *right.* HICKEY *bustles down to the left end
of table*) I'll sit here at the foot.

(*He sits, with* CORA *on his left and* JOE *on her left.* ROCKY *and*
CHUCK *appear from the bar, each bearing a big tray laden with
schooners of champagne which they start shoving in front of
each member of the party*)

ROCKY (*With forced cheeriness*) Real champagne, bums! Cheer
up! What is dis, a funeral? Jees, mixin' champagne wid Harry's
redeye will knock yuh paralyzed! Ain't yuh never satisfied?
(*He and* CHUCK *finish serving out the schooners, grab the last
two themselves and sit down in the two vacant chairs remaining
near the middle of the table. As they do so,* HICKEY *rises, a
schooner in his hand*)

HICKEY (*Rapping on the table for order when there is nothing but
a dead silence*) Order! Order, Ladies and Gents! (*He catches*
LARRY's *eyes on the glass in his hand*) Yes, Larry, I'm going to
drink with you this time. To prove I'm not teetotal because I'm
afraid booze would make me spill my secrets, as you think.
(LARRY *looks sheepish.* HICKEY *chuckles and goes on*) No, I gave
you the simple truth about that. I don't need booze or anything
else any more. But I want to be sociable and propose a toast in
honor of our old friend, Harry, and drink it with you. (*His eyes
fix on* HUGO, *who is out again, his head on his plate— To* CHUCK,
*who is on* HUGO's *left*) Wake up our demon bomb-tosser, Chuck.
We don't want corpses at this feast.

CHUCK (*Gives* HUGO *a shake*) Hey, Hugo, come up for air! Don't
yuh see de champagne?

(HUGO *blinks around and giggles foolishly*)

HUGO Ve vill eat birthday cake and trink champagne beneath the
villow tree! (*He grabs his schooner and takes a greedy gulp—
then sets it back on the table with a grimace of distaste—in a
strange, arrogantly disdainful tone, as if he were rebuking a
butler*) Dis vine is unfit to trink. It has not properly been iced.

HICKEY (*Amusedly*) Always a high-toned swell at heart, eh,
Hugo? God help us poor bums if you'd ever get to telling us where
to get off! You'd have been drinking our blood beneath those
willow trees! (*He chuckles.* HUGO *shrinks back in his chair,
blinking at him, but* HICKEY *is now looking up the table at*
HOPE. *He starts his toast, and as he goes on he becomes more
moved and obviously sincere*) Here's the toast, Ladies and
Gents! Here's to Harry Hope, who's been a friend in need to

every one of us! Here's to the old Governor, the best sport and the kindest, biggest-hearted guy in the world! Here's wishing you all the luck there is, Harry, and long life and happiness! Come on, everybody! To Harry! Bottoms up!

(*They have all caught his sincerity with eager relief. They raise their schooners with an enthusiastic chorus of "Here's how, Harry!" "Here's luck, Harry!" etc., and gulp half the wine down,* HICKEY *leading them in this*)

HOPE (*Deeply moved—his voice husky*) Bejees, thanks, all of you. Bejees, Hickey, you old son of a bitch, that's white of you! Bejees, I know you meant it, too.

HICKEY (*Moved*) Of course I meant it, Harry, old friend! And I mean it when I say I hope today will be the biggest day in your life, and in the lives of everyone here, the beginning of a new life of peace and contentment where no pipe dreams can ever nag at you again. Here's to that, Harry!

(*He drains the remainder of his drink, but this time he drinks alone. In an instant the attitude of everyone has reverted to uneasy, suspicious defensiveness*)

ROCKY (*Growls*) Aw, forget dat bughouse line of bull for a minute, can't yuh?

HICKEY (*Sitting down—good-naturedly*) You're right, Rocky, I'm talking too much. It's Harry we want to hear from. Come on, Harry! (*He pounds his schooner on the table*) Speech! Speech! (*They try to recapture their momentary enthusiasm, rap their schooners on the table, call "Speech," but there is a hollow ring in it.* HOPE *gets to his feet reluctantly, with a forced smile, a smoldering resentment beginning to show in his manner*)

HOPE (*Lamely*) Bejees, I'm no good at speeches. All I can say is thanks to everybody again for remembering me on my birthday. (*Bitterness coming out*) Only don't think because I'm sixty I'll be a bigger damned fool easy mark than ever! No, bejees! Like Hickey says, it's going to be a new day! This dump has got to be run like other dumps, so I can make some money and not just split even. People has got to pay what they owe me! I'm not running a damned orphan asylum for bums and crooks! Nor a God-damned hooker shanty, either! Nor an Old Men's Home for lousy Anarchist tramps that ought to be in jail! I'm sick of being played for a sucker! (*They stare at him with stunned, bewildered hurt. He goes on in a sort of furious desperation, as if he hated himself for every word he said, and yet couldn't stop*) And don't think you're kidding me right now, either! I know damned well you're giving me the laugh behind my back, thinking to yourselves, The old, lying, pipe-dreaming faker, we've heard his bull about taking a walk around the ward for years, he'll never make it! He's yellow, he ain't got the guts, he's scared he'll find out— (*He glares around at them almost with hatred*) But I'll show you, bejees! (*He glares at* HICKEY) I'll show you, too, you son of a bitch of a frying-pan-peddling bastard!

HICKEY (*Heartily encouraging*) That's the stuff, Harry! Of course you'll try to show me! That's what I want you to do!

(HARRY *glances at him with helpless dread—then drops his eyes and looks furtively around the table. All at once he becomes miserably contrite*)

HOPE (*His voice catching*) Listen, all of you! Bejees, forgive me. I lost my temper! I ain't feeling well! I got a hell of a grouch on! Bejees, you know you're all as welcome here as the flowers in May!

(*They look at him with eager forgiveness.* ROCKY *is the first one who can voice it*)

ROCKY Aw, sure, Boss, you're always aces wid us, see?

HICKEY (*Rises to his feet again. He addresses them now with the simple, convincing sincerity of one making a confession of which he is genuinely ashamed*) Listen, everybody! I know you are sick of my gabbing, but I think this is the spot where I owe it to you to do a little explaining and apologize for some of the rough stuff I've had to pull on you. I know how it must look to you. As if I was a damned busybody who was not only interfering in your private business, but even sicking some of you on to nag at each other. Well, I have to admit that's true, and I'm damned sorry about it. But it simply had to be done! You must believe that! You know old Hickey. I was never one to start trouble. But this time I had to—for your own good! I had to make you help me with each other. I saw I couldn't do what I was after alone. Not in the time at my disposal. I knew when I came here I wouldn't be able to stay with you long. I'm slated to leave on a trip. I saw I'd have to hustle and use every means I could. (*With a joking boastfulness*) Why, if I had enough time, I'd get a lot of sport out of selling my line of salvation to each of you all by my lonesome. Like it was fun in the old days, when I traveled house to house, to convince some dame, who was sicking the dog on me, her house wouldn't be properly furnished unless she bought another wash boiler. And I could do it with you, all right. I know every one of you, inside and out, by heart. I may have been drunk when I've been here before, but old Hickey could never be so drunk he didn't have to see through people. I mean, everyone except himself. And, finally, he had to see through himself, too. (*He pauses. They stare at him, bitter, uneasy and fascinated. His manner changes to deep earnestness*) But here's the point to get. I swear I'd never act like I have if I wasn't absolutely sure it will be worth it to you in the end, after you're rid of the damned guilt that makes you lie to yourselves you're something you're not, and the remorse that nags at you and makes you hide behind lousy pipe dreams about tomorrow. You'll be in a today where there is no yesterday or tomorrow to worry you. You won't give a damn what you are any more. I wouldn't say this unless I knew, Brothers and Sisters. This peace is real! It's a fact! I know! Because I've got it! Here! Now! Right in front of you! You see the difference in me! You remember how I used to be! Even when I had two quarts of rotgut under my belt and joked and sang "Sweet Adeline," I still felt like a guilty skunk. But you can all see that I don't give a damn about anything now. And I promise you, by the time this day is over, I'll have every one of you feeling the same way! (*He pauses. They stare at him fascinatedly. He adds with a grin*) I guess that'll be about all from me, boys and girls—for the present. So let's get on with the party.

(*He starts to sit down*)

LARRY (*Sharply*) Wait! (*Insistently—with a sneer*) I think it would help us poor pipe-dreaming sinners along the sawdust trail to salvation if you told us now what it was happened to you that converted you to this great peace you've found. (*More and more with a deliberate, provocative taunting*) I notice you didn't deny it when I asked you about the iceman. Did this great revelation of the evil habit of dreaming about tomorrow come to you after you found your wife was sick of you?

(*While he is speaking the faces of the gang have lighted up vindictively, as if all at once they saw a chance to revenge themselves. As he finishes, a chorus of sneering taunts begins, punctuated by nasty, jeering laughter*)

HOPE Bejees, you've hit it, Larry! I've noticed he hasn't shown her picture around this time!

MOSHER He hasn't got it! The iceman took it away from him!

MARGIE  Jees, look at him! Who could blame her?

PEARL  She must be hard up to fall for an iceman!

CORA  Imagine a sap like him advisin' me and Chuck to git married!

CHUCK  Yeah! He done so good wid it!

JIMMY  At least I can say Marjorie chose an officer and a gentleman.

LEWIS  Come to look at you, Hickey, old chap, you've sprouted horns like a bloody antelope!

WETJOEN  Pigger, py Gott! Like a water buffalo's!

WILLIE  (*Sings to his Sailor Lad tune*)

"Come up," she cried, "my iceman lad,
   And you and I'll agree—"

(*They all join in a jeering chorus, rapping with knuckles or glasses on the table at the indicated spot in the lyric*)

"And I'll show you the prettiest (*Rap, rap, rap*)
   That ever you did see!"

(*A roar of derisive, dirty laughter. But* HICKEY *has remained unmoved by all this taunting. He grins good-naturedly, as if he enjoyed the joke at his expense, and joins in the laughter*)

HICKEY  Well, boys and girls, I'm glad to see you getting in good spirits for Harry's party, even if the joke is on me. I admit I asked for it by always pulling that iceman gag in the old days. So laugh all you like. (*He pauses. They do not laugh now. They are again staring at him with baffled uneasiness. He goes on thoughtfully*) Well, this forces my hand, I guess, your bringing up the subject of Evelyn. I didn't want to tell you yet. It's hardly an appropriate time. I meant to wait until the party was over. But you're getting the wrong idea about poor Evelyn, and I've got to stop that. (*He pauses again. There is a tense stillness in the room. He bows his head a little and says quietly*) I'm sorry to tell you my dearly beloved wife is dead.

(*A gasp comes from the stunned company. They look away from him, shocked and miserably ashamed of themselves, except* LARRY *who continues to stare at him*)

LARRY  (*Aloud to himself with a superstitious shrinking*)  Be God, I felt he'd brought the touch of death on him! (*Then suddenly he is even more ashamed of himself than the others and stam-*)

*mers*) Forgive me, Hickey! I'd like to cut my dirty tongue out!
(*This releases a chorus of shamefaced mumbles from the crowd.
"Sorry, Hickey." "I'm sorry, Hickey." "We're sorry, Hickey."*)

HICKEY (*Looking around at them—in a kindly, reassuring tone*)
Now look here, everybody. You mustn't let this be a wet blanket
on Harry's party. You're still getting me all wrong. There's no
reason— You see, I don't feel any grief. (*They gaze at him
startledly. He goes on with convincing sincerity*) I've got to feel
glad, for her sake. Because she's at peace. She's rid of me at last.
Hell, I don't have to tell you—you all know what I was like. You
can imagine what she went through, married to a no-good
cheater and drunk like I was. And there was no way out of it
for her. Because she loved me. But now she is at peace like she
always longed to be. So why should I feel sad? She wouldn't
want me to feel sad. Why, all that Evelyn ever wanted out of
life was to make me happy.
(*He stops, looking around at them with a simple, gentle
frankness. They stare at him in bewildered, incredulous confusion*)

*Curtain*

# ACT THREE

SCENE: *Barroom of* HARRY HOPE'S, *including a part of what had been the back room in Acts One and Two. In the right wall are two big windows, with the swinging doors to the street between them. The bar itself is at rear. Behind it is a mirror, covered with white mosquito netting to keep off the flies, and a shelf on which are barrels of cheap whiskey with spigots and a small show case of bottled goods. At left of the bar is the doorway to the hall. There is a table at left, front, of barroom proper, with four chairs. At right, front, is a small free-lunch counter, facing left, with a space between it and the window for the dealer to stand when he dishes out soup at the noon hour. Over the mirror behind the bar are framed photographs of Richard Croker and Big Tim Sullivan, flanked by framed lithographs of John L. Sullivan and Gentleman Jim Corbett in ring costume.*

*At left, in what had been the back room, with the dividing curtain drawn, the banquet table of Act Two has been broken up, and the tables are again in the crowded arrangement of Act One. Of these, we see one in the front row with five chairs at left of the barroom table, another with five chairs at left-rear of it, a third back by the rear wall with five chairs, and finally, at extreme left-front, one with four chairs, partly on and partly off stage, left.*

*It is around the middle of the morning of* HOPE'S *birthday, a hot summer day. There is sunlight in the street outside, but it does not hit the windows and the light in the back-room section is dim.*

JOE MOTT *is moving around, a box of sawdust under his arm, strewing it over the floor. His manner is sullen, his face set in gloom. He ignores everyone. As the scene progresses, he finishes his sawdusting job, goes behind the lunch counter and cuts loaves of bread.* ROCKY *is behind the bar, wiping it, washing glasses, etc. He wears his working clothes, sleeves rolled up. He looks sleepy, irritable and worried. At the barroom table, front,* LARRY *sits in a*

*chair, facing right-front. He has no drink in front of him. He stares
ahead, deep in harried thought. On his right, in a chair facing right,*
HUGO *sits sprawled forward, arms and head on the table as usual,
a whiskey glass beside his limp hand. At rear of the front table
at left of them, in a chair facing left,* PARRITT *is sitting. He is
staring in front of him in a tense, strained immobility.*

*As the curtain rises,* ROCKY *finishes his work behind the bar. He
comes forward and drops wearily in the chair at right of* LARRY's
*table, facing left.*

ROCKY  Nuttin' now till de noon rush from de Market. I'm goin' to
rest my fanny. (*Irritably*) If I ain't a sap to let Chuck kid me
into workin' his time so's he can take de mornin' off. But I got
sick of arguin' wid 'im. I says, "Aw right, git married! What's it to
me?" Hickey's got de bot' of dem bugs. (*Bitterly*) Some party
last night, huh? Jees, what a funeral! It was jinxed from de start,
but his tellin' about his wife croakin' put de K.O. on it.

LARRY  Yes, it turned out it wasn't a birthday feast but a wake!

ROCKY  Him promisin' he'd cut out de bughouse bull about peace
—and den he went on talkin' and talkin' like he couldn't stop!
And all de gang sneakin' upstairs, leavin' free booze and eats like
dey was poison! It didn't do dem no good if dey thought dey'd
shake him. He's been hoppin' from room to room all night. Yuh
can't stop him. He's got his Reform Wave goin' strong dis
mornin'! Did yuh notice him drag Jimmy out de foist ting to get
his laundry and his clothes pressed so he wouldn't have no
excuse? And he give Willie de dough to buy his stuff back from
Solly's. And all de rest been brushin' and shavin' demselves wid
de shakes—

LARRY  (*Defiantly*)  He didn't come to my room! He's afraid I
might ask him a few questions.

ROCKY  (*Scornfully*)  Yeah? It don't look to me he's scared of yuh.
I'd say you was scared of him.

LARRY  (*Stung*)  You'd lie, then!

PARRITT  (*Jerks round to look at* LARRY—*sneeringly*)  Don't let
him kid you, Rocky. He had his door locked. I couldn't get in,
either.

ROCKY  Yeah, who d'yuh tink yuh're kiddin', Larry? He's showed
you up, aw right. Like he says, if yuh was so anxious to croak,
why wouldn't yuh hop off your fire escape long ago?

LARRY  (*Defiantly*)  Because it'd be a coward's quitting, that's why!

PARRITT   He's all quitter, Rocky. He's a yellow old faker!

LARRY   (*Turns on him*)   You lying punk! Remember what I warned you—!

ROCKY   (*Scowls at* PARRITT)   Yeah, keep outta dis, you! Where d'yuh get a license to butt in? Shall I give him de bum's rush, Larry? If you don't want him around, nobody else don't.

LARRY   (*Forcing an indifferent tone*)   No. Let him stay. I don't mind him. He's nothing to me.

(ROCKY *shrugs his shoulders and yawns sleepily*)

PARRITT   You're right, I have nowhere to go now. You're the only one in the world I can turn to.

ROCKY   (*Drowsily*)   Yuh're a soft old sap, Larry. He's a no-good louse like Hickey. He don't belong. (*He yawns*) I'm all in. Not a wink of sleep. Can't keep my peepers open.

(*His eyes close and his head nods.* PARRITT *gives him a glance and then gets up and slinks over to slide into the chair on* LARRY'S *left, between him and* ROCKY. LARRY *shrinks away, but determinedly ignores him*)

PARRITT   (*Bending toward him—in a low, ingratiating, apologetic voice*)   I'm sorry for riding you, Larry. But you get my goat when you act as if you didn't care a damn what happened to me, and keep your door locked so I can't talk to you. (*Then hopefully*) But that was to keep Hickey out, wasn't it? I don't blame you. I'm getting to hate him. I'm getting more and more scared of him. Especially since he told us his wife was dead. It's that queer feeling he gives me that I'm mixed up with him some way. I don't know why, but it started me thinking about Mother—as if she was dead. (*With a strange undercurrent of something like satisfaction in his pitying tone*) I suppose she might as well be. Inside herself, I mean. It must kill her when she thinks of me—I know she doesn't want to, but she can't help it. After all, I'm her only kid. She used to spoil me and made a pet of me. Once in a great while, I mean. When she remembered me. As if she wanted to make up for something. As if she felt guilty. So she must have loved me a little, even if she never let it interfere with her freedom. (*With a strange pathetic wistfulness*) Do you know, Larry, I once had a sneaking suspicion that maybe, if the truth was known, you were my father.

LARRY   (*Violently*)   You damned fool! Who put that insane idea in your head? You know it's a lie! Anyone in the Coast crowd could tell you I never laid eyes on your mother till after you were born.

PARRITT  Well, I'd hardly ask them, would I? I know you're right, though, because I asked her. She brought me up to be frank and ask her anything, and she'd always tell me the truth. (*Abruptly*) But I was talking about how she must feel now about me. My getting through with the Movement. She'll never forgive that. The Movement is her life. And it must be the final knockout for her if she knows I was the one who sold—

LARRY  Shut up, damn you!

PARRITT  It'll kill her. And I'm sure she knows it must have been me. (*Suddenly with desperate urgency*) But I never thought the cops would get her! You've got to believe that! You've got to see what my only reason was! I'll admit what I told you last night was a lie—that bunk about getting patriotic and my duty to my country. But here's the true reason, Larry—the only reason! It was just for money! I got stuck on a whore and wanted dough to blow in on her and have a good time! That's all I did it for! Just money! Honest!

(*He has the terrible grotesque air, in confessing his sordid baseness, of one who gives an excuse which exonerates him from any real guilt*)

LARRY  (*Grabs him by the shoulder and shakes him*)  God damn you, shut up! What the hell is it to me?

(*ROCKY starts awake*)

ROCKY  What's comin' off here?

LARRY  (*Controlling himself*)  Nothing. This gabby young punk was talking my ear off, that's all. He's a worse pest than Hickey.

ROCKY  (*Drowsily*)  Yeah, Hickey— Say, listen, what d'yuh mean about him bein' scared you'd ask him questions? What questions?

LARRY  Well, I feel he's hiding something. You notice he didn't say what his wife died of.

ROCKY  (*Rebukingly*)  Aw, lay off dat. De poor guy— What are yuh gettin' at, anyway? Yuh don't tink it's just a gag of his?

LARRY  I don't. I'm damned sure he's brought death here with him. I feel the cold touch of it on him.

ROCKY  Aw, bunk! You got croakin' on de brain, Old Cemetery. (*Suddenly ROCKY's eyes widen*) Say! D'yuh mean yuh tink she committed suicide, 'count of his cheatin' or something?

LARRY  (*Grimly*)  It wouldn't surprise me. I'd be the last to blame her.

ROCKY (*Scornfully*) But dat's crazy! Jees, if she'd done dat, he wouldn't tell us he was glad about it, would he? He ain't dat big a bastard.

PARRITT (*Speaks up from his own preoccupation—strangely*) You know better than that, Larry. You know she'd never commit suicide. She's like you. She'll hang on to life even when there's nothing left but—

LARRY (*Stung—turns on him viciously*) And how about you? Be God, if you had any guts or decency—!
(*He stops guiltily*)

PARRITT (*Sneeringly*) I'd take that hop off your fire escape you're too yellow to take, I suppose?

LARRY (*As if to himself*) No! Who am I to judge? I'm done with judging.

PARRITT (*Tauntingly*) Yes I suppose you'd like that, wouldn't you?

ROCKY (*Irritably mystified*) What de hell's all dis about? (*To* PARRITT) What d'you know about Hickey's wife? How d'you know she didn't—?

LARRY (*With forced belittling casualness*) He doesn't. Hickey's addled the little brains he's got. Shove him back to his own table, Rocky. I'm sick of him.

ROCKY (*To* PARRITT, *threateningly*) Yuh heard Larry? I'd like an excuse to give yuh a good punch in de snoot. So move quick!

PARRITT (*Gets up—to* LARRY) If you think moving to another table will get rid of me! (*He moves away—then adds with bitter reproach*) Gee, Larry, that's a hell of a way to treat me, when I've trusted you, and I need your help.
(*He sits down in his old place and sinks into a wounded, self-pitying brooding*)

ROCKY (*Going back to his train of thought*) Jees, if she committed suicide, yuh got to feel sorry for Hickey, huh? Yuh can understand how he'd go bughouse and not be responsible for all de crazy stunts he's stagin' here. (*Then puzzledly*) But how can yuh be sorry for him when he says he's glad she croaked, and yuh can tell he means it? (*With weary exasperation*) Aw, nuts! I don't get nowhere tryin' to figger his game. (*His face hardening*) But I know dis. He better lay off me and my stable! (*He pauses—then sighs*) Jees, Larry, what a night dem two pigs give me! When de party went dead, dey pinched a coupla bottles and brung dem up deir room and got stinko. I don't get a wink of sleep, see? Just as I'd drop off on a chair here, dey'd come down lookin' for trouble. Or else dey'd raise hell upstairs, laughin' and singin', so I'd get scared dey'd get de joint pinched and go up to tell dem to can de noise. And every time dey'd crawl my frame wid de same old argument. Dey'd say, "So yuh agreed wid Hickey, do yuh, yuh dirty little Ginny? We're whores, are we? Well, we agree wid Hickey about you, see! Yuh're nuttin' but a lousy pimp!" Den I'd slap dem. Not beat 'em up, like a pimp would. Just slap dem. But it don't do no good. Dey'd keep at it over and over. Jees, I get de earache just thinkin' of it! "Listen," dey'd say, "If we're whores we gotta right to have a reg'lar pimp and not stand for no punk imitation! We're sick of wearin' out our dogs poundin' sidewalks for a double-crossin' bartender, when all de thanks we get is he looks down on us. We'll find a guy who really needs us to take care of him and ain't ashamed of it. Don't expect us to work tonight, 'cause we won't, see? Not if de streets was blocked wid sailors! We're goin' on strike and yuh can like it or lump it!" (*He shakes his head*) Whores goin' on strike! Can yuh tie dat? (*Going on with his story*) Dey says, "We're takin' a holiday. We're goin' to beat it down to Coney Island and shoot the chutes and maybe we'll come back and maybe we won't. And you can go to hell!" So dey put on deir lids and beat it, de bot' of dem stinko. (*He sighs dejectedly. He seems grotesquely like a harried family man, henpecked and browbeaten by a nagging wife.* LARRY *is deep in his own bitter preoccupation and hasn't listened to him.* CHUCK *enters from the hall at rear. He has his straw hat with the gaudy band in his hand and wears a Sunday-best blue suit with a high stiff collar. He looks sleepy, hot, uncomfortable and grouchy*)

CHUCK (*Glumly*) Hey, Rocky. Cora wants a sherry flip. For her noives.

ROCKY (*Turns indignantly*) Sherry flip! Christ, she don't need nuttin' for her noive! What's she tink dis is, de Waldorf?

CHUCK Yeah, I told her, what would we use for sherry, and dere wasn't no egg unless she laid one. She says, "Is dere a law yuh can't go out and buy de makings, yuh big tramp?" (*Resentfully puts his straw hat on his head at a defiant tilt*) To hell wid her! She'll drink booze or nuttin'!
(*He goes behind the bar to draw a glass of whiskey from a barrel*)

ROCKY (*Sarcastically*) Jees, a guy oughta give his bride anything she wants on de weddin' day, I should tink! (*As* CHUCK
*comes from behind the bar,* ROCKY *surveys him derisively*) Pipe de
bridegroom, Larry! All dolled up for de killin'!

(LARRY *pays no attention*)

CHUCK Aw, shut up!

ROCKY One week on dat farm in Joisey, dat's what I give yuh!
Yuh'll come runnin' in here some night yellin' for a shot of booze
'cause de crickets is after yuh! (*Disgustedly*) Jees, Chuck, dat
louse Hickey's coitinly made a prize coupla suckers outa youse.

CHUCK (*Unguardedly*) Yeah. I'd like to give him one sock in de
puss—just one! (*Then angrily*) Aw, can dat! What's he got to
do wid it? Ain't we always said we was goin' to? So we're goin'
to, see? And don't give me no argument! (*He stares at* ROCKY
*truculently. But* ROCKY *only shrugs his shoulders with weary disgust and* CHUCK *subsides into complaining gloom*) If on'y Cora'd
cut out de beefin'. She don't gimme a minute's rest all night.
De same old stuff over and over! Do I really want to marry her?
I says, "Sure, Baby, why not?" She says, "Yeah, but after a week
yuh'll be tinkin' what a sap you was. Yuh'll make dat an excuse
to go off on a periodical, and den I'll be tied for life to a no-good
soak, and de foist ting I know yuh'll have me out hustlin' again,
your own wife!" Den she'd bust out cryin', and I'd get sore.
"Yuh're a liar," I'd say. "I ain't never taken your dough 'cept when
I was drunk and not workin'!" "Yeah," she'd say, "and how long
will yuh stay sober now? Don't tink yuh can kid me wid dat
water-wagon bull! I've heard it too often." Dat'd make me sore and
I'd say, "Don't call me a liar. But I wish I was drunk right now,
because if I was, yuh wouldn't be keepin' me awake all night
beefin'. If yuh opened your yap, I'd knock de stuffin' outa yuh!"
Den she'd yell, "Dat's a sweet way to talk to de goil yuh're goin'
to marry." (*He sighs explosively*) Jees, she's got me hangin' on de
ropes! (*He glances with vengeful yearning at the drink of
whiskey in his hand*) Jees, would I like to get a quart of dis
redeye under my belt!

ROCKY Well, why de hell don't yuh?

CHUCK (*Instantly suspicious and angry*) Sure! You'd like dat,
wouldn't yuh? I'm wise to you! Yuh don't wanta see me get married and settle down like a reg'lar guy! Yuh'd like me to stay
paralyzed all de time, so's I'd be like you, a lousy pimp!

ROCKY (*Springs to his feet, his face hardened viciously*) Listen! I don't take dat even from you, see!

CHUCK (*Puts his drink on the bar and clenches his fists*) Yeah? Wanta make sometin' of it? (*Jeeringly*) Don't make me laugh! I can lick ten of youse wid one mit!

ROCKY (*Reaching for his hip pocket*) Not wid lead in your belly, yuh won't!

JOE (*Has stopped cutting when the quarrel started—expostulating*) Hey, you, Rocky and Chuck! Cut it out! You's ole friends! Don't let dat Hickey make you crazy!

CHUCK (*Turns on him*) Keep outa our business, yuh black bastard!

ROCKY (*Like* CHUCK, *turns on* JOE, *as if their own quarrel was forgotten and they became natural allies against an alien*) Stay where yuh belong, yuh doity nigger!

JOE (*Snarling with rage, springs from behind the lunch counter with the bread knife in his hand*) You white sons of bitches! I'll rip your guts out!

(CHUCK *snatches a whiskey bottle from the bar and raises it above his head to hurl at* JOE. ROCKY *jerks a short-barreled, nickel-plated revolver from his hip pocket. At this moment* LARRY *pounds on the table with his fist and bursts into a sardonic laugh*)

LARRY That's it! Murder each other, you damned loons, with Hickey's blessing! Didn't I tell you he'd brought death with him? (*His interruption startles them. They pause to stare at him, their fighting fury suddenly dies out and they appear deflated and sheepish*)

ROCKY (*To* JOE) Aw right, you. Leggo dat shiv and I'll put dis gat away.

(JOE *sullenly goes back behind the counter and slaps the knife on top of it.* ROCKY *slips the revolver back in his pocket.* CHUCK *lowers the bottle to the bar.* HUGO, *who has awakened and raised his head when* LARRY *pounded on the table, now giggles foolishly*)

HUGO Hello, leddle peoples! Neffer mind! Soon you vill eat hot dogs beneath the villow trees and trink free vine— (*Abruptly in a haughty fastidious tone*) The champagne vas not properly iced. (*With guttural anger*) Gottamned liar, Hickey! Does that prove I vant to be aristocrat? I love only the proletariat! I vill lead them! I vill be like a Gott to them! They vill be my slaves! (*He stops in bewildered self-amazement—to* LARRY *appealingly*)

I am very trunk, no, Larry? I talk foolishness. I am so trunk, Larry, old friend, am I not, I don't know vhat I say?

LARRY (*Pityingly*) You're raving drunk, Hugo. I've never seen you so paralyzed. Lay your head down now and sleep it off.

HUGO (*Gratefully*) Yes. I should sleep. I am too crazy trunk. (*He puts his head on his arms and closes his eyes*)

JOE (*Behind the lunch counter—brooding superstitiously*) You's right, Larry. Bad luck come in de door when Hickey come. I's an ole gamblin' man and I knows bad luck when I feels it! (*Then defiantly*) But it's white man's bad luck. He can't jinx me! (*He comes from behind the counter and goes to the bar—addressing ROCKY stiffly*) De bread's cut and I's finished my job. Do I get de drink I's earned? (*ROCKY gives him a hostile look but shoves a bottle and glass at him. JOE pours a brimful drink—sullenly*) I's finished wid dis dump for keeps. (*He takes a key from his pocket and slaps it on the bar*) Here's de key to my room. I ain't comin' back. I's goin' to my own folks where I belong. I don't stay where I's not wanted. I's sick and tired of messin' round wid white men. (*He gulps down his drink—then looking around defiantly he deliberately throws his whiskey glass on the floor and smashes it*)

ROCKY Hey! What de hell—!

JOE (*With a sneering dignity*) I's on'y savin' you de trouble, White Boy. Now you don't have to break it, soon's my back's turned, so's no white man kick about drinkin' from de same glass. (*He walks stiffly to the street door—then turns for a parting shot—boastfully*) I's tired of loafin' 'round wid a lot of bums. I's a gamblin' man. I's gonna get in a big crap game and win me a big bankroll. Den I'll get de okay to open up my old gamblin' house for colored men. Den maybe I comes back here sometime to see de bums. Maybe I throw a twenty-dollar bill on de bar and say, "Drink it up," and listen when dey all pat me on de back and say, "Joe, you sure is white." But I'll say, "No, I'm black and my dough is black man's dough, and you's proud to drink wid me or you don't get no drink!" Or maybe I just says, "You can all go to hell. I don't lower myself drinkin' wid no white trash!" (*He opens the door to go out—then turns again*) And dat ain't no pipe dream! I'll get de money for my stake today, somehow, somewheres! If I has to borrow a gun and stick up some white man, I gets it! You wait and see!

(*He swaggers out through the swinging doors*)

CHUCK (*Angrily*) Can yuh beat de noive of dat dinge! Jees, if I wasn't dressed up, I'd go out and mop up de street wid him!

ROCKY Aw, let him go, de poor old dope! Him and his gamblin' house! He'll be back tonight askin' Harry for his room and bummin' me for a ball. (*Vengefully*) Den I'll be de one to smash de glass. I'll loin him his place!

(*The swinging doors are pushed open and* WILLIE OBAN *enters from the street. He is shaved and wears an expensive, well-cut suit, good shoes and clean linen. He is absolutely sober, but his face is sick, and his nerves in a shocking state of shakes*)

CHUCK Another guy all dolled up! Got your clothes from Solly's, huh, Willie? (*Derisively*) Now yuh can sell dem back to him again tomorrow.

WILLIE (*Stiffly*) No, I—I'm through with that stuff. Never again. (*He comes to the bar*)

ROCKY (*Sympathetically*) Yuh look sick, Willie. Take a ball to pick yuh up.

(*He pushes a bottle toward him*)

WILLIE (*Eyes the bottle yearningly but shakes his head—determinedly*) No, thanks. The only way to stop is to stop. I'd have no chance if I went to the D.A.'s office smelling of booze.

CHUCK Yuh're really goin' dere?

WILLIE (*Stiffly*) I said I was, didn't I? I just came back here to rest a few minutes, not because I needed any booze. I'll show that cheap drummer I don't have to have any Dutch courage— (*Guiltily*) But he's been very kind and generous staking me. He can't help his insulting manner, I suppose. (*He turns away from the bar*) My legs are a bit shaky yet. I better sit down a while. (*He goes back and sits at the left of the second table, facing* PARRITT, *who gives him a scowling, suspicious glance and then ignores him.* ROCKY *looks at* CHUCK *and taps his head disgustedly.* CAPTAIN LEWIS *appears in the doorway from the hall*)

CHUCK (*Mutters*) Here's anudder one.

(LEWIS *looks spruce and clean-shaven. His ancient tweed suit has been brushed and his frayed linen is clean. His manner is full of a forced, jaunty self-assurance. But he is sick and beset by katzenjammer*)

LEWIS Good morning, gentlemen all. (*He passes along the front of bar to look out in the street*) A jolly fine morning, too. (*He turns back to the bar*) An eye-opener? I think not. Not required, Rocky, old chum. Feel extremely fit, as a matter of fact. Though can't say I slept much, thanks to that interfering ass, Hickey, and that stupid bounder of a Boer. (*His face hardens*) I've had about all I can take from that fellow. It's my own fault, of course, for allowing a brute of a Dutch farmer to become familiar. Well, it's come to a parting of the ways now, and good riddance. Which reminds me, here's my key. (*He puts it on the bar*) I shan't be coming back. Sorry to be leaving good old Harry and the rest of you, of course, but I can't continue to live under the same roof with that fellow.

(*He stops, stiffening into hostility as* WETJOEN *enters from the hall, and pointedly turns his back on him.* WETJOEN *glares at him sneeringly. He, too, has made an effort to spruce up his appearance, and his bearing has a forced swagger of conscious physical strength. Behind this, he is sick and feebly holding his booze-sodden body together*)

ROCKY (*To* LEWIS—*disgustedly putting the key on the shelf in back of the bar*) So Hickey's kidded the pants offa you, too? Yuh tink yuh're leavin' here, huh?

WETJOEN (*Jeeringly*) Ja! Dot's vhat he kids himself.

LEWIS (*Ignores him—airily*) Yes, I'm leaving, Rocky. But that ass, Hickey, has nothing to do with it. Been thinking things over. Time I turned over a new leaf, and all that.

WETJOEN He's going to get a job! Dot's what he says!

ROCKY What at, for Chris' sake?

LEWIS (*Keeping his airy manner*) Oh, anything. I mean, not manual labor, naturally, but anything that calls for a bit of brains and education. However humble. Beggars can't be choosers. I'll see a pal of mine at the Consulate. He promised any time I felt an energetic fit he'd get me a post with the Cunard—clerk in the office or something of the kind.

WETJOEN Ja! At Limey Consulate they promise anything to get rid of him vhen he comes there tronk! They're scared to call the police and have him pinched because it vould scandal in the papers make about a Limey officer and chentleman!

LEWIS As a matter of fact, Rocky, I only wish a post temporarily. Means to an end, you know. Save up enough for a first-class passage home, that's the bright idea.

WETJOEN He's sailing back to home, sveet home! Dot's biggest pipe dream of all. What leetle brain the poor Limey has left, dot isn't in whiskey pickled, Hickey has made crazy!

(LEWIS' *fists clench, but he manages to ignore this*)

CHUCK (*Feels sorry for* LEWIS *and turns on* WETJOEN—*sarcastically*) Hickey ain't made no sucker outa you, huh? You're too foxy, huh? But I'll bet you tink yuh're goin' out and land a job, too.

WETJOEN (*Bristles*) I am, ja. For me, it is easy. Because I put on no airs of chentleman. I am not ashamed to vork vith my hands. I vas a farmer before the war ven ploody Limey thieves steal my country. (*Boastfully*) Anyone I ask for job can see with one look I have the great strength to do work of ten ordinary mens.

LEWIS (*Sneeringly*) Yes, Chuck, you remember he gave a demonstration of his extraordinary muscles last night when he helped to move the piano.

CHUCK Yuh couldn't even hold up your corner. It was your fault de damned box almost fell down de stairs.

WETJOEN My hands vas sweaty! Could I help dot my hands slip? I could de whole veight of it lift! In old days in Transvaal, I lift loaded oxcart by the axle! So vhy shouldn't I get job? Dot longshoreman boss, Dan, he tell me any time I like, he take me on. And Benny from de Market he promise me same.

LEWIS You remember, Rocky, it was one of those rare occasions when the Boer that walks like a man—spelled with a double o, by the way—was buying drinks and Dan and Benny were stony. They'd bloody well have promised him the moon.

ROCKY Yeah, yuh big boob, dem boids was on'y kiddin' yuh.

WETJOEN (*Angrily*) Dot's lie! You vill see dis morning I get job! I'll show dot bloody Limey chentleman, and dot liar, Hickey! And I need vork only leetle vhile to save money for my passage home. I need not much money because I am not ashamed to travel steerage. I don't put on first-cabin airs! (*Tauntingly*) Und *I can* go home to my country! Vhen I get there, they vill let *me* come in!

LEWIS (*Grows rigid—his voice trembling with repressed anger*) There was a rumor in South Africa, Rocky, that a certain Boer officer—if you call the leaders of a rabble of farmers officers—kept advising Cronje to retreat and not stand and fight—

WETJOEN And I vas right! I vas right! He got surrounded at Poardeberg! He had to surrender!

LEWIS (*Ignoring him*) Good strategy, no doubt, but a suspicion grew afterwards into a conviction among the Boers that the officer's caution was prompted by a desire to make his personal escape. His countrymen felt extremely savage about it, and his family disowned him. So I imagine there would be no welcoming committee waiting on the dock, nor delighted relatives making the veldt ring with their happy cries—

WETJOEN (*With guilty rage*) All lies! You Gottamned Limey— (*Trying to control himself and copy* LEWIS's *manner*) I also haf heard rumors of a Limey officer who, after the war, lost all his money gambling vhen he vas tronk. But they found out it was regiment money, too, he lost—

LEWIS (*Loses his control and starts for him*) You bloody Dutch scum!

ROCKY (*Leans over the bar and stops* LEWIS *with a straight-arm swipe on the chest*) Cut it out!
(*At the same moment* CHUCK *grabs* WETJOEN *and yanks him back*)

WETJOEN (*Struggling*) Let him come! I saw them come before— at Modder River, Magersfontein, Spion Kopje—waving their silly swords, so afraid they couldn't show off how brave they vas!—and I kill them vith my rifle so easy! (*Vindictively*) Listen to me, you Cecil! Often vhen I am tronk and kidding you I say I am sorry I missed you, but now, py Gott, I am sober, and I don't joke, and I say it!

LARRY (*Gives a sardonic guffaw—with his comically crazy, intense whisper*) Be God, you can't say Hickey hasn't the miraculous touch to raise the dead, when he can start the Boer War raging again!
(*This interruption acts like a cold douche on* LEWIS *and* WETJOEN. *They subside, and* ROCKY *and* CHUCK *let go of them.* LEWIS *turns his back on the Boer*)

LEWIS (*Attempting a return of his jaunty manner, as if nothing had happened*) Well, time I was on my merry way to see my chap at the Consulate. The early bird catches the job, what? Good-bye and good luck, Rocky, and everyone.
(*He starts for the street door*)

WETJOEN Py Gott, if dot Limey can go, I can go!
(*He hurries after* LEWIS. *But* LEWIS, *his hand about to push the swinging doors open, hesitates, as though struck by a sudden paralysis of the will, and* WETJOEN *has to jerk back to avoid bumping into him. For a second they stand there, one behind the other, staring over the swinging doors into the street*)

ROCKY Well, why don't yuh beat it?

LEWIS (*Guiltily casual*) Eh? Oh, just happened to think. Hardly

the decent thing to pop off without saying good-bye to old
Harry. One of the best, Harry. And good old Jimmy, too. They
ought to be down any moment. (*He pretends to notice* WETJOEN
*for the first time and steps away from the door—apologizing as to
a stranger*)
Sorry. I seem to be blocking your way out.

WETJOEN (*Stiffly*) No. I vait to say good-bye to Harry and Jimmy,
too.
(*He goes to right of door behind the lunch counter and looks
through the window, his back to the room.* LEWIS *takes up a
similar stand at the window on the left of door*)

CHUCK Jees, can yuh beat dem simps! (*He picks up* CORA's *drink
at the end of the bar*) Hell, I'd forgot Cora. She'll be trowin' a
fit.
(*He goes into the hall with the drink*)

ROCKY (*Looks after him disgustedly*) Dat's right, wait on her and
spoil her, yuh poor sap!
(*He shakes his head and begins to wipe the bar mechanically*)

WILLIE (*Is regarding* PARRITT *across the table from him with an
eager, calculating eye. He leans over and speaks in a low confidential tone*) Look here, Parritt. I'd like to have a talk with
you.

PARRITT (*Starts—scowling defensively*) What about?

WILLIE (*His manner becoming his idea of a crafty criminal lawyer's*)
About the trouble you're in. Oh, I know. You don't admit it.
You're quite right. That's my advice. Deny everything. Keep
your mouth shut. Make no statements whatever without first consulting your attorney.

PARRITT Say! What the hell—?

WILLIE But you can trust me. I'm a lawyer, and it's just occurred
to me you and I ought to co-operate. Of course I'm going to see
the D.A. this morning about a job on his staff. But that may take
time. There may not be an immediate opening. Meanwhile it
would be a good idea for me to take a case or two, on my own,
and prove my brilliant record in law school was no flash in the
pan. So why not retain me as your attorney?

PARRITT You're crazy! What do I want with a lawyer?

WILLIE That's right. Don't admit anything. But you can trust me,
so let's not beat about the bush. You got in trouble out on the
Coast, eh? And now you're hiding out. Any fool can spot that.
(*Lowering his voice still more*) You feel safe here, and maybe

you are, for a while. But remember, they get you in the end. I know from my father's experience. No one could have felt safer than he did. When anyone mentioned the law to him, he nearly died laughing. But—

PARRITT You crazy mutt! (*Turning to* LARRY *with a strained laugh*) Did you get that, Larry? This damned fool thinks the cops are after me!

LARRY (*Bursts out with his true reaction before he thinks to ignore him*) I wish to God they were! And so should you, if you had the honor of a louse!

(PARRITT *stares into his eyes guiltily for a second. Then he smiles sneeringly*)

PARRITT And you're the guy who kids himself he's through with the Movement! You old lying faker, you're still in love with it!

(LARRY *ignores him again now*)

WILLIE (*Disappointedly*) Then you're not in trouble, Parritt? I was hoping— But never mind. No offense meant. Forget it.

PARRITT (*Condescendingly—his eyes on* LARRY) Sure. That's all right, Willie. I'm not sore at you. It's that damned old faker that gets my goat. (*He slips out of his chair and goes quietly over to sit in the chair beside* LARRY *he had occupied before—in a low, insinuating, intimate tone*) I think I understand, Larry. It's really Mother you still love—isn't it?—in spite of the dirty deal she gave you. But hell, what did you expect? She was never true to anyone but herself and the Movement. But I understand how you can't help still feeling—because I still love her, too. (*Pleading in a strained, desperate tone*) You know I do, don't you? You must! So you see I couldn't have expected they'd catch her! You've got to believe me that I sold them out just to get a few lousy dollars to blow in on a whore. No other reason, honest! There couldn't possibly be any other reason!

(*Again he has a strange air of exonerating himself from guilt by this shameless confession*)

LARRY (*Trying not to listen, has listened with increasing tension*) For the love of Christ will you leave me in peace! I've told you you can't make me judge you! But if you don't keep still, you'll be saying something soon that will make you vomit your own soul like a drink of nickel rotgut that won't stay down! (*He pushes back his chair and springs to his feet*) To hell with you!

(*He goes to the bar*)

PARRITT (*Jumps up and starts to follow him—desperately*) Don't go, Larry! You've got to help me!

(*But* LARRY *is at the bar, back turned, and* ROCKY *is scowling at him. He stops, shrinking back into himself helplessly, and turns away. He goes to the table where he had been before, and this time he takes the chair at rear facing directly front. He puts his elbows on the table, holding his head in his hands as if he had a splitting headache*)

LARRY Set 'em up, Rocky. I swore I'd have no more drinks on Hickey, if I died of drought, but I've changed my mind! Be God, he owes it to me, and I'd get blind to the world now if it was the Iceman of Death himself treating! (*He stops, startledly, a superstitious awe coming into his face*) What made me say that, I wonder. (*With a sardonic laugh*) Well, be God, it fits, for Death was the Iceman Hickey called to his home!

ROCKY Aw, forget dat iceman gag! De poor dame is dead. (*Pushing a bottle and glass at* LARRY) Gwan and get paralyzed! I'll be glad to see one bum in dis dump act natural.

(LARRY *downs a drink and pours another.* ED MOSHER *appears in the doorway from the hall. The same change which is apparent in the manner and appearance of the others shows in him. He is sick, his nerves are shattered, his eyes are apprehensive, but he, too, puts on an exaggeratedly self-confident bearing. He saunters to the bar between* LARRY *and the street entrance*)

MOSHER Morning, Rocky. Hello, Larry. Glad to see Brother Hickey hasn't corrupted you to temperance. I wouldn't mind a shot myself. (*As* ROCKY *shoves a bottle toward him he shakes his head*) But I remember the only breath-killer in this dump is coffee beans. The boss would never fall for that. No man can run a circus successfully who believes guys chew coffee beans because they like them. (*He pushes the bottle away*) No, much as I need one after the hell of a night I've had— (*He scowls*) That drummer son of a drummer! I had to lock him out. But I could hear him through the wall doing his spiel to someone all night long. Still at it with Jimmy and Harry when I came down just now. But the hardest to take was that flannel-mouth, flatfoot Mick trying to tell me where I got off! I had to lock him out, too. (*As he says this,* MCGLOIN *comes in the doorway from the hall. The change in his appearance and manner is identical with that of* MOSHER *and the others*)

MCGLOIN He's a liar, Rocky! It was me locked him out!

(MOSHER *starts to flare up—then ignores him. They turn their backs on each other.* MCGLOIN *starts into the back-room section*)

WILLIE　Come and sit here, Mac. You're just the man I want to see. If I'm to take your case, we ought to have a talk before we leave.

MCGLOIN (*Contemptuously*)　We'll have no talk. You damned fool, do you think I'd have your father's son for my lawyer? They'd take one look at you and bounce us both out on our necks! (WILLIE *winces and shrinks down in his chair.* MCGLOIN *goes to the first table beyond him and sits with his back to the bar*) I don't need a lawyer, anyway. To hell with the law! All I've got to do is see the right ones and get them to pass the word. They will, too. They know I was framed. And once they've passed the word, it's as good as done, law or no law.

MOSHER　God, I'm glad I'm leaving this madhouse! (*He pulls his key from his pocket and slaps it on the bar*) Here's my key, Rocky.

MCGLOIN (*Pulls his from his pocket*)　And here's mine. (*He tosses it to* ROCKY) I'd rather sleep in the gutter than pass another night under the same roof with that loon, Hickey, and a lying circus grifter! (*He adds darkly*) And if that hat fits anyone here, let him put it on!

(MOSHER *turns toward him furiously but* ROCKY *leans over the bar and grabs his arm*)

ROCKY　Nix! Take it easy! (MOSHER *subsides.* ROCKY *tosses the keys on the shelf—disgustedly*) You boids gimme a pain. It'd soive you right if I wouldn't give de keys back to yuh tonight.
(*They both turn on him resentfully, but there is an interruption as* CORA *appears in the doorway from the hall with* CHUCK *behind her. She is drunk, dressed in her gaudy best, her face plastered with rouge and mascara, her hair a bit disheveled, her hat on anyhow*)

CORA (*Comes a few steps inside the bar—with a strained bright giggle*)　Hello, everybody! Here we go! Hickey just told us, ain't it time we beat it, if we're really goin'. So we're showin' de bastard, ain't we, Honey? He's comin' right down wid Harry and Jimmy. Jees, dem two look like dey was goin' to de electric chair! (*With frightened anger*) If I had to listen to any more of Hickey's bunk, I'd brain him. (*She puts her hand on* CHUCK's *arm*) Come on, Honey. Let's get started before he comes down.

CHUCK (*Sullenly*)　Sure, anyting yuh say, Baby.

CORA (*Turns on him truculently*) Yeah? Well, I say we stop at de foist reg'lar dump and yuh gotta blow me to a sherry flip—or four or five, if I want 'em!—or all bets is off!

CHUCK Aw, yuh got a fine bun on now!

CORA Cheap skate! I know what's eatin' you, Tightwad! Well, use my dough, den, if yuh're so stingy. Yuh'll grab it all, anyway, right after de ceremony. I know you! (*She hikes her skirt up and reaches inside the top of her stocking*) Here, yuh big tramp!

CHUCK (*Knocks her hand away—angrily*) Keep your lousy dough! And don't show off your legs to dese bums when yuh're goin' to be married, if yuh don't want a sock in de puss!

CORA (*Pleased—meekly*) Aw right, Honey. (*Looking around with a foolish laugh*) Say, why don't all you barflies come to de weddin'? (*But they are all sunk in their own apprehensions and ignore her. She hesitates, miserably uncertain*) Well, we're goin', guys. (*There is no comment. Her eyes fasten on* ROCKY—*desperately*) Say, Rocky, yuh gone deef? I said me and Chuck was goin' now.

ROCKY (*Wiping the bar—with elaborate indifference*) Well, goodbye. Give my love to Joisey.

CORA (*Tearfully indignant*) Ain't yuh goin' to wish us happiness, yuh doity little Ginny?

ROCKY Sure. Here's hopin' yuh don't moider each odder before next week.

CHUCK (*Angrily*) Aw, Baby, what d'we care for dat pimp? (ROCKY *turns on him threateningly, but* CHUCK *hears someone upstairs in the hall and grabs* CORA's *arm*) Here's Hickey comin'! Let's get outa here!

(*They hurry into the hall. The street door is heard slamming behind them*)

ROCKY (*Gloomily pronounces an obituary*) One regular guy and one all-right tart gone to hell. (*Fiercely*) Dat louse Hickey oughta be croaked!

(*There is a muttered growl of assent from most of the gathering. Then* HARRY HOPE *enters from the hall, followed by* JIMMY TOMORROW, *with* HICKEY *on his heels.* HOPE *and* JIMMY *are both putting up a front of self-assurance, but* CORA's *description of them was apt. There is a desperate bluff in their manner as they walk in, which suggests the last march of the condemned.* HOPE *is dressed in an old black Sunday suit, black tie, shoes, socks, which give him the appearance of being in mourning.* JIMMY's *clothes*)

*are pressed, his shoes shined, his white linen immaculate. He has
a hangover and his gently appealing dog's eyes have a boiled
look.* HICKEY's *face is a bit drawn from lack of sleep and his
voice is hoarse from continual talking, but his bustling energy
appears nervously intensified, and his beaming expression is one
of triumphant accomplishment*)

HICKEY    Well, here we are! We've got this far, at least! (*He pats*
JIMMY *on the back*) Good work, Jimmy. I told you you weren't
half as sick as you pretended. No excuse whatever for post-
poning—

JIMMY    I'll thank you to keep your hands off me! I merely mentioned I would feel more fit tomorrow. But it might as well be
today, I suppose.

HICKEY    Finish it now, so it'll be dead forever, and you can be free!
(*He passes him to clap* HOPE *encouragingly on the shoulder*)
Cheer up, Harry. You found your rheumatism didn't bother you
coming downstairs, didn't you? I told you it wouldn't. (*He winks
around at the others. With the exception of* HUGO *and* PARRITT,
*all their eyes are fixed on him with bitter animosity. He gives*
HOPE *a playful nudge in the ribs*) You're the damnedest one for
alibis, Governor! As bad as Jimmy!

HOPE    (*Putting on his deaf manner*)    Eh? I can't hear— (*Defiantly*) You're a liar! I've had rheumatism on and off for twenty
years. Ever since Bessie died. Everybody knows that.

HICKEY    Yes, we know it's the kind of rheumatism you turn on
and off! We're on to you, you old faker!
(*He claps him on the shoulder again, chuckling*)

HOPE    (*Looks humiliated and guilty—by way of escape he glares
around at the others*)    Bejees, what are all you bums hanging
round staring at me for? Think you was watching a circus!
Why don't you get the hell out of here and 'tend to your own
business, like Hickey's told you?
(*They look at him reproachfully, their eyes hurt. They fidget as
as if trying to move*)

HICKEY    Yes, Harry, I certainly thought they'd have had the guts
to be gone by this time. (*He grins*) Or maybe I did have my
doubts. (*Abruptly he becomes sincerely sympathetic and earnest*) Because I know exactly what you're up against, boys. I
know how damned yellow a man can be when it comes to making
himself face the truth. I've been through the mill, and I had to
face a worse bastard in myself than any of you will have to in

yourselves. I know you become such a coward you'll grab at any
lousy excuse to get out of killing your pipe dreams. And yet, as
I've told you over and over, it's exactly those damned tomorrow
dreams which keep you from making peace with yourself. So
you've got to kill them like I did mine. (*He pauses. They glare
at him with fear and hatred. They seem about to curse him, to
spring at him. But they remain silent and motionless. His manner
changes and he becomes kindly bullying*) Come on, boys! Get
moving! Who'll start the ball rolling? You, Captain, and you,
General. You're nearest the door. And besides, you're old war
heroes! You ought to lead the forlorn hope! Come on, now,
show us a little of that good old battle of Modder River spirit
we've heard so much about! You can't hang around all day
looking as if you were scared the street outside would bite you!

LEWIS (*Turns with humiliated rage—with an attempt at jaunty
casualness*) Right you are, Mister Bloody Nosey Parker! Time
I pushed off. Was only waiting to say good-bye to you, Harry,
old chum.

HOPE (*Dejectedly*) Good-bye, Captain. Hope you have luck.

LEWIS Oh, I'm bound to, Old Chap, and the same to you.
(*He pushes the swinging doors open and makes a brave exit,
turning to his right and marching off outside the window at
right of door*)

WETJOEN Py Gott, if dot Limey can, I can!
(*He pushes the door open and lumbers through it like a bull
charging an obstacle. He turns left and disappears off rear, outside the farthest window*)

HICKEY (*Exhortingly*) Next? Come on, Ed. It's a fine summer's
day and the call of the old circus lot must be in your blood!
(*MOSHER glares at him, then goes to the door. MCGLOIN jumps up
from his chair and starts moving toward the door. HICKEY claps
him on the back as he passes*) That's the stuff, Mac.

MOSHER Good-bye, Harry.
(*He goes out, turning right outside*)

MCGLOIN (*Glowering after him*) If that crooked grafter has the
guts—
(*He goes out, turning left outside. HICKEY glances at WILLIE who,
before he can speak, jumps from his chair*)

WILLIE Good-bye, Harry, and thanks for all your kindness.

HICKEY (*Claps him on the back*) That's the way, Willie! The

D.A.'s a busy man. He can't wait all day for you, you know.
(WILLIE *hurries to the door*)

HOPE (*Dully*) Good luck, Willie.

(WILLIE *goes out and turns right outside. While he is doing so,*
JIMMY, *in a sick panic, sneaks to the bar and furtively reaches
for* LARRY's *glass of whiskey*)

HICKEY And now it's your turn, Jimmy, old pal. (*He sees what*
JIMMY *is at and grabs his arm just as he is about to down the
drink*) Now, now, Jimmy! You can't do that to yourself. One
drink on top of your hangover and an empty stomach and you'll
be oreyeyed. Then you'll tell yourself you wouldn't stand a chance
if you went up soused to get your old job back.

JIMMY (*Pleads abjectly*) Tomorrow! I will tomorrow! I'll be in
good shape tomorrow! (*Abruptly getting control of himself—with
shaken firmness*) All right. I'm going. Take your hands off me.

HICKEY That's the ticket! You'll thank me when it's all over.

JIMMY (*In a burst of futile fury*) You dirty swine!

(*He tries to throw the drink in* HICKEY's *face, but his aim is poor
and it lands on* HICKEY's *coat.* JIMMY *turns and dashes through
the door, disappearing outside the window at right of door*)

HICKEY (*Brushing the whiskey off his coat—humorously*) All set for
an alcohol rub! But no hard feelings. I know he feels. I wrote
the book. I've seen the day when if anyone forced me to face
the truth about my pipe dreams, I'd have shot them dead.
(*He turns to* HOPE—*encouragingly*) Well, Governor, Jimmy made
the grade. It's up to you. If he's got the guts to go through with
the test, then certainly you—

LARRY (*Bursts out*) Leave Harry alone, damn you!

HICKEY (*Grins at him*) I'd make up my mind about myself if I
was you, Larry, and not bother over Harry. He'll come through
all right. I've promised him that. He doesn't need anyone's bum
pity. Do you, Governor?

HOPE (*With a pathetic attempt at his old fuming assertiveness*)
No, bejees! Keep your nose out of this, Larry. What's Hickey
got to do with it? I've always been going to take this walk, ain't
I? Bejees, you bums want to keep me locked up in here 's if I
was in jail! I've stood it long enough! I'm free, white and twenty-
one, and I'll do as I damned please, bejees! You keep your nose
out, too, Hickey! You'd think you was boss of this dump, not
me. Sure, I'm all right! Why shouldn't I be? What the hell's to
be scared of, just taking a stroll around my own ward? (*As he*

*talks he has been moving toward the door. Now he reaches it)* What's the weather like outside, Rocky?

ROCKY Fine day, Boss.

HOPE What's that? Can't hear you. Don't look fine to me. Looks 's if it'd pour down cats and dogs any minute. My rheumatism— *(He catches himself)* No, must be my eyes. Half blind, bejees. Makes things look black. I see now it's a fine day. Too damned hot for a walk, though, if you ask me. Well, do me good to sweat the booze out of me. But I'll have to watch out for the damned automobiles. Wasn't one of them around the last time, twenty years ago. From what I've seen of 'em through the window, they'd run over you as soon as look at you. Not that I'm scared of 'em. I can take care of myself. *(He puts a reluctant hand on the swinging door)* Well, so long— *(He stops and looks back— with frightened irascibility)* Bejees, where are you, Hickey? It's time we got started.

HICKEY *(Grins and shakes his head)* No, Harry. Can't be done. You've got to keep a date with yourself alone.

HOPE *(With forced fuming)* Hell of a guy, you are! Thought you'd be willing to help me across the street, knowing I'm half blind. Half deaf, too. Can't bear those damned automobiles. Hell with you! Bejees, I've never needed no one's help and I don't now! *(Egging himself on)* I'll take a good long walk now I've started. See all my old friends. Bejees, they must have given me up for dead. Twenty years is a long time. But they know it was grief over Bessie's death that made me— *(He puts his hand on the door)* Well, the sooner I get started— *(Then he drops his hand—with sentimental melancholy)* You know, Hickey, that's what gets me. Can't help thinking the last time I went out was to Bessie's funeral. After she'd gone, I didn't feel life was worth living. Swore I'd never go out again. *(Pathetically)* Somehow, I can't feel it's right for me to go, Hickey, even now. It's like I was doing wrong to her memory.

HICKEY Now, Governor, you can't let yourself get away with that one any more!

HOPE *(Cupping his hand to his ear)* What's that? Can't hear you. *(Sentimentally again but with desperation)* I remember now clear as day the last time before she— It was a fine Sunday morning. We went out to church together.

*(His voice breaks on a sob)*

HICKEY *(Amused)* It's a great act, Governor. But I know better, and so do you. You never did want to go to church or any place else with her. She was always on your neck, making you have ambition and go out and do things, when all you wanted was to ⋏ get drunk in peace.

HOPE (*Falteringly*) Can't hear a word you're saying. You're a Goddamned liar, anyway! (*Then in a sudden fury, his voice trembling with hatred*) Bejees, you son of a bitch, if there was a mad dog outside I'd go and shake hands with it rather than stay here with you!

(*The momentum of his fit of rage does it. He pushes the door open and strides blindly out into the street and as blindly past the window behind the free-lunch counter*)

ROCKY (*In amazement*) Jees, he made it! I'd a give yuh fifty to one he'd never— (*He goes to the end of the bar to look through the window—disgustedly*) Aw, he's stopped. I'll bet yuh he's comin' back.

HICKEY Of course, he's coming back. So are all the others. By to-night they'll all be here again. You dumbbell, that's the whole point.

ROCKY (*Excitedly*) No, he ain't neider! He's gone to de coib. He's lookin' up and down. Scared stiff of automobiles. Jees, dey ain't more'n two an hour comes down dis street, de old boob!

(*He watches excitedly, as if it were a race he had a bet on, oblivious to what happens in the bar*)

LARRY (*Turns on* HICKEY *with bitter defiance*) And now it's my turn, I suppose? What is it I'm to do to achieve this blessed peace of yours?

HICKEY (*Grins at him*) Why, we've discussed all that, Larry. Just stop lying to yourself—

LARRY You think when I say I'm finished with life, and tired of watching the stupid greed of the human circus, and I'll welcome closing my eyes in the long sleep of death—you think that's a coward's lie?

HICKEY (*Chuckling*) Well, what do you think, Larry?

LARRY (*With increasing bitter intensity, more as if he were fighting with himself than with* HICKEY) I'm afraid to live, am I?—and even more afraid to die! So I sit here, with my pride drowned on the bottom of a bottle, keeping drunk so I won't see myself shaking in my britches with fright, or hear myself whining and praying: Beloved Christ, let me live a little longer at any price! If it's only for a few days more, or a few hours even, have mercy,

Almighty God, and let me still clutch greedily to my yellow heart this sweet treasure, this jewel beyond price, the dirty, stinking bit of withered old flesh which is my beautiful little life! (*He laughs with a sneering, vindictive self-loathing, staring inward at himself with contempt and hatred. Then abruptly he makes* HICKEY *again the antagonist*) You think you'll make me admit that to myself?

HICKEY (*Chuckling*) But you just did admit it, didn't you?

PARRITT (*Lifts his head from his hands to glare at* LARRY—*jeeringly*) That's the stuff, Hickey! Show the old yellow faker up! He can't play dead on me like this! He's got to help me!

HICKEY Yes, Larry, you've got to settle with him. I'm leaving you entirely in his hands. He'll do as good a job as I could at making you give up that old grandstand bluff.

LARRY (*Angrily*) I'll see the two of you in hell first!

ROCKY (*Calls excitedly from the end of the bar*) Jees, Harry's startin' across de street! He's goin' to fool yuh, Hickey, yuh bastard! (*He pauses, watching—then worriedly*) What de hell's he stoppin' for? Right in de middle of de street! Yuh'd tink he was paralyzed or somethin'! (*Disgustedly*) Aw, he's quittin'! He's turned back! Jees, look at de old bastard travel! Here he comes! (*Hope passes the window outside the free-lunch counter in a shambling, panic-stricken run. He comes lurching blindly through the swinging doors and stumbles to the bar at* LARRY's *right*)

HOPE Bejees, give me a drink quick! Scared me out of a year's growth! Bejees, that guy ought to be pinched! Bejees, it ain't safe to walk in the streets! Bejees, that ends me! Never again! Give me that bottle! (*He slops a glass full and drains it and pours another— To* ROCKY, *who is regarding him with scorn— appealingly*) You seen it, didn't you, Rocky?

ROCKY Seen what?

HOPE That automobile, you dumb Wop! Feller driving it must be drunk or crazy. He'd run right over me if I hadn't jumped. (*Ingratiatingly*) Come on, Larry, have a drink. Everybody have a drink. Have a cigar, Rocky. I know you hardly ever touch it.

ROCKY (*Resentfully*) Well, dis is de time I do touch it! (*Pouring a drink*) I'm goin' to get stinko, see! And if yuh don't like it, yuh know what yuh can do! I gotta good mind to chuck my job, anyways. (*Disgustedly*) Jees, Harry, I thought yuh had some guts! I was bettin' yuh'd make it and show dat four-flusher up. (*He nods at* HICKEY—*then snorts*) Automobile, hell! Who d'yuh tink yuh're kiddin'? Dey wasn' no automobile! Yuh just quit cold!

HOPE (*Feebly*) Guess I ought to know! Bejees, it almost killed me!

HICKEY (*Comes to the bar between him and* LARRY, *and puts a hand on his shoulder—kindly*) Now, now, Governor. Don't be foolish. You've faced the test and come through. You're rid of all that nagging dream stuff now. You know you can't believe it any more.

HOPE (*Appeals pleadingly to* LARRY) Larry, you saw it, didn't you? Drink up! Have another! Have all you want! Bejees, we'll go on a grand old souse together! You saw that automobile, didn't you?

LARRY (*Compassionately, avoiding his eyes*) Sure, I saw it, Harry. You had a narrow escape. Be God, I thought you were a goner!

HICKEY (*Turns on him with a flash of sincere indignation*) What the hell's the matter with you, Larry? You know what I told you about the wrong kind of pity. Leave Harry alone! You'd think I was trying to harm him, the fool way you act! My oldest friend! What kind of a louse do you think I am? There isn't anything I wouldn't do for Harry, and he knows it! All I've wanted to do is fix it so he'll be finally at peace with himself for the rest of his days! And if you'll only wait until the final returns are in, you'll find that's exactly what I've accomplished! (*He turns to* HOPE *and pats his shoulder—coaxingly*) Come now, Governor. What's the use of being stubborn, now when it's all over and dead? Give up that ghost automobile.

HOPE (*Beginning to collapse within himself—dully*) Yes, what's the use—now? All a lie! No automobile. But, bejees, something ran over me! Must have been myself, I guess. (*He forces a feeble smile—then wearily*) Guess I'll sit down. Feel all in. Like a corpse, bejees. (*He picks a bottle and glass from the bar and walks to the first table and slumps down in the chair, facing left-front. His shaking hand misjudges the distance and he sets the bottle on the table with a jar that rouses* HUGO, *who lifts his head from his arms and blinks at him through his thick spectacles.* HOPE *speaks to him in a flat, dead voice*) Hello, Hugo. Coming up for air? Stay passed out, that's the right dope. There ain't any cool willow trees—except you grow your own in a bottle. (*He pours a drink and gulps it down*)

HUGO (*With his silly giggle*) Hello, Harry, stupid proletarian monkey-face! I vill trink champagne beneath the villow— (*With a change to aristocratic fastidiousness*) But the slaves must ice it properly! (*With guttural rage*) Gottamned Hickey! Peddler pimp for nouveau-riche capitalism! Vhen I lead the jackass mob to the sack of Babylon, I vill make them hang him to a lamppost the first one!

HOPE (*Spiritlessly*) Good work. I'll help pull on the rope. Have a drink, Hugo.

HUGO (*Frightenedly*) No, thank you. I am too trunk now. I hear myself say crazy things. Do not listen, please. Larry vill tell you I haf never been so crazy trunk. I must sleep it off. (*He starts to put his head on his arms but stops and stares at* HOPE *with growing uneasiness*) Vhat's matter, Harry? You look funny. You look dead. Vhat's happened? I don't know you. Listen, I feel I am dying, too. Because I am so crazy trunk! It is very necessary I sleep. But I can't sleep here with you. You look dead.

(*He scrambles to his feet in a confused panic, turns his back on* HOPE *and settles into the chair at the next table which faces left. He thrusts his head down on his arms like an ostrich hiding its head in the sand. He does not notice* PARRITT, *nor* PARRITT *him*)

LARRY (*To* HICKEY *with bitter condemnation*) Another one who's begun to enjoy your peace!

HICKEY Oh, I know it's tough on him right now, the same as it is on Harry. But that's only the first shock. I promise you they'll both come through all right.

LARRY And you believe that! I see you do! You mad fool!

HICKEY Of course, I believe it! I tell you I know from my own experience!

HOPE (*Spiritlessly*) Close that big clam of yours, Hickey. Bejees, you're a worse gabber than that nagging bitch, Bessie, was. (*He drinks his drink mechanically and pours another*)

ROCKY (*In amazement*) Jees, did yuh hear dat?

HOPE (*Dully*) What's wrong with this booze? There's no kick in it.

ROCKY (*Worriedly*) Jees, Larry, Hugo had it right. He does look like he'd croaked.

HICKEY (*Annoyed*) Don't be a damned fool! Give him time. He's coming along all right. (*He calls to* HOPE *with a first trace of underlying uneasiness*) You're all right, aren't you, Harry?

HOPE (*Dully*) I want to pass out like Hugo.

LARRY (*Turns to* HICKEY—*with bitter anger*) It's the peace of death you've brought him.

HICKEY (*For the first time loses his temper*) That's a lie! (*But he controls this instantly and grins*) Well, well, you did manage to get a rise out of me that time. I think such a hell of a lot of Harry— (*Impatiently*) You know that's damned foolishness. Look at me. I've been through it. Do I look dead? Just leave Harry alone and wait until the shock wears off and you'll see. He'll be a new man. Like I am. (*He calls to* HOPE *coaxingly*) How's it coming, Governor? Beginning to feel free, aren't you? Relieved and not guilty any more?

HOPE (*Grumbles spiritlessly*) Bejees, you must have been monkeying with the booze, too, you interfering bastard! There's no life in it now. I want to get drunk and pass out. Let's all pass out. Who the hell cares?

HICKEY (*Lowering his voice—worriedly to* LARRY) I admit I didn't think he'd be hit so hard. He's always been a happy-go-lucky slob. Like I was. Of course, it hit me hard, too. But only for a minute. Then I felt as if a ton of guilt had been lifted off my mind. I saw what had happened was the only possible way for the peace of all concerned.

LARRY (*Sharply*) What was it happened? Tell us that! And don't try to get out of it! I want a straight answer! (*Vindictively*) I think it was something you drove someone else to do!

HICKEY (*Puzzled*) Someone else?

LARRY (*Accusingly*) What did your wife die of? You've kept that a deep secret, I notice—for some reason!

HICKEY (*Reproachfully*) You're not very considerate, Larry. But, if you insist on knowing now, there's no reason you shouldn't. It was a bullet through the head that killed Evelyn.

(*There is a second's tense silence*)

HOPE (*Dully*) Who the hell cares? To hell with her and that nagging old hag, Bessie.

ROCKY Christ. You had de right dope, Larry.

LARRY (*Revengefully*) You drove your poor wife to suicide? I knew it! Be God, I don't blame her! I'd almost do as much myself to be rid of you! It's what you'd like to drive us all to— (*Abruptly he is ashamed of himself and pitying*) I'm sorry, Hickey. I'm a rotten louse to throw that in your face.

HICKEY (*Quietly*) Oh, that's all right, Larry. But don't jump at conclusions. I didn't say poor Evelyn committed suicide. It's the last thing she'd ever have done, as long as I was alive for her to take care of and forgive. If you'd known her at all, you'd never get such a crazy suspicion. (*He pauses—then slowly*) No, I'm sorry to have to tell you my poor wife was killed.

(LARRY *stares at him with growing horror and shrinks back along the bar away from him.* PARRITT *jerks his head up from his hands and looks around frightenedly, not at* HICKEY, *but at* LARRY. ROCKY's *round eyes are popping.* HOPE *stares dully at the table top.* HUGO, *his head hidden in his arms, gives no sign of life*)

LARRY (*Shakenly*) Then she—was murdered.

PARRITT (*Springs to his feet—stammers defensively*) You're a liar, Larry! You must be crazy to say that to me! You know she's still alive!

(*But no one pays any attention to him*)

ROCKY (*Blurts out*) Moidered? Who done it?

LARRY (*His eyes fixed with fascinated horror on* HICKEY—*frightenedly*) Don't ask questions, you dumb Wop! It's none of our damned business! Leave Hickey alone!

HICKEY (*Smiles at him with affectionate amusement*) Still the old grandstand bluff, Larry? Or is it some more bum pity? (*He turns to* ROCKY—*matter-of-factly*) The police don't know who killed her yet, Rocky. But I expect they will before very long. (*As if that finished the subject, he comes forward to* HOPE *and sits beside him, with an arm around his shoulder—affectionately coaxing*) Coming along fine now, aren't you, Governor? Getting over the first shock? Beginning to feel free from guilt and lying hopes and at peace with yourself?

HOPE (*With a dull callousness*) Somebody croaked your Evelyn, eh? Bejees, my bets are on the iceman! But who the hell cares? Let's get drunk and pass out. (*He tosses down his drink with a lifeless, automatic movement—complainingly*) Bejees, what did you do to the booze, Hickey? There's no damned life left in it.

PARRITT (*Stammers, his eyes on* LARRY, *whose eyes in turn remain fixed on* HICKEY) Don't look like that, Larry! You've got to believe what I told you! It had nothing to do with her! It was just to get a few lousy dollars!

HUGO (*Suddenly raises his head from his arms and, looking straight in front of him, pounds on the table frightenedly with his small fists*) Don't be a fool! Buy me a trink! But no more vine! It is not properly iced! (*With guttural rage*) Gottamned stupid proletarian slaves! Buy me a trink or I vill have you shot! (*He collapses into abject begging*) Please, for Gott's sake! I am not trunk enough! I cannot sleep! Life is a crazy monkey-face! Always there is blood beneath the villow trees! I hate it and I am afraid! (*He hides his face on his arms, sobbing muffledly*) Please, I am crazy trunk! I say crazy things! For Gott's sake, do not listen to me!

(*But no one pays any attention to him.* LARRY *stands shrunk back against the bar.* ROCKY *is leaning over it. They stare at* HICKEY. PARRITT *stands looking pleadingly at* LARRY)

HICKEY (*Gazes with worried kindliness at* HOPE) You're beginning to worry me, Governor. Something's holding you up somewhere. I don't see why— You've faced the truth about yourself. You've done what you had to do to kill your nagging pipe dreams. Oh, I know it knocks you cold. But only for a minute. Then you see it was the only possible way to peace. And you feel happy. Like I did. That's what worries me about you, Governor. It's time you began to feel happy—

*Curtain*

# ACT FOUR

SCENE: *Same as Act One—the back room with the curtain separating it from the section of the barroom with its single table at right of curtain, front. It is around half past one in the morning of the following day.*

*The tables in the back room have a new arrangement. The one at left, front, before the window to the yard, is in the same position. So is the one at the right, rear, of it in the second row. But this table now has only one chair. This chair is at right of it, facing directly front. The two tables on either side of the door at rear are unchanged. But the table which was at center, front, has been pushed toward right so that it and the table at right, rear, of it in the second row, and the last table at right in the front row, are now jammed so closely together that they form one group.*

*LARRY, HUGO and PARRITT are at the table at left, front. LARRY is at left of it, beside the window, facing front. HUGO sits at rear, facing front, his head on his arms in his habitual position, but he is not asleep. On HUGO's left is PARRITT, his chair facing left, front. At right of table, an empty chair, facing left. LARRY's chin is on his chest, his eyes fixed on the floor. He will not look at PARRITT, who keeps staring at him with a sneering, pleading challenge.*

*Two bottles of whiskey are on each table, whiskey and chaser glasses, a pitcher of water.*

*The one chair by the table at right, rear, of them is vacant.*

*At the first table at right of center, CORA sits at left, front, of it, facing front. Around the rear of this table are four empty chairs. Opposite CORA, in a sixth chair, is CAPTAIN LEWIS, also facing front. on his left, MCGLOIN is facing front in a chair before the middle table of his group. At right, rear, of him, also at this table, GENERAL WETJOEN sits facing front. In back of this table are three empty chairs.*

*At right, rear, of WETJOEN, but beside the last table of the group, sits* WILLIE. *On* WILLIE'S *left, at rear of table, is* HOPE. *On* HOPE'S *left, at right, rear, of table, is* MOSHER. *Finally, at right of table is* JIMMY TOMORROW. *All of the four sit facing front.*

*There is an atmosphere of oppressive stagnation in the room, and a quality of insensibility about all the people in this group at right. They are like wax figures, set stiffly on their chairs, carrying out mechanically the motions of getting drunk but sunk in a numb stupor which is impervious to stimulation.*

*In the bar section,* JOE *is sprawled in the chair at right of table, facing left. His head rolls forward in a sodden slumber.* ROCKY *is standing behind his chair, regarding him with dull hostility.* ROCKY'S *face is set in an expression of tired, callous toughness. He looks now like a minor Wop gangster.*

ROCKY (*Shakes* JOE *by the shoulder*) Come on, yuh damned nigger! Beat it in de back room! It's after hours. (*But* JOE *remains inert.* ROCKY *gives up*) Aw, to hell wid it. Let de dump get pinched. I'm through wid dis lousy job, anyway! (*He hears someone at rear and calls*) Who's dat? (CHUCK *appears from rear. He has been drinking heavily, but there is no lift to his jag; his manner is grouchy and sullen. He has evidently been brawling. His knuckles are raw and there is a mouse under one eye. He has lost his straw hat, his tie is awry, and his blue suit is dirty.* ROCKY *eyes him indifferently*) Been scrappin', huh? Started off on your periodical, ain't yuh?

(*For a second there is a gleam of satisfaction in his eyes*)
CHUCK Yeah, ain't yuh glad? (*Truculently*) What's it to yuh?
ROCKY Not a damn ting. But dis is someting to me. I'm out on my feet holdin' down your job. Yuh said if I'd take your day, yuh'd relieve me at six, and here it's half past one A.M. Well, yuh're takin' over now, get me, no matter how plastered yuh are!
CHUCK Plastered, hell! I wisht I was. I've lapped up a gallon, but it don't hit me right. And to hell wid de job. I'm goin' to tell Harry I'm quittin'.
ROCKY Yeah? Well, I'm quittin', too.
CHUCK I've played sucker for dat crummy blonde long enough, lettin' her kid me into woikin'. From now on I take it easy.
ROCKY I'm glad yuh're gettin' some sense.
CHUCK And I hope yuh're gettin' some. What a prize sap you been, tendin' bar when yuh got two good hustlers in your stable!

ROCKY Yeah, but I ain't no sap now. I'll loin dem, when dey get back from Coney. (*Sneeringly*) Jees, dat Cora sure played you for a dope, feedin' yuh dat marriage-on-de-farm hop!

CHUCK (*Dully*) Yeah. Hickey got it right. A lousy pipe dream. It was her pulling sherry flips on me woke me up. All de way walkin' to de ferry, every ginmill we come to she'd drag me in to blow her. I got tinkin', Christ, what won't she want when she gets de ring on her finger and I'm hooked? So I tells her at de ferry, "Kiddo, yuh can go to Joisey, or to hell, but count me out."

ROCKY She says it was her told you to go to hell, because yuh'd started hittin' de booze.

CHUCK (*Ignoring this*) I got tinkin', too, Jees, won't I look sweet wid a wife dat if yuh put all de guys she's stayed wid side by side, dey'd reach to Chicago. (*He sighs gloomily*) Dat kind of dame, yuh can't trust 'em. De minute your back is toined, dey're cheatin' wid de iceman or someone. Hickey done me a favor, makin' me wake up. (*He pauses—then adds pathetically*) On'y it was fun, kinda, me and Cora kiddin' ourselves— (*Suddenly his face hardens with hatred*) Where is dat son of a bitch, Hickey? I want one good sock at dat guy—just one!—and de next buttin' in he'll do will be in de morgue! I'll take a chance on goin' to de Chair—!

ROCKY (*Starts—in a low warning voice*) Piano! Keep away from him, Chuck! He ain't here now, anyway. He went out to phone, he said. He wouldn't call from here. I got a hunch he's beat it. But if he does come back, yuh don't know him, if anyone asks yuh, get me? (*As* CHUCK *looks at him with dull surprise he lowers his voice to a whisper*) De Chair, maybe dat's where he's goin'. I don't know nuttin', see, but it looks like he croaked his wife.

CHUCK (*With a flash of interest*) Yuh mean she really was cheatin' on him? Den I don't blame de guy—

ROCKY Who's blamin' him? When a dame asks for it— But I don't know nuttin' about it, see?

CHUCK Is any of de gang wise?

ROCKY Larry is. And de boss ought to be. I tried to wise de rest of dem up to stay clear of him, but dey're all so licked, I don't know if dey got it. (*He pauses—vindictively*) I don't give a damn what he done to his wife, but if he gets de Hot Seat I won't go into no mournin'!

CHUCK Me, neider!

ROCKY    Not after his trowin' it in my face I'm a pimp. What if I
am? Why de hell not? And what he's done to Harry. Jees, de
poor old slob is so licked he can't even get drunk. And all de
gang. Dey're all licked. I couldn't help feelin' sorry for de poor
bums when dey showed up tonight, one by one, lookin' like
pooches wid deir tails between deir legs, dat everyone'd been
kickin' till dey was too punch-drunk to feel it no more. Jimmy
Tomorrow was de last. Schwartz, de copper, brung him in. Seen
him sittin' on de dock on West Street, lookin' at de water and
cryin'! Schwartz thought he was drunk and I let him tink it. But
he was cold sober. He was tryin' to jump in and didn't have de
noive, I figgered it. Noive! Jees, dere ain't enough guts left in de
whole gang to battle a mosquito!

CHUCK    Aw, to hell wid 'em! Who cares? Gimme a drink. (ROCKY
*pushes the bottle toward him apathetically*) I see you been
hittin' de redeye, too.

ROCKY    Yeah. But it don't do no good. I can't get drunk right.
(CHUCK *drinks.* JOE *mumbles in his sleep.* CHUCK *regards him resentfully*) Dis doity dinge was able to get his snootful and pass
out. Jees, even Hickey can't faze a nigger! Yuh'd tink he was
fazed if yuh'd seen him come in. Stinko, and he pulled a gat and
said he'd plug Hickey for insultin' him. Den he dropped it and
begun to cry and said he wasn't a gamblin' man or a tough guy
no more; he was yellow. He'd borrowed de gat to stick up someone, and den didn't have de guts. He got drunk panhandlin'
drinks in nigger joints, I s'pose. I guess dey felt sorry for him.

CHUCK    He ain't got no business in de bar after hours. Why don't
yuh chuck him out?

ROCKY    (*Apathetically*) Aw, to hell wid it. Who cares?

CHUCK    (*Lapsing into the same mood*) Yeah. I don't.

JOE    (*Suddenly lunges to his feet dazedly—mumbles in humbled
apology*) Scuse me, White Boys. Scuse me for livin'. I don't
want to be where I's not wanted.
(*He makes his way swayingly to the opening in the curtain at
rear and tacks down to the middle table of the three at right,
front. He feels his way around it to the table at its left and gets
to the chair in back of* CAPTAIN LEWIS)

CHUCK    (*Gets up—in a callous, brutal tone*) My pig's in de back
room, ain't she? I wanna collect de dough I wouldn't take dis
mornin', like a sucker, before she blows it.
(*He goes rear*)

ROCKY (*Getting up*) I'm comin', too. I'm trough woikin'. I ain't no lousy bartender.

(CHUCK *comes through the curtain and looks for* CORA *as* JOE *flops down in the chair in back of* CAPTAIN LEWIS)

JOE (*Taps* LEWIS *on the shoulder—servilely apologetic*) If you objects to my sittin' here, Captain, just tell me and I pulls my freight.

LEWIS No apology required, old chap. Anybody could tell you I should feel honored a bloody Kaffir would lower himself to sit beside me.

(JOE *stares at him with sodden perplexity—then closes his eyes.* CHUCK *comes forward to take the chair behind* CORA'S, *as* ROCKY *enters the back room and starts over toward* LARRY'S *table*)

CHUCK (*His voice hard*) I'm waitin', Baby. Dig!

CORA (*With apathetic obedience*) Sure. I been expectin' yuh. I got it all ready. Here. (*She passes a small roll of bills she has in her hand over her shoulder, without looking at him. He takes it, glances at it suspiciously, then shoves it in his pocket without a word of acknowledgment.* CORA *speaks with a tired wonder at herself rather than resentment toward him*) Jees, imagine me kiddin' myself I wanted to marry a drunken pimp.

CHUCK Dat's nuttin,' Baby. Imagine de sap I'da been, when I can get your dough just as easy widout it!

ROCKY (*Takes the chair on* PARRITT'S *left, facing* LARRY—*dully*) Hello, Old Cemetery. (LARRY *doesn't seem to hear. To* PARRITT) Hello, Tightwad. You still around?

PARRITT (*Keeps his eyes on* LARRY—*in a jeeringly challenging tone*) Ask Larry! He knows I'm here, all right, although he's pretending not to! He'd like to forget I'm alive! He's trying to kid himself with that grandstand philosopher stuff! But he knows he can't get away with it now! He kept himself locked in his room until a while ago, alone with a bottle of booze, but he couldn't make it work! He couldn't even get drunk! He had to come out! There must have been something there he was even more scared to face than he is Hickey and me! I guess he got looking at the fire escape and thinking how handy it was, if he was really sick of life and only had the nerve to die! (*He pauses sneeringly.* LARRY'S *face has tautened, but he pretends he doesn't hear.* ROCKY *pays no attention. His head has sunk forward, and he stares at the table top, sunk in the same stupor as the other occupants of the room.* PARRITT *goes on, his tone becoming more insistent*) He's

been thinking of me, too, Rocky. Trying to figure a way to get out
of helping me! He doesn't want to be bothered understanding.
But he does understand all right! He used to love her, too.
So he thinks I ought to take a hop off the fire escape! (*He
pauses,* LARRY's *hands on the table have clenched into fists, as his
nails dig into his palms, but he remains silent.* PARRITT *breaks
and starts pleading*) For God's sake, Larry, can't you say something? Hickey's got me all balled up. Thinking of what he must
have done has got me so I don't know any more what I did or
why. I can't go on like this! I've got to know what I ought to
do—

LARRY (*In a stifled tone*) God damn you! Are you trying to make
me your executioner?

PARRITT (*Starts frightenedly*) Execution? Then you do think—?

LARRY I don't think anything!

PARRITT (*With forced jeering*) I suppose you think I ought to die
because I sold out a lot of loud-mouthed fakers, who were
cheating suckers with a phony pipe dream, and put them where
they ought to be, in jail? (*He forces a laugh*) Don't make me
laugh! I ought to get a medal! What a damned old sap you
are! You must still believe in the Movement! (*He nudges* ROCKY
*with his elbow*) Hickey's right about him, isn't he, Rocky? An
old no-good drunken tramp, as dumb as he is, ought to take a
hop off the fire escape!

ROCKY (*Dully*) Sure. Why don't he? Or you? Or me? What de
hell's de difference? Who cares? (*There is a faint stir from all the
crowd, as if this sentiment struck a responsive chord in their
numbed minds. They mumble almost in chorus as one voice, like
sleepers talking out of a dully irritating dream,* "The hell with
it!" "Who cares?" *Then the sodden silence descends again on the
room.* ROCKY *looks from* PARRITT *to* LARRY *puzzledly. He mutters*)
What am I doin' here wid youse two? I remember I had something on my mind to tell yuh. What—? Oh, I got it now. (*He
looks from one to the other of their oblivious faces with a strange,
sly, calculating look—ingratiatingly*) I was tinking how you was
bot' reg'lar guys. I tinks, ain't two guys like dem saps to be
hangin' round like a coupla stew bums and wastin' demselves.
Not dat I blame yuh for not woikin'. On'y suckers woik. But dere's
no percentage in bein' broke when yuh can grab good jack for
yourself and make someone else woik for yuh, is dere? I mean,
like I do. So I tinks, Dey're my pals and I ought to wise up two

good guys like dem to play my system, and not be lousy barflies, no good to demselves or nobody else. (*He addresses* PARRITT *now —persuasively*) What yuh tink, Parritt? Ain't I right? Sure, I am. So don't be a sucker, see? Yuh ain't a bad-lookin' guy. Yuh could easy make some gal who's a good hustler, an' start a stable. I'd help yuh and wise yuh up to de inside dope on de game. (*He pauses inquiringly.* PARRITT *gives no sign of having heard him.* ROCKY *asks impatiently*) Well, what about it? What if dey do call yuh a pimp? What de hell do you care—any more'n I do.

PARRITT (*Without looking at him—vindictively*) I'm through with whores. I wish they were all in jail—or dead!

ROCKY (*Ignores this—disappointedly*) So yuh won't touch it, huh? Aw right, stay a bum! (*He turns to* LARRY) Jees, Larry, he's sure one dumb boob, ain't he? Dead from de neck up! He don't know a good ting when he sees it. (*Oily, even persuasive again*) But how about you, Larry? You ain't dumb. So why not, huh? Sure, yuh're old, but dat don't matter. All de hustlers tink yuh're aces. Dey fall for yuh like yuh was deir uncle or old man or someting. Dey'd like takin' care of yuh. And de cops 'round here, dey like yuh, too. It'd be a pipe for yuh, 'specially wid me to help yuh and wise yuh up. Yuh wouldn't have to worry where de next drink's comin' from, or wear doity clothes. (*Hopefully*) Well, don't it look good to yuh?

LARRY (*Glances at him—for a moment he is stirred to sardonic pity*) No, it doesn't look good, Rocky. I mean, the peace Hickey's brought you. It isn't contented enough, if you have to make everyone else a pimp, too.

ROCKY (*Stares at him stupidly—then pushes his chair back and gets up, grumbling*) I'm a sap to waste time on yuh. A stew bum is a stew bum and yuh can't change him. (*He turns away—then turns back for an afterthought*) Like I was sayin' to Chuck, yuh better keep away from Hickey. If anyone asks yuh, yuh don't know nuttin', get me? Yuh never even hoid he had a wife. (*His face hardens*) Jees, we all ought to git drunk and stage a celebration when dat bastard goes to de Chair.

LARRY (*Vindictively*) Be God, I'll celebrate with you and drink long life to him in hell! (*Then guiltily and pityingly*) No! The poor mad devil— (*Then with angry self-contempt*) Ah, pity again! The wrong kind! He'll welcome the Chair!

PARRITT (*Contemptuously*) Yes, what are you so damned scared of death for? I don't want your lousy pity.

ROCKY Christ, I hope he don't come back, Larry. We don't know nuttin' now. We're on'y guessin', see? But if de bastard keeps on talkin'—

LARRY (*Grimly*) He'll come back. He'll keep on talking. He's got to. He's lost his confidence that the peace he's sold us is the real McCoy, and it's made him uneasy about his own. He'll have to prove to us—

(*As he is speaking* HICKEY *appears silently in the doorway at rear. He has lost his beaming salesman's grin. His manner is no longer self-assured. His expression is uneasy, baffled and resentful. It has the stubborn set of an obsessed determination. His eyes are on* LARRY *as he comes in. As he speaks, there is a start from all the crowd, a shrinking away from him*)

HICKEY (*Angrily*) That's a damned lie, Larry! I haven't lost confidence a damned bit! Why should I? (*Boastfully*) By God, whenever I made up my mind to sell someone something I knew they ought to want, I've sold 'em! (*He suddenly looks confused —haltingly*) I mean— It isn't kind of you, Larry, to make that kind of crack when I've been doing my best to help—

ROCKY (*Moving away from him toward right—sharply*) Keep away from me! I don't know nuttin' about yuh, see?

(*His tone is threatening but his manner as he turns his back and ducks quickly across to the bar entrance is that of one in flight. In the bar he comes forward and slumps in a chair at the table, facing front*)

HICKEY (*Comes to the table at right, rear, of* LARRY's *table and sits in the one chair there, facing front. He looks over the crowd at right, hopefully and then disappointedly. He speaks with a strained attempt at his old affectionate jollying manner*) Well, well! How are you coming along, everybody? Sorry I had to leave you for a while, but there was something I had to get finally settled. It's all fixed now.

HOPE (*In the voice of one reiterating mechanically a hopeless complaint*) When are you going to do something about this booze, Hickey? Bejees, we all know you did something to take the life out of it. It's like drinking dishwater! We can't pass out! And you promised us peace.

(*His group all join in in a dull, complaining chorus, "We can't pass out! You promised us peace!"*)

HICKEY (*Bursts into resentful exasperation*) For God's sake, Harry, are you still harping on that damned nonsense! You've kept it up all afternoon and night! And you've got everybody else singing the same crazy tune! I've had about all I can stand— That's why I phoned— (*He controls himself*) Excuse me, boys and girls. I don't mean that. I'm just worried about you, when you play dead on me like this. I was hoping by the time I got back you'd be like you ought to be! I thought you were deliberately holding back, while I was around, because you didn't want to give me the satisfaction of showing me I'd had the right dope. And I did have! I know from my own experience. (*Exasperatedly*) But I've explained that a million times! And you've all done what you needed to do! By rights you should be contented now, without a single damned hope or lying dream left to torment you! But here you are, acting like a lot of stiffs cheating the under-taker! (*He looks around accusingly*) I can't figure it—unless it's just your damned pigheaded stubbornness! (*He breaks—miserably*) Hell, you oughtn't to act this way with me! You're my old pals, the only friends I've got. You know the one thing I want is to see you all happy before I go— (*Rousing himself to his old brisk, master-of-ceremonies manner*) And there's damned little time left now. I've made a date for two o'clock. We've got to get busy right away and find out what's wrong. (*There is a sodden silence. He goes on exasperatedly*) Can't you appreciate what you've got, for God's sake? Don't you know you're free now to be yourselves, without having to feel remorse or guilt, or lie to yourselves about reforming tomorrow? Can't you see there is no tomorrow now? You're rid of it forever! You've killed it! You don't have to care a damn about anything any more! You've finally got the game of life licked, don't you see that? (*Angrily exhorting*) Then why the hell don't you get pie-eyed and celebrate? Why don't you laugh and sing "Sweet Adeline"? (*With bitterly hurt accusation*) The only reason I can think of is, you're putting on this rotten half-dead act just to get back at me! Because you hate my guts! (*He breaks again*) God, don't do that, gang! It makes me feel like hell to think you hate me. It makes me feel you suspect I must have hated you. But that's a lie! Oh, I know I used to hate everyone in the world who wasn't as rotten a bastard as I was! But that was when I was still living in hell—before I faced the truth and saw the one possible way to free poor Evelyn and give her the peace she'd always dreamed about.

(*He pauses. Everyone in the group stirs with awakening dread and they all begin to grow tense on their chairs*)

CHUCK (*Without looking at* HICKEY—*with dull, resentful viciousness*) Aw, put a bag over it! To hell wid Evelyn! What if she was cheatin'? And who cares what yuh did to her? Dat's your funeral. We don't give a damn, see? (*There is a dull, resentful chorus of assent, "We don't give a damn."* CHUCK *adds dully*) All we want outa you is keep de hell away from us and give us a rest.

(*A muttered chorus of assent*)

HICKEY (*As if he hadn't heard this—an obsessed look on his face*) The one possible way to make up to her for all I'd made her go through, and get her rid of me so I couldn't make her suffer any more, and she wouldn't have to forgive me again! I saw I couldn't do it by killing myself, like I wanted to for a long time. That would have been the last straw for her. She'd have died of a broken heart to think I could do that to her. She'd have blamed herself for it, too. Or I couldn't just run away from her. She'd have died of grief and humiliation if I'd done that to her. She'd have thought I'd stopped loving her. (*He adds with a strange impressive simplicity*) You see, Evelyn loved me. And I loved her. That was the trouble. It would have been easy to find a way out if she hadn't loved me so much. Or if I hadn't loved her. But as it was, there was only one possible way. (*He pauses—then adds simply*) I had to kill her.

(*There is a second's dead silence as he finishes—then a tense indrawn breath like a gasp from the crowd, and a general shrinking movement*)

LARRY (*Bursts out*) You mad fool, can't you keep your mouth shut! We may hate you for what you've done here this time, but we remember the old times, too, when you brought kindness and laughter with you instead of death! We don't want to know things that will make us help send you to the Chair!

PARRITT (*With angry scorn*) Ah, shut up, you yellow faker! Can't you face anything? Wouldn't I deserve the Chair, too, if I'd— It's worse if you kill someone and they have to go on living. I'd be glad of the Chair! It'd wipe it out! It'd square me with myself!

HICKEY (*Disturbed—with a movement of repulsion*) I wish you'd get rid of that bastard, Larry. I can't have him pretending there's something in common between him and me. It's what's in your heart that counts. There was love in my heart, not hate.

PARRITT (*Glares at him in angry terror*) You're a liar! I don't hate her! I couldn't! And it had nothing to do with her, anyway! You ask Larry!

LARRY (*Grabs his shoulder and shakes him furiously*) God damn you, stop shoving your rotten soul in my lap!

(PARRITT *subsides, hiding his face in his hands and shuddering*)

HICKEY (*Goes on quietly now*) Don't worry about the Chair, Larry. I know it's still hard for you not to be terrified by death, but when you've made peace with yourself, like I have, you won't give a damn. (*He addresses the group at right again— earnestly*) Listen, everybody. I've made up my mind the only way I can clear things up for you, so you'll realize how contented and carefree you ought to feel, now I've made you get rid of your pipe dreams, is to show you what a pipe dream did to me and Evelyn. I'm certain if I tell you about it from the beginning, you'll appreciate what I've done for you and why I did it, and how damned grateful you ought to be—instead of hating me. (*He begins eagerly in a strange running narrative manner*) You see, even when we were kids, Evelyn and me—

HOPE (*Bursts out, pounding with his glass on the table*) No! Who the hell cares? We don't want to hear it. All we want is to pass out and get drunk and a little peace!

(*They are all, except* LARRY *and* PARRITT, *seized by the same fit and pound with their glasses, even* HUGO, *and* ROCKY *in the bar, and shout in chorus, "Who the hell cares? We want to pass out!"*)

HICKEY (*With an expression of wounded hurt*) All right, if that's the way you feel. I don't want to cram it down your throats. I don't need to tell anyone. I don't feel guilty. I'm only worried about you.

HOPE What did you do to this booze? That's what we'd like to hear. Bejees, you done something. There's no life or kick in it now. (*He appeals mechanically to* JIMMY TOMORROW) Ain't that right, Jimmy?

JIMMY (*More than any of them, his face has a wax-figure blank-ness that makes it look embalmed. He answers in a precise, com-pletely lifeless voice, but his reply is not to* HARRY's *question, and he does not look at him or anyone else*) Yes. Quite right. It was all a stupid lie—my nonsense about tomorrow. Naturally, they

would never give me my position back. I would never dream of
asking them. It would be hopeless. I didn't resign. I was fired for
drunkenness. And that was years ago. I'm much worse now.
And it was absurd of me to excuse my drunkenness by pretending it was my wife's adultery that ruined my life. As Hickey
guessed, I was a drunkard before that. Long before. I discovered
early in life that living frightened me when I was sober. I have
forgotten why I married Marjorie. I can't even remember now if
she was pretty. She was a blonde, I think, but I couldn't swear to
it. I had some idea of wanting a home, perhaps. But, of course,
I much preferred the nearest pub. Why Marjorie married me,
God knows. It's impossible to believe she loved me. She soon
found I much preferred drinking all night with my pals to being
in bed with her. So, naturally, she was unfaithful. I didn't blame
her. I really didn't care. I was glad to be free—even grateful to
her, I think, for giving me such a good tragic excuse to drink as
much as I damned well pleased.

(*He stops like a mechanical doll that has run down. No one
gives any sign of having heard him. There is a heavy silence.
Then* ROCKY, *at the table in the bar, turns grouchily as he hears
a noise behind him. Two men come quietly forward. One,*
MORAN, *is middle-aged. The other,* LIEB, *is in his twenties. They
look ordinary in every way, without anything distinctive to
indicate what they do for a living*)

ROCKY (*Grumpily*)  In de back room if yuh wanta drink.

(MORAN *makes a peremptory sign to be quiet. All of a sudden*
ROCKY *senses they are detectives and springs up to face them,
his expression freezing into a wary blankness.* MORAN *pulls back
his coat to show his badge*)

MORAN (*In a low voice*)  Guy named Hickman in the back room?

ROCKY  Tink I know de names of all de guys—?

MORAN  Listen, you! This is murder. And don't be a sap. It was
Hickman himself phoned in and said we'd find him here around
two.

ROCKY (*Dully*)  So dat's who he phoned to. (*He shrugs his
shoulders*) Aw right, if he asked for it. He's de fat guy sittin'
alone. (*He slumps down in his chair again*) And if yuh want a
confession all yuh got to do is listen. He'll be tellin' all about
it soon. Yuh can't stop de bastard talkin'.

(MORAN *gives him a curious look, then whispers to* LIEB, *who disappears rear and a moment later appears in the hall doorway of*

*the back room. He spots* HICKEY *and slides into a chair at the left of the doorway, cutting off escape by the hall.* MORAN *goes back and stands in the opening in the curtain leading to the back room. He sees* HICKEY *and stands watching him and listening*)

HICKEY (*Suddenly bursts out*) I've got to tell you! Your being the way you are now gets my goat! It's all wrong! It puts things in my mind—about myself. It makes me think, if I got balled up about you, how do I know I wasn't balled up about myself? And that's plain damned foolishness. When you know the story of me and Evelyn, you'll see there wasn't any other possible way out of it, for her sake. Only I've got to start way back at the beginning or you won't understand. (*He starts his story, his tone again becoming musingly reminiscent*) You see, even as a kid I was always restless. I had to keep on the go. You've heard the old saying, "Ministers' sons are sons of guns." Well, that was me, and then some. Home was like a jail. I didn't fall for the religious bunk. Listening to my old man whooping up hell fire and scaring those Hoosier suckers into shelling out their dough only handed me a laugh, although I had to hand it to him, the way he sold them nothing for something. I guess I take after him, and that's what made me a good salesman. Well, anyway, as I said, home was like jail, and so was school, and so was that damned hick town. The only place I liked was the pool rooms, where I could smoke Sweet Caporals, and mop up a couple of beers, thinking I was a hell-on-wheels sport. We had one hooker shop in town, and, of course, I liked that, too. Not that I hardly ever had entrance money. My old man was a tight old bastard. But I liked to sit around in the parlor and joke with the girls, and they liked me because I could kid 'em along and make 'em laugh. Well, you know what a small town is. Everyone got wise to me. They all said I was a no-good tramp. I didn't give a damn what they said. I hated everybody in the place. That is, except Evelyn. I loved Evelyn. Even as a kid. And Evelyn loved me.

(*He pauses. No one moves or gives any sign except by the dread in their eyes that they have heard him. Except* PARRITT, *who takes his hands from his face to look at* LARRY *pleadingly*)

PARRITT I loved Mother, Larry! No matter what she did! I still do! Even though I know she wishes now I was dead! You believe that, don't you? Christ, why can't you say something?

HICKEY (*Too absorbed in his story now to notice this—goes on in a*

*tone of fond, sentimental reminiscence*) Yes, sir, as far back
as I can remember, Evelyn and I loved each other. She always
stuck up for me. She wouldn't believe the gossip—or she'd pretend she didn't. No one could convince her I was no good.
Evelyn was stubborn as all hell once she'd made up her mind.
Even when I'd admit things and ask her forgiveness, she'd make
excuses for me and defend me against myself. She'd kiss me and
say she knew I didn't mean it and I wouldn't do it again. So I'd
promise I wouldn't. I'd have to promise, she was so sweet and
good, though I knew darned well— (*A touch of strange bitterness comes into his voice for a moment*) No, sir, you couldn't
stop Evelyn. Nothing on earth could shake her faith in me. Even
I couldn't. She was a sucker for a pipe dream. (*Then quickly*)
Well, naturally, her family forbid her seeing me. They were one
of the town's best, rich for that hick burg, owned the trolley line
and lumber company. Strict Methodists, too. They hated my
guts. But they couldn't stop Evelyn. She'd sneak notes to me
and meet me on the sly. I was getting more restless. The town
was getting more like a jail. I made up my mind to beat it. I knew
exactly what I wanted to be by that time. I'd met a lot of
drummers around the hotel and liked 'em. They were always
telling jokes. They were sports. They kept moving. I liked their
life. And I knew I could kid people and sell things. The hitch
was how to get the railroad fare to the Big Town. I told Mollie
Arlington my trouble. She was the madame of the cathouse.
She liked me. She laughed and said, "Hell, I'll stake you, Kid!
I'll bet on you. With that grin of yours and that line of bull,
you ought to be able to sell skunks for good ratters!" (*He
chuckles*) Mollie was all right. She gave me confidence in myself.
I paid her back, the first money I earned. Wrote her a kidding
letter, I remember, saying I was peddling baby carriages and
she and the girls had better take advantage of our bargain offer.
(*He chuckles*) But that's ahead of my story. The night before
I left town, I had a date with Evelyn. I got all worked up, she was
so pretty and sweet and good. I told her straight, "You better
forget me, Evelyn, for your own sake. I'm no good and never
will be. I'm not worthy to wipe your shoes." I broke down and
cried. She just said, looking white and scared, "Why, Teddy?
Don't you still love me?" I said, "Love you? God, Evelyn, I love
you more than anything in the world. And I always will!" She
said, "Then nothing else matters, Teddy, because nothing but

death could stop my loving you. So I'll wait, and when you're
ready you send for me and we'll be married. I know I can
make you happy, Teddy, and once you're happy you won't
want to do any of the bad things you've done any more." And
I said, "Of course, I won't, Evelyn!" I meant it, too. I believed it.
I loved her so much she could make me believe anything.
(*He sighs. There is a suspended, waiting silence. Even the two
detectives are drawn into it. Then* HOPE *breaks into dully exasperated, brutally callous protest*)

HOPE   Get it over, you long-winded bastard! You married her, and
you caught her cheating with the iceman, and you croaked her,
and who the hell cares? What's she to us? All we want is to pass
out in peace, bejees! (*A chorus of dull, resentful protest from all
the group. They mumble, like sleepers who curse a person who
keeps awakening them,* "What's it to us? We want to pass out in
peace!" HOPE *drinks and they mechanically follow his example.
He pours another and they do the same. He complains with a
stupid, nagging insistence*) No life in the booze! No kick! Dishwater. Bejees, I'll never pass out!

HICKEY   (*Goes on as if there had been no interruption*)   So I beat
it to the Big Town. I got a job easy, and it was a cinch for me to
make good. I had the knack. It was like a game, sizing people
up quick, spotting what their pet pipe dreams were, and then
kidding 'em along that line, pretending you believed what they
wanted to believe about themselves. Then they liked you, they
trusted you, they wanted to buy something to show their
gratitude. It was fun. But still, all the while I felt guilty, as if I
had no right to be having such a good time away from Evelyn. In
each letter I'd tell her how I missed her, but I'd keep warning
her, too. I'd tell her all my faults, how I liked my booze every
once in a while, and so on. But there was no shaking Evelyn's
belief in me, or her dreams about the future. After each letter of
hers, I'd be as full of faith as she was. So as soon as I got enough
saved to start us off, I sent for her and we got married. Christ,
wasn't I happy for a while! And wasn't she happy! I don't
care what anyone says, I'll bet there never was two people
who loved each other more than me and Evelyn. Not only
then but always after, in spite of everything I did— (*He
pauses—then sadly*) Well, it's all there, at the start, everything
that happened afterwards. I never could learn to handle
temptation. I'd want to reform and mean it. I'd promise

Evelyn, and I'd promise myself, and I'd believe it. I'd tell her, it's the last time. And she'd say, "I know it's the last time, Teddy. You'll never do it again." That's what made it so hard. That's what made me feel such a rotten skunk—her always forgiving me. My playing around with women, for instance. It was only a harmless good time to me. Didn't mean anything. But I'd know what it meant to Evelyn. So I'd say to myself, never again. But you know how it is, traveling around. The damned hotel rooms. I'd get seeing things in the wall paper. I'd get bored as hell. Lonely and homesick. But at the same time sick of home. I'd feel free and I'd want to celebrate a little. I never drank on the job, so it had to be dames. Any tart. What I'd want was some tramp I could be myself with without being ashamed—someone I could tell a dirty joke to and she'd laugh.

CORA (*With a dull, weary bitterness*) Jees, all de lousy jokes I've had to listen to and pretend was funny!

HICKEY (*Goes on obliviously*) Sometimes I'd try some joke I thought was a corker on Evelyn. She'd always make herself laugh. But I could tell she thought it was dirty, not funny. And Evelyn always knew about the tarts I'd been with when I came home from a trip. She'd kiss me and look in my eyes, and she'd know. I'd see in her eyes how she was trying not to know, and then telling herself even if it was true, he couldn't help it, they tempt him, and he's lonely, he hasn't got me, it's only his body, anyway, he doesn't love them. I'm the only one he loves. She was right, too. I never loved anyone else. Couldn't if I wanted to. (*He pauses*) She forgave me even when it all had to come out in the open. You know how it is when you keep taking chances. You may be lucky for a long time, but you get nicked in the end. I picked up a nail from some tart in Altoona.

CORA (*Dully, without resentment*) Yeah. And she picked it up from some guy. It's all in de game. What de hell of it?

HICKEY I had to do a lot of lying and stalling when I got home. It didn't do any good. The quack I went to got all my dough and then told me I was cured and I took his word. But I wasn't, and poor Evelyn— But she did her best to make me believe she fell for my lie about how traveling men get things from drinking cups on trains. Anyway, she forgave me. The same way she forgave me every time I'd turn up after a periodical drunk. You all know what I'd be like at the end of one. You've seen me. Like something lying in the gutter that no alley cat would lower itself to drag in—something they threw out of the D.T. ward in Bellevue along with the garbage, something that ought to be dead and isn't! (*His face is convulsed with self-loathing*) Evelyn wouldn't have heard from me in a month or more. She'd have been waiting there alone, with the neighbors shaking their heads and feeling sorry for her out loud. That was before she got me to move to the outskirts, where there weren't any next-door neighbors. And then the door would open and in I'd stumble—looking like what I've said—into her home, where she kept everything so spotless and clean. And I'd sworn it would never happen again, and now I'd have to start swearing again this was the last time. I could see disgust having a battle in her eyes with love. Love always won. She'd make herself kiss me, as if nothing had happened, as if I'd just come home from a business trip. She'd never complain or bawl me out. (*He bursts out in a tone of anguish that has anger and hatred beneath it*) Christ, can you imagine what a guilty skunk she made me feel! If she'd only admitted once she didn't believe any more in her pipe dream that some day I'd behave! But she never would. Evelyn was stubborn as hell. Once she'd set her heart on anything, you couldn't shake her faith that it had to come true—tomorrow! It was the same old story, over and over, for years and years. It kept piling up, inside her and inside me. God, can you picture all I made her suffer, and all the guilt she made me feel, and how I hated myself! If she only hadn't been so damned good—if she'd been the same kind of wife I was a husband. God, I used to pray sometimes she'd —I'd even say to her, "Go on, why don't you, Evelyn? It'd serve me right. I wouldn't mind. I'd forgive you." Or course, I'd pretend I was kidding—the same way I used to joke here about her being in the hay with the iceman. She'd have been so hurt if I'd said it seriously. She'd have thought I'd stopped loving her. (*He pauses —then looking around at them*) I suppose you think I'm a liar, that no woman could have stood all she stood and still loved me so much—that it isn't human for any woman to be so pitying and forgiving. Well, I'm not lying, and if you'd ever seen her, you'd realize I wasn't. It was written all over her face, sweetness and love and pity and forgiveness. (*He reaches mechanically for the inside pocket of his coat*) Wait! I'll show you. I always carry her picture. (*Suddenly he looks startled. He stares before him, his hand falling back—quietly*) No, I'm forgetting I tore it up—afterwards. I didn't need it any more.

*(He pauses. The silence is like that in the room of a dying man where people hold their breath, waiting for him to die)*

CORA *(With a muffled sob)* Jees, Hickey! Jees!

*(She shivers and puts her hands over her face)*

PARRITT *(To* LARRY *in a low insistent tone)* I burnt up Mother's picture, Larry. Her eyes followed me all the time. They seemed to be wishing I was dead!

HICKEY It kept piling up, like I've said. I got so I thought of it all the time. I hated myself more and more, thinking of all the wrong I'd done to the sweetest woman in the world who loved me so much. I got so I'd curse myself for a lousy bastard every time I saw myself in the mirror. I felt such pity for her it drove me crazy. You wouldn't believe a guy like me, that's knocked around so much, could feel such pity. It got so every night I'd wind up hiding my face in her lap, bawling and begging her forgiveness. And, of course, she'd always comfort me and say, "Never mind, Teddy, I know you won't ever again." Christ, I loved her so, but I began to hate that pipe dream! I began to be afraid I was going bughouse, because sometimes I couldn't forgive her for forgiving me. I even caught myself hating her for making me hate myself so much. There's a limit to the guilt you can feel and the forgiveness and the pity you can take! You have to begin blaming someone else, too. I got so sometimes when she'd kiss me it was like she did it on purpose to humiliate me, as if she'd spit in my face! But all the time I saw how crazy and rotten of me that was, and it made me hate myself all the more. You'd never believe I could hate so much, a good-natured, happy-go-lucky slob like me. And as the time got nearer to when I was due to come here for my drunk around Harry's birthday, I got nearly crazy. I kept swearing to her every night that this time I really wouldn't, until I'd made it a real final test to myself—and to her. And she kept encouraging me and saying, "I can see you really mean it now, Teddy. I know you'll conquer it this time, and we'll be so happy, dear." When she'd say that and kiss me, I'd believe it, too. Then she'd go to bed, and I'd stay up alone because I couldn't sleep and I didn't want to disturb her, tossing and rolling around. I'd get so damned lonely. I'd get thinking how peaceful it was here, sitting around with the old gang, getting drunk and forgetting love, joking and laughing and singing and swapping lies. And finally I knew I'd have to come. And I knew if I came this time, it was the finish. I'd never have the guts to go back and be forgiven again, and that would break Evelyn's heart because to her it would mean I didn't love her any more. (*He pauses*) That last night I'd driven myself crazy trying to figure some way out for her. I went in the bedroom. I was going to tell her it was the end. But I couldn't do that to her. She was sound asleep. I thought, God, if she'd only never wake up, she'd never know! And then it came to me—the only possible way out, for her sake. I remembered I'd given her a gun for protection while I was away and it was in the bureau drawer. She'd never feel any pain, never wake up from her dream. So I—

HOPE (*Tries to ward this off by pounding with his glass on the table —with brutal, callous exasperation*) Give us a rest, for the love of Christ! Who the hell cares? We want to pass out in peace! (*They all, except* PARRITT *and* LARRY, *pound with their glasses and grumble in chorus: "Who the hell cares? We want to pass out in peace!"* MORAN, *the detective, moves quietly from the entrance in the curtain across the back of the room to the table where his companion,* LIEB, *is sitting.* ROCKY *notices his leaving and gets up from the table in the rear and goes back to stand and watch in the entrance.* MORAN *exchanges a glance with* LIEB, *motioning him to get up. The latter does so. No one notices them. The clamor of banging glasses dies out as abruptly as it started.* HICKEY *hasn't appeared to hear it*)

HICKEY (*Simply*) So I killed her.
(*There is a moment of dead silence. Even the detectives are caught in it and stand motionless*)

PARRITT (*Suddenly gives up and relaxes limply in his chair—in a low voice in which there is a strange exhausted relief*) I may as well confess, Larry. There's no use lying any more. You know, anyway. I didn't give a damn about the money. It was because I hated her.

HICKEY (*Obliviously*) And then I saw I'd always known that was the only possible way to give her peace and free her from the misery of loving me. I saw it meant peace for me, too, knowing she was at peace. I felt as though a ton of guilt was lifted off my mind. I remember I stood by the bed and suddenly I had to laugh. I couldn't help it, and I knew Evelyn would forgive me. I remember I heard myself speaking to her, as if it was something I'd always wanted to say: "Well, you know what you can do with your pipe dream now, you damned bitch!" (*He stops with a horrified start, as if shocked out of a nightmare, as if he couldn't believe he heard what he had just said. He stammers*) No I never—!

PARRITT (*To* LARRY—*sneeringly*)  Yes, that's it! Her and the damned old Movement pipe dream! Eh, Larry?

HICKEY (*Bursts into frantic denial*)  No! That's a lie! I never said—! Good God, I couldn't have said that! If I did, I'd gone insane! Why, I loved Evelyn better than anything in life! (*He appeals brokenly to the crowd*) Boys, you're all my old pals! You've known old Hickey for years! You know I'd never— (*His eyes fix on* HOPE) You've known me longer than anyone, Harry. You know I must have been insane, don't you, Governor?

HOPE (*At first with the same defensive callousness—without looking at him*)  Who the hell cares? (*Then suddenly he looks at* HICKEY *and there is an extraordinary change in his expression. His face lights up, as if he were grasping at some dawning hope in his mind. He speaks with a groping eagerness*) Insane? You mean—you went really insane?

(*At the tone of his voice, all the group at the tables by him start and stare at him as if they caught his thought. Then they all look at* HICKEY *eagerly, too*)

HICKEY  Yes! Or I couldn't have laughed! I couldn't have said that to her!

(MORAN *walks up behind him on one side, while the second detective,* LIEB, *closes in on him from the other*)

MORAN (*Taps* HICKEY *on the shoulder*)  That's enough, Hickman. You know who we are. You're under arrest. (*He nods to* LIEB, *who slips a pair of handcuffs on* HICKEY's *wrists.* HICKEY *stares at them with stupid incomprehension.* MORAN *takes his arm*) Come along and spill your guts where we can get it on paper.

HICKEY  No, wait, Officer! You owe me a break! I phoned and made it easy for you, didn't I? Just a few minutes! (*To* HOPE— *pleadingly*) You know I couldn't say that to Evelyn, don't you, Harry—unless—

HOPE (*Eagerly*)  And you've been crazy ever since? Everything you've said and done here—

HICKEY (*For a moment forgets his own obsession and his face takes on its familiar expression of affectionate amusement and he chuckles*)  Now, Governor! Up to your old tricks, eh? I see what you're driving at, but I can't let you get away with— (*Then, as* HOPE's *expression turns to resentful callousness again*

*and he looks away, he adds hastily with pleading desperation)*
Yes, Harry, of course, I've been out of my mind ever since! All
the time I've been here! You saw I was insane, didn't you?

MORAN (*With cynical disgust*) Can it! I've had enough of your
act. Save it for the jury. (*Addressing the crowd, sharply*) Listen,
you guys. Don't fall for his lies. He's starting to get foxy now and
thinks he'll plead insanity. But he can't get away with it.
(*The crowd at the grouped tables are grasping at hope now. They
glare at him resentfully*)

HOPE (*Begins to bristle in his old-time manner*) Bejees, you dumb
dick, you've got a crust trying to tell us about Hickey! We've
known him for years, and every one of us noticed he was nutty
the minute he showed up here! Bejees, if you'd heard all the
crazy bull he was pulling about bringing us peace—like a bughouse preacher escaped from an asylum! If you'd seen all the
damned-fool things he made us do! We only did them because—
(*He hesitates—then defiantly*) Because we hoped he'd come
out of it if we kidded him along and humored him. (*He looks
around at the others*) Ain't that right, fellers?
(*They burst into a chorus of eager assent: "Yes, Harry!"
"That's it, Harry!" "That's why!" "We knew he was crazy!" "Just
to humor him!"*)

MORAN A fine bunch of rats! Covering up for a dirty, cold-blooded
murderer.

HOPE (*Stung into recovering all his old fuming truculence*) Is that
so? Bejees, you know the old story, when Saint Patrick drove the
snakes out of Ireland they swam to New York and joined the
police force! Ha! (*He cackles insultingly*) Bejees, we can believe
it now when we look at you, can't we, fellers? (*They all growl
assent, glowering defiantly at* MORAN. MORAN *glares at them,
looking as if he'd like to forget his prisoner and start cleaning out
the place.* HOPE *goes on pugnaciously*) You stand up for your
rights, bejees, Hickey! Don't let this smart-aleck dick get funny
with you. If he pulls any rubber-hose tricks, you let me know!
I've still got friends at the Hall! Bejees, I'll have him back in
uniform pounding a beat where the only graft he'll get will be
stealing tin cans from the goats!

MORAN (*Furiously*) Listen, you cockeyed old bum, for a plugged
nickel I'd— (*Controlling himself, turns to* HICKEY, *who is oblivious
to all this, and yanks his arm*) Come on, you!

HICKEY (*With a strange mad earnestness*) Oh, I want to go, Officer. I can hardly wait now. I should have phoned you from the house right afterwards. It was a waste of time coming here. I've got to explain to Evelyn. But I know she's forgiven me. She knows I was insane. You've got me all wrong, Officer. I want to go to the Chair.

MORAN  Crap!

HICKEY  (*Exasperatedly*)  God, you're a dumb dick! Do you suppose I give a damn about life now? Why, you bonehead, I haven't got a single damned lying hope or pipe dream left!

MORAN  (*Jerks him around to face the door to the hall*)  Get a move on!

HICKEY  (*As they start walking toward rear—insistently*)  All I want you to see is I was out of my mind afterwards, when I laughed at her! I was a raving rotten lunatic or I couldn't have said— Why, Evelyn was the only thing on God's earth I ever loved! I'd have killed myself before I'd ever have hurt her!
(*They disappear in the hall.* HICKEY's *voice keeps on protesting*)

HOPE  (*Calls after him*)  Don't worry, Hickey! They can't give you the Chair! We'll testify you was crazy! Won't we, fellers?
(*They all assent. Two or three echo* HOPE's *"Don't worry, Hickey." Then from the hall comes the slam of the street door.* HOPE's *face falls—with genuine sorrow*)  He's gone. Poor crazy son of a bitch! (*All the group around him are sad and sympathetic, too.* HOPE *reaches for his drink*)  Bejees, I need a drink. (*They grab their glasses.* HOPE *says hopefully*)  Bejees, maybe it'll have the old kick, now he's gone.
(*He drinks and they follow suit*)

ROCKY  (*Comes forward from where he has stood in the bar entrance —hopefully*)  Yeah, Boss, maybe we can get drunk now.
(*He sits in the chair by* CHUCK *and pours a drink and tosses it down. Then they all sit still, waiting for the effect, as if this drink were a crucial test, so absorbed in hopeful expectancy that they remain oblivious to what happens at* LARRY's *table*)

LARRY  (*His eyes full of pain and pity—in a whisper, aloud to himself*)  May the Chair bring him peace at last, the poor tortured bastard!

PARRITT  (*Leans toward him—in a strange low insistent voice*)  Yes, but he isn't the only one who needs peace, Larry. I can't feel sorry for him. He's lucky. He's through, now. It's all decided for him. I wish it was decided for me. I've never been any good at deciding things. Even about selling out, it was the tart the detective agency got after me who put it in my mind. You remember what Mother's like, Larry. She makes all the decisions. She's always decided what I must do. She doesn't like anyone to be free but herself. (*He pauses, as if waiting for comment, but* LARRY *ignores him*) I suppose you think I ought to have made those dicks take me away with Hickey. But how could I prove it, Larry? They'd think I was nutty. Because she's still alive. You're the only one who can understand how guilty I am. Because you know her and what I've done to her. You know I'm really much guiltier than he is. You know what I did is a much worse murder. Because she is dead and yet she has to live. For a while. But she can't live long in jail. She loves freedom too much. And I can't kid myself like Hickey, that she's at peace. As long as she lives, she'll never be able to forget what I've done to her even in her sleep. She'll never have a second's peace. (*He pauses—then bursts out*) Jesus, Larry, can't you say something? (LARRY *is at the breaking point.* PARRITT *goes on*) And I'm not putting up any bluff, either, that I was crazy afterwards when I laughed to myself and thought, "You know what you can do with your freedom pipe dream now, don't you, you damned old bitch!"

LARRY (*Snaps and turns on him, his face convulsed with detestation. His quivering voice has a condemning command in it*) Go! Get the hell out of life, God damn you, before I choke it out of you! Go up—!

PARRITT (*His manner is at once transformed. He seems suddenly at peace with himself. He speaks simply and gratefully*) Thanks, Larry. I just wanted to be sure. I can see now it's the only possible way I can ever get free from her. I guess I've really known that all my life. (*He pauses—then with a derisive smile*) It ought to comfort Mother a little, too. It'll give her the chance to play the great incorruptible Mother of the Revolution, whose only child is the Proletariat. She'll be able to say: "Justice is done! So may all traitors die!" She'll be able to say: "I am glad he's dead! Long live the Revolution!" (*He adds with a final implacable jeer*) You know her, Larry! Always a ham!

LARRY (*Pleads distractedly*) Go, for the love of Christ, you mad tortured bastard, for your own sake!

(HUGO *is roused by this. He lifts his head and peers uncomprehendingly at* LARRY. *Neither* LARRY *nor* PARRITT *notices him*)

PARRITT (*Stares at* LARRY. *His face begins to crumble as if he were going to break down and sob. He turns his head away, but reaches out fumblingly and pats* LARRY's *arms and stammers*) Jesus, Larry, thanks. That's kind. I knew you were the only one who could understand my side of it.

(*He gets to his feet and turns toward the door*)

HUGO (*Looks at* PARRITT *and bursts into his silly giggle*) Hello, leedle Don, leedle monkey-face! Don't be a fool! Buy me a trink!

PARRITT (*Puts on an act of dramatic bravado—forcing a grin*) Sure, I will, Hugo! Tomorrow! Beneath the willow trees!

(*He walks to the door with a careless swagger and disappears in the hall. From now on,* LARRY *waits, listening for the sound he knows is coming from the backyard outside the window, but trying not to listen, in an agony of horror and cracking nerve*)

HUGO (*Stares after* PARRITT *stupidly*) Stupid fool! Hickey make you crazy, too. (*He turns to the oblivious* LARRY—*with a timid eagerness*) I'm glad, Larry, they take that crazy Hickey avay to asylum. He makes me have bad dreams. He makes me tell lies about myself. He makes me want to spit on all I have ever dreamed. Yes, I am glad they take him to asylum. I don't feel I am dying now. He vas selling death to me, that crazy salesman. I think I have a trink now, Larry.

(*He pours a drink and gulps it down*)

HOPE (*Jubilantly*) Bejees, fellers, I'm feeling the old kick, or I'm a liar! It's putting life back in me! Bejees, if all I've lapped up begins to hit me, I'll be paralyzed before I know it! It was Hickey kept it from— Bejees, I know that sounds crazy, but he was crazy, and he'd got all of us as bughouse as he was. Bejees, it does queer things to you, having to listen day and night to a lunatic's pipe dreams—pretending you believe them, to kid him along and doing any crazy thing he wants to humor him. It's dangerous, too. Look at me pretending to start for a walk just to keep him quiet. I knew damned well it wasn't the right day for it. The sun was broiling and the streets full of automobiles. Bejees, I could feel myself getting sunstroke, and an automobile damn near ran over me. (*He appeals to* ROCKY, *afraid of the result, but daring it*) Ask Rocky. He was watching. Didn't it, Rocky?

ROCKY (*A bit tipsily*) What's dat, Boss? Jees, all de booze I've mopped up is beginning to get to me. (*Earnestly*) De automo-

bile, Boss? Sure, I seen it! Just missed yuh! I thought yuh was a goner. (*He pauses—then looks around at the others, and assumes the old kidding tone of the inmates, but hesitantly, as if still a little afraid*) On de woid of a honest bartender!
(*He tries a wink at the others. They all respond with smiles that are still a little forced and uneasy*)

HOPE (*Flashes him a suspicious glance. Then he understands— with his natural testy manner*) You're a bartender, all right. No one can say different. (ROCKY *looks grateful*) But, bejees, don't pull that honest junk! You and Chuck ought to have cards in the Burglars' Union! (*This time there is an eager laugh from the group.* HOPE *is delighted*) Bejees, it's good to hear someone laugh again! All the time that bas— poor old Hickey was here, I didn't have the heart— Bejees, I'm getting drunk and glad of it! (*He cackles and reaches for the bottle*) Come on, fellers. It's on the house. (*They pour drinks. They begin rapidly to get drunk now.* HOPE *becomes sentimental*) Poor old Hickey! We mustn't hold him responsible for anything he's done. We'll forget that and only remember him the way we've always known him before—the kindest, biggest-hearted guy ever wore shoe leather. (*They all chorus hearty sentimental assent: "That's right, Harry!" "That's all!" "Finest fellow!" "Best scout!" etc.* HOPE *goes on*) Good luck to him in Matteawan! Come on, bottoms up! (*They all drink. At the table by the window* LARRY's *hands grip the edge of the table. Unconsciously his head is inclined toward the window as he listens*)

LARRY (*Cannot hold back an anguished exclamation*) Christ! Why don't he—!

HUGO (*Beginning to be drunk again—peers at him*) Vhy don't he what? Don't be a fool! Hickey's gone. He vas crazy. Have a trink. (*Then as he receives no reply—with vague uneasiness*) What's matter vith you, Larry? You look funny. What you listen to out in backyard, Larry?
(CORA *begins to talk in the group at right*)

CORA (*Tipsily*) Well, I thank Gawd now me and Chuck did all we could to humor de poor nut. Jees, imagine us goin' off like we really meant to git married, when we ain't even picked out a farm yet!

CHUCK (*Eagerly*) Sure ting, Baby. We kidded him we was serious.

JIMMY (*Confidently—with a gentle, drunken unction*) I may as well say I detected his condition almost at once. All that talk of his about tomorrow, for example. He had the fixed idea of the insane. It only makes them worse to cross them.

WILLIE (*Eagerly*) Same with me, Jimmy. Only I spent the day in the park. I wasn't such a damned fool as to—

LEWIS (*Getting jauntily drunk*) Picture my predicament if I *had* gone to the Consulate. The pal of mine there is a humorous blighter. He would have got me a job out of pure spite. So I strolled about and finally came to roost in the park. (*He grins with affectionate kidding at* WETJOEN) And lo and behold, who was on the neighboring bench but my old battlefield companion, the Boer that walks like a man—who, if the British Government had taken my advice, would have been removed from his fetid kraal on the veldt straight to the baboon's cage at the London Zoo, and little children would now be asking their nurses: "Tell me, Nana, is that the Boer General, the one with the blue behind?"

(*They all laugh uproariously.* LEWIS *leans over and slaps* WET-JOEN *affectionately on the knee*) No offense meant, Piet, old chap.

WETJOEN (*Beaming at him*) No offense taken, you damned Limey! (WETJOEN *goes on—grinningly*) About a job, I felt the same as you, Cecil.

(*At the table by the window* HUGO *speaks to* LARRY *again*)

HUGO (*With uneasy insistence*) What's matter, Larry? You look scared. What you listen for out there?

(*But* LARRY *doesn't hear, and* JOE *begins talking in the group at right*)

JOE (*With drunken self-assurance*) No, suh, I wasn't fool enough to git in no crap game. Not while Hickey's around. Crazy people puts a jinx on you.

(MCGLOIN *is now heard. He is leaning across in front of* WETJOEN *to talk to* ED MOSHER *on* HOPE's *left*)

MCGLOIN (*With drunken earnestness*) I know you saw how it was, Ed. There was no good trying to explain to a crazy guy, but it ain't the right time. You know how getting reinstated is.

MOSHER (*Decidedly*) Sure, Mac. The same way with the circus. The boys tell me the rubes are wasting all their money buying food and times never was so hard. And I never was one to cheat for chicken feed.

HOPE (*Looks around him in an ecstasy of bleary sentiment con-*

*tent*) Bejees, I'm cockeyed! Bejees, you're all cockeyed! Bejees, we're all all right! Let's have another!

(*They pour out drinks. At the table by the window* LARRY *has unconsciously shut his eyes as he listens.* HUGO *is peering at him frightenedly now*)

HUGO (*Reiterates stupidly*) What's matter, Larry? Why you keep eyes shut? You look dead. What you listen for in backyard?
(*Then, as* LARRY *doesn't open his eyes or answer, he gets up hastily and moves away from the table, mumbling with frightened anger*) Crazy fool! You vas crazy like Hickey! You give me bad dreams, too.
(*He shrinks quickly past the table where* HICKEY *had sat to the rear of the group at right*)

ROCKY (*Greets him with boisterous affection*) Hello, dere, Hugo! Welcome to de party!

HOPE Yes, bejees, Hugo! Sit down! Have a drink! Have ten drinks, bejees!

HUGO (*Forgetting* LARRY *and bad dreams, gives his familiar giggle*) Hello, leedle Harry! Hello, nice, leedle, funny monkey-faces!
(*Warming up, changes abruptly to his usual declamatory denunciation*) Gottamned stupid bourgeois! Soon comes the Day of Judgment! (*They make derisive noises and tell him to sit down. He changes again, giggling good-naturedly, and sits at rear of the middle table*) Give me ten trinks, Harry. Don't be a fool.
(*They laugh.* ROCKY *shoves a glass and bottle at him. The sound of* MARGIE's *and* PEARL's *voices is heard from the hall, drunkenly shrill. All of the group turn toward the door as the two appear. They are drunk and look blowsy and disheveled. Their manner as they enter hardens into a brazen defensive truculence*)

MARGIE (*Stridently*) Gangway for two good whores!

PEARL Yeah! And we want a drink quick!

MARGIE (*Glaring at* ROCKY) Shake de lead outa your pants, Pimp! A little soivice!

ROCKY (*His black bullet eyes sentimental, his round Wop face grinning welcome*) Well, look who's here! (*He goes to them unsteadily, opening his arms*) Hello, dere, Sweethearts! Jees, I was beginnin' to worry about yuh, honest!
(*He tries to embrace them. They push his arms away, regarding him with amazed suspicion*)

PEARL What kind of a gag is dis?

HOPE (*Calls to them effusively*) Come on and join the party, you broads! Bejees, I'm glad to see you!

(*The girls exchange a bewildered glance, taking in the party and the changed atmosphere*)

MARGIE Jees, what's come off here?

PEARL Where's dat louse, Hickey?

ROCKY De cops got him. He'd gone crazy and croaked his wife. (*The girls exclaim, "Jees!" But there is more relief than horror in it.* ROCKY *goes on*) He'll get Matteawan. He ain't responsible. What he's pulled don't mean nuttin'. So forget dat whore stuff. I'll knock de block off anyone calls you whores! I'll fill de bastard full of lead! Yuh're tarts, and what de hell of it? Yuh're as good as anyone! So forget it, see?

(*They let him get his arms around them now. He gives them a hug. All the truculence leaves their faces. They smile and exchange maternally amused glances*)

MARGIE (*With a wink*) Our little bartender, ain't he, Poil?

PEARL Yeah, and a cute little Ginny at dat!

(*They laugh*)

MARGIE And is he stinko!

PEARL Stinko is right. But he ain't got nuttin' on us. Jees, Rocky, did we have a big time at Coney!

HOPE Bejees, sit down, you dumb broads! Welcome home! Have a drink! Have ten drinks, bejees! (*They take the empty chairs on* CHUCK's *left warmly welcomed by all.* ROCKY *stands in back of them, a hand on each of their shoulders, grinning with proud proprietorship.* HOPE *beams over and under his crooked spectacles with the air of a host whose party is a huge success, and rambles on happily*) Bejees, this is all right! We'll make this my birthday party, and forget the other. We'll get paralyzed! But who's missing? Where's the Old Wise Guy? Where's Larry?

ROCKY Over by de window, Boss. Jees, he's got his eyes shut. De old bastard's asleep (*They turn to look.* ROCKY *dismisses him*) Aw, to hell wid him. Let's have a drink.

(*They turn away and forget him*)

LARRY (*Torturedly arguing to himself in a shaken whisper*) It's the only way out for him! For the peace of all concerned, as Hickey said! (*Snapping*) God damn his yellow soul, if he doesn't soon, I'll go up and throw him off!—like a dog with its guts ripped out you'd put out of misery!

(*He half rises from his chair just as from outside the window*

*comes the sound of something hurtling down, followed by a muf-
fled, crunching thud.* LARRY *gasps and drops back on his chair,
shuddering, hiding his face in his hands. The group at right
hear it but are too preoccupied with drinks to pay much attention*)

HOPE (*Wonderingly*) What the hell was that?

ROCKY Aw, nuttin'. Someting fell off de fire escape. A mattress,
I'll bet. Some of dese bums been sleepin' on de fire escapes.

HOPE (*His interest diverted by this excuse to beef—testily*) They've
got to cut it out! Bejees, this ain't a fresh-air cure. Mattresses cost
money.

MOSHER Now don't start crabbing at the party, Harry. Let's drink
up.

(HOPE *forgets it and grabs his glass, and they all drink*)

LARRY (*In a whisper of horrified pity*) Poor devil! (*A long-for-
gotten faith returns to him for a moment and he mumbles*)
God rest his soul in peace. (*He opens his eyes—with a bitter self-
derision*) Ah, the damned pity—the wrong kind, as Hickey said!
Be God, there's no hope! I'll never be a success in the grandstand
—or anywhere else! Life is too much for me! I'll be a weak fool
looking with pity at the two sides of everything till the day I die!
(*With an intense bitter sincerity*) May that day come soon!
(*He pauses startledly, surprised at himself—then with a sardonic
grin*) Be God, I'm the only real convert to death Hickey made
here. From the bottom of my coward's heart I mean that now!

HOPE (*Calls effusively*) Hey there, Larry! Come over and get
paralyzed! What the hell you doing, sitting there? (*Then as
LARRY doesn't reply he immediately forgets him and turns to the
party. They are all very drunk now, just a few drinks ahead of the
passing-out stage, and hilariously happy about it*) Bejees, let's
sing! Let's celebrate! It's my birthday party! Bejees, I'm
oreyeyed! I want to sing!

(*He starts the chorus of "She's the Sunshine of Paradise Alley,"
and instantly they all burst into song. But not the same song.
Each starts the chorus of his or her choice.* JIMMY TOMORROW's
is "A Wee Dock and Doris"; ED MOSHER's, "Break the News to
Mother"; WILLIE OBAN's the Sailor Lad ditty he sang in Act
One;* GENERAL WETJOEN's, "Waiting at the Church"; MCGLOIN's,
"Tammany"; CAPTAIN LEWIS's, "The Old Kent Road"; JOE's, "All
I Got Was Sympathy"; PEARL's and MARGIE's, "Everybody's Doing
It"; ROCKY's, "You Great Big Beautiful Doll"; CHUCK's, "The Curse

*of an Aching Heart"; CORA's, "The Oceana Roll"; while HUGO jumps to his feet and, pounding on the table with his fist, bellows in his guttural basso the French Revolutionary "Carmagnole." A weird cacophony results from this mixture and they stop singing to roar with laughter. All but HUGO, who keeps on with drunken fervor)*

HUGO

Dansons la Carmagnole!
Vive le son! Vive le son!
Dansons la Carmagnole!
Vive le son des canons!

*(They all turn on him and howl him down with amused derision. He stops singing to denounce them in his most fiery style)* Capitalist svine! Stupid bourgeois monkeys! *(He declaims)* "The days grow hot, O Babylon!" *(They all take it up and shout in enthusiastic jeering chorus)* "'Tis cool beneath thy willow trees!" *(They pound their glasses on the table, roaring with laughter, and HUGO giggles with them. In his chair by the window, LARRY stares in front of him, oblivious to their racket)*

*Curtain*

EUGENE O'NEILL was born on October 16, 1888, in New York City. His father was James O'Neill, the famous dramatic actor; and during his early years O'Neill traveled much with his parents. In 1909 he went on a gold-prospecting expedition to South America; he later shipped as a seaman to Buenos Aires, worked at various occupations in the Argentine and tended mules on a cattle steamer to South Africa. He returned to New York destitute, then worked briefly as a reporter on a newspaper in New London, Connecticut, at which point an attack of tuberculosis sent him for six months to a sanitarium. This event marked the turning point in his career, and shortly after, at the age of twenty-four, he began his first play. His major works include *The Emperor Jones*, 1920; *The Hairy Ape*, 1921; *Desire Under the Elms*, 1924; *The Great God Brown*, 1925; *Strange Interlude*, 1926, 1927; *Mourning Becomes Electra*, 1929, 1931; *Ah, Wilderness*, 1933; *Days Without End*, 1934; *A Moon for the Misbegotten*, 1945; *The Iceman Cometh*, 1946; and several plays produced posthumously, including *Long Day's Journey into Night*, *A Touch of the Poet* and *Hughie*. Eugene O'Neill died in 1953.